Cognitive Science

Handbook of Perception and Cognition

2nd Edition

Series Editors
Edward C. Carterette
and **Morton P. Friedman**

Cognitive Science

Edited by

Benjamin Martin Bly

Department of Psychology
Rutgers University
Newark, New Jersey

David E. Rumelhart

Department of Psychology
Stanford University
Stanford, California

Academic Press
San Diego   London   Boston
New York   Sydney   Tokyo   Toronto

Academic Press
a division of Harcourt Brace & Company
525 B Street, Suite 1900, San Diego, California 92101-4495, USA
http://www.apnet.com

Academic Press
24-28 Oval Road, London NW1 7DX, UK
http://www.hbuk.co.uk/ap/

Library of Congress Catalog Card Number: 99-60977

International Standard Book Number: 0-12-601730-1

PRINTED IN THE UNITED STATES OF AMERICA
99   00   01   02   03   04   BB   9   8   7   6   5   4   3   2   1

Contents

3   *Categorization*

Douglas L. Medin and Evan Heit

4 Reasoning

Kenneth J. Kurtz, Dedre Gentner, and Virginia Gunn

5 Cognitive Development

Susan Carey and Ellen M. Markman

6   *The Brain Basis of Syntactic Processes: Architecture, Ontogeny, and Phylogeny*

Michael D. Patterson and Benjamin Martin Bly

7   *The Cognitive Neuroscience Approach*

Kevin N. Ochsner and Stephen M. Kosslyn

8   Emotion

George Mandler

Contributors

Numbers in parentheses indicate the pages on which the authors' contributions begin.

Benjamin Martin Bly (255)
Department of Psychology
Rutgers University
Newark, New Jersey 07102

Susan Carey (201)
Department of Psychology
New York University
New York, New York 10003

C. R. Gallistel (1)
Department of Psychology
University of California, Los Angeles
Los Angeles, California 90095

Dedre Gentner (145)
Department of Psychology
Northwestern University
Evanston, Illinois 60208

Virginia Gunn (145)
Department of Psychology
Northwestern University
Evanston, Illinois 60208

Evan Heit (99)
Department of Psychology
Northwestern University
Evanston, Illinois 60208

Stephen M. Kosslyn (319)
Department of Psychology
Harvard University
Cambridge, Massachusetts 02138

Kenneth J. Kurtz (145)
Department of Psychology
Northwestern University
Evanston, Illinois 60208

David LaBerge[1] (43)
Department of Cognitive Sciences
University of California, Irvine
Irvine, Califronia 92697

George Mandler (367)
Department of Psychology
University of California, San Diego
La Jolla, California 92093

[1] Present address: South Egremont, Massachusetts 01258.

Ellen M. Markman (201)
Department of Psychology
Stanford University
Stanford, California 94305

Douglas L. Medin (99)
Department of Psychology
Northwestern University
Evanston, Illinois 60208

Kevin N. Ochsner (319)
Department of Psychology
Harvard University
Cambridge, Massachusetts 02138

Michael Patterson (255)
Department of Psychology
Rutgers University
Newark, New Jersey 07102

Foreword

The problem of perception and cognition is in understanding how the organism transforms, organizes, stores, and uses information arising from the world in sense data or memory. With this definition of perception and cognition in mind, this handbook is designed to bring together the essential aspects of this very large, diverse, and scattered literature and to give a précis of the state of knowledge in every area of perception and cognition. The work is aimed at the psychologist and the cognitive scientist in particular, and at the natural scientist in general. Topics are covered in comprehensive surveys in which fundamental facts and concepts are presented, and important leads to journals and monographs of the specialized literature are provided. Perception and cognition are considered in the widest sense. Therefore, the work treats a wide range of experimental and theoretical work.

The *Handbook of Perception and Cognition* should serve as a basic source and reference work for those in the arts or sciences, indeed for all who are interested in human perception, action, and cognition.

Edward C. Carterette and Morton P. Friedman

Preface

Cognitive science is the study of mental representations and computations and of the physical systems that support those processes. Cognitive science includes cognitive psychological examination of thinking, but also much more. It includes investigations of the ways in which the human brain and other systems, natural or artificial, make possible complex behavior that depends on internal system states. These states and processes may not be amenable to direct measurement, either because they are not accessible to instruments or because they are not, per se, equivalent to any specific measurable state of matter or energy. Such an intangible object of inquiry seems to preclude the possibility of external, objective validation or to take cognitive science out of the realm of empirical sciences altogether. In fact, it does neither.

The success of science in using empirical measurements to test detailed predictions about the world has drawn particular attention to the act of measurement as a distinguishing characteristic of the scientific method. But the fact that scientific arguments often depend on careful measurement does not mean that science depends on measurement alone; indeed, it could not. No measurement is so free of conceptions that it consists only and entirely of the actuality of a thing. Does this mean that all views are equally correct? On the contrary: the success of science depends on the fact that some ways of conceiving of measurements and their implications correspond with the world better than others. As scientists, we seek a collection of conceptions that coheres and covers the facts of the world, as we observe them. Not all observations are equally true, as the proverbial cliff quickly proves.

This metaphysical issue is a hoary philosophical chestnut and it will not be settled by cognitive scientists. But as we sensibly flee from the argument, we should not pretend that we have avoided it by including only objective measurements as constraints on our theories. To think that this is what we, or indeed any scientist, have done is to adopt a rather unrealistic view of science altogether. Physics might be thought to concern only measurables and measurements, but of course this is not and has never been true. All general claims go beyond the scope of a brute fact, as they depend on language and concepts for their very formulation. It is only that in the case of cognitive science we face the doubly complex problem that the object of our interest is the very instrument of our scientific inquiry: the mind itself.

Exactly because theories of cognition can only be inferred by a potentially recursive exploration of the most intricate physical properties and outrageously conplex behavior of organisms, cognitive science is both interesting and hard. Faced with this daunting problem, cognitive science has often revisited familiar debates and rehearsed carefully polarized dichotomies, hoping to find conclusive, orderly answers to its deep questions. The chapters in this volume confront some of these issues, but it should be noted that in all cases, the aim is to eschew heat in favor of light.

Twenty years ago, a handbook of cognitive science would have included chapters on philosophy, cognitive psychology, linguistics, and computer science. An unusual volume might have included a chapter on neuroscience, but more likely, one chapter or more would have explained that a science of the mind need not be overly concerned with the implementational details of human cognition. The chapters would have put forward somewhat distinct perspectives, separated by each field's very different notions of what is important and in certain cases even what is true. Cognitive science today includes ideas from a number of fields, but it has moved beyond an interdisciplinary hodge-podge to become the locus of a more coherent collection of concepts. Still, few scientists identify themselves primarily as "cognitive scientists" and even fewer come from departments of cognitive science. Why? This is partly because in spite of tremendous progress, cognitive science has not converged on rigorous, overarching theories of the mind: this goal is universally acknowledged to be one of the most difficult topics science can confront. In part it is because the methodological ties and foundational assumptions of the various intersecting disciplines related to cognitive science are strong, even for scientists whose work is entirely concerned with the study of cognition. Perhaps most simply, for any individual scientist, it is difficult to identify with a field that is changing so fundamentally, and so rapidly. Even as cognitive science has emerged as a discipline, it has changed radically with changing ideas about the nature of the mind, particularly the introduction of neuroscientific, connectionist, and, more recently, evolutionary perspectives on the mind and the brain.

In constructing this volume, we have sought to avoid presenting an assembly of connected but conflicting approaches to studying cognition. Rather we have asked the contributing authors to address problems central to the understanding of cognition, drawing as broadly as possible on the ideas that have been infused into cognitive science from a number of disciplines. The resulting volume includes chapters on action, attention, categorization, cognitive development, language, reasoning, and emotion. All of these chapters focus on a domain and aim to present what might be called "broad cognitive scientific view" of that domain. In addition, we have included a chapter on the cognitive neuroscience approach to the study of cognition because cognitive neuroscience now occupies a central position in the understanding of cognition and that represents a change that has occurred gradually since the early 1980s, one that we believe warrants particular attention.

It is an editor's privilege to introduce the work of the scientists who contribute to a collected volume such as this, and I thank the authors individually and collectively for their efforts. They are an unusual group of scholars, able to provide intriguing, often idiosyncratic, but ultimately nondogmatic presentations of the subjects they have undertaken. These presentations are authoritative without being doctrinaire, a difficult balance to strike.

Because the subject matter of cognitive science seems to defy grand theory building, because it often founders in debating polarities rather than finding novel alternatives, because it seems always on the verge of fracturing into disconnected, irreconcilable branches, this volume aims to do something unusual. This aim arises out of one scientist's vision and practice, and it is reflected clearly in his lifetime of fundamental contributions to the field in which he labored. Any success, and no element of failure, in this effort is due to David E. Rumelhart, who is that rare person: a cognitive scientist.

Benjamin Martin Bly

CHAPTER 1

Coordinate Transformations in the Genesis of Directed Action

C. R. Gallistel

I. INTRODUCTION

A paradox of psychology is that the analytic difficulty of a problem may be inversely related to the phenomenological difficulty. Things that seem trivially easy to do are often the most difficult to understand analytically, whereas things that seem difficult—things that require "real brains"—have been rather successfully modeled with modest effort. We can program computers to do many things that we find conceptually challenging—inverting matrices, solving partial differential equations—but we are a long way from being able to program machines to do what we find so easy that it requires no thought—for example, reaching out to pick up a pencil.

The deep difficulty in understanding basic aspects of perception is widely appreciated. It has proved extraordinarily difficult to program a computer to segment a visual image into components that correspond to objects in the three-dimensional space from which the image is projected. Thus, the first deep problem that prevents the manufacture of robots that can pick up pencils is getting them to pick out the relevant portion(s) from the image of a scene. Less widely appreciated are the deep difficulties of trying to understand how the brain generates simple directed actions. Given that the brain has somehow determined *where* it wants the limb to go, how can it control the pattern of motor neuron firing to make something as mechanically intractable as a vertebrate forelimb move there?

I will attempt to bring conceptual order and coherence to some interesting recent findings by arguing first that the problem of controlling the trajectory of a limb is a problem in computing a series of coordinate transformations. Second, there is evidence that anatomically localized stages of the neural circuitry perform computationally distinct coordinate transformations. This suggests that the nervous system itself treats the problem as if it had the substructure of a series of coordinate transformations. Third, the control of the eye's movement is, for good reasons, the most intensively studied simple movement: moving the eye is mechanically simpler than moving a limb, yet several of the fundamental problems that arise in considering the muscular control of simple directed movements appear to be present even within the simplified mechanical situation provided by the eye. Thus, the study of oculomotor control is of central interest in developing and refining our understanding of the control of directed actions. Finally, the computation of coordinate transformations is the foundation of other important capacities, for example, the capacity to navigate. An understanding of the neurobiological basis of the brain's ability to compute coordinate transformations in the control of simple directed actions may yield principles that have broad application in cognitive neuroscience.

A. Coordinate Transformations

A coordinate transformation, in the very general sense in which I will use it here, is an operation that maps or relates points specified by coordinates in one "space" to points specified by coordinates in a different framework. "Space" is in quotes because it will often refer to something that is a space only in the mathematical sense of a metric space. A metric space is a collection of points on which a distance relation is defined, so that it is possible to say how far apart points in the space are.[1] The dimensionality of a metric space is the number of variables whose values must be specified in order to specify a point in that space—one for a one-dimensional space (a line), two for a plane, three for ordinary physical space, and n for an n-dimensional space. The dimensions of an abstract space need not and often do not correspond to the dimensions of a physical space. Coordinate transformations take the vector (string of numbers or quantities) that specifies a point in one space and generate the vector for a corresponding point in another space. The only restriction on the transformations I consider under the heading of coordinate transformations is that the transformation carries nearby points in one framework to nearby points in the other framework. Thus, points that lie close to each other in the first space cannot correspond to points that are sprinkled all over the place in the second space.

In directed limb movements, the primary sensory input arises in one framework while the movement is effected in a different framework, which is, generally speaking, of higher dimensionality than the primary sensory space. This is illustrated in Figure 1, which is based on a well-known experiment by Fukson, Berkinblit, and Feldman (1980) demonstrating that the spinal frog solves a variable coordinate trans-

---

[1] A distance is defined if there is a procedure that, given any two points p, q in the space, specifies a quantity (a scalar) $d \geq 0$, such that $d(p,q) = d(q,p)$, $d(p,q) + d(q,r) \geq d(p,r)$ and $d(p,q) = 0$ if $p = q$.

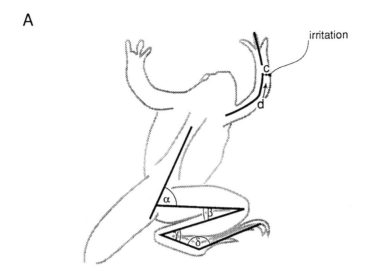

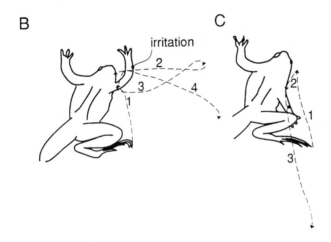

FIGURE 1 Tracings from filmstrips of the wiping motions of the hind limb of a high spinal frog wiping at an irritation of the elbow of its forelimb (small black square). (A) The sensory coordinate framework for the forelimb skin surface is the framework in which the primary sensory message is encoded $<d$ = distance along forelimb, c = circumferential distance$>$. The joint space coordinate framework $<\alpha, \beta, \gamma, \delta>$ is the framework within which kinematic planning takes place, because muscle actions change joint angles. (B and C) The spinal frog corrects its scratching motion to take into account the change in the position of its forelimb. Thus, the generation of the scratching movements requires a coordinate transformation that combines the skin-surface position signal with signals indicating the positions of the limbs relative to the body. The numbers indicate the sequence of discrete movements of the tips of the digits. (Redrawn with permission from O. I. Fukson, M. B. Berkinblit, and A. G. Feldman (1980). The spinal frog takes into account the scheme of its body during the wiping reflex. *Science, 209,* 1261–1263. Copyright © 1980 American Association for the Advancement of Science.)

formation problem when it directs the scratching action of its hind foot toward an irritated spot on the skin of its foreleg. The sensory signal from the irritation specifies the location of the target in a coordinate framework anchored to the forelimb. The axes of this two-dimensional forelimb-skin space are indicated by the lines labeled d and c in Figure 1, for distance down the limb and position around its circumference. A coordinate system like this, which is defined by (or anchored to) a one- or two-dimensional sensory surface such as the skin of a forelimb, or the retina, or the basilar membrane, I call a *sensory space*.

The coordinate system within which the action must be effected is *suggested* by the angles of the hind limb joint, labeled α, β, γ, δ. Such a system, where points are defined by joint angles (or, in reference to the eye, rotation angles) will hereafter be called a *joint space* (even when speaking of the eye, which, of course, has no joints, but behaves like the ball part of a ball joint). In the present case, the real joint space is only suggested by the illustration, because it shows each hind limb joint as having only one variable angle. As a result, the joint space portrayed in Figure 1 has only four dimensions, four angles that must be controlled or specified by the motor outflow. The actual joint space of the hind limb would be four-dimensional only if the joints were all hinge joints; that is, only if there were only one possible axis of rotation per joint. In fact, however, some of the joints have more degrees of freedom than a hinge. For example, in the figure, it appears that the upper leg can only move forward and backward at the hip joint, but in fact it can also be raised and lowered, and it can be rotated. (In other words, the hip joint is a ball joint with three degrees of freedom.) Thus, during a movement of the real hind limb, three angles must be controlled at the first joint alone. The diagram of all the variable angles in a multijointed limb is too complex for present purposes, so let us pretend that this is a two-dimensional frog, in which case the angles of the four joints of its hind limb define a four-dimensional metric space.[2]

To scratch the right spot, the frog must adjust the angles α, β, γ, and δ so as to place the tip of its hind foot on the irritated patch. In the language of coordinate transforms, its neuromuscular system must effect a transformation that maps the point $<d_i, c_i>$ in sensory space to an appropriate point $<\alpha_i, \beta_i, \gamma_i, \delta_i>$ in joint space. What makes this particularly challenging is that, as indicated in the lower half of Figure 1, the relation between these two coordinate frameworks changes as the position of the forelimb changes. The transformation that maps points in forelimb-skin space into hind limb-joint space must vary as a function of the position of the forelimb.

The experiment of Fukson et al. (1980) shows that the spinal cord of the frog adjusts the motor output to the hind limb to compensate for the change in the position of the forelimb; that is, it in effect computes this variable coordinate transfor-

---

[2] This simplification is the more appropriate in that in some of the work to be discussed later, involving microstimulation of motor centers in the spinal frog, the movements of the leg were (generally but not always) constrained to the horizontal plane.

mation (lower part of Figure 1). The problem is to understand how it does so. Are the neural processes in the spinal cord organized in terms of a series of coordinate transforms? If so, which coordinate transforms are performed, and where? When the transformations go from a space of lower dimensionality to a space of higher dimensionality, what further constraints does the nervous system impose in order to obtain a unique mapping? What structural aspects of the circuitry and what properties of the cellular level events within that circuitry effect the transformation (the mapping)?

Or, if the nervous system does not organize its operations in terms of a series of coordinate transformations, then by what principles can we understand what the nervous system is doing?

B. Two Contrasting Conceptions

Although it may be natural for someone with a standard mathematical training to think about the frog's problem in terms of coordinate transformations, it does not follow that this conceptualization of what is happening will lead to an understanding of how the nervous system accomplishes what it accomplishes. In fact, theories about how the nervous system solves this problem may be contrasted on the basis of the extent to which they assume that conceptualizing the problem this way leads to valid insights about the underlying processes. This may be illustrated by considering two extreme positions. Although the views to be contrasted here are more extreme than would probably be defended by any contemporary theorist, the first view is roughly the view that an engineer with experience in the design of robot arms might bring to the problem (e.g., Hollerbach, 1982), whereas the second view would be more congenial to a connectionist modeler (e.g., Smolensky, 1988). In fact, of course, the views of individual scientists are apt to evolve over time, so variants of both views may be found in the work of a single influential figure (Robinson, 1975, 1985, 1992).

1. One Transformation after the Other: An Engineer's View

In this conceptualization, there is a separate stage of computation for each of the stages that arise in a conventional physical analysis of the problem, such as would be made by an engineer trying to make a robot that did what the neural tissue in the spinal cord of a frog so readily does.

First, both the primary sensory coordinates for the irritation (in forelimb–skin space) and the primary sensory coordinates that specify the position of the hind foot in joint space are mapped (transformed) into the same three-dimensional space, for example, the Cartesian coordinate framework with the rostro-caudal, medio-lateral, and dorso-ventral axes used by anatomists to describe positions relative to a body. Hereafter, I refer to this coordinate system as *body-centered space*. Coordinate frameworks like the framework for body-centered space are also called extrinsic coordinates to distinguish them from intrinsic coordinate systems, which are defined by joints or muscles. The transformation of the forelimb-skin point into a point in body-centered space requires, in addition to the signal from the irritated patch of skin, signals that specify a point in forelimb-joint space, the point defined by the current position of the forelimb. Thus, this sensory transformation combines a point in forelimb-joint space with a point in forelimb-skin space to yield a point in extrinsic or body-centered space.

In this conception, mapping the two points into a common extrinsic system of coordinates (body-centered space) is a precondition for planning the *path* of the movement that will bring the tip of the hind foot to the irritated patch of skin. The planning algorithm must also specify the *time course* of the movement, where it will be along the path at successive moments. The path in body-centered space is a set of points in that three-dimensional space constituting what a geometer would call the "curve" connecting the starting point to the end point (curves in this usage include straight lines), while the *trajectory* in body-centered space is a set of points (curve) in four-dimensional space, the fourth dimension being the temporal dimension. Thus, a path has no temporal dimension, whereas a trajectory does. The planning of the trajectory of a movement is commonly called *kinematic* planning.

When a trajectory in body-centered space has been specified, the planned trajectory is realized by means of a series of transformations, each of which may be conceived of as a mapping from points specified in one system of coordinates to points specified in a different system of coordinates, in other words, as a coordinate transformation. First, there is the *inverse kinematics* transformation of the trajectory. This transformation carries a trajectory in body-centered space, which by definition has three nontemporal dimensions, into a trajectory in the higher dimensional joint space. This transformation poses a knotty problem, because it carries points into a higher dimensional space. All of the transformations considered so far carried points from a space of higher dimensionality into a space of lower dimensionality. These higher-to-lower transformations were realizable by functions, in the mathematical sense, that is, operations or processes that produce for any given input one and only one output. For a point in hind limb-joint space (that is, for specified values of the variable angles of the joints of the hind limb), there is one and only one point where the tip of the foot can be. Thus, there is a function that carries points in the joint space into points in the body-centered space. (This is the *forward kinematics* transformation.) The reverse is not true. For a point in body-centered space, there are many corresponding points in hind limb-joint space; that is, there are many different combinations of angles for the hind limb joints, all of which place the tip of the foot at the same point in body-centered space. You can verify this by reaching out to touch a point on your desk, then varying the configuration (hence, the joint angles) of your forearm while keeping your finger on that same point.

This lower-to-higher mapping problem, first highlighted by Bernstein (1967), is called the *degrees of freedom* problem. It means that the problem of finding *the* trajectory in joint space corresponding to a trajectory in body-centered space is not well defined. The nervous system must make it well defined by imposing restrictions on trajectories in joint space, restrictions that reduce the variety of possible trajectories to one actual trajectory. The question then becomes, what restrictions does the nervous system impose in computing this transformation?

The inverse kinematic transformation specifies the values of the joint angles as a function of time. The final stage in computing the time course of the signals to be sent to the muscles is to solve the *inverse dynamics* problem, which is, given the time courses of the desired changes in joint angles, find the time course of the force to be exerted by each relevant muscle. The pulling forces exerted by muscles are not pure torques, that is, they are not directed perpendicular to the direction of joint rotation. Also, they are related in extremely complicated ways to the torques that do develop (Zajac & Gordon, 1989). Finding the inverse dynamics can also be considered a coordinate transformation problem, this time from trajectories in joint space to trajectories in muscle space. The dimensionality of muscle space is the number of muscles that move the limb. Because this number is greater than the dimensionality of joint space—there are more muscles controlling a limb than there are degrees of freedom in its joints—the degrees of freedom problem arises again. Its reappearance, together with the strong nonlinearities in the biomechanics of limb and muscle, makes the inverse dynamics an intimidating problem (Saltzman, 1979). It is impossible to derive analytic expressions for the requisite functions (Hasan, 1991). At this point the engineer may begin to wonder how the nervous system could compute this particular, very messy transformation and whether it can in some sense avoid doing so.

2. One Big Look-up Table: A Radical Connectionist's View

Because the inverse transformations required in the above conceptualization of the problem are refractory to analytic treatment, one questions whether the conceptualization in terms of a series of coordinate transformations conforms at all to what actually occurs in the nervous system. A connectionist modeler might be inclined to reject this kind of computational decomposition of the problem into a sequence of transformations and think instead of a single overall mapping from sensory vectors (the array of signals in the first-order sensory axons) to motor vectors (the array of signals in the motor neurons). On this view, the connections in the network of interneurons (the hidden layer) intervening between the sensory neurons (input layer) and the motor neurons (output layer) have been adjusted by error-correcting feedback processes so that different patterns of input evoke optimized outputs (optimal by some criterion defined by the feedback process). The nervous system may act as a gigantic look-up table, a table that specifies outputs given inputs, but not by an analytically describable process.

In this view, the relevant inputs—primary visual afferents, primary somatosensory afferents, primary muscle and joint afferents, and so on—come from many different frameworks, so they cannot be conceived of as together defining points in any one space. Also, one school of connectionism has tended to emphasize the possibility that within the hidden layer (the network of interneurons), there may be no pattern in the activity of individual neurons or in pools of neurons that would relate in any systematic way to the kinds of coordinate frameworks that an engineer uses to conceptualize the problem (Hasan, 1991; Kalaska & Crammond, 1992; Lehky, Sejnowski, & Desimone, 1992; Lockery & Sejnowski, 1993; Smolensky, 1988). Indeed, the pattern of connectivity and of interneuron activity that arises under the influence of error-correcting feedback may vary radically from one network to the next due to variations in the initial conditions of the network. In this case, knowledge of the pattern of intervening neuronal activity in one network that solves the problem might offer no insight into what is going on in another network that solves the same problem, even though both networks developed their structure under the impact of the same experiences and the same error-correcting feedback process.

If the radical connectionist vision gives an accurate conception of how the nervous system solves the problem of directed action, then the attempt to describe what is going on in the nervous system in terms of a series of coordinate transformations is doomed from the outset. Einstein once remarked that the most incomprehensible thing about the universe was that it was comprehensible—by which he meant mathematically describable. Perhaps the nervous system's way of solving difficult problems is not mathematically describable.

There are, of course, compromises between the two extremes just described. One interesting compromise treats connectionist networks as nonanalytic function approximators, that is, physical devices that can be tuned to approximate almost any function, including functions for which it is impossible to derive an analytic expression, such as the inverse dynamics function in the control of a multijoint limb. Networks may even be conceived of as linearizing strongly nonlinear dynamic control problems, so as to present to the higher levels of the nervous system a set of basis functions from which any desired kinematics may be realized by additive composition (more about this later).

II. DIRECTED LIMB MOVEMENTS

A. Kinematics

1. Path Characteristics

The kinematics of the wrist during directed human arm movements have been studied in a variety of experiments. For a movement between two points, there is very little variability in the trajectory, regardless of the speed of the motion or the load (weight) carried by the hand (Atkeson & Hollerbach, 1985; Flash & Hogan, 1985; Lacquaniti, Soechting, & Terzuolo, 1982, 1986; Morasso, 1981; Soechting & Lacquaniti, 1981). The trajectories are usually straight (or at least only moderately curved) lines in either body-centered space (Morasso, 1981) or joint space (Hollerbach & Atkeson, 1987). (A straight line in joint space means that the ratios of the angular velocities of the joints are maintained throughout the movement.) In general, a trajectory cannot be straight in joint space if it is straight in body-centered space, and vice versa, although there is an important exception, namely, when the trajectory in body-centered space lies along a straight line through the shoulder (Hollerbach & Atkeson, 1987).

Because maximum kinematic smoothness is realized by straight paths (Hogan & Flash, 1987), one might hope to deduce from the straightness or lack of straightness of the trajectories in the two kinematic spaces whether the trajectory is planned in body-centered space or joint space (or neither). The fact that the trajectory can be strongly curved in either one space or the other depending on the work space (the region of body-centered space within which the starting and ending points of a trajectory are found) does not permit an unequivocal decision in favor of either planning space (Hollerbach, 1990).

The fact that freely chosen trajectories are curved in some parts of either body-centered space or joint space might even be thought to favor the third alternative—that is, there is no planning space, the radical connectionist view. However, it is not clear why in a radical connectionist view, the trajectories should tend toward straightness in most of the work space, nor why they should be so similar between subjects. The answer would presumably lie in something about the criteria that the error-correcting feedback process uses to determine error. One suspects, however, that the specification of this criterion would amount to assuming that the "teacher" (the feedback-determining process) has a space in which it evaluates trajectories; that is, the teacher does more than assess whether or not the desired endpoint was reached. There is also a question whether the teacher can teach in the absence of internal models of the dynamics (Atkeson, 1989; Jordan, 1994a). Internal models are the sort of thing that a *radical* connectionist eschews, but they are the sort of thing that a moderate connectionist might imagine that a neural network provides.

It has also been suggested that the variety of trajectories observed in body-centered and joint space might be a by-product of optimizing the smoothness of joint torques (Uno, Kawato, & Suzuki, 1989); that is, it may be a by-product of dynamic rather than kinematic planning. (Maximizing smoothnss means minimizing jerk, which is the third derivative of position as a function of time.) In short, the data on kinematics per se do not point unequivocally to a particular system of coordinates in which the planning of limb trajectories are carried out.

2. Evidence from Endpoint Variability

Results by Gordon, Ghilardi, and Ghez (1994) on the variability of movement endpoints suggest a stage in which the trajectory is planned in body-centered space, rather than joint space. Gordon et al. found that the directional variability in the endpoint (that is, the dispersion of the directions of the endpoints of repeated trajectories around the mean direction relative to the starting point) was constant and independent of the length of the trajectory. This constancy held for patterns involving different joints and for both slow and fast movements. By contrast, endpoint variability along the axis of the trajectory (that is, variability in the length of a repeated trajectory) increased markedly but nonlinearly with distance. Gordon et al. argue that their results imply that the direction and extent of the movement in body-centered space are independently computed. In vector terms, the orientation and length of the movement vector in body-centered space are separately computed and make separable contributions to the error in the endpoint.

3. Trajectory Adaptation Experiments

Strong evidence that trajectories are planned in body-centered space comes from recent adaptation experiments by Wolpert, Ghahramani, and Jordan (1995). They used an ingenious setup in which the subjects moved a computer mouse on a digitizing tablet toward a target. While doing so, they looked at an illusory view of a spot that seemingly marked the position of their hand relative to the target square. The target and the hand spot were projected via a computer-controlled system onto a mirror interposed between the subject's head and hand, creating a virtual image in the plane of the hand's movement (an image that appeared to originate from the surface of the digitizing tablet along which the hand was moving). This arrangement enabled them to provide erroneous visual information about the hand's position during the course of the movement, without an error at the beginning and end of the movement. That is, they were able to make straight trajectories appear curved and vice versa, while keeping the perception of the location of the beginning and ends of the trajectories constant.

They had subjects make repeated back and forth movements that were either transverse (for some subjects) or sagittal (for other subjects)—that is, either perpendicular to or in the sagittal plane of body-centered space. During the first 80 such movements, the trajectory was made to appear more curved. During the final 20 trials, the subjects made the same movement in the absence of visual feedback, so that the experimenters could assess the aftereffect of the adaptation experience.

A purely dynamic planning process—a process that computed the time course of the muscle forces required to bring the hand from its starting position to its ending position without regard to the trajectory through three-dimensional body-centered space—would not be affected by this artificial alteration in the apparent trajectory of the hand during the adaptation phase. If, however, there is a stage that plans the trajectory in body-centered space, and if that stage takes visual input as a reliable indicator of position in body-centered space, then this stage should register a trajectory error. This trajectory error might then be used to make adjustments in the inverse kinematics transformation so as to offset the error in the trajectory through body-centered space. This was what they in fact found: In the 20 movements made in the absence of visual feedback following the adaptation phase, the subjects' trajectories showed a significant increase in curvature, a curvature that straightened the apparent trajectory. This is strong evidence for a stage that plans a trajectory in body-centered space.

In these experiments, the subjects' preadaptation trajectories were gently curved rather than perfectly straight. In companion experiments (Wolpert, Ghahramani, & Jordan, 1994), the authors show that this curvature is predicted by errors in the visual perception of the straightness of the trajectory. Subjects perceived a straight trajectory of a moving spot as in fact curved; to get them to perceive the trajectory as straight, the actual trajectory had to be curved. There was a highly significant correlation between the curvature a subject perceived as straight and the curvature of the subject's actual hand movements.

Not all trajectory curvature can be explained as a consequence of the misperception of straightness in body-centered space. When subjects move their hand from a position in front of them to a position not far above their shoulder, the curvature in the trajectory is much too great to be explained in this way. The pronounced curvature in the trajectory through body-centered space that is observed in this case (arguably a special case) is presumably dictated by the greater simplicity or smoothness of the trajectory in joint space. Thus, it appears, that planning in body-centered space is not obligatory; plans may be constructed in joint space.

4. Velocity Profiles

The velocity profiles of directed trajectories are bell shaped: the wrist accelerates smoothly along its path to reach a maximal tangential velocity midway in the movement, then decelerates just as smoothly, so that the second half of the velocity profile is nearly the mirror image of the first (Figure 2). These Gaussian velocity profiles minimize the jerk (Hogan & Flash, 1987), which suggests that smoothness considerations play an important role in planning the trajectory. Although it is not at all intuitively obvious, these smoothness considerations also dictate straight-line trajectories in body-centered space (Flash & Hogan, 1985). Smoothness considerations in joint space may also play a fundamental role in specifying unique solutions for the inverse kinematics transformation; that is, the nervous system may pick out the smoothest trajectory in joint space that realizes the already planned trajectory in body-centered space.

B. Dynamics

A separable stage of dynamic planning, working to achieve a prespecified kinematics, is suggested by the fact that the velocity profiles are invariant (except for scaling) in the face of substantial changes in the speed at which the movement is executed and the weight carried by the hand (Figure 2). Changing the speed and the weight carried changes substantially the forces that must be applied to achieve these profiles. Because of the nonlinear biomechanics of the arm, the changes in the required forces are not a simple scaling up in the forces required at lower speeds or

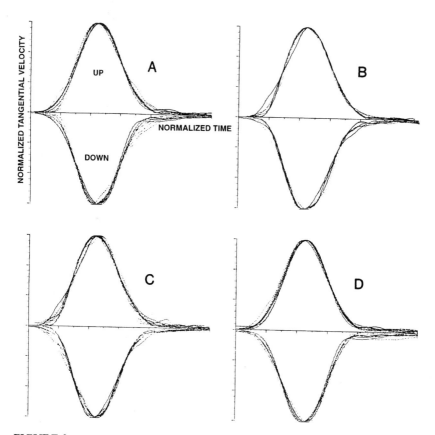

FIGURE 2   Tangential velocity profiles for the wrist during point-to-point reaching movements in the sagittal plane, normalized for speed and distance and aligned at their peaks. Each panel superimposes several profiles between which one or another parameter of the reach varied (speed, load, trajectory, or subject). The principal thing to note is that despite the variations in speed, load and trajectory—which variations have important consequences for which muscles must be contracted, when, and how strongly—the normalized tangential velocity profiles are all essentially the same (they superimpose). The upward profiles in each panel are for reaching in one direction (from point 1 to point 2); the downward deflections for reaching in the opposite direction (from point 2 to point 1). (A) Different speeds (duration of a constant-distance movement ≈ 400, 800, or 1200 ms). (B) Different loads (unloaded hand vs. 2- or 4-lb weight in hand). (C) Different trajectories. (The following descriptions of the different trajectories give the relation between the starting point and ending point; the actual trajectories were not always straight: straight-up and straight-down, straight-out and straight-back, up-and-out and down-and-in, up-and-in and down-and-out.) (D) Different subjects. (Reproduced from Atkeson and Hollerbach, 1985, p. 2326, with permission of the author and publisher.)

when carrying less weight. The pattern of required forces—the *relative* strengths of the forces that must be applied and the relative times at which they must be applied—must be altered in order to maintain the same profile as speed and load vary. This suggests that the kinematics of the movement are specified independently

sent to the muscles in advance function to develop the torques required to offset these reactive forces. This has led to the suggestion that in order to generate those components of the motor signal that reflect the need to offset the reactive forces, the trajectory planning process transiently specifies bogus equilibrium points well beyond the desired endpoint (Hogan et al., 1987). This bogus trajectory, which deviates from the actually intended trajectory in a manner that generates the torque components required to offset the reactive forces is called a virtual trajectory. The complex equilibrium-point trajectories observed by Gomi and Kawato (1996) might be interpreted as evidence of such complex virtual trajectories. However, it is not clear how the system could choose an appropriate virtual trajectory without solving the inverse kinematics and inverse dynamics problem, the problems that this model was intended to finesse.

Another problem with the moving-equilibrium-point hypothesis is that it does not support efficient adaptive modification of motor commands during practice, modifications that overcome changes in limb dynamics produced by growth, pathology, and working with implements that have substantial inertia (hammers, stones, spears, poles, tennis rackets, etc.; Atkeson, 1989). The problem is that because the nervous system has no representation of the relation between the kinematics and the dynamics, it has no way of relating the errors, which are kinematic (deviations from planned trajectories), to the dynamics (the pattern of forces that generated the trajectory). Thus, it cannot use observed trajectory errors to make goal-directed changes in the planning process; it can only proceed by random trial and error.

2. Adaptation to Artificially Manipulated Dynamics

Although roboticists have not yet made computer-controlled robots that can reach and wipe as well as a frog can, they have nonetheless made enough progress to permit highly instructive experimental manipulations of the forces that a human arm encounters during a reach. Shadmehr & Mussa-Ivaldi (1994) had subjects make targeted reaching movements while grasping a handle on the end of a low-inertia robot arm. The robot arm had computer-controlled torque motors at its joints, which enabled the computer to generate forces on the hand as it moved. Sensors in the joints gave the computer moment-by-moment information on the angular position and velocity of its joints, from which it could calculate the position and velocity of the subject's hand in body-centered space or the corresponding values in joint-angle space (that is, the angular position and velocity of the subject's joints) by just the sort of coordinate transformations that are the focus of this review. This arrangement enabled the experimenters to program the computer to generate novel velocity-dependent force fields. Because these forces were velocity-dependent (like the forces that oppose the stirring of molasses), they did not exist until the hand began to move.

The subjects made control reaches with the same hand in two different work spaces, one on their right and one on their left, before the velocity-dependent force fields were introduced. Then they made 1,000 reaches in the right work space in the presence (mostly) of the artificial velocity-dependent force field. When the subjects first encountered the novel forces, their trajectories veered far from the straight lines characteristic of normal reaches, and the velocity profiles were multimodal rather than bell-shaped. However, as they practiced making reaches in this bizarre dynamic environment, the trajectories again became straight and the velocity profiles bell-shaped.

During the subjects' adaptation to the artificially imposed force fields, a few trials where inserted on which the field was turned off. On these trials, the subjects' trajectories veered away from the normative in ways more or less opposite and equal to the veers induced by the artificial force field when they first encountered it. These veers are the aftereffects of the adaptation. They show that the nervous system is sending signals to the muscles that anticipate and counteract forces that will develop during the course of the planned movement. When the anticipated forces do not materialize, the muscle forces intended to counteract those forces cause veers.

The aftereffects prove that muscular forces designed to offset forces that will develop during the movement are programmed in advance into the signals sent to the muscles. In other words, the problem of generating the requisite forces is not solved primarily by feedback control; it is solved by feed-forward control. This same conclusion—that trajectory constancy is not obtained by stiffening the limb—follows from the finding that as subjects adapt to experimentally imposed perturbations in limb movements, limb stiffness declines rather than increases (Milner & Cloutier, 1993; van Emmerik, 1991). The nervous system tries to minimize deviations from programmed trajectories by increasing the gain of the visco-elastic feedback control loop only at first, before it has learned to compensate for the new reactive forces by feed-forward control.

The fact that the nervous system learns to compensate for new reactive forces by feed-forward control strongly suggests that it has a modifiable dynamic model of the limb (Jordan, 1994a, 1994b), which enables it to solve the inverse dynamics problem, the problem of calculating the forces required to implement a given trajectory and velocity profile. The model of the limb's dynamics has feedback-adjustable parameters. When the world changes so as to invalidate the model, the resulting error signals adjust the parameters of the model to make it once again a usable model of the limb's dynamics. The model may even be context-specific; that is, when you pick up a familiar implement like a tennis racket or a hammer, the central nervous system may switch in a different model of the limb's dynamics, a model that incorporates the contributions of the implement.

Perhaps the most elegant aspect of the Shadmehr and Mussa-Ivaldi (1994) experiment is that they trained their subjects with velocity-dependent force fields defined in the two different kinematic spaces: body-centered space and joint-angle space. For one group, the velocities and the resulting artificial forces were specified in joint-angle space, while for another group, they were specified in body-centered space. The force fields were chosen so that they were essentially identical when the hand was moving in the right work space, where the adaptation training took place. Thus, there was no way for the subject to know which space defined the artificial force field to which he was adapting. That is, there was no way of knowing whether a given force (with a certain magnitude and direction) was evoked by a joint-angle velocity or by the resulting velocity of the hand in body-centered space. However, when the adapted subjects moved their hand over into the left work space, the force fields produced by the two different programs were no longer identical in body-centered space. In fact, they were nearly orthogonal; that is, the force produced by one program in response to a given velocity of the hand in body-centered space was almost perpendicular to the force produced by the other program in response to the same velocity.

When the subjects shifted their reaches over to the left work space, they were tested with both field-generating programs and also with the imposed force field turned off. This allowed a decisive test of two important questions: (a) Did the adaptation transfer from one work space to another? (b) If so, did the transfer occur in body-centered space or in joint-angle space?

The adaptation did transfer from the right work space to the left one, and the transfer clearly occurred in joint-angle space, not body-centered space. When there was no force-imposing program in the left work space (the space in which they had not practiced), both groups of subjects showed strong and very similar veers (adaptation aftereffects). When the force field that depended on velocities in body-centered space was present in the transfer work space, the subjects showed strong veers, regardless of which program they had adapted to. The adaptation they had learned in the training work space did not enable them to compensate properly for the "same" forces in the new work space, where *same* means same if defined in body-centered space. By contrast, when the force field that depended on the joint-angle velocity vector was operative in the new work space, both groups of subjects compensated well. They did not make veers in the new work space when they encountered the "same" velocity-dependent forces they had encountered in the previous work space, where *same* now means same if defined in joint-angle space.

The fact that proper compensation transferred only when the force fields were defined with reference to joint-angle space not body-centered space is strong evidence that the inverse dynamics are computed after an inverse kinematics transformation. What the subjects learned were the forces required to implement a given trajectory (and velocity profile) in joint-angle space. How they could learn this if the trajectory in joint-angle space were not represented in the nervous system is unclear. The experiments by Wolpert et al. (1995) showing adaptation to false-visual curvature give strong evidence for trajectory planning in body-centered space. The Shadmehr and Mussa-Ivaldi results give strong evidence that the dynamics are computed from a trajectory specified in joint space. Together, these experiments argue for the succession of transformations envisioned by the engineering analysis: first a trajectory in body-centered space; then a derived trajectory in joint space (the inverse kinematics computation); finally, a derived feed-forward trajectory in muscle-force space (the inverse dynamics computation).

The transfer of the adaptation to the new work space implies that the inverse dynamics are not computed by means of a look-up table. A look-up table gives an output (e.g., a pattern of motor-neuron signals) for each input (e.g., a set of sensory signals indicating limb position and velocity and a set of command signals indicating a desired trajectory). The values of the signals that come into a look-up table do not define a position in a space, at least if the look-up table is what is called a "dumb" look-up table, one that does not do interpolation. With a dumb look-up table, there is no sense in which one incoming pattern of signals is close to (similar to) another pattern. Because there is no sense in which patterns recognized as distinct inputs are close or distant from one another, the dumb look-up table neither interpolates nor extrapolates.

Interpolation implies that inputs may be ordered along various continuous dimensions; that is, that they are points in a space on which a metric may be defined. (Look-up tables that do interpolation are called smart look-up tables.) Extrapolation implies not only that the inputs and outputs to the mapping are points in metric spaces, but also that the mapping between one region of the input space and its corresponding region in the output space defines the mapping for other regions of the input space. This is something akin to analyticity in the theory of functions, and, indeed, neural networks that specify a function over its entire domain are called function approximators. (A function is analytic if its behavior over any region of its domain [input] defines its behavior over its entire domain.)

The subjects in the Shadmehr and Mussa-Ivaldi (1994) experiment extrapolated the adaptation they learned during training in the right work space to the left work space. Moreover, and particularly to be remarked, this extrapolation was on the mark. The extrapolated control signals enabled them to produce straight trajectories in body-centered space in a new region of joint space (and body-centered space), provided that the force field was programmed in joint space. Anyone who has used a polynomial function to fit nonlinear data should be impressed by this, because the best-fitting polynomial generally deviates wildly from any plausible further data as soon as it gets outside the region for which one already has data. In other words, polynomial functions fitted to observations seldom correctly anticipate what will happen in a new region of the space being experimentally explored; they do not extrapolate correctly. The Shadmehr and Mussa-Ivaldi transfer results imply that in generating the motor commands from the joint-space kinematics, the nervous system operates with something akin to analytic functions, which are sufficiently accurate reflections of the limb's biomechanics that they yield valid extrapolations.

3. Dynamic Basis Functions

One of the most important ideas in the theory of metric spaces is the concept of a basis function, which may be thought of as a generalization of the notion of the basis for a vector space, one of the fundamental ideas in linear algebra. Recent experimental results suggest that this idea may have relevance to our understanding of how the nervous system generates the muscle commands that induce a limb to follow a planned trajectory (Bizzi & Mussa-Ivaldi, 1995; Giszter, Mussa-Ivaldi, & Bizzi, 1993; Mussa-Ivaldi, Giszter, & Bizzi, 1994).

A basis for a vector space is a set of points (that is, vectors) that may be scaled (multiplied by a scaling factor) and combined (by vector addition) to yield any point (any vector) in the space. The traditional basis for any three-dimensional physical space, such as the body-centered space, are the vectors that specify a point one arbitrarily chosen metric unit along each of the orthogonal axes—the x, y, and z axes by reference to which the positions of points in the space are defined. These orthogonal unit vectors are <1, 0, 0>, <0, 1, 0>, and <0, 0, 1>. Scaling one of these vectors means multiplying each of its components by some scaling factor, which can be any real number. Adding scaled vectors means adding (in the conventional arithmetic sense) corresponding components (the first component of one to the first component of the other, the second to the second, and the third to the third). Obviously, by these two operations applied to these orthogonal unit vectors, one can generate any sequence of three real numbers one wants, which is to say any point in the space. Thus, for example, the point <3.2, $\sqrt{2}$, π> is obtained by scaling the first basis vector by 3.2, the second by $\sqrt{2}$, and the third by π, then adding these scaled orthogonal unit vectors.

A basis function generalizes this idea to the (infinite) sets of points that constitute curves, that is, trajectories. (*Curves* in this usage include straight lines.) Probably the most generally familiar basis for continuous function space are the sine and cosine curves used in the Fourier decomposition and synthesis of a function. Roughly speaking, the Fourier theorem asserts that: (a) one may obtain any continuous curve (thus, any trajectory) by scaling and adding to each other (superimposing) some set of sine and cosine curves; and (b) for any given function, the requisite set and the required scaling factors are unique. Thus, the sine and cosine functions constitute a basis for a trajectory space—you can get any trajectory you want by scaling them and superimposing them, adding them up point by point. (For an illustrated introduction to the superimposing of sine and cosine curves, see Gallistel, 1980.) Technically speaking, it requires an infinite set of sine and cosine curves to make a basis for continuous function space, but, practically speaking, a good approximation to almost any trajectory can be achieved by scaling and superimposing a modest fixed set of sine and cosine curves—a set containing on the order of 50 curves. Thus, a finite set of sine and cosine curves can serve as a practical basis for generating any trajectory one wants.

The sine and cosine curves are by no means the only basis for trajectory space. There are many other possibilities, some of which offer appreciable advantages over the Fourier set in some contexts (e.g., wavelets, see Strang, 1994). The importance of the Fourier basis set in the present context is only to serve as an illustration of the general idea of a set of basis functions.

This short introduction to the concept of a set of basis functions is by way of preamble to a review of the results obtained by Giszter et al. (1993) and Mussa-Ivaldi et al. (1994), working with the spinal frog. They mapped out the force fields produced by brief (0.3 s) trains of low intensity (1–10 µÅ, 1-ms wide) anodal stimulating pulses delivered at 40 Hz through a microelectrode to interneuron pools in the spinal cord. To map the force field induced by the stimulation (the active force field), they anchored the ankle to a 6-axis force transducer on an x–y positioning stage and moved the foot to different points in body-centered space. At each position of the foot, they noted the force vector exerted by the limb before and during stimulation. By subtracting the force vector before stimulation from the force vector that developed during stimulation, they derived the *active* force vector as a function of time since the onset of stimulation.

The force vectors obtained from a gridwork of points in body-centered space define a force field. The static force field observed in the absence of stimulation and the active field developed during stimulation were generally *convergent*. That is, there was a point in space at which there was no force—the *equilibrium point*—and at all other points, the force vectors pointed along curves that converged on this equilibrium point. The static equilibrium point was the position to which the unstimulated frog's ankle would return if released from the positioning device, in other words, its resting posture. The active equilibrium point was the point to which the ankle would move during stimulation if it were free to move and if the static, pre-stimulation force field were absent. Not surprisingly, the strength of the vectors in the active field increased during stimulation.

The total force field acting on the ankle at any moment during the stimulating train was the superimposition (sum) of the static field and of the active field. The active field grew stronger over time since the onset of stimulation. Therefore, the equilibrium point of the summated force field moved during stimulation—to a point that was intermediate between the static and the active equilibrium points. The stronger the active field became relative to the static field, the nearer the equilibrium point of the summated field approached that of the active field. The authors term the trajectory of this moving equilibrium point of the summated field the *virtual trajectory*, to distinguish it from an actual trajectory the ankle would trace out if it were free to move. When they did allow the ankle to move from its resting position during stimulation, its actual trajectory was generally close to this virtual trajectory.

When they determined the active force fields produced at different depths as they moved the stimulating electrode deeper into the lateral portion of the cord at any given point along the anterior–posterior axis of the cord, they found that the force fields were very similar at different depths—a finding reminiscent of the columnar structure of receptive fields in sensory areas of the cortex. When they varied the strength (stimulating current) or duration of the train of pulses, they found that both of these manipulations served chiefly to change the lengths of the force vectors not their orientation nor the time course of their development. If the stimulating train is itself conceived of as a "pulse" input whose height is defined by the strength of stimulation (current $\times$ pulse frequency) and whose width is defined by train duration, then we can say that varying the energy in the pulse (its area) by varying either its width or height scales the active force field. The importance of this is that scaling the basis functions is one of the two operations by which other functions are synthesized from basis functions.

More interestingly—from the standpoint of where we are headed, which is toward a concept of dynamic basis set—they found that the active force fields from many different stimulating sites fell into only about four distinct classes of fields. Stimulation at sites in one class created a force field that moved the tip of the leg forward and out, stimulation at sites in another class moved it back and in, and so on. Most interestingly, when Mussa-Ivaldi et al. (1994) measured the force fields produced by stimulating simultaneously through two different electrodes that produced different classes of force fields, they found that the resulting active force field was the superimposition (the adding up) of the component active force fields. That is, for any given position of the frog's ankle in space and at any moment in time after stimulation onset, they could predict the active force vector by adding the active force vectors at that point and time obtained when stimulating at each field individually.[3]

Because the force fields superimposed, Mussa-Ivaldi et al. (1994) could predict the virtual trajectory produced by stimulating the two classes of interneuron pools simultaneously. Note, however, that it was not the virtual trajectory itself that could be obtained by superimposing the two virtual trajectories; rather it was the force field that could be obtained by superimposing the two force fields. Thus, if these different classes of force field-producing interneuron pools are basis functions for the generation of trajectories—which is what Mussa-Ivaldi et al. (1994) suggest they are—then the space for which they constitute a basis set is a dynamic space not a trajectory space.

These interneuron pools in the spinal cord may be a fundamental part of the neural machinery that computes the inverse dynamics. In fact, they could be the part whose output is modified during adaptation to novel dynamics, although it should be borne in mind that evidence of such adaptations has not been obtained in the frog. The system could use information about trajectory errors to alter the parameters of the circuits that create the force fields. This adaptive capacity at the level of the dynamic basis functions would make changes in the dynamics "transparent" to higher planning stages—something that they did not have to take into consideration in carrying out their coordinate transformations. However, as already

---

[3] A surprising finding in this research was the superimposition (additive combination) of the force fields elicited by direct stimulation of muscles in a limb whose inverse kinematics were not experimentally constrained (i.e., where many different points in joint space could correspond to a single point in anatomical space). This suggests that the biomechanics of limbs are not as intractably nonlinear as they are sometimes supposed to be. The muscles appear to insert in such a way that their effects combine additively even though they need not.

noted, this kind of adaptation requires that the nervous system have a model of the limb's dynamics, a model that represents the relation between force as a function of time and position as a function of time.

Dynamic basis functions may simplify the control problem from the standpoint of the higher stages of motor planning in two ways: (a) by reducing the degrees of freedom, the number of variables whose values need to be specified in order to obtain the desired output; and (b) by linearizing the "apparent" dynamics. They may, in effect, give the next stage up four control levers (assuming four basis functions) to "pull" on—for example, one giving a forward-and-outward force field converging on a stable position at the forwardmost and outermost limit of reach; a second giving a backward-and-outward force also converging on a stable limb position, that is, an equilibrium point; a third giving a backward-and-inward force (likewise convergent); and a fourth giving a forward-and-inward force (again convergent). Because the force fields superimpose when the next stage up pulls on more than one lever at a time, the consequences of various combinations of lever pulls are easily computed or modeled. This is the advantage of having a stage that linearizes the apparent dynamics.

C. Conclusions

The behavioral evidence—particularly the evidence from adaptation experiments—favors the view that there are three separable stages in the planning of a directed limb movement: a stage that plans the trajectory in three-dimensional body-centered space; an inverse kinematics stage, which translates this into a trajectory in joint space; and, finally, an inverse dynamics stage, which translates the joint-space trajectory into a dynamic, convergent force field.

A convergent force field is defined in that subspace of body-centered space consisting of all the positions that may be occupied by the endpoint of the limb. The force vectors acting on the end point of the limb at the positions in this space are all directed along curves that converge on a single equilibrium point, a point where the force vector is zero. In a dynamic, convergent force field, the equilibrium point traces out a trajectory; that is, it changes position over time. Thus, a dynamic convergent force field is a force field with an equilibrium point whose position changes over time.

Evidence from spinal cord microstimulation in the frog suggests that the inverse dynamics may be implemented by means of a modest set of interneuron pools, with each pool producing a dynamic basis function. These basis functions are the primitives from which all dynamic convergent force fields are synthesized by superimposition—the point-by-point addition of the force vectors. Concurrent activation of these interneuron pools generates the dynamic, convergent force field required to implement a joint-space trajectory. Thus, the problem of computing the inverse dynamics becomes the problem of determining which combinations of these basis functions must be activated and in what temporal sequence in order to produce the joint-space trajectory.

In humans at least, the system that computes the inverse dynamics adapts to an altered dynamic environment, an environment in which the viscous force (the velocity-dependent force) opposing the movement of a limb is artificially manipulated. This adaptation is not realized by stiffening the limb. The adaptation is invariant under translations of the altered dynamics computed in joint space but not under translations computed in body-centered space. That is, when the arm is in a new region of both joint space and body-centered space (when the joints have angles different from any they had during adaptation and, as a result, the hand is in a different location in body-centered space), the adapted nervous system nonetheless correctly anticipates the artificially altered forces that will oppose a reaching movement, *provided* that the artificial alterations in opposing viscous force are computed on the basis of the movements of the joints rather than the movements of the hand. (In other words, the system behaves as if it concluded that the joints had altered viscosity, rather than that the hand was moving through a medium with an altered viscosity.) When the artificial alterations in the forces that oppose the movement of the limb in this new part of the work space are computed on the basis of the direction in which the hand moves, rather than on the basis of the movement of the joints, then the adapted nervous system does not correctly anticipate the alterations in the apparent viscous force. This is an elegant and important result. It appears to be strong evidence that the joint-space trajectory is explicitly computed in the course of generating a movement, evidence, that is, that movements are represented both in body-centered space and in joint space.

The ability of the system to adapt to these perturbations in apparent viscosity with feed-forward corrections—that is, by programming forces that are calculated in advance to offset the alteration in the forces that will oppose the programmed movement—is thought to require at least a crude internal model of the dynamics, called a model of the "plant" (Atkeson, 1989; Jordan, 1994a). An internal model of the plant is a neural network that generates from a copy of the control signals sent to the muscles the expected pattern of signals from the sensors that report the limb trajectory actually achieved. In other words, the neural model is a stand-in for the limb itself; it mimics the manner in which the limb converts motor signals into sensory signals, signals that indicate the consequences of the muscle forces developed in response to the motor signals. Such a model is thought to be required in order for the system to make appropriate adjustments in the inverse dynamics mapping when the trajectories actually achieved deviate systematically and repeatedly from the trajectories specified by the planning process.

In planning trajectories in body-centered space, the system generally adopts trajectories that maximize smoothness, which is to say trajectories that minimize the jerk (the first derivative of acceleration). Jerk-minimizing trajectories are straight lines. This straightness is not a by-product of some other planning goal (e.g., a purely dynamic goal), because if the trajectories actually produced are made to appear curved when they in fact are not, the subject adapts; he begins to produce trajectories that are in fact curved but appear straight.

In computing the inverse kinematics (changes in joint angles required to move the hand through the specified trajectory in body-centered space), the nervous system must impose additional constraints to make the problem well posed, that is, to insure that there is a unique solution. Additional constraints must be imposed because there are infinitely many joint-space trajectories that will implement any given trajectory in body-centered space (the degrees of freedom problem). The further constraint that is imposed may again be a smoothness constraint; that is, the inverse kinematics transformation may pick out from this infinitude of joint-space trajectories the one that minimizes the jerk in joint space. It should be noted that this joint-space trajectory will not (necessarily) be the smoothest possible joint-space trajectory; rather, it will be the smoothest joint-space trajectory that implements the required body-centered trajectory. In other words, the system may first plan the smoothest possible body-centered trajectory, then plan the smoothest joint-space trajectory consistent with this body-centered trajectory (sequential constraint satisfaction).

III. SACCADIC EYE MOVEMENTS

A saccadic eye movement is a high-speed ballistic movement of the eyes from one direction of gaze to another. It may be directed to a punctate visual target; or, it may be elicited by an auditory stimulus and directed toward the computed position of the source; or, its direction may be specified by purely internal processes in the absence of any punctate target stimulus. It functions to bring the image of the source position (the position of the distal stimulus in head-centered space) onto the fovea. The movement is ballistic in the sense that it is not influenced by the movement of the visual field across the retina that ordinarily occurs during a saccade, that is, retinal feedback. Manipulating retinal feedback experimentally, for example, by stabilizing the retinal image, does not alter the trajectory of a saccade.

Although there is much that remains to be understood about the control of saccadic eye movements, this is nonetheless the best understood system from a neurobiological standpoint, and the one that provides the most compelling evidence for neuroanatomically distinct stages of coordinate transformation.

A. Integrator Coordinates: A Neurally Imposed Framework

One of the coordinate transformations that the saccade-generating neural circuitry must compute is necessitated by the peculiarities of rotational kinematics, namely, the nonorthogonality of rotations about orthogonal axes. A ball rotating in a socket has three degrees of rotational freedom: it can rotate horizontally (to the left or to the right about a vertical axis); it can rotate vertically (up or down about a transverse axis in the horizontal plane); and it can rotate torsionally clockwise or counterclockwise about a sagittal axis in the horizontal plane, an axis that passes through the pupil when the eye looks straight ahead).[4] To appreciate the nonorthogonality of positional changes in a three-dimensional rotational framework, imagine that the eye rotates horizontally 90° away from straight-ahead gaze. This rotation brings the pupil of the eye to the point where the transverse axis of rotation enters the eyeball. (Such an extreme rotation is anatomically impossible, but the consequences of this rotation are easy to visualize, and the conclusions that follow apply in intermediate degree for any intermediate rotation.) Now imagine that the eye rotates 45° "vertically," that is, about the transverse axis, which now passes through the pupil of the eye. During this rotation, the pupil remains in the horizontal plane (because it coincides with the axis of the rotation) and a cross drawn on the pupil rotates into an x. Imagine that the eye subsequently rotates 90° horizontally back to a straight-ahead gaze. In this sequence, the eye never rotated about the chosen torsional axis, but it has nonetheless undergone a 45° torsional rotation. Thus, a retinal receptive field that had a vertical orientation before we started will now be oriented 45° away from vertical. Two equal and opposite rotations about our vertical axis (90° to one side and then 90° back) with an intervening rotation about our transverse axis yield a change in eye position that could have been produced by a single rotation about the torsional axis and no rotation about the transverse axis. This is weird. It happens, because as soon as the eye rotates horizontally by any amount away from the straight-ahead position, then any rotation about the transverse axis (the axis for 'vertical' rotations) becomes to some extent also a rotation about the torsional axis.

Donders law says that torsional changes in the eye's position in the socket do not occur during saccades. That is, at any moment during a saccade the eye occupies a position that could have been reached from the straight-ahead, zero-torsion primary position of the eye by a rotation about an axis that lies in the plane defined by transverse and vertical axes perpendicular to the direction of gaze when the eye is in the primary position. These axes define a transverse plane that divides the eye into a front half and a back half. This plane—the plane perpendicular to the primary direction of gaze—is sometimes called Listing's plane. All eye positions reachable from the primary position by a rotation about an axis in this plane have the property that the images of vertical lines align with vertical meridians on the retina (great circles intersecting at the vertical axis) and the images of horizontal lines align with horizontal meridians (great circles intersecting at the transverse axis). Thus, the

---

[4] The consequences of a sequence of such rotations can be hard to visualize. To follow this exposition, the reader may find it useful to take the ball out of a computer mouse and mark a cross at the "pupil" of this ball, taking care to distinguish the horizontal and vertical bars of this cross. The axis for horizontal rotations passes vertically through the center of the ball. When the ball is held with a fingertip on top and the thumb on the bottom, it rotates about this axis. The axis for vertical rotations passes transversely through the center of the ball. Holding the ball at the points where a transverse axis intersects its surface, allows one to rotate it vertically. To make pure torsional rotations, you have to place the fingertip on the pupil and the thumb diametrically opposite the pupil, so that the axis of rotation lies in the sagittal plane, rather than the transverse plane.

orientations in inertial space of the lines to which simple cells in V1 are most sensitive are the same for all such positions of the eye. A receptive field that is vertical on the retina will be maximally stimulated by a vertical line, no matter what the direction of gaze nor how that direction was reached.

The eye's position is specified in a three-dimensional rotational space, all of whose dimensions are angular (degrees of rotation). Often, the positions of the eye during saccades are said to lie in Listing's plane, because Listing's plane may also be conceived of as the zero-torsion plane in rotational space.[5] The dual meaning of the term *Listing's plane* is confusing, because the two planes referred to are not the same. In fact, they are planes in two different, nonisomorphic spaces. One plane, which I will hereafter call Listing's axes plane, is defined by a set of axes of rotation in a Cartesian head-centered space. The other, which I will call Listing's position plane, is defined by a set of eye positions in a rotational space. Listing's coordinates specify two-dimensional eye positions (that is, directions of 0-torsion gazes) in terms of the direction in which the gaze is imagined to depart from the primary position (the origin of the system of coordinates) and the magnitude of the rotation made in this direction.

Donder's law, which is sometimes called Listing's law, has sometimes been thought to be a consequence of the biomechanics of the eye. However, the eye occupies positions that are not in Listing's position plane during the smooth portions of vestibular nystagmus (Crawford & Vilis, 1991), during smooth pursuit eye movements (Westheimer & McKee, 1973), and during sleep (Nakayama, 1975). This implies that the eye is not biomechanically constrained always to occupy a position in Listing's position plane. Moreover, whenever the eye is not in its primary position at the start of a saccade, then the axis of rotation during that saccade does not lie in Listing's axes plane (Tweed & Vilis, 1990). When the eye deviates α degrees from the primary position at the start of the saccade, then the axis of rotation for the saccade lies in a plane that is tilted by $\alpha/2°$ away from Listing's axes plane in the direction of α (Villis & Tweed, 1991). In other words, the axes of rotation that maintain the eye in Listing's position plane only lie in Listing's axes plane if the starting point of the saccade is the primary position. For other starting positions, the axis of the rotation lies outside Listing's axes plane. Thus, the eye is certainly not biomechanically constrained to rotate only about axes that lie in Listing's axes plane. Finally, and most tellingly, Listing's axes plane varies substantially within a subject over time. It varies more widely than can plausibly be attributed to variations in biomechanics (Crawford, 1994; Ferman, Collewijn, & Van den Berg, 1987; Tweed & Villis, 1990).

---

[5] This is a plane in the mathematical sense not the physical sense. Mathematically, a 'plane' is an (infinite) two-dimensional set of points in a three-dimensional space. A two-dimensional set of points is a set of three-dimensional position vectors (points in a 3-dimensional space) that do not vary along one of the three dimensions after an appropriate rotation of the framework. Thus, the set of all positions in rotational space that have zero torsion constitute a plane in the mathematical sense.

One often imagines that coordinate frameworks are imposed on the nervous system by our analysis—that the framework is in the mind of the theorist, or in the practical necessities of the experimentalist, not in the brain of the subject (Robinson, 1992). In implementing Donders' law, however, the nervous system establishes a coordinate framework of its own, because the positions that the eye assumes during saccadic eye movements have zero torsion only if one correctly identifies the primary position of the eye, and it is the nervous system that determines what that primary position is. Recall that Listing's axes plane is by definition the transverse plane through the center of the eye *orthogonal to the direction of gaze when the eye is in its primary position.* If the experimenter assumes a primary position of the eye that is not the one the nervous system specifies, then the experimenter's measurements of eye position during saccades will yield points (three-angle eye-position vectors) that do not have zero torsion in the experimenter's system of coordinates.[6] The positions assumed by the eye as it jumps around has zero-torsion only when the experimenter correctly identifies the primary position of the eye. In fact, this is in essence how one determines the primary direction of gaze and hence, the orientation of Listing's position plane: one rotates the coordinate-framework in which the measured eye positions are expressed until one finds the orientation that minimizes the departures from 0 along the torsional dimension (Tweed, Cardera, & Villis, 1990). The primary position of the eye varies widely between subjects—by as much as 30°—and it also varies substantially within subjects over time—by as much as 14° (Crawford, 1994; Ferman et al., 1987; Tweed et al., 1990).

Crawford (1994) demonstrated that the neural integrators that maintain static eye positions establish an intrinsic coordinate system for eye positions. His experiments exploited two aspects of our extensive knowledge of the neurobiology of oculomotor control. *First,* the motor signals that govern the eye muscles during and after a saccade are programmed in a pulse-and-step pattern (Robinson, 1975). The pulse is an initial burst of motor neuron firing, which generates the force required to accelerate the eye to the peak velocity that it reaches during the saccade. The greater the magnitude of the saccade, the greater the peak velocity, and the stronger this initial burst of firing. (The size of the pulse also varies as a function of the position of the eye in the orbit at the beginning of the saccade.) The step is the sustained change in firing required to maintain the eye in its new position. Remarkably, the nervous system computes the step by integrating the pulse (Robinson, 1989). Thus, the change in the sustained rate of motor neuron firing is proportional to the area of the pulse. *Second,* the nervous system decomposes sustained changes in eye position (position steps) into horizontal and vertical-torsional components, which are realized by distinct integrators. The integrator for the horizontal component is in the nucleus prepositus hypoglossi (Cannon & Robinson, 1987; Cheron & Godaux, 1987; Straube, Kurszan, & Büttner, 1991), whereas the integrators for

[6] Clinicians refer to torsions that arise from choosing a coordinate system other than the zero-torsion Listing's system as "false torsions."

the vertical-torsional components are in the interstitial nucleus of Cajal (Buttner, Buttner-Ennever, & Henn, 1977; Crawford & Villis, 1991, 1993; King & Moore, 1991).

It is possible to knock out an integrator and hence the step change in firing that it produces without knocking out the pulse that determines the saccadic trajectory. When the pulse remains but the step is gone, the eye jumps to its new position in response to the burst of motor neuron firing that constitutes the pulse, but then, because the step change in firing is absent, it drifts back to the origin (0-point) of the integrator's axis, following an exponential time course.

Crawford (1994) reasoned—and confirmed by simulation—that if he knocked out the vertical-torsional integrators but not the horizontal integrator, then the eye would drift back to a resting position on the horizontal axis of Listing's plane after each saccade. Following saccades with different horizontal components, the eye would come to rest at different points along the horizontal axis. Also the postsaccadic drift trajectories would parallel the vertical axis of the intrinsic coordinate system. Thus, from the static resting positions to which the eye drifted, one could determine the horizontal axis of the integrator-imposed coordinate system; and from the drift trajectories, one could determine the orientation of the vertical axis. In short, knocking out the vertical-torsional integrators makes both axes of the neurally imposed coordinate framework manifest in the postsaccadic drifts in eye position. These two axes define a plane. If Listing's zero-torsion coordinate framework is imposed by the neural integrators in the intact preparation, then the orientation of the plane determined by drift trajectories after knocking out the vertical-torsional integrators should agree with the orientation determined from the eye positions observed in the intact preparation.

Crawford made repeated experiments on the same monkeys. In each experiment, he first determined Listing's position plane from the positions assumed by the eye during normal saccades and then he temporarily knocked out the vertical-torsional integrators by injecting muscimol into the interstitial nucleus of Cajál (which is a midline structure). The axes established by the postsaccadic drifts observed after temporarily knocking out the vertical-torsional integrators defined a plane that aligned closely with the zero-torsion plane derived from preinjection saccades. Moreover, the orientations of the planes defined in these two different ways showed strong day-to-day within-subject covariation. The primary position of the eyes (the origin of Listing's zero-torsion coordinate system) changed substantially from day to day—by as much as 14°. This change was seen both in the orientation of the zero-torsion plane in the intact subject and in the orientation of the plane defined by the drift trajectories after muscimol injection.

It is important to bear in mind that the axes of the integrator coordinate system are not the axes of Listing's coordinates. The axes of Listing's coordinates are direction (angle with respect to the horizontal plane) and amplitude (angle of rotation from the primary position in the specified direction). There is no vertical axis in the coordinate framework that Listing suggested for describing torsion-free eye positions. By contrast, the axes of the integrator's coordinates are horizontal and vertical. This means that the horizontal and vertical-torsional pulses that cause saccadic eye movements must be computed in such a way as to maintain the eye in the zero-torsion positions demanded by Donders' law. To do this, the circuitry that generates these motor pulses must take into account the position of the eye at the start of the saccade. The burst of motor neuron firing that produces the same *change* in eye position (e.g., 10° to the right and 5° up) differs depending on the starting position of the eye. In other words, the innervation received by the eye muscles must specify a change from one absolute position of the eye to another, not simply a relative change in position (Nakayama, 1975; Westheimer, 1981).

By specifying saccadic changes in eye position in a zero-torsion coordinate framework of its own devising, the oculomotor system reduces the degrees of freedom in saccadic eye movements from three to two. This neurally imposed reduction in the degrees of freedom of a joint is not unique to the eye. The orientation of the head during combined head and eye gaze shifts and the orientation of the wrist during pointing are similarly constrained (Hepp & Hepp-Reymond, 1989; Tweed & Vilis, 1992). Thus, it may be possible to discover neurally imposed coordinate systems at other joints with three degrees of rotational freedom.

B. The Representation of Saccades in the Superior Colliculus

Whereas the brain stem circuits generating the motor neuron firing that moves the eye must reckon with the position of the eye in the orbit as well as the desired change in its position, the superior colliculus simply specifies the desired change in the direction of gaze in a coordinate system whose origin is the current direction of gaze. The activity of neurons in the deep layers of the superior colliculus specify the deviation between the direction of gaze and the target. Target positions computed in other coordinate frameworks—the retinal framework in the case of visual inputs, a head-centered coordinate framework in the case of auditory inputs—are mapped to this common coordinate system for the production of saccadic changes in the direction of gaze.

1. The Mapping of Computed Gaze Error

A fascinating aspect of this coordinate system is that there is a topographic mapping of computed gaze error onto anatomical dimensions of the superior colliculus, so that adjacent neurons (or adjacent columns of neurons) in the superior colliculus represent adjacent positions of the distal target in a gaze-centered coordinate system (Sparks & Groh, 1995). This mapping of gaze error is unlike other familiar topographic mappings, such as the mapping of the retina onto V1 or the mapping of the cochlear membrane onto the primary auditory cortex, in that it is not a topographic mapping of a sensory surface. A stimulus falling anywhere on the retina or vibrating any point along the basilar membrane of the cochlea can activate any position in the deep collicular mapping of gaze error. In fact, because units in this mapping of gaze-error space may be driven by either visual or auditory input, the firing of units in this mapping does not necessarily indicate which sensory epithelium (retinal or cochlear) was stimulated, let alone the position on one of those sensory surfaces excited by the proximal stimulus. In short, this is a mapping of the position of the distal stimulus, not of the position(s) of the proximal stimulus(i).

The topographic mapping of gaze error is delineated by the results of microstimulation at different sites in the superior colliculus and by recordings from neurons at those sites. Stimulating a site in the colliculus elicits a saccade that is a systematic function of the position stimulated. The elicited saccade shows only a weak dependence on the position of the eye in the orbit. Thus, for example, if the stimulation elicits a saccade of magnitude 5° directed up and to the right at an angle of 45° from the horizontal when the eye is initially in the primary position, then renewed or continued stimulation will elicit a second such saccade, at the end of which the eye is roughly 10° away from the primary position along the 45° direction line. A roughly but not exactly equivalent statement is that both saccades will have horizontal and vertical components of about 3.5°.

Figure 3 shows the motor map obtained by Robinson (1972) in one such study. The appropriate coordinate framework for describing these results is an interesting question, with computational and neurobiological implications. Robinson described the saccades he elicited in terms of their direction and magnitude. His map of the effects of stimulation is given in Figure 3B. As he moved his stimulating electrode from the rostral margin of the left superior colliculus back to the caudal margin along a line that bisected the collicular surface, he elicited horizontal saccades of increasing magnitude. If he moved his stimulating electrode away from this central axis toward the dorsomedial margin of the colliculus, the saccades elicited were directed upward as well as laterally. The closer the electrode was to the dorsomedial margin, the more the direction of the saccade deviated from the horizontal direction. Thus, the direction of the elicited saccade (its deviation from horizontal) varied as a function of how far the electrode was from the horizontal axis (the line of stimulating positions that elicited purely horizontal saccades).

Another way of describing the same results is to say that the horizontal components of the elicited saccades were determined by the position of the stimulating electrode along a rostro-caudal axis, whereas the vertical components were determined by its position along a dorsomedial to ventrolateral axis. The coordinate framework for this alternative description is given in Figure 3C.

At this same time, Schiller and Stryker (1972) published the results of an experiment in alert monkeys in which they immobilized one eye, so that they could determine the "receptive field" of units at a given position in the superior colliculus. They left the other eye mobile, so that they could determine the saccade elicited by stimulating through the electrode used for recording. They found that when, for example, the units at a given position were sensitive to stimuli located 10° lateral to the fovea and 10° above the horizontal, then stimulation at that site elicited a sac-

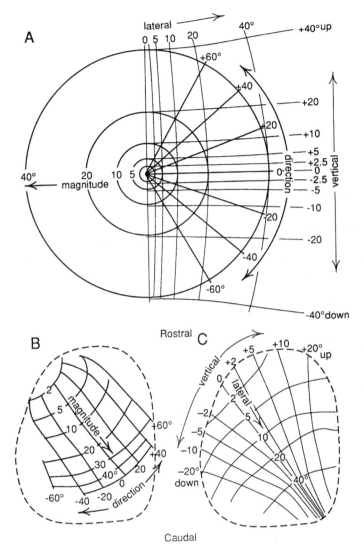

FIGURE 3 (A) Two coordinate frameworks for representing saccades—the magnitude-direction framework and the horizontal-vertical framework (also called the lateral-vertical, or azimuth-elevation framework). The concentric circles represent saccades of equal magnitude (2.5, 5, 10, 20, or 40°) in the magnitude-direction framework. The radial lines represent saccades in the same direction. The bowed vertical lines represent saccades whose horizontal component has a given magnitude. The bowed horizontal lines represent saccades whose vertical component has a given magnitude. Formulae for converting m–d coordinates to h–v coordinates frameworks are: $v = \sin^{-1}[\sin(d)\sin(m)]$ and $h = \tan^{-1}[\cos(d)\tan(m)]$. Formulae for the reverse conversion are $m = \cos^{-1}[\cos(h)\cos(v)]$ and $d = \tan^{-1}[\tan(v)/\sin(h)]$. (B) The results of Robinson's microstimulation experiment represented with the m–d system of coordinates. (Reprinted from *Vision Research, 12,* D. A. Robinson, Eye movements evoked by collicular stimulation in the alert monkey, pp. 1795–1808, © 1972, with permission from Elsevier Science. (C) Approximately how Robinson's results would look if they were represented in h–v coordinates.

cade with a $10°$ horizontal component and a $10°$ vertical component; that is, a saccade whose direction $(45°)$ and magnitude $(14°)$ were such as to foveate a stimulus at the distal position to which the units at that site were most sensitive.

The term *receptive field* is enclosed in quotes above, because subsequent work by Mays and Sparks (1980) showed that visually sensitive units in the deeper layers of the superior colliculus do not have retinal receptive fields in the ordinary meaning of the term. There is no fixed area of the retina where a stimulus must fall in order to elicit firing from these deeper units, because the deep layers combine retinal position information with eye position information to map the position of visual sources in a gaze-centered coordinate system. Mays and Sparks used a double-saccade paradigm to dissociate the retinal position of the proximal stimulus from the gaze error of the distal stimulus position at the time the foveating saccade is made.

In the double-saccade paradigm, there are two brief flashes. The second flash is delivered before the eye initiates the saccade that foveates the first flash. Both flashes are gone before the eye makes any saccade. In response to the two flashes, the monkey makes two saccades—an initial saccade that foveates the position from which the first flash originates and a second saccade that foveates the position from which the second flash originates. Suppose that one records from a site that is ordinarily excited by a stimulus $10°$ to the right and $10°$ above the direction of gaze. Suppose one delivers a first flash that is $10°$ to the left and $10°$ below the direction of gaze and a second flash that is directly in the direction of gaze. The second flash falls on the fovea, not on the putative receptive field of the units one is recording from. However, the first flash elicits a saccade $10°$ to the left and $10°$ down. After this saccade, the gaze error for the distal position from which the second flash came is now $10°$ right and $10°$ up. A flash from this position would activate the recording site. However, the second flash came and went before the eye made the first saccade, and, as already noted, this second flash in fact fell on the fovea, well outside the putative receptive field of the units recorded from. Nonetheless, the units show a response to the second flash, but this response develops only after the eye makes the first saccade. The units respond to the second flash only when the distal position from which that flash originated comes to occupy the position in a gaze-centered framework to which these units are sensitive. Thus, their response to a flash is jointly determined by information from the sensory epithelium, indicating where the flash fell on the retina (in this case, the fovea), and by a position signal, indicating the intervening displacement of the eye. The signal giving the eye's displacement vector and the signal giving the retinal position of the proximal stimulus (the retinal position vector) are combined in such a way as to make the units in the deep layers of the superior colliculus sensitive to the position of the distal stimulus in a coordinate framework centered on the current direction of gaze. The combinatorial operation is equivalent to vector subtraction.

Units in these same deep layers are also sensitive to the distal position (azimuth and elevation) of an auditory stimulus source. This position is computed in head-centered coordinates by a sequence of operations that use small differences in the intensity and time of arrival of sound waves at the two ears. The sequence of computations culminates in a head-centered topographic map of auditory space in the external nucleus of the *inferior* colliculus (Konishi, 1995).[7] This map is then relayed to the superior colliculus, where it is transformed into a gaze-centered map of auditory space. Because the mapping of auditory space in the superior colliculus is gaze-centered rather than head-centered, a coordinate transformation is required. An eye displacement vector must be subtracted from the head-centered auditory position vector to yield a gaze-centered auditory position vector. A consequence of this coordinate transform is that the position in the deep layers of the superior colliculus excited by a sound source at a given head-centered position changes as the eyes change position in the orbit (Jay & Sparks, 1987). Equivalently, the position in head-centered coordinates of the *auditory* stimulus source to which a unit in the deep layers of the superior colliculus is most sensitive changes as the *eye* changes its position in the orbit.

The transformations demonstrated neurobiologically by the work of Sparks and his collaborators are the sorts of transformations that we inferred from the ability of the spinal frog to scratch its elbow with its hind limb regardless of the relative position of the two limbs (Figure 1). In that case, the sensory epithelium was the surface of the forelimb rather than the retina. The displacements that had to be combined with this sensory signal to determine the direction in which the hind limb had to move were the changes in the angular positions of the two limbs. The great importance of the work on the superior colliculus—and similar work in other areas (Bruce, 1990; Bruce & Goldberg, 1990; Gnadt & Andersen, 1988; Russo & Bruce, 1994)—is that it demonstrates that these sorts of coordinate transformations are explicitly carried out in the operation of the nervous system. The nervous system carries out the inferred coordinate transformations and creates electrophysiologically observable topographic mappings of the resulting spaces. It does not *"act as if"* it carried out such transformations; it really does them.

2. The Position or Displacement Signal Comes from Corollary Discharge

The eye-position or eye-displacement vector that is used in computing the current gaze error does not come from sensory receptors, because animals in which this sensory input has been eliminated nonetheless compensate for changes in eye position (Guthrie, Porter, & Sparks, 1983). This finding has implications similar to the finding that the reaching system can adapt to artificial dynamic perturbations with feedforward corrections, forces that are programmed in anticipation of forces that will arise during a movement. The adaptation findings imply that the system has an internal model of the dynamics. The finding that the eye position or displacement vector is based on corollary discharge or efference copy implies that the system has

---

[7] This is the case, at least in the barn owl, where work on the neurobiology of auditory scene analysis is most extensive. An equivalent analysis has yet to be done in a primate.

an internal model of the relation between these command discharges and the changes in position that they may be expected to produce. Recall that to generate the enduring discharge of motor neurons that holds the eye in place after a saccade, the nervous system integrates the initial "pulse," the brief burst of firing that specifies the velocity and duration of the saccade. Thus, the displacement signal in these coordinate transformations derives from integrating a velocity signal with respect to time.

3. Computational Implications of Choosing Different Coordinates

The units in the deep layers of the superior colliculus are broadly tuned, like units in the many other topographic mappings in sensory–perceptual areas. Each unit has a best direction, a gaze error for which it fires most vigorously, but it also fires to some extent prior to saccades in a cluster of directions centered around its best direction. Thus, prior to any saccade, there is a substantial population of active neurons. Each active neuron may be thought of from a computational perspective as a vector pointing at a particular gaze error, the gaze error represented by its position in the topographic mapping of gaze-error space. Two questions arise: (a) What is the combinatorial operation that determines the resulting saccade from the activity of a population of adjacent active neurons each of which codes for a slightly different gaze error? (b) What are the computationally meaningful coordinates for describing the position of a unit in gaze-error space?

Two simple kinds of combinatorial decision processes might decide the direction: (a) Winner take all—the saccade made is determined by the coordinates of the most active unit, or (b) a vector-combining operation in which the gaze error that determines the saccade is derived from the coordinates of all the active units, weighting the contribution of each according to how active it is. Lee, Rohrer, and Sparks (1988) and Sparks, Lee, and Rohrer (1990) report results that point toward the second alternative. In a winner-take-all scheme, inactivating with lidocaine the center of the active population—that is, temporarily knocking out the units that are firing most vigorously—should alter the direction and magnitude of the resulting saccade, because it should knock out the "winner," shifting the site of greatest activity (hence, the location of the winner) away from the center of the population. Conversely, inactivating units on the margin of the active population—units that are less active than units at the center—should have no effect on the direction and magnitude of the resulting saccade, because the activity level of the winning position is unaffected by such an injection. However, Lee et al. (1988) showed that inactivating the center of the population did not alter the direction and magnitude of the saccade, although it did greatly reduce its velocity (see also Sparks et al., 1990). They further showed that inactivating units on the margin of the active population moved the resulting saccade away from the saccades coded for by the area that was inactivated. Thus, if the center of the active population coded for purely lateral (0-direction) saccades of magnitude 10°, and one inactivated cells coding for saccades lying above and to the left of that in gaze-error space, then the resulting saccade was down and to the right of the saccade that one would have observed in the absence of the inactivation. This shows that the activity of units on the margin of the active population helps to determine the saccade, which implies that the gaze errors indicated by all the active units are summed or averaged to determine the saccade.

But which is it—summing or averaging? In describing the Lee et al. (1988) experiment, I mixed two distinct frames of reference that may be used to describe gaze errors and the resulting saccades. I referred to the center of the active population in terms of the direction (0°) and magnitude (10°) of the indicated gaze error. Direction and magnitude are the coordinates in Figure 3B. However, in the same sentence, I referred to the inactivated cells as lying above and to the left of the gaze error indicated by the center of the active population. The lateral (to the left, to the right) and vertical (above, below) dimensions are the coordinates used in Figure 3C. This highlights the fact that it is not obvious simply from the data what kinds of vectors we should use to represent a unit's contribution to the determination of the saccade vector.

From the standpoint of the computations needed to specify a saccade, it matters which framework we use. If we use a two-dimensional direction-and-magnitude framework, then we have to assume that the combinatorial operation is equivalent to vector averaging. Moreover, we have to imagine a conversion somewhere else from the direction-and-magnitude specification of the saccade vector to a specification in terms of the horizontal and vertical components of the saccade, because we know that there are separate brain stem nuclei for the horizontal and vertical components. Finally, we have to use a different combinatorial operation to specify saccade velocity from the overall level of activity in the population.

On the other hand, if we think of active units as equivalent to three-dimensional vectors, then we have to assume only simple vector summation as the combinatorial operation that specifies the saccade and this same operation gives the velocity of the saccade. Moreover, if we assume that the positions of units in the superior colliculus specify the horizontal and vertical components of saccades (Figure 3C), rather than their direction and magnitude (Figure 3B), then this same operation gives what the next stage needs, namely, the horizontal and vertical components of the required saccade.

If we follow the conventional practice of thinking of vectors as arrows, then in a two-dimensional, direction-and-magnitude framework, an active unit is at the point of an arrow whose tail is at the origin of the coordinate system. The origin of the direction-magnitude coordinate system is the upper left corner of Figure 3B, the point toward which the direction lines are converging. This point corresponds to the current direction of gaze. The activity of the unit (how fast it is firing) is not a dimension of the vector in this scheme; it serves merely to determine the relative weight that will be given to that vector when the error vectors are averaged. Thinking of the active units as arrows lying on the collicular surface makes it obvious why we cannot combine the vectors for active units by simple summation. Vector summation is equivalent to moving one of the arrows so that its tail coincides with the point of the other. The position of the point of the moved arrow is then the vector sum. Thus, summing two adjacent units, both specifying a saccade of 0° direction and magnitude 10° would yield a gaze error of 0° direction and a magnitude of roughly 30° (as may be verified by carrying out this operation on Figure 3B). Thus, the vectors resulting from simple summation are much too long; they specify impossibly big saccades. To make the results of the combinatorial operation plausible, the sum of the weighted error vectors must be normalized by the sum of the weights, that is, the nervous system must compute not the vector sum but the vector average. In computing this average, it must first scale each vector by its firing rate, then sum the scaled vectors, then divide that sum by the sum of all the firing rates.

However, we need not think of the active units as corresponding to two-dimensional vectors. It takes three numbers to describe an active unit—two to specify its position in the superior colliculus and one to specify its firing rate. This encourages us to think of active units as three-dimensional vectors. To visualize *these* vectors as arrows, we may think of the surface in Figure 3C as wrapped on a globe. The origin of the coordinate system, where the vector tails are pinned, is not on the surface shown in Figure 3C, it is at the center of the globe. The three-dimensional vector corresponding to an active unit does not lie on the surface of Figure 3C; rather it penetrates that surface. Where it penetrates the surface gives a position in gaze-error space. The third dimension of these vectors—their length—is the firing rate of the unit. The greater the length of one of these vectors, the farther it projects beyond the gaze-error surface. This length may be thought of as the vigor with which an active unit urges the eye to make the move indicated by the unit's position in gaze-error space. This vigor translates into the velocity of the saccade; the more vigorously the unit fires, the faster the saccade it calls for. If these are the neurobiologically meaningful coordinates for describing positions in the superior colliculus's mapping of gaze-error space, then the specification of the horizontal and vertical components of the saccade *and* its velocity require only the equivalent of vector summation—the summation of the vectors corresponding to all the units in the active population. The point where the resultant vector penetrates the surface gives the lateral and vertical components of the saccade. The length of the resultant vector specifies its velocity.

The vector-summation model, which replaces vector averaging with vector summation by treating the vectors as three dimensional rather than two dimensional, gives a computationally simpler explanation of the results of the lidocaine experiment.[8] Lidocaine injected into the center of the population will not alter the position at which the resultant vector penetrates the surface, because the direction

[8] One of the schemes proposed by Sparks and Mays (1990) for extracting the horizontal component of a saccade from the activity of a population of units in the superior colliculus implicitly assumes that the horizontal–vertical framework is the appropriate framework (see Figure 1 in Sparks & Mays, 1990).

of the resultant (where it penetrates the surface) will not be altered by knocking out arrows distributed symmetrically around the resultant. However, by removing the longest contributors to the resultant (the most active units), the injection will reduce the length of the resultant. And, the length of the resultant specifies velocity. Thus, knocking out vectors in the center of the active population should reduce the velocity of the saccade without altering its direction and magnitude. Lidocaine injected to one side of the population center will shift the point at which the resultant vector penetrates the surface away from the site of injection by removing the contribution of the vectors pointing to the positions where the lidocaine was injected. If the lidocaine is injected on the caudal (more lateral) margin of the population, it will shift the direction of the resultant medially towards gaze errors of smaller magnitude, resulting in hypometric saccades, saccades that are shorter than they should be. If it is injected on the rostral (more medial) margin, it will shift the resultant laterally toward gaze errors of greater magnitude, producing hypermetric saccades, saccades that are bigger than they should be. These are the results that Lee et al. (1988) in fact obtained.

IV. CONCLUDING REMARKS

Behavioral and neurobiological data support the conclusion that the positions of targets, the trajectories of target-directed movements, and the trajectories of forces required to drive those movements are represented in the nervous system in a sequence of different, explicitly computed coordinate frameworks. Thus, an understanding of the circuitry and cellular mechanisms by which coordinate transforms of various kinds may be computed is a fundamental goal of integrative neuroscience. The behavioral analysis of the coordinate transformations that mediate directed actions has a major role to play in the description and elucidation of these mechanisms, because the behavioral analysis tells us what transformations to look for.

In many cases, the computed spaces are realized through the topographic arrangement of units tuned to different positions in the space. Units at a given location in these topographic mappings of abstract spaces become excited when the target or trajectory occupies the region of that space to which the unit is tuned. The center of this region, the position that corresponds to the maximum firing, is the best position of the unit. The mapping of positions in the space to which neurons are tuned is said to be topographic when units that are adjacent neuroanatomically are tuned to adjacent best positions.[9] *Adjacent* here has a purely mathematical meaning, because some of the spaces that may be topographically mapped may not have

---

[9] The term *topographic*, which has become standard in the neurobiological literature, may have arisen from a confounding of *topographic* with *topological*. In mathematics, a topological mapping is one that preserves adjacency but not distance and angle. A topographic map, on the other hand, is a map of (some part of) the earth's surface that encodes elevations as well as horizontal locations (latitudes and longitudes). In neurobiology, however, topographic mapping means a mapping that preserves adjacency.

a simple physical interpretation. An example of a space without a simple physical interpretation of adjacency would be a trajectory space. "Points" in such a space specify trajectories formed by the superposition of basis functions. The different basis functions constitute the axes of such a space. The dimensionality of the space is equal to the number of basis functions from which trajectories are synthesized. The values along these dimensions give the scaling values for the basis function—how much of this basis function to use when adding up the various contributions to determine the resultant function. Points in such a space are adjacent if the scaling values for corresponding basis functions are all adjacent; that is, if the value of each dimension in one vector is adjacent to the value for the same dimension in the other vector. As psychologists become more sophisticated about coordinate transforms and basis functions, these sorts of highly abstract "spaces" are likely to play a more prominent role in our analysis of directed actions.

Directed action has been treated here in a circumscribed and literal sense—to refer to actions in which the optical axis of the eye is to be directed to a given target or a hand or foot is to be moved to a given target. Directed action in a more general sense—action that accomplishes some goal—requires for its analysis a much broader range of principles and mechanisms. Some of those mechanisms—the different kinds of elementary units of behavior, how they are coordinated into complex units of behavior, the hierarchical structure of the resulting complex units, and the mechanisms for coordination within that hierarchy—have been described and illustrated elsewhere (Gallistel, 1980, 1994).

The coordinate transformations that mediate simple directed actions may prove directly relevant to another aspect of directed action—navigation, moving the whole animal to a target. Navigation depends on the construction and use of a cognitive map. Both the construction of a map and its use require coordinate transformations strikingly similar to those discussed here (Gallistel, 1998, 1990; Gallistel & Cramer, 1996). To construct a cognitive map, the brain combines a position vector in a body-centered coordinate framework—the position of a terrain feature relative to the animal—with a displacement vector (the animal's displacement in the geocentric coordinate framework). Similarly, the superior colliculus combines the position of a stimulus in a retinal or head-centered coordinate framework with a vector indicating the displacement of that coordinate framework relative to a larger framework. In the construction of a cognitive map, the displacement vector arises from dead reckoning—the integration of the animal's velocity with respect to time to yield the body's displacement vector. Similarly, the signals that specify the eye's displacement vector appear to arise from the integration of eye velocity signals with respect to time.

When the brain adds a vector that specifies a terrain feature in a body-centered coordinate system to the body-displacement vector from the animal's dead-reckoning mechanism, it maps the position of the terrain feature into a geocentric coordinate framework. By routinely doing this coordinate transformation, the animal builds up a representation of the different terrain features in its environment in a common geocentric coordinate system, even though those features may have been viewed at widely differing times and places.

Using the map involves the inverse transformation, mapping from the position of a goal on the geocentric map to the position of the goal in a body-centered framework. It is this inverse transformation that enables the animal to orient toward goals it cannot currently perceive by reference to its cognitive map and its own position and orientation on that map. Thus, the study of coordinate transformations and their neurobiological implementation is of broad significance for our understanding of the computational processes that underlie higher cognitive function.

References

Atkeson, C. G. (1989). Learning arm kinematics and dynamics. *Annual Review of Neuroscience, 12,* 157–184.

Atkeson, C. G., & Hollerbach, J. M. (1985). Kinematic features of unrestrained vertical movements. *Journal of Neuroscience, 5,* 2318–2330.

Berkinblit, M. V., Gelfand, I. M., & Feldman, A. G. (1986). Model of the control of movements of a multijoint limb. *Biophysics, 31,* 142–153.

Bernstein, N. (1967). *The coordination and regulation of movements.* Oxford, England: Pergamon Press.

Bizzi, E., & Mussa-Ivaldi, F. A. (1990). Muscle properties and the control of arm movement. In D. O. Osherson, S. M. Kosslyn, & J. M. Hollerbach (Eds.), *An invitation to cognitive science: Vol. 2. Visual cognition and action* (pp. 213–242). Cambridge, MA: MIT Press.

Bizzi, E., & Mussa-Ivaldi, A. (1995). Toward a neurobiology of coordinate transformations. In M. S. Gazzaniga (Ed.), *The cognitive neurosciences* (pp. 495–506). Cambridge, MA: MIT Press.

Bizzi, E., Mussa-Ivaldi, F. A., & Giszter, S. (1991). Computations underlying the execution of movement: A biological perspective. *Science, 253,* 287–291.

Bruce, C. J. (1990). Integration of sensory and motor signals for saccadic eye movements in the primate frontal eye fields. In *Signal and sense: Local and global order in perceptual maps* (pp. 261–314). New York: Wiley-Liss.

Bruce, C. J., & Goldberg, M. E. (1990). Primate frontal eye fields: III. Maintenance of a spatially accurate saccade signal. *Journal of Neurophysiology, 64,* 489–508.

Buttner, U., Buttner-Ennever, J. A., & Henn, V. (1977). Vertical eye movement related unit activity in the rostral mesencephalic reticular formation of the alert monkey. *Brain Research, 130,* 239–252.

Cannon, S. C., & Robinson, D. A. (1987). Loss of the neural integrator of the oculomotor system from brainstem lesions in the monkey. *Journal of Neurophysiology, 57,* 1383–1409.

Cheron, G., & Godaux, E. (1987). Disabling of the oculomotor integrator by kainic acid injections in the prepositus-vestibular complex of the cat. *Journal of Physiology (London), 394,* 267–290.

Crawford, J. D. (1994). The oculomotor neural integrator uses a behavior-related coordinate system. *Journal of Neuroscience, 14*(11, Pt. 2), 6911–6923.

Crawford, J. D., & Vilis, T. (1991). Axes of eye rotation and Listing's law during rotations of the head. *Journal of Neurophysiology, 65,* 407–423.

Crawford, J. D., & Vilis, T. (1993). Modularity and parallel processing in the oculomotor integrator. *Experimental Brain Research, 96,* 443–456.

Feldman, A. G. (1974). Change of muscle length due to shift of the equilibrium point of the muscle-load system. *Biofizika, 19,* 534–538.

Ferman, L., Collewijn, H., and Van den Berg, A. V. (1987). A direct test of Listing's law. I. Human ocular torsion measured in static tertiary positions. *Vision Research, 27,* 929–938.

Flash, T., & Hogan, N. (1985). The coordination of arm movements: An experimentally confirmed mathematical model. *Journal of Neuroscience, 5,* 1688–1703.

Fukson, O. I., Berkinblit, M. B., & Feldman, A. G. (1980). The spinal frog takes into account the scheme of its body during the wiping reflex. *Science, 209,* 1261–1263.

Gallistel, C. R. (1980). *The organization of action: A new synthesis.* Hillsdale, NJ: Erlbaum.

Gallistel, C. R. (1990). *The organization of learning.* Cambridge, MA: Bradford Books/MIT Press.

Gallistel, C. R. (1994). Elementary and complex units of behavior. In G. d'Ydewalle, P. Celen, & P. Bertelson (Eds.), *Current advances in psychological science: An international perspective* (pp. 157–175). Hillsdale, NJ: Erlbaum.

Gallistel, C. R. (1998). Symbolic processes in the brain: The case of insect navigation. In D. Osherson (Series Ed.) & S. Sternberg & D. Scarborough (Vol. Eds.), *Methods, models, and conceptual issues: Vol. 4. Invitation to cognitive science* (2nd ed.) (pp. 1–51). Cambridge, MA: MIT Press.

Gallistel, C. R., & Cramer, A. E. (1996). Computations on metric maps in mammals: Getting oriented and choosing a multi-destination route. *Journal of Experimental Biology, 199,* 211–217.

Giszter, S. F., Mussa-Ivaldi, F. A., & Bizzi, E. (1993). Convergent force fields organized in the frog's spinal cord. *Journal of Neuroscience, 13*(2), 467–491.

Gnadt, J. W., & Andersen, R. A. (1988). Memory related motor planning activity in posterior parietal cortex of macaque. *Experimental Brain Research, 70,* 216–220.

Gomi, H., & Kawato, M. (1996). Equilibrium-point control hypothesis examined by measured arm stiffness during multijoint movement. *Science, 271,* 117–120.

Gordon, J., Ghilardi, M. F., & Ghez, C. (1994). Accuracy of planar reaching movements: I. Independence of direction and extent variability. *Experimental Brain Research, 99,* 97–111.

Guthrie, B. L., Porter, J. D., & Sparks, D. L. (1983). Corollary discharge provides accurate eye position information to the oculomotor system. *Science, 221,* 1193–1195.

Hasan, Z. (1991). Biomechanics and the study of multijoint movements. In D. R. Humphrey & H.-J. Freund (Eds.), *Motor control: Concepts and issues* (pp. 75–84). New York: Wiley.

Hasan, Z., & Stuart, D. G. (1988). Animal solutions to problems of movement control: The role of proprioceptors. *Annual Review of Neuroscience, 11,* 199–223.

Hepp, K., & Hepp-Reymond, M.-C. (1989). *Donders' and Listing's Law for reaching and grasping arm synergies.* Abstracts of the 15th annual meeting of the Society for Neuroscience, p. 604.

Hogan, N., & Flash, T. (1987). Moving gracefully: Quantitative theories of motor coordination. *Trends in NeuroSciences, 10,* 170–174.

Hogan, N., Bizzi, E., & Mussa-Ivaldi, F. A. (1987). Controlling multijoint motor behavior. *Exercise and Sport Sciences Review, 15,* 153–190.

Hollerbach, J. M. (1982). Computers, brains, and the control of movement. *Trends in NeuroSciences, 5,* 189–192.

Hollerbach, J. M. (1990). Planning of arm movements. In D. O. Osherson, S. M. Kosslyn, & J. M. Hollerbach (Eds.), *An invitation to cognitive science: Vol. 2. Visual cognition and action* (pp. 183–211). Cambridge, MA: MIT Press.

Hollerbach, J. M., & Atkeson, C. G. (1987). Deducing planning variables from experimental arm trajectories: Pitfalls and possibilities. *Biological Cybernetics, 56,* 279–292.

Jay, M. F., & Sparks, D. L. (1987). Sensorimotor integration in the primate superior colliculus. II. Coordinates of auditory signals. *Journal of Neurophysiology, 57,* 35–55.

Jordan, M. I. (1994a). Computational aspects of motor control and motor learning. In H. Heuer & S. Keele (Eds.), *Handbook of perception and action: Motor skills* New York: Academic Press.

Jordan, M. I. (1994b). Computational motor control. In M. S. Gazzaniga (Ed.), *The cognitive neurosciences* (pp. 597–609). Cambridge, MA: MIT Press.

Kalaska, J. F., & Crammond, D. J. (1992). Cerebral cortical mechanisms of reaching movements. *Science, 255,* 1517–1523.

King, A. J., & Moore, D. R. (1991). Plasticity of auditory maps in the brain. *Trends in NeuroSciences, 14*(1), 31–36.

Konishi, M. (1995). Neural mechanisms of auditory image formation. In M. S. Gazzaniga (Ed.), *The cognitive neurosciences* (pp. 269–277). Cambridge, MA: MIT Press.

Lacquaniti, F., Soechting, J. F., & Terzuolo, C. A. (1982). Some factors pertinent to the organization and control of arm movement. *Brain Research, 252,* 394–397.

Lacquaniti, F., Soechting, J. F., & Terzuolo, C. A. (1986). Path constraints on point-to-point arm movements in three-dimensional space. *Neuroscience, 17,* 313–324.

Lee, C., Rohrer, W. H., & Sparks, D. L. (1988). Population coding of saccadic eye movements by neurons in the superior colliculus. *Nature (London), 332,* 357–360.

Lehky, S. R., Sejnowski, T. J., & Desimone, R. (1992). Predicting responses of nonlinear neurons in monkey striate cortex to complex patterns. *Journal of Neuroscience, 12*(9), 3568–3581.

Lockery, S. R., & Sejnowski, T. J. (1993). The computational leech. *Trends in NeuroSciences, 16*(7), 283–290.

Loeb, G. E. (1987). Hard lessons in motor control from the mammalian spinal cord. *Trends in Neuro-Sciences, 10,* 108–113.

Mays, L. E., & Sparks, D. L. (1980). Dissociation of visual and saccade-related responses in superior colliculus neurons. *Journal of Neurophysiology, 43,* 207–232.

Milner, T. E., & Cloutier, C. (1993). Compensation for mechanically unstable loading in voluntary wrist movements. *Experimental Brain Research, 94,* 522–532.

Morasso, P. (1981). Spatial control of arm movements. *Experimental Brain Research, 42,* 223–237.

Mussa-Ivaldi, F. A., Giszter, S. F., & Bizzi, E. (1994). Linear combinations of primitives in vertebrate motor control. *Proceedings of the National Academy of Sciences of the U.S.A., 91*(16), 7534–7538.

Nakayama, K. (1975). Coordination of extra-ocular muscles. In G. Lennerstrand & P. Bach-y-Rita (Eds.), *Basic mechanisms of ocular motility and their clinical implications* (pp. 193–208). Oxford, England: Pergamon Press.

Robinson, D. A. (1972). Eye movements evoked by collicular stimulation in the alert monkey. *Vision Research, 12,* 1795–1808.

Robinson, D. A. (1975). Oculomotor control signals. In P. Bach-y-Rita & G. Lennerstrand (Eds.), *Basic mechanisms of ocular motility and their clinical implications* (pp. 337–374). Oxford, England: Pergamon Press.

Robinson, D. A. (1985). The coordinates of neurons in the vestibulo-ocular reflex. In A. Berthoz & M. Jones (Eds.), *Adaptive mechanisms in gaze control. Facts and theories* (pp. 297–311). New York: Elsevier.

Robinson, D. A. (1989). Integrating with neurons. *Annual Review of Neuroscience, 12,* 33–46.

Robinson, D. A. (1992). Implications of neural networks for how we think about brain function. *Behavior and Brain Science, 15,* 644–655.

Russo, G. S., & Bruce, C. J. (1994). Frontal eye field activity preceding aurally guided saccades. *Journal of Neurophysiology, 71,* 1250–1253.

Saltzman, E. (1979). Levels of sensorimotor representation. *Journal of Mathematical Psychology, 20,* 91–163.

Schiller, P. H., & Stryker, M. (1972). Single-unit recording and stimulation in superior colliculus of the alert rhesus monkey. *Journal of Neurophysiology, 35,* 915–924.

Shadmehr, R., & Mussa-Ivaldi, F. A. (1994). Adaptive representation of dynamics during learning of a motor task. *Journal of Neuroscience, 14*(5, Pt.2), 3208–3224.

Smolensky, P. (1988). On the proper treatment of connectionism. *Behavioral and Brain Sciences, 11,* 1–74.

Soechting, J. F., & Lacquaniti, F. (1981). Invariant characteristics of a pointing movement in man. *Journal of Neuroscience, 1,* 710–720.

Sparks, D. L., & Groh, J. F. (1995). The superior colliculus: A window for viewing issues in integrative neuroscience. In M. S. Gazzaniga (Ed.), *The cognitive neurosciences* (pp. 565–584). Cambridge, MA: MIT Press.

Sparks, D. L., Lee, C., & Rohrer, W. H. (1990). Population coding of the direction, amplitude, and velocity of saccadic eye movements by neurons in the superior colliculus. *Cold Spring Harbor Symposia on Quantitative Biology, 55,* 805–811.

Sparks, D. L., & Mays, L. E. (1990). Signal transformations required for the generation of saccadic eye movements. *Annual Review of Neuroscience, 13,* 309–336.

Strang, G. (1994). Wavelets. *American Scientist, 82,* 250–255.

Straube, A., Kurszan, R., & Büttner, U. (1991). Differential effects of bicuculine and muscimol microinjections into the vestibular nuclei on simian eye movements. *Experimental Brain Research, 86,* 347–358.

Tweed, D., Cardera, W., & Vilis, T. (1990). Computing three dimensional eye position quaternions and eye velocity from search coil signals. *Vision Research, 30,* 97–110.

Tweed, D., & Villis, T. (1990). Geometric relations of eye position and velocity vectors during saccades. *Vision Research, 30,* 111–127.

Tweed, D., & Vilis, T. (1992). Listing's law for gaze-directing head movements. In A. Berthoz, W. Graf, & P. P. Vidal (Eds.), *The head-neck sensory-motor system* (pp. 387–391). Chichester: Wiley.

Uno, Y., Kawato, M., & Suzuki, R. (1989). Formation and control of optimal trajectory in human multijoint arm movement. *Biological Cybernetics, 61,* 89–101.

van Emmerik, R. E. A. (1991). Kinematic adaptations to perturbations as a function of practice in rhythmic drawing movements. *Journal of Motor Behavior, 24,* 117–131.

Villis, T., & Tweed, D. (1991). What can rotational mechanics tell us about the neural control of eye movements? In D. R. Humphrey & H.-J. Freund (Eds.), *Motor control: Concepts and issues* (pp. 85–99). New York: Wiley.

Westheimer, G. (1981). Donders', Listing's, and Hering's laws and their implications. In B. L. Zuber (Ed.), *Models of oculomotor behavior and control* (pp. 149–160). Boca Raton, FL: CRC Press.

Westheimer, G., & McKee, S. P. (1973). Failure of Donders' law during smooth pursuit eye movement. *Vision Research, 13,* 2145–2153.

Wolpert, D. M., Ghahramani, Z., & Jordan, M. I. (1994). Perceptual distortion contributes to the curvature of human reaching movements. *Experimental Brain Research, 98,* 153–156.

Wolpert, D. M., Ghahramani, Z., & Jordan, M. I. (1995). Are arm trajectories planned in kinematic or dynamic coordinates? An adaptation study. *Experimental Brain Research, 103,* 460–470.

Zajac, F. E., & Gordon, M. E. (1989). Determining muscle's force and action in multi-articular movement. *Exercise and Sport Science Reviews, 17,* 187–230.

CHAPTER 2

Attention

David LaBerge

This chapter addresses the ways cognitive science disciplines have inquired into the attention process. Resting on the seminal work of William James (1890), the discipline of cognitive psychology has developed most of the current concepts of attention in conjunction with the invention of new behavioral tasks that evoke particular aspects of the attention process. The discipline of neuroscience, in turn, has adopted many of these behavioral tasks to produce attentional states in monkeys and humans that can be measured by various physiological techniques such as single-cell recordings, evoked response potentials (ERPs), positron emission topography (PET), and functional magnetic resonance imaging (fMRI).

As ongoing experimental work in psychology and neuroscience sharpen our notions of attentional processing we can expect them to be used increasingly in the discipline of philosophy to illuminate issues concerned with the nature of the mind, including the long-standing problem of consciousness and the current problem of distinguishing human minds from computer "minds."

Over the past half-century, psychologists have offered the following surprising variety of descriptions of the attention process: a filter (Broadbent, 1958), effort (Kahneman, 1973), a control process of short-term memory (Shiffrin & Schneider, 1977), resources (Shaw, 1978), orienting (Posner, 1980), conjoining object attributes (Treisman & Gelade, 1980), a spotlight (Tsal, 1983), a gate (Reeves & Sperling, 1986), a zoom lens (C. W. Eriksen & St. James, 1986), both selection and preparation (LaBerge & Brown, 1989), and as intensified activity in cortical columns

Cognitive Science

(LaBerge, 1998). Many of these views of attention have appeared over the past two decades in surveys and reviews of the field by Allport (1989), Johnston and Dark (1986), Kinchla (1992), LaBerge (1995b), Naatanen (1992), Parasuraman (1998), Parasuraman and Davies (1984), Pashler (1998), Posner and Petersen (1990), Shiffrin (1988), and Wright (1998).

Given the current heterogeneous concepts of what attention is and what it does (sadly, one is reminded of the story of the four blind men describing an elephant), it is difficult to provide a broad review across cognitive science disciplines that has useful integrative aspects without first establishing some conceptual framework within which the attention process is to be examined. Of course, there are drawbacks in choosing a particular conceptual formulation in that it may require some readers to put forth extra effort to look at a familiar phenomenon in a relatively new way, and it may not embrace all of the data that some readers regard as important to the field. However, it is hoped that these hazards may be at least partly offset if the framework provides some useful integrations of contributions from the variety of disciplines under consideration.

This chapter treats attention mainly in the context of visual perception because the empirical and theoretical literature in visual perception has contributed most of the concepts that have led to the ways that the attention process is presently understood by scientists. However, current research in attention is also gaining ground in the domain of internal actions, particularly actions that control attention. Therefore, an attempt is made here to relate some of the developing concepts in this domain to the more traditional concepts that have their roots in visual attention.

To begin, a cross-disciplinary framework for inquiry into attention will be described, followed by an overview of developmental issues. In the interest of maintaining some continuity across the developmental life span, studies of adult attention will be inserted between the studies of infant development and aging. Thus, the development section will be somewhat larger than the other sections of this chapter. After this overview of developmental changes in attentional processes, separate sections are devoted to evolutionary, cultural, and computational issues of attention, and the chapter ends with philosophical treatments of the attention process. The neuroscience approach to attention is addressed within the discussions of the other topics, owing to its key role in defining the expression, mechanisms, and controls of attention.

I. A COGNITIVE NEUROSCIENCE FRAMEWORK FOR VIEWING ATTENTION

The framework that is adopted here for examining attention bears some similarities to the research framework proposed by Marr (1982) for the study of vision, and it combines methods of several cognitive science disciplines. The framework of inquiry is directed at the process of attention, but its applicability to scientific research in general can be observed by substituting the process of memory or breathing for the process of attention.

The first questions posed by the framework concern the goals of the attention process. What does the attention process do for the individual; that is, in what ways do attentional operations provide adaptive advantages within a complex environment, and, more specifically, how does attention operate in satisfying the individual's personal goals? The answer to these questions can be described appropriately in cognitive or behavioral terms. The next question asks what problems must be solved by the processing system in order to achieve these advantages. The answer to this question requires that the physical processing system be described at an appropriate level somewhere, say, between the molecular activity in neurons and psychological behavior. Without taking the space for justification, it is simply stated that the appropriate level for describing attention is the activity within neural circuits (LaBerge, 1997, 1998), which often can be viewed alternatively as the flow of information along brain pathways.

A. Goals of Attention

Three classes of attentional goals are defined here in cognitive terms. The classification scheme is made quite general in an attempt to include the attention goals indicated or implied in most of the attention literature. The first class of goals is the accurate perception of particular objects, and accurate execution of particular actions (internal as well as external), especially when other objects or actions are available. Simple examples from perception are identifications of objects one at a time in a cluttered field, as occurs in search and reading; examples from action are choosing a verb that is associated with a presented noun, or executing a particular sequence of finger movements. All of these examples require a process that selects a part of the information simultaneously available in the stimulus array or in memory.

The second class of goals is an increase in the speed of perceptions and executions of actions (internal and external), by preparing the system to process these stimuli and/or actions. Examples in perception are the speeded identification of an object, which is produced by preparing to perceive the shape, color, and/or motion of the object (e.g., a food object or a predator); examples in actions are the speeded assembly of action plans when the form of the response is anticipated in advance (e.g., choosing words to express a sentence, or preparing to process a rapid series of displays on a trial of an experiment). Preparations for perceptions and actions may be accompanied by sustaining their components in working memory so that the components may be accurately and quickly converted to appropriate executive commands as events unfold.

The third class of goals is the sustaining of attention to perception or action over a relatively long time interval for its own sake, that is, without the expectation of using it instrumentally in the near future to effectively perceive some upcoming object or to perform some action. Examples are the prolonging of aesthetic (viewing a painting), consummatory (tasting food), and repetitive actions, such as humming a tune repeatedly or doodling with a pencil. This manner of sustaining attention differs from the other two classes of goals (accurate and speeded responding) in that it confers no immediate adaptive benefit to the individual. A possible remote benefit of maintaining attention to a pleasant activity is that the resulting elevation of mood could promote more effective responding to upcoming environmental challenges. Yet, the prospect of being able to extend our experiencing of aesthetic and consummatory processing motivates many of our daily human actions. The goal of simple maintenance of a particular kind of processing apparently calls upon the same mechanisms of attention as the directly adaptive goals of fast and accurate processing. Nevertheless, it appears that these examples of maintaining attention to affective processes resist satisfactory descriptions and evaluations in computational terms (see discussions of "qualia" by Dennett, 1991; but also see Johnson-Laird, 1988).

B. Manifestations of Attention

The three major goals of attention listed here are indicative of the ways that attentional processing is observed or inferred in behavioral and cognitive situations. When a judgment of an object in a field cluttered with salient objects is made correctly, or one of a set of alternative responses is chosen, it is inferred that selective attention has successfully removed or attenuated the influence of the extraneous and confusing information. For example, identifying the center letter in the word COG requires that information arising from the locations near the center letter be prevented from entering the module (or sets of modules) that performs a judgment of identification. If selection by location does not occur, the entire word COG will presumably enter the identification module and be identified instead of the letter O. On the action side of cognition, selection of information from working memory is assumed to occur when pressing a particular function key on a computer keyboard when other keys are available, and during speaking when a particular word is chosen from alternative words as we pause before emphasizing a point. This manifestation of attention, then, may be referred to as simple selection.

When we observe a substantial increase in speed of responding to the onset of a given stimulus following the presentation of a predictive cue, it is inferred that attention has been concentrated prior to the onset of the stimulus on some processing module or area in the pathways between perception of the stimulus and evocation of the response. Modules that have been shown to be sensitive to predictive cuing are perception of the stimulus (as in cuing the location, color, and shape of an object), response generation (as in cuing a particular response), and working memory (as in cuing a word in a lexical decision task). The resulting effect of directing attention to a processing module is presumed to be a shortening of the time to process the appropriate information at the time when target stimulus information arrives at that module.

James (1890) described the latter case as "preprocessing" of the stimulus, and used it as a prototypical example of attentional "anticipation" or "preparation." In this chapter, this particular manifestation of attention will be denoted as preparation.

It should be noted that preparatory attention is usually directed to a particular feature of a stimulus, or to a particular response unit, or to a particular intervening operation, so that selective processing is required for this manifestation of attention as well as for the simple selection manifestation. However, it is the prolonged aspect of preparatory attention that marks it off from simple selective attention, which can be initiated quickly and without preparation, as in examining successive objects during search.

Preparation to process a stimulus, response, or mental operation almost always involves an expectation of an upcoming time at which the prepared-for processing is to be initiated. This temporal expectation is presumed to be represented in working memory along with a representation of the stimulus attribute or action plan that is to receive preparatory attention. For example, if we are preparing to see a green light flash at a street intersection, we not only have in working memory an expectation of when the light will occur, but we also have in working memory some representation of the green light, perhaps in verbal form. However, preparatory attention requires that an additional step be taken, which is that the representation of the green light in working memory must command a perceptual preparation for the green light, and/or command a motor preparation for pressing the gas pedal. Hence, when a person prepares for a particular type of processing, (from either external or internal instructions), it may not be clear to the person or to an observer whether the preparation is represented only abstractly in working memory as an expectation or is represented also as a preparatory state of the processing component itself. When instructions induce preparation at the site of the processing component, one expects faster processing than when instructions only induce a storage in working memory of the expected perception or action plan.

A third manifestation of the attention process corresponds closely to the third goal of attention considered here, which is the simple maintenance of processing without an accompanying expectation of an upcoming event. Inferring the presence of this particular manifestation of attention is more difficult than inferring the presence of preparatory or selective attention.

However, from the point of view of introspective experience of one's own attentional states, maintenance attention would appear to be as directly observable as are the attentional processes of preparation or selection. Other kinds of measurement methods available to the cognitive scientist, such as brain imaging by PET, fMRI, and electroencephalogram (EEG) could presumably provide more objective bases for inferring maintenance attention. However, currently the most effective methods of brain imaging are based on subtraction of measurements across carefully constructed behavioral tasks, which almost always involve specific behavioral goals.

As was the case for preparatory attention, maintenance attention almost always requires selection among items in sensory and memory sources. It appears then that selective processing is a property that unifies all three manifestations of attention.

The three manifestations of attention, selection, preparation, and maintenance, all apparently occur within a trial of a typical behavioral–cognitive experiment. An illustrative example of these manifestations is a trial of the word association task, in which a word is presented and the subject is required to generate the opposite of the stimulus word. Prior to the stimulus the subject's attention is manifest as preparation for perceiving a visual word in a particular location on a screen, and preparation for making a spoken response. as well as a preparation to process the stimulus word as an opposite. When the stimulus word is presented, the subject selects from a set of stored alternative associates, which involves a relatively brief operation of simple selective attention, and emits a verbal response. The response is then evaluated as to its appropriateness and feedback is given explicitly or implicitly. The subject then may shift attention to contemplate the feedback or to process his or her "feelings about the feedback" in the maintenance mode of attention.

Of the three manifestations of attention considered here, two of them, selection and preparation, seem to have been studied experimentally more than maintenance (for a review, see LaBerge, 1995b). This state of affairs may not seem surprising owing to the difficulty of measuring maintenance attention using the typical form of a laboratory task. In his famous chapter on attention, William James (1890) described the "two physiological" processes of attention as "the accommodation or adjustment of the sensory organs" and "the anticipatory preparation from within the ideational centers concerned with the object to which the attention is paid" (Vol. 1, p. 434). Moray (1959) listed selection and concentration (mental set) as the two different aspects of attention, and Posner and Boies (1971) listed alertness (general preparation) and selectivity along with processing capacity as the three components of attention. More recently Posner and Petersen (1990) described three major functions of attention as: (1) orienting to sensory events; (2) detecting signals for focal (conscious) processing, and (3) the maintenance of a vigilant or alert state.

C. Problems To Be Solved by Attentional Processing

In order to achieve the goals just described, attention must be able to restrict the processing of the enormous array of information that is continuously available from sensory and memory sources. Ambiguous and extraneous information can lead not only to inaccurate responses, but also can lengthen the time to respond. This problem exists not only for the system regarded as a whole, but also for particular modules that participate in cognitive processing, such as modules that specialize in processing location information and shape information on the stimulus side, and modules that specialize in configuring external and internal actions on the response side.

Another problem for attention to solve is to prolong the selection of information in the sensory and memory arrays until a particular anticipated action or event occurs, or simply for its own sake without anticipating some future action or event. But under some circumstances sustained attention may be counter-adaptive, as in the example of the animal attending exclusively to eating while being stalked by a predator. Therefore, to be adaptive, the attentional processes must be subject to interrupts. An interrupt may be regarded as prioritizing attentional selection toward a particular class of events. The clearest examples of interrupts are sudden changes in luminance or sound produced by the abrupt appearance of objects (Yantis, 1993; Yantis & Jonides, 1990), which frequently signal highly significant events in the daily life of animals and humans. An object that signals its presence by an abrupt onset may subsequently become the target of sustained attention, but then attention to this object in turn becomes vulnerable to interruption by sudden changes in the sights and sounds of still other objects.

The three problems just described, restricting of processing to specific inputs, prolonging this restriction, and interrupting such restrictions, do not exhaust the hurdles that confront an attention process if it is to do its job and be an effective part of the processing system, but they would appear to be among the major ones. Other problems for attention are prompt termination of selective processing of one object once an appropriate judgment has been made (e.g., with respect to its identity or color); rapid shifts to selectively process another object, preferably an object that has not yet been scanned, as apparently occurs in rapid search and in rapid, fluent reading; and rapid shifts between two or more tasks that require simultaneous monitoring.

D. Summary of the Present Cognitive Neuroscience Framework for Understanding the Attention Process

This initial section of the chapter provides a framework for inquiry into the attention process by combining concepts and methods of the cognitive science disciplines of cognitive psychology and neurobiology. The first question deals with the goals of the individual's processing system that are met by attention, and the second question deals with the set of problems to be solved by attentional operations if they are to benefit the life of the individual. Three goals of the attention process were stated: accurate and fast judgments of objects and ideas and the sustaining of desired mental processing. Attention was said to meet these three goals with three corresponding manifestations of attention: simple selection, preparation, and maintenance. Common to all three manifestations of attention is the selective property, but the duration of selection is typically more prolonged in the manifestations of attentional preparation and attentional maintenance.

II. DEVELOPMENTAL ISSUES AND METHODS IN THE STUDY OF VISUAL ATTENTION

Two main questions that arise when attention is viewed developmentally concern (a) the time periods in the life of the individual when attention-related structures and functions become increasingly effective and when they become less effective, and (b) the relative contributions of genetic, environment, and self-regulatory factors to this timing and to the particular structural and functional forms exhibited by an individual. Present measurement techniques have only begun to suggest answers to these questions, and of the several promising lines of research in this area, a few are described here whose methods of inquiry appear to cross the boundaries of cognitive science disciplines. Although this section of the chapter will emphasize attention-related processing in infancy and late adulthood, some of the issues related to methodology and brain structures will refer to the literature on the adult period of the developmental life span.

The Russian psychologist, Luria (1973), viewed attention as having two major subsystems that are particularly distinguishable in the developing infant. In the few months following birth, the involuntary attention system enables a visual stimulus to direct a child's head and eyes toward the location of that stimulus, and in later months the voluntary attention system enables the child to control these movements from internal sources. Today, the involuntary influence of external stimuli on both orienting and attentional processing has been termed "exogenous" control, and the largely voluntary influence by internal memory sources have been termed "endogenous" control (e.g., Klein, Kingstone, & Pontefract, 1992). One way to view the development of attention toward the adult competence level (Rothbart, Posner, & Boylan, 1990) is in terms of the increasing degree to which orienting can be controlled by endogenous sources.

Visual orienting can be directly observed when it involves the overt positioning or movements of the eyes, head, or trunk of the body. However, visual orienting can also occur independently of eye, head, or trunk movements (Posner, 1980), and the term *covert orienting* is used to distinguish this case from the observable *overt orienting*. Eye movements can often serve as a fairly reliable indicator that a covert shift in orientation has occurred because the typical saccadic eye movement to a target location appears to be preceded by a faster movement of covert orientation to (or near to) the target location (Posner, 1988; Remington, 1980).

The goals of both overt and covert orienting appear to be to guide the attention process, which in turn enables correct and rapid detection of an object or event. The specific goal of overt orienting may be viewed as the alignment of sensory receptors to the location of an object in the environment. In vision, the foveation of a target object results in finer resolution of detail that can increase accuracy of object discrimination and identification. The specific goal of covert orienting, by definition, is not directly observed. The view of this chapter is that covert orienting's goal is to increase the activity of specific locations in spatial maps of the cortex. Cuing of a particular location for adults increases the speed of detecting an object that subsequently appears in that location (Bachinski & Bachrach, 1984; Downing, 1988) as well as increases the speed of responses (C. W. Eriksen & Hoffman, 1972; Hawkins, Shafto, & Richardson, 1988; Posner, Snyder, & Davidson, 1980). Also, because multiple cues can activate several locations in the spatial map simultaneously, perceptual processing of an upcoming object is facilitated when that object falls in any one of the several cued locations (Wright, 1994). Thus, owing to its capability of guiding the prospective spatial locations of attention, orienting may be said to be the gateway to spatial attention.

A. Theory of Orienting

In order to meet the goals of sensory receptor alignment and preactivating of cortically coded locations, several problems must be solved by the neural circuitry serving these events. Some of these problems may be addressed broadly within Posner's theory of the orienting process (Posner, 1988; Posner, Petersen, Fox, & Raichle, 1988), which involves three major processes: disengagement, movement, and engagement. These three events correspond to three easily observed events of an eye movement, in which the eyeball leaves a current angle of gaze, rotates, and comes to a stop at a new angle of gaze.

Overt orienting, viewed as disengagement, movement, and engagement of the eye, apparently occurs independently of the current location of attention. Covert orienting experiments demonstrate that individuals can attend to locations away from the direction of gaze (e.g., C. W. Eriksen & Hoffman, 1972; Posner & Cohen, 1984). Furthermore, when several locations are cued simultaneously and attention is subsequently directed to an object in one of these cued locations, activity apparently continues for a time at the other cued locations (LaBerge, Carlson, Williams, & Bunney, 1997). Therefore, the activation of one or several separate locations in cortical spatial maps, which is assumed here to be the specific goal of covert orienting, contrasts with the specific goal of attention, which is to activate one particular location (which may be narrow or wide in spatial extent).

In view of these considerations, it would appear that the neural circuitry serving overt and covert orienting is not sufficient by itself to produce an attentional event in the brain. Attention to visuospatial locations is assumed here to require top-down activations of parietal areas from frontal cortical areas, which amplify and prolong the activations initially produced by abrupt onsets of a stimulus. Later in this section of the chapter the development of frontal cortical areas will be examined in view of available experimental findings.

The term *orienting,* in both the covert and overt senses, has been used in two principal ways, particularly in the infant attention literature. One use of the term refers to the sustaining of attention to a particular object: an example is the "obligatory attention" to a stimulus observed in infants at 1 month of age (Stechler & Latz, 1966); another example is the maintenance of attention to a particular object in the preferential looking task by infants over 3 months of age (for a review, see Olson & Sherman, 1983). A second main use of orienting refers to the process of shifting attention to another location. Often the spatial distance between the "old" and "new" objects used in testing is well over 5° of visual angle. For example, before age 4 infants have difficulty shifting their gaze from a centrally located stimulus to a peripherally located stimulus 34° to the right or left (Johnson, 1994), and they also have difficulty in using the central target to predict the side where the peripheral target will appear (Johnson, Posner, & Rothbart, 1991).

Whereas the first use of orienting as "sustained orienting" involves attention (controlled from frontal cortex) to one location or object, the second use of orienting as "shift orienting" may involve attentional processing at two locations: the location of the "old" object and the location of the "new" object. The ease with which attention is shifted from an old to a new location appears to depend on the strength with which attention is sustained at the old location or object (e.g., Richards, 1989). Richards used decelerations in heart rate of infants as the indicator of sustained attention in a 5–15-s period following the onset of a complex stimulus. He found that the time taken for a peripheral flashing light to induce a shift of gaze away from the complex stimulus was substantially increased during the sustained attention period as compared with baseline periods in 3 and 6 months of age but not at 2 months of age.

A similar technique was used by LaBerge (1973) with adult subjects who were cued to prepare to see a yellow square and varied strength of preparatory attention to the yellow square by presenting catch trials that were either red squares or yellow-orange squares. Occasionally tones were presented to probe the strength of preparatory attention to the yellow square, and the data showed longer mean response times to the tone on trial blocks in which yellow was discriminated against yellow-orange than on trial blocks in which yellow was discriminated against red.

These results are consistent with the increased activity in V4 cells found by Spitzer, Desimone, and Moran (1988) and by Haenny and Schiller (1988) when the color or orientation of an object is discriminated against an object of similar (vs. less similar) objects. In both the Richards and LaBerge experiments, the strength of attention directed to the "old" stimulus was measured by its effect on shifting attention away from it to a "new" stimulus.

Shift orienting is also affected by endogenously produced attentional preparations at peripheral locations. Johnson et al. (1991) tested 2-, 3-, and 4-month-old infants with a central stimulus (an array of moving dots with a regular beeping sound vs. a looming box with an irregular beeping sound) that could be used to cue the side at which a peripheral stimulus would appear. The central stimulus was somewhat similar to the endogenous arrow cue used with adults in orienting tasks. Test trials were occasionally presented in which the peripheral target, a flashing green diamond above a pink rectangle (3° in width), appeared simultaneously on each side. The 4-month-old infants looked more frequently to the cued side than the uncued side, whereas the 2- and 3-month-old infants looked equally to the cued and uncued sides. These findings indicate that prior to the shift of attention, infants of 4 months show ability to control their shifts of attention from learned contingencies between a central stimulus and the location of a peripheral stimulus.

B. Brain Models of Visual Orienting

This chapter attempts to portray an interactive collaboration of behavioral/cognitive studies with data and models of brain structures believed to be crucial to attentional processing (see Figure 1). One current view of neural circuit development on infant changes in visual orienting, taken by Posner and his colleagues (Clohessy,

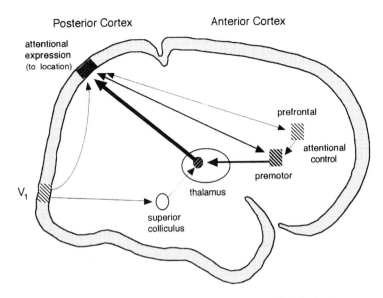

FIGURE 1   Schematic drawing of cortical and subcortical areas of the brain that are assumed to produce the expression of orienting and the expression of attention. The input signals to the superior colliculus, which evoke the expression of orienting, originate in V1 and retinal ganglion cells. The expression of attention is produced by signals from control sites (prefrontal storage and premotor executive) in the anterior cortex; these signals are amplified by the thalamus within the triangular circuit of attention.

Posner, Rothbart, & Vecera, 1991; Rothbart et al., 1990), emphasizes the maturation of the parietal cortex (PC), the superior colliculus (SC), and pulvinar (see Figure 1), which are the brain areas assumed to mediate the disengage, move, and engage components of covert attention shifting. Another view, taken by Johnson (1990, 1994), emphasizes the maturation of the brain areas believed to support oculomotor control. These areas include the SC, area V5 (MT) magnocellular motion pathway, the frontal eye field (FEF) pathway, and the inhibitory pathways arising from the pars reticulata sector of the substantia nigra in the basal ganglia (Schiller, 1985). Visual signals in all of these pathways arise from V1, and therefore depend crucially on the development of circuits in the superficial, middle, and deep layers of area V1.

The interconnections among the SC, V5, FEF, PC, V1, and thalamic areas constitute a parallel circuitry serving eye movement control that is somewhat resistant to effects of lesioning some of its components (for a review, see Colby, 1991). These component areas of the oculomotor system develop with separate time courses in the infant, and the appearance of functional characteristics of visually guided behavior should correspond to the times in which these component structures mature. Ideally, if the progressive anatomical development of these structures could be set in correspondence to the appearance of behavioral characteristics during development of the child, we would be closer to determining how specific circuits determine the functions manifest in orienting and attention.

Indicators of the degree to which a neural circuit has reached functional maturity involve measures of the size of the soma, length of dendrites, density of dendritic spines, and the degree of axon myelination. Maturity of function also depends on the development of synaptic microstructures, including the functional presence of axon terminals from neuromodulatory structures of the brain stem and forebrain, and at present our knowledge of synaptic microstructure is incomplete, though expanding rapidly (Churchland & Sejnowski, 1992). It is expected, however, that some neural circuits may function with varying degrees of effectiveness prior to complete development. Present measures of cell morphologies offer some comparisons of anatomical development of these structures and their interconnections (for reviews, see Atkinson, 1984; Bronson, 1974; Johnson, 1990, 1994). Pathways that connect the retina to the superior colliculus develop before pathways that connect the retina to cortical area V1 (via the lateral geniculate nucleus). Deep layers of V1 whose cells project to the SC and pulvinar mature prior to the superficial layers whose cells project directly to V5 and indirectly to the posterior PC (PPC) and FEF. The different rates of development in the deep and superficial layers of V1 have been proposed by Johnson (1990) as a major determinant of development of visually guided behavior in the infant. However, because newborns recognize some patterns (Slater, Morison, & Somers, 1988) and discriminate orientations (Atkinson, Hood, Wattam-Bell, Anker, & Tricklebank, 1988), some sectors of the temporal visual pathways must have begun to mature prior to the full maturity of V1 cells.

C. Enhancements of Activity in Brain Structures Serving Eye Movements

An early study by Goldberg and Wurtz (1972) showed an enhancement of cell firing in brain structures associated with eye movements. A peripheral visual stimulus was presented in the receptive field of a cell in the SC superficial layers (cells that drive eye-movement generators in the brain stem lie in the intermediate layers of the monkey SC [Ma, Graybiel, & Wurtz, 1991]) of a monkey who was trained to release a lever when the stimulus began to dim. These SC cells discharged more vigorously to the stimulus when a behavioral response was to be made than when no response was made to the stimulus. Subsequently, Wurtz and Mohler (1976) found similar enhancement effects when the behavioral response was an eye movement to the stimulus when it dimmed. Another study used a matching-to-sample task to reveal enhancement of cell firing to a stimulus in the absence of eye movements (Gattass & Desimone, 1991). In their task, the test display contained both a target (to be matched to the preceding cue) and a distractor, and SC superficial layer cells showed enhanced firing when the attended target stimulus was inside their receptive fields, but showed no enhancement when an unattended distractor was inside their receptive fields.

Enhancement of cell firings when a peripheral stimulus is a target of an impend-ing eye movement have also been demonstrated in the FEF (Goldberg & Bushnell, 1981), the basal ganglia (Hikosaka & Wurtz, 1983), the pulvinar (Petersen, Robin-son, & Keys, 1985), and in extrastriate areas (Fischer & Bock, 1981). Enhancements of neural activity in the PPC in monkeys (corresponding to the superior PC in humans) has been amply demonstrated (e.g., Gnadt & Andersen, 1988; Goldman-Rakic, Chafee, & Friedman, 1993; Mountcastle, Andersen, & Motter, 1981; Robin-son, Goldberg, & Stanton, 1978). These single-cell effects have been supplemented by ERP studies with humans in which simultaneous MRI scans of individual sub-ject's brains showed increased negativity over the PPC 150–190 ms after a visual stimulus occurred in a cued location (Mangun, Hillyard, & Luck, 1992) and cere-bral blood flow studies that indicate increased activation in the superior PC during a spatial cuing task (Corbetta, Miezin, Shulman, & Petersen, 1993).

Therefore, it appears that in the typical shift-orienting experiment, the onset of a peripheral stimulus induces a particular set of cells in many oculomotor-related areas to discharge more vigorously when the stimulus location has been cued in advance. These orienting enhancements of activity could be regarded as the expres-sion of orienting in the several brain structures in which they are found. In the cor-tex of the present framework, the enhancements in cortical structures would seem to be particularly important for attentional processing when these enhancements are subsequently prolonged and intensified by signals from frontal cortical areas.

D. Enhancement of Activity in Brain Maps of Spatial Location

The PC contains areas that register or index the location of a visual stimulus (e.g., Colby, 1991), and lesions in this region reduce the ability to shift orientation to objects in the contralateral visual field (Heilman, Bowers, Coslett, Whelan, & Wat-son, 1985; Posner, Walker, Friedrich, & Rafal, 1984). Because the areas of the PC connect richly to many areas of the posterior and anterior cortices (Goldman-Rakic, 1988), it seems plausible to conjecture that the parietal area contains a "mas-ter map" of spatial location (Koch & Ullman, 1985; Treisman, 1988) in which a rel-ative enhancement of cell discharges expressing attention to a specific object location may be reciprocally connected to corresponding cells in spatial maps of attributes of that object. Attributes of objects that form singletons in a display may induce pop out, which is presumed to signal a location by enhancing the discharge of parietal cells that code object location. This "preattentive parsing" of the visual field has been observed in infants (also in infant monkeys of 3–4 months) by Rovee-Collier, 1984, suggesting that connections are intact between the PPC and areas that code object attributes.

Given the large receptive fields found in these parietal areas, it is not surprising that single-cell recordings indicate that the coding of location information is dis-tributed across large numbers of cells in many (but not all) subareas of PPC (Ander-sen, 1989; Mazzoni, Andersen, & Jordan, 1993; Zipser & Andersen, 1988). In con-trast, the coding of object locations in V1 and V4 is usually more local (Desimone and Schein, 1987), and in the inferotemporal (IT) area face information appears to be coded by clusters of cells (Young & Yamane, 1992). O'Reilly, Kosslyn, Marsolek, and Chabris (1990) simulated the operation of networks of PPC and IT cells and showed that location information could be coded more accurately with the more distributed code of the PC network.

In the early months of development, the SC movement system may be the dominant mechanism that produces the appropriate enhancements in the PC, whereas in later months of development the FEF may begin to compete and be the dominant mechanism that produces these effects in PC.

The controls on the oculomotor mechanisms in the SC are presumed to be retinal inputs that project directly to the superficial SC layers or project indirectly through V1 or through V1-V2-V5 (the motion pathway). These cells in the superficial layers of the SC project via the pulvinar to the PC (and other cortical areas) and therefore are in a position to control the enhancement of the PC cells coding the location of the visual stimulus beyond the level induced via the cortical pathway from V1 to PC. In this way the pattern of cell enhancements in PC is presumed to be exogenously controlled.

E. Prefrontal Cortical Influences on Visuospatial Orienting

Controls of visuospatial orienting from prefrontal areas have been termed endogenous or top-down controls. Endogenous controls on the indexing of object locations can be produced through the FEF-to-PC connections that are parallel to the FEF-to-SC (deeper layers) that drive the oculomotor generators in the brain stem (Fries, 1984; Graham, Lin, & Kaas, 1979). The FEF cells show enhanced responses to stimuli that will be a target for eye movements (Wurtz & Mohler, 1976), and the FEF appears to operate as a mechanism that induces eye movements in response to frontal sources of control such as those serving associative and working memory. Associative controls of motor responses may serve as the basis of the anticipatory alternation behavior observed after infants reach 4 months of age (Johnson et al., 1991), and associative controls on perceptual expectations may serve as the basis of the contingency learning by which infants of 4 months predict the location of a peripheral stimulus on the basis of the information in a central cue (Johnson et al., 1991). Circuits that underlie associative memory are generally believed to involve hippocampal pathways (e.g., Squire et al., 1992; Zola-Morgan & Squire, 1986), and the foregoing infant studies of associative learning suggest some degree of maturation of these pathways by 4 months of age. However, anatomical studies show relatively late hippocampal maturation at about 15–18 months, with myelination continuing into years 3–5 (Brody, Kinney, Kloman, & Gilles, 1987; Kretschmann, Kammradt, Krauthausen, Sauer, & Wingert, 1986). However, one should allow for the possibility that some computations may be carried out by the hippocampal circuits earlier than others.

Whereas infants of 3 months remember a cue-response association for hours or days (Rovee-Collier, 1984), infants' memory in the delayed response task does not exceed 2- or 3-s delay between hiding and retrieval until after 8 months, and thereafter the length of the delay increases about 2 s through the 12th month (Diamond & Doar, 1989). In contrast, infant monkeys during their third month showed a progression from 6 to 12 seconds in the delay that could be tolerated in this task, and lesions of the dorsolateral prefrontal cortex at 4.5 months eliminated successful performance at delays above 2 s (Diamond, 1990). The dorsolateral prefrontal cortex (DLPFC), which develops late (Goldman-Rakic, 1987), has been strongly implicated in performance of the delayed response task by an impressive array of studies (for a brief review, see Diamond, 1990), including the oculomotor delayed response (Funahashi, Bruce, & Goldman-Rakic, 1989; Wilson, O'Scalaidhe, & Goldman-Rakic, 1993). Goldman-Rakic (1987) has reviewed a wide array of evidence that implicates DLPFC circuitry in working memory (see also Goldman-Rakic & Friedman, 1991; Wilson et al., 1993).

Therefore, the sources of endogenous control of visual orienting would seem to involve hippocampal structures in the case of associative memory for visual locations, and the DLPFC in the case of working memory for visual locations. When eye movements are called upon to exhibit this memory, the hippocampal and DLPFC structures presumably project activity to a spatial map in the FEF, which in turn projects to eye-movement generators in the SC directly and indirectly through the PPC. The projections from the FEF eye-movement mechanism to the PPC presumably produce an endogenous expression of attention in the PPC by inducing an enhancement of activity in cell populations representing a location in visual space. Also, direct projections existing between the DLPFC and the PC cells (Goldman-Rakic, Chafee, & Friedman, 1993) may produce an endogenous expression of attention in the PC by prolonging the activation begun by the abrupt onset of a stimulus.

F. A Neural View of Attentional Shifts in Visual Space

The foregoing review of infant and adult studies suggest that attentional expression in visual shift orienting between well-separated spatial locations can be viewed as top-down enhancements in particular cells of the PC, whose initial activity is produced by abrupt onsets. The mechanisms that generate these initial activities (particularly when several objects are presented simultaneously) are presumed to be oculomotor-related circuits within the SC and the FEF, while the mechanisms that prolong the activities are working-memory-related circuits within the frontal cortex. Circuits within the thalamus are presumed to contribute to subsequent attentional expression by amplifying the activity in the parietal areas coding for location.

The controlling sources for the infant that determine what will be attended and the length of time attention will be given appear to be (a) characteristics of the exogenous stimuli and (b) activity in endogenous structures within the prefrontal cortex that subserve associative and working memory (Goldman-Rakic, Chafee, & Friedman, 1993). For the adult, there may well be several additional controlling sources (e.g., the anterior cingulate area) (Posner & Petersen, 1990), that are concerned with organizational processing that influences how attention is expressed both in anterior and posterior cortical regions.

Infants change in their ability to orient to the onset of a peripheral stimulus while they are sustaining attention at the center location. In the Johnson et al. (1991) task already described, the central "attractor" stimulus remained while the peripheral stimulus was presented, and the percentage of trials in which infants shifted their gaze to the peripheral stimulus (within 8 s) went from about 40% to about 90% between 2 and 4 months of age. In the shift-orienting task, it is assumed that two locations are marked in oculomotor system maps by enhanced cellular activity, one at the site corresponding to the central object location and the other at the site corresponding to the peripheral object location. The site with the stronger activity would be expected to win in the control of gaze direction.

The competition for control of eye movements prior to 3 months of age occurs mainly in the SC, where cells in the rostral part of the SC fire strongly and inhibit caudally located "saccade" cells when animals maintain their gaze on an object of interest (Munoz & Wurtz, 1993a). These "fixation" cells reduce their firings when the animal makes a saccadic eye movement to another object location. After 4 months of age, the competition between central and peripheral object locations in orienting tasks may also take place in the PPC, where cells corresponding to the central and peripheral locations are assumed also to compete by the strength of their enhancements. Fixation cells have also been found in area 7a of the PPC (Mountcastle, Lynch, Georgopoulos, Sakata, & Acuna, 1975; Sakata, Shibutani, & Kawano, 1980), and although the temporal patterns of firing differ somewhat from SC fixation cells, the fixation cells may be part of a fixation system (Munoz & Wurtz, 1993b) that sustains attention in the manner observed in 3 and 6 month olds by Richards (1989).

Posner and his colleagues (1988) have emphasized the role of the PC in the "disengagement" of gaze and attention from a current object location. The ease with which an infant of 4 months shifts its gaze to a peripheral stimulus onset suggests that computations in the PC override the tendency for SC fixation cells to sustain attention at a central stimulus. If it is assumed that the center and peripheral stimuli produce enhanced firing in PC cells that code the spatial locations of these stimuli, then one may ask what happens in the PC to allow the activity of cells that code the peripheral site to dominate the activity of cells that code the central site. One characteristic of the PC mapping at this age is that the PC-to-FEF reciprocal connections may be sufficiently intact to enable the frontal cortex to sustain the activity in the PC induced by a sudden onset of a peripheral object, and thereby increase its chance of winning over the activity existing at the center object. However, if the FEF-to-PC activity is already sufficiently strong, then even in adults a peripheral stimulus may not induce a shift of attention (e.g., Yantis, 1993).

Another possible factor that would potentiate the effect of a peripheral stimulus on a shift of orienting is a buildup over trials of residual activation in the PPC at locations of recently attended events (e.g., objects presented at some location to the left or right of center), that can increase the effectiveness of a peripheral stimulus (LaBerge & Brown, 1986, 1989; LaBerge, Carlson, Williams, & Bunney, 1997).

Thus, a case could be made that the expression of spatial attention during orienting waits upon the development of the PC, and that prior to that time, the SC will not release the gaze from a centrally located object when it is strongly fixated. However, on occasions when a central object location is not strongly fixated, one might expect that the SC could allow a saccade to a peripheral object, following the fixation-saccade cell interaction scheme proposed by Munoz and Wurtz (1993b). A related phenomenon in the adult, presumably based on the same fixation-saccade cell scheme, is the generation of a short-latency express saccade. The express saccade occurs apparently only when the peripheral stimulus is located at least 2° from fixation, and when central fixation is released before the onset of a peripheral target by a blank period (Fischer & Ramsperger, 1986; Reuter-Lorenz, Hughes, & Fendrich, 1991). Another way in which a release from fixation may come about after 3 months of age is the development of the inhibitory pathway from the substantia nigra pars reticulata (SNr) to the SC. However, few cells in the SNr project selectively to the rostral area in the SC where the fixation cells were found (Munoz & Wurtz, 1993a).

Thus, in the shift-orienting task, the tendency to shift to a peripheral object location while orientation is being sustained at a central location would seem to depend upon the competitive effects induced by several relatively sophisticated computations within the PC areas as it matures. These computations include (a) the sustaining (and/or enhancing) of stimulus-induced cell activity in either location by frontal structures; (b) the potentiation of stimulus-induced cell activity by the memory residue of prior object locations; (c) the projected activity from cells at corresponding object-location sites in the SC; and (d) the possible modulatory effects of the thalamic circuitry that is involved when frontal areas and the SC project to the PC. When a peripheral cue and a central object compete for attention, frontal cells that code the central or peripheral locations may sustain activity in cells at one or the other corresponding site in the PC. It is the latter sustained enhancements that are assumed to express spatial attention at the central or peripheral object location. Meanwhile, the cell activity at the nondominant sites in the frontal, SC, and PC areas is reduced. To what extent this reduction in activity comes about by passive decay as opposed to active inhibition between the dominant and nondominant cells within a given area is not clear at present.

Both overt and covert shifts in orienting would seem to be produced by enhanced activity in cells at one object-location site while activity subsides in cells at the other site. During shifts of orienting, no changes of activity are assumed to occur in cells corresponding to locations between the two object-location sites. Hence the shift orienting is deemed to be discrete, and the only analog movements that occur in the body are the mechanical movements of the eyes in their orbits. Furthermore, a shift of activation sites from one object location to another in the SC, frontal, and PC maps does not imply a "transfer" of cellular activity from one location to another, but rather the rapid buildup of activity at a new location while the activity at the old location subsides or is suppressed (LaBerge & Brown, 1989; LaBerge, Carlson, Williams, & Bunney, 1997).

A phenomenon related to the control of shift orienting that has been studied in the young infant is the inhibition of return (for a review, see Johnson, 1994), which is a reduction in the tendency to orient toward a previously attended visual location. This inhibitory effect, which can follow a shift of orienting, is believed to be carried out mainly by the SC, because it is closely related to preparation for an eye movement to that location (Rafal, Calabresi, Brennan, & Sciolto, 1989), and can be abolished by midbrain lesions (Posner, Rafal, Choate, & Vaughan, 1985; Rafal, Posner, Friedman, Inhoff, & Berstein, 1988). The adaptive benefits of the inhibition of return is that it biases attention toward novel locations (Posner & Cohen, 1984). Rapid development of this phenomenon apparently takes place between 3 and 6 months (Clohessy et al., 1991). This finding poses a problem for a purely SC account of inhibition of return, since the SC is believed to be relatively mature at birth (Atkinson, 1984; Chugani, Phelps, & Mazziotta, 1987).

G. Selective Attention in Adults

Most orienting tasks studied in the laboratory involve simple detection of the presence of an object that is well separated from distractors. In contrast many attention tasks require the discrimination or identification of a target object that is displayed with distractors positioned nearby. In these tasks, the location of the target relative to the distractors (e.g., the location of the mother's face in a group of faces) may be known prior to the onset of the display, or the location may be unknown and search operations are required to find the location of the target. During search, selective operations are presumed to operate as each item in the display is individually examined in succession, as is typically the case when targets are identified by a conjunction of features (Treisman & Gelade, 1980) or when targets and distractors have similar attributes (Nagy & Sanchez, 1990).

When objects are located close to one another, large receptive fields such as those found in parietal areas would seem to preclude the resolving of attention to the small spatial area of one object. Examples are attending to a letter within a word or a nose on a face when the word and face subtend less than 2 or 3° of visual angle.

One way that large receptive fields may be constricted to sharpen the resolution of a spatial location code involves the thalamic circuitry that is interconnected with cortical sites that code locations of target and distractor objects. Simulations of the thalamic circuit (LaBerge, Carter, & Brown, 1992) suggest that the sharpening of input contrasts is produced mainly by activity enhancement of target pathways, accompanied by some degree of activity suppression of distractor pathways. Hence, the intensity of attentional activity in thalamocortical circuits would be expected to increase when distractors are placed near the target object; evidence from a PET study in which distractors were placed close to a target object (separations were less than a degree) showed increases in neural activity in the pulvinar nucleus of the thalamus (LaBerge & Buchsbaum, 1990). Also, the intensity of attentional activity would be expected to increase as the target-distractor similarity increases; evidence from another PET study that varied similarity of distractors to the target stimulus (the letters G and Q surrounding a target letter O versus line slashes surrounding the target letter O) showed increases in pulvinar activity (Liotti, Fox, & LaBerge, 1994). Conceivably, outputs from the PC to the V1-to-IT pathway can be sharpened by the parallel connections that traverse the pulvinar. Hence, the thalamic nuclei could serve as a mechanism of attention that increases the activity differences in cortical columns that represent closely spaced objects.

Several recent studies support the hypothesis that the thalamus is involved in expressing attentional selectivity. Frith and Friston (1996) showed that the right midthalamus is activated when subjects attend to sounds while ignoring visual stimuli. Morris, Friston, and Dolan (1997) found that increases in salience of emotionally expressive faces increased activation in the right pulvinar nucleus. A review of nine PET studies of visual processing (Shulman, et al., 1997) superimposed the PET activations obtained from tasks of discrimination, search, language, memory and imagery, and found consistent activations in the thalamus and cerebellum, but no consistent activation of particular cortical areas (except for the striate area—Area V1).

The course of development of the ability to concentrate attention to closely positioned objects or to a small part of an object apparently has not received much systematic investigation. Given that the PC involvement in orienting (to objects separated by 30° or so) begins at approximately 3 months, one would expect that the ability to orient to an object at smaller separations would develop in the following months or possibly years.

It is known that the projections to the PC from the SC synapse in the pulvinar; consequently, the amplification capability of the pulvinar circuitry may serve to enhance the bottom-up signaling between the SC and the PC when abrupt stimulus onsets index a new location in PC sites. Orienting to a new location is regarded as an "engage" operation (Posner, 1988; Posner & Petersen, 1990), and lesions of the posterior thalamus in adults have been shown to disturb orienting to visual signals (Rafal & Posner, 1987). The engagement of orienting would appear not to be the same as the operation of selecting a target from distractors, because the operation of shrinking receptive fields of target and distractors apparently requires intense and relatively prolonged top-down activation of the pulvinar circuitry. Thus, orienting to a new location is assumed to produce activation sites in cortical areas that can then be further activated by the top-down controlled attentional circuitry to resolve target and distractor locations during the selection process.

Development of thalamic mechanisms serving selection and orienting also involves the concurrent development of the cortical areas to which they project, because the thalamic circuitry critically involves returning fibers from the cortical area to which it projects. A much more appropriate label for "thalamic circuitry" is therefore "thalamocortical circuitry." Cortical areas of particular importance in spatial attention to objects, with or without distractors being present, are the posterior PC and areas V4 and IT in which spatial attention is presumed to select which objects are discriminated or identified. Although the development of thalamic projections to a cortical area develops early (Rakic, 1995), the cortical cells that receive these projections and those that return the projections develop later, and the parietal cortex apparently continues to mature through the early years of adolescence (Lecours, 1975). Therefore it would be expected that attentional processing that depends upon later stages of maturation of the thalamo-cortical circuitry would continue to show improvement during childhood years, while attentional processing that depends upon earlier stages of circuit maturation would have shown its greatest improvement during infancy.

H. Selective Attention in the Child

We turn now to studies of selective attention in the child. Akhtar and Enns (1989) added a filtering (selectivity) component to the standard two-location orienting task developed by Posner (1978) and tested subjects 5, 7, and 24 years of age. The cue was a dot that appeared to the right or left of center, and subjects responded to one of two targets (a cross or a square) that was displayed in isolation or was displayed with a distractor on each side. The overall results showed appreciable improvement in performance (ratio of response time [RT] to percent correct) with age, and a reduction of the difference between valid and invalid cue conditions with age. For valid cue conditions the effect of the distractor was relatively constant for the 5, 7, and 20 year olds, but for invalid cue conditions the effect of the distractor decreased with age.

These results suggest that shifting visual attention to a new location shows substantial improvement between the ages of 5 and 20. However, selection of the middle object of a three-object ensemble does not improve when it appears in cued locations, where activation is initially low, but does improve in uncued locations where activation is already high. Tipper and McLaren (1990) used a four-location task with subjects from grade 1, grade 6, and college undergraduates and found overall decreases in RT with age. The effect of distractors showed a consistent trend with age, but the interaction was not significant.

The sustaining and shifting of orienting to auditory and somatosensory stimuli is presumed to develop in the infant along with visual orienting, but less systematic research has been carried out with the ear and touch senses owing to the fact that the structures responsive to manipulations by verbal instructions and measurements by relative fine motor movements are not yet developed at those ages (Olson & Sherman, 1983).

I. Development of Attention to Actions

From 6–12 months the infant shows progress in grasping, reaching for, locomoting toward, and manipulating objects and persons in the environment. According to Olson and Sherman (1983), these responses are guided largely by what the infant is currently learning to attend to in the social and the physical world. The responses, in turn, change the sensory inputs, which in turn change the momentary focus of attention. But as locomoting and manipulative skills develop, the infant soon becomes faced with the problem of doing more than one thing at a time, for example, walking around an obstacle while holding a glass of water upright.

To successfully perform two or more tasks at a time requires the management or coordination of attention to task goals and task operations. These organizational, or "executive" functions are believed to depend crucially on computations carried out in the frontal lobes of the brain (Baddeley, 1986; Duncan, 1995; Norman & Shallice, 1980). A complex problem-solving task (e.g., problems in standard intelligence tests) can usually be analyzed into subproblems, each of which may define its solution in terms of a goal, and a particular subproblem may be further analyzed into its subproblems, each of which may define its solution in terms of a goal, so that the entire problem may be conceptualized and remembered as a hierarchy of goals (Duncan, 1995). When the individual has solved the problem and gone through it several times, each remembered subgoal may itself index in memory the operations (internal or external actions) that are performed to achieve it.

During the performance of organized problem solving the individual is presumed to employ attention in selecting the appropriate subgoal among a clutter of remembered subgoals, selecting the operation(s) that will achieve that subgoal, and then sustain selective attention to each particular operation to insulate it from interfering information in other concurrent operations. For example, when two operations are coordinated, as the operations in the two hands must be in playing the violin or piano, or setting the feet before throwing a ball, the control over an automatic sequence of operations is presumed to be shifted rapidly between the limbs. During the time intervals that control is directed to the operations the information flow of that control must be protected from crosstalk arising from the other operation (Allport, 1989).

It would seem reasonable to presume that expression of selective attention is required for the successful choosing of goals, their associated operations, and the protective insulating of operational control. The expression of this attention is assumed to be the relative enhancement of activity in cortical sites corresponding to the attended goal or operation. This conceptualization of attentional selection in the organizational management of "executive" actions is essentially the same as the conceptualization of attentional selection in the modulation of incoming stimulus information: enhanced activation of the target site relative to activation of distractor sites.

The brain areas in which attentional expression is crucial for the selection of goals and actions is presumed to be the frontal areas. PET measures of blood flow in tasks that involve the management of multiple operations (Corbetta, Miezin, Dobmeyer, Shulman, & Petersen, 1991; Frith, Friston, Liddle, & Frackowiak, 1991; Pardo, Pardo, Janer, & Raichle, 1990; Petersen, Fox, Posner, Minton, & Raichle,

1988) reveal that the anterior cingulate area of the midfrontal cortex is active in these tasks as compared with simple tasks in which little if any processing is devoted to the selection of subgoals and their contingent operations. For example, in the Corbetta et al. (1991) experiment, one of the simple tasks required subjects to determine whether or not the color of an array of moving rectangles matched the color of the array that had just been cued, another task required the matching of the rectangle shapes to the shapes in the cue, and the third simple task required the matching of the velocity of movement to that of the shapes in the cue. Within a block of trials the goal was the same: match only the color, or only the shape, or only the movement velocity. In the complex task, the subjects were instructed to determine which of the three attributes matched the cue, and now the subject had to manage the goal and operation of more than one subtask on each trial. The PET measures showed that the anterior cingulate was more active than in passive control conditions during the complex task but not during the simple tasks.

If selective attention is expressed in frontal pathways when goals and operations are being managed in complex tasks, then what are the sources of control that determine which goals will be selected? One way to prioritize a set of alternative goals is to compute their motivational value or interest to the individual. It could be conjectured that circuits in the frontal cortex, which appear to be crucial to goal-directed processing (e.g., Fuster, 1989; Goldman-Rakic, 1987) are connected to cortico-basal ganglia-thalamo-cortico circuits (Alexander & Crutcher, 1990), which may enable the motivation-sensitive basal ganglia to regulate the level of activity in the frontal cortex through the thalamo-cortical loop (LaBerge, 1998). This cortico-basal ganglia-thalamo-cortical circuitry does not exist in the posterior cortex, suggesting that the processing of perceptions is not as directly affected by motivational interests as is the processing of actions (LaBerge, 1998). Thus, anatomical connectivity of the anterior cortical areas with the basal ganglia suggest one way that goals might be prioritized in anterior cortical areas during the management of complex tasks.

J. Developmental Aging

As the adult ages, the neuroanatomy changes in several ways: neurons in some areas are lost, dendritic shafts and spines are fewer, there is a general increase in glia cells and various inactive substances within the neuron, and the level of neurotransmitter substances available at synapses decreases (Timiras, 1988). Many of these changes affect the ways that neural circuits of the brain process information. The issue in this section of the chapter concerns the effects of these structural changes on attentional processing, specifically, on the expression, mechanisms, and control of attention.

Although many older adult drivers are skilled in driving, as a group they have more traffic convictions, crashes, and fatalities per mile than any other adult age group (National Highway Traffic Safety Administration, 1989). Self-reports by aging adults indicate that, with age, it is more difficult to read signs, locate a sign among other signs, read a sign while moving, and read credits on TV (Kosnik, Winslow, Kline, Rasinski, & Sekuler, 1988). Changes in visual acuity are only weakly correlated with vehicle crashes (e.g., K. Ball, Owsley, Sloane, Roenker, & Bruni, 1993; Hills & Burg, 1977), and age differences in detection of an object in the peripheral field do not increase with eccentricity of the object's location unless other objects also appear in the field (K. K. Ball, Beard, Roenker, Miller, & Griggs, 1988) so that the causes of decline with age in these and other visual skills have been sought elsewhere, particularly in a general cognitive slowing with age (e.g., Cerella, 1985; Salthouse, 1985) and possibly in a decline in attentional processing.

A recent thorough review of the literature on attentional changes in aging by Hartley (1992) identified a consensus for strong age-related effects for the following attention-related phenomena: in semantic priming, larger RT benefits; for Stroop-type effects, larger benefits and costs produced by irrelevant stimuli; in visual search, larger conjunction search rates; in memory search, larger RT changes due to set size; in dichotic listening and dual tasks, decreased performance. Some investigators (e.g., Cerella, 1991) have suggested that all age-related effects can be accounted for by a general slowing of processing, but the amount by which absolute response times in these and other tasks increases with age is not always found in the analysis of the components of a task, such as the time course of priming and cuing (see the review by Hartley, 1992).

D'Aloisio and Klein (1990) compared the attentional performance of young (17 to 25 years of age) and older (55 to 75 years of age) on three frequently used experimental paradigms. The search task was one employed by Treisman and Souther (1985), in which the subject was to decide whether a circle was present in an array of circles having gaps; the filtering (selection) task involved placing distractors at varying distances from the target (the digit 1 or 2) following the design of B. A. Eriksen and Eriksen (1974), and the attention range (preparatory attention) task focused attention narrowly or widely across five letters and used the digit 1 or 2 as the probe, following the design of LaBerge (1983) and LaBerge and Brown (1986, 1989). The results of the search task showed that older adults search at a slower rate than younger adults, which is consistent with the search results of Plude and Hoyer (1985), and may be due to a general slowing of processing rather than a deficit in attention (Salthouse, 1980). In both the attentional selection and the narrow-broad attentional preparation tasks, performance appeared to be the same for the two adult groups. In the young adults, the selection and preparation measures showed a significant correlation ($r = -.53$), but there was no significant correlation between these two tasks and the search task. In the older adults, no pair of tasks showed a significant correlation.

One pattern that seems to emerge from reviewing studies of aging effects on attention is that the age effects are relatively small in tasks where attention is directed to perceiving the location of an object, but relatively large when attention is directed to the performing of more than one task currently. This classification scheme corresponds to a possibly oversimplified, but useful, neuroanatomical division of cognitive processing in which perceptual processing is assumed to be carried out largely by the posterior cortex, and action processing is carried out largely by the anterior cortex. Posner and Petersen (1990) have proposed that attentional processing in each of these two regions involves different attentional systems. The posterior attentional system includes the parietal cortex, superior colliculus, and thalamus, which respectively mediate the disengagement, movement, and engagement of attention during overt and covert (shift) orienting, whereas the anterior attentional system contains the anterior cingulate area, which mediates the management of multiple operations during concurrent tasks.

The attentional perspective described in this chapter suggests a possible refinement of the anterior–posterior cortical scheme of attentional processing. The expression of attention as the relative enhancement of information flow in cortical pathways is presumed to hold for both posterior and anterior cortical processing, with the attentional expression of perceptual processing taking place mainly in posterior cortical streams and the attentional expression of operations taking place mainly in anterior cortical streams. The voluntary controls for both perceptual and operational attention are assumed to be located in anterior areas (e.g., prefrontal areas), whereas the thalamic mechanism that is hypothesized to increase and sharpen enhancements of attentional expressions is available not only to posterior cortical fields but also to virtually all anterior cortical fields as well (Jones, 1985).

However, the anterior cingulate circuits would appear also to influence the expression of attention in anterior cortices in some way (e.g., by place marking) when goals and operations are being managed in concurrent task situations, and therefore this mechanism also constitutes a distinguishing component of attentional processing in the anterior and posterior systems. PET measures taken while subjects are engaged in concurrent tasks, both of which require attention, have consistently shown enhanced activity in anterior cingulate and prefrontal areas.

An instructive example of an aging study that was guided by the Posner and Petersen (1990) anterior–posterior cortical scheme is given by Hartley (1993). He varied the displays of a Stroop-type task so that for one type of display the anterior attentional mechanism would dominate processing, and for the other type of display the posterior mechanism would dominate processing. In one condition, the display was the traditional Stroop display, in which the words *blue* and *green* were printed in blue or green ink, which presumably requires the management of the two tasks of color and lexical processing. In the other condition, the word *blue* or *green* was printed in black ink and positioned either above or below a blue or green rectangle so that spatial orienting could select the colored rectangle and allow the color-processing task to dominate processing. For both conditions, the display was located either to the left or right of a central fixation point, and cues were presented either centrally by an arrow, or peripherally by a black rectangular outline. The results at stimulus onset asymmetry (SOA) ranging from 100–300 ms showed no appreciable difference between the 18–21-year-old adults and the 68–86-year-old adults for the word-adjacent-to-color condition, but a strong difference between the young and old adults for the standard colored word Stroop condition. This contrasting pattern of outcomes observed within the same experimental situation is consistent with age-related findings found in the different experimental situations that employed location-coding tasks (D'Aoisio & Klein, 1990; Nissen & Corkin, 1985; Plude & Hoyer, 1985) on the one hand and dual tasks (e.g., Madden & Plude, 1993; McDowd & Birren, 1990) on the other. These findings support the hypothesis that advanced aging produces deficits when selective attention is directed to one of several task operations (presumed to be mediated mainly by anterior cortical systems), but preserves selective attention to one of several available object locations (presumed to be mediated mainly by posterior cortical systems).

III. THE EVOLUTION OF ATTENTIONAL STRUCTURES

The preceding section of this chapter compared human adults and children of various ages in attentional capabilities. In this section the human adult is compared with adults of other species with respect to the attentional operations they can potentially call upon. Because the most salient index of a species is generally its structural morphology, it would seem appropriate to organize comparisons of a particular information-processing capability across species around the differences in the neural structures that are deemed to be crucial to that type of information processing. Therefore, this section will draw heavily on what is known and frequently conjectured about the neural substrates of attention while considering how the expression, mechanisms, and control of attentional processes change across phyla.

The brain structures relevant to attentional processing that have shown the most dramatic phylogenetic changes may be conveniently classed into two groups, anterior and posterior areas. The anterior cortical areas and the particular thalamic nuclei that amplify activity in these areas express attention to actions, but also presumably control attentional expressions of perception in the posterior cortical areas through the thalamic pulvinar nucleus. These cortical and thalamic areas vary dramatically across species, and presumably are thereby mainly responsible for the differences in attentional capabilities across species.

A. Anterior Brain Structures: Attention to Actions

Probably the most objective indicator that some kind of selective processing is going on in an animal is simply the occurrence of a single overt response. Given the large number of alternative responses that are in the repertoire of the normal animal, some operation or set of operations within the animal determines that one and not some other response will be emitted at any given moment. The processes that determine which response is selected have been used by one tradition of attention theories, the late-selection theories, as the basis for the attention process (Deutsch & Deutsch, 1963; Duncan, 1980; Norman, 1968). The classes of events commonly believed to induce a response are (a) an immediate stimulus, with which a response may be associated innately or through learning, and (b) an internal neural event, which is sometimes regarded as the triggering component of voluntary action. It is said that combinations of external and internal influences converge when a stimulus "sets the occasion for a response," for example, when a response associated with a particular stimulus is emitted or not emitted according to the current motivational state of the individual. Not only external responses but also internal responses or covert actions (e.g., rehearsing a telephone number) can also be produced by a similar combination of external and internal events.

The selection of an action and its execution over time may or may not be modulated by attentional operations; many reflex actions and well-learned actions may be initiated and run off automatically. Thus, attention to actions seem to be involved whenever responses are not governed by routine.

Attention to actions (e.g., moving the fingers in particular sequences) appears to be expressed chiefly in anterior cortical areas, whereas attention to perceptions (e.g., colors, faces, etc.) appears to be expressed chiefly in posterior cortical areas. Of particular importance to this chapter is the special internal action that commands attention to perceptions and actions. Thus, the anterior cortical area contains both the executive or command aspect of attentional control as well as sites for the expression of attention to actions.

The executive aspect of attentional control is currently viewed as one part of the working memory system (a part that includes encoding and retrieval), whereas the other part of the working memory system stores information in a highly accessible form over a short period of time (Baddeley, 1995). Cross-species comparisons of working memory storage have been reported in the literature much more frequently than cross-species comparisons of attentional control. However, if the range of what can be controlled attentionally from working memory depends upon the range of what can be stored in working memory, then experimental evidence of what a species is capable of storing over delay intervals may provide some indication of what the animal is capable of attending to.

The location of structures in the anterior cortex that serve working memory lie forward of the primary motor cortex (Area 4), the strip that lies anterior and adjacent to the lateral fissure, and it is here that the execution of an overt response is expressed as an increase in firing rates of the particular pyramidal cells that drive muscle groups. In front of the motor strip lies the premotor cortex (Area 6), which is closely associated with the motor cortex, and apparently is involved in processing motor plans. Both strips extend ventrally from the top (dorsal) part of the brain to a point on or close to the Sylvian fissure.

In front of these areas lies the prefrontal cortex, which, unlike the motor and premotor areas, does not contain a somatotopic map of the body, and does not contain cells that directly connect to the spinal cord and/or brain stem motor nuclei, and does not evoke muscle movements when stimulated electrically (for a review, see Goldman-Rakic, 1987). Nevertheless, the prefrontal cortex contains subdivisions that are believed to influence responses by sustaining response-related information in working memory over short periods of time after a stimulus has been withdrawn (see reviews by Fuster, 1989; Goldman-Rakic, 1987; Passingham, 1985).

The monkey prefrontal cortex contains anatomically distinct regions in which neurons that are active during the delays between a sample display and a test display are selectively responsive to spatial locations, and the shape and color of objects (Wilson et al., 1993), and to the identity of faces (O'Scalaidhe, Wilson, & Goldman-Rakic, 1997). A PET study with humans showed anatomically different working memory systems for spatial, object, and verbal information with the verbal system localized more in the left hemisphere and the spatial system localized more in the right hemisphere (Smith, Jonides, & Koeppe, 1996).

The executive control part of working memory may be located in areas adjacent to the prefrontal areas, where the storage part of working memory is believed to be located. Recent spatial working memory studies (Haxby et al., 1994; Jonides et al., 1993) have shown activity in regions that contain both the premotor (Area 6) and frontal eye fields (Area 8). Attention-related activations have also been shown in premotor areas in several PET studies (Corbetta et al., 1993; Liotti, Fox, & LaBerge, 1994; Nobre et al., 1997).

The kind of information sustained in prefrontal areas of working memory may under certain circumstances take precedence over immediate external stimuli in determining what response is evoked. Goldman-Rakic and Friedman (1991) have stated that the ability of the brain to hold information "in the absence of direct stimulation may be its inherently most flexible mechanism and its evolutionarily most significant achievement" (p. 73).

B. The Evolution of the Prefrontal Cortex and Attention

During the evolution of primates, the prefrontal cortex greatly increased in size, and in the human it occupies approximately 30% of the cerebral cortex surface (Brodmann, 1925). The human prefrontal cortex is marked by a granularity in layer IV that is less apparent in other frontal cortical areas, whereas the prefrontal cortical layers of other mammals (e.g., carnivores, marsupials, and rodents) exhibit agranularity throughout (Akert, 1964).

A major behavioral indicator of prefrontal function across species is the delayed response task (Hunter, 1913), in which the animal observes a stimulus object being placed in one location, after which the object is concealed for an interval of time before the animal can make a response. Hunter (1913) compared the maximum delays that could be tolerated in this task across several species and found these delays to be 10 s for rats, 25 s for raccoons, 5 min for dogs, and 25 min for an 8-year-old girl. Lesions of the prefrontal cortex of monkeys have been known to produce severe impairments in the performance of spatial-delayed tasks since the early experiments of Jacobsen (1936), and many studies since then have established that these tasks are successfully performed only if the DLPFC in both hemispheres is intact (for a review, see Goldman-Rakic, 1987). Taken together with Hunter's findings, these results strongly suggest that the delayed response task measures the capacity of prefrontal circuitry to sustain response-relevant information over short periods of time.

Caution must be exercised in concluding what kind of information is being stored during the delays; if the subjects can maintain a postural orientation toward the location of the target object during the delay, then the "content" or type of working memory would seem to be mainly motoric, but if postural orientations are prevented, then it would appear that spatial location may dominate as the type of working memory involved during the delay. If the subjects can store motoric and/or location information in working memory, they also may be able to use this information to command preparatory attention to these types of information. In the case of motoric working memory, the preparatory attention to respond and the storage of the response may overlap considerably, whereas for spatial working memory, the storage of the location may be independent of the preparatory attention to it (see Figure 1).

Phylogenetically, working memory for location in prefrontal areas may have developed in association with motoric preparation in adjacent premotor areas. If this is the case, then the control of attentional preparation for a perception or action would seem to have preceded phylogenetically the storage in working memory of the perception or action.

C. The Evolution of the Supplemental Motor Area and the Anterior Cingulate Cortex

More dorsal and medial to the prefrontal area are the supplemental motor area (SMA) and the anterior cingulate areas, which have been strongly implicated in executive control functions for complex tasks (LaBerge, 1990a; Posner & Petersen, 1990; Posner & Raichle, 1994). As the prefrontal areas of the anterior cortex expanded during evolution, the anterior cingulate area and SMA also expanded. The contribution of the anterior portion of the cingulate area and SMA to the adaptive abilities of the animal and human appears to concern the management of more than one simple task operation.

An example of operations management is learning to move the fingers of one hand in a particular order (Jueptner et al., 1997; Roland, 1985). Imaging this task without performing it overtly activates the SMA (for a review of several brain-imaging studies involving many different voluntary tasks, see Roland, 1985), which suggest that the SMA is crucially involved in the expression of attention to action plans.

The anterior cingulate area, on the other hand, may be crucial for the storage component of working memory for complex voluntary tasks. In a PET experiment by Corbetta et al. (1991), subjects were to decide whether an array of moving colored rectangles differed in velocity, color, or shape. The PET measures taken during the task showed increased blood flow in the right anterior cingulate area (a region on the medial surface of the cortex above and at the forward end of the corpus callosum), and in the right dorsolateral prefrontal area. However, these areas did not show increased blood flow in an additional task condition that used the same stimuli and response assignments but required that only one operation be performed over a series of trials.

Other tasks whose working-memory demands appear to induce enhanced activity in the anterior cingulate area, as measured by PET, are the Stroop task (Pardo et al., 1990) and the verb-generation task (Petersen et al., 1988), in which a noun is given and the subject must generate an associated verb (e.g., water-drink). All of these tasks appear to involve consideration of more than one operation on a trial, which implies that the anterior cingulate and SMA computations may be required to prioritize action routines (management of actions with respect to goals) while they are temporarily sustained in working memory (LaBerge, 1990b).

Recently ERP studies (e.g., Gehring, Gos, Coles, Meyer, & Donchin, 1993) and an fMRI study (Carter et al., 1998) have implicated the anterior cingulate area in the processing of errors during performance of tasks. Whether the error processing involves comparisons of the just-performed erroneous response with the correct response or involves competing response tendencies, it would appear that working memory for the component task operations is necessary to carry out either of these error-correcting processes. During these rapid considerations or comparisons, attention is presumed to be directed to single components of the tasks, so that the executive command to attend to the particular operation is presumed to be required. Owing to its action property, the command component of attentional control would seem to lie nearer the premotor areas than the memory component of control, both for multiple-action tasks and for simple action tasks.

A somewhat similar view of executive control of attention emphasizes the participation of the anterior cingulate area within a network of areas, which includes the anterior cingulate area, the SMA, and portions of the basal ganglia that supply dopamine to the frontal lobe (Posner & Petersen, 1990; Posner & Raichle, 1994; Posner & Tudela, 1997). The executive network is assumed to increase its activation during the performance of complex discrimination tasks, and but is also presumed to be responsible for anticipating the location of a target (Murtha, Chertkow, Dixon, Beauregard, & Evans, 1996). The network is assumed to be activated during tasks involving "supervisory control" (Norman & Shallice, 1980), for example, planning, novelty and error detection, resolution of conflict, and increased task difficulty (see Posner & DiGirolamo, in press, for a review of PET and fMRI evidence).

To briefly summarize this section, attentional control is viewed here as an action, which is generated from information held in working memory storage of a perception or an action plan. Crucial parts of the circuitry underlying the executive controlling action are expected to be found at or near the premotor area, and crucial parts of the circuitry of working memory store are expected to be found more anterior in the prefrontal cortex for simple actions and in the anterior cingulate areas for multiple actions. Expressions of attention-to-action plans are assumed to be crucially dependent on the SMA, and are assumed to be triggered from the premotor area. Additional research is needed to design tasks that allow clearer functional separation of these several frontal sites that underlie the working memory, attentional command, and attentional expressive functions in tasks that involve a simple action and in tasks that involve a complex set of operations.

Observed across phylogenetic stages of evolution, the increase in the prefrontal, SMA, and anterior cingulate area of the frontal cortex can be seen to contribute to the increase variety of simple perceptions and complex task operations that can be held in working memory. Because the contents of working memory available to a species may set limits on what executive commands can be generated, working memory structures in that species may indicate the range of perception and task operations that can potentially be attended to by the species.

D. The Evolution of Posterior Brain Structures

At the same time that the "association" areas of the anterior cortex of the brain (areas other than the primary motor area) enlarged phylogenetically, the "association" areas of the posterior cortex of the brain (areas other than the primary sensory areas) also expanded. In primates, the enlargement of cortical surfaces in the inferotemporal area apparently provided the neural substrate for identifying complex objects such as faces, and the enlargement of the posterior parietal cortical areas apparently provided the neural substrates for more complex spatial computations, such as fine resolutions and relationships between object locations. Although the delayed-response task enabled cross-species comparisons corresponding to prefrontal expansion, no behavioral task has yet provided as effective a means of comparing the abilities of species to identify complex objects or to compute complex location information. A possible candidate for a cross-species location task is the double saccade task (Sparks & Mays, 1980), in which the animal moves the eyes twice to two locations that were cued. Presumably, along with the evolution of posterior cortical circuits that can process complex attributes and finer granularity of spatial information there was an evolution of structures that made it possible to attend selectively to these richer perceptual aspects of objects.

One evolutionarily old brain structure that has been regarded as a mechanism of visual attention is the superior colliculus (Posner, 1988; Rafal et al., 1988), whose structure does not appear to have significantly advanced in performing this function during the evolution of higher mammals. Rather, it appears that the expansion of other structures, particularly the posterior parietal cortex and the frontal eye fields have provided elaboration (as well as duplication) of the processes that move the eyes in a variety of situations. For example, like cells in the SC, some cells of the PPC apparently code the location of a visual stimulus presented in the periphery of the eye in terms of the amplitude and direction of an eye movement that would bring the stimulus to the center of the eye. But more cells of the PPC than the SC hold location information for a time after the stimulus has gone off, suggesting that attention to location in the absence of object landmarks may be more likely to be mediated by the PPC than the SC.

A study with monkeys compared covert shifting of attention to well-separated object locations (Bowman, Brown, Kertzman, Schwarz, & Robinson, 1993). Using displays with two target locations, each 15° to the left and right of a center fixation dot, they found that shifts of orientation peripheral (exogenous) cues were similar to those shown by humans. However, unlike humans (Enns & Brodeur, 1989; Jonides, 1980), monkeys responded to the cue in much the same way regardless of its validity; that is, they did not use the cue in the 20% validity condition to predict the target location on the opposite side endogenously. After careful training, however, monkeys learned to use an arrow cue at the fovea to endogenously predict the target, and the obtained cue effects were larger than those obtained with peripheral cues. When landmarks were removed, the monkeys showed no significant effect of cues on performance, whereas for humans the absence of landmarks reduced but did not eliminate the cue effect (Mangun, Hansen, & Hillyard, 1987). Taken together, these findings indicate that the attention-shifting mechanisms of monkeys and humans may not differ appreciably, but humans show a substantially greater tendency to use a cue to induce predictive processing, which presumably involves computations lying outside the SC-PPC-FEF network.

When objects or parts of objects are located within a few degrees of each other, then some mechanism is presumably needed to sharpen the expression of attention in cortical pathways (LaBerge, 1995a, 1995b), and the thalamo-cortical circuit is anatomically situated to perform this function. The thalamo-cortical circuits that serve the posterior cortical association areas are located mainly in the pulvinar nucleus of the thalamus (Jones, 1985). During the evolution of mammals, the relative size of the pulvinar to the whole thalamus kept pace with the increase in relative size of the posterior cortical association areas to the whole cortex. The pulvinar is virtually nonexistent in the rat, whereas in the cat it is so small that it is usually grouped with the lateral posterior thalamic nucleus into the "lateral posterior-pulvinar complex" (LP-P complex). In the human brain, the pulvinar is the largest nucleus in the thalamus, accounting for approximately two-fifths of the thalamic volume.

One of the conjectured functions of the pulvinar is to increase the saliency of a visual object (Robinson & Petersen, 1992), which is directly related to the degree of "pop-out" attributed to an object embedded in a cluttered field. This effect is regarded in this chapter as an indicator of the degree of attentional control exerted by external stimuli on the expression of attention in posterior cortical pathways. An increase in saliency in the visual processing of an object may be interpreted in exactly the same way as attention is expressed in a brain pathway: that is, as an increase in the difference in information flow in the target pathways relative to the information flow in surrounding pathways. Furthermore, the way in which this difference is amplified within the pulvinar is similar for both saliency and attentional expression; by imposing on an input (to the pulvinar) a relatively small difference in information flow between the target object site and the sites of surrounding objects and delivering as an output (to the cortex) a relatively large difference in information flow between these sites. In the context of visual information flow through areas V1, V2, and so on, successive saliency increases could be produced by the involvement of thalamo-cortical pathways when one visual area projects to another visual area.

It has been proposed (LaBerge, 1995a, 1995b, 1997, 1998) that cortical areas are interconnected by triangular circuits, in which one connection is a direct one that projects from Area A to Area B, and the other connection is an indirect one that projects to the thalamic relay neuron that projects to Area B. According to the simulations carried out on models of the thalamic circuit (LaBerge et al., 1992), the route from Area A to Area B through the thalamic circuit is capable of enhancing and sharpening the differences in information flow between a target site and surrounding sites. In view of these considerations, it is possible that circuits in the pulvinar that connect with many visual areas of the posterior cortex could participate through the indirect route of a triangular circuit every time that information is projected from one area to another.

One way to view the evolutionary changes in the posterior cortical and posterior thalamic (pulvinar) structures is in terms of the advantages in perceptual emphasis that these structures can confer on an important object that is vulnerable to camouflage by the presence of other objects in the visual field. At the surface of the visual receptor, retinal circuitry emphasizes the border of objects by a process of lateral inhibition. At the next processing structure in the visual stream, the lateral geniculate nucleus, the thalamic circuitry can emphasize luminance changes further by using a combination of lateral inhibition and recurrent positive feedback (Sherman & Koch, 1986; Steriade, Jones, & Llinas, 1990) that could serve to emphasize certain pathways by enhancement effects (e.g., LaBerge et al., 1992). Triangular circuits (LaBerge, 1995a,b) involving the pulvinar may repeatedly emphasize particular attributes of objects as the visual information flows from V1 to V2 and higher areas, resulting in emphasis as saliency increases (Robinson & Petersen, 1992). However, in many of the same early visual areas in which emphasis is imposed by saliency, further emphasis of a potentially high strength may be produced from triangular circuits originating in the prefrontal cortex that could elevate the existing enhanced activity in posterior cortical pathways to levels of attention that William James described as "possessing the mind" (James, 1890).

The ability to choose to attend intensely to one among other closely spaced salient objects apparently rests to a large degree on the PC, PFC, and pulvinar, structures that have increased in size so dramatically during primate evolution. At the same time, evolutionary enlargement and elaboration of the PFC and other areas of the anterior cortex have enabled attention to be directed to the processing of complex internal operations, which in turn has led to the development of high-level self-organizing skills that characterize the human information processor.

IV. CULTURAL INFLUENCES ON ATTENTION

Few people would question the statement that culture affects the way a person attends to events in the physical, social, and mental worlds. But before addressing detailed questions about which cross-cultural variables account for differences in attentional processing and how such variables manage to shape the internal and private attentional operations of an individual group member, it would seem helpful to separate attention processing into its expression, mechanisms, and sources of control. In previous sections of this chapter, the effects of individual development and species evolution were evaluated principally by means of neuroanatomical changes in the brain of the individual. It was assumed there that these structural changes determined the mechanisms of attention available to the individual as well as the brain pathways in which the expression of attention takes place. In the present framework of viewing attention, however, it would seem reasonable to assume that both the mechanisms and manner in which attention is expressed neurophysiologically are independent of cultural influence; that is, these aspects of attention are virtually completely biologically determined, and the aspect of attention that appears to be influenced by culture lies in the matter of the control of attention.

The major sources of attentional control are assumed to be (a) incoming stimuli arising from the external world and (b) the representations and procedures arising from internal memories, including working memories and long-term memories. External stimuli may attract attention by the highly transient activity produced when they appear, but their power to sustain attention to themselves depends strongly on their interest to the individual, and most of what interests an individual is what was learned during the process of socialization in the presence of caretakers, peers, and other members of the culture to which the individual belongs.

Learned interests, learned skills and rituals, and learned modes of self-regulation are among the many culturally determined factors that determine what objects, words, ideas, and actions will receive attention and for how long. The sequence of operations constituting a skill or routine often involves the careful timing of attention shifts from operation to operation, and although interest may be a dominant factor at the time of choosing to perform a skill or ritual at that time, the attentional operations involved in the series of actions may not be closely linked to states of interest, but presumably run off "ballistically." Therefore, when attentional operations become part of the actions of the skill or routine, the learned routine controls them rather than their being controlled directly by the current interest state of the individual each time they occur.

In advanced stages of skill learning, sequences of actions are believed to run off automatically, that is, without attention to their component operations. But few skills can be performed over extended durations of time without the involvement of attention, particularly at the beginning of a new action unit or action group within the skill. When a skill or routine is regarded as a relatively routinized sequence of actions joined by the use of relatively routinized operations of attention, then during many moments during a typical day, the attention of an individual is controlled by routinized behaviors that were shaped within a cultural context, and are initiated daily within a cultural context. Examples are dressing in the morning, preparing food, playing basketball, courting a mate, going to a restaurant, and making music with others.

Another way that culture molds what is attended to and for how long is through frequently used "cultural units" that symbolize important shared concepts of a social group. Dawkins calls these semantic units *memes,* and examples are tunes, catchphrases, clothing fashions, ideas, ways of making pots, etc. (Dawkins, 1976). When a meme is seen or heard by a member of the meme's culture (in words, pictorially, in song, etc.) or when a meme is simply thought of in connection with something else, it would seem to capture and sustain attention of an individual, owing to the associations that the meme evokes that arouse the individual's interest. Because the daily communications between members of a culture abound with these cultural units, it would be expected that, whenever a meme is experienced, the attention of the recipient would be sustained for a longer time than in the case of the sudden onset of a stimulus with little cultural significance.

An example of an attention-controlling communication medium in our culture is television. It may be instructive to consider the various methods used by television programmers and advertisers to capture and sustain the attention of its viewers. Although programs generally seek to hold the viewer's attention for extended periods of at least 30 min, advertisers need to hold the viewers' attention only for the 10 or 15 s needed to communicate their short message. Controlling attention over short time periods can be accomplished by a series of abrupt and intense stimulus onsets (which could be called the building blocks of "hype"), which may rivet attention reflexively to the TV screen. The high-activity transients are mediated through posterior cortical mechanisms of spatial orientation and attribute salience, and capture prefrontal activity for the time needed to store the message that follows. Brief clusters of memes, in spoken or pictoral form, can automatically engage anterior voluntary structures and sustain them longer through the interest already associated with the memes. For controlling attention over longer time periods, larger units of meaning such as the unfolding of stories are deemed to be appropriate, in which the viewer may sometimes have an opportunity to control their momentary attention themselves on the basis of the ideas they have generated on their own.

In most cultures certain individuals appear to have exceptional power to control the attention of members of their group. Often described as "charismatic," these individuals sustain attention of people around them for long durations of time while they tell stories, give political speeches, sing songs, tell a series of jokes, or host a talk show. It is not clear exactly what features of their behavior are responsible for the unusual control they exert over the attention of viewers, but a careful analysis of their actions could be helpful in understanding how attention operates at these highly sustained and possibly high-intensity levels in the people of these cultures.

Thus, early socialization of the individual could be said to shape the interests that control to a large degree what objects and events will be attended to during the daily experiences of an individual. As these socially induced controls are exercised repeatedly in the life of an individual, the influence of socially related signals on attention mechanisms become more automatic and therefore more direct, so that attention in many situations comes to be controlled in a "reflexlike" manner. However, the individual is presumed to have the capability of breaking this automatic control by accessing self-reflective and self-organizing processes that allow the individual to evaluate the interest value of a given socially related stimulus event before attention is sustained further on the stimulus event.

V. COMPUTATIONAL CONCEPTUALIZATIONS AND MODELS OF ATTENTION

Traditionally, computer scientists treat a cognitive process such as learning or decision making with one of two general goals in mind. One goal uses that process to solve computational problems so that a system may adapt to an environment in an optimal way, and the other goal seeks to mimic the algorithms employed by the brain when it exhibits that process. The first goal, characteristic of artificial intelligence, may take hints from algorithms suggested by brain anatomy and physiology, but these considerations do not constrain the algorithms ultimately chosen to do the job. The second goal searches for algorithms within the constraints imposed by known anatomy and physiology of the brain, usually with the aim of understanding how the brain processes some task.

A. Is Attentional Processing Dispensible in Principle?

From the viewpoint of artificial intelligence, one of the first questions that might be asked about the cognitive process of attention is whether or not in some universal sense attention is a necessary component of information-processing systems when these systems reach a sufficiently high level of proficiency and complexity (Hurlbert and Poggio, 1986). Could massively parallel computers dispense with attention as it is known in human information processing? Is the seriality or the one-at-a-timeness of selective attention simply a consequence of the seriality typically imposed by the human agent's response topography (we cannot speak more than one word at a time nor can we clap our hands while holding a glass of water), or is a selection algorithm required to process attributes of objects and events as unified entities, and thereby provides the basis for the representation of knowledge in a mind? Could a massively parallel system synthesize subsets of available information into units according to varying scales or window sizes and analyze parts of units without a selective algorithm? In short, does a superrobot need to attend the way a human brain attends?

Obtaining informative answers to these and related questions would seem to require a clear formulation of the attention process; in particular it must first be known what attention does for the individual, how it is expressed in information-processing terms, what algorithms give rise to the expression, and what kinds of events control the input to these algorithms. These issues, which lie in the background of this chapter's investigative framework, are still in the process of being resolved by researchers.

B. Computational Models of Attention

The main issue addressed by this section of the chapter concerns how adequately current computational methods can be used to model the attention process as it is known to operate in living organisms. One class of models that makes explicit use of computational concepts and methods in building relatively detailed simulations of attentional operations are connectionist models. During the following brief review of some current connectionist models of attention, one might consider the following questions. Do these models adequately simulate the input–output relationships involved in attentional selection, preparation, and maintenance? To what extent do the simulation algorithms mimic the ways brain structures are believed to transform inputs into these attentional outcomes?

One of the first connectionist models of attention (Cohen, Dunbar, & McClelland, 1990) was developed within the parallel distributed processing (PDP) framework (Rumelhart & McClelland, 1986). The purpose of the model was to account for data obtained from experiments on the Stroop effect, and the pathways representing color naming and word reading were represented by two different pathways having the usual connectionist structure. The speed of processing and interference effects depend upon the strength of processing within each pathway, and attentional operations modulate these strengths so that competition between pathways is avoided and one is selected.

Attention was represented in their model by an additional source of input to the color and word pathways that shifts the resting levels of units in these pathways so that units in these pathways can respond differently to the same stimulus input. A unit in the selected pathway was made more responsive by shifting its resting level toward the middle of the dynamic range of its nonlinear activation function, where small changes of its net input produces a large change in output. At the same time, a unit in the unselected pathway was made less responsive by shifting its resting level toward the lower end of the activation function, where changes in the net input produce small changes in the output. Thus, in this model attention is expressed by shifting of the resting level of units, and the mechanism that produces this shift is a fixed amount of activation flowing from one of the two "task demand" units, which in turn was controlled by the intention to name colors or to read words.

It is difficult to conceive of an attentional mechanism that could be simpler than the fixed outputs of the task-demand units. The fixed-output property of these attention modules put little constraint on the class of algorithms: the outputs could operate on the resting states of pathway units by adding activation to the selected pathway, subtracting activation from the unselected pathway, or both. Nevertheless, this model implements both the selective and preparatory manifestations of attention in the Stroop task.

More complex computations are carried out in the attention module of the connectionist network of Sandon (1990) that uses spatial location as a basis for selecting which features (e.g., oriented edges) of a stimulus array will be processed for identification. The underlying network represents location and features in a hierarchical structure that performs translation-invariant object recognition. The attention module contains one or two levels, depending upon the level of intensity resolution of the image. Subregions of space are defined for the first level (e.g., the overall strength of activity of the edges of an oriented bar), and a "winner-take-all" (WTA) algorithm (Hinton & Lang, 1985) drives all but the strongest response in that subregion to zero. The selected features in each subregion are then sent to the next level of the attention module, where a WTA operation is performed on specific edges of a bar to select the bar with the edge showing the strongest activity. The activity from this selected region is then sent on to the object-recognition processor. Thus, at each level of the attention module, multiple images compete with each other through a WTA mechanism for access to higher-order processing modules.

Attention is expressed in the Sandon model by higher activity in the pathways of a particular spatial region relative to the activities in other regions. The mechanism within the attention module that produces the activity contrast is the WTA procedure, which operates by suppressing the activity in the nondominant regions. The attention module is placed directly in the line of flow of stimulus input to the object recognition module, whereas in the Cohen et al. (1990) model and most other models (see also Mozer & Behrmann, 1992; Niebur & Koch, 1994) the attention module operates outside this line of information flow. Although the attention modules of the Sandon (1990) model carry out more sophisticated operations than those of the Cohen et al. (1990) model, the controlling influences made explicit in simulations of the Sandon model are entirely bottom-up; that is, the spatial region that is selected depends only on the combination of features contained in the stimulus input (although there are bidirectional arrows in the flow-diagram of the attention module that potentially could mediate top-down priming). In contrast, selection in the simulations of the Cohen et al. (1990) model are controlled entirely top-down by the "intention" of the subject. Hence, although both models exhibit selective attention during stimulus processing, the Cohen et al. model emphasizes top-down preparatory attention by setting selection parameters prior to the onset of the stimulus.

A model that is somewhat similar to the spatial selection model of Sandon, but that places the attention units outside instead of inside the information-processing pathway, is the neurobiologically based model of Olshausen, Anderson, and Von Essen (1993). This model contains transformations that are more biologically informed and are described in more detail than is the case in most early models. The transformations shift and rescale the representation of an object within the attended area as activity flows from retinal maps to object-centered maps in higher levels of processing. The strengths of connections between units in the stimulus-processing pathways is modulated by outputs from the attention units, which in effect create a "dynamic routing circuit" within these pathways. The attention units lie outside the pathways and are presumed to be neurons within the pulvinar nucleus of the thalamus. The controls on these neurons are assumed to arise bottom-up from early visual areas (e.g., V1, V2) and top-down from the posterior parietal areas.

The algorithm in the Olshausen et al. (1993) model that governs how the attention units interact with each other to produce an output pattern of activation is apparently quite general, so that the expression of attention as relatively higher strength in attended pathways could come about by facilitation at the attended pathway, suppression at the unattended pathways, or both.

A similar biologically motivated computational model of attention by LaBerge et al. (1992) is based on known connectivity of the pulvinar nucleus with areas PPC and V4 and what is known of the connectivity of neurons within the pulvinar. Although the Olshausen et al. (1993) model emphasizes computational details of attentional expression within the stimulus processing pathways, the LaBerge et al. (1992) model emphasizes computational details of the pulvinar mechanism that is assumed by both models to produce these effects. Spatial relationships within this model are preserved within the attended area of varying sizes, so that objects requiring a large attention window, for example, the five-letter word, *STONE,* can be successfully identified, as well as nested objects, for example the letter *O* at the center of that word (LaBerge, 1983) and the word *TON.* Analysis of the pulvinar circuitry (LaBerge et al., 1992) indicates that selection occurs mainly by enhancement of activity at the site of the attended area, whereas the activity at nearby unattended sites undergoes either a decrement, no change, or even a small increment. Control of the pulvinar mechanism in spatial attention is assumed to arise from bottom-up sources and especially from top-down sources, particularly by circuits connecting the DLPFC to the PPC (see also LaBerge, 1995a, 1995b).

More recently an analytic version (LaBerge, Carlson, & Williams, 1997) of the neural network connectionist model of pulvinar function (LaBerge et al., 1992) was described, in which the predicted trajectories of target and distractor activities resembled closely the trajectories predicted by the connectionist model. One advantage of the analytic model is that the closed-form differential equations could be solved directly, whereas the sets of equations in the neural network model could be solved only by numerical integration. Another advantage of the analytical model is that the number of free parameters is 4 compared to the 24 free parameters of the connectionist model.

C. The Problem of Attentional Maintenance

One of the three manifestations of attention described in this chapter, attentional maintenance, has apparently been omitted in most or all of the known computational models. In the first section of this chapter it was pointed out that maintenance attention does not seem to have a "computational goal" in the same sense that selection and preparation do. Selection and preparation lead to accurate and fast identifications and other judgments of objects and events, and thereby serve the adaptation of the individual. But it is not apparent how simply sustaining attention to an object, idea, or action for its own sake has adaptive value. Yet the prospects of sustaining attention on the process of watching ocean waves, hearing music, contemplating ideas, tasting food and wine, and relaxing with a favorite pet nearby, all serve to motivate a large portion of a person's daily actions. The specific operations involved in maintaining attention over a period of time are shared with those that sustain preparatory attention over time, particularly the controlling operations by certain prefrontal areas upon attentional mechanisms. The only difference between maintenance and preparatory attention appears to be that while sustaining preparatory attention there is stored in working memory an expectation of some impending event that is being prepared for, usually the appearance of a stimulus.

From a computational point of view the existence of maintenance attention in humans (and perhaps on occasion in animals) presents a puzzle, because what is computed during maintenance attention does not appear to solve any problem related to adaptability of the individual. Therefore what reason could there be to design this manifestation of attention into the construction of any conceivable robot?

Perhaps the case could be made that the kinds of processing that are maintained in this way involve "feelings," which some philosophers (e.g., Ziff, 1959) have argued as one of the distinguishing states of organic as opposed to inorganic systems. Other philosophers (e.g., Putnam, 1960) and cognitive psychologists (e.g., Johnson-Laird, 1988) regard feelings as computational states that function as non-symbolic ways of guiding behavior, but they do not distinguish between the preparatory attention to feeling involved in guiding behavior to some expected outcome and maintenance attention to feelings for their own sake. Nevertheless, it is clear that humans frequently engage in this kind of attentional processing and doing so appears to enhance the quality of their life experiences.

The root of this question may lie in the way the attentional state is defined. In this chapter (and elsewhere (LaBerge, 1997, 1998) the expression of attention is defined as the prolonged increase in activity in particular cortical columns that represent the event attended to. The heightened activity is presumed to produce mental experience, and part of that experience is the processing of perceptions, conceptions, actions, and feelings without consideration of their adaptive advantages in the competitive world of Darwin. In contrast, the computer is designed to optimize particular input–output relationships (problem–solution relationships), and the internal states of the computer are constructed to serve this optimization. Hence, the basic hardware of computers is not designed to prolong heightened electrical activity within the mainframe, but rather to produce one of two voltage states in the pathways that process information in an input-to-output manner.

Apparently it is only the biologically constructed brain that produces the appropriately magnified electrical states that are assumed to constitute the expression of attention.

IV. PHILOSOPHICAL APPROACHES TO ATTENTION

Among the disciplines gathered under the umbrella of cognitive sciences is the discipline of philosophy, in particular, the philosophy of mind. What has philosophy contributed to our understanding of attention, and what might it be expected to contribute in the future?

Any attempt to locate the topic of attention within traditional and modern philosophy is distracted by the tendency on the part of philosophers to view attention as a part of consciousness. On this view, it would seem that the process of attention cannot be clearly explicated without having first explained consciousness. Although the issue of consciousness has relentlessly challenged many philosophers (and nonphilosophers as well) over the centuries, there is today still no general agreement about the right questions to ask and the right methods to use in investigating the topic. However, my view is that considerations of attention can be treated separately from considerations of notions of consciousness, and that philosophical questions and methods of inquiry can contribute to our progressive understanding of attention.

Four philosophical methods and a survey of traditional and current philosophical views of attention will be briefly presented here. The four methods addressed are the synoptic perspective, understanding, geography of concepts, and formal explanation.

A. Philosophy's Synoptic Perspective

The consideration of a topic such as attention from a wider perspective than that found in one scientific discipline or one level of description is a hallmark of cognitive science, and therefore the traditional synoptic perspective of philosophy should be a congenial one to cognitive scientists. Researchers who concentrate their daily efforts at one level of description often find themselves looking both to lower and upper levels to provide a broader context within which to consider issues and problems. Sometimes it turns out that the best way to approach a given research goal described at a particular level is to incorporate methods at adjacent levels of description, as when a cognitive psychologist takes a behavioral task into a PET scan laboratory, or computer scientist wonders what cognitive purposes could be served by a newly discovered network algorithm.

Productive researchers are typically confronted with a large number of alternative experiments that they could undertake, and often the greatest problem is to determine which experiment is the best one to perform next. Theories that are formulated at levels higher than the level at which a researcher is currently working provide a broader perspective with which to prioritize prospective experiments. But there are also factors that work against glancing upward along the descriptive levels. Reductionistic orientations direct the vision downward, and a run of successes at one level may concentrate the vision at that level. A current example of this influence may be the perspective taken by some current researchers in the field of molecular biology, where dramatic contributions at the cellular level has apparently drawn the emphasis of the field of physiology away from its traditionally central problem of understanding the whole organism and the overall "logic of life," as denoted by the meaning of the word *physiology* (Boyd & Noble, 1993).

Philosophy offers a combination of the upward and downward views along the descriptive hierarchy with its synoptic vision of the mind. One example of the synoptic vision of philosophy that seems particularly appropriate to cognitive science is the naturalistic principle of "reflective equilibrium," described by Rawls (1971) and more recently by Flanagan (1992). This principle favors equal consideration of three levels of description of cognition: phenomenology (how things seem to our experience), psychological information processing (how mental life works), and neuroscience (how mental life may be realized in biological hardware). The emphasis on balance of the three levels opposes a reductive approach that gives priority to concepts at the neuroscience level. Hence, from a "reflective equilibrium" perspective, the search for explanations of cognitive phenomena avoids the elimination of that which is to be explained during the analytic steps involved in the process of explanation.

B. Philosophical Understanding of Attention

To understand a phenomenon in the philosophical sense, some philosophers require knowledge of at least three properties (e.g., Searle, 1990): its mode of existence (ontology), what it does (causation), and how we find out about it (epistemology). In the case of attention its mode of existence is assumed here to be elevated activity in particular cortical areas. What it does is to select pathways of neural signaling for specialized processing, but also, the elevated activities in cortical areas could be said to be cognitive events that constitute mental life. How we find out about it is by giving subjects appropriate tasks and observing their activities with measures that are behavioral (response frequency and response time), physiological (e.g., ERP, PET, fMRI, single-cell recordings), and phenomenological (experiential reports).

Examples of questions that fall under the three categories of understanding are as follows: the question of whether attention can exist in non-biological devices is an issue of ontology; the question of whether maintenance attention has adaptive effects is related to the issue of causation; and the question of the informative value of phenomenological reports is an issue of epistemology.

C. Philosophy's Geography of Concepts

How does philosophy treat a concept like attention? One of the first things that many philosophers attempt to do when presented with a concept is to clarify its meaning, which involves examining the concept from the "largest" viewpoint (i.e., *sub specie aeternitatis*) and interrelating the concept with other concepts. In effect, the philosopher "locates" the concept within a "geography" of significant concepts by showing how the propositions in which it is embedded are consistent or inconsistent with other propositions, and what other propositions are related to them by inference (Ryle, 1949; White, 1964). The resulting clusters of closely related concepts could be said to form fields of inquiry, such as ethics, logic, political theory, aesthetics, theory of mind, memory, attention, and so on.

Within the field of attention there are many terms denoting concepts without well-defined meanings, a state of affairs that produces undesired ambiguity, but at the same time may suggest to the researcher unnoticed aspects of attention that could be fruitfully investigated. Ryle (1949) assembled a list of attention-related terms he called "heed" words; examples are noticing, taking care, concentrating, applying one's mind, putting one's heart into something, thinking of what one is doing, trying, and doing something studiously, vigilantly, conscientiously, pertinaciously and with alertness, interest, and intentness. In contrast, it is without (or with little) attention that one behaves carelessly, absentmindedly, inadvertently, or with negligence. The attention-related terms have in common the notion of "activity," that is, the "doing of something" by an agent, as opposed to the notion of "something happening to" an agent, such as being conscious of something. This active–passive distinction between attention and consciousness could contribute to the justification of treating them as separable processes, as is being done in this chapter.

Part of the ambiguity in "heed" words stems from the fact that they do not tell us what particular activity the individual is engaged in. Unlike the "specific activity" concepts of walking, breathing, and counting, attention concepts are "polymorphous activity" concepts that take a variety of "forms," which may differ when attention is employed in learning, remembering, perceiving, practicing, or thinking. Some philosophers question whether terms like *noticing* or *detecting* denote the process of attending, because the noticing of something can be delayed while attention has been shifted elsewhere, and because noticing is a relatively brief event, whereas attention typically occurs over a longer duration of time (White, 1964). The distinction between the durations of attending to and noticing of an object, reached by philosophical analysis, apparently has a counterpart in a current neurophysiological notion of attention being expressed in a sustained mode of preparation, dominated by right hemisphere structures, as opposed to being expressed in a brief mode of simple selection, dominated by left hemisphere structures (e.g., Liotti et al., 1994).

Another distinction examined by philosophers is attending as a spectator versus attending as an agent. When we engage in an activity such as driving a car, we can watch ourselves do it as we would watch someone else doing the same thing, and we can direct our attention to the perceptions and actions involved in performing the act. Attending as a spectator is characteristic of introspection, and it is presumed that this kind of attention provides the kinds of knowledge required for self-perception (e.g., LaBerge, 1997), and for self-organization of executive procedures (Allport, 1989; Duncan, 1995) that underlie effective problem solving.

The terrain of attention concepts could be described as rather muddled compared to the relatively well-ordered geography of simpler bodily activities such as breathing. The main reason for the clarity of breathing concepts is that, owing to the fact that breathing is much more accessible to observation and simpler in operation, the breathing process has become better understood with respect to its expression (movements of air), mechanism (bellows function of the lungs), and controlling influences (brain stem circuits). By analogy, it is expected that the concepts of attention will become clearer and more universally agreed upon as research reveals more about how it is processed in the brain. However, although few philosophers doubt the importance of cognitive and neuroscience research in understanding the attention process, others seem to question the degree to which scientific findings can or should reshape the traditional meanings of the phenomenologically based attention concepts that were handed down to us by our cultural heritage.

D. Formal Methods of Explanation

Throughout the foregoing descriptions of philosophical approaches to attention, the term *understanding* has been used almost as a primitive concept, that is, a concept whose meaning is not further analyzed into other concepts. However, some philosophers have regarded understanding as a too vaguely defined goal of scientific endeavors, and have substituted the term *explanation* for understanding. Then they have proceeded to "explain" the occurrence and properties of an event by deducing it logically from a set of axioms (e.g., Suppes, 1969). In formal treatments of a phenomenon or process, all concepts are defined set theoretically (e.g., a stimulus may be defined as a set of elements, attention as a sampled subset of stimulus elements, a class of responses as a vector, learning as a function relating sampled sets of elements to responses, etc.).

Theoretical statements relating a process such as attention to a stimulus or a response in some particular situation can often be expressed in the form of mathematical equations (e.g., LaBerge, Carlson, & Williams, 1997; Sperling & Weichselgartner, 1995). The benefit is that theoretical predictions in specific experimental situations are more detailed and unambiguous, and therefore more capable of being evaluated by empirical tests. Also, when mathematical language connects the theoretical predictions more tightly to the theoretical assumptions, experimental findings can speak more directly and decisively to the validity of the assumptions. In this manner, axiomatically formulated theories can promote agreement among researchers as to when a particular process or phenomenon has been "explained."

E. Traditional Philosophical Views of Attention

A survey of philosophical history reveals scant treatment of the process of attention. In the philosophy of mind, in particular, it might be expected that attention would feature in both ontological and epistemological issues. Ontology concerns what exists, and the momentary slices of experience that some believe carry prima facie validity to their existence are themselves highly sculpted by how we choose to attend to them. Epistemology concerns what is known and how it comes to be known, and it would seem that the selective character of attention has a tremendous influence on what parts of stimulus inputs from the external (and internal) worlds are received, reflected upon, and become part of the individual's belief system. However, these philosophical considerations of attention apparently escaped the notice of such famous philosophers as Descartes, Kant, and the British empiricists.

One of the few references to attention by Kant can be found in the *Critique of Pure Reason* (Kant, 1787/1929), in which a reference to attention can be found in a footnote under section #24:

> I do not see why so much difficulty should be found in admitting that our inner sense is affected by ourselves. Such affection finds exemplification in each and every act of attention. In every act of attention the understanding determines inner sense, in accordance with the combination which it thinks, to that inner intuition which corresponds to the manifold in the synthesis of the understanding.

One interpretation of this comment (Allison, 1983) is that attention actively participates in transforming raw mental contents into cognitions. For example, the received appearances of object aspects (color, spatial location, etc.) are collected by attention into an object representation that is then comprehended as a synthesized whole, in a manner reminiscent of Treisman's Feature Integration Theory of Attention (Treisman & Gelade, 1980).

Although Kant held that the mind is not transparent to itself, Descartes and Berkeley believed that mental contents are grasped directly and typically without error. Berkeley, Locke, and other British empiricists viewed perception as the means by which the mind became a "mirror of nature," and apparently they believed that the "mirror" that represented the pure products of experience would be distorted by placing an active selection device between the world and the mind. William James summed up this state of affairs in the opening sentence of the chapter on attention in his *Principles of Psychology* (1890):

> Strange to say, so patent a fact as the perceptual presence of selective attention has received hardly any notice from psychologists of the English empiricist school. The Germans have explicitly treated it, either as a faculty or as a resultant, but in the pages of such writers as Locke, Hume, Hartley, the Mills, and Spencer, the word hardly occurs, or if it does so, it is parenthetically and as if by inadvertence. (Vol. I, p. 402)

It could be said that the main reason for the neglect of attention on the part of traditional philosophers is that they tacitly assimilated attention into the topic of consciousness, where it was invoked only to describe cases in which consciousness is particularly strongly concentrated on a perception or idea. Apparently, attention came into its own within philosophy when it was treated separately from the concept of consciousness in the hands of William James at the turn of the century.

James was an empiricist who believed that mental experiences are not reducible to events described at lower physical levels, and who believed that an individual could determine moment-by-moment what perception or idea will dominate cognition simply by the act of voluntarily choosing to attend to that perception or idea. Thus, the individual has the potential to influence actively what she or he will experience, in contrast to being a passive recipient of whatever sensory inputs happen to be produced by the environment. The attention process itself was not regarded by James as a "first cause," but as a resultant mainly of the "subjective interest" of the perception or idea to which attention is directed. In his most speculative moments, James averred that other yet-to-be-discovered influences could extend or shorten the duration of attention to an idea which, through its direct effect on the will, enabled an individual to act upon the course of world events independently of the deterministic forces of physical history. Thus, the momentary operation of attention was central to his philosophical view of how an individual may exercise choice in a "free" manner.

James (1890) described two "physiological" processes of attention: "the accommodation or adjustment of sensory organs; and the anticipatory preparation from within of the ideational centres concerned with the object to which the attention is paid" (p. 434). These two descriptions appear to correspond to current views of the manifestations of attention. The "adjustment of sensory organs" is similar to the orientation of attention (e.g., Posner, 1980) and the selectivity of attention (e.g., Broadbent, 1958), and the "anticipatory preparation" is similar to the effects produced by cuing and priming (e.g., LaBerge, Van Gelder, & Yellott, 1970; Posner & Snyder, 1975). Much of the attention research in psychology over the past century can be classified under these two manifestations of attention (LaBerge, 1990a,b).

Although James did not have a classification for maintenance attention, this manifestation of attention featured strongly in his many descriptions of personal phenomenological observations. Given the difficulty that maintenance attention presents for computational views of attention and the ease in which it is accommodated by the phenomenological views, it could turn out that a concerted effort to understand maintenance attention will bring about a closer interaction between the computational and phenomenological approaches.

F. Current Philosophical Approaches to Attention

Among the several philosophies of mind being actively developed today, few have treated the process of attention in a direct and comprehensive manner. As in traditional philosophic positions the concept of attention is currently being viewed as an aspect of consciousness more than as a process in its own right. However, it may be instructive to review briefly a sample of current philosophies of mind that appear to be particularly appropriate for a philosophical treatment of attention within the broad context of cognitive science. The three positions are computational functionalism, eliminative materialism, and constructive naturalism. Two sources of illuminating comparisons of these positions are Churchland (1986) and Flanagan (1992).

Cognitive scientists frequently employ the computational metaphor to illuminate how a cognitive process like attention functions to achieve goals set by an organic or inorganic system. Explanations of how a cognitive process works are couched in terms of computational operations on functional states, which are usually defined independently of the physical properties of the hardware in which they could be implemented. Examples of the main functional states are beliefs and desires, and to this pair of states one could add the state of considering something. The functional state of consideration could be said to capture the notion of attention. Thus, in certain situations, a cognitive account of the information processing of an individual could be described in terms of the causal relations among beliefs, desires, and momentary considerations. The three types of cognitive states differ in their temporal properties; beliefs tend to endure over long periods of time, some desires endure as long as beliefs whereas others change cyclically in a matter of hours (as in hunger), and considerations tend to fluctuate rapidly within a few seconds or fraction of a second.

One objection to the functionalist approach is that the concepts arising from the computer metaphor do not necessarily presage the concepts that will arise from knowledge of brain processing levels (Churchland, 1986). Concepts such as beliefs, desires, and considerations have roots in culturally induced ways of talking and thinking about inner processes, and this "folk psychology" that we learned from our culture is vulnerable to the same kinds of error as the folk theories of astronomy, chemistry, and medicine that misled much of humanity before scientific discoveries provided "hard" definitions for the basic concepts in these fields.

On this account, the attention concept is highly vulnerable to the influences of folk psychology because, unlike the concept, say, of electricity, it has for centuries been frequently expressed in the forms of many different words in daily social interactions. Examples of these are the "heed" words described in an earlier part of this section on philosophy. The remedy, suggested by the eliminative materialist, is to let neuroscience findings shape the concept or concepts that are presently vaguely pointed to by the "heed" words.

However, it would be inaccurate to state that that eliminative materialism in the hands of the Churchlands denies the value of viewing a process like attention from higher levels. In her book, *Neurophilosophy*, Patricia Churchland (1986) describes a co-evolutionary research approach to attention that combines the notion of a spotlight framed at the psychological level (e.g., Treisman & Gelade, 1980) with the notion of thalamic neural activity framed at the neurobiological level (Crick, 1984). The role of philosophy is believed to provide a "synoptic vision" within which questions are formulated not for philosophy, nor for neuroscience, nor for psychology, but about the brain-mind (Churchland, 1986).

Although eliminative materialism confers sovereignty to the neurobiological level in framing the concept of attention, the "natural method" proposed by Flanagan (1992) adds phenomenology to the psychological and neurobiological approaches of Churchland's co-evolutionary method and gives each of the three approaches an equal weight, producing a "reflective equilibrium." He argues that none of these views can do the job alone. Phenomenology has no means of indicating how scientific measurements could reveal "what attention is like" to introspection; psychological models of mind-brain could proliferate endlessly unless constrained by knowledge of brain anatomy and physiology; and neuroscience needs psychological and phenomenological descriptions in order to determine how specific neural circuits contribute to the function of the mind. Together, however, phenomenology, psychology, and neuroscience may provide the appropriate approach to understanding attention.

VII. FINAL COMMENT

Of the many kinds of cognitive processes that are being studied by cognitive scientists, attention would appear to be among the ones that could profit substantially by a cross-disciplinary perspective. The philosophical approach to attention that has just been addressed provides a synoptic context for concluding remarks about attention from the broad perspective of the cognitive sciences. Both Churchland (1986) and Flanagan (1992) emphasize the present importance of neuroscience in understanding a cognitive process such as attention, and this chapter has heavily utilized neurobiological concepts to define the core issues of how attention is expressed, what mechanisms produce this expression, and what brain structures control these mechanisms. The reader might come away with the impression that the importance of neuroscience is overemphasized here with respect to other cognitive science domains, but it could be said that, owing to the relatively recent appearance of cognitive research in neuroscience, some emphasis is needed to bring neuroscience into an equal status with the more traditional and familiar concepts of attention provided by personal phenomenology and cognitive psychology.

References

Akert, K. (1964). Comparative anatomy of frontal cortex and thalamo-frontal connections. In J. M. Warren & K. Akert (Eds.), *The frontal granular cortex and behavior.* New York: McGraw-Hill.

Akhtar, N., & Enns, J. T. (1989). Relations between covert orienting and filtering in the development of visual attention. *Journal of Experimental Child Psychology, 48,* 315–334.

Alexander, G. E., & Crutcher, M. D. (1990). Functional architecture of basal ganglia circuits: Neural substrates of parallel processing. *Trends in Neurosciences, 13,* 266–271.

Allison, H. E. (1983). *Kant's transcendental idealism: An interpretation and defense.* New Haven, CT: Yale University Press.

Allport, A. (1989). Visual attention. In M. I. Posner (Ed.), *The foundations of cognitive science* (pp. 631–682). Cambridge, MA: MIT Press.

Andersen, R. A. (1989). Visual and eye movement functions of the posterior parietal cortex. *Annual Reviews of Neuroscience, 12,* 377–403.

Atkinson, J. (1984). Human visual development over the first six months of life: A review and a hypothesis. *Human Neurobiology, 3,* 61–74.

Atkinson, J., Hood, B., Wattam-Bell, J., Anker, S., & Tricklebank, J. (1988). Development of orientation discrimination in infants. *Perception, 17,* 587–595.

Bachinski, H. S., & Bachrach, V. R. (1980). Enhancement of perceptual sensitivity as the result of selectively attending to spatial locations. *Perception & Psychophysics, 28,* 241–248.

Baddeley, A. (1986). *Working memory.* New York: Oxford University Press.

Baddeley, A. (1995). Working memory. In M. Gazzaniga (Ed.), *The cognitive neurosciences* (pp. 755–764). Cambridge, MA: MIT Press.

Ball, K., Owsley, C., Sloane, M. E., Roenker, D. L., & Bruni, J. R. (1993). Visual attention problems as a predictor of vehicle crashes in older drivers. *Investigative Ophthalmology and Visual Science, 34,* 3110–3123.

Ball, K. K., Beard, B. L., Roenker, D. I., Miller, R. L., & Griggs, D. S. (1988). Age and visual search: Expanding the useful field of view. *Journal of the Optical Society of America, A, 5,* 2210–2219.

Bowman, E. M., Brown, V. J., Kertzman, C., Schwarz, U., & Robinson, D. L. (1993). Covert orienting of attention in macaques. I. Effects of behavioral context. *Journal of Neurophysiology, 70,* 431–443.

Boyd, C. A. R., & Noble, D. (1993). *The logic of life: The challenge of integrative physiology.* New York: Oxford University Press.

Broadbent, D. A. (1958). *Perception and communication.* London: Pergamon Press.

Brodmann, K. (1925). *Vergleichende Lokalisationslehre der Grosshirnrinde.* Leipzig: Barth.

Brody, F. A., Kinney, H. C., Kloman, A. S., & Gilles, F. H. (1987). Sequence of central nervous system myelination in human infancy. I. An autopsy study of myelination. *Journal of Neuropathology and Experimental Neurology, 46,* 283–301.

Bronson, G. W. (1974). The postnatal growth off visual capacity. *Child Development, 45,* 873–890.

Carter, C. S., Braver, R. S., Barch, D. M., Botvinick, M. M., Noll, D., & Cohen, J. D. (1998). Anterior cingulate cortex, error detection, and the online monitoring of performance. *Science, 280,* 747–749.

Cerella, J. (1985). Information processing rates in the elderly. *Psychological Bulletin, 98,* 67–83.

Cerella, J. (1991). Age effects may be global, not local: Comments on Fisk and Rogers (1991). *Journal of Experimental Psychology: General, 120,* 215–223.

Chugani, H., Phelps, M. E., & Mazziotta, J. C. (1987). Positron emission tomography study of human brain functional development. *Annals of Neurology, 22,* 487–497.

Churchland, P. S. (1986). *Neurophilosophy.* Cambridge, MA: MIT Press.

Churchland, P. S., & Sejnowski, T. J. (1992). *The computational brain.* Cambridge, MA: MIT Press.

Clohessy, A. B., Posner, M. I., Rothbart, M. K., & Vecera, S. P. (1991). The development of inhibition of return in early infancy. *Journal of Cognitive Neuroscience, 3,* 335–344.

Cohen, J. D., Dunbar, K., & McClelland, J. L. (1990). On the control of automatic processes: A parallel distributed processing account of the Stroop effect. *Psychological Review, 97,* 332–361.

Colby, C. L. (1991). The neuroanatomy and neurophysiology of attention. *Journal of Child Neurology,* S90–S118.

Corbetta, M., Miezin, F. M., Dobmeyer, S., Shulman, G. L., & Petersen, S. (1991). Selective and divided attention during visual discrimination of shape, color, and speed: Functional anatomy by positron emission tomography. *Journal of Neuroscience, 11,* 2383–2402.

Corbetta, M., Miezin, F. M., Shulman, G. L., and Petersen, S. E. (1993). A PET study of visuopatial attention. *Journal of Neuroscience, 13,* 1202–1226.

Crick, F. (1984). The function of the thalamic reticular complex: The searchlight hypothesis. *Proceedings of the National Academy of Sciences of the U.S.A., 81,* 4586–4590.

D'Aloisio, A., & Klein, R. M. (1990). Aging and the deployment of visual attention. *Advances in Psychology, 69,* 447–466.

Dawkins, M. S. (1976). *The selfish gene.* Oxford, England: Oxford University Press.

Dennett, D. C. (1991). *Consciousness explained.* Boston: Little, Brown.

Desimone, R., & Schein, S. J. (1987). Visual properties of neurons in area V4 of the macaque: Sensitivity to stimulus form. *Journal of Neurophysiology, 57,* 835–868.

Deutsch, J. A., & Deutsch, D. (1963). Attention; Some theoretical considerations. *Psychological Review, 70,* 80–90.

Diamond, A. (1990). The development and neural bases of memory functions as indexed by the AB and delayed response tasks in human infants and infant monkeys. *Annals of the New York Academy of Sciences, 608,* 268–317.

Diamond, A., & Doar, F. (1989). The performance of human infants on a measure of frontal cortex function, the delayed response task. *Developmental Psychobiology, 22,* 271–294.

Downing, C. (1988). Expectancy and visual-spatial attention: Effects on perceptual quality. *Journal of Experimental Psychology: Human Perception and Performance, 14,* 188–202.

Duncan, J. (1980). The locus of interference in the perception of simultaneous stimuli. *Psychological Review, 87,* 272–300.

Duncan, J. (1995). Attention, intelligence, and the frontal lobes. In M. S. Gassaniga (Ed.), *The cognitive neurosciences* (pp. 721–734), Cambridge, MA: MIT Press.

Enns, J. T., & Brodeur, D. A. (1989). A developmental study of covert orienting to peripheral visual cues. *Journal of Experimental Child Psychology, 48,* 171–189.

Eriksen, B. A., & Eriksen, C. W. (1974). Effects of noise letters upon the identification of a target letter in a nonsearch task. *Perception & Psychophysics, 16,* 143–149.

Eriksen, C. W., & Hoffman, J. E. (1972). Temporal and spatial characteristics of selective encoding from visual displays. *Perception & Psychophysics, 12,* 201–204.

Eriksen, C. W., & St. James, J. D. (1986). Visual attention within and around the field of focal attention: A zoom lens model. *Perception & Psychophysics, 40,* 225–240.

Fischer, B., & Bock, R. (1981). Enhanced activation of neurons in prelunate cortex before visually guided saccades of trained rhesus monkeys. *Experimental Brain Research, 44,* 129–137.

Fischer, B., & Ramsperger, E. (1986). Express-saccades of the monkey: Effects of daily training on probability of occurrence and reaction time. *Experimental Brain Research, 55,* 232–242.

Flanagan, O. (1992). *Consciousness reconsidered.* Cambridge, MA: MIT Press.

Fries, W. (1984). Cortical projections to the superior colliculus in the macaque monkey: A retrograde study using horseradish peroxidase. *Journal of Comparative Neurology, 230,* 55–76.

Frith, C. D., Friston, K., Liddle, P. F., & Frackowiak, R. S. J. (1991). Willed action and the prefrontal cortex in man: A study with PET. *Proceedings of the Royal Society of London, Series B, 244,* 241–246.

Funahashi, S., Bruce, C. J., Goldman-Rakic, P. S. (1989). Mnemonic coding of visual space in the monkey's dorsolateral prefrontal cortex. *Journal of Neurophysiology, 61,* 331–349.

Fuster, J. M. (1989). *The prefrontal cortex: Anatomy, physiology, and neuropsychology of the frontal lobe* (2nd ed.). New York: Raven Press.

Gattass, R., & Desimone, R. (1991). Attention-related responses in the superior colliculus of the macaque. *Society for Neuroscience Abstracts, 17,* 545.

Gehring, W. J., Gos, B., Coles, M. G. H., Meyer, D. E., & Donchin, E. (1993). A neural system for error detection and compensation. *Psychological Science, 4,* 385–390.

Gnadt, J. W., & Andersen, R. A. (1988). Memory related motor planning activity in posterior parietal cortex of macaque. *Experimental Brain Research, 70,* 216–220.

Goldberg, M. E., & Bushnell, M. C. (1981). Behavioral enhancement of visual responses in monkey cerebral cortex. II. Modulation in frontal eye fields specifically related to saccades. *Journal of Neurophysiology, 46,* 773.

Goldberg, M. E., & Wurtz, R. H. (1972). Activity of superior colliculus in behaving monkey. II. Effect of attention on neuronal responses. *Journal of Neurophysiology, 35,* 560–574.

Goldman-Rakic, P. S. (1987). Circuitry of primate prefrontal cortex and regulation of behavior by representational memory. In F. Plum (Ed.), *Handbook of physiology* (Sect. 1, Vol. 5, pp. 373–417). Bethesda, MD: American Physiological Society.

Goldman-Rakic, P. S. (1988). Topography of cognition: Parallel distributed networks in primate association cortex. *Annual Review of Neuroscience, 11,* 137–156.

Goldman-Rakic, P. S., Chafee, M., & Friedman, H. (1993). Allocation of spatial function in distributed circuits. In T. Ono, L. R. Squire, M. E. Raichle, D. I. Perrett, & M. Fukuda (Eds.), *Brain mechanisms of perception and memory: From neuron to behavior* (pp. 445–456). New York: Oxford University Press.

Goldman-Rakic, P. S., & Friedman, H. R. (1991). The circuitry of working memory revealed by anatomy and metabolic imagery. In H. S. Levin, H. M. Eisenberg, and A. L. Benton (Eds.), *Frontal lobe function and dysfunction.* New York: Oxford University Press, pp. 72–91.

Graham, J., Lin, C. S., & Kaas, J. H. (1979). Subcortical projections of six visual cortical areas in the owl monkey, *Aotus trivirgatus. Journal of Comparative Neurology, 187,* 557–580.

Haenny, P. E., & Schiller, P. H. (1988). State dependent activity in monkey visual cortex: I. Single cell activity in V1 and V4 on visual tasks. *Experimental Brain Research, 69,* 225–244.

Hartley, A. (1992). Attention. In F. I. M. Craik & T. A. Salthouse (Eds.), *The handbook of aging and cognition.* Hillsdale, NJ: Erlbaum.

Hartley, A. (1993). Evidence for the selective preservation of spatial selective attention in old age. *Psychology and Aging, 8,* 371–379.

Hawkins, H. L., Shafto, M. G., & Richardson, K. (1988). Effects of target luminance and cue validity on the latency of visual detection. *Perception & Psychophysics, 44,* 484–492.

Haxby, J. V., Horwitz, B., Ungerleider, L. G., Maisog, J. M., Pietrini, P., & Grady, C. L. (1994). The functional organization of human extrastriate cortex: A PET-rCBF study of selective attention to faces and locations. *Journal of Neuroscience, 14,* 6336–6353.

Heilman, K. M., Bowers, D., Coslett, H. B., Whelan, H., & Watson, R. T. (1985). Directional hypokinesia: Prolonged reaction times for leftward movements in patients with right hemisphere lesions and neglect. *Neurology, 35,* 855–859.

Hikosaka, O., & Wurtz, R. H. (1983). Visual and oculomotor functions of monkey substantia nigra pars reticulata IV. Relation of substantia nigra to superior colliculus. *Journal of Neurophysiology, 49,* 1285–1301.

Hills, B. L., & Burg, A. (1977). *A re-analysis of California driver vision data: General findings* (Rep. No. 768). Crowthorne, England: Transport and Road Research Laboratory.

Hinton, G. E., & Lang, K. J. (1985). *Shape recognition and illusory conjunctions.* Paper presented at the ninth International Joint conference on Artificial Intelligence, Los Angeles.

Hunter, W. S. (1913). The delayed reaction in animals and children. *Behavior Monographs, 2,* 1–86.

Hurlbert, A., & Poggio, T. (1986). Do computers need attention? *Nature (London), 321,* 651–652.

Jacobsen, C. F. (1936). Studies of cerebral function in primates. *Comparative Psychology Monographs, 13,* 1–68.

James, W. (1890). *Principles of psychology* (Vols. 1 and 2). New York: Holt.

Johnson, M. H. (1990). Cortical maturation and the development of visual attention in early infancy. *Journal of Cognitive Neuroscience, 2,* 81–95.

Johnson, M. H. (1994). Visual attention and the control of eye movements in early infancy. In C. Umilta & M. Moscovitch (Eds.), *Attention and performance XV* (pp. 291–310). Cambridge, MA: MIT Press.

Johnson, M. H., Posner, M. I., & Rothbart, M. K. (1991). Components of visual orienting in early infancy: Contingency learning, anticipatory looking, and disengaging. *Journal of Cognitive Neuroscience, 3,* 335–344.

Johnson-Laird, P. N. (1988). *The computer and the mind: An invitation to cognitive science.* Cambridge, MA: Harvard University Press.

Johnston, W. A., & Dark, V. J. (1986). Selective attention. *Annual Review of Psychology, 37,* 43–75.

Jones, E. G. (1985). *The thalamus.* New York: Plenum Press.

Jonides, J. (1980). Towards a model of the mind's eye's movement. *Canadian Journal of Psychology, 34,* 103–112.

Jonides, J., Smith, E. E., Koeppe, R. A., Awh, E., Minoshima, S., & Mintun, M. A. (1993). Spatial working memory in humans as revealed by PET. *Nature (London), 363,* 623–625.

Jueptner, M., Stephan, K. M., Frith, C. D., Brooks, D. J., Frackowiak, R. S., & Passingham, R. E. (1997). Anatomy of motor learning. I. Frontal cortex and attention to action. *Journal of Neurophysiology, 77*, 1313–1324.

Kahneman, D. (1973). *Attention and effort.* Englewood Cliffs, NJ: Prentice-Hall.

Kant, I. (1929). *Critique of pure reason* (N. Kemp-Smith, Trans.) New York: St. Martin's Press. (Original work published 1787).

Kinchla, R. A. (1992). Attention. *Annual Reviews of Psychology, 43*, 711–742.

Klein, R. M., Kingstone, A., & Pontefract, A. (1992). Orienting of visual attention. In K. Rayner (Ed.), *Eye movements and visual cognition: Scene perception and reading.* New York: Springer-Verlag.

Koch, C., & Ullman, S. (1985). Shifts in selective visual attention: Towards the underlying neural circuitry. *Human Neurobiology, 4*, 219–227.

Kosnik, W., Winslow, I., Kline, D., Rasinski, K., & Sekuler, R. (1988). Visual changes in daily life throughout adulthood. *Journals of Gerontology: Psychological Sciences, 43*, 63–70.

Kretschmann, H. J., Kammradt, F., Krauthausen, I., Sauer, B., & Wingert, F. (1986). Growth of the hippocampal formation in man. *Bibliotheca Anatomica, 28*, 27–52.

LaBerge, D. (1973). Attention and the measurement of perceptual learning. *Memory & Cognition, 1*, 268–276.

LaBerge, D. (1983). The spatial extent of attention to letters and words. *Journal of Experimental Psychology: Human Perception and Performance, 9*, 371–379.

LaBerge, D. (1990a). Attention. *Psychological Science, 1*, 156–162.

LaBerge, D. (1990b). Thalamic and cortical mechanisms of attention suggested by recent positron emission tomographic experiments. *Journal of Cognitive Neuroscience, 2*, 358–372.

LaBerge, D. (1994). Quantitative models of attention and response processes in shape identification tasks. *Journal of Mathematical Psychology, 38*, 198–243.

LaBerge, D. (1995a). Computational and anatomical models of selective attention in object identification. In M. Gassaniga (Ed.), *The cognitive neurosciences* (pp. 649–663). Cambridge, MA: MIT Press.

LaBerge, D. (1995b). *Attention: The brain's art of mindfulness.* Cambridge, MA: Harvard University Press.

LaBerge, D. (1997). Attention, awareness, and the triangular circuit. *Consciousness and Cognition, 6*, 149–181.

LaBerge, D. (1998). Attention as the intensification of cortical activity. *Revue de Neuropsychologie, 8*, 54–81.

LaBerge, D., & Brown, V. (1986). Variations in size of the visual field in which targets are presented: An attentional range effect. *Perception & Psychophysics, 40*, 188–200.

LaBerge, D., & Brown, V. (1989). Theory of attentional operations in shape identification. *Psychological Review, 96*, 101–124.

LaBerge, D., & Buchsbaum, M. S. (1990). Positron emission tomographic measurements of pulvinar activity during an attention task. *Journal of Neuroscience, 10*, 613–619.

LaBerge, D., Carlson, R. D., & Williams, J. K. (1997). Toward an analytic model of attention to visual shape. In A. A. J. Marley (Ed.), *Choice, decision and measurement.* Mahwah, NJ: Erlbaum, pp. 389–410.

LaBerge, D., Carlson, R. L., Williams, J. K., & Bunney, B. G. (1997). Shifting attention in visual space: Tests of moving-spotlight models versus an activity-distribution model. *Journal of Experimental Psychology: Human Perception and Performance, 23*, 1380–1392.

LaBerge, D., Carter, M., & Brown, V. (1992). A network simulation of thalamic circuit operations in selective attention. *Neural Computation, 4*, 318–331.

LaBerge, D., Van Gelder, P., & Yellott, J. I. (1970). A cueing technique in choice reaction time. *Perception & Psychophysics, 7*, 57–62.

Lecours, A. R. (1975). Myelogenetic correlates of the development of speech and language. In E. H. Lenneberg & E. Lenneberg (Eds.), *Foundations of language development: A multidisciplinary approach* (Vol. 1, pp. 121–135. New York: Academic Press.

Liotti, M., Fox, P. T., & LaBerge, D. (1994). PET measurements of attention to closely spaced visual shapes. *Society for Neurosciences Abstracts, 20*, 354.

Luria, A. R. (1973). *The working brain: An introduction to neuropsychology.* New York: Basic Books.

Ma, T. P., Graybiel, A. M., & Wurtz, R. H. (1991). Location of saccade-related neurons in the macaque superior colliculus. *Experimental Brain Research, 85,* 21–35.

Madden, D. J., and Plude, D. J. (1993). Selective preservation of selective attention. In J. Cerella, J. M. Rybash, W. Hoyer, and M. L. Commons (Eds.). *Adult information processing: Limits on loss.* San Diego: Academic Press, pp. 273–300.

Mangun, G. R. Hillyard, S. A., & Luck, S. J. (1992). Electrocortical substates of visual selective attention. In D. Meyer & S. Kornblum (Eds.), *Attention and performance XIV.* Hillsdale, NJ: Erlbaum.

Marr, D. (1982). *Vision.* San Francisco: Freeman.

Mazzoni, P., Andersen, R. A., & Jordan, M. I. (1993). A more biologically plausible learning rule for neural networks. *Proceedings of the National Academy of Sciences of the U.S.A., 88,* 4433–4437.

McDowd, J. M., & Birren, J. E. (1990). Aging and attentional processes. In J. E. Birren and K. W. Schaie (Eds.), *The handbook of aging.* San Diego: Academic Press, pp. 222–233.

Moray, N. (1959). Attention in dichotic listening: Affective cues and the influence of instructions. *Quarterly Journal of Experimental Psychology, 11,* 56–60.

Morris, B. C., Friston, K., & Dolan, R. J. (1997). Neural responses to salient visual stimuli. *Proceedings of the Royal Society of London, Series B, 264,* 769–775.

Mountcastle, V. B., Andersen, R. A., & Motter, B. C. (1981). The influence of attentive fixation upon the excitability of the light-sensitive neurons of the posterior parietal cortex. *Journal of Neuroscience, 1,* 1218–1235.

Mountcastle, V. B., Lynch, J. C., Georgopoulos, A., Sakata, H., & Acuna, C. (1975). Posterior parietal association cortex of the monkey: Command functions for operations within extrapersonal space. *Journal of Neurophysiology, 38,* 871–907.

Mozer, M. C., & Behrmann, M. (1992). Reading with attentional impairments: A brain-damaged model of neglect and attentional dyslexias. In R. G. Reilley & N. E. Sharkey (Eds.), *Connectionist approaches to natural language processing* (pp. 409–460). Hillsdale, NJ: Erlbaum.

Munoz, D. P., & Wurtz, R. H. (1993a). Fixation cells in monkey superior colliculus I. Characteristics of cell discharge. *Journal of Neurophysiology, 70,* 559–575.

Munoz, D. P., & Wurtz, R. H. (1993b). Fixation cells in monkey superior colliculus II. Reversible activation and deactivation. *Journal of Neurophysiology, 79,* 576–589.

Murtha, S., Chertkow, H. K., Dixon, R., Beauregard, M., & Evans, A. (1996). Anticipation causes increased blood flow to the anterior cingulate cortex. *Human Brain Mapping, 4,* 103–112.

Naatanen, R. (1992). *Attention and brain function.* Hillsdale, NJ: Erlbaum.

Nagy, A. L., & Sanchez, R. R. (1990). Critical color differences determined with a visual search task. *Journal of the Optical Society of America, 7,* 1209–1217.

National Highway Traffic Safety Administration (1989). *Conference on Research and Development Needed to Improve Safety and Mobility of Older Drivers* (Report DOT 807 554). Washington, DC: U.S. Department of Transportation, Department of Transportation.

Niebur, E., & Koch, C. (1994). A model for the neuronal implementation of selective visual attention based on temporal correlation among neurons. *Journal of Computational Neuroscience, 1,* 141–158.

Nissen, M. J. K., and Corkin, S. (1985). Effectiveness of attentional cueing in older and younger adults. *Journal of Gerontology, 40,* 185–191.

Nobre, A. C., Sebestyen, G. N., Gitelman, D. R., Mesulam, M. M., Frackowiak, R. S., & Frith, C. D. (1997). Functional localization of the system for visuospatial attention using positron emission tomography. *Brain, 120,* 515–533.

Norman, D. A. (1968). Toward a theory of memory and attention. *Psychological Review, 75,* 522–536.

Norman, D. A., & Shallice, T. (1980). *Attention to action: Willed and automatic control of behavior* (Rep. No. 8006). San Diego: University of California, Center of Human Information Processing.

Olshausen, B. A., Anderson, C. H., & Van Essen, D. C. (1993). A neurobiological model of visual attention and invariant pattern recognition based on dynamic routing of information. *Journal of Neuroscience, 13,* 4700–4719.

Olson, G. M., & Sherman, T. (1983). Attention, learning, and memory in infants. In P. Mussen (Ed.), *Handbook of child psychology: Vol. 2. Infancy and developmental psychobiology* (pp. 1001–1080). New York: Wiley.

O'Reilly, R. C., Kosslyn, S. M., Marsolek, C. J., & Chabris, C. F. (1990). Receptive field characteristics that allow parietal lobe neuron to encode spatial properties of visual input: A computational analysis. *Journal of Cognitive Neuroscience, 2,* 141–155.

O'Scalaidhe, S. P., Wilson, F. A., & Goldman-Rakic, P. S. (1997). Areal segregation of face-processing neurons in prefrontal cortex. *Science, 278,* 1135–1138.

Parasuraman, R. (Ed.). (1998). *The attentive brain.* Cambridge, MA: MIT Press.

Parasuraman, R., and Davies, D. R. (Eds.). (1984). *Varieties of attention.* New York: Academic Press.

Pardo, J. V., Pardo, P. J., Janer, K. W., & Raichle, M. E. (1990). The anterior cingulate cortex mediates processing selection in the Stroop attentional conflict paradigm. *Proceedings of the National Academy of Sciences of the U.S.A., 87,* 256–259.

Pashler, H. E. (1998). *The psychology of attention.* Cambridge, MA: MIT Press.

Passingham, R. E. (1985). Cortical mechanisms and cues for action. *Philosophical Transactions of the Royal Society of London, Series B, 308,* 101–111.

Petersen, S. E., Fox, P. T., Posner, M. I., Minton, M., and Raichle, M. E. (1988). Positron emission tomographic studies of the cortical anatomy of single word processing. *Nature (London), 331,* 585–589.

Petersen, S. E., Robinson, D. L., & Keys, W. (1985). Pulvinar nuclei of the behaving rhesus monkey: Visual responses and their modulation. *Journal of Neurophysiology, 54,* 867–886.

Plude, D. J., & Hoyer, W. J. (1985). Attention and performance: Identifying and localizing age deficits. In N. Charness (Ed.), *Aging and human performance.* (pp. 47–99). New York: Wiley.

Posner, M. I. (1978). *Chronometric explorations of mind.* Englewood Heights, NJ: Erlbaum.

Posner, M. I. (1980). Orienting of attention. *Quarterly Journal of Experimental Psychology, 32,* 3–25.

Posner, M. I. (1988). Structures and functions of selective attention. In T. Boll & B. Bryant (Eds.), *Master lectures in clinical neuropsychology* (pp. 173–202). Washington, DC: American Psychological Association.

Posner, M. I., & Boies, S. J. (1971). Components of attention. *Psychological Review, 78,* 391–408.

Posner, M. I., & Cohen, Y. (1984). Components of performance. In H. Bouma & D. Bowhuis (Eds.), *Attention and performance* (pp. 531–556). Hillsdale, NJ: Erlbaum.

Posner, M. I., & DiGirolamo, G. J. (1998). Conflict, target detection and cognitive control. In R. Parasuraman (Ed.), *The attentive brain.* Cambridge, MA: MIT Press.

Posner, M. I., & Petersen, S. E. (1990). The attention system of the human brain. *Annual Review of Neuroscience, 13,* 25–41.

Posner, M. I., Petersen, S. E., Fox, P. T., & Raichle, M. E. (1988). Localization of cognitive functions in the human brain. *Science, 240,* 1627–1631.

Posner, M. I., & Raichle, M. E. (1994). *Images of mind.* New York: Scientific American Library.

Posner, M. I., Rafal, R. D., Choate, L. S., & Vaughan, J. (1985). Inhibition of return: Neural basis and function. *Cognitive Neuropsychology, 2,* 211–228.

Posner, M. I., & Snyder, C. R. R. (1975). Facilitation and inhibition in the processing of signals. In P. M. A. Rabbitt & S. Dornic (Eds.), *Attention and performance V* (pp. 669–681). New York: Academic Press.

Posner, M. I., Snyder, C. R. R., & Davidson, B. J. (1980). Attention and the detection of signals. *Journal of Experimental Psychology: General, 109,* 160–174.

Posner, M. I., & Tudela. (1997). Imaging resources. *Biological Psychology, 45,* 95–107.

Posner, M. I., Walker, J. A., Friedrich, F. J., & Rafal, R. D. (1984). Effects of parietal injury on covert orienting of visual attention. *Journal of Neuroscience, 4,* 1863–1874.

Putnam, H. (1960). Minds and machines. In S. Hook (Ed.), *Dimensions of mind.* New York: New York University Press.

Rafal, R. D., Calabresi, P. A., Brennan, C. W., & Sciolto, R. K. (1989). Saccade preparation inhibits reorienting to recently attended locations. *Journal of Experimental Psychology: Human Perception and Performance, 15,* 673–685.

Rafal, R. D., & Posner, M. I. (1987). Deficits in human visual spatial attention following thalamic lesions. *Proceedings of the National Academy of Sciences of the U.S.A., 84,* 7349–7353.

Rafal, R. D., Posner, M. I., Friedman, J. H., Inhoff, A. W., & Berstein, E. (1988). Orienting of visual attention in progressive supranuclear palsy. *Brain, 111,* 267–280.

Rakic, P. (1995). Corticogenesis in human and nonhuman primates. In M. Gazzaniga (Ed.), *The cognitive neurosciences* (pp. 127–146). Cambridge, MA: MIT Press.

Rawls, J. (1971). *A theory of justice.* Cambridge, MA: Harvard University Press.

Reeves, A., and G. Sperling. (1986). Attention gating in short-term visual memory. *Psychological Review, 93,* 180–206.

Remington, R. (1980). Attention and saccadic eye movement. *Journal of Experimental Psychology: Human Perception and Performance, 6,* 726–744.

Reuter-Lorenz, P. A., Hughes, H. C., & Fendrich, R. (1991). The reduction of saccadic latency by prior offset of the fixation point: An analysis of the gap effect. *Perception & Psychophysics, 49,* 167–175.

Richards, J. E. (1989). Sustained visual attention in 8-week old infants. *Infant Behavior Development, 12,* 425–436.

Robinson, D. L., Goldberg, M. E., & Stanton, G. B. (1978). Parietal association cortex in the primate: Sensory mechanisms and behavioral modulations. *Journal of Neurophysiology, 41,* 910–932.

Robinson, D. L., & Petersen, S. E. (1992). The pulvinar and visual salience. *Trends in Neurosciences, 15,* 127–132.

Roland, P. E. (1985). Cortical organization of voluntary behavior in man. *Human Neurobiology, 4,* 155–167.

Rothbart, M. K., Posner, M. I., & Boylan, A. (1990). Regulatory mechanisms in infant temperament. In J. Enns (Ed.), *The development of attention: Research and theory* (pp. 47–66). Amsterdam: North-Holland.

Rovee-Collier, C. K. (1984). The ontogeny of learning and memory in human infancy. In R. Kail & N. E. Spear (Eds.), *Comparative perspectives on the development of memory* (pp. 103–134). Hillsdale, NJ: Erlbaum.

Rumelhart, D. E., & McClelland, J. L. (Eds.). (1986). *Parallel distributed processing: Explorations in the microstructure of cognition* (Vol. 1). Cambridge, MA: MIT Press/Bradford Books.

Ryle, G. (1949). *The concept of mind.* NY: Harper and Row.

Sakata, H., Shibutani, H., & Kawano, K. (1980). Spatial properties of visual fixation neurons in posterior parietal association cortex of the monkey. *Journal of Neurophysiology, 43,* 1654–1672.

Salthouse, T. A. (1980). Age and memory: Strategies for localizing the loss. In L. W. Poon, J. L. Fozard, L. Cermak, D. Arenberg, & L. W. Thompson (Eds.), *Human aging and behavior.* New York: Academic Press.

Salthouse, T. A. (1985). Speed of behavior and its implications for cognition. In J. F. Birren & K. W. Schaie (Eds.), *Handbook of the psychology of aging* (2nd ed., pp. 400–426). New York: Van Nostrand-Reinhold.

Sandon, P. A. (1990). Simulating visual attention. *Journal of Cognitive Neuroscience, 2,* 213–231.

Schiller, P. H. (1985). A model of the generation of visually guided saccadic eye movements. In D. Rose & V. G. Dobson (Eds.), *Models of the visual cortex.* Chichester, England: Wiley.

Searle, J. R. (1990). Consciousness, explanatory inversion, and cognitive science. *Behavioral and Brain Sciences, 13,* 585–642.

Shaw, M. L. (1978). A capacity allocation model for reaction time. *Journal of Experimental Psychology: Human Perception and Performance, 4,* 596–598.

Sherman, S. M., & Koch, C. (1986). The control of retinogeniculate transmission in the mammalian lateral geniculate nucleus. *Experimental Brain Research, 63,* 1–20.

Shiffrin, R. M. (1988). Attention. In R. C. Atkinson, R. J. Herrnstein, G. Lindsey, & R. D. Luce (Eds.), *Steven's Handbook of experimental psychology* (2nd ed.). New York: Wiley.

Shiffrin, R. M., & Schneider, W. (1977). Controlled and automatic human information processing. II. Perceptual learning, automatic attending, and a general theory. *Psychological Review, 84,* 127–190.

Shulman, G. L., Corbetta, M., Buckner, R. D., Fiez, J. A., Miezin, F. M., Raichle, M. E., & Petersen, S. E. (1997). Common blood flow changes across visual tasks: I. Increases in subcortical structures and cerebellum but not in nonvisual cortex. *Journal of Cognitive Neuroscience, 9,* 624–647.

Slater, A. M., Morison, V., & Somers, M. (1988). Orientation discrimination and cortical function in the human newborn. *Perception, 17,* 597–602.

Smith, E. E., Jonides, J., & Koeppe, R. A. (1996). Dissociating verbal and spatial working memory using PET. *Cerebral Cortex, 6,* 11–20.

Sparks, D., & Mays, L. (1980). Movement fields of saccade-related burst neurons in the monkey superior colliculus. *Brain Research, 190,* 39–50.

Sperling, G., & Weichselgartner, E. (1995). Episodic theory of the dynamics of spatial attention. *Psychological Review, 102,* 503–532.

Spitzer, H., Desimone, R., & Moran, J. (1988). Increased attention enhances both behavioral and neuronal performance. *Science, 240,* 338–340.

Squire, L. R., Ojemann, J. G., Miezin, F. M., Petersen, S. E., Videen, T. O., & Raichle, M. E. (1992). Activation of the hippocampus in normal humans: A functional anatomical study of memory. *Proceedings of the National Academy of Sciences of the U.S.A., 89,* 1837–1841.

Stechler, G., & Latz, E. (1966). Some observations on attention and arousal in the human infant. *Journal of the American Academy of Child Psychiatry, 5,* 517–525.

Steriade, M., Jones, E. G., & Llinas, R. R. (1990). *Thalamic oscillations and signaling.* New York: Wiley.

Suppes, P. (1969). *Studies in the methodology and foundations of science: Selected papers from 1951 to 1969.* Dordrecht, The Netherlands: Reidel.

Timiras, P. S. (1988). *Physiological basis of geriatrics.* New York: Macmillan.

Tipper, S. P., & McLaren, J. (1990). Evidence for efficient visual selectivity in children. In J. T. Enns (Ed.), *The development of attention: Research and theory.* Amsterdam: Elsevier.

Treisman, A. (1988). Features and objects: The fourteenth Bartlett memorial lecture. *Quarterly Journal of Experimental Psychology, 40A,* 201–237.

Treisman, A., & Gelade, G. (1980). A feature integration theory of attention. *Cognitive Psychology, 12,* 97–136.

Treisman, A., & Souther, J. (1985). Search asymmetry: A diagnostic for preattentive processing of separable features. *Journal of Experimental Psychology: General, 114,* 285–310.

Tsal, Y. (1983). Movement of attention across the visual field. *Journal of Experimental Psychology: Human Perception and Performance, 9,* 523–530.

White, A. R. (1964). *Attention.* Oxford, England: Blackwell.

Wilson, F. A. W., O'Scalaidhe, S. P., & Goldman-Rakic, P. S. (1993). Dissociation of object and spatial processing domains in primate prefrontal cortex. *Science, 260,* 1955–1958.

Wright, R. D. (1994). Shifts of visual attention to multiple simultaneous location cues. *Canadian Journal of Experimental Psychology, 48,* 1–12.

Wright, R. D. (Ed.). (1998). *Visual Attention.* New York: Oxford University Press.

Wurtz, R. H., & Mohler, C. W. (1976). Organization of monkey superior colliculus: Enhanced visual responses of superficial layer cells. *Journal of Neurophysiology, 39,* 745–762.

Yantis, S. (1993). Stimulus-driven attentional capture. *Current Directions in Psychological Science, 2,* 156.

Yantis, S., & Jonides, J. (1990). Abrupt visual onsets and selective attention: Voluntary versus automatic allocation. *Journal of Experimental Psychology; Human Perception and Performance, 16,* 121–134.

Young, M. P., & Yamane, S. (1992). Sparse population coding of faces in the inferotemporal cortex. *Science, 256,* 1327–1331.

Ziff, P. (1959). The feelings of robots. *Analysis, 19,* 64–68.

Zipser, D., & Andersen, R. A. (1988). A back-propagation programmed network that simulates response properties of a subset of posterior parietal neurons. *Nature (London), 331,* 697–684.

Zola-Morgan, S., & Squire, L. R. (1986). Memory impairment in monkeys following lesions of the hippocampus. *Behavioral Neuroscience, 100,* 155–160.

CHAPTER 3

Categorization

Douglas L. Medin
Evan Heit

I. OVERVIEW

A. Current State of Affairs

The study of categorization is not unlike the cooperative algorithms associated with neural net models. That is to say, there is a synergy between the various areas associated with cognitive science that makes categorization research dynamic and exciting. Individual subdisciplines have matured to the degree that they are interacting with one another more extensively than perhaps ever before. Consider the question of the extent to which categorizing in any particular situation is based on the application of abstract rules or on the retrieval of specific memories. For example, is categorizing a novel item (e.g., "X is an instance of Disease Y") driven by checking the consistency with abstract rules or deciding that the item is sufficiently similar to a remembered instance of a category (e.g., Rips, 1989; E. E. Smith & Sloman, 1994)? It turns out that memory-based categorization in cognitive psychology is closely related to a development in artificial intelligence (AI) known as case-based reasoning. And the question of memories versus rules is highly relevant to issues in philosophy concerning concept stability. Finally, the long-held belief in linguistics that knowledge of a grammar is represented by linguistic rules has been challenged by connectionist researchers who hold that knowledge is far more specific than rules. In short, there are strong motivations for mutual interaction across traditionally distinct research areas.

Of course, the various cognitive science subdisciplines approach a given issue from different, complementary perspectives. Our review of current work in categorization reflects these diverse methods of inquiry. It also reflects the fact that we are cognitive psychologists; cognitive scientists from other areas would no doubt have different patterns of emphasis and organization.

B. Brief History

One of the most central questions in categorization concerns the structure of concepts. By *concept* we mean a mental representation of a category serving multiple functions, one of which is to allow for the determination of whether or not something belongs to a class. Following E. E. Smith and Medin (1981), one can distinguish three positions on conceptual structure. The *classical view* holds that all instances of a category share common properties that are necessary and sufficient conditions for defining the concept. The *probabilistic view* denies that there are defining properties and instead claims that concepts are organized in terms of properties that are only characteristic of category instances. Membership in a category can thus be graded rather than all-or-none, where the better members have more characteristic properties than the poorer ones. Perhaps the most exciting development in the psychology of concepts in the 1970s was the shift from the classical to the probabilistic view, importantly motivated by Eleanor Rosch's studies of natural object categories (see Mervis & Rosch, 1981; Medin & Smith, 1984, for reviews, and Margolis, 1994, for a recent critique; E. Rosch, 1978; e.g., E. Rosch & Mervis, 1975; E. E. Smith, Shoben, & Rips, 1974). The third view of conceptual structure, the *exemplar view,* agrees with the claim that concepts need not contain defining properties, but further claims that categories may be represented by their individual exemplars, and that classification is determined by whether the instance is sufficiently similar to one or more of the category's known exemplars (e.g., Brooks, 1978; Medin & Schaffer, 1978).

It is obvious that views of conceptual structure constrain models of category processing. For example, hypothesis testing or rule-based models are more compatible with classically defined than with probabilistic categories. Hypotheses would correspond to conjectures about the defining properties, and if there are no defining properties, any conjunctive rule would need to have a procedure for dealing with exceptions. A learning procedure that abstracts the central tendency of category examples, such as prototype formation (e.g., Posner & Keele, 1968), is especially compatible with the probabilistic view. In fact the probabilistic view is sometimes referred to as the prototype view. At a more general level, all three views of conceptual structure are consistent with similarity-based models of category learning. For purposes of illustration we could assume some generic similarity model where similarity is some weighted function of shared and distinctive properties. Classical view category structures would correspond to the special case of the similarity model, where the defining features receive all the weight. Probabilistic view category structures could be learned as a system that also weights important or characteristic features regardless of whether or not they are defining. Finally, the exemplar view explicitly assumes that similarity to examples *is* the processing system determining classification. We belabor this point about similarity because similarity-based models of category learning have recently come under criticism (e.g., Murphy & Medin, 1985; Schank, Collins, & Hunter, 1986).

One challenge for similarity-based models of categorization is adequately constraining the notion of similarity. According to Tversky's (1977) contrast model, for example, similarity is a weighted function of matching and mismatching features. Therefore, the similarity between two entities depends crucially on which features enter into comparison for matches and mismatches and on the weights assigned to the features being compared. Potentially, then, similarity is an empty notion devoid of explanatory power (Goodman, 1972). To make similarity meaningful, there must be constraints on the features and their weighting. In that event, however, it is the constraints that are performing the explanatory work, not the abstract notion of similarity (e.g., Medin, 1989). Of course, one might argue that the human perceptual system has evolved to select the right kinds of similarity, namely, those that give useful categorization schemes (Murphy & Medin, 1985). The success of similarity-based learning models suggests that this is at least part of the story.

Another source of constraints might be theories and other forms of knowledge that pick out and weight relevant features. In AI this approach to categorization is referred to as explanation-based learning (e.g., Dejong, 1988). The idea is that prior knowledge in the form of a domain theory can be used to explain *why* some example is a member of a category and then can be used to generalize the concept appropriately. For example, if the explanation for why some example is a *cup* does not include the color of the cup as part of the explanation, then the generalization will not contain color as a relevant feature (Mitchell, Keller, & Kedar-Cabilli, 1986). Therefore, if the example were a red cup, the system would show no tendency to act as if other red things might be cups.

Later on we shall have much more to say about both similarity-based learning (SBL) and explanation-based learning (EBL). For now we simply note that a great deal of current research and theory in categorization is directed both at contrasts between these two approaches and, more significantly, at ways of integrating or combining them.

C. Ecological Validity and Artificial versus Natural Categories

Anyone who starts reading psychological research on categorization will quickly notice that studies using natural object categories and those using artificially constructed categories are both prominently represented. By natural object categories we mean categories with lexical entries (e.g., *bird*) whose instances correspond to entities in the world (e.g., *robin, turkey, pigeon*). Artificially constructed categories typically involve novel stimuli where the constituent features or properties of examples are familiar, but where the experimenter specifically manipulates the properties of examples and the assignment of examples to categories to create some particular category structure of interest. Neither the examples nor the categories need necessarily correspond to real-world entities.

There is both interplay and tension between work using natural categories and that using artificial categories (e.g., see Murphy, 1993, for a discussion). On the one hand, it seems straightforward that the closer an experimental situation is to real-world contexts, the more readily one may generalize to those contexts. Results from artificial categories may be apropos of nothing. A counter-argument is that real-world contexts are characterized by numerous correlated (and, therefore, confounded) variables and that artificial categories are needed to run properly controlled experiments capable of isolating variables relevant to categorization. We believe that both positions have validity; researchers may profitably and explicitly violate ecological validity for certain purposes, but they cannot ignore it. Let's take a quick look at two examples of an effective interplay between the artificial and the natural (see Medin & Thou, 1992, for further examples and discussion).

One general rationale for using artificial categories is to identify some variable or structural property of natural categories, incorporate that property into artificially constructed categories, and then conduct experiments to evaluate the role and importance of that property in categorization. This strategy allows one to control for a variety of extraneous variables that might affect performance with natural categories. Consider, for example, Rosch's pioneering research on goodness of example or typicality effects (e.g., E. Rosch, 1973; E. Rosch & Mervis, 1975). Rosch proposed that natural categories have a *family resemblance* structure giving rise to typicality effects. Under the family resemblance principle, category members considered the most typical are those with the most properties in common with other category members and the fewest attributes in common with members of contrasting categories. E. Rosch and Mervis (1975) employed a variety of measures that converged to suggest that natural categories have a family resemblance structure. They then created artificial categories according to a family resemblance principle, ran learning and category verification studies, and observed the same pattern of goodness-of-example effects that had been observed earlier. This replication reinforces the claim that family resemblance structure rather than some other factor, such as familiarity, is responsible for typicality results.

The interplay between the natural and the artificial can also flow in the other direction. For example, Lee Brooks and his colleagues (e.g., Allen & Brooks, 1991; Brooks, 1987; Reagher & Brooks, 1993) have used artificial stimuli and categories to study the influence of specific item similarity on categorization. One striking result is that even when participants are explicitly asked to employ a straightforward rule to categorize, their responses are influenced by irrelevant (from the perspective of the rule) similarities. That is, people are slower and less accurate at classifying an example as a noninstance of the rule if it shares rule-irrelevant similarities with specific examples that do instantiate the rule. These specific item similarity influences are interesting in their own right, but Brooks and his associates have also used natural categories to pursue the implications and generality of their results (e.g., Brooks, Norman, & Allen, 1991). In the domain of dermatology, Brooks et al. (1991) found that the diagnosis of skin disorder was facilitated by similar cases previously seen in the same context. In short, episodic influences on categorization are quite robust (see also Weber, Bockenholt, Hilton, & Wallace, 1993).

We believe that the above two instances are examples worth imitating. Without some concern with real-world contexts, there is always the risk that critical variables are being ignored (critics of similarity-based models of categorization might argue that the influence of prior knowledge on categorization is one such variable). But progress often requires controlled observations, and artificially created categories are an important tool for doing so.[1]

D. Summary

Although we have alluded to a parallel, interactive pattern of categorization research activity, we necessarily are constrained to describe it in a serial manner. Our review will be organized around methods of inquiry, and certain themes and issues will recur in virtually every section. We begin with evolutionary considerations and then turn to philosophical perspectives. Next, we review developmental and cross-cultural research, followed by a focus on computational models, and finally by observations from neuroscience. Our survey will necessarily not be comprehensive but we hope to at least convey the flavor and some of the strong points of each of these methodologies. In the last section of this chapter, our goal is to provide a summary and integration by discussing challenges and opportunities in categorization research.

II. METHODS OF INQUIRY

A. Evolutionary

Although human cognition presumably is adaptive, until recently cognitive psychologists have placed little emphasis on the purpose or function of cognitive activities. One reason for this neglect is that it is far from clear how one might go about testing or providing independent evidence bearing on hypotheses about function. Cognitive scientists such as Marr (1982), however, have demonstrated the value of multiple levels of analysis, including the broad question of what an intelligent system is trying to compute. In the domain of categorization one clear benefit of an

[1]Of course the distinction between artificial and natural categories can to some extent be blurred. Researchers may create artificial categories from natural stimuli (e. g., photographs of faces) or employ stimulus materials where prior knowledge comes into play (e. g., Wattenmaker, Dewey, Murphy, & Medin, 1986). Nonetheless, we think it is important to keep the potential trade-offs between artificiality and generalizability in mind in evaluating research and theory in categorization.

evolutionary perspective is the realization that concepts serve multiple functions and a focus on a single function comes at the risk of developing theories that are too narrow to do the work they ultimately will be asked to do (see Matheus, Rendell, Medin, & Goldstone, 1989, for applications in both AI and cognitive psychology). We begin with a brief summary of conceptual functions and some research directly linked to evolutionary analysis. Of course the reader will want to keep these functions in mind as they are also relevant to subsequent sections of this review.

1. Conceptual Functions

We distinguish eight distinct functions of concepts: categorization, understanding, learning, inference, explanation, conceptual combination, planning, and communication. By the *categorization* function of concepts we refer to the fact that mental representations are used to determine the category membership of entities. Indeed, psychologists are sometimes accused (perhaps correctly) of assuming that the *only* function of concepts is to classify, and that conceptual representations include little more than procedures for identifying category membership (e.g., Mandler, 1993). But categorization must be more than an end in itself.

Categorization is also a procedure for relating new to old. Even when objects or events are novel, the cognitive system is capable of bringing relevant knowledge to bear in the service of *understanding.* For example, as a result of categorizing some object as a *telephone,* people understand its relevant parts and how they might interact with it.

A critical conceptual function is to *support learning.* New entities are understood in terms of old, but the new also feeds back to modify or update the knowledge used in categorization. This broad function is itself associated with a variety of critical questions concerning adaptation and adaptiveness. For example, updating must balance the need to be relevant to contemporary contexts with the danger of discarding accumulated wisdom. Furthermore, given that instances partake of multiple category memberships (e.g., some white fury thing can be categorized as a poodle, a dog, a mammal, a pet, a domestic animal, and so on) should each experience modify all possible categories or just some relevant subset?

A fourth important function of concepts is *inference.* Having categorized some entity we can make predictions concerning its behavior. In the domain of medicine, diagnostic categories allow the physician to predict what sort of treatment might prove effective. As we shall see, there has been a recent upsurge of research and theory on category-based inferencing.

Concepts are critically involved in *explanation* and *reasoning.* Having categorized a young man who is cleaning a sidewalk with a toothbrush as a *fraternity pledge* one can provide a reason for his strange behavior. Furthermore, sometimes concepts may be used to persuade; we are all familiar, for example, with the use of labels in political campaigns.

By combining concepts we can use a limited number of concepts to create an unlimited number of new concepts. Just how people modify constituent concepts in order to comprehend combined concepts remains a significant challenge. For example, we understand *car repair* as repair of a car but *expert repair* as repair by an expert (Murphy, 1988).

Additionally, we use categories to instantiate goals in planning. For example, one might think about what sort of food one would like for dinner or what things one ought to bring along on a camping trip (e.g., Barsalou, 1983).

Finally, we use concepts for communication. The interpersonal aspect of concepts places constraints on virtually every other conceptual function. We will not cover this function in detail in this review, but we wish to make the distinction clear between communication and other functions. For example, a speaker might first categorize some object as a *Toyota Tercel,* then refer in conversation to this object as either a *vehicle,* a *car,* a *foreign car,* or a *Toyota,* depending on the speaker's communicative goals (Grice, 1957). (See Malt, 1990, 1994, for further discussion of the distinction between categorization and naming.)

These above functions may place competing demands on conceptual organization. For example, one can maximize prediction from category memberships by developing very narrow categories. The cost of this precision is that new examples may frequently fall into no preexisting category, undermining the understanding function of concepts. We turn now to some specific applications and ideas inspired by the evolutionary framework.

2. Purpose of Categorization

a. Anderson's Rational Model

One clear example of an evolutionary or ecological approach to categorization is Anderson's rational model (Anderson, 1990, 1991). Anderson argues that the human mind is a rational, (close to) optimal system, and that one can construct models that are excellent approximations to human performance by analyzing what is optimal. He assumes that what is being optimized in categorization is predictability of features or properties (i.e., what we have referred to as the inference function of concepts). The next step in his analysis is to describe the structure of information in the environment. This analysis leads to three main conclusions or hypotheses: (a) features are probabilistically associated with categories; (b) categories are a (nearly) disjoint partitioning of objects in the world; and (c) features or properties within a category are (approximately) independently distributed.

The third step in Anderson's rational analysis is to derive the optimal function, taking into account the costs associated with different functions. The ideal algorithm would keep track of all possible partitions to select the partition with maximum predictability. However, in the case of categorization, the optimal procedure cannot be run on a computer because there are too many possible partitionings (there's a combinatorial explosion for all but the smallest number of objects). As an alternative, Anderson developed an iterative algorithm in which members are con-

sidered incrementally and classified into the category that maximizes the predictability of the resulting partitioning (see Anderson, 1990, for details).

The prediction rule of the rational model works as follows: When some novel
object is presented and the system has to predict whether some feature k is present,
the algorithm calculates the probability that the object is in each of its categories
multiplied by the probability of each category having feature k. The sum of this
cumulative function is the predicted probability that the novel object has feature k.

Anderson's rational model is quite successful at predicting the results of a number of category learning experiments using artificial categories. To apply the model
to the classification of examples, one treats the category label simply as another feature that one is trying to predict.

Is Anderson's rational model superior to alternative categorization models? For
a variety of reasons the answer is not obvious. Nosofsky (1991) provided a formal
proof that the rational model is a generalization of an exemplar model of categorization, the Medin and Schaffer (1978) context theory. Nosofsky examined 11 sets
of transfer data from categorization experiments and found that the general form
of the rational model failed to provide an account of transfer superior to the special case corresponding to the context model. Heit (1992) extended the context
theory to prediction and inference tasks (rather than just categorization) and to reasoning using chains of examples. This extended context model successfully predicted the results of several experiments in which subjects made predictions about
transfer stimuli. Heit also applied the rational model to these data on inferences, and
it provided no improvement over the multiple-step context model.

As Murphy (1993) notes, the rational model does not make much use of its categories in prediction in that it sums categorization and feature probabilities over all
categories. Ahn and Medin (1992) directly evaluated the rational model's predictions concerning category construction. They presented people with sets of examples and asked them to create categories, in some cases according to certain constraints (e.g., two categories of equal size). The examples had a feature structure that
could be used to create family resemblance categories. Ahn and Medin observed
family resemblance sorting under some conditions, but the rational model was
unable to predict when family resemblance sorting would or would not occur. The
results were consistent with a two-stage model, which assumes that people impose
more structure than the examples support in the first stage, and that the second stage
adjusts for this difference between perceived and preferred structure (see also Medin,
Wattenmaker, & Michalski, 1987, for analogous results in a rule induction task).

Thau (1992) also has evidence that people actively organize categories. He
employed an incremental clustering task where instances are presented one at a
time; a key experimental manipulation was the order in which the examples were
presented. His goal was to create a situation where two distinct orders would yield
the identical category structure after n examples. The question was whether the n
+ 1 example would be categorized the same way for the two orders. Many incremental clustering models, including the rational model, predict no effect of order.

Thau observed clear order effects that were consistent with the idea that selective attention or weighting is given to dimensions used to organize early examples. Again this is consistent with active organization rather than an unbiased weighting of probabilistic structures.

b. Critique

Anderson's rational model illustrates both the potential strengths and shortcomings of an evolutionary or ecological analysis. Each step in the analysis offers challenges and potential problems. For example, although prediction is an important function of concepts, we would argue that it is far from being the only one. Murphy (1993) provides a detailed criticism of each of Anderson's assumptions concerning the structure of information in the environment. Murphy points out that categories (a) often have multiple overlapping membership functions (e.g., *dog, pet*) rather than being disjoint; (b) that questions about feature structure may be meaningless unless one can provide constraints on features; and (c) that features within a category may be correlated rather than independent (e.g., Malt & Smith, 1984). Finally, Murphy argues that because optimal functions need to consider computational constraints, one needs a fairly concrete process model, as different models for the same task can require very different constraints.

The upshot of these criticisms is that an ecological analysis is difficult—not that it should not or cannot be done. Indeed, Murphy (1993) argues in favor of an ecological analysis that focuses on real-world concept learning and use. He suggests that such analysis will include attention to the learner as well as to the environment by itself. For example, conceptual domains may be organized by theories and may change with expertise, according to Murphy.

c. Shepard's Universal Law of Generalization

As another illustration of the evolutionary approach to concepts, we will briefly describe work by Shepard (1987). Shepard argues that all organisms are faced with the task of *generalization;* because no stimulus ever recurs in exactly the same way, organisms constantly have to categorize novel stimuli and make other inferences about them. In Shepard's terminology, a learner has to decide what is the *consequential region* for an observed stimulus. In other words, after observing an object located at some point in multidimensional psychological space, the learner must assume that other objects within an enclosed region of psychological space near the first object will have the same consequences as that original object. (For example, if a bird eats a caterpillar then gets sick, the bird may generalize that other caterpillars of similar color and markings are also poisonous.) From these basic assumptions about categorization and prediction, Shepard derived a mathematical account of the functional form of generalization in humans and other species. In particular, for a variety of possible shapes of consequential regions, and regardless of the size of the consequential region, the probability of generalizing from an old observation to a new observation is a negative exponential function of the psychological distance between the two stimuli. Shepard (1987) reviewed many studies on generalization that indeed showed just this functional form. Importantly, some recent models of categorization make predictions about generalization similar to Shepard's evolutionary account (Gluck, 1991).

d. Summary

Clearly the rational analysis by Anderson has been valuable in serving as the basis for analysis of critical issues in categorization. The contrast between Anderson and Murphy illustrates the differences in perspective of similarity-based and explanation-based approaches to categorization. A key question is whether we have these concepts because of the way the world is structured or because of the way human minds are structured. Likewise, Shepard's account of categorization and prediction was derived by considering the basic tasks faced by any organism, and notably Shepard's account is similar to descriptive psychological models of categorization. We think the observation of William James (1890) is most apt: "mind and world have evolved together, and in consequence are something of a mutual fit" (p. 47). Within the broad spectrum of that something of a fit, however, is room for a great deal of exciting debate and interaction. Asking and addressing questions about conceptual functions has been and, in our opinion, will continue to be a key organizing principle for categorization research.

B. Philosophical

The contributions of philosophical perspectives to categorization research have been substantial and have taken a variety of forms. For present purposes we will focus on some observations concerning reference and meaning and their implications for conceptual structure.

1. Reference

Psychologists have tended to assume that concept representations mediate the link between words and the things to which they refer. For example, one's concept of *triangle* contains information that determines reference—the things that are or are not triangles. Putnam, however, has argued that words may refer more directly (see Rey, 1983). Borrowing an example from Komatsu (1992), a person who knows nothing about *sassafras* may ask, "What is sassafras?" thereby referring to sassafras, without having any conceptual representation of it. If a mental representation is not necessary as a mediator in this example, direct reference may also be possible in situations where a conceptual representation is available (e.g., when one is somewhat familiar with sassafras). Putnam claims that for some types of nouns, such as natural kind terms (e.g., *gold, water,* biological kinds), individual people's conceptual representations do *not* establish reference. Instead, the reference of natural kind terms is ultimately a matter of discovery. That is, it is a matter for science to determine the true nature of things like *gold* and *water.*

Putnam's view has attracted a great deal of attention and debate. One issue concerns just which kinds of concepts entail direct reference (e.g., Dupré, 1981, Losonsky, 1990; Schwartz, 1977). Malt (1990) examined the acceptability of linguistic hedges as a means of evaluating people's beliefs about categories. The hedges included phrases like "according to experts," "technically speaking," "by definition," and "loosely speaking." Her results are consistent with the idea that concepts may differ from one another not only in the properties represented in the concept, but also in the belief held about the completeness and validity of these properties as a description of their referents. For instance, the hedge "according to experts" was much more acceptable for natural kind examples than for artifacts, whereas the reverse held for the hedge, "loosely speaking." Malt's observations are consistent with the idea that theories and beliefs play a role in conceptual organization not captured by constituent properties per se.

In related work, cognitive psychologists have shown that judgments of category membership are critically affected by theories about the underlying natures of entities. For example, Rips (1989) gave people scenarios where an animal changed from having bird-like properties to having insect-like properties so that, perceptually, it became much more like an insect than a bird. The transformation was framed in terms of normal development or as a response to hazardous chemicals. People judged that animal from the first stage more likely to be truly a bird when the transformation was an accident than when it was part of normal development (see also Keil, 1989).

Researchers have also worried about the extent to which laypeople do defer to science. Although we are willing to categorize whales as mammals despite their superficial similarity to fish, we continue to employ our concept of *tree* even though taxonomists point out that trees do not comprise a kind. Malt (1994) has studied the set of fluids that people call *water*. Contrary to Putnam, she finds that although some amount of H_2O may be necessary for something to be called water, the percentage of H_2O in a liquid is a rather poor predictor of what people will call water.

If reference can change as our beliefs change, then what gives our concepts stability? (See Rey, 1983, E. E. Smith, Medin, & Rips, 1984, for a more detailed discussion of this issue.) Rips (in press) proposes a distinction between mental representations *of* a category from mental representations *about* a category. He suggests that the former need only consist of node or marker, functioning to provide both intra- and interindividual concept stability. The part of the representation that is about the category consists of theories and beliefs that themselves may change within an individual or be different across individuals.

2. Kinds of Categories

Another important aspect of Putnam's analysis is the idea that there are distinct *kinds* of categories. Putnam maintains that the reference of natural kind terms is based on underlying natures and is a matter of discovery. In contrast, the reference of nominal kind terms such as *bachelor* is established by convention (see also Donnellan,

1977). Artifact categories may be intermediate in their dependence on convention versus discovery. Although these distinctions may involve more of a continuum than a dichotomy, they do emphasize two important dimensions of conceptual structure that are central to theories of conceptual change. Consider the situation where some entity is categorized as belonging to some category and that the entity then manifests some surprising property or properties. At this point there is tension between modifying one's concept versus one's belief that the entity is, in fact, a member of that category.

3. Meaning

To the extent that reference is a matter for experts to determine and to the extent that meaning includes relations between concepts and referents, the study of concepts does not provide a full account of meaning (Fodor, 1983). To clarify this point we need to distinguish between metaphysics and epistemology. Metaphysics is concerned with issues about how the world is, whereas epistemology is concerned with how we know, believe, or infer that the world is. Reference for natural kinds is presumably a matter of metaphysics; psychological studies of categorization are confined to epistemological questions. For example, the classical view of concepts represents a claim about mental representations of categories, not the categories themselves. Things in nature may have an underlying nature that people remain ignorant of, or conversely, people may believe that certain concepts (e.g., of a species or biological kind) have a shared underlying essence even though science fails to support this view (e.g., Mayr, 1982).

4. Summary

Our treatment of the philosophical perspective on categorization research necessarily has been limited. We hope it is clear that questions about relationships among category representations, reference, and meaning are central to our understanding of categorization. The possibility that there are distinct kinds of categories is one important by-product of these analyses.

C. Developmental

Developmental research has had a truly major impact on the psychology of categorization. Questions about learning and the role of similarity versus theories in conceptual organization are sharply focused in developmental studies. The chapter 5 (this volume) by Carey and Markman describes much of this body of work, and we will only touch on a few high points.

1. Similarity and Development

A number of researchers have suggested that there are developmental changes in similarity processing that have straightforward linkages to categorization. One way to characterize the shift is to propose that young children process stimuli holistically and that older children are more analytic (e.g., Kemler, 1982, 1983; Kemler-Nelson, 1988; Shepp & Swartz, 1976; L. B. Smith & Kemler, 1977, 1978; but see also Ward, Vela, & Hass, 1990). Linda Smith (1989) offered a mathematical model of similarity processing where the central claim was that relative to younger children, older children are more likely to selectively weight dimensions and more likely to give greater weight to matching values on a dimension.

Gentner and Ratterman (1991) argue for a shift from processing focusing on simple attributes or properties (one-place predicates: e.g., "X is green") to attention to relational properties (multiplace predicates: e.g., "X is above Y" or "X causes Y"). Keil and Batterman (1984) report a developmental shift in categorization from a reliance on characteristic features to a greater emphasis on more central or defining characteristics. These two sets of observations converge if more central properties tend to be more relational in character.

These various distinctions all seem to point toward a story whereby younger children employ SBL that is later integrated with theory-based learning. Theories seem to involve analytical processes, selective weighting, and relational predicates or properties, each of which seems to appear later in development. But this is only part of the story, and many of the authors we have cited would disagree with it. Let's take a closer look.

2. Constraints, Theories, and Development

Keil (1989) refers to the above story about SBL being followed (developmentally) by theory-based reasoning as the "doctrine of original sim" and he rejects it. Instead, he claims that even very young children's category learning is constrained by domain-specific theoretical biases. He is not alone in this view. Carey (1985) argues that there is a development shift in children's biological reasoning from being organized in terms of a naive psychology to being based on a naive biology. For example, she has evidence that young children's inductive inferences are guided by similarity to humans, not an unbiased overall similarity. That is, they are more confident that a *bee* has some novel property if they are told that *people* have it than if they are told *bugs* have it.

There is evidence that babies are sensitive to the animate–inanimate distinction (e.g., Leslie, 1984) and that young children use animacy as an organizing principle even when it conflicts with overall similarity (R. Gelman, 1990; S. A. Gelman & Wellman, 1991). In short, it does not appear that there is a stage of development where similarity has the turf to itself.

Of course, researchers do not necessarily assume that children hold theories that have all the properties of scientific theories. So what do they mean? As one example, let's look at the notion of *psychological essentialism* (e.g., Atran, 1990; S. A. Gelman & Wellman, 1991; Keil, 1989; Medin & Ortony, 1989). The main idea is that (at least for the domain of biological things and events) people act as if things in the world have a true underlying nature that imparts category identity. Furthermore, this essence is thought to be the causal mechanism that generates visible properties. Therefore, surface features provide clues but are not infallible indicators of category membership. We refer to this view as *psychological* essentialism because it is concerned with people's *assumptions* about how the world is, not how the world truly is.

Developmental psychologists (especially Susan Gelman and Frank Keil) have provided evidence consistent with the view that children reason in an essentialist manner (S. A. Gelman, Coley, & Gottfried, 1994; S. A. Gelman & Wellman, 1991; Keil, 1989; Springer & Keil, 1991). Four types of evidence seem especially relevant: (a) appeal to invisible causal mechanisms to explain appearance and changes associated with growth; (b) the assumption of innate dispositions or inborn capacities to explain capacities that emerge later in life; (c) belief in the maintenance of identity despite changes in superficial appearance; and (d) the assumption that members of a category share a large number of other properties that may be hidden or unknown. S. A. Gelman et al. (1994) review extensive supportive evidence for each of these assumptions (see also Shipley, 1993, for a cogent discussion of induction potential).

There is clear evidence that category labels are treated by children as especially significant for reasoning. For example, S. A. Gelman and Markman (1986) pitted category membership against perceptual similarity in an inductive reasoning task. Young children were first shown pictures of two animals and taught that different novel properties were true of them. Then they were asked which property was true of a pictured new example. The new example was perceptually similar to one of the first pictures, but it shared category membership with the other (which was not similar to the new example). Children judged that the new example would have the property of the animal that was of the same category but perceptually different. Even for young children, similarity acts as a general guideline that can be overridden by other forms of knowledge.

This emphasis on the role of theories in category development is not a universal assumption. For a recent critique see S. S. Jones and Smith (1993) and the associated commentaries (Barsalou, 1993; S. A. Gelman & Medin, 1993; Mervis, Johnson, & Scott, 1993).

3. Category Labels and Learning

Our discussion so far has treated category learning as straightforward and ignored some difficult problems associated with learning the referent or extension of concepts. As Quine (1960) noted in his discussion of translation, there is an inherent ambiguity in reference. When a parent points to a rabbit and says "rabbit" the situation is much more complex than might first appear. The word could refer to "small" or "white," or "furry" or "hopping," or a proper name or "pet" or "animal," or any of an unlimited number of other things. The learning situation is seriously underconstrained. So how do children learn what's what?

Ellen Markman (1989, 1990) has suggested three constraints that children place on reference and provided empirical support for each of them. One bias is that children tend to assume that a novel term applies to the entire object rather than to its parts or properties. Another is that children act as if they expect objects to have only one label. Note that this assumption is objectively incorrect, but may nonetheless be helpful in initial stages of language learning. For example, suppose a child sees two objects and hears a novel label. If the child knows the label for one of the objects he or she might assume that the novel label applies to the other object (Markman, 1992; Markman & Wachtel, 1988). A third bias is to assume that labels refer to objects of like kind rather than to objects that are contextually or thematically related. In related work, Landau, Smith, and Jones (1988) have found that children's assumptions about "like kind" shift from overall similarity to shape similarity as one moves from a nonlinguistic context to a linguistic context.

4. Kindhood and the Basic Level

Earlier we mentioned that a given entity may have numerous category memberships. One may ask whether any of these is privileged with respect to notions of like kind or kindhood. Rosch's innovative studies of natural object concepts included an analysis of the vertical component of categories. For example, an object being driven down the highway might be alternatively referred to as a convertible, a car, or a vehicle. In a seminal paper, E. Rosch, Mervis, Gray, Johnson, and Boyes-Braem (1976) singled out one level in such hierarchies, which they called the *basic level,* as playing a central role in many cognitive processes associated with categorization. For example, the categories *chair, car,* and *dog* are generally considered to be basic level, and they contrast with more specific *subordinate* concepts (e.g., *recliner, convertible, poodle*) and more general *superordinate* concepts (e.g., *furniture, vehicle, animal*). E. Rosch et al. educed a variety of criteria, each of which converged on a common basic level. For example, the basic level is (a) the preferred in naming, (b) the most abstract level, where members share numerous perceptual properties including overall shape, and (c) the level at which people can categorize most rapidly. It also appears that children learn basic-level categories faster than other levels of categories (e.g., Anglin, 1977; Horton & Markman, 1980; E. Rosch et al., 1976). In short, notions of kindhood may correspond to the basic level.

Of course, observations on the basic level could also be used to buttress similarity-based models of categorization. One could argue (as Rosch did) that objects in the world form natural clusters (at the basic level) and that human cognition is sensitive to these chunks. Presumably, the perceptual system has evolved such that its notion of similarity picks out the basic level as significant (more on this when we consider computational models). A central question, therefore, is whether the basic level changes with development or expertise. If the basic level changes, then its significance may be more in terms of human conceptual processing than facts about the world. Mervis (1987) has argued that the acquisition of new knowledge makes adult-basic-level categories at least somewhat different from child-basic categories, and there is some suggestive evidence for changes with expertise (Mervis et al., 1993; Tanaka & Taylor, 1991). Finally, Mandler, Bauer, and McDonough (1991) have argued that the first categories acquired by children are more global than earlier work had suggested. For example, the first categorization of animals might be into land, air, and sea animals. Mandler (1992, 1993) suggests that global categories reflect the influence of more abstract conceptual notions, such as animate motion (Mandler & McDonough, 1993). So the debate continues.

5. Domain Specificity and Cross-Domain Interactions

Although there is considerable discussion of the domain specificity of conceptual organization in development (e.g., Carey & Gelman, 1991; Hirschfeld & Gelman, 1994; Keil, 1989), space limitations only allow us to do little more than allude to this issue. Most of the research on psychological essentialism has examined biological kinds. One may also ask whether children and adults also believe in a true underlying nature for artifacts, personality traits, occupations, and other sorts of categories. There is evidence that to varying extents they do (Hirschfeld, 1994; Keil, 1989; Rothbart & Taylor, 1992; Yuill, 1992). This raises a variety of important questions concerning cross-domain interactions. Do children start out as essentialists about biological kinds and then generalize by analogy to other domains (e.g., naturalizing social kinds) or do children start out as essentialists about everything and narrow this assumption as domain-specific knowledge is acquired? For differing perspectives on this question see Atran (1998), S. A. Gelman et al. (1994), and Hirschfeld (1995).

6. Summary

Given the significance of learning to theories of categorization, it is easy to see the central role of developmental research in this area. We hesitate to draw any strong conclusions, but it is obvious that key questions about the integration of knowledge (theories) and experience in learning are sharply focused in studies of conceptual development.

D. Cross-Cultural Comparisons

Cross-cultural comparisons represent something of an approach–avoidance conflict for categorization researchers. They may be (logistically) difficult to perform, almost certain to be confounded (in multiple ways) from the point of view of good experimental design, and they often leave the experimenter wondering if a slight difference in procedures might have produced dramatically different results. On the other hand, they provide a powerful test of the generality of some observation or principle. If the same results appear in the face of all the differences between cultures, the results are robust indeed. Furthermore, systematic variation across cultures can likewise be informative. Categorization research has only taken advantage of cross-cultural comparisons in a limited way; nonetheless, the work that has been done has had an important impact.

1. Basic Levels

Rosch's analyses of basic levels reflected a salient influence of cross-cultural comparisons. Berlin, Breedlove, and Raven (1966, 1973) examined folk biological categories across a variety of cultures and argued that there was strong cross-cultural agreement at what one might call the folk generic level. This level more or less corresponds to the genus level of scientific taxonomy. Frequently, the locally represented genus is monospecific, in which case species and genus would be coextensive. This folk generic level of naming biological kinds appears to be a cross-cultural universal. Ethnobiologists have suggested that the basis for this consistency is that organisms possess bundles of correlated features that create natural groupings. Berlin (1992) goes so far as to say that these clusters are "crying out to be named."

The folk generic level may correspond to what E. Rosch et al. (1976) (see also E. H. Rosch, 1975) referred to as the basic level. Indeed the E. Rosch et al. (1976) studies extended the observations about basicness from biological kinds to human artifacts, such as clothing and vehicles. There is, however, a puzzle that remains to be explained. The biological taxonomies that E. Rosch et al. anticipated would be basic level by anthropological (naming) criteria acted like subordinates by the E. Rosch et al. criteria. Rather than *maple, oak, trout, cardinal,* and *eagle* being basic E. Rosch et al. found that *tree, fish,* and *bird* met their criteria for basicness.

Why do the ethnobiological and psychological measures of the basic level disagree? One possibility is that Berkeley undergraduates know little about biological categories relative to the people studied in the anthropological investigations. That is, the basic level may change with expertise (again see Tanaka & Taylor, 1991, for partial support for this idea). A second possibility is that the different measures pick out different levels. Ethnobiological studies tend to use naming or linguistic criteria for basicness, whereas E. Rosch et al. (1976) relied heavily on perceptual criteria. Interestingly, the clearest changes with expertise in the Tanaka and Taylor (1991) studies involved naming preferences. In short, the question of whether the difference is one of expertise or a matter of divergent criteria remains an open one—open and yet central to addressing the question of why we have the categories we have. As we shall see, this question carries over to the next issue.

2. Similarity-Based versus Theory-Driven Learning

Cross-cultural comparisons ought to provide ideal testing grounds for SBL, EBL contrasts. The logic is as follows. People in different cultures have the more or less the same perceptual system (presumably) but differ in knowledge, theories, and beliefs. Therefore, similar categorization systems reinforce the role of SBL, whereas differences support contributions of theory-driven categorization.

But things aren't so simple. First of all, SBL models are sensitive to the distribution of types, and many are sensitive to token frequency. Therefore, differences in categorization may be attributable to differential familiarity or experience with category members. For example, Schwanenflugel and Rey (1986) found that the correlation between typicality ratings for members of common object categories by monolingual English speakers and monolingual Spanish speakers is significantly higher when the contribution of familiarity to judgments is partialed out (see also Boster, 1988). So differences cannot automatically be assigned to the theory side of things. Conversely, similarities do not imply that theory is not in play. People in different cultures may create the same theories (or at least the same kinds of theories). Atran (1987, 1990, 1998) has argued that an essentialist stance toward biological kinds is a cross-cultural universal. These caveats notwithstanding, there have been a number of intriguing cross-cultural comparisons only a tiny sample of which can be presented here (but see Barkow, Cosmides, & Tooby, 1992; Hirschfeld & Gelman, 1994; Premack, 1994; also see Malt, 1995, for a review).

How does one gauge agreement and disagreement across cultures (or even within cultures for that matter)? One very useful tool has been the cultural consensus model (CCM) of Romney, Weller, and Batchelder (1986). The CCM assumes that the agreement between informants is a function of the extent to which each knows the culturally defined consensus or truth. The model assumes a single consensus, that informants' answers are independent, and that each individual can be characterized by a competence parameter that reflects the probability of their knowing the consensus for a given item of information (more knowledgeable people would have a higher competence parameter than less knowledgeable people). If these conditions are met, then a minimum residual factor analysis of the agreement matrix should yield a single-factor solution such that the first latent root should be substantially higher than all other latent roots.

The application of the CCM to categorization is straightforward. If the classification judgment of two distinct groups yields a single consensus (i.e., the CCM model fits the data with a single factor), then a common categorization system is supported. Differences may be observed in at least two ways. First of all the CCM may fail, implying a lack of shared knowledge (e.g., Weller, 1987). Alternatively, the CCM may be generally supported but may not provide a full account of the data. The CCM may be used to calculate the expected agreement between informants, compare it with the observed agreement, and then see if the residual agreement reflects systematic deviations from the consensus. Boster (1986) used this latter technique to evaluate agreement between Aguaruna Jivaro (a South American Indian group) in manioc identification (manioc is a perennial shrub with starchy roots that are an important part of their diet). He observed strong general agreement with the CCM, but also systematic residual deviations from consensus that were correlated with the kinship distance of the participants.

Much of the anthropological work on culture and categorization has focused on biological kinds. On a general level, there is a striking amount of cross-cultural consistency in categorization (e.g., Boster, 1987; Boster & D'Andrade, 1989; Malt,

1995) and substantial agreement of folk biology with scientific taxonomy (e.g., Atran, 1998; Boster, Berlin, & O'Neill, 1986). Interestingly, in their studies of similarity comparison by fish experts (peoples who fished for a living) and novices, Boster and Johnson (1989) found that expertise was associated with *decreased* agreement with scientific taxonomy. Boster and Johnson suggest that knowledge of function influenced the judgments of experts and led to at least some category reorganization.

The categorization function is only one aspect of conceptual behavior. Unfortunately, there has been very little work on the use of categories in reasoning. Walker (1992) examined preservation-of-identity judgments by rural, urban poor, and urban wealthy Nigerian adults. Participants heard stories describing changes where one natural kind came to appear like another (as in the studies of Keil and of Rips described earlier). Furthermore, these changes were described as taking place either in a ritual context or a nonritual context. Walker found that the Nigerian participants preserved identity of category membership essentially all the time in nonritual contexts and the vast majority of the time in ritual contexts. She also observed that nonpreservation judgments varied as a function of the centrality of the concept to ritual practices (dogs are more central than chickens, and there were more nonpreservation judgments involving dogs than chickens). These latter findings suggest that adults' natural kind concepts may be at least partially influenced by belief systems other than the biological (see also Boyer, 1990, for further discussions of the interplay between biological reasoning and religious/cultural beliefs).

Atran (1998) has recently examined relationships between categorization and reasoning, using both the CCM and the Osherson, Smith, Wilkie, Lopez, and Shafir (1990) category-based induction model. His preliminary results suggest a close correspondence between folk biological taxonomy and hypothetical reasoning about reproduction among the Itza Maya of Guatemala. For example, Atran finds both similarity and typicality effects in inductive reasoning. It also appears, however, that the basis for typicality may deviate from central tendencies for the Maya. For example, the most typical bird is the *turkey,* priced for its meat and culturally significant, and the most typical snake is the *fer-de-lance,* the most poisonous of snakes. In short, for some categories typicality may be driven by proximity to an ideal rather than an average (as in Barsalou's, 1985, observations with goal-derived categories). The fact that typicality effects are observed on the induction task suggests that the cultural differences are not based on misunderstandings about the meaning of "typicality." Given that most college students are not especially knowledgeable about biological kinds, it is possible that the cultural differences in the basis for typicality (ideals versus central tendencies) should be attributed to differences in knowledge and expertise.

3. Summary

We end this section on an optimistic note. It appears that cross-cultural similarities in categorization are strong enough to avoid the confusion that might have been created by a morass of differences. This backdrop of agreement permits focused questions about differences, and the CCM and category-based induction model provide important methodological tools for these analyses. Cross-cultural comparisons are not a panacea for working out relationships between similarity and theory, but they do represent a fruitful avenue for exploration.

E. Computational

1. Issues and Purposes of Modeling

In research on categorization, there is a widespread tradition of implementing theoretical ideas as computational or mathematical models. This development of models of categorization has had several purposes. Foremost, a categorization model is a precise statement of an account of categorization. Modeling may be thought of as a language for describing theories of categorization. Stating differing accounts of categorization within this common language makes it easier to compare them. As previously mentioned, Nosofsky (1991) showed that when Anderson's rational theory (1990) and Medin's context theory (Medin & Schaffer, 1978) are compared, the context theory is equivalent to a special case of the rational theory. Also, describing categorization with the language of modeling has an advantage over, say, the language of English. Models run.

Modeling provides some insurance against potential errors of human reasoning; it is often difficult for a researcher to know what some theory will predict until the theory is implemented as a model (Hintzman, 1991). For example, Medin and Schaffer (1978) discovered that an exemplar model of categorization can predict prototypicality effects; that is, new prototypical category examples may be categorized more accurately than old, less central category members. This conclusion was surprising because exemplar models do not assume that a category prototype is explicitly represented in memory. Therefore, findings of prototypicality effects in experimental data need not be interpreted as indicating that people form prototypes.

It is important to note that no computational model (so far) has been presented as a complete account of categorization. For example, many models assume that category members are represented in terms of lists of features, but these models do not provide an account of how people learn to use these features. Sometimes it is a virtue of modeling that it allows us to focus on critical aspects of theory, while keeping other issues in the background. To give an extreme example, Busemeyer, Myung, and McDaniel (1993) derived predictions for a set of connectionist models of category learning, which are largely independent of how features are represented and of the specific algorithm for learning. Busemeyer et al. showed that none of these models can account for a phenomenon in human category learning known as the *cue competition effect,* in which learning about a valid cue is overshadowed by knowledge of another valid cue. What is critical about these models is that they all learn optimal associations between cues (or features) and categories, but the cue competition effect results from suboptimal learning. Busemeyer et al. suggested modifications for these models that would allow them to better approximate human learning.

A final general point we will make is that categorization models, ideally, will not be isolated accounts of a particular task or experiment but instead will dovetail with other theoretical accounts of cognition. We believe that categorization is an important topic, but it is a topic that is intertwined with the study of learning, memory, and reasoning (among other topics). One example of the potential synergy between categorization models and other computational models of cognition is the compatibility between exemplar models of categorization and multiple-trace models of memory (Gillund & Shiffrin, 1984; Hintzman, 1986, 1988). Multiple-trace models assume that a memory judgment, such as a recognition decision, depends on evaluating the total similarity of a test item to memory traces of particular stimuli (see C. M. Jones & Heit, 1993, for a review). Likewise, exemplar models assume that a decision whether to place a test item in one category or another depends on evaluating the similarity of the test item to memory traces for members of each category. Much research has capitalized on this connection between categorization and memory, and has led to the development of unified accounts of not only categorization but also other memory abilities, such as recognition, frequency judgment, and recall (Estes, 1993, 1994; Heit, 1993, 1994; Hintzman, 1986, 1988). Note that such a synergy between models of different, related tasks need not be limited to the common framework of exemplar models and multiple-trace models. For example, connectionist modeling provides another framework for developing general models of categorization and other cognitive abilities.

2. Learning

Now it is time to discuss and compare particular models of categorization. Most of these models fit into one of two broad categories: SBL or EBL. Briefly, what SBL models have in common is the assumption that a judgment about how to categorize something depends on its similarity to previously observed category members. The SBL models differ mainly in how the information about past category members is represented in memory (e.g., in terms of summary statistics in an abstraction model or in terms of association strengths in a neural network model). In contrast, the fundamental criterion for categorization in EBL models is that a category must provide an explanation, just as a theory provides an explanation for observed data. To use a well-known example from Murphy and Medin (1985), a fully clothed person who jumps in a swimming pool may be categorized as a fraternity pledge, because *fraternity pledge* provides an explanation for this person's odd behavior. In this example, it seems difficult to explain the categorization of this person in terms of similarity to other pledges.

a. Similarity-Based Learning

i. Abstraction models   One attractive idea about how to represent concepts is to store an abstraction, that is, summary information about category members. For example, to categorize cows, you might keep in memory what an average cow looks like. Most cows that you will see probably resemble this cow prototype (e.g., in terms of shape overlap). The parsimony of this approach is appealing. Indeed, some computer schemes for object recognition (Ullman, 1989) rely on templates to represent average category members. In addition, prototype models are important historically in cognitive psychology. Posner and Keele (1968) found that subjects, after viewing members of a category of dot patterns, were quite likely to say that the prototype (i.e., the central tendency of the category) was also an observed category member even when the prototype had not been presented. This result is certainly suggestive of the claim that people form abstractions of central tendencies. (For a review of successful applications of prototype models, see Hampton, 1993.) However, psychological research has progressed beyond pure prototype models, mainly because it is known that people learn more about categories than just their central tendencies.

In addition to the central tendency of a category, people can learn about the variability of a category. For example, Fried and Holyoak (1984) taught subjects about two categories of painting where for each category, the members were distortions of the category's central prototype. However, one category of paintings had quite variable members, and the members of the other category were close to its prototype. In the critical test questions, subjects were asked to categorize a new painting that was midway between the prototypes of the two categories. Most people placed the new painting in the more variable category. If subjects had simply remembered the central tendency of each test item, then they would have been indifferent between the two categories. Fried and Holyoak concluded that an abstraction model that only stored central tendencies was untenable. They suggested that abstraction models could be improved so that people would learn about variability as well (e.g., they learn summary information about means and variances for each dimension; see also Flannagan, Fried, & Holyoak, 1986).

Much more elaborate abstraction models have also been developed. According to general recognition theory (Ashby & Gott, 1988), a perceptual category is represented in memory by a specification of a multidimensional probability density function. The category description is probabilistic because the same category member may be processed in somewhat different ways on different observations, due to error or noise in the perceptual system. The representational system of general recognition theory is powerful; a category description may contain information about expected means and variances of various stimulus dimensions as well as correlations between dimensions. In addition to these representational assumptions, the framework of general recognition theory allows a variety of processing assumptions about how people make categorization decisions. In one version of the theory, a person sets a decision boundary, such as a line or curve, between two categories. For observations that fall exactly on this boundary, it is equally likely that the observation comes from each of the two multidimensional distributions corresponding to the two categories. However, most stimuli will fall on one side of the categorization boundary or the other, so their category membership will be clear.

ii. Exemplar models The modeling framework that seems diametrically opposed to abstraction models is exemplar models. Rather than representing a concept as a summary of what the category members are like, in exemplar models the concept is represented by memories of particular category members. Note that exemplar models of categorization by humans do not necessarily assume that all category members are remembered, or that each category member is stored veridically. We know that human memory is not perfect. Still, there are reasons to suggest that people represent categories not simply with abstract summary information but with information about specific instances.

Some of the best arguments for the plausibility of exemplar representation have been provided by Brooks (1978). First, he suggests that some categories may not have an obvious abstract representation, so remembering exemplars of the category would be an attractive alternative. Likewise, other factors such as time pressure during learning might make deriving a summary difficult. Second, category learning may occur in the pursuit of other goals that would require learning about particular instances. For example, when we learn about social categories, such as categories of people with various occupations, we are often interested in learning about these people as individuals as well. It is plausible that this information about individuals could be accessed during judgments about categories. Certain learning conditions, such as repeated experiences with the same individual, would also facilitate exemplar memory. Finally, remembering exemplars allows for maximal flexibility for conceptual organization in the future. We might need to form different concepts on different occasions or for different goals (see Barsalou, 1983). For example, information in memory about a particular pet dog could later be used for judgments about the categories *pet* and *dog*. (See Heit, 1992, for an application of an exemplar model to studies in which subjects first learned exemplars and later made multiple categorization judgments.)

One widely tested exemplar model of categorization is the *context model* (Medin & Schaffer, 1978). Consider the task of deciding whether some stimulus, x, belongs in category A or category B. According to the context model, the probability of categorizing x as an A rises with the similarity of x to members of A and falls with the similarity of x to the members of B. In the context model, stimuli are represented as vectors of features. For example, in a study of simulated medical classification by Medin, Altom, Edelson, and Freko (1982), it was assumed that exemplars of categories of people with a certain disease were represented by a list of symptoms, such as *swollen eyelids* and *discolored gums*. The similarity between two stimuli is assessed by counting their numbers of matching and mismatching features. In general, similarity is assumed to be monotonically related to the number of matches, but the critical assumption of the context model, known as the *multiplicative similarity rule,* is that perfectly matching stimuli or near-perfect matches will be considered much more similar than pairs that mismatch on several features. Thus, in the categorization of *x,* exemplars that are close matches to *x* will especially influence categorization.

One implication of the high impact of close matches is that the context model predicts that people can readily learn categories that are not *linearly separable.* That is, the distributions of the members of two categories may overlap, so that it would be impossible to draw a straight-line boundary that segregates the members of one category from the other. The context model predicts that people can learn to distinguish between such categories because a new stimulus that is a close match to an old exemplar will likely be placed in the same category as that exemplar, whether or not the two categories overlap. In contrast, abstraction models such as prototype models or simple linear classifiers (both special cases of the Ashby & Gott, 1988, framework) predict that people cannot learn to distinguish correctly between categories that are not linearly separable. It is clear that people can learn nonlinearly separable categories (Medin & Schwanenflugel, 1981), although more recent evidence (e.g., Wattenmaker, 1995) suggests that people's relative ability to learn linearly separable versus nonlinearly separable categories may vary across domains.

One limitation of the context model is its simple representation of stimuli as vectors of features. Consider learning about the people you meet, including their physical appearances and their intellectual abilities. It would seem valuable to represent continuous information such as height in inches and probably IQ, rather than just features such as *short* and *intelligent.* Nosofsky (1986) has proposed a *generalized context model* (GCM) that is more flexible in how it represents stimuli and in how similarity is evaluated. According to the GCM, stimuli are represented as points in multidimensional space. For example, a short intelligent person might be represented with a point near 50″ on a height axis and near 140 on IQ axis. As in the context model, in the GCM, categorization decisions are made by comparing a stimulus to exemplars retrieved from memory. Nosofsky has evaluated several rules for assessing the similarity between stimuli described in terms of multiple continuous dimensions. For example, one consideration is whether the dimensions are separable (as in the case of height and intelligence) or perceptually integral (such as hue and saturation of colored objects, see Garner, 1974) (Nosofsky, 1987). Together, the context model and the GCM has been applied successfully to the results of many laboratory studies on categorization (see Nosofsky, 1988, 1992, for reviews).

To complete the discussion of exemplar models, we will briefly mention two additional applications of exemplar theory. First, recent work by Eliot Smith (E. R. Smith, 1990; E. R. Smith & Zarate, 1992) has applied exemplar models to the domain of social cognition. This research has demonstrated with computer simulations that many phenomena in social psychology, such as the influence of knowledge about social categories (i.e., stereotypes) on judgments about individuals persons, can be explained in terms of exemplar models. Furthermore, people evaluate the similarity between individuals in a somewhat flexible manner. In some contexts, making a judgment about some person might lead to retrieval of memories of other persons of the same gender, and in other contexts, memories of persons of the same racial group might be retrieved instead. However, the issue of flexibility of similarity is not an entirely solved problem; it is still largely an open question how people's learning and reasoning processes lead them to focus on certain dimensions on certain occasions.

Second, exemplar theory also provides the basis for a successful technique in AI models, case-based reasoning (Bareiss, 1989; Hammond, 1989; Riesbeck & Schank, 1989). A case-based reasoning program can make inferences about a new case by retrieving similar cases from memory. For example, the computer program MEDI-ATOR attempts to solve international conflicts by retrieving case studies of similar past conflicts and determining a solution from the past conflicts and how they were resolved (Kolodner & Simpson, 1989). Comparing instances also provides the opportunity for developing representations intermediate between exemplars and fully abstract representations (e.g., Medin & Edelson, 1988; Ross & Kennedy, 1990; Ross, Perkins, & Tenpenny, 1990; Spalding & Ross, 1994). One challenge for case-based reasoning models is known as the *indexing problem*. How shall memory be organized so that in reasoning about some new situation, the most helpful or relevant past cases will be considered? The indexing problem is a version of the problem faced by all similarity-based models of categorization. If categorization depends on similarity to a representation of known category members, then what features or dimensions of the representation are counted in evaluating similarity (Murphy & Medin, 1985)?

iii. Connectionist models   An increasingly popular framework for developing computational models is *connectionist,* or *neural network,* models (McClelland & Rumelhart, 1986; Rumelhart & McClelland, 1986). Connectionist models of categorization usually consist of a set of input nodes corresponding to features on stimuli to be categorized, a set of output nodes corresponding to possible response categories, and a network of connections between the input and output nodes. This network of connections stores associative information about the relations between inputs and output (i.e., between stimulus features and categories). These connections may have a simple structure, such as one connection between each input node and each output node, or the structure may be more complex, with multiple layers of connections as well as additional nodes, known as hidden traits. Learning takes place by adjusting the connection strengths according to a learning rule (much current research on connectionist modeling addresses the development of learning rules). Typically, the degree of learning about a stimulus is proportional to a measure of categorization error. If the connection strengths already allow a particular stimulus to be categorized perfectly, then the connections would not be adjusted after an observation of this stimulus.

One particular application of connectionist principles to categorization is Kruschke's (1992) ALCOVE model. As in other connectionist models, ALCOVE has input nodes corresponding to the dimensions of variation of stimuli and output nodes corresponding to response categories. In addition, ALCOVE has two kinds of connections. First, attentional connections run from the input nodes to a set of hidden units that correspond to representations of specific exemplars in memory. For example, if the input nodes corresponding to *small* and *red* are activated, then exemplars of hidden units corresponding to small, red things will be especially activated. In this way, ALCOVE is an exemplar-based connectionist model, a hybrid between neural nets and traditional exemplar models. Second, connections run from the hidden units to the output nodes. These connections are adjusted as in other connectionist models so that ALCOVE can learn correct categorizations.

The novel contribution of ALCOVE lies in the first kind of connections, which corresponds to attentional weights on different dimensions. For example, if the attentional connections for color input nodes are stronger than connections for size input nodes, then an input of *small and red* would tend to activate *red* units more than *small* units. Because ALCOVE is a connectionist network, these attentional strengths are learned by the model. Previous work on attention in category learning (e.g., Nosofsky, 1986) has shown that people selectively attend to diagnostic dimensions, but previous models have not provided an account of the process by which selective attention is applied. In contrast, ALCOVE provides an account of how people learn to attend to the dimensions of stimuli that are most useful or diagnostic for learning categories. For some examples of successful applications of ALCOVE to studies of categorization, see Kruschke (1992), Nosofsky and Kruschke (1992), and Nosofsky, Kruschke, and McKinley (1992).

An alternative connectionist model for category learning has been proposed by Gluck and Bower (1988b). In this model, input nodes are connected directly to the output nodes, without any hidden units. One advantage of this relatively simple scheme is that it makes it possible to derive the predictions of the model without running extensive simulations. For example, Markman (1989) derived mathematical predictions of how sensitive this model will be to base rates (i.e., the relative frequencies of categories). Although Gluck and Bower's model does not have the hidden units, or the separate component for attentional learning of the ALCOVE model, it has still been quite successful (see Gluck & Bower, 1988a, 1988b, for examples of applying this model to particular studies). One problem with the original model is that it can only learn linearly separable categories (recall that Medin and Schwanenflugel [1981] found that people can learn categories whether or not they are linearly separable). This limitation of the model follows directly from its lack of hidden units; certain patterns of categorization require hidden units (Minsky & Papert, 1988). Even with hidden units many network models predict that linearly separable categories should be easier to learn than nonlinearly separable categories, a prediction for which there is little or no support. More recently, Gluck and Bower (1990) have proposed an extension known as the *configural cue model*. In the configural cue model, input nodes may correspond not only to features of stimuli but also to pairs of features, triples of features, and in most extreme case, all possible *n*-tuples of features. In this extreme case, the input to the model would correspond to an exemplar representation, because each possible stimulus would have its own input node (see also Barsalou, 1990).

iv. Rule-based models   Rule-based approaches to categories and concepts have had an uneven history. They received a lot of attention in the 1960s and early 1970s when experimenters implicitly or explicitly acted as if categories are well defined. Interest was in the relative difficulty of different forms of logical rules (e.g., Bourne, 1970). If categories are fuzzy or ill defined, then most such logical rules will not work. Consequently, one by-product of the shift to the probabilistic view was severely diminished attention to rule-based models.

In principle, however, fuzzy structures do not rule out rules. Indeed many participants in laboratory studies of categorization report that they are trying to develop rules and they often succeed (by forming disjunctive rules or rules with exceptions). Therefore, ignoring rule learning may come at some risk (Martin & Caramazza, 1980; Medin, 1986). Nosofsky, Palmeri, and McKinley (1994) have shown that a rule-based model can account for a wide range of categorization phenomena associated with fuzzy artificial categories, so this view needs to be taken seriously.

Any one category partitioning is consistent with a virtually limitless set of rules or inductive generalizations. Michalski (1983a, 1983b) has developed an AI system for inducing rules from partitioned examples where the aim is to have rules that are psychologically comprehensible. Michalski's INDUCE system works by selecting an example and describing it in alternative ways according to certain generalization rules. The goal of these generalization rules is that the description will apply to other examples of the same category and not to examples of contrasting categories. The process is recursive such that if the best rule is consistent (does not have any counterexamples) but not complete (fails to apply to all category), an example that is not covered by the rule is selected and generalization rules applied to it. Therefore, the general form of rules will be a disjunction of conjunctions. Michalski has found that INDUCE shows very good accuracy in classifying new examples after inducing a rule from a modest set of training examples (e.g., Michalski, Mozetic, Hong, & Lavrac, 1986; also see Michalski, 1993, for more recent applications of the same general framework).

Medin et al. (1987) compared the rules developed by INDUCE with those of people, again using preclassified examples. They observed both general agreement and systematic differences. In particular, people often develop initial rules that are overly general and then restrict them by adding clauses that eliminate counterexamples (e.g., a rule such as "X and Y" that applies to some examples of the alternative category may be patched up by adding the hedge "and not Z"). Medin et al. suggested that this rule formation strategy facilitates the inference function of concepts.

There are other similarity-based AI classification systems that are conceptually close to rule-based models. For example, discrimination net models that involve a series of branching tests (of feature values) can be construed as rule generators (see also Rendell & Cho, 1990). Increasingly, these models are being applied to human categorization data (e.g., Ahn & Medin, 1992; Richman, 1991; and especially Fisher & Langley, 1990, and Fisher & Yoo, 1993). A good recent review of relevant work in this area is provided by the volume edited by Fisher, Pazzani, and Langley (1991).

v. Comparing and developing models   For the most part, we have emphasized the development of the similarity-based models within single frameworks, such as the progression from the prototype model of Posner and Keele (1968) to the abstraction models of Ashby and Gott (1988), the progression from the exemplar model of Medin and Schaffer (1978) to the exemplar model of Nosofsky (1986), and the progression from the connectionist model of Gluck and Bower (1988b) to the configural cue version of this model (1990), rather than emphasizing comparisons between frameworks, such as whether exemplar models are better than abstraction models. This emphasis reflects a bias of our own, that computational modeling is a language that is particularly useful for expressing and developing theories of categorization. To continue the language metaphor, different kinds of modeling, such as connectionist models and exemplar models, may be thought of as different languages. It is easier to compare two models within the same framework than two models in different frameworks, just as it is easier to compare two short stories in one language than two stories in different languages. Certainly it is also valuable to compare models from different frameworks; for example, Nosofsky (1992) has shown that certain abstraction, exemplar, and connectionist models are formally equivalent. One implication of these analyses is that you can't tell a model by its label—an exemplar model and a connectionist model may be much more similar than two connectionist or two exemplar models. Furthermore, a complete description of a particular model must refer not only to its form of representation but also must develop its processing assumptions (Barsalou, 1990).

b. Explanation-Based Learning

i. Arguments for theory effects   What the similarity-based models (abstraction, exemplar, connectionist, and rule-based) described so far have in common is that they form categories with bottom-up, data-driven processes. Murphy and Medin (1985) have argued that such accounts of category learning are incomplete, because the concepts that people form cannot be predicted only from what people observe (see also Schank et al., 1986). People bring to bear many forms of prior knowledge that also influence concept formation, from simple expectations about what will be in a category and what features will be relevant for evaluating similarity, to more elaborate causal knowledge (or theories) about the relations between category members and the relations between categories. Many recent studies have demonstrated the influence of prior knowledge on category learning (e.g., Hayes & Taplin, 1992; Heit, 1994; S. S. Jones, Smith, & Landau, 1991; Lamberts, 1994; Murphy & Wisniewski, 1989; Pazzani, 1991; Wattenmaker et al., 1986; Wisniewski & Medin, 1991, 1994a; see Murphy, 1993, for a review). For example, Wattenmaker et al.

(1986) showed that prior knowledge of occupations helped subjects learn about novel categories of occupations. Together, these studies have made it clear that it is easier to learn new categories that are consistent with prior knowledge than categories that are inconsistent with prior knowledge. In addition, people's beliefs about newly formed categories reflect knowledge from outside of these categories; that is, people show assimilation effects.

ii. AI models of EBL A number of proposals for addressing the role of prior knowledge and theories have been developed in the domain of machine learning under the banner of EBL (Dejong, 1988; Ellman, 1989; Mooney, 1993). Typically, an explanation-based system uses its background knowledge (in the form of a domain theory) to explain or prove why a training example is a member of a given category. It then generalizes the explanation so that it will apply to future examples. An advantage over SBL approaches is that appropriate abstraction may take place on the basis of experience with only a single example.

There have been some promising recent applications of EBL to psychological experiments (e.g., Ahn, Brewer, & Mooney, 1992; Pazzani, 1991). AI research in the EBL framework has been very active, addressing a variety of issues, such as the problem of incomplete or incorrect theories (e.g., Porter, Bareiss, & Holte, 1990; Rajamoney, 1990). These and other analyses (e.g., Dietterich, 1986) have led to a growing interest in methods for integrating theory and data (EBL and SBL) a topic to which we now turn.

iii. Merging SBL and EBL An alternative to these pure EBL accounts is to develop existing SBL models to address the effects of prior knowledge, leading to what may be considered mixed models. As one example, we describe in some detail a recent similarity-based model of category learning that has been modified to address the effects of prior knowledge (Heit, 1994). The *integration* model is an exemplar model that is a variant of context theory (Medin & Schaffer, 1978). The novel assumption of the integration model is that two kinds of exemplars influence judgment of whether some stimulus belongs in a category: both exemplars of that category as well as *prior examples,* from other categories. For example, imagine that you move to a new city and you are looking for friends to join you in jogging. In effect, you are trying to learn about a new category: joggers in this city. In your early observations of residents of the city, your categorization judgments about whether these persons are joggers will be influenced by similarity to prior examples of joggers from other contexts (e.g., joggers from where you previously lived). Eventually, with more observations, your categorization judgments will be influenced much more by observed examples of joggers in your new city and less by the prior examples. In this way, the integration model is similar to Bayesian models of statistical estimation (Edwards, Lindman, & Savage, 1963). For several experiments simulating this experience of category learning in a new context where subjects were knowledgeable about prior examples, Heit (1994) found that the integration model gave a good qualitative and quantitative account.

In addition to the integration of prior examples and observed examples, Heit distinguished other possible processes by which prior knowledge might affect category learning. First, prior knowledge may lead to selective weighting of category members so observations that fit prior knowledge are remembered best. For example, you might be more successful at learning about joggers who own expensive running shoes than about joggers who do not own expensive running shoes. Second, prior knowledge may lead to selective weighting of features. In learning to categorize joggers in your new city, you might attend to people's shoes rather than hair color. Third, prior knowledge may have a distortion effect; for example, a jogger without expensive running shoes might be misremembered as a jogger with expensive running shoes or even as a nonjogger. Although these additional processes all seem plausible, the results of Heit (1994) could be explained without any of them (i.e., by the integration model alone). Thus, providing distinctive evidence for when these other processes occur in addition to integration will be a task for future research.

Of course, there are a number of other ways of integrating EBL and SBL. For example, Lebowitz describes a system, UNIMEM, where SBL is used to determine regularities, and then UNIMEM attempts to explain these commonalities with its domain theory. The goal of the explanatory component is to separate causally relevant features from those that are spurious or coincidental. Other AI systems such as Induction over the Unexplained (IOU) (Mooney, 1993), or Induction over the Explained (IOE) (Flann and Dietterich, 1989), and EXOR (Fisher & Yoo, 1993; Yoo & Fisher, 1991) operate in essentially the opposite manner. For example, IOU first applies EBL on training items, and features that do not enter into explanations are input to an SBL component. The target concept is then augmented with these unexplained regularities. The SBL component allows the system to acquire predictive features that are not covered by the domain component. IOE develops explanations for each of a series of training examples and then employs empirical learning (SBL) to detect frequently occurring substructures and patterns of features across explanatory trees. For a review and analysis of integrated systems, see Mooney (1993) and Wisniewski and Medin (1991).

A generalization that applies to almost all integrated SBL–EBL systems is that the interaction between the empirical and explanatory components is unidirectional and indirect. In a number of systems the first component acts as a filter for the second component by reducing the number of features input to the second component. Wisniewski and Medin (1991, 1994a, 1994b) have argued, however, that more tightly coupled systems are needed, at least in the case of psychological process models. They used categorization and rule induction paradigms where the same examples (children's drawings) were associated with different domain theories (e.g., in one case people might be told the drawings were done by creative versus noncreative children; in another that the drawings were done by emotionally disturbed versus mentally healthy children). A number of findings point to the need for greater interaction between theory and data. First of all, it may not always be reasonable to assume a space of prespecified unambiguous features. Wisniewski and

Medin noted that the features comprising subjects' rules varied as a function of domain theory and that the same aspect of a drawing was interpreted differently for different category labels. Participants also sometimes reinterpret features when given feedback about category membership. Finally, participants' rules often involve abstract features that are operationalized differently as a function of learning history (e.g., one might expect creative children to draw detailed pictures, but how detailed does a drawing have to be to qualify as "detailed"?). On the basis of these observations, Wisniewski and Medin argued that relatively modular ways of incorporating prior knowledge into categorization models are inadequate.

3. Induction

The extent of the previous section reflects that most work on computational models of concept use has focused on one conceptual function, namely categorization. However, other work on computational models has addressed the inference and inductive reasoning function of concepts. The category-based induction (CBI) model (Osherson et al., 1990; Osherson, Stern, Wilkie, Stob, & Smith, 1991) addresses the issue of how we infer novel properties of categories. For example, given the premise that cows have sesamoid bones, how likely is the conclusion that dogs also have sesamoid bones? According to the CBI model, two factors influence how people evaluate the inductive soundness of such inferences. First, the similarity between the premise category (e.g., *cow*) and the conclusion category (e.g., *dog*) is critical. To the extent that people believe that the premise and conclusion categories share other properties, people will be willing to project a new property from the premise to the conclusion. So if the premise is that elephants (instead of cows) have sesamoid bones, it would seem less likely that dogs have sesamoid bones, because dogs and cows are more similar than dogs and elephants.

The second factor in the CBI model is the *coverage* of the premise, that is the similarity between the category or categories in the premise and members of the superordinate category that encompasses the categories in the premise and conclusion. A few examples should make coverage clear. Consider again an inductive inference from *cow* to *dog*. The most specific superordinate category that includes cows and dogs is *mammal*. Now, *cow* is fairly similar to other members of the category *mammal;* cows are moderately typical mammals. Thus, if cows have sesamoid bones, it is moderately plausible that all mammals have sesamoid bones. In turn, if all mammals have this property, than so must dogs have the property. In the CBI model, the two sources of evaluating inferences, similarity and coverage, are just added together. Category members that are atypical do not contribute much to coverage; for example, *aardvark* would provide little coverage for the superordinate category *mammal* (see also Rips, 1975). The CBI model also provides an elegant way to evaluate the coverage of arguments with multiple premises. For example, given the premises that both horses and squirrels have sesamoid bones, it seems likely that all mammals have sesamoid bones, because horses and squirrels are quite diverse members of the superordinate, *mammals*. On the other hand, the premises that horses and mules have some property does not lend as much support to the belief that all mammals have the property, because horses and mules do not cover the superordinate category *mammals* much better than just horses alone.

The CBI model provides an intuitively pleasing account of how people use similarity and category information to make inferences, and gives a good explanation for many empirical results at both a qualitative and quantitative level (see Osherson et al., 1990, 1991). The CBI model focuses on the role of categories in inductive reasoning, but it does not provide an account of the role of properties. Most of the Osherson et al. (1990, 1991) studies used "blank properties" such as *has sesamoid bones* and *has an ulnar artery* that seem biologically related but are otherwise unfamiliar. Heit and Rubinstein (1994) have proposed that one systematic effect of the property being inferred is that it leads people to focus on certain other relevant properties when evaluating similarity. For example, Heit and Rubinstein found that for the anatomical properties such as *has a liver with two chambers,* subjects were more willing to make an inference from *mouse* to *bat* than from *sparrow* to *bat.* Thus, for an anatomical property, people are influenced by the common biological properties of *mouse* and *bat*. In contrast, when subjects evaluated inferences about behavioral properties, they appeared to evaluate similarity in terms of other behavioral characteristics, such as method of locomotion. For example, for the behavioral property *travels shorter distances in extreme heat,* subjects favored inferences between *sparrow* and *bat* over inferences between *mouse* and *bat*. Presently, the CBI model does not address the part of inductive reasoning by which we determine which properties are relevant to evaluating similarity, nor does any other model address this issue.

4. Conceptual Combination

Finally, we address the computational modeling of another important function of knowledge of categories, conceptual combination. Conceptual combination is important because it allows us to be productive in our use of concepts, so that we can create and understand a potentially unlimited set of new concepts. For example, we are only rarely faced with the task of understanding a single concept in isolation; much more commonly we need to interpret a set of concepts combined to form a phrase or sentence. Yet most categorization models do not address the phenomena related to combined concepts (Rips, 1995). One exception is the selective modification model (E. E. Smith & Osherson, 1984; E. E. Smith, Osherson, Rips, & Keane, 1988), which is a specialized account of the understanding of adjective-noun combinations such as brown apple. According to the selective modification model, to understand this term a person would retrieve the prototype of apple, pay extra attention to the dimension of color, and replace the default value of red for apples with the value brown. In effect, the person would be constructing a new prototype for brown apple by modifying the apple prototype. Then, judgments such as categorization decisions and typicality ratings could use the brown apple prototype in accordance with an ordinary prototype model of categorization.

But conceptual combination is more complex than the selective modification model (or any other current model) suggests. One complication is that the people also use their general knowledge about relations between features. For example, in interpreting the combined concept *large spoon,* people not only modify their spoon prototype to make it larger, but they also seem to make inferences about other features, such as that a large spoon is likely to be made of wood (Medin & Shoben, 1988). Interestingly, conceptual combination sometimes leads to inferences about emergent features (i.e., features of the combined concept that are not considered as features of either constituent concept) (Hampton, 1987; Hastie, Schroeder, & Weber, 1990; Kunda, Miller, & Claire, 1990; Murphy, 1988; Rips, 1995). For example, many people would expect a Harvard-educated carpenter to be a nonconformist, but this feature is not as often expected for either of the constituent categories, Harvard-educated people and carpenters (Kunda et al., 1990). These two findings, regarding feature relations and regarding emergent features, indicate that conceptual combination could be a compositional process, as assumed by the selective modification model (as well as the model of Hampton, 1987, 1988) but that other sources of knowledge influence understanding. In other words, you cannot fully interpret a combination of two concepts by simply combining what you know about each concept alone. Instead, additional knowledge outside of the two constituent concepts must also be brought to bear (Hampton, 1988; Kunda et al., 1990; Murphy, 1988; Rips, in press).

5. Summary

Our summary paragraphs in this review may be seen as not only modular but interchangeable. Again we see the tension between SBL and theory-based category learning and a number of attempts to reconcile the two. We don't think it is speculative to predict that the integration of SBL and EBL will be a recurrent theme in future research (see the edited volume by Nakamura, Taraban, & Medin, 1993, for a number of examples).

F. Neuroscience

Opportunities to link categorization research with observations from neuroscience have only recently begun to be exploited. In this section we provide only a single example, but one that shows the potential interplay of neuroscience with categorization.

It appears that brain damage can lead to category-specific impairments of semantic memory. Warrington and Shallice (1984) reported that some patients were much worse at identifying plants and animals than nonliving things (see also Sartori & Job,

1988). Impaired knowledge of nonliving things relative to living things has also been observed (Warrington & McCarthy, 1987). These observations suggest that knowledge of living kinds versus inanimate objects are represented in distinct submodules of semantic memory. Warrington and her associates (e.g., Warrington & McCarthy, 1983) have raised the alternative possibility that semantic memory is organized in terms of modality. They note that living kinds are distinguished primarily by their perceptual sensory features, whereas artifacts are distinguished in terms of functional properties (e.g., intended use). In brief, the selective impairment of knowledge about living versus nonliving things may be based on an underlying perceptual versus functional information loss.

Farah and McClelland (1991) have recently described support for Warrington's view in the form of computational modeling. They developed a parallel distributed processing model organized by modality (perceptual vs. functional) and demonstrated that simulated lesions to either the functional or visual area of the network could reproduce impaired knowledge of living things versus artifacts. Furthermore, the simulations provided a detailed account of more subtle aspects of these deficits (e.g., differences between probing knowledge visually vs. verbally).

The neuroscience observations and the explorations with artificial neural networks operate hand in hand. Neuroscience provides hypotheses to be investigated as well as constraints on models. The models, in turn, allow one to go beyond a macroscopic level of analysis, and their explanatory power can feedback to suggest further relevant observations. We anticipate that categorization research increasingly will benefit from these sorts of interdisciplinary analyses.

III. CHALLENGES AND OPPORTUNITIES

A. Challenges

It is perhaps a sign of our optimism that we would not be unhappy with a straight line projection of current states of affairs in categorization research. By projection we mean continuing to follow promising paths, not exactly more of the same. Our sanguine attitude does, however, recognize certain significant challenges.

1. Questions of Features

Although it is often advantageous to use stimulus materials where the constituents or features are readily described, little progress has been made in understanding how features come into existence. In the case of certain visual features one might claim that they are hardwired into the perceptual system, but this sort of analysis is unlikely to work for more conceptual properties. There is some work on feature construction in neural network models (e.g., Rumelhart & Zipser, 1985), but so far there has been little by way of application to categorization. We need to understand how features come into play and how they are developed and modified as a function of knowledge structures and experience (see Wisniewski and Medin, 1994b, for more discussion).

2. Question of Kinds

Any research program that focuses on a narrow range of stimulus materials or tasks faces the twin dangers of narrow generality or misattribution. With respect to the latter, the combination of a single task and stimulus type creates an ambiguity as to whether the performance observed is triggered by the task, by the stimuli, or by some interaction of the two. Lee Brooks and his associates (e.g., Brooks et al., 1991; Reagher & Brooks, 1993; Whittlesea, 1933) have repeatedly demonstrated powerful interactions of stimuli with processing tasks. More generally, categorization research has tended to focus primarily on nominal, natural kind, and artifact categories. It is not clear how or how much our perspective might change if there were corresponding efforts to study actions, events, or any of a variety of other types of categories. For example, Gentner (1981) and Huttenlocher and Lui (1979) described many differences between noun categories and verb categories, yet many accounts of research on concepts (including the present chapter) focus on noun categories. (For some recent examples of research on verb categories or event categories, especially in language acquisition, see Behrend, 1990; Kersten & Billman, 1992; Naigles, 1990; Nelson, 1986).

3. Questions of Structure

One anomalous observation, in our opinion, is that little attention has been directed to relational properties and their role in creating structure. For example, computational approaches to object recognition (e.g., Hummel & Biederman, 1992; Ullman, 1989) directly or indirectly incorporate structure. Given that EBL entails relational properties and structure, it might prove more feasible to integrate SBL and EBL if similarity models took a more structural view (e.g., Gentner, 1989; Goldstone and Medin, 1994a, 1994b). In addition to structural relations between features, we think that it will also be important to consider structural relations between category members. A concept is more than an unstructured collection of exemplars. For example, it is certainly true that priests, bishops, and nuns are members of the category *clergy*, but critical to understanding the *clergy* concept are the relations among these members. Some recent work has considered the relations between category members, suggesting that some categories have radial or chained structures (Lakoff, 1987; Malt, 1994).

4. Questions of Learning

Some of the most important research in categorization stems from the area of cognitive development. Observations on conceptual change lend important insight into categorization. Our review has notably failed to include a linguistic perspective on categorization, but surely language plays a critical role in determining what categories are learned and how they are learned (e.g., Landau & Gleitman, 1985; Pinker, 1992).

B. Opportunities

As we said earlier, we are guilty of optimism, and we think it's time for categorization research to become more ambitious. More ambitious in the sense that each of the perspectives we have reviewed (and others such as linguistics and computational vision) has methods, models, and insights that could effectively contribute in an integration of approaches. Each perspective can claim exciting developments, but each could be more powerful if it could borrow from its neighbors. We think it will happen.

Acknowledgments

Preparation of this chapter was supported by National Science Foundation grant 91-10245 to Douglas Medin. We are grateful to Lance Rips and Edward Wisniewski for comments on this chapter.

References

Ahn, W., Brewer, W. F., & Mooney, R. J. (1992). Schema acquisition from a single example. *Journal of Experimental Psychology: Learning, Memory, and Cognition, 18,* 391–413.

Ahn, W., & Medin, D. L. (1992). A two-stage model of category construction. *Cognitive Science, 16,* 81–121.

Allen, S. W., & Brooks, L. R. (1991). Specializing the operation of an explicit rule. *Journal of Experimental Psychology: General, 120,* 3–19.

Anderson, J. R. (1990). *The adaptive character of thought.* Hillsdale, NJ: Erlbaum.

Anderson, J. R. (1991). The adaptive nature of human categorization. *Psychological Review, 98,* 409–429.

Anglin, J. (1977). *Word, object, and conceptual development.* New York: Norton.

Ashby, F. G., & Gott, R. E. (1988). Decision rules in the perception and categorization of multidimensional stimuli. *Journal of Experimental Psychology: Learning, Memory, and Cognition, 14,* 33–53.

Atran, S. (1987). Origins of the species and genus concepts. *Journal of the History of Biology, 20,* 195–279.

Atran, S. (1990). *Cognitive foundations of natural history: Towards an anthropology of science.* Cambridge, England: Cambridge University Press.

Atran, S. (1998). Folk biology and the anthropology of science, cognitive universals, and cultural particulars. *Behavioral and Brain Sciences, 21,* 547–609.

Bareiss, R. (1989). *Exemplar-based knowledge acquisition: A unified approach to concept representation, classification, and learning.* Boston: Academic Press.

Barkow, J. H., Cosmides, L., & Tooby, J. (1992). *The adapted mind: Evolutionary psychology and the generation of culture.* New York: Oxford University Press.

Barsalou, L. W. (1983). Ad hoc categories. *Memory & Cognition, 11,* 211–217.

Barsalou, L. W. (1985). Ideas, central tendency, and frequency of instantiation as determinants of graded structure in categories. *Journal of Experimental Psychology: Learning, Memory, and Cognition, 11,* 629–649.

Barsalou, L. W. (1990). On the indistinguishability of exemplar memory and abstraction in memory representation. In T. K. Srull & R. S. Wyer (Eds.), *Advances in social cognition* (pp. 61–88). Hillsdale, NJ: Erlbaum.

Barsalou, L. W. (1993). Structure, flexibility, and linguistic vagary in concepts: Manifestations of a compositional system of perceptual systems. In A. C. Collins, S. E. Gathercole, & M. A. Conway (Eds.), *Theories of memory* (pp. 61–88). London: Erlbaum.

Behrend, D. A. (1990). The development of verb concepts: Children's use of verbs to label familiar novel events. *Child Development, 61,* 681–697.

Berlin, B. (1992). *Ethnobiological classification: Principles of categorization of plants and animals in traditional societies.* Princeton, NJ: Princeton University Press.

Berlin, B., Breedlove, D., & Raven, P. (1966). Folk taxonomies and biological classification. *Science, 154,* 273–275.

Berlin, B., Breedlove, D., & Raven, P. (1973). General principles of classification and nomenclature in folk biology. *American Anthropologist, 74,* 214–242.

Boster, J. S. (1986). Exchange of varieties and information between aguaruna manioc cultivators. *American Anthropologist, 88,* 429–436.

Boster, J. S. (1987). Agreement between biological classification systems is not dependent on cultural transmission. *American Anthropologist, 89,* 914–920.

Boster, J. S. (1988). Natural sources of internal category structure: Typicality, familiarity, and similarity of birds. *Memory & Cognition, 16,* 258–270.

Boster, J. S., Berlin, B., & O'Neill, J. (1986). The correspondence of Jivaroan to Scientific ornithology. *American Anthropologist, 88,* 569–586.

Boster, J. S., & D'Andrade, R. (1989). Natural and human sources of cross-cultural agreement in ornithological classification. *American Anthropologist, 91,* 132–142.

Boster, J. S., & Johnson, J. C. (1989). Form or function: A comparison of expert and novice judgments of similarities among fish. *American Anthropologist, 91,* 866–889.

Bourne, L. E., Jr. (1970). Knowing and using concepts. *Psychological Review, 77,* 546–556.

Boyer, P. (1990). *Tradition as truth and communication: A cognitive description of traditional discourse.* Cambridge, England: Cambridge University Press.

Brooks, L. R. (1978). Nonanalytic concept formation and memory for instances. In E. Rosch & B. B. Lloyd (Eds.), *Cognition and categorization.* pp. 169–211. New York: Wiley.

Brooks, L. R. (1987). Decentralized control of categorization: The role of prior processing episodes. In U. Neisser (Ed.), *Concepts and conceptual development: The ecological and intellectual factors in categorization* (pp. 141–174). Cambridge, England: Cambridge University Press.

Brooks, L. R., Norman, G. R., & Allen, S. W. (1991). Role of specific similarity in a medical diagnosis task. *Journal of Experimental Psychology: General, 120,* 278–287.

Busemeyer, J. R., Myung, I. J., & McDaniel, M. A. (1993). Theoretical implications for adaptive network learning models. *Psychological Science, 4,* 196–203.

Carey, S. A. (1985). *Conceptual change in childhood.* Cambridge, MA: Bradford Books.

Carey, S. A., & Gelman, R. (Eds.). (1991). *Epigenesis of mind: Studies in biology and cognition.* Hillsdale, NJ: Erlbaum.

Dejong, G. F. (1988). An introduction to explanation-based learning. In H. Shrobe (Ed.), *Exploring artificial intelligence* (pp. 45–81). San Mateo, CA: Morgan Kaufmann.

Dietterich, T. G. (1986). Learning at the knowledge level. *Machine Learning, 1,* 287–316.

Donnellan, K. S. (1977). Reference and definite descriptions. In S. P. Schwartz (Ed.), *Naming, necessity, and natural kinds* (pp. 42–65). Ithaca, NY: Cornell University Press.

Dupré, J. (1981). Natural kinds and biological taxa. *Philosophical Review, 90,* 66–90.

Edwards, W., Lindman, H., & Savage, L. J. (1963). Bayesian statistical inferences for psychological research. *Psychological Review, 70,* 193–242.

Ellman, T. (1989). Explanation-based learning: A survey of programs and perspectives. *Computing Surveys, 21,* 163–221.

Estes, W. K. (1993). Concepts, categories, and psychological science. *Psychological Science, 4,* 143–154.

Estes, W. K. (1994). *Classification and cognition* (pp. 161–163). Oxford, England: Oxford University Press.

Farah, M. J., & McClelland, J. L. (1991). A computational model of semantic memory impairment: Modality specificity and emergent category specificity. *Journal of Experimental Psychology: General, 120,* 339–358.

Fisher, D. H., & Langley, P. (1990). The structure and formation of natural categories. In G. H. Bower (Ed.), *The psychology of learning and motivation* (Vol. 26, pp. 241–284). San Diego, CA: Academic Press.

Fisher, D. H., Pazzani, M. J., & Langley, P. (Eds.). (1991). *Concept formation: Knowledge and experience in unsupervised learning*. San Mateo, CA: Morgan Kaufmann.

Fisher, D. H., & Yoo, J. P. (1993). Categorization, concept learning, and problem solving: A unifying view. In G. V. Nakamura, R. Taraban, & D. L. Medin (Eds.), *The psychology of learning and motivation: Categorization by humans and machines* (Vol. 29, pp. 219–255). San Diego, CA: Academic Press.

Flann, N. S., & Dieterich, T. G. (1989). A study of explanation-based methods for inductive learning. *Machine Learning, 4*, 187–226.

Flannagan, M. J., Fried, L. S., & Holyoak, J. K. (1986). Distributional expectations and the induction of category structure. *Journal of Experimental Psychology: Learning, Memory, and Cognition, 12*, 241–256.

Fodor, J. A. (1983). *The modularity of mind*. Cambridge, MA: MIT Press.

Fried, L. S., & Holyoak, K. J. (1984). Induction of category distributions: A framework for classification learning. *Journal of Experimental Psychology: Learning, Memory, and Cognition, 10*, 234–257.

Garner, W. R. (1974). *The processing of information and structure*. Hillsdale, NJ: Erlbaum.

Gelman, R. (1990). First principles organize attention to and learning about relevant data: Number and the animate-inanimate distinction as examples. *Cognitive Science, 14*, 79–106.

Gelman, S. A., Coley, J. D., & Gottfried, G. M. (1994). Essentialist beliefs in children: The acquisition of concepts and theories. In L. A. Hirschfeld & S. A. Gelman (Eds.), *Mapping the mind* (pp. 341–367). Cambridge, England: Cambridge University Press.

Gelman, S. A., & Markman, E. M. (1986). Categories and induction in young children. *Cognition, 23*, 183–209.

Gelman, S. A., & Medin, D. L. (1993). What's so essential about essentialism? A different perspective on the interaction of perception, language, and conceptual knowledge. *Cognitive Development, 8*, 157–167.

Gelman, S. A., & Wellman, H. M. (1991). Insides and essence: Early understandings of the non-obvious. *Cognition, 38*, 213–244.

Gentner, D. (1981). Some interesting differences between verbs and nouns. *Cognition and Brain Theory, 4*, 161–178.

Gentner, D. (1989). The mechanisms of analogical learning. In S. Vosniadou & A. Ortony (Eds.), *Similarity and analogical reasoning* (pp. 199–241). Cambridge, England: Cambridge University Press.

Gentner, D., & Ratterman, M. J. (1991). Language and the career of similarity. In S. A. Gelman & J. P. Byrnes (Eds.), *Perspective on thought and language: Interrelations in development* (pp. 225–277). Cambridge, England: Cambridge University Press.

Gillund, G., & Shiffrin, R. M. (1984). A retrieval model for both recognition and recall. *Psychological Review, 91*, 1–67.

Gluck, M. A. (1991). Stimulus generalization and representation in adaptive network models of category learning. *Psychological Science, 2*, 50–55.

Gluck, M. A., & Bower, G. H. (1988a). Evaluating an adaptive network model for human learning. *Journal of Memory and Language, 27*, 166–195.

Gluck, M. A., & Bower, G. H. (1988b). From conditioning to category learning: An adaptive network model. *Journal of Experimental Psychology: General, 117*, 227–247.

Gluck, M. A., & Bower, G. H. (1990). Component and pattern information in adaptive networks. *Journal of Experimental Psychology: General, 119*, 105–109.

Goldstone, R. L., & Medin, D. L. (1994a). Similarity, interactive activation, and mapping: An overview. In K. Holyoak & J. Barnden (Eds.), *Advances in connectionist and neural computation theory: Connectionist approaches to analogy, metaphor, and case-based reasoning* (Vol. 2, pp. 321–362). Norwood, NJ: Ablex.

Goldstone, R. L., & Medin, D. L. (1994b). Time course of comparison. *Journal of Experimental Psychology: Learning, Memory, and Cognition, 20*, 29–50.

Goodman, N. (1972). Seven strictures on similarity. In N. Goodman (Ed.), *Problems and projects* (pp. 437–447). New York: Bobbs-Merrill.

Grice, H. P. (1957). Meaning. *Philosophical Review, 66*, 377–388.

Hammond, K. J. (1989). *Case-based planning: Viewing planning as a memory task.* San Diego, CA: Academic Press.

Hampton, J. A. (1987). Inheritance of attributes in natural concept conjunctions. *Memory & Cognition, 15,* 55–71.

Hampton, J. A. (1988). Overextension of conjunctive concepts: Evidence for a unitary model of concept typicality and class inclusion. *Journal of Experimental Psychology: Learning, Memory, and Cognition, 14,* 12–32.

Hampton, J. A. (1993). Prototype models of concept representation. In I. V. Mechelen, J. Hampton, R. Michalski, & P. Theuns (Eds.), *Categories and concepts: Theoretical views and inductive data analysis* (pp. 67–88). San Diego, CA: Academic Press.

Hastie, R., Schroeder, C., & Weber, R. (1990). Creating complex social conjunction categories from simple categories. *Bulletin of the Psychonomic Society, 28,* 242–247.

Hayes, B. K., & Taplin, J. E. (1992). Developmental changes in categorization processes: Knowledge and similarity-based models of categorization. *Journal of Experimental Child Psychology, 54,* 188–212.

Heit, E. (1992). Categorization using chains of examples. *Cognitive Psychology, 24,* 341–380.

Heit, E. (1993). Modeling the effects of expectations on recognition memory. *Psychological Science, 4,* 244–252.

Heit, E. (1994). Models of the effects of prior knowledge on category learning. *Journal of Experimental Psychology: Learning, Memory, and Cognition, 20,* 1264–1282.

Heit, E., & Rubinstein, J. (1994). Similarity and property effects in inductive reasoning. *Journal of Experimental Psychology: Learning, Memory, and Cognition, 20,* 411–422.

Hintzman, D. L. (1986). "Schema abstraction" in a multiple-trace memory model. *Psychological Review, 93,* 411–428.

Hintzman, D. L. (1988). Judgments of frequency and recognition memory in a multiple-trace memory model. *Psychological Review, 95,* 528–551.

Hintzman, D. L. (1991). Why are formal models useful in psychology? In W. E. Hockley & S. Lewandowsky (Eds.), *Relating theory and data: Essays on human memory in honor of Bennet B. Murdock* (pp. 39–56). Hillsdale, NJ: Erlbaum.

Hirschfeld, L. A. (1994). The child's representation of human groups. In D. L. Medin (Ed.), *The psychology of learning and motivation* (Vol. 31, pp. 133–184). San Diego, CA: Academic Press.

Hirschfeld, L. A. (1995). Anthropology, psychology, and the meanings of social causality. In A. Premack, D. Premack, & D. Sperber (Eds.), *Causal cognition: A multidisciplinary debate* (pp. 313–350). New York: Oxford University Press.

Hirschfeld, L. A., & Gelman, S. A. (1994). *Mapping the mind.* Cambridge, England: Cambridge University Press.

Horton, M. S., & Markman, E. M. (1980). Developmental differences in the acquisition of basic and superordinate categories. *Child Development, 51,* 708–719.

Hummel, J. E., & Biederman, I. (1992). Dynamic binding in a neural network for shape recognition. *Psychological Review, 99,* 480–517.

Huttenlocher, J., & Lui, F. (1979). The semantic organization of some simple nouns and verbs. *Journal of Verbal Learning and Verbal Behavior, 18,* 141–162.

James, W. (1890). *Principles of Psychology* (Vol. 1). New York: Holt.

Jones, C. M., & Heit, E. (1993). An evaluation of the total similarity principle: Effects of similarity on frequency judgments. *Journal of Experimental Psychology: Learning, Memory, and Cognition, 19,* 799–812.

Jones, S. S., & Smith, L. B. (1993). The place of perception in children's concepts. *Cognitive Development, 8,* 113–140.

Jones, S. S., & Smith, L. B., & Landau, B. (1991). Object properties and knowledge in early lexical learning. *Child Development, 62,* 499–516.

Keil, F. C. (1989). *Concepts, kinds, and cognitive development.* Cambridge, MA: MIT Press.

Keil, F. C., & Batterman, N. (1984). A characteristic-to-defining shift in the development of word meaning. *Journal of Verbal Learning and Behavior, 23,* 221–236.

Kemler, D. G. (1982). Classification in young and retarded children: The primacy of overall similarity relations. *Child Development, 53,* 768–779.

Kemler, D. G. (1983). Exploring and reexploring issues of integrality, perceptual sensitivity, and dimensional salience. *Journal of Experimental Child Psychology, 36,* 365–379.

Kemler-Nelson, D. G. (1988). When category learning is holistic: A reply to Ward and Scott. *Memory & Cognition, 16,* 79–84.

Kersten, A. W., & Billman, D. O. (1992). *The role of correlational structure in learning event categories.* Proceedings of the 14th annual conference of the Cognitive Science Society, Bloomington, Indiana, pp. 432–437.

Kolodner, J. L., & Simpson, R. L. (1989). The MEDIATOR: Analysis of an early case-based problem solver. *Cognitive Science, 13,* 507–549.

Komatsu, L. K. (1992). Recent views of conceptual structure. *Psychological Bulletin, 112,* 500–526.

Kruschke, J. K. (1992). ALCOVE: An exemplar-based connectionist model of category learning. *Psychological Review, 99,* 22–44.

Kunda, Z., Miller, D. T., & Claire, T. (1990). Combining social concepts: The role of causal reasoning. *Cognitive Science, 14,* 551–577.

Lakoff, G. (1987). *Women, fire, and dangerous things: What categories reveal about the mind.* Chicago: University of Chicago Press.

Lamberts, K. (1994). Flexible tuning of similarity in exemplar-based categorization. *Journal of Experimental Psychology: Learning, Memory, and Cognition, 20,* 1003–1021.

Landau, B., & Gleitman, L. R. (1985). *Language and experience: Evidence from the blind child.* Cambridge, MA: Harvard University Press.

Landau, B., Smith, L. B., & Jones, S. S. (1988). The importance of shape in early lexical learning. *Cognitive Development, 3,* 299–321.

Leslie, A. M. (1984). Spatiotemporal continuity and the perception of causality in infants. *Perception, 13,* 287–305.

Losonksy, M. (1990). The nature of artifacts. *Philosophy, 65,* 81–89.

Malt, B. C. (1990). Features and beliefs in the mental representations of categories. *Journal of Memory and Language, 29,* 289–315.

Malt, B. C. (1994). Water is not H_2O. *Cognitive Psychology, 27,* 41–70.

Malt, B. C. (1995). Category coherence in cross-cultural perspectives. *Cognitive Psychology, 29,* 85–148.

Malt, B. C., & Smith, E. E. (1984). Correlated properties in natural categories. *Journal of Verbal Learning and Verbal Behavior, 23,* 250–269.

Mandler, J. M. (1992). How to build a baby: II. Conceptual primitives. *Psychological Review, 99,* 587–604.

Mandler, J. M. (1993). On concepts. *Cognitive Development, 8,* 141–148.

Mandler, J. M., Bauer, P. J., & McDonough, L. (1991). Separating the sheep from the goats: Differentiating global categories. *Cognitive Psychology, 23,* 263–298.

Mandler, J. M., & McDonough, L. (1993). Concept formation in infancy. *Cognitive Development, 8,* 291–318.

Margolis, E. (1994). A reassessment of the shift from the classical theory of concepts to prototype theory. *Cognition, 51,* 73–89.

Markman, E. M. (1989). *Categorization and naming in children: Problems of induction.* Cambridge, MA: MIT Press.

Markman, E. M. (1990). Constraints children place on word meanings. *Cognitive Science, 14,* 57–77.

Markman, E. M. (1992). Constraints on word learning: Speculations about their nature, origins, and domain specificity. In M. R. Gunnar & M. Maratsos (Eds.), *Modularity and constraints in language and cognition* (pp. 59–102). Hillsdale, NJ: Erlbaum.

Markman, E. M., & Wachtel, G. R. (1988). Children's use of mutual exclusivity to constrain the meaning of two words. *Cognitive Psychology, 20,* 121–157.

Marr, D. (1982). *Vision.* San Francisco: Freeman.

Martin, R. C., & Caramazza, A. (1980). Classification of well-defined and ill-defined categories: Evidence for common processing strategies. *Journal of Experimental Psychology: General, 109*, 320–353.

Matheus, C. J., Rendell, L. R., Medin, D. L., & Goldstone, R. C. (1989). *Purpose and conceptual functions: A framework for concept representation and learning in humans and machines.* Proceedings of the 7th annual conference of the Society for the Study of Artificial Intelligence and Simulation of Behavior. T. Cohn (Ed.). Sussex, England: Pitmen Publishing.

Mayr, E. M. (1982). *The growth of biological thought: Diversity, evolution, and inheritance.* Cambridge, MA: Harvard University Press.

McClelland, J. L., & Rumelhart, D. E. (Eds.). (1986). *Parallel distributed processing: Explorations in the microstructure of cognition: Psychological and biological models* (Vol. 2). Cambridge, MA: MIT Press.

Medin, D. L. (1986). Comment on "Memory storage and retrieval processes in category learning." *Journal of Experimental Psychology: General, 115*, 373–381.

Medin, D. L. (1989). Concepts and conceptual structure. *American Psychologist, 44*, 1469–1481.

Medin, D. L., Altom, M. W., Edelson, S. M., & Freko, D. (1982). Correlated symptoms and simulated medical classification. *Journal of Experimental Psychology: Learning, Memory, and Cognition, 8*, 37–50.

Medin, D. L., & Edelson, S. E. (1988). Problem structure and the use of base-rate information from experience. *Journal of Experimental Psychology: General, 117*, 68–85.

Medin, D. L., & Ortony, A. (1989). Psychological essentialism. In S. Vosniadou & A. Ortony (Eds.), *Similarity and analogical reasoning.* Cambridge, England: Cambridge University Press.

Medin, D. L., & Schaffer, M. M. (1978). Context theory of classification learning. *Psychological Review, 85*, 207–238.

Medin, D. L., & Schwanenflugel, P. J. (1981). Linear separability in classification learning. *Journal of Experimental Psychology: Human Learning and Memory, 7*, 355–368.

Medin, D. L., & Shoben, E. J. (1988). Context and structure in conceptual combination. *Cognitive Psychology, 20*, 158–190.

Medin, D. L., & Smith, E. E. (1984). Concepts and concept formation. *Annual Review of Psychology, 35*, 113–138.

Medin, D. L., & Thau, D. M. (1992). Theories, constraints, and cognition. In H. L. Pick, P. Van Den Broek, & D. C. Knill (Eds.), *Cognition: Conceptual and methodological issues* (pp. 165–188). Washington, DC: American Psychological Association.

Medin, D. L., Wattenmaker, W. D., & Michalski, R. S. (1987). Constraints and preferences in inductive learning: An experimental study of human and machine performance. *Cognitive Science, 11*, 299–339.

Mervis, C. B. (1987). Child-basic object categories and early lexical development. In U. Neisser (Ed.), *Concepts and conceptual development: Ecological and intellectual factors in categorization* (pp. 201–233). New York: Cambridge University Press.

Mervis, C. B., Johnson, K. E., & Scott, P. (1993). Perceptual knowledge, conceptual knowledge, and expertise: Comment on Jones and Smith. *Cognitive Development, 8*, 149–155.

Mervis, C. B., & Rosch, E. (1981). Categorization of natural objects. *Annual Review of Psychology, 32*, 89–115.

Michalski, R. S. (1983a). A theory and methodology of inductive learning. *Artificial Intelligence, 20*, 111–161.

Michalski, R. S. (1983b). A theory and methodology of inductive learning. *Artificial Intelligence, 2*, 111–163.

Michalski, R. S. (1993). Inferential learning theory as a conceptual basis for multistrategy learning. *Machine Learning, 11*, 111–151.

Michalski, R. S., Mozetic, I., Hong, J., & Lavrac, N. (1986). The multipurpose incremental learning system AQ15 and its testing application to three medical domains. In *Proceedings of the Fifth Annual Conference on Artificial Intelligence* (pp. 1041–1045). Philadelphia: Morgan Kaufmann.

Minsky, M. L., & Papert, S. A. (1988). *Perceptrons.* Cambridge, MA: MIT Press.

Mitchell, T. M., Keller, R., & Kedar-Cabelli, S. (1986). Explanation-based generalization: A unifying view. *Machine Learning, 10,* 79–110.

Mooney, R. J. (1993). Integrating theory and data in category learning. In G. V. Nakamura, R. Taraban, & D. L. Medin (Eds.), *The psychology of learning and motivation: Categorization by humans and machines* (Vol. 29, pp. 189–219). San Diego, CA: Academic Press.

Murphy, G. L. (1988). Comprehending complex concepts. *Cognitive Science, 12,* 529–562.

Murphy, G. L. (1993). Theories and concept formation. In I. V. Mechelen, J. Hampton, R. Michalski, & P. Theuns (Eds.), *Categories and concepts: Theoretical views and inductive data analysis* (pp. 173–200). London: Academic Press.

Murphy, G. L., & Medin, D. L. (1985). The role of theories in conceptual coherence. *Psychological Review, 92,* 289–316.

Murphy, G. L., & Wisniewski, E. J. (1989). Categorizing objects in isolation and in scenes: What a superordinate is good for. *Journal of Experimental Psychology: Learning, Memory, and Cognition, 15,* 572–586.

Naigles, L. (1990). Children use syntax to learn verb meanings. *Journal of Child Language, 17,* 357–374.

Nakamura, G. V., Taraban, R., & Medin, D. L. (Eds.). (1993). *The psychology of learning and motivation: Categorization by humans and machines* (Vol. 29). San Diego, CA: Academic Press.

Nelson, K. (1986). *Event knowledge: Structure and function in development.* Hillsdale, NJ: Erlbaum.

Nosofsky, R. M. (1986). Attention, similarity and the identification-categorization relationship. *Journal of Experimental Psychology: General, 115,* 39–57.

Nosofsky, R. M. (1987). Attention and learning processes in the identification and categorization of integral stimuli. *Journal of Experimental Psychology: Learning, Memory, and Cognition, 13,* 87–108.

Nosofsky, R. M. (1988). Exemplar-based accounts of relations between classification, recognition, and typicality. *Journal of Experimental Psychology: Learning, Memory, and Cognition, 14,* 700–708.

Nosofsky, R. M. (1991). Tests of an exemplar model for relating perceptual classification and recognition in memory. *Journal of Experimental Psychology: Human Perception and Performance, 17,* 3–27.

Nosofsky, R. M. (1992). Exemplar-based approach to relating categorization, identification, and recognition. In F. G. Ashby (Ed.), *Multidimensional models of perception and cognition* (pp. 363–393). Hillsdale, NJ: Erlbaum.

Nosofsky, R. M., & Kruschke, J. K. (1992). Investigations of an exemplar-based connectionist model of category learning. In D. L. Medin (Ed.), *The psychology of learning and motivation* (Vol. 28, pp. 207–250). New York: Academic Press.

Nosofsky, R. M., Krushke, J. K., & McKinley, S. C. (1992). Combining exemplar-based category representations and connectionist learning rules. *Journal of Experimental Psychology: Learning, Memory, and Cognition, 18,* 211–233.

Nosofsky, R. M., Palmeri, T. J., & McKinley, S. C. (1994). Rule-plus-exception model of classification learning. *Psychological Review, 101,* 53–79.

Osherson, D. N., Smith, E. E., Wilkie, O., Lopez, A., & Shafir, E. (1990). Category-based induction. *Psychological Review, 97,* 185–200.

Osherson, D. N., Stern, J., Wilkie, O., Stob, M., & Smith, E. E. (1991). Default probability. *Cognitive Science, 15,* 251–269.

Pazzani, M. J. (1991). Influence of prior knowledge on concept acquisition: Experimental and computational results. *Journal of Experimental Psychology: Learning, Memory, and Cognition, 17,* 416–432.

Pinker, S. (1992). Language and species. *Language, 68,* 375–383.

Porter, B. W., Bareiss, R., & Holte, R. C. (1990). Concept learning and heuristic classification in weak-theory domains. *Artificial Intelligence, 45,* 229–263.

Posner, M. I., & Keele, S. W. (1968). On the genesis of abstract ideas. *Journal of Experimental Psychology, 77,* 353–363.

Premack, A. (Ed.). (1994). *Causal understanding in cognition and culture.* New York: Oxford University Press.

Quine, W. V. O. (1960). *Word and object.* Cambridge, MA: MIT Press.

Rajamoney, S. A. (1990). A computational approach to theory revision. In J. Shrager & P. Langley (Eds.),

Computational models of scientific discovery and theory formation (pp. 225–254). San Mateo, CA: Morgan Kaufmann.

Reagher, G., & Brooks, L. R. (1993). Perceptual manifestations of an analytic structure: The priority of holistic individuation. *Journal of Experimental Psychology: General, 122,* 92–114.

Rendell, L. A., & Cho, H. (1990). Empirical learning as a function of concept character. *Machine Learning, 5,* 267–298.

Rey, G. (1983). Concepts and stereotypes. *Cognition, 15,* 237–262.

Richman, H. (1991). Discrimination net models of concept formation. In D. Fisher, M. Pazzani, & P. Langley (Eds.), *Concept formation: Knowledge and experience in unsupervised learning* (pp. 103–125). San Mateo, CA: Morgan Kaufmann.

Riesbeck, C. K., & Schank, R. C. (1989). *Inside case-based reasoning.* Hillsdale, NJ: Erlbaum.

Rips, L. J. (1975). Inductive judgments about natural categories. *Journal of Verbal Learning and Verbal Behavior, 14,* 665–681.

Rips, L. J. (1989). Similarity, typicality and categorization. In S. Vosniadou & A. Ortony (Eds.), *Similarity and analogical reasoning* (pp. 21–59). Cambridge, England: Cambridge University Press.

Rips, L. (1995). The current status of research on conceptual combination. *Mind and Language, 10,* 72–104.

Romney, A. K., Weller, S. C., & Batchelder, W. H. (1986). Culture as consensus: A theory of culture and informant accuracy. *American Anthropologist, 88,* 318–338.

Rosch, E. (1973). Natural categories. *Cognitive Psychology, 4,* 328–350.

Rosch, E. (1978). Principles of categorization. In E. Rosch, & B. B. Lloyd (Eds.), *Cognition and categorization* (pp. 27–48). Hillsdale, NJ: Erlbaum.

Rosch, E., & Mervis, C. B. (1975). Family resemblances: Studies in the internal structure of categories. *Cognitive Psychology, 7,* 573–605.

Rosch, E., Mervis, C. B., Gray, W., Johnson, D., & Boyes-Braem, P. (1976). Basic objects in natural categories. *Cognitive Psychology, 8,* 573–605.

Ross, B. H., & Kennedy, P. T. (1990). Generalizing from the use of earlier examples in problem solving. *Journal of Experimental Psychology: Learning, Memory, and Cognition, 16,* 42–55.

Ross, B. H., Perkins, S. J., & Tenpenny, P. L. (1990). Reminding-based category learning. *Cognitive Psychology, 22,* 460–492.

Rothbart, M., & Taylor, M. (1992). Category labels and social reality: Do we view social categories as natural kinds? In G. Semin & K. Fielder (Eds.), *Language, interaction and social cognition* (pp. 11–36). Beverly Hills, CA: Sage.

Rumelhart, D. E., & McClelland, J. R. (Eds.). (1986). Parallel distributed processing. *Explorations in the microstructure of cognition: Foundations* (Vol. 1). Cambridge, MA: MIT Press.

Rumelhart, D. E., & Zipser, D. (1985). Feature discovery by competitive learning. *Cognitive Science, 19,* 75–112.

Sartori, G., & Job, R. (1988). The oyster with four legs: A neuropsychological study on the interaction of visual and semantic information. *Cognitive Neuropsychology, 15,* 105–132.

Schank, R. C., Collins, G. C., & Hunter, L. E. (1986). Transcending inductive category formation in learning. *Behavioral and Brain Sciences, 9,* 639–651.

Schwanenflugel, P. J., & Rey, M. (1986). Interlingual semantic facilitation: Evidence for a common representational system in the bilingual lexicon. *Journal of Memory and Language, 25,* 605–618.

Schwartz, S. P. (1977). *Naming, necessity, and natural kinds.* Ithaca, NY: Cornell University Press.

Shepard, R. N. (1987). Toward a universal law of generalization for psychological science. *Science, 237,* 1317–1323.

Shepp, B. E., & Swartz, K. B. (1976). Selective attention and the processing of integral and non-integral dimensions: A developmental study. *Journal of Experimental Child Psychology, 22,* 73–85.

Shipley, E. F. (1993). Categories, hierarchies, and induction. In D. L. Medin (Ed.), *The psychology of learning and motivation* (Vol. 30, pp. 265–301). San Diego, CA: Academic Press.

Smith, E. E., & Medin, D. L. (1981). *Categories and concepts.* Cambridge, MA: Harvard University Press.

Smith, E. E., Medin, D. L., & Rips, L. J. (1984). A psychological approach to concepts: Comments on Rey's "Concepts and stereotypes." *Cognition, 17,* 265–274.

Smith, E. E., & Osherson, D. N. (1984). Conceptual combination with prototype concepts. *Cognitive Science, 8,* 337–361.

Smith, E. E., Osherson, D. N., Rips, L. J., & Keane, M. (1988). Combining prototypes: A selective modification model. *Cognitive Science, 12,* 485–527.

Smith, E. E., Shoben, E. J., & Rips, L. J. (1974). Structure and process in semantic memory: A featural model for semantic decisions. *Psychological Review, 81,* 214–241.

Smith, E. E., & Sloman, S. (1994). Similarity-versus rule-based categorization. *Memory & Cognition, 22,* 377–386.

Smith, E. R. (1990). Content and process specificity in the effects of prior experiences. In T. K. Srull & R. S. Wyer, Jr. (Eds.), *Advances in social cognition* (pp. 1–59). Hillsdale, NJ: Erlbaum.

Smith, E. R., & Zarate, M. A., Exemplar-based models of social judgment. *Psychological Review, 99,* 3–21.

Smith, L. B. (1989). A model of perceptual classification in children and adults. *Psychological Review, 96,* 125–144.

Smith, L. B., & Kemler, D. G. (1977). Developmental trends in free classification: Evidence for a new conceptualization of perceptual development. *Journal of Experimental Child Psychology, 24,* 279–298.

Smith, L. B., & Kemler, D. G. (1978). Levels of experienced dimensionality in children and adults. *Cognitive Psychology, 10,* 502–532.

Spalding, T. L., & Ross, B. H. (1994). Comparison-based learning: Effects of comparing instances during category learning. *Journal of Experimental Psychology: Learning, Memory, and Cognition, 20,* 1251–1263.

Springer, K., & Keil, F. C. (1991). Early differentiation of causal mechanisms appropriate to biological and nonbiological kinds. *Child Development, 62,* 767–785.

Tanaka, J. W., & Taylor, M. (1991). Object categories and expertise: Is the basic level in the eye of the beholder? *Cognitive Psychology, 23,* 457–482.

Thau, D. M. (1992). *Primacy effects and selective attention incremental clustering.* Proceedings of the 14th annual conference of the Cognitive Science Society, Bloomington, Indiana, pp. 219–223.

Tversky, A. (1977). Features of similarity. *Psychological Review, 84,* 327–352.

Ullman, S. (1989). Aligning pictorial descriptions: An approach to object recognition. *Cognition, 32,* 193–254.

Walker, S. J. (1992). Supernatural beliefs, natural kinds, and conceptual structure. *Memory & Cognition, 20,* 655–662.

Ward, T. B., Vela, E., & Hass, S. D. (1990). Children and adults learn family-resemblance categories analytically. *Child Development, 61,* 393–406.

Warrington, E. K., & McCarthy, R. (1983). Category specific access dysphasia. *Brain, 106,* 859–878.

Warrington, E. K., & McCarthy, R. (1987). Categories of knowledge: Further fractionation and an attempted integration. *Brain, 110,* 1237–1296.

Warrington, E. K., & Shallice, T. (1984). Category specific semantic impairments. *Brain, 107,* 829–854.

Wattenmaker, W. D. (1995). Knowledge structures and linear separability: Integrating information in object and social categorization. *Cognitive Psychology, 28,* 273–328.

Wattenmaker, W. D., Dewey, G. I., Murphy, T. D., & Medin, D. L. (1986). Linear separability and concept learning: Context, relational properties, and concept naturalness. *Cognitive Psychology, 18,* 158–194.

Weber, E. U., Bockenholt, U., Hilton, D. J., & Wallace, B. (1993). Determinants of diagnostic hypothesis generation: Effects of information, base rates, and experience. *Journal of Experimental Psychology: Learning, Memory, and Cognition, 19,* 1131–1165.

Weller, S. C. (1987). Shared knowledge, intracultural variation, and knowledge aggregation. *American Behavioral Scientist, 31,* 178–193.

Whittlesea, B. W. (1993). Illusions of familiarity. *Journal of Experimental Psychology: Learning, Memory, and Cognition, 19*, 1235–1254.

Wisniewski, E. J., & Medin, D. L. (1991). Harpoons and long sticks: The interaction of theory and similarity in rule induction. In D. H. Fisher, M. J. Pazzani, & P. Langley (Eds.), *Concept formation: Knowledge and experience in unsupervised learning* (pp. 237–278). San Mateo, CA: Morgan Kaufmann.

Wisniewski, E. J., & Medin, D. L. (1994a). The fiction and nonfiction of features. In R. S. Michalski & G. Tecuci (Eds.), *Machine learning* (Vol. 4, pp. 63–84). San Mateo, CA: Morgan Kaufmann.

Wisniewski, E. J., & Medin, D. L. (1994b). On the interaction of theory and data in concept learning. *Cognitive Science, 18*, 221–281.

Yoo, J., & Fisher, D. H. (1991). Concept formation over problem-solving experience. In D. H. Fisher, M. J. Pazzani, & P. Langley (Eds.), *Concept formation: Knowledge and experience in unsupervised learning* (pp. 279–303). San Mateo, CA: Morgan Kaufmann.

Yuill, N. (1992). Children's conception of personality traits. *Human Development, 35*, 265–279.

CHAPTER 4

Reasoning

Kenneth J. Kurtz
Dedre Gentner
Virginia Gunn

I. REASONING

Human reasoning can be broadly described as a set of cognitive processes by which people take an initial set of information and generate inferences that extend beyond the original data. In this sense, the expectations, generalizations, and assertions people reach in interpreting events and situations can all be considered the result of reasoning. The inferences people produce can range from conclusions justified by formal procedures to sketchy hunches supported by varying degrees of evidence. Reasoning ranges from the really "hard" thinking it takes to formulate an answer to a difficult question or resolve a complex situation to the nearly automatic inferences and predictions that occur in the planning and execution of everyday activities. Reasoning is multifaceted, ubiquitous, and fundamental to human cognition.

A. An Introductory Framework

Reasoning can be broken down into three basic components: the available information, the cognitive processes brought to bear, and generated inferences. These are naturally expressed in terms of a simple, abstract description of the processing of information underlying human reasoning:

This research was supported by the National Science Foundation, grant number SBR-95-11757.

Cognitive Science

$$y = F(x) \tag{1}$$

In this formulation, x is the initial available information; the function F is a summary of the set of computational tools used to manipulate, recombine, or transform the input information; and y is the inferential product of the reasoning process, which might take the form of a judgment, conclusion, or prediction. In certain kinds of reasoning, people draw not only on the presented information x, but also on represented information—memory traces from personal experience or general conceptual knowledge. To reflect this, we can introduce a component k, which refers to the stored knowledge used in reasoning:

$$y = F(x,k) \tag{2}$$

The component k lends additional richness and flexibility to the construction of inferences by allowing reasoning processes to access domain knowledge and particular cases. By way of clarifying the nature of the k component, Wisniewski (1995) draws a useful distinction between knowledge and experience. *Knowledge* is the synthesis of abstracted principles, constraints, or organizations that comprise understanding of the world. Such knowledge might be organized as theory-like explanatory frameworks that can guide understanding and inference (Murphy & Medin, 1985). *Experience* is stored information collected in a bottom-up fashion from empirical observation. It is relatively unfashioned and may be represented by statistical summaries or memory traces themselves in the form of exemplars or cases.

Accounts of human reasoning can be characterized according to either Equation (1) or Equation (2) as well as by their particular instantiations of the variables. To be clear, an explanation of reasoning must specify:

1. How the available information x is represented
2. How the information x is related to computational tools F (and stored knowledge k)
3. How inferences y beyond the available information are generated

B. Kinds of Reasoning

Human reasoning is a well-trodden area, and there are many excellent reviews (e.g., Evans, Newstead, & Byrne, 1993; Rips, 1990). Rather than following the divisions authors have found convenient in the past, we have tried to select "cuts" through the conceptual space that build on earlier progress and offer new perspectives. Before presenting our framework, we briefly visit the traditional distinction between deductive and inductive forms of reasoning. In *deductive reasoning*, conclusions are entailed or follow directly from the application of logical forms to the premises. An additional usage of the term refers to a top-down direction of inferencing from abstractions to specific cases. Two corresponding meanings are linked to the notion of induction. *Inductive reasoning* refers to the generation of inferences that are not guaranteed within a formal system. These inferences are essentially guesses made probable by a set of evidence. Induction also refers to the bottom-up construction of high-level abstractions derived from observation of specific cases. This duality of meaning can lead to confusions in usage. Furthermore, the very issue of directionality between general and specific can become slippery. For example, consider the generalization of a concept (e.g., dog) to a novel instance "Spot." From the top-down, the abstract concept is used to interpret and make inferences about "Spot"—from the bottom-up, the concept representation is updated to reflect properties of the new member.

Rips (1990) presents an alternative general framework in his treatment of human reasoning. He structures his discussion around a contrast between what he terms the *strict* and *loose* views of reasoning. The strict view calls upon algorithmic processes involving the ordered application of abstract procedures to produce definitive conclusions. The loose view calls upon specific associations, stored instances, statistical summaries, and heuristics that generate continuous-valued predictions or best guesses. The strict–loose distinction concerns both the way in which processing occurs and the inferential products that result.

Equations (1) and (2) above suggest a related but slightly more precise way to differentiate among approaches to reasoning: the degree to which content or domain knowledge, the k component, is used in the reasoning process. Reasoning methods based on Equation (1) involve domain-general computational procedures applied to the available information to generate inferences. Reasoning methods based on Equation (2) rely on bringing to bear stored knowledge or experience of the world that can be used to draw inferences beyond the available data. In considering a related set of issues, Gentner and Medina (1998) made use of a distinction between strong and weak methods of reasoning originally proposed by Newell and Simon (1972). *Weak methods* are general strategies that can operate without special knowledge of a domain. Examples include methods such as means-ends analysis or an inference rule like modus ponens. *Strong methods* make intensive use of specific or abstract represented knowledge. Weak methods are valuable because of their generality; they provide a means of operating on novel or knowledge-poor domains. However, as Newell and Simon noted, strong methods are often superior when the appropriate knowledge is present. We will classify forms of reasoning such as logical deduction that fit Equation (1) as weak methods and forms of reasoning based on knowledge of a concept or stored analog consistent with Equation (2) as strong methods. Note that while the *process* of mapping a target to a base or classifying an instance as a category member may be domain-general, it is the role of specific knowledge content that makes these methods strong.

A second issue that follows from the weak–strong distinction is how the reasoning system connects to the rest of higher-order cognition. Traditionally, deductive reasoning is largely modularized in that there is a lack of explicit dependencies or interactions with other cognitive processes. Typically, other cognitive processes are referred to primarily in order to explain poor reasoning performance in terms of the input to or readout from the reasoning system. The phenomena to be accounted for are often considered to be a clearly circumscribed set of problems and puzzles (e.g., syllogisms) that seem to represent a fairly narrow slice of human reasoning phenomena. Reasoning is treated in a modularized fashion as a unique facet of cognitive function (though see Rips, 1994a, for an attempt to place rule-based deduction in a prominent role for general cognition). Strong methods of reasoning place a greater emphasis on the context of the rest of cognition. Relating reasoning to learning, memory, and knowledge organization leads to a view of inferential processes that can be consistent with, or even share, processes and representations underlying the acquisition, organization, and use of knowledge. Differences in reasoning performance with learning and development or across domains can be linked to conceptual change and variation in the amount, nature, and structure of the available knowledge. This perspective in some ways compliments a "constructive" view of cognition that blurs the distinctions between reasoning and processes, like perception and memory, which can be mediated by knowledge-based constraints and expectations.

There is another important source of variation among reasoning approaches that Rips (1990) captures effectively with the strict–loose distinction. Some methods of reasoning are more closely specified in procedural terms than others. Methods vary in the degree to which one could trace and justify the way in which a particular inference was reached. In a strict approach, the steps are precisely determined and formulated; the history of each computation and result effectively documents the reasoning process. In loose forms of reasoning, multiple kinds of processing are permitted, and the overall process can be difficult to trace because intermediate states are usually not represented explicitly. The computation may be distributed across many processing elements and may be probabilistic in nature—leaving little in the way of accountability. This dimension of *process specificity* cross-cuts to a degree the distinction we make between weak and strong methods of reasoning.

How do these different variations on reasoning fit together? Here are three general possibilities: (a) there are only weak methods or only strong methods of reasoning; (b) there are two separate systems; or (c) strong and weak methods can be fit within a unifying framework. The one-system view has two manifestations—the extreme positions of all-strong or all-weak reasoning. These may be the most difficult positions to defend because an entire proposed system of reasoning must be done away with. To dispense with strong reasoning methods requires explaining away the role of world knowledge and specific problem content in reasoning. To set aside weak reasoning methods involves disproving the use of explicit, content-blind processes. Rips (1990) points out that "if you take the position that there is only one relevant process, then your task is to specify the details of the process and to show how it is responsible for the different manifestations of reasoning" (p. 326). This risks broadening the descriptions to the point of vacuity.

In one version of the *separate systems view,* Sloman (1996) adopts a dichotomy much like that of Rips (1990), but takes the view that loose reasoning based on similarity and strict reasoning based on rules are two separate, and essentially competing, systems. One is associative and largely automatic while the other is logical and effortful. Sloman argues from cases of *simultaneous contradictory belief* that two separate systems operate independently to produce different solutions to the same problem at the same time. Another version of the separate systems view takes one set of methods to function as a backup in case of failure of the primary system. Rips (1995) notes the possibility that heuristics or probabilistic procedures may be called into play when logical deductions exceed some threshold of difficulty for the natural logic system. Rumelhart (1989) takes the view that the dominant system is reasoning by similarity instantiated as pattern matching in a parallel processing system. Formal reasoning is a special case for complex or novel problems. Rumelhart also points toward a possible unifying basis—formal reasoning may be derived from the internalization of sensorimotor interactions with external representations.

The third possible "big picture" of reasoning involves unifying strong and weak methods within a common framework. In explicating the strict–loose distinction, Rips (1990) pays particular attention to *special structure*. He argues that strict reasoning depends upon special components of representations, such as, "implies" and "or." Rips speculates that analogy (often considered a loose approach) may in fact be a matter of special structure because of the central importance assigned to certain higher-order relational structures (such as causality) in analogical processing (Gentner, 1983, 1989). In the framework we have presented, analogical processing stands out as well: it is a strong form of reasoning with high process specificity. This powerful combination leads us to consider a unifying perspective on reasoning that emphasizes the explanatory potential of structured comparison processes.

II. REASONING BY FORMAL SYSTEMS: WEAK METHODS

There is a substantial body of research on formal reasoning—what we describe as weak methods with highly specified processing functioning in a generally modularized reasoning system. The longest standing view of reasoning is essentially a syntactic view with an emphasis on explicit prescriptions for the lawful combination and transformation of propositions. This view has produced accounts of reasoning based on weak methods (e.g., natural logic) that specify the conclusions that follow from a set of premises without regard for the particular content of the represented information being operated upon.

A. Reasoning with Propositions: Basic Phenomena

Although the traditional domain of "deductive" reasoning includes phenomena involving quantificational and relational forms of deduction, we will concentrate on reasoning with propositions (statements using "not," "if," "and," and "or"). For example, consider the following conditional rule (from Evans et al., 1993):

If the ignition key is turned then the engine runs.

In the abstract case, this would be:

if p then q

What conclusions can be drawn from such a rule? Given this rule as a premise and an additional premise (p, q, not-p, or not-q) there are four classical types of inferences:

Valid
modus ponens	The key is turned; therefore the engine is running.
	(if p then q; p; therefore, q)
modus tollens	The engine is not running; therefore the key is not turned.
	(if p then q; not-q; therefore, not-p)

Invalid
denial of the antecedent	The key is not turned; therefore the engine is not running.
	(if p then q; not-p; therefore, not-q)
affirmation of the consequent	The engine is running; therefore the key is turned.
	(if p then q; q; therefore, p)

Evans et al. (1993) summarize behavioral studies of deductive performance on conditional rules. Adult participants are almost universally correct with modus ponens, but not with modus tollens (41–81%). Incorrect inference rates for denial of the antecedent and affirmation of the consequent are highly variable across studies (25–75%). This range might reflect differences in the materials used and the presentation of the task (such as whether or not forced choice).

Another important pattern of results stems from Watson's (1966) selection task involving an open-ended conditional syllogism. In the standard abstract form of the task (Wason & Johnson-Laird, 1972), participants see four cards that they are told have a letter on one side and a number on the other. A conditional statement is given, such as, "If there is an A on one side of the card, then there is a 3 on the other side." The values on the sides of the cards facing the participant include two that match the elements in the rule (A and 3) and two differing values (e.g., D and 7). Participants are told to turn over the necessary cards to test the rule. The rule is an instance of the classic conditional "if p then q," and the cards correspond to "p," "q," "not-p," and "not-q."

Although the logically correct response to this task is to turn over the A and 7 cards ("p" and "not-q"), only a minority of participants (6–33%) choose the correct two cards (Evans, 1982; Wason, 1968, 1969; Wason & Johnson-Laird, 1970). The majority of participants choose only the A (p) card or the A and D cards (p and q). This may be due to selection based on a match between the rule and the cards. When conditional statements contain negated antecedents and/or consequents, participants seem to ignore the negation and simply match their selections to the cards mentioned in the premises (Evans, 1989). Additionally, the potentially falsifying 7 ("not-*q*") is rarely selected. In a reduced array version (only *q* and not-*q* as choices) performance improves; possibly because participants' attention is directed to the need to test not-*q* (Johnson-Laird & Wason, 1970).

The question arises whether performance would be facilitated when the selection task is taken out of the abstract. Wason and Shapiro (1971) obtained 62% correct selection using a specific rule grounded in a thematic context ("Every time I go to Manchester, I go by car") and a set of cards representing various destinations and modes of transport. However, this result failed to replicate. In a different study, the rule involved an arbitrary relation between specific objects ("Every time I eat haddock, then I drink gin") and resulted in no facilitation relative to the low level of performance with the abstract, arbitrary conditions (Manktelow & Evans, 1979).

Rather than specificity, it might be that familiarity and prior experience are at the heart of these content effects. Griggs and Cox (1982) found strong facilitation using a highly familiar rule such as, "If a person is drinking beer, then the person must be over 19 years of age." This result has been replicated, but may require explicitly establishing a police officer scenario involving "looking for violators" (Griggs & Cox, 1982; Pollard & Evans, 1987). Improvement up to 81% correct was found using a postal rule ("If a letter is sealed, then it has a 50 lire stamp on it") along with a set of actual envelopes (sealed and unsealed, with a 50 lire or a 40 lire stamp) as materials; critically, the facilitation is dependent on participant familiarity with the rule (Cheng & Holyoak, 1985; Johnson-Laird, Legrenzi, & Legrenzi, 1972). These studies suggest that the source of facilitation is prior experience with the rule and counter-examples to the rule, but facilitation was also found by D'Andrade (cited in Evans et al., 1993) in a case where there is no direct real-world experience ("If a purchase exceeds $30 than the receipt must be approved by the departmental manager"). However, it is possible that participants in this study were able to generalize from personal experience of a highly similar nature. We return to the issue of transfer effects with the selection task later in our discussion.

With these basic findings in mind, we now move to consider the most influential attempts to account for the major patterns of correct versus fallacious reasoning: rule-based models (also called mental logic or natural logic) and the mental model theory of reasoning. Additionally, we will discuss a third class of theories known as the deontic reasoning models, including pragmatic reasoning schemas and social contract theories.

B. Rule-Based Theories

Although the focus and details vary somewhat across different rule-based theories (e.g., Braine, 1978; Braine & O'Brien, 1991; Osherson, 1975; Rips, 1983), there is a basic consensus. Rule-based accounts fit the framework of weak methods of reasoning represented by Equation (1), $y = F(x)$; where x is the available evidence, F

is the set of rules, and γ is the set of logical inferences. The rule-based account proposes that people possess explicit mental inference rules that operate on and transform propositions in working memory. These mental rules are similar, but not identical, to the deductive laws of formal systems of logic. The goal of rule theories of reasoning is to provide a psychological version of traditional logic that accounts for systematic patterns of successful and unsuccessful inferencing. Such a "natural logic" (Braine, 1978) is thus constrained by the demands of normative deductive steps as well as the vagaries of human performance.

1. Reasoning by Rules

Rule-based systems are characteristically discrete and syntactic. The assertions within a logical system are all-or-none, with no distinctions among degrees of validity or likelihood. This makes rule-based systems clear and consistent in their use and interpretation. Logical rule systems are weak methods of reasoning in that the processing is syntactic; blind to content. The rules specify the allowable ways in which information, *any* information, can be put together, related, and structured. The rules instantiate a mental logic with specifications of (a) the conditions under which they are applicable and (b) their entailments when brought to bear. For example, recall modus ponens, which is fundamental to every rule-based account:

$$\text{if A, then B}$$
$$\underline{\text{A}}$$
$$\text{therefore, B}$$

The rule applies universally without regard to the semantic reference of A and B. There are two key advantages to this domain-generality: (a) the reasoning procedure is performed objectively and reliably, and (b) the reasoning procedure is robust and can be applied to any situation.

Reasoning by rules has been applied most often to the realm of propositional logic. First, the premises are encoded to extract the underlying logical form. This translation taps into a predicate calculus language of propositions composed of symbols and connectives. As characterized by Rips (1994a), the premises are then stored in working memory. Second, the application of rules is coordinated by a reasoning program that searches for and produces appropriate inferences by constructing and linking steps in a mental proof. This chaining process may proceed forward or backward in a constrained way and may involve building assertion trees in working memory (Rips, 1983, 1994a). To limit working memory load, inferences are drawn only when needed for a direct answer to a problem or a subgoal to an answer. The set of deductive inferences comprises an implicit mental proof that validates the conclusions that are finally translated back into the content of the premises. Some accounts allow for a role of nonlogical processes (such as heuristic approaches or strong methods of reasoning) if logical processes fail to produce a straightforward conclusion (Braine, 1978; Rips, 1995).

2. Support for Rule-Based Theories

E. E. Smith, Langston, and Nisbett (1992) propose a set of criteria by which to specify and evaluate rule-based accounts. The authors emphasize that the criteria should distinguish between reasoning performance that is rule-governed versus that which is rule-described. Rules are often convenient ways to characterize a general pattern of performance or processing steps. Rule-based theories require that the rules are explicitly represented and activated during processing; that they be the causal force in the reasoning process. We focus here on two key predictions from the E. E. Smith et al. (1992) framework. In accord with the content-blind, universal quality of formal logical rules, rule-driven reasoning should exhibit no variation in performance due to the degree of familiarity or level of abstraction of the information. Second, following from the process-level description of rule-driven reasoning, the quality and ease of performance should be predicted by the number of rules required in the implicit deductive proof. In addition, some rules may be more easily retrieved than others (Rips, 1983).

Marcus and Rips (1979) found that participants confirm the validity of modus ponens arguments regardless of the content of the problems. Furthermore, most participants perform logically on modus ponens problems across levels of abstractness (Evans, 1977) and familiarity of items (Byrne, 1991). However, these findings do *not* extend reliably beyond modus ponens. Rule-based theories have received some support for predictions involving perceived difficulty. Problems are rated as more difficult when more applications of a rule are needed to formulate a proof (Braine, Reiser, & Rumain, 1984; Rips, 1983, 1989). Greater variety of rules and greater complexity of rules may likewise increase difficulty. Rips (1994a) reports longer reaction times for participants to evaluate conclusions for two-rule arguments than one-rule arguments. On higher-level deduction problems (so-called knight–knave puzzles), larger-step problems took longer to solve than did smaller-step problems (Rips, 1989).

Rule theories must also be evaluated according to their account of reasoning failures. Errors can occur if a logical rule does not exist, if there is a failure to apply rules appropriately, or if the complexity of the task exceeds processing or capacity limitations (Rips, 1995). The actual circumstances of such failures are not well-specified, although limits on working memory and problems with the control mechanism responsible for applying the rules are potential contributing factors. Several researchers have attempted to argue that "actual reasoning" is logical, but errors may arise in the initial comprehension/encoding stage or in the final translation stage (Braine & O'Brien, 1991; Henle, 1962; Marcus & Rips, 1979; Rumain, Connell, & Braine, 1983). There is some evidence that comprehension errors may occur separately from the reasoning process per se (see Braine & O'Brien, 1991; Evans et al., 1993; Henle, 1962; Rumain et al., 1983). For example, the term *if* might be interpreted as a biconditional, as opposed to a conditional due to an everyday usage of the English word *if* that is compatible with Gricean maxims of informativity and relevance (Rips, 1988). Logical reasoning may also be hampered at the outset if people are not encoding the logically pertinent aspects of the input. Researchers have posited that an availability bias (Pollard, 1982) or relevance heuristic (Evans, 1989) may lead people to focus on the salience of certain features and associated memories that can lead them astray.

Even if reasoning proceeds logically from encoding through the application of inference procedures, participants may still fall prey to errors in the statement or interpretation of conclusions. The most common of these errors is the belief bias (Evans, 1989; Evans, Barston, & Pollard, 1983; Henle, 1962). Belief bias occurs when participants evaluate the validity of an argument based on whether the conclusion is compatible with prior beliefs, rather than on logical entailment. Because the effects of belief bias are more pronounced with arguments that are not deducible, Rips (1995) suggests that this may be a strategy that participants use when they are unable to find a proof. In addition, participants may misinterpret their task as one of evaluating confidence in a conclusion, rather than evaluating strict entailment.

3. Learning and Transfer of Rules

Where do the rules of natural logic come from? Rips (1994a) argues for innateness of basic logical abilities. He notes, however, that innateness does not necessitate perfection in application of rules, nor does it preclude the possibility of learning and improvement. E. E. Smith et al.'s (1992) criteria for rule-based accounts include two that are particularly relevant to learning and transfer: (a) successive uses of the same rule should show priming effects or positive transfer, and (b) performance should improve with training on relevant rules. E. E. Smith et al. (1992) found more correct tests (using the Wason paradigm) of a permission rule following another permission rule than following an obligation rule. However, the transfer may have been due to shared surface similarities in the problem, which only helped when the rules were of the same type. Johnson-Laird et al. (1972) collected think-aloud protocols in a study of transfer in the selection task and found that only 2 of 24 participants recognized the underlying similarity between specific and abstract problems. This evidence contradicts the rule priming prediction as well as the general claim that the level of abstraction of problem content should not matter.

There are mixed results on the issue of training. In one study, extensive training on propositional logic rules (including modus tollens) failed to improve performance on the Wason selection task (Cheng, Holyoak, Nisbett, & Oliver, 1986). A semester course in logic was equally ineffective. However, others (e.g., Fong, Krantz, & Nisbett, 1986) have found that abstract rule training, such as a course in statistics, did improve reasoning on problems involving the Law of Large Numbers (that larger samples are more representative of a population). Hoch and Tschirgi (1985; described in Evans, 1989) also report that master's students perform better on this task than do bachelor's students.

4. Criticisms of the Rule-Based Account

Although the rule-based view is appealing and advantageous in some ways, the basic tenets of the view have been strongly challenged. General objections to rule-based theories include the observations that people make invalid inferences and that errors do not tend to be the trivial, irrelevant, or useless inferences that syntactic logic might predict (Johnson-Laird, Byrne, & Schaeken, 1992). Along these lines, Rips (1994a) incorporates goals and subgoals to constrain rule-driven inferencing. The very idea that deductive reasoning is a matter of syntactic rule application has been questioned by researchers led by Johnson-Laird (1983), who suggest an alternative approach based on the notion of mental models. Evidence shows that it is not always the case that a greater number of rules leads to a more difficult problem—for example, modus tollens is easier from a biconditional than a conditional (Johnson-Laird & Byrne, 1991; Johnson-Laird et al., 1992; Johnson-Laird, Byrne, & Schaeken, 1994).

The syntactic, content-blind character of logical rules as a weak method of reasoning has been challenged by researchers (including Cheng & Holyoak, 1985) in response to a number of findings of content effects in reasoning behavior. People perform quite poorly on the abstract version of the Wason selection task (Wason & Johnson-Laird, 1972) described above. The facilitatory effects of content on this task and the lack of transfer from content to abstract problems are not effectively explained. Furthermore, the matching bias (matching the terms of the conclusion to the terms of the premises) only occurs with abstract or arbitrary materials, not content problems (Evans, 1992; Griggs & Cox, 1983; Manktelow & Evans, 1979; Reich & Ruth, 1982). Rips (1990, 1995) suggests that content effects may be at least partially accounted for by the use of modal and deontic logics (containing operators such as PERMISSIBLE, OBLIGATORY), as well as nonlogical operations, availability effects, and analogical reasoning.

The "flawed comprehension stage" explanations of errors have inspired a number of criticisms. Johnson-Laird (1983) notes that this comprehension component remains underspecified, and as such, may be a buffer against potentially falsifying results. Further, if prior knowledge interferes with correct abstract encoding, then people should do better on abstract tasks than content-specific tasks—but clearly they do not. Lastly, positing a faulty comprehension stage does not lessen the need to prove that people reason by natural logic (for instance, Evans, 1989, describes a heuristic-analytic model where faulty encoding is followed by manipulations of mental models). Such a criticism may also be applied to the "flawed end processes" explanation of errors. If knowledge effects (e.g., belief bias) alter performance even at the end stage of reasoning, then content-free abstract rules seem less plausible (Evans et al., 1993).

C. Reasoning by Mental Models

We begin this section with a brief clarification: the term *mental models* has been used in different ways. The mental models approach to deductive reasoning of Johnson-

Laird (1983) and his colleagues should be distinguished from the use of mental models for reasoning in knowledge-rich domains (Gentner & Stevens, 1983). The latter version focuses on the representation and application of long-term beliefs about domains and devices. Although the two theories share some similarities, they differ in their representational and processing assumptions as well as in the core phenomena they aim to explain. In this section the term *mental models* will refer to the kinds of *analog* mental models described by Johnson-Laird and his colleagues; in cases where we contrast the two kinds of mental models, we will use the terms *analog mental models* and *causal mental models* for the sake of clarity.

1. Reasoning by Models

According to the mental models theory of reasoning (Johnson-Laird, 1983; Johnson-Laird & Byrne, 1991; Johnson-Laird et al., 1994), human reasoning is more concerned with the truth conditions in the world (semantics) than about logical form (syntax). The argument is that people do not reason using abstract rules, but rather they construct and combine mental models and generate inferences consistent with those models. The models are based on the given premises and on general semantic knowledge including the meaning of quantifiers and connectives. Models consist of symbolic tokens that represent the properties of entities and preserve the relations between entities. These models are essentially envisioned situations representing the truth conditions of propositions, but they are not assumed to take on any particular subjective form (perceptual, propositional, etc.); rather, it is the structure of the models that is important.

Mental model theory was originally formulated to explain syllogistic reasoning, but it has been extended fairly broadly. The reasoning process begins with the formation of models representing situations based on the premises. Consider the following deduction (from Johnson-Laird et al., 1994):

> Either there is a student or a professor in the room.
> Actually, there is no professor in the room.
> Therefore, there is a student in the room.

The initial model structure of the premises might be represented as:

where *s* refers to a situation involving a student in the room, and *p* refers to a situation involving a professor in the room. Each separate row represents a separate model to indicate that either one or the other condition is true in the world. When one model is ruled out in the second statement, then the other model can be used as the basis for a valid conclusion.

For more complex situations with heavy demands on working memory and for reasoning with conditionals, possible models may be represented implicitly by a "mental footnote." These footnotes constrain the content of alternate models if they need to be made explicit. As an example of explicit and implicit models, consider the conditional, "If there is an A on the board, then there is a 2 on the board" (from Johnson-Laird et al., 1994). One may need to represent only the premises in an explicit model:

$$[A] \quad 2$$
$$\ldots$$

The ellipses represent other implicit possibilities, such as the possible existence of a model of the world that contains only a 2. The brackets represent noting that any further models must not contain an A because A is exhaustively represented in the first model.

Once the explicit mental models are formed, they are then combined with one another to form the most parsimonious description of possible situations in the world. This revision process to reduce redundancy and eliminate inconsistencies is carried out according to a program of *procedural* rules. Mental model theorists emphasize that these rules are not the same as abstract, deductive rules. Instead, these rules serve to translate verbal propositions to a spatial or symbolic array representation. After the explicit models have been formed and combined, conclusions can be formulated based on what holds true in the models. Useful conclusions may arise featuring information not explicitly stated in the premises. However, a conclusion is not accepted until a search for alternative models has been carried out. The specifics of this search mechanism remain sketchy (see Johnson-Laird, 1989, for a possibility). If no alternative model is found, then the conclusion is accepted as valid. Conversely, discovering an alternative means returning to the process of formulating a conclusion based on the updated models.

The criteria for evaluating the mental model theory are similar to those put forth for rule-based theories. In particular, mental model theory needs to be able to account for situations in which people reason correctly or make mistakes. It should also explain the pattern of those mistakes, as well as the existence of content effects and biases, and the determinants of difficulty and reaction time in solving problems. The mental model account posits that people are generally logical, but may fail to validate conclusions using alternate models or may construct models poorly (that is, they fail to flesh them out when required). Errors that occur should not be random, but rather should match incomplete models. People should make more errors, and take longer to solve problems that require the construction of more explicit models (since each must be checked for inconsistencies with the others). Such measures should also correlate with the complexity of the models required, which requires more working memory load and a longer processing time as well. In the Wason task, mental model theory predicts that reasoners will only consider those cards that are represented in their explicit models, and will choose only those cards whose hidden sides appear relevant to establishing the truth or falsity of the rule (Evans et al., 1993). Hence, the logically correct falsifying card will only be chosen when models have been fleshed out to include that card; some content domains will facilitate this process more than others.

2. Support for the Mental Model Theory of Reasoning

Evidence that people can reason across levels of abstractness and familiarity (Byrne, 1991; Evans, 1977; Marcus & Rips, 1979) can be taken as support for both rule-based and mental model theories. The use of mental models is quite general, in that it only requires a knowledge of the connective or quantificational terms present in the premises and conclusions. Yet it is purported to account for specific knowledge effects as well. The mental model account is consistent with reports of matching bias, if as claimed, negative premises tend to elicit representations of corresponding positive situations (Evans et al., 1993). Likewise, the facilitative versions of the Wason task may be describable as facilitating explicit representations of negative instances. This explanation is most convincing when applied to particular manipulations, such as the reduced-array task and facilitative versions with explicit "look for violators" instructions (Griggs & Cox, 1982; Johnson-Laird & Wason, 1970; Pollard & Evans, 1987). Evans (1989) concludes that the belief bias is a result of "selective scrutiny"; hence, one could imagine that certain versions of both rule-based and mental model theories could accommodate it.

There is some evidence that problems are rated as more difficult when a greater number of models is required (Johnson-Laird et al., 1992). Difficulty is also linked to the complexity of the initial model (Johnson-Laird & Byrne, 1989). Bauer and Johnson-Laird (1993) report that a diagrammatic format of premises (that makes alternate possibilities more explicit) leads to faster and more valid conclusions than does a verbal format of premises. In the domain of discourse, participants remembered passages of text that called for a single model of a spatial layout more easily than those that were consistent with more than one model (Johnson-Laird, 1989). Additionally, participants' errors on discourse memory have been found to be consistent with the formation of mental models of described situations (Bransford, Barclay, & Franks, 1972).

The predictions of the mental model theory at times seem difficult to distinguish from those of the rule-based theories. However, the mental models theory, but not the rule-based theory, can explain certain findings—such as the fact that modus tollens problems are easier to solve in biconditional than in conditional form, and the greater difficulty of inferences based on exclusive, rather than inclusive, disjunction (Bauer & Johnson-Laird, 1993; Evans et al., 1993; Johnson-Laird & Byrne, 1991; Johnson-Laird et al., 1994). Likewise, the observation that people will suppress both invalid and valid inferences when encouraged to think about alternate causes of a consequent can be seen to support mental model theory, but not the rule-based theory (Byrne, 1989; Johnson-Laird & Byrne, 1991).

3. Learning and Transfer with Mental Models

Mental models can indeed be taught, according to Johnson-Laird (1989). He points to studies of representation of beliefs about natural phenomena (Forbus, 1983; Gentner & Gentner, 1983; Kempton, 1986; McClosky, Caramazza, & Green, 1980) to imply that a novice-to-expert shift involves mental models. However, as noted earlier, Johnson-Laird's theory of reasoning by mental models is not interchangeable with the mental model theories under consideration in the research cited above. The different mental models theories—while not completely unrelated—make different assumptions about representation, use distinct notational systems, and make use of different expectations about the role of world knowledge in models. Nonetheless, the mental models theory of reasoning leaves room for learning and improvement. For example, Bauer and Johnson-Laird (1993) note that diagrams may help people reason because they make alternate possibilities explicit.

On the issue of development, Johnson-Laird and Byrne (1991) posit that what is innate is a capacity to build mental models of the world and search for alternative models. Linguistic abilities, the capacity of working memory, and metacognition develop through learning and maturation. The authors cite evidence that syllogistic reasoning is hampered in 7-year-olds by a lack of understanding of quantificational terms, and that somewhat older children can reason with one, but not with multiple models (Inhelder & Piaget, 1964, described in Johnson-Laird & Byrne, 1991; Johnson-Laird, Oakhill, & Bull, 1986). Rips (1994a), however, counters that basic logical operations (such as "and") could hardly be learned if one did not already possess some kind of understanding of what "and" entails.

4. Criticisms of the Mental Model Account

Studies have not always upheld the mental model prediction that difficulty is related to the number of explicit models needed (Byrne & Handley, 1992; Rips, 1990). Worse, it is not always clear how to count models in a consistent way (e.g., Bonatti, 1994). Much of the time, predictions about difficulty really do not distinguish between the mental model and rule-based theories. There have also been reported cases where the number of models needed would be intractable, but people avoid fallacies and draw inferences (O'Brien, Braine, & Yang, 1994).

Many of the criticisms of mental model theory relate either to its lack of specificity or to the possibility that procedures for manipulating models are essentially rule-based and syntactic at heart. On the first point, critics have argued that the mechanisms for comparing and falsifying models are left unspecified (Polk, 1993; Rips, 1994b). The theory is similarly vague about how people retrieve counterexamples and at what point they flesh out their models. Another area of difficulty is the nature of the representations used. In contrast to causal mental models (e.g., Gentner & Stevens, 1983; Halford, 1993; Kempton, Boster, & Hartley, 1994; Kieras & Bovair, 1984; McCloskey, 1983; Miyake, 1986; Schwartz & Black, 1996; B. Tversky, 1991), which use explicit representational conventions derived from predicate calculus or from qualitative reasoning to represent beliefs, mental models in the deductive reasoning tradition rely largely on an intuitive set of spatial conventions. For example, the statement "there is a tiger and there is an ox" would be notated in the same way as the statement "the tiger is on the left of the ox" or even "the tiger is hungrier than the ox:"

T	O

This representational indeterminacy means that much of the interpretation is external to the actual model: there must be distinct processes not reflected in the model representation to deal with different logical interpretations of the same surface form. In essence, the mental models theory has been accused of making assumptions that are not represented in the models themselves. Johnson-Laird and his colleagues have responded to these charges (Johnson-Laird & Byrne, 1990, 1991, 1993), noting that all representation models require interpretation. Nonetheless, the representational indeterminacy makes it difficult to connect these analog mental models with long-term belief systems (in which "left of" and "hungrier than" are distinct relations). In response researchers in the analog mental models tradition can maintain that their interest is in on-line processing, not in long-term storage. Finally, the question arises how implicit models can be unconscious yet in working memory (Braine & O'Brien, 1991; Rips, 1989). Johnson-Larid and Byrne (1993) counter that reasoning processes should not be expected to be fully introspectible. Holyoak and Spellman (1993) argue that the very notion of an implicit model is at odds with the "vivid" quality of mental models.

Critics have also asserted that mental models are essentially rule-based. Johnson-Laird and his colleagues claim that procedural rules for manipulating models are not abstract inference rules. But routines for manipulating models can be seen as abstract rules (Braine, 1993; Rips, 1988, 1990), as, for example, they must be general enough to recognize identity between any two tokens connected by " = ." Rips (1994b) points out that mental model representations of some entailments are isomorphic to natural logical propositions and can be manipulated to the same effect. The two camps have also clashed on the issue of whether mental models are really semantically privileged (see Johnson-Laird, 1989; Rips, 1994b). Lastly, Rips (1994a) has issued a challenge for mental model theorists to demonstrate their usefulness and predictive power over and above that of rule-based theories, as (he argues) mental model accounts fare no better than rule-based accounts on the issues of learnability and the use of world knowledge.

D. Pragmatic Reasoning Schemas

The theory of pragmatic reasoning schemas (PRS) (Cheng & Holyoak, 1985, 1989; Holyoak & Cheng, 1995) draws on many of the same assumptions as *causal* mental models—including structured representations and complex inferential processes that operate over them. The theory arose in response to growing interest in content effects in the Wason selection task and has been tested almost exclusively within this paradigm. According to the PRS approach, content effects in deductive reasoning reflect the centrality of goals and knowledge structures. People do not reason with content-free syntactic rules, nor with analog mental models, when faced with realistic situations; rather, they access and apply certain generalized sets of procedures that are organized by classes of goals. PRS are abstract rule sets induced by prior experience. Unlike purely syntactic rules, PRS are context-sensitive and may be extended to interpret both logical (e.g., "if–then") and nonlogical terms (e.g., "predict").

1. Reasoning by Pragmatic Reasoning Schemas

Although PRS include knowledge structures evoked by "obligations," "causations," "precautions," and others, the prototypical and most frequently studied PRS is that of "permissions." The Drinking Age problem described above ("If a person is drinking beer, then the person must be over 19 years of age") is an example of a permission schema. Permission schemas contain a core of four abstract rules (Cheng & Holyoak, 1985):

> Rule 1: If an action is to be taken, then the precondition must be satisfied.
> Rule 2: If the action is not to be taken, then the precondition need not be satisfied.
> Rule 3: If the precondition is satisfied, then the action may be taken.
> Rule 4: If the precondition is not satisfied, then the action must not be taken.

These rules become available when a permission schema is evoked by the context of a problem or situation. Once evoked, such rules lead to inferences that facilitate performance on schema-relevant forms of the Wason task (such as the Drinking Age problem). Facilitation is likely because Rules 2 and 3 above prevent certain fallacies (denial of the antecedent, affirmation of the consequent) that tend to occur with abstract and arbitrary versions of the Wason task. Note, however, that facilitation is not a foregone conclusion: logically correct performance depends on which schema is evoked (if one is evoked at all). Schemas are cued when the purpose of a rule statement becomes recognized. Specifically, permission–obligation schemas apply to rules with a social purpose imposed by authority.

The PRS view claims to account for the pattern of content effects observed in the Wason task. Familiar contexts (e.g., the Postal rule for people in countries with such a rule) are the most strongly facilitative because of past specific experience with such rules. However, performance with unfamiliar, but realistic, rules may still be facilitated—the appropriate schema is likely to be recognizable as a general type even though the specific rule has never been encountered. For example, the Sears problem ("If a purchase exceeds $30 then the receipt must be approved by the departmental manager") is not likely to be specifically present in memory, nor is it particularly likely to cue counterexamples as some researchers have suggested as a possible explanation (Griggs & Cox, 1982; Manktelow & Evans, 1979; Reich & Ruth, 1982). Rather, the Sears problem evokes a general permission schema that may be familiar to many people. Arbitrary or abstract problems (e.g., the haddock/gin rule, the original Wason task) do not evoke a schema and thus produce few logically correct responses. There is evidence that in the face of many abstract problems, participants may resort to nonlogical strategies, such as matching the form of the conclusion to that of the premises (Manktelow & Evans, 1979; Reich & Ruth, 1982). Indeed, we have noted above that the matching bias occurs with abstract problems, but is quite unlikely to occur in problems with realistic content.

The PRS approach does not account for those occasions when participants reason logically on abstract problems. PRS theorists acknowledge that syntactic knowledge structures exist, but assert that the pragmatic level takes priority in reasoning (Cheng & Holyoak, 1985). Presumably, PRS would also take precedence over any domain-independent analog mental model procedures—though little is said on this point.

2. Support for Pragmatic Reasoning Schemas

Cheng and Holyoak (1985) attempted to facilitate performance on a conditional reasoning task by providing a rationale for problems that might otherwise appear arbitrary. They used a variant of the Postal rule ("If an envelope is sealed, then it must have a 20 cent stamp") and what they termed the Cholera rule ("If a passenger's form says 'Entering' on one side, then the other side must include 'cholera' "). They also varied the familiarity of the problem content by using two populations of participants—one of which was familiar with such postal rules. Both rules were presented with context (e.g., "You are a postal clerk working in a foreign country . . .") and either with or without a rationale (e.g., "The rationale for this regulation is to increase profit from personal mail, which is nearly always sealed . . .").

The pattern of results confirmed predictions: the rationale versions were highly facilitatory for both populations of participants, while the no-rationale version of the Postal rule was facilitatory only for participants familiar with the rule. Thus, in the absence of specific experience with a domain, the presence of schema-evoking context resulted in a higher percentage (about 88%) of correct responses than did the exact problem without such context (about 60%). More striking were the results of a permission problem given an abstract form ("If one is to take action 'A' then one must first satisfy precondition 'P' "). While 61% of participants correctly solved the permission problem, only 19% solved a modified version of the letters and numbers Wason task that presumably did not evoke a permission schema (Cheng & Holyoak, 1985; see also Jackson & Griggs, 1990).

Instructions to check for "violations" of a rule were found to be more facilitatory than instructions to determine truth or falsity of a rule—but only for those problems with some meaningful content (Griggs, 1983; Yachanin, 1986). Thus, highlighting potential violations may make permission–obligation schemas easier to evoke in realistic problems. However, the impact of PRS goes beyond mere violation checking. Cheng and Holyoak (1985) found that when participants were asked to rephrase rules (from "only-if" to "if-then", or vice versa), they were more likely to insert a model (e.g., "can," "must") for permission statements than arbitrary statements. This task was linguistic in nature and involved accessing declarative knowledge. Lastly, due to the semantic nature of PRS rules, this approach can account for differences in acceptability between contrapositives (switching p and q: "If not everyone will die, then the bomb does not explode"). The rule-based approach must appeal to interference from pragmatic knowledge to account for this result.

3. Learning and Transfer of Pragmatic Reasoning Schema

As for causal mental models in general, PRS theorists claim that these knowledge structures are acquired through ordinary life experiences. Indeed, performance on selection tasks with realistic content increases systematically between 10 and 18 years of age (Girotto, Light, & Colbourn, 1988; Overton, Ward, Noveck, Black, & O'Brien, 1987; Ward & Overton, 1990). Six- and seven-year olds can perform respectably on a reduced array (binary) permission version, and 10–11-year-olds and 14–15-year-olds show high facilitation for a full (4-card) permission version (Girotto, Gilly, Blaye, & Light, 1989). Cheng and Holyoak (1985) found that training adults on formal rules was ineffectual, but training on the nature of obligations facilitated performance on conditional rules that could be seen as evoking an obligation schema (but also see Fong et al., 1986).

The transfer performance seen on the Wason task (from content problem to content problem and abstract problem to abstract problem, but usually not from one problem type to the other) has implications for PRS and rule-based theories. As noted earlier, Cox and Griggs (1982) found that an unfamiliar rule, "If a person is wearing blue, then the person must be over 19," is facilitatory only when presented after the Drinking Age problem. The Clothing Age rule is not in itself a clear permission rule—it may be interpreted as simple co-occurrence, which would not facilitate reasoning performance. However, when the Clothing Age problem is presented after the Drinking Age problem, participants may reason by analogy to the earlier problem and thus interpret the second problem in terms of permission.

4. Criticisms of the Pragmatic Reasoning Schemas Account

As mentioned earlier, the PRS view cannot account for above-chance performance on abstract tasks (Evans, 1991). Furthermore, it has been argued that permission rules are reducible to logical rules (Rips, 1988). However, such a stance becomes difficult to defend in light of findings that (a) realistic content improves reasoning performance—so much so that children perform better with permission versions than adults do with abstract versions; (b) participants rephrase PRS and abstract versions of rules differently; (c) differences in acceptability occur for different phrasings with the same logical syntactic form; and (d) and PRS training and formal logical training lead to different levels of improvement on the selection task. PRS adherents emphasize that although PRS are indeed made up of abstract procedural rules of propositional form, these rules are context-sensitive in nature. Critics have also argued that the PRS account is insufficiently specified (Oaksford & Chater, 1993) and that PRS are not the only ways that knowledge can be organized and applied (Johnson-Laird & Byrne, 1991). Manktelow and Over (1991) suggest that a more likely division between facilitative and nonfacilitative content might be between deontic (if-may/must) and indicative (if-then) conditionals. Almor and Sloman (1996) assert that even nondeontic contexts that evoke "clear expectations" can be facilitatory. Rips (1990) has noted that modal logics already have terms with which to handle these types of problems (the operators PERMISSABLE and OBLIGATORY).

Another line of criticism centers around a possible confound in Cheng and Holyoak's design (Cosmides, 1989; Griggs & Cox, 1982; Jackson & Griggs, 1990). Although the PRS rule contained explicit negatives for not-p and not-q (e.g., "has not taken action 'A' "), the original Wason task contained only implicit negatives. This is potentially a serious confound since Evans et al. (1983) have shown that explicit negatives facilitate logical performance and reduce matching bias. Jackson and Griggs (1990) found that facilitation on abstract permission and obligation rules disappeared when implicit negatives were used (though the use of explicit negatives did not facilitate performance on the arbitrary rules). However, this criticism overlooks the fact that Cheng and Holyoak (1985) adapted the arbitrary Wason rule to fit the explicit logical form of their permission rule.

In sum, PRS occupy a middle ground between the storage of specific content knowledge and content-free abstractions. Although they are triggered by context, the reasoning rules themselves are abstract and propositional in nature. They are brought about by general learning processes that may be the same as those underlying the acquisition of categories and general memory schemas, but PRS rules are restricted in application to certain deontic contexts. PRS rules have been presented as an endpoint—no account has been offered of how learning could proceed beyond the schemas toward content-free abstractions.

E. Social Contract Theory

The social contract theory (SCT) (Cosmides, 1989) was developed as an alternative to the PRS account of content effects in reasoning. According to Cosmides (1989), other theories fall short because they appeal to content-independent processes to explain content-dependent behavior (even the PRS theory posits that content-independent processes of induction are used to include content-specific schemas). In contrast, the SCT proposes a content-specific module that is specially adapted for reasoning about social contract problems (that is, those dealing with cooperation between two parties for mutual benefit). The idea is that SC schemas came about evolutionarily due to adaptation pressures resulting from living in social groups. Human beings innately possess mechanisms and procedures that exist specifically to reason about SCs and to detect cheaters—to ensure that no benefits are taken without the appropriate costs. Because SC reasoning is modular and innate, improvements due to learning and development are difficult to reconcile.

When triggered by appropriate content, these specialized mechanisms function by calling up procedural knowledge that leads to content-appropriate inferences. As with PRS, SC schemas generate inferences that may or may not be consistent with logic. According to Cosmides (1989), the problem contents that are consistently facilitatory are those that invoke the cost-benefit structure of social contracts. Such content would induce the reasoner to look for the "cost not paid" and the "benefit accepted" cards in order to investigate potential cheaters. When these cards are the same as the logically correct cards ("p" and "not-q"), performance will be facilitated. Proponents of SCT argue that SC rules are not reducible to logical rules. They further argue that PRS owe their facilitatory effects to the presence, stated or implied, of cost-benefit structure. SC reasoning is not simple memory cuing because it occurs with unfamiliar problems that have cost-benefit structure.

Cosmides (1989) manipulated familiarity and context in four experiments to pit the SCT against rule-based and availability (memory cuing) theories. SC rules (in the form of "If you take the benefit (p) then you pay the cost (q)") were contrasted with switched SC rules (in the form of "If you pay the cost (p) then you take the benefit (q)"). For SC rules, the cards corresponding to p and not-q were both relevant to cheater detection and logically correct. However, for switched SC rules, the cards corresponding to not-p and q were relevant for cheater detection, but logically incorrect. Rules were presented in the context of rather lengthy stories that varied in terms of familiarity and cost-benefit structure (SC/switched SC/non-SC). Cosmides found high facilitation for unfamiliar SC problems, but little facilitation for unfamiliar non-SC problems—ruling out pure memory cuing hypotheses and contrary to predictions of rule-based views. Additional experiments (Cosmides, 1989) pitted the SCT against the PRS theory. An SC rule was tested along with a non-SC permission rule with a social purpose (that is, the rule had the action-precondition representation, but no cost-benefit structure). SC responses were about twice as frequent for the SC rules than for the non-SC permission rules—suggesting a privileged status for reasoning about social contracts. It was concluded that facilitation on permission rules in past experiments occurred because the permission rules' context led them to be interpreted as social contracts.

In the selection task, participants performed better with instructions to look for "violators," which encourages a search for cheaters (Gigerenzer & Hug, 1992; Griggs, 1983; Yachanin & Tweney, 1982). Further, the Clothing Age rule discussed above was not facilitatory unless it was presented after the Drinking Age rule. Proponents of SCT have taken this to mean that the cost-benefit structure of the second rule was made apparent by comparison to the first. Lastly, for rules such as "If an employee gets a pension, then that employee must have worked for the firm for at least 10 years," participants turned over different cards depending on whether they took the perspective of the employer or the employee—this corresponds to the predictions of SCT, but not formal logic or PRS (Gigerenzer & Hug, 1992; Manktelow & Over, 1991; Politzer & Nguyen-Xuan, 1992).

Despite this evidence, the SCT account faces a number of serious criticisms. Evans et al. (1993) point out that even though non-SC permission rules led to less facilitation than SC rules (Cosmides, 1989; Gigerenzer & Hug, 1992); non-SC rules still led to a much higher percentage of correct choices than in a standard abstract Wason task. Thus, SCT does not provide a full account. A major point of debate is Cosmides's classification of some PRS problems as SCs. As Cheng and Holyoak (1989) point out, Cosmides (1989) wavers between a definition of a social contract as an exchange situation where a cost must be paid and one where a requirement must be met. By this latter criteria, permission rules are somewhat questionably reclassified as SCs. For example, Cosmides classifies the Drinking Age problem as an SC, though attaining a certain age cannot easily be seen as paying a cost to an individual or group. In the Cholera problem (inoculation for protection against disease) and other examples, the rule is more of a conditional obligation than a paid cost. These cases facilitate performance reliably (Cheng & Holyoak, 1985; Evans, 1982; Griggs & Cox, 1982), but are not convincing as SCs. Manktelow and Over (1990) found facilitation for PRS rules that are clearly not SC rules such as, "If you clean up spilt blood, then you must wear rubber gloves." Such a rule does not, in any sense, imply a cost-benefit exchange or opportunity for cheater detection. Cheng and Holyoak (1989) claim that even Cosmides's own examples (such as "If a man eats cassava root, then he must have a tattoo on his face") may be more comfortably classified as permission rules than cost-benefit exchanges. Cosmides and Tooby (1992) counter that the "benefit" and "cost" terms do not presuppose the values that the parties in the exchange assign to the terms.

III. REASONING BY SIMILARITY: STRONG METHODS

A sizable share of the reasoning situations that people encounter do not seem to be resolved by formal abstract procedures, but instead by strong methods that rely heavily on content knowledge to support predictive inferences (Rumelhart, 1989). Such methods are characterized by Equation (2) in which the knowledge component k plays a critical role in the flow from evidence to inferences. The evidence is often assumed to be represented in terms of the presence or absence of features or values along dimensions (but see section IV.A for an alternative assumption that the evidence is represented structurally). Categorization and statistical likelihood estimation are examples of mechanisms that operate over stored knowledge or experience.

Similarity is frequently posited as the key psychological construct underlying strong methods (e.g., Sloman, 1996). Hahn and Chater (1998) suggest that similarity-based reasoning can be distinguished from rule-based reasoning by its use of *partial matches*. Although situations vary in the extent to which they match a stored example or category, there is no way to partially trigger a rule. Strong methods gain power and flexibility by relying on best matches rather than perfect matches. But as the quality of the match varies, so might the quality of the resulting inference. Weak forms of reasoning have a high threshold for activation (e.g., matching a rule to the evidence), but the logical validity of the resulting inference is guaranteed.

We focus our discussion of strong methods on a subset of knowledge-driven approaches, including (a) reasoning driven by the use of category representations, (b) reasoning driven by computations over data (i.e., statistical and connectionist approaches), and (c) reasoning as a set of heuristics and biases. In section IV, we focus on the strong method of reasoning by analogy and consider wider implications of comparison processes.

A. Reasoning by Categorization

Categorization itself can be thought of as a reasoning process in which the category assignment is the conclusion and the featural evidence serves as premises (Holland, Holyoak, Nisbett, & Thagard, 1986) or in which the properties of an instance count as evidence to be explained by a theory-based category (Murphy & Medin, 1985). However, we focus in this section on the property-level inferences that can be made by assigning instances to categories. Once category membership has been established, the knowledge stored in the category representation becomes a resource for generating inferences about the new member.

This inductive potential varies with the nature of the category representation. The number, kind, and validity of candidate inferences depend on how categories are structured (see Medin & Heit, Chapter 3, this volume, for detailed discussion of the various accounts). Some theorists posit that categories consist of sets of defining criteria. An alternative representational assumption is that categories are structured by prototypes that store information about the central tendency across members. In this case, the candidate inferences are based on which features are likely to be present or what values the dimensions tend toward; but these are reasonable guesses with no guarantee of validity. A third view is that category representation is exemplar-based; membership is determined by similarity to one or more specific exemplars. In this case, properties of particular exemplars are candidate inferences. A more recent viewpoint considers categories to be intuitive theories made up of properties organized by explanatory principles. In this case, candidate inferences may be warranted by convincing causal links rather than correlational history.

The theory view of categories has provided a framework for investigations of what kinds of inferences are drawn about what kinds of categories. It has been argued (Carey, 1985; Keil, 1989) that people's understanding of natural kind categories, such as biological categories, is grounded in theories that specify the causal basis or nature of the category. Gelman and Coley (1991) suggest six properties that characterize natural kinds categories: (a) rich inductive potential—the capacity to generate inferences; (b) nonobvious basis—they capture deep similarities that might not otherwise be noted; (c) essence—a unique core property responsible for the surface properties (see also Medin & Ortony, 1989); (d) existence of anomalies—reflecting the idea that core properties, not surface properties, constitute the essence of natural kinds; (e) division of linguistic labor—the recognition that expert knowledge of a category's basis may exceed one's own; and (f) corrigibility—the belief that as theories are revised, theory-laden categories can change. In contrast, artifact concepts—such as bicycle and grater—are typically structured around functional characteristics and, along with nominal kinds—such as triangle, bachelor, and pet—offer a narrower range of inductive potential than natural kinds (Keil, 1989, 1991b).

Within a domain, instances can be categorized at multiple levels of abstraction. Rosch, Mervis, Gray, Johnson, and Boyes-Braem (1976) interpreted the superordinate, basic, and subordinate levels of categorization in terms of varying degrees of informativity (these levels may be specific to American undergraduates; see Medin & Heit, Chapter 3, this volume, for more about differing taxonomies). According to Rosch, the more specific the categorization, the more inferences are made, though the subordinate level does not add much beyond the privileged basic level. The few inferences made at more superordinate levels (e.g., if X is an animal, then it has a body) may be the most likely to be valid, but the least likely to be useful.

Although it is commonly assumed that taxonomic inheritance from superordinate to subordinate categories is a basic and relatively general reasoning process, recent evidence suggests that the story may be more complex. Sloman (1998) found that participants tested on inductive projections with arbitrary properties did not, in fact, consistently follow taxonomic inference rules. For example, they might fail to infer that a property true of a superordinate category (e.g., electronic equipment) was true of its subordinate category (e.g., stereos). Instead, the similarity of the two categories predicted judgments. Sloman argues that this calls into question the inferential strategy of the rule "It belongs to Category X, so it must have the properties of Category X" and instead prompts consideration of a similarity-based strategy such as "It is like Example X, so it is likely to have the properties of Example X."

B. Reasoning across Categories: Category-Based Induction

Categories can also be useful for reasoning about other categories. Say a reasoner needs to know whether a particular property is true of dogs, but no relevant information is included within their concept of dogs. If the status of the property is known with regard to another category (e.g., cats), this other category can serve as a basis for inductive reference. The reasoning process in this case is not a matter of categorizing an instance as a cat (as described above), but instead amounts to using what is known about cats to evaluate a possible property of dogs.

Gelman and her colleagues have carried out extensive research on the development of category-based induction (CBI) (e.g., Davidson & Gelman, 1990; Gelman,

1988, 1989; Gelman & Coley, 1991; Gelman & Markman, 1986, 1987). For example, Gelman and Markman (1986) studied children's inductions using a paradigm in which a target instance was given the same label as one standard, but was highly similar in appearance to a second standard. The task pits perceptual similarity against category membership (as indicated by the common label) in order to ask whether children would use inductive projection based on the category given the two standards. Young children (like adults) tended to extend the property from the case with the shared label—demonstrating reliance on category membership as an inferential basis. Perceptual similarity was a factor, but shared category dominated.

Davidson and Gelman (1990) obtained a different pattern of results using novel objects (e.g., a gnu-like animal), novel labels, and unfamiliar properties (e.g., "has four stomachs"). Children were taught a property of one animal, and then asked whether or not the property would be present in another animal. The researchers found that 4- and 5-year-old children made more inferences for animals that were perceptually similar to the standard (about 75%) than for those that were perceptually dissimilar to the standard (about 45%). There was no effect of shared labels whether novel or familiar. In a version in which the correlation between similarity and common label in the stimulus set was increased, common label did have an effect when supported by appearances. When there was a conflict between labels and appearances, children based their inferences on appearances. Children's inductions appear to be influenced both by perceptual similarity and by common category labels.

Osherson, Smith, Wilkie, Lopez, and Shafir (1990) conducted an extensive study of adult CBI using arguments of the form "Cats have property P. Therefore mammals have property P." Inductive arguments of this kind can be classified as *general* or *specific*. In *general* arguments, like the one above, the conclusion category is more general than (i.e., includes) the premise category/ies. In *specific* arguments, the conclusion category lies at the same level of specificity as the premise and belongs to the same superordinate category/ies (Osherson et al., 1990). An example is: "Cats have a left aortic arch. Therefore, badgers have a left aortic arch."

The dependent measure in this paradigm is the strength of the argument that the property is true of the conclusion given that it is true of the premise(s). Note that the property in question is unlikely to be part of the representation of the conclusion category. The use of *blank* predicates (Osherson et al., 1990) sets up the task as a comparison between the premise and conclusion categories rather than evaluation of the validity of the property relative to the conclusion category. Although this clearly qualifies as a strong method of reasoning because the results are heavily dependent on category representations, it is (by design) less knowledge-intensive and more reliant on general processes than reasoning by categorization—the semantic content of the inference (the blank predicate) is disconnected from the semantic content of the conclusion category.

Osherson et al. (1990) have identified a constellation of phenomena in which the strength of category-based inductive arguments varies systematically with the nature of the premise and conclusion categories and the relationship between them. In the *similarity* phenomenon, greater similarity between the premise and conclusion categories leads to greater argument strength. For example, given that mice have a property, one is more likely to attribute the property to rats than to elk. In addition, general arguments are stronger when they are based on more typical premises. This *typicality* phenomenon extends Rips's (1975) finding of increased likelihood of generalization with greater typicality of the premise category. General arguments are also stronger with more homogeneous conclusion categories. Thus, in the *homogeneity* phenomenon, more specific conclusion categories lead to greater argument strength (robin → bird is stronger than robin → animal). However, Shafir, Smith, and Osherson (1990) describe an effect called the *inclusion fallacy*, according to which more general conclusions seem stronger than specific ones. In normative terms, people should be less willing to make a more wide-ranging conclusion, but given a premise about robins, the inductive argument for ostriches is sometimes considered weaker than the argument for birds (all birds including ostriches!).

Using multiple premises, Osherson et al. (1990) collected evidence for a further set of phenomena that apply to both general and specific arguments. They found that the *diversity* of the premise categories predicts argument strength. If a property is known to be true for a set of far-ranging creatures (e.g., wasp and deer), it is more likely to apply to a new case than if it is known to be true of a cluster of more similar creatures (e.g., antelope and deer). Also, adding an additional premise at the lowest level category that includes the other premises and conclusions increases argument strength. This is called the *monotonicity* phenomenon since more evidence leads to greater argument strength. For example, collies, poodles, dalmations → dogs is stronger than an argument based on only two of the three premises. On the other hand, given a third premise from an outside category (collies, poodles, *dragonflies* → dogs), then the argument is often judged to be weaker than (collies, poodles → dogs). This phenomenon is known as *nonmonotonicity* because the argument strength decreases with the additional premise.

Osherson et al. (1990) propose a *similarity-plus-coverage* model to account for this set of findings. The strength of an argument depends, first, on the similarity of the premise and conclusion categories. In addition to accounting for the similarity phenomena described above, the similarity component of the model can account for the inclusion fallacy if the similarity between the general conclusion category (birds) and the premise category (robins) is greater than the similarity between the specific conclusion category (ostriches) and the premise category (robins). The second component in the model is *coverage,* the average similarity of the premise categories to the lowest-level category that spans both the premise and conclusion categories. Intuitively, argument strength increases with the extent to which the categories in the premises cover different areas within the space of the inclusive category (Lopez, Gelman, Gutheil, & Smith, 1992). In an argument such as (robins → bluejays), the degree of coverage is the average similarity of robins to exemplars of the lowest inclusive category, bird. An argument like (trout → bluejay) should be less persuasive than (robins → bluejays) because the coverage between trout and animal—the lowest inclusive category in this case—is low. Coverage is critical to explaining the multiple-premise effects. Monotonicity is explained by assuming that the additional within-category premise increases the coverage of the inclusive category. Nonmonotonicity (as in the example used above) occurs because the additional premise from outside the category (dragonflies) forces the lowest-level inclusive category up to the level of animals rather than dogs. The category of animals is less well covered (by collies, poodles, and dragonflies) than the category of dogs is by collies and poodles alone. Less coverage means less argument strength, despite the greater number of premises.

Sloman (1993) offers a different interpretation of this set of reasoning phenomena, based on comparison of features, not categories. His *feature-based* induction model is instantiated as a connectionist model. The premises of an argument are encoded in terms of the strength of associations from input units representing the features of the premise categories to an output unit representing belief in the predicate. The strength of an argument is tested by applying the features of the conclusion category to the input vector to determine the degree of activation of the output unit. The prediction is that the degree of feature overlap between the premise and conclusion category determines the argument strength. Similarity implicitly guides the process since like inputs lead to like outputs, but there is no explicit computation of similarity.

Sloman (1993) successfully modeled most of the core phenomena demonstrated by Osherson et al. (1990). For example, he explained diversity effects in terms of feature overlap, rather than by category coverage. Diverse premises lead to stronger arguments because they provide greater coverage of the feature space (more of the excitatory feature-to-output connections are activated). Sloman's model predicts an additional phenomenon related to diversity called *feature exclusion*. Using a same-level conclusion category (weasel) rather than superordinate (mammal), diverse premises (foxes and rhinos) do not lead to greater argument strength than clustered premises (foxes and deer) because the premises do not provide broader coverage of the feature space of the conclusion category.

Sloman argues that the feature-overlap model is superior because (a) it is not dependent on the existence of stable category structures or explicit similarity computations, and (b) the core phenomena are explained by a unified account rather than requiring the two components of similarity and category-coverage. However, the feature-based approach does not account for the nonmonotonicity phenomenon (without an additional assumption of feature competition). Additionally, critics point out that Sloman's emphasis on features is a somewhat dangerous move because there is no satisfying basis for determining the set of representing features. Furthermore, recent arguments in the study of conceptual structure (Markman & Wisniewski, 1997; Murphy & Medin, 1985) and comparison processes (Markman & Gentner, 1993a; Medin, Goldstone, & Gentner, 1993) have emphasized the importance of structured representations of causal and relational information. We will return to the role of structured representations and comparison processes in section IV.

C. Statistical Inference

Associative or statistical accounts of reasoning are based on the updating of statistical parameters via observational learning. In this manner, prior experience is used as a basis for prediction. Statistical regularities such as feature occurrences (frequencies) and co-occurrences (correlations) can be applied to predict unknowns as a function of the presence or absence of other features. Stored associations based on keeping track of occurrences or observable properties are an alternative to explicit knowledge structures such as rules, schemas, or concepts. Apparent subjectivity in people's interpretations of the statistical structure of a domain challenges the assumption that people construct accurate statistical models of the environment. For example, Chapman and Chapman (1969) found effects such as *illusory correlations* in which participants consider a correlation to be stronger or weaker than its objective basis due to the mediating influence of a prior belief or goal.

Bayes's theorem provides a formal framework for generating optimal inferences based on probability information. Any proposition (or feature, hypothesis, event, etc.) can be assigned a prior probability of being true. This likelihood of the proposition in a neutral context provides a base rate for prediction. Bayesian inference is the process of computing likelihoods as a function of the priors along with conditional probabilities representing the likelihood of a proposition being true given that one or more other propositions are true. Because there is a complex network of dependencies and interactions among propositions, effective prediction often involves a process of maximum likelihood estimation over a set of parameters.

Anderson (1991) explored the use of such a Bayesian framework as a psychological account grounded in evolutionary adaptation. In his "rational analysis," category membership is treated like any other feature that could be predicted via conditional probabilities. Category structure is constrained by the overall goal of optimizing inference performance. Predictions are made by combining the likelihoods of all possible classifications and their subsequent inferences. Anderson's model predicts a number of behavioral results in human categorization (e.g., prototype effects, linear separability, base-rate effects, and more), but the Bayesian framework requires the simplifying assumptions that features are independent of one another and that categories are nonoverlapping. The psychological plausibility of this approach has been questioned by Ross and Murphy (1996), who show that participants generally make inferences on the basis of one best-fitting category, instead of using a probabilistic summation across multiple possible categories.

Statistical accounts of reasoning are challenged by evidence that people often fail to conform to the prescriptions of Bayesian inference. A classic example is base-rate neglect or the failure to take appropriate account of the prior probability in assessing a likelihood (Kahneman, Slovic, & Tversky, 1982; A. Tversky & Kahneman, 1981). For example, even if someone is 90% certain they just saw a duck-billed platypus, before believing them, it would be worth considering how likely it is in general for such a creature to make an appearance. In probability estimation tasks, it has been shown that participants tend to respond as though the base rate information were not present or did not matter. However, Holyoak and Spellman (1993) suggest this phenomenon may not be robust. There are a variety of circumstances involving increased salience or causal relevance of the base-rate information in which proper use of base rates is made (e.g., Bar-Hillel & Fischoff, 1981). Additionally, much of the empirical evidence for base-rate neglect uses the methodological approach of establishing the base rates by providing summaries rather than a range of experience to allow statistical learning. Manis, Dovalina, Avis, and Cardoze (1980) show that base rates acquired through presentation of exemplars are used effectively.

D. Reasoning by Heuristics

Cognition may be effectively characterized as informal and subject to a variety of biases. A. Tversky and Kahneman (1973, 1983) have carried out an important research program exploring natural reasoning heuristics. They have shown that people do not always follow normative processes in their judgments and decisions. Instead of optimal performance (as established by either statistical or logical frameworks), reasoning often reflects the use of heuristic approaches that provide reasonable resolutions at minimal cost of time and processing resources. These shortcuts are not guaranteed to provide a correct answer (or any answer), and they are often linked to systematic biases in performance. Barsalou (1992) suggests that reasoning phenomena may best be explained in terms of the interaction between a system capable of deductive logic and three pervasive cognitive biases that reflect the way information is compared (representativeness), brought to bear (availability), and stored (in organizing knowledge frames).

Much of the evidence for these effects comes from studies of probability estimation in which the outcome of the reasoning process is not a new belief, but a degree of confidence in a particular belief. We briefly discuss two such phenomena that reflect the role of stored knowledge. One example is the *conjunction fallacy* (A. Tversky & Kahneman, 1983), in which people seem to rely on a *representativeness* heuristic rather than probability theory to make a judgment. The likelihood of a conjunctive event that is typical of its kind is judged as greater than the likelihood of one of the single constituent events by itself. Despite the fact that logically the co-occurrence of two events cannot be more likely than the occurrence of one of the events alone, people judge (for example) that it's more likely that Bjorn Borg lost the first game but won the set than that he lost the first game. In this case, knowledge about representative cases take precedence over an analysis grounded in formal likelihood estimation or logic. Another example is the *availability* heuristic—

the use of easily accessible knowledge to make a judgment (A. Tversky & Kahneman, 1973). For example, in judging the probability of a car being blue, experience with blue cars that is recent or salient often increases the probability estimate. Again, people's ability to collect and apply probability information objectively is called into question. In these examples, the reasoning process seems to reflect reliance on knowledge content rather than strict use of domain-general principles.

E. Connectionist Inference

Connectionist models provide several interesting interpretations of reasoning within the framework of parallel, distributed processing. In such systems, a large number of simple processing units loosely inspired by the networks of neurons in the brain take on activation values as a function of input from the environment along with weighted signals from other connected units. Recently, the statistical nature of connectionist models has been emphasized (see Smolensky, Mozer, & Rumelhart, 1996) to demonstrate the formal groundwork on which the models operate. This emphasis reflects the challenges connectionism has faced, such as (a) it is difficult or impossible to tell exactly how or why the models do what they do, and (b) they can be made to do nearly anything so they are uninteresting. Jacobs, Jordan, Nowlan, and Hinton (1991) describe a connectionist design principle for creating systems known as *mixture models* that instantiate principles of Bayesian inference.

   Connectionist models are also intriguing to many researchers for their psychological and neurobiological plausibility rather than as a way of doing statistics. Such models are often trained using a learning algorithm to perform pattern association or a function mapping between a set of inputs to a set of outputs. These systems produce inferences by generalizing from training experience. A novel input is treated like (or leads to the same output as) the training instance(s) with which it shares the most in common or a configuration of particularly critical features—similar inputs lead to similar outputs (Rumelhart, Durbin, Golden, & Chauvin, 1996).

   Connectionist models based on recurrent architectures perform a type of processing known as *constraint satisfaction* involving a series of small, local adjustments toward eventually settling at a stable global state. Examples of such systems as psychological models include Holyoak and Thagard's (1989) ACME model of analogical mapping and Rumelhart, Smolensky, McClelland, and Hinton's (1986) account of schema-based processing (see Holyoak & Spellman, 1993, for further discussion of connectionist vs. symbolic paradigms in thinking and hybrid connectionist-symbolic accounts such as ACME). In these *settling systems,* the activation level of processing units represent degree of belief in hypotheses about properties of the environment. Connections between units represent associations or the degree to which one property is consistent with or predicts the other. The activations of the units of the system are continually updated to effect small increases in the overall goodness (consistency of the configuration of global activation with prior knowledge as stored in the connections between units) of the interpretation of an input. Such systems, along with pattern association devices, have the interesting properties of completing partial patterns of input activation with inferred values in a manner reflecting the statistical structure of the training data and even overturning incongruous hypotheses. Rumelhart (1989) discusses how a settling system of this sort featuring a soft clamping mechanism on the inputs will naturally exhibit a range of performance along a continuum from memory to reasoning. Depending on the match between the input and the knowledge stored in the weights, the system will amplify a recognized pattern, complete a partial pattern, or generalize from appropriately similar examples to a novel variation.

IV. STRUCTURAL ALIGNMENT IN REASONING

Analogy can be defined as the perception of relational commonalities between domains that may be dissimilar on the surface, or as a kind of reasoning based on the assumption that two things that are similar in some ways will be similar in others. In fact, the two definitions are related. Relational correspondences between a base and target often lead to further candidate inferences. Rips (1990) noted that analogy occupies an intermediate position with respect to his strict–loose criteria, as discussed above. Analogy also holds an intermediate position in the weak–strong framework for reasoning we have set forth. Because it is clearly knowledge-intensive, it qualifies as a form of strong reasoning, yet the processing mechanisms are fairly well specified and are relatively independent of other cognitive processes. (Of course, as with other forms of reasoning, the representations over which it operates are influenced by other processes.)

In this section, we begin by outlining the characteristics of analogy and its relative, similarity, with a particular focus on the underlying mechanism of structural alignment and mapping. Then we consider how these processes can inform our understanding of the strong and weak methods discussed above. The perspective raised by this consideration of comparison processes suggests a general view of reasoning as a continuum from strong to weak methods, rather than a dichotomy between systems. We speculate on the unifying claim that structural alignment processes may not only guide strong forms of reasoning, but may contribute to the development of weak methods as well.

A. Reasoning by Analogy

Analogy research has focused mainly on the mapping process used to establish correspondences between two situations. A familiar situation, referred to as the base or source analog, is used as a model from which to map inferences to the unfamiliar situation or target. Such mappings can be decomposed into two subprocesses: (a) alignment of the two representational structures, and (b) projection of inferences from one to the other. The subprocesses are intimately linked because the nature of the alignment process constrains the candidate inferences that result. We present a basic overview of analogical mapping and inference. In addition, we explore how the structural alignment account of analogy can be extended to other comparison processes such as similarity. Lastly, because the process of reasoning by analogy about a target domain often depends on accessing potential base analogs stored in memory, we briefly discuss the retrieval component of analogical thinking.

1. Analogy: Theoretical Claims and Models

According to Gentner's (1983, 1989; Gentner & Markman, 1997) structure-mapping theory, analogical mapping is a matter of establishing a *structural alignment* between two represented situations and then projecting inferences. The theory assumes the existence of structured representations made up of properties (such as objects and attributes) and relations connecting the properties. An alignment consists of an explicit set of correspondences between the sets of representational elements of two situations with a focus on matching relational predicates. The alignment is determined according to a set of constraints that guarantee structural consistency: (a) there must be one-to-one correspondence between the mapped elements in the base and target, and (b) there must be parallel connectivity such that the arguments of corresponding predicates also correspond. In addition, the selection of an alignment is guided by the *systematicity principle:* a system of relations connected by higher-order constraining relations such as causal relations is more preferred in mapping than an equal number of independent matches. Thus, if analogical similarity is a matter of common relational structure, then a base domain with a richly linked system of connected relations can yield candidate inferences by guiding completion of the corresponding structure in the target (Bowdle & Gentner, 1997). The systematicity principle underscores a preference for coherence and causal predictive power in analogical processing. Table 1 (adapted from Gentner & Markman, 1997) lists seven key phenomena of analogical mapping.

Structure-mapping theory is instantiated in a computational model of human analogy processing. The Structure-Mapping Engine (SME) of Falkenhainer, Forbus, and Gentner (1989) begins by finding all possible local matches between the elements of two potential analogs. The system combines these into structurally consistent kernels and then combines the kernels into the largest and deepest connected systems of matches. As a natural outcome of the alignment, other propositions connected to the common system in the base become candidate inferences about the target. Holyoak and Thagard's (1989) ACME (Analogical Constraint Mapping Engine) uses a similar local-to-global algorithm, but in the form of a winner-take-all connectionist system that implements multiple soft constraints: structural consistency, semantic similarity, and pragmatic bindings. The multiconstraint system permits a highly flexible mapping process, but has the disadvantage that it often arrives at structurally inconsistent mappings with indeterminate candidate inferences. Markman (1997) found that this kind of indeterminacy was rarely experi-

TABLE 1 Seven Phenomena of Analogy[a]

1. Structural consistency	Analogical mapping involves one-to-one correspondence and parallel connectivity.
2. Candidate inferences	Analogical inferences are generated via structured completion.
3. Systematicity	People prefer connected relations rather than collections of isolated relations.
4. Relational focus	Relational matches are made whether or not the objects making up the relations also match.
5. Interactive interpretation	The interpretation of an analogy depends on both terms; the same term yields different interpretations in different comparisons.
6. Multiple interpretations	Analogy allows multiple interpretations of a single comparison.
7. Cross-mapping	Adults generally perceive both interpretations of a cross-mapping and typically prefer the relational interpretation.

[a] Adapted from Gentner and Markman, 1997.

enced by people solving analogies. Another variant of the local-to-global algorithm is Hofstadter and Mitchell's (1994) Copycat system for perceptual analogies. Hummel and Holyoak's (1997) LISA model is an account of analogical processing that attempts to unify mapping and access using temporal synchrony to bind distributed representational elements. Lastly, IAM (Incremental Analogy Machine) is a "projection-first" model that operates by finding or deriving an abstraction in the base and projecting it to the target (Keane & Brayshaw, 1988). Additional matches are added incrementally—this allows the system to model effects of processing order.

These models demonstrate various accounts (with a common theoretical grounding) of the core analogical reasoning process. Turning a candidate inference into an actual hypothesis about the target also depends on a process of judging the acceptability of the analogy. At least three criteria are involved in the evaluation. The first is *structural soundness:* whether the alignment and the projected inferences are structurally consistent. The second criterion is the *factual validity* of the projected inferences in the target. Because analogy is not a deductive mechanism, the candidate inference is not guaranteed to be correct. Finally, in problem-solving situations, an additional criterion is *goal relevance*—checking whether the analogical inferences are relevant to the current goals. Models of analogy differ in when and how goal relevance is invoked during the process. Holyoak and Thagard (1989) assign it a central role in mapping, while Gentner (1989) proposes that goals influence the input representations and the postmapping evaluation process, but not the mapping itself.

As part of the mapping process, analogy can act as a mechanism for learning or knowledge change through *re-representation* of the constituent predicates of the analogs or *highlighting* the common structure between analogs (C. A. Clement & Gentner, 1991; J. Clement, 1988; Gentner, 1989; Holyoak & Thagard, 1989). Re-representation (or adaptation) involves altering the representation of one or both analogs to improve the quality of the match (see Holyoak, Novick, & Melz, 1994; Kass, 1994; Keane, 1996; Kotovsky & Gentner, 1996). Schema abstraction occurs when a common system arrived at in understanding an analogy is rendered salient—thereby increasing the possibility that it will be used again later (Gick & Holyoak, 1983; Hayes-Roth & McDermott, 1978). Through these mechanisms, analogy can promote the formation of new relational categories and abstract rules.

2. Systematicity as a Constraint on Inference

The role of relational structure in analogical processing is more specific than a global preference for relational commonalities over attribute or object matches. As noted above, the analogical interpretation process seeks matches consisting of interconnected systems of relations. This preference for interpretations of analogies that align systems of predicates connected by higher-order constraining relations is known as the *systematicity* principle (Gentner, 1983, 1989). This claim that comparison acts to promote systems of interrelated knowledge is crucial to analogy's viability as a reasoning process. If the comparison process generated a set of isolated features, there would be no natural basis by which to constrain the inferences derived from the match.

A useful experimental methodology for observing the effects of structure in comparison takes advantage of *cross-mappings* in which structural commonalities conflict with object matches (Gentner & Toupin, 1986; Goldstone & Medin, 1994a; Markman & Gentner, 1993b; Ross, 1987). For example, in a comparison between "Spot bit Fido" and "Fido bit Rover," Fido is cross-mapped. When presented with cross-mapped comparisons, participants can compute both alignments (see Table 1). Adults (though not young children) typically prefer the relational alignment. The preference becomes more emphatic when the cross-mapping includes higher-order relational structure (Gentner & Rattermann, 1991; Gentner & Toupin, 1986; Markman & Gentner, 1993c).

In order to test the role of systematicity as a constraint on inference, C. A. Clement and Gentner (1991) showed participants analogous scenarios and asked them to judge which of two lower-order assertions shared by the base and target was most important to the match. Participants chose the assertion that was connected to matching causal antecedents—their choice was based not only on the goodness of the local match, but also on whether it was connected to a larger matching system. In addition, inferences projected from one scenario to the other were governed by systematicity—inferences were made in order to complete a causal system.

3. Similarity Is Like Analogy

The framework developed for analogy extends naturally to literal similarity (Gentner & Markman, 1993, 1995, 1997; Goldstone, 1994b; Goldstone, Medin, & Gentner, 1991; Markman & Gentner, 1993a,c; Medin et al., 1993). Specifically, the alignment of relational structure is also crucial to similarity comparisons. The distinction between analogy and literal similarity can be thought of within a similarity space defined by the degree of object-attribute similarity and the degree of relational similarity (Gentner, 1989). Analogy occurs when comparisons exhibit a high degree of relational similarity with very little attribute similarity. As the amount of attribute similarity increases, the comparison shifts towards literal similarity. Literal similarity matches are easier to make than analogy because the alignment of relational structure is supported by object matches.

Markman and Gentner (1993b) found evidence that similarity comparison induces a structural alignment. Participants viewed pairs of pictures—in one scene, a woman was shown *giving* food to a squirrel; in the other, a similar-looking woman was shown *receiving* food from a man. One group of participants rated how similar the two scenes were to each other, while a control group rated the two scenes' aesthetic value. All participants were then asked to map the woman in the first picture to an element of the second. Participants who had first rated the similarity of the scenes made significantly more relational mappings (i.e., woman to squirrel) than did participants in the control condition. The very act of carrying out a similarity comparison can induce a structural alignment and increase the likelihood of making matches on the basis of shared relations rather than object similarity.

In addition to relational focus, the critical finding that systematically guides inference (C. A. Clement & Gentner, 1991) also carries over to similarity comparisons. Bowdle and Gentner (1997) gave participants pairs of similar scenarios (without distinguishing a base or target) and asked for inferences. It was found that participants preferred to make inferences from a systematic structure to a less systematic structure and also judged comparisons to be more informative in this direction than the reverse.

4. Analogical Retrieval

So far our focus has been on analogical mapping once the base and target have been established. Explaining the use of analogy and similarity in reasoning requires some account of how potential analogs are accessed in long-term memory. There is considerable evidence that similarity-based retrieval, unlike the mapping process, is more influenced by surface similarity than structural similarity. Strong similarity and content effects seem to dominate remindings and to limit the transfer of learning across domains (Gentner, Ratterman, & Forbus, 1993; Holyoak & Koh, 1987; Keane, 1988; Novick, 1988a, 1988b; Reed, 1987; Ross, 1984, 1987, 1989).

In Gick and Holyoak's (1980, 1983) classic studies, participants often failed to access potentially useful analogs. The rate of successful solution of a very difficult problem tripled (from a baseline of 10%) for participants given an analogous story prior to the problem; but even so, the majority of participants failed to benefit from the analogy. However, when these nonsolvers were given a hint to think about the story they had heard, the solution rate approximately tripled again to 80–90%.

Because no new information was given about the story, it can be concluded that the analog was available in memory, but was not spontaneously retrieved. The structural similarity between the story and the problem was sufficient to carry out the mapping with both analogs present in working memory, but not sufficient to produce spontaneous retrieval.

To test this functional distinction between kinds of similarity, Gentner et al. (1993) gave participants a large set of stories to remember and then later provided new stories that varied in their surface and relational similarity to the originals. Participants were asked to write out any original stories they were reminded of—the remindings that resulted were strongly governed by surface commonalities such as similar characters. However, when asked to rate the similarity and inferential soundness of pairs of stories, the same participants relied primarily on higher-order relational commonalities, such as matching causal structure. Participants even rated their own surface-similar remindings as poor matches. This disassociation is also found in problem-solving tasks: remindings of prior problems are strongly influenced by surface similarity, but structural similarity better predicts success in solving the problem (e.g., Ross, 1987).

B. Reasoning by Categories Revisited

At the outset of this chapter, we suggested that structural alignment could serve as a unifying framework for a discussion of reasoning. We now begin our effort to make good on this proposal. We have seen how the comparison processes of analogy and similarity can function as a mechanism for extending knowledge. Similarity and categorization are quite intricately and somewhat controversially linked to one another—in ways ranging from accounts of one in terms of the other to dissociations between them (see Medin & Heit, this volume). We leave the debate aside except to note that if similarity as structural alignment is "explanatory" as a source of constraints on category coherence (Goldstone, 1994a) and hierarchical organization (Markman & Wisniewski, 1997), then inferences that arise from categorization (as in section III.A) may in fact be derived from structured comparison between instances and category representations (see Kurtz & Gentner, 1998). The use of CBI (section III.B) to extrapolate knowledge on the basis of category structure is generally considered distinct from similarity-based inference (the projection of knowledge from one specific instance to another). Nonetheless, viewing CBI from the vantage of structural alignment yields some useful insights.

1. Comparison and Category-Based Induction

Most models of CBI utilize a notion of similarity as the degree of match between sets of features. Evidence suggests that adults' property induction is guided by structural similarity rather than flat similarity (as in Osherson, et al., 1990) or featural overlap (as in Sloman, 1993). Lassaline (1996) found that argument strength increased when there was a causally connected inference that could be carried over as a candidate inference. For example, adding the relational premise "For Animal B, a weak immune system causes an acute sense of smell" increased the strength of the following argument:

Animal A has a weak immune system, skin that has no pigment, and dry flaky skin
Animal B has a weak immune system and an acute sense of smell

---

therefore, Animal A also has an acute sense of smell

Further evidence that people are sensitive to connected systems of relations in induction comes from Heit and Rubinstein (1994). They found that participants make stronger inferences when the kind of property to be inferred (anatomical or behavioral) matches the kind of similarity between the animals (anatomical or behavioral). For example, participants made stronger behavioral inferences from tuna to whales (because both swim) than from bears to whales. Stronger anatomical inferences were made from whales to bears (because both are mammals). If we assume that anatomy and behavior are represented by different systems of semantic relations, then these findings support the claim that adults are strongly influenced by relational focus and systematicity in drawing inductive inferences.

Wu and Gentner (1998) found further evidence for structural alignment effects in category-based inference. Participants were given descriptions of two standard animals and a target animal and asked to make an inference about the target based on one of the standards. The target shared one property with Animal A and two properties with Animal B; thus its featural similarity was higher with B than with A. However, the description of Animal A also included the information that the shared property *causes* an additional property. Participants strongly preferred the inference connected to causal structure (from Animal A) despite the greater feature overlap favoring the inference from Animal B. The pattern of findings suggests that people carry out structural alignment during CBI.

Given this evidence, the question arises whether structural alignment might also explain the patterns of responding found in studies of CBI discussed above. We focus our discussion on the nonmonotonicity effect (Osherson et al., 1990; Lopez et al., 1992) in which inference strength goes down with the addition of a distant premise. For example, Argument 1 below is stronger than argument 2:

Argument 1: (crow, peacock) → bird
Argument 2: (crow, peacock, rabbit → bird)

This runs contrary to the monotonicity prediction that increasing the number of premises should increase inductive strength. Osherson et al. (1990) argue that nonmonotonicity effects are due to category coverage. By enlarging the size of the covering category, the average similarity of the argument categories to the covering category is diluted. However, consider Sloman's (1993) example in which Argument 1 is stronger than Argument 2:

Argument 1: (crocodile) → alligator

Argument 2: (crocodile and king snake) → alligator

This effect is not predicted by coverage. Note, however, that crocodile has a richer match with alligator than that arising from the alignment of crocodile and king snake. Some instances of nonmonotonicity may reflect structural alignment of the premise categories (Gentner & Medina, 1998). Consider again the "bird" example from above. In Argument 1, the premises (crow and peacock) are strongly alignable—yielding a rich "premise schema" that can project inferences to the conclusion category with which this schema is also strongly alignable. The addition of a difficult-to-align premise (rabbit) in Argument 2 invites a retreat from strong alignment-based reasoning. The reasoning process could rely on this less forceful alignment—one that must incorporate rabbit in with crow and peacock—or instead shift to taxonomic reasoning. This shift can be seen as going from a strong reasoning process (close alignment) to a somewhat more domain-general (or less strong) reasoning process (category-based inheritance). Category-based inheritance is less dependent on the specific knowledge structures associated with the entities than is literal similarity alignment. For example, tiger and paramecium are equally entitled to inherit the properties of animal, even though tiger yields a more satisfying alignment with animal than does paramecium.

2. Analogical Induction in Development

Even more than adults, children often need to reason in the absence of useful background knowledge. Indeed, it is sometimes stated that the inductive processes used by children are comparison based—as opposed to the CBI used by adults (Carey, 1985; Inagaki, 1989). Lopez et al. (1992) used inductive inference problems like those of Osherson et al. (1990) to demonstrate a developmental pattern of early reliance on similarity with category-based reasoning entering later. Both kindergarteners and second graders showed similarity-driven effects such as the influence of premise-conclusion similarity and typicality of the premise. However, only the second graders showed category coverage effects such as premise diversity and monotonicity. As in the Osherson et al. studies, it was found that adults appeared to use both comparison-based and category-based processes. Adults with different kinds of expertise showed different patterns of inductive reasoning in the domain of trees (Medin, Lynch, & Coley, 1997). Participants with expert ecological or causal knowledge (maintenance workers and landscapers) tended not to use diversity to guide their reasoning. This may reflect direct comparison of sophisticated knowledge structures rather than the use of the more domain-general (weaker) method.

Carey (1985) asked children to make inductive inferences about properties. For example, children were told that a dog had a spleen and then asked if bugs were likely to have a spleen. She found that before age 10, children tended to base their inductive attributions of biological properties on the similarity of the target object to humans. This pattern suggests that children might be using a well-understood species (i.e., their own species) to reason about less familiar species; that is, they were drawing an analogy. The research program of Inagaki, Hatano and colleagues (Inagaki, 1989, 1990; Inagaki & Hatano, 1987, 1991; Inagaki & Sugiyama, 1988) suggests that (a) children use structure-mapping processes in inducing new features of animals, but (b) the flexibility and sophistication of their reasoning is limited by incomplete domain representations. Inagaki and Hatano (1987) examined children's spontaneous use of analogy in inductive problems from the biological domain. They asked 5–6-year-old children questions like, "What would happen if a rabbit were continually given more water?" As in Carey (1985), the children often made explicit analogies to humans such as: "We can't keep it [the rabbit] forever in the same size. Because, like me, if I were a rabbit, I would be 5 years old and become bigger and bigger." The personification responses were often reasonable and tended to be more correct than nonpersonification responses. When asked questions for which the analogy with humans would yield incorrect responses, children were far less likely to use the analogy. In addition, children were more likely to use the analogy to humans for target entities more similar to humans. This is consistent with high similarity facilitating alignment and inference projection.

Viewing this process as analogy suggests that children based their inferences on knowledge of humans because their knowledge of humans is deeper and more systematic than their knowledge of other animals. If this is the correct account, then the same pattern should hold for other animals about which children possess expertise. Inagaki (1990) found that children who raised goldfish were highly likely to use their knowledge about goldfish to make analogical inferences about unfamiliar aquatic animals such as frogs. Interestingly, the goldfish-raising children also used the person analogy for frogs almost twice as often as the control subjects. It is possible that the experience of raising goldfish had led the children to compare humans and goldfish and to abstract underlying commonalities. Goldfish raisers were more likely to draw analogies from people to goldfish than non-goldfish raisers, despite the fact that they demonstrably knew more about goldfish. Deeper knowledge about animals apparently made children better able to notice and use cross-species analogies (see also Kotovsky & Gentner, 1996). Developmental gains in inductive accuracy may result through increasingly sophisticated analogical comparison rather than a shift from comparison to category use. The distinction lies between comparison based on overall similarity and more informed analogical comparison in which similarity with respect to specific causal or functional systems determines the common system and the projected inference.

C. Reasoning by Rules Revisited

Deductive inference rules are the quintessential case of a purely syntactic, content-independent (weak) form of reasoning. Their operation is in principle unaffected by the semantic content of the representations to which they apply. Does comparison have any role to play in such processes? One suggestion from norm theory (Kahneman & Miller, 1986) is that people use analogical reasoning to compare a target situation to ad hoc counterfactual alternatives (see also E. E. Smith & Osherson, 1989). In this section we seek to establish three links between structural alignment and deductive rules (Gentner & Medina, 1997, 1998). First, we suggest that rule application typically entails structural alignment. Second, people are often more accurate with concrete analogies than with the structurally equivalent rule. Third, alignment processes may provide a route to acquiring deductive rules.

1. Structural Alignment in Rule Application

The use of rules in reasoning may actually depend on comparison processes. Wittgenstein's (1953) discussion of rule following emphasizes the interdependence of similarity and rules. He argues that it is a mistake to think similarity can be established independently of rule-governed activities because similarity is unconstrained. For example, given the series "2, 4, 6, 8, . . . ," it is indeterminate what should come next. Our sense of similarity alone might suggest monotonic increase, even numbers, or single-digit numbers. A rule such as "+2" is what provides a constrained basis for continuing the number sequence. Goodman (1972) adopted this line of argument to attack similarity as a basis for concepts. However, Wittgenstein argued the converse point as well—similarity plays a role in the application of rules. A represented rule like "+ 2" lacks a basis for determining when and how to apply the rule to specific instances (see Gentner & Medina, 1998, for more on this and related points).

   The application for a deductive rule requires a firm structural binding of the abstract components of the rule with the specific premise and conclusion assertions. This binding or unification of rule and evidence can be seen as an alignment process. Imagine a continuum from analogy to relational abstraction. Both involve overlap in relational structure, but they vary in the concreteness of the base domain. In analogical mapping the objects of the concrete base must be aligned with the objects and relations of the target. When an abstraction acts as the base, there are only variables to fill rather than concrete objects to overcome. Thus, an abstract rule that is clearly represented by the learner should be easy to align.

2. Analogies as Surrogates for Rules

E. E. Smith et al. (1992) note that deductive rule following should be at least as accurate with abstract or unfamiliar materials. This assumption is challenged by content effects in reasoning. Participants given Wason's (1968) selection task typically fail in the application of conditional inference rules to abstract and unfamiliar material, but perform far better if familiar concrete materials are used. Additionally, an important pattern of transfer effects has been established using the selection task. The canonical result is that subjects revert to poor performance when they receive the abstract (i.e., letters and numbers) version of the task, even following a facilitating content problem, such as the Drinking Age problem (Cox & Griggs, 1982; Johnson-Laird et al., 1972; Wason & Shapiro, 1971). However, Cox and Griggs (1982) also demonstrated that an arbitrary specific rule, such as a Clothing Age rule ("If a person is wearing blue then the person must be over 19") shows facilitation after presentation of the Drinking Age rule.

The facilitation effects found in the Wason task are usually ascribed to "familiarity" with the rule and material used. Our framework allows us to be more specific and distinguish two different sources of facilitation: (a) transparency—the overall similarity between the prior knowledge representation and the representation of the conditional statement to be tested; and (b) systematicity, or the availability of higher-order structure that supports the application of the conditional inference. The role of transparency, or overall similarity, is straightforward. Successful transfer hinges on recognizing that the two problems are similar. As discussed above, analogical transfer between two specific problems is rare without surface similarity (or explicit hints). Thus, the high similarity between the Drinking Age scenario and the Clothing Age scenario leads to analogical reminding of the former given the latter, and facilitates positive transfer. But when subjects are given a specific case followed by an abstract case, the surface similarity may be insufficient to lead to a reminding.

The second factor is systematicity—being reminded of a stored scenario is only useful if that scenario contains a system of higher-order relations that is correlated with the structure of the rule (Gentner et al., 1993; Holyoak & Koh, 1987; Ross, 1987, 1989). For example, Wason and Shapiro's thematic rule "Every time I go to Manchester I travel by car" produces facilitation because people have well-established planning schemas that link particular destinations with modes of transport; and these schemas have the desired implicative structure (One is not tempted to infer $q \rightarrow p$: "If I am traveling by car I am going to Manchester"). These can be mapped onto the conditional scenario to provide the appropriate constraint. In contrast, a rule such as "Every time I go into the kitchen I wear my brown shoes"—even though it contains highly familiar elements—should produce little if any facilitation for the conditional rule, perhaps in part because $p \rightarrow q$ and $q \rightarrow p$ are equally plausible (or implausible) in this scenario. Maximal facilitation requires not only familiar elements but appropriate relations among the elements.

Although experimental studies that demonstrate strong facilitation effects typically combine transparency and systematicity (e.g., Griggs and Cox's drinking task and Johnson-Laird et al.'s postal rule task), these effects are conceptually separable (Gentner & Toupin, 1986). For example, Johnson-Laird and Shapiro (using a different set of reasoning problems) found that realistic relations facilitate performance when they correlate with the logical structure of the problem, but hinder the deduction process when they do not (Wason & Johnson-Laird, 1972).

As expected on this account, children are highly sensitive to content in reasoning tasks. Girotto et al. (1988) gave children a simplified version of the selection task. Following Cheng and Holyoak's (1985) paradigm, they used obligation and permission rules accompanied with brief rationales, as well as arbitrary rules. All the rules were unfamiliar to the children, and they were introduced in a game situation with toy bees and an imaginary beehive. An obligation rule, for instance, was "If a bee buzzes, then it must stay outside," followed by the rationale that the queen bee wanted to avoid spreading the disease to baby bees. An arbitrary rule was, for example, "If a bee buzzes, then it is outside." Children were then asked which of the bees should be checked (i.e., those inside, those outside, those that buzz, those that don't). As expected, children performed better with meaningful rules than with arbitrary rules (70% vs. 11% correct in 9- and 10-year-olds).

3. Structural Alignment and the Acquisition of Rules

Analogies during learning can lead to highlighting and abstraction of common structural systems; thus comparison can orient learners towards systems of interconnected knowledge (e.g., systems linked by higher-order causal, mathematical, or perceptual relations). We suggest a progression from reasoning based on overall, literal similarity to reasoning based on higher-level abstract similarity—that is, in the limit on rule-application. With repeated alignment and abstraction, similarity comparisons evolve from being initially perceptual and context-bound to become increasingly framed in terms of common higher-order structure. The structural alignment and mapping process grades naturally from highly concrete and literally similar comparisons to purely abstract comparisons. This predicted pattern parallels a developmental trend from overall similarity to relational similarity and abstract mappings, which Gentner and Rattermann (1991) called *the career of similarity*. As Quine puts it (1969, p. 167), we "retain different similarity standards . . . for use in different contexts." Of course, comparison is only one of many learning mechanisms involved in the route to abstract cognition, but its potential role in bridging strong and weak methods of reasoning is unique. In the current framework, rule-governed processes are based on abstract structural similarity, but they may coexist with processes governed by more concrete alignments.

Kotovsky and Gentner (1996; Gentner, Rattermann, Markman, & Kotovsky, 1995) investigated the possibility that comparison processes might promote children's learning about higher-order perceptual relations such as symmetry or monotonic increase. In particular, they focused particularly on the ability to perceive cross-dimensional matches, which require an abstract appreciation of common relational structure. Prior research shows a relational shift: preschool children are generally unable to appreciate higher-order perceptual patterns such as symmetry and monotonicity (Chipman, 1977; Halford, 1987, 1992; Smith, 1984, 1989, 1993). The materials were perceptual patterns—groups of simple shapes that could be perceived readily—so that higher-order relational commonalities could be manipulated independently of object similarity. Children were shown a standard embodying some relational structure such as *symmetry* (e.g., XoX) and were asked to say which of two other figures it was most similar to. The two alternatives were (a) the relational (correct) choice, which shared a higher-order relation (e.g., symmetry) with the standard (HiH); and (b) a foil that was composed of the same elements as the relational choice, but was rearranged to remove the higher-order pattern (iHH). Since both choices were equally dissimilar to the standard in terms of object attributes, and the relational choice exceeded in relational overlap, it was (by adult standards) the clear winner.

The key variable was the degree of concrete lower-order similarity between the standard and the relational choice. For same-dimension triads, the relational choice had the same dimension of change as the standard: the match was concrete and easily perceivable (e.g., big-little-big/big-little-big). In cross-dimension triads, the match was solely at the abstract higher-order level (e.g., big-little-big/dark-light-dark). When given mixed sets of these similarity triads (without feedback), 4-year-olds were correct on the within-dimension (close similarity) triads, but chose randomly on the cross-dimension triads. However, simply presenting children with concrete "easy" matches before the abstract cross-dimensional matchers led to significantly better performance on the cross-dimensional matches. Kotovsky and Gentner (1996) suggest a mechanism of *progressive alignment* whereby initially concrete, dimensionally specific representations are rendered more abstract by comparison and alignment. Even for novices, close matches are easy to perceive because they are, in a sense, automatically aligned. This alignment results in a slight highlighting of the common relational structure. After repeating such alignments, the higher-order relational structure becomes strong enough so that a partial match can be made even in a cross-dimensional pairing.

Applying this notion of progressive alignment to deductive reasoning leads to the prediction that content effects should occur at a range of different levels of abstraction from highly specific through progressively more abstract. The level of abstraction achieved will vary with learner and with topic or domain. This predicts that facilitation can occur not only with highly specific scenarios, as discussed above, but also with abstract schemas. This seems to be the case. As Cheng and Holyoak (1985, 1989) have argued, the higher-order relation of permissibility can be abstractly represented in a schema that would include rules such as "If Action A is taken, then Precondition P must be satisfied." Cheng and Holyoak (1985) tested performance on a selection problem that described a permission situation abstractly, using the rule "If one is to take action A, then one must first satisfy precondition P." Subjects gave 61% correct answers in the abstract permission problem, in contrast with a 19% success rate in the Wason card problem for the same subjects. This facilitation effect of systematicity with abstract stimuli was almost as strong as that obtained with concrete similarity (e.g., 81% in Johnson-Laird et al., 1972).

Cheng and Holyoak's proposal that pragmatic reasoning schemas are "abstract knowledge structures induced from ordinary life experiences" (p. 395) is consistent with our proposal of a continuum of abstraction. However, there are some differences between their pragmatic approach and the present framework. First, they contend that the schematic structures that guide everyday reasoning derive primarily from experience with classes of goal-related situations. We suggest more broadly that the essential element is a well-established higher-order relational schema that supports conditional reasoning. The pragmatic dimension per se is not the source of facilitation. Goal-oriented contexts are undoubtedly a rich source of meaningful schemas, but (a) many regularities are learned across a variety of different goal scenarios, making it unlikely that their structure is derived from one particular type of goal; and (b) humans attend to many kinds of regularities in the world, not just to those that influence goal achievement. We learn many higher-order relational sche-mas that are not fundamentally goal-oriented (e.g., causality, perceptual higher-order relations, mathematical relatedness, and so on). For example, consider this rule:

If a pattern is symmetric, it has some identical components.

Although this rule could hardly be described as goal-driven, it seems likely to result in correct performance in a selection task. It is reasonably intuitive to resist the "affirming the consequent" fallacy—that is, to see that "some identical components" does not imply "symmetric"; and it is also intuitive to accept the contrapositive ("denying the consequent," the correct inference)—that is, to see that "no identical components" implies "not symmetric."

A second difference is that we do not suggest that pragmatic reasoning schemas are the end point of learning. With experience and instruction, people can and do develop abstract schemas that are not embedded in pragmatic contexts. For example, Rips and Conrad (1983) found that a one-quarter course in elementary logic substantially improved subjects' ability to evaluate propositional arguments, many of which contained conditionals. For subjects sufficiently trained in conditional logic, the implications of complex rules may be readily available. Finally, whereas Cheng and Holyoak assume no special role for language in this evolution, Gentner and Medina (1998) suggest that the acquisition of relational language may play an important role in analogical processing (Gentner & Rattermann, 1991) and relational abstraction (Kotovsky & Gentner, 1996).

D. How Do the Different Views of Reasoning Fit Together?

We have organized our discussion of reasoning around a continuum with two extremes. Weak methods of deductive reasoning consist of the application of content-free syntactic inference rules that operate on the logical form of representations. Strong methods of reasoning rely heavily on specific experience and knowledge representations. Some researchers have proposed that similarity-based and rule-based processes are both important in human cognition, but that they function as different cognitive systems. Smolensky (1988) draws a distinction between two different mechanisms: a conscious rule interpreter that functions algorithmically, and an intuitive processor that operates at the subsymbolic level. Perhaps the most clearly articulated proposal is Sloman's (1996) argument for the existence of two separate systems of reasoning that operate independently and in parallel. The associative system encodes covariation of features in the environment and makes predictions based on statistical regularities. Sloman's account restricts similarity to these associative, subsymbolic processes, while the rule-based system operates on structured symbolic representations.

As evidence for the existence of two independent systems of reasoning, Sloman cites the inclusion fallacy and the conjunction fallacy, where similarity and rules lead to contradictory conclusions (Shafir et al., 1990; E. E. Smith & Osherson, 1989; A. Tversky & Kahneman, 1983). In the "Linda the bank teller" example of the conjunction fallacy (A. Tversky & Kahneman, 1983), participants judged that Linda (who, as a student, "was deeply concerned with issues of discrimination and social justice") was more likely to be "a bank teller and active in the feminist movement" than "a bank teller." One explanation of this phenomenon is that participants were swayed by the greater similarity of the description of Linda to a "feminist bank teller" than to the typical bank teller (E. E. Smith & Osherson, 1989). Sloman notes that people are often simultaneously attracted to both of two contradictory conclusions—the correct "bank teller" solution and also "the feminist bank teller" solution—and interprets this as evidence for two parallel systems of reasoning.

However, as Gentner and Medina (1998) note, contradictory responses can be generated within a single comparison-based reasoning system in at least three ways. First, the retrieval process may produce more than one possibility for a given contextual cue. Second, even after the pair to be aligned has been selected, the local-to-global alignment process (see section IV.A.1) can lead to contradictory responses over time. Early responses are dominated by local object matches, whereas later responses reflect an alignment of relational structure (Falkenhainer et al., 1989; Goldstone & Medin, 1994b; Ratcliff & McKoon, 1989). Goldstone (1994a) found evidence for this temporal shift from object matches to relational matches using a deadline same-different task. A third way that contradictory responses may arise is that the same comparison (even with the same correspondences) can give rise to alternative interpretations. For example, the statement that a given battle "is the mother of battles" could mean that it is the biggest (as a parent is larger than her offspring) or that it will engender a host of others (which may be larger than the parent). People can experience simultaneous awareness of these possibilities. In all three of these cases, the contradictory responses arise within one system.

A more fundamental difficulty with Sloman's proposal is that classifying all similarity with association neglects the evidence that the comparison process is structure-sensitive (Gentner & Clement, 1988; Gentner & Markman, 1994, 1997; Goldstone & Medin, 1994a; Markman & Gentner, 1993c, 1996; Medin et al., 1993).

When similarity is considered as structural alignment, a range of reasoning performance can be understood as a continuum between strong and weak methods. Furthermore, structural comparison can act as a bridge by which similarity-based processes lead to the development of abstract rules. This view of gradual abstraction of initially conservative, context-specific representations is consistent with the proposal that abstractions can arise from comparison across highly specific instances (Cheng & Holyoak, 1985; Elio & Anderson, 1981; Forbus & Gentner, 1986; Gentner & Medina, 1998; Gick & Holyoak, 1983; Medin & Ross, 1989). As Gentner and Medina argue, there is a graceful learning continuum from a fully concrete mapping, in which the objects transparently match their intended correspondents, to an analogical mapping in which a relational structure is imported to a new domain with no support (or even with conflict) from the object matches, to a fully abstract mapping in which the base domain contains variables, the target contains objects, and the mapping qualifies as rule application.

V. SUMMARY AND DISCUSSION

Before closing it is worth briefly noting the rise of new approaches that may lead to rapid change in the field. First, research in cognitive neuroscience may eventually make it possible to link the higher-order representations and processes posited in psychological accounts of reasoning to their neurobiological instantiations. At this point the exact form of the connection and which techniques (e.g., neuroimaging) will provide constraints on theories of high-level cognition are hard to predict.

A second area from which accounts of reasoning stand to benefit is cross-cultural research. Strong forms of reasoning would be expected to show cultural and developmental differences due to variations in the knowledge brought to bear. For example, Lopez, Atran, Coley, Medin, and Smith (1997) found that inductive reasoning among the Itzaj-Mayans was much like that of American subjects in making heavy use of similarity and typicality, but differed in that Mayans did not make use of premise diversity. When premise variability was high, Mayans often drew on their ecological knowledge concerning relations among the creatures. The pattern of performance differences may reflect Mayans' superior knowledge of their ecology. Choi, Nisbett, and Smith (1999) found that Koreans were less likely than Americans to use categories for inductive inference when presented with specific arguments in which the covering category must be generated. Nisbett and his colleagues suggest that this difference may reflect different reasoning styles: in particular, a general pattern of greater reliance on categories among Europeans and Americans than among East Asians. As another example, East Asians have been found to focus relatively more on situational factors than Europeans and Americans in making causal attributions (Choi, Nisbett, & Norenzayan, 1997).

Weak methods might be expected to be more stable and universal, because they are domain-independent and, according to some researchers, originate innately.

However, cross-cultural research suggests caution in the belief that particular weak methods are fundamental or universal in cognition. For example, Carraher, Carraher, and Schliemann (1985) used naturalistic methods to study mathematical knowledge in real-world contexts. Brazilian schoolchildren who worked as street vendors were skilled at arithmetic performance in the marketplace when the problems were formulated in the context of fruit sales, but could not solve equivalent problems in the abstract version used in formal instruction. The mathematical ability of these children seemed to be situated in a particular context.

Within and across cultures, there is evidence for both strong and weak methods of reasoning. Neither form can be relegated to a peripheral role in reasoning. It is clear that people can and do apply domain-general rules such as modus ponens; it is equally clear that they are not the whole story. As Newell and Simon noted, when stored data from relevant experience is available, people typically rely on it rather than invoking a more abstract, universal algorithm. Strong methods driven by cases, categories, statistical summaries, and heuristics are a useful way to get on with the goals of understanding and prediction. We agree with Holyoak and Spellman (1993) that "the psychological difficulty of inferences seems to depend more on the relationship between the content of the premises and prior knowledge than on the logical form of the reasoning involved" (p. 292).

The structural alignment view points toward a way of linking strong and weak methods. Structural alignment and projection can guide the application of either concrete or abstract prior knowledge to new situations, yielding inferences beyond the available evidence. Progressive alignment processes can also lead to the development of new abstract forms. Comparison-based computation takes advantage of stored knowledge as a strong method, but with a specificity of processing usually associated only with weak methods. This potential for compatibility among various methods may be a promising sign for a unified account of human reasoning.

References

Almor, A., & Sloman, S. A. (1996). Is deontic reasoning special? *Psychological Review, 103*(2), 374–380.

Anderson, J. R. (1991). The adaptive nature of human categorization. *Psychological Review, 98*(3), 409–429.

Bar-Hillel, M., & Fischoff, B. (1981). When do base rates affect predictions? *Journal of Personality and Social Psychology, 41*, 671–680.

Barsalou, L. W. (1992). *Cognitive psychology: An overview for cognitive scientists.* Hillsdale, NJ: Erlbaum.

Bauer, M. J., & Johnson-Laird, P. N. (1993). How diagrams can improve reasoning. *Psychological Science, 4*, 372–378.

Berry, D. C. (1983). Metacognitive experience and transfer of logical reasoning. *Quarterly Journal of Experimental Psychology, 35A*(1), 39–49.

Bonatti, L. (1994). Why should we abandon the mental logic hypothesis? *Cognition, 50*(1–3), 17–39.

Bowdle, B., & Gentner, D. (1997). Informativity and asymmetry in comparisons. *Cognitive Psychology, 34*(3), 244–286.

Braine, M. D. S. (1978). On the relation between the natural logic of reasoning and standard logic, *Psychological Review, 85*, 1–21.

Braine, M. D. S. (1993). Mental models cannot exclude mental logic, and make little sense without it. *Behavioral and Brain Sciences, 16.*

Braine, M. D. S., & O'Brien, D. P. (1991). A theory of if: A lexical entry, reasoning program, and pragmatic principles. *Psychological Review, 98*(2), 182–203.

Braine, M. D. S., Reiser, B. J., & Rumain, B. (1984). Some empirical justification for a theory of natural propositional logic. In G. H. Bower (Ed.), *The psychology of learning and motivation* (Vol. 18). New York: Academic Press.

Bransford, J. D., Barclay, J. R., & Franks, J. J. (1972). Sentence memory: A constructive versus interpretive approach. *Cognitive Psychology, 3*(2), 193–209.

Byrne, R. M. J. (1989). Suppressing valid inferences with conditionals. *Cognition, 31,* 61–83.

Byrne, R. M. J. (1991). Can valid inferences be suppressed. *Cognition, 39,* 71–78.

Byrne, R. M. J., & Handley, S. J. (1992). Reasoning strategies. *Irish Journal of Psychology, 13*(2), 111–124.

Carey, S. (1985). *Conceptual change in childhood.* Cambridge, MA: MIT Press.

Carraher, T. N., Carraher, D. W., & Schliemann, A. D. (1985). Mathematics in the streets and in the schools. *British Journal of Developmental Psychology, 3,* 21–29.

Chapman, L. J., & Chapman, J. P. (1969). Illusory correlation as an obstacle to the use of valid psychodiagnostic signs. *Journal of Abnormal Psychology, 74,* 272–280.

Cheng, P. W., & Holyoak, K. J. (1985). Pragmatic reasoning schemas. *Cognitive Psychology, 17,* 391–416.

Cheng, P. W., & Holyoak, K. J. (1989). On the natural selection of reasoning theories. *Cognition, 33,* 285–313.

Cheng, P. W., Holyoak, K. J., Nisbett, R. E., & Oliver, L. M. (1986). Pragmatic versus syntactic approaches to training deductive reasoning. *Cognitive Psychology, 18*(3), 293–328.

Chipman, S. F. (1977). Complexity and structure in visual patterns. *Journal of Experimental Psychology: General, 106,* 269–301.

Choi, I., Nisbett, R. E., & Norenzayan, A. (1999). Causal attribution across cultures: Variation and universality. *Psychological Bulletin, 125*(1), 47–63.

Choi, I., Nisbett, R. E., & Smith, E. E. (1997). Culture, category salience, and inductive reasoning. *Cognition, 65*(1), 15–32.

Chrostowski, J. J., & Griggs, R. A. (1985). The effects of problem content, instructions, and verbalization procedure on Wason's selection task. *Current Psychological Research and Reviews, 4*(2), 99–107.

Clement, C. A., & Gentner, D. (1991). Systematicity as a selection constraint in analogical mapping. *Cognitive Science, 15,* 89–132.

Clement, J. (1988). Observed methods for generating analogies in scientific problem solving. *Cognitive Science, 12*(4), 563–586.

Cosmides, L. (1989). The logic of social exchange: Has natural selection shaped how humans reason? Studies with the Wason selection task. *Cognition, 31*(3), 187–276.

Cosmides, L., & Tooby, J. (1992). Cognitive adaptations for social exchange. In J. H. Barkow, L. Cosmides, & J. Tooby (Eds.), *The adapted mind: Evolutionary psychology and the generation of culture.* New York: Oxford University Press.

Cox, J. R., & Griggs, R. A. (1982). The effects of experience on performance in Wason's selection task. *Memory & Cognition, 10,* 496–502.

Davidson, N. S., & Gelman, S. A. (1990). Inductions from novel categories: The role of language and conceptual structure. *Cognitive Development, 5,* 151–176.

Elio, R., & Anderson, J. R. (1981). The effect of category generalizations and instance similarity on schema abstraction. *Journal of Experimental Psychology: Human Learning and Memory, 7,* 397–417.

Evans, J. St. B. T. (1977). Toward a statistical theory of reasoning. *Quarterly Journal of Experimental Psychology, 29*(4), 621–635.

Evans, J. St. B. T. (1982). *The psychology of deductive reasoning.* London: Routledge & Kegan Paul.

Evans, J. St. B. T. (1989). *Bias in human reasoning: Causes and consequences.* Hove, UK: Erlbaum.

Evans, J. St. B. T. (1991). Review of 'Deduction'. *Quarterly Journal of Experimental Psychology, 43A,* 916–919.

Evans, J. St. B. T. (1992). Reasoning with bounded rationality. *Theory and Psychology, 2,* 237–242.

Evans, J. St. B. T., Barston, J. L., & Pollard, P. (1983). On the conflict between logic and belief in syllogistic reasoning. *Memory & Cognition, 11,* 295–306.

Evans, J. St. B. T., Newstead, S. E., & Byrne, R. M. J. (1993). *Human reasoning: The psychology of deduction.* Hove, UK: Erlbaum.

Falkenhainer, B., Forbus, K. D., & Gentner, D. (1989). The structure-mapping engine: Algorithm and examples. *Artificial Intelligence, 41,* 1–63.

Fong, G. T., Krantz, D. H., & Nisbett, R. E. (1986). The effects of statistical training on thinking about everyday problems. *Cognitive Psychology, 18,* 253–292.

Forbus, K. D. (1983). Qualitative reasoning about space and motion. In D. Gentner & A. L. Stevens (Eds.), *Mental models* (pp. 53–73). Hillsdale, NJ: Erlbaum.

Forbus, K. D., & Gentner, D. (1986). Causal reasoning about quantities. *Proceedings of the Eighth Annual Meeting of the Cognitive Science Society,* 196–207.

Gelman, S. A. (1988). The development of induction with natural kind and artifact categories. *Cognitive Psychology, 20,* 65–95.

Gelman, S. A. (1989). Children's use of categories to guide biological inferences. *Human Development, 32,* 65–71.

Gelman, S. A., & Coley, J. D. (1991). Language and categorization: The acquisition of natural kind terms. In S. A. Gelman & J. P. Byrnes (Eds.), *Perspectives in language and thought: Interrelations in development* (pp. 146–196). Cambridge, England: Cambridge University Press.

Gelman, S. A., & Markman, E. M. (1986). Categories and induction in young children. *Cognition, 23,* 183–209.

Gelman, S. A., & Markman, E. M. (1987). Young children's inductions from natural kinds: The role of categories and appearances. *Child Development, 58,* 1532–1541.

Gentner, D. (1983). Structure-mapping: A theoretical framework for analogy. *Cognitive Science, 7,* 155–170.

Gentner, D. (1989). The mechanisms of analogical learning. In S. Vosniadou & A. Ortony (Eds.), *Similarity and analogical reasoning* (pp. 199–241). London: Cambridge University Press. (Reprinted in *Knowledge Acquisition and Learning,* 1993, pp. 673–694)

Gentner, D., & Clement, C. (1988). Evidence for relational selectivity in the interpretation of analogy and metaphor. In G. H. Bower (Ed.), *The psychology of learning and motivation, advances in research and theory* (Vol. 22, pp. 307–358). New York: Academic Press.

Gentner, D., & Gentner, D. R. (1983). Flowing waters or teeming crowds: Mental models of electricity. In D. Gentner & A. L. Stevens (Eds.), *Mental models* (pp. 99–129). Hillsdale, NJ: Erlbaum. (Reprinted in *Cognitive functions: Classic readings in representation and reasoning,* M. J. Brosnan, Ed., Eltham, London: Greenwich University Press)

Gentner, D., & Markman, A. B. (1993). Analogy—Watershed or Waterloo? Structural alignment and the development of connectionist models of cognition. In S. J. Hanson, J. D. Cowan, & C. L. Giles (Eds.), *Advances in neural information processing systems, 5* (pp. 855–862). San Mateo, CA: Morgan Kauffmann.

Gentner, D., & Markman, A. B. (1994). Structural alignment in comparison: No difference without similarity. *Psychological Science, 5*(3), 152–158.

Gentner, D., & Markman, A. B. (1995). Similarity is like analogy: Structural alignment in comparison. In C. Cacciari (Ed.), *Similarity in language, thought and perception* (pp. 111–147). Brussels: BREPOLS.

Gentner, D., & Markman, A. B. (1997). Structure mapping in analogy and similarity. *American Psychologist, 52,* 45–56.

Gentner, D., & Medina, J. (1997). Comparison and the development of cognition and language. *Cognitive Studies: Bulletin of the Japanese Cognitive Science Society, 4*(1), 112–149.

Gentner, D., & Medina, J. (1998). Similarity and the development of rules. *Cognition, 65,* 263–297.

Gentner, D., & Rattermann, M. J. (1991). Language and the career of similarity. In S. A. Gelman & J. P.

Brynes (Eds.), *Perspectives on thought and language: Interrelations in development* (pp. 225–277). London: Cambridge University Press.

Gentner, D., Rattermann, M. J., & Forbus, K. D. (1993). The roles of similarity in transfer: Separating retrievability and inferential soundness. *Cognitive Psychology, 25,* 524–575.

Gentner, D., Rattermann, M. J., Markman, A. B., & Kotovsky, L. (1995). Two forces in the development of relational similarity. In T. J. Simon & G. S. Halford (Eds.), *Developing cognitive competence: New approaches to process modeling* (pp. 263–313). Hillsdale, NJ: Erlbaum.

Gentner, D., & Stevens, A. L. (Eds.). (1983). *Mental models.* Hillsdale, NJ: Erlbaum.

Gentner, D., & Toupin, C. (1986). Systematicity and surface similarity in the development of analogy. *Cognitive Science, 10,* 277–300.

Gentner, D., & Wolff, P. (in press). Metaphor and knowledge change. In E. Dietrich & A. Markman (Eds.), *Cognitive dynamics: Conceptual change in humans and machines.* Cambridge, MA: MIT Press.

Gick, M. L., & Holyoak, K. J. (1980). Analogical problem solving. *Cognitive Psychology, 12,* 306–355.

Gick, M. L., & Holyoak, K. J. (1983). Schema induction and analogical transfer. *Cognitive Psychology, 15,* 1–38.

Gigerenzer, G., & Hug, K. (1992). Domain-specific reasoning: Social contracts, cheating and perspective change. *Cognition, 43,* 127–171.

Girotto, V., Gilly, M., Blaye, A., & Light, P. (1989). Children's performance on the selection task: Plausibility and familiarity. *European Bulletin of Cognitive Psychology, 9,* 227–231.

Girotto, V., Light, P., & Colbourn, C. (1988). Pragmatic schemas and conditional reasoning in children. *Quarterly Journal of Experimental Psychology, 40A*(3), 469–482.

Girotto, V., Mazzacco, A., & Cherubini, P. (1992). Judgments of deontic relevance in reasoning: A reply to Jackson and Griggs. *Quarterly Journal of Experimental Psychology, 45A,* 547–574.

Goldstone, R. L. (1994a). The role of similarity in categorization: Providing a groundwork. *Cognition, 52*(2), 125–157.

Goldstone, R. L. (1994b). Similarity, interactive activation, and mapping. *Journal of Experimental Psychology: Learning, Memory, and Cognition, 20*(1), 3–28.

Goldstone, R. L., & Medin, D. L. (1994a). Similarity, interactive-activation and mapping: An overview. In K. J. Holyoak & J. A. Barnden (Eds.), *Advances in connectionist and neural computation theory: Vol. 2. Analogical connections* (pp. 321–362). Norwood, NJ: Ablex.

Goldstone, R. L., & Medin, D. L. (1994b). Time course of comparison. *Journal of Experimental Psychology: Learning, Memory, and Cognition, 20*(1), 29–50.

Goldstone, R. L., Medin, D. L., & Gentner, D. (1991). Relational similarity and the nonindependence of features in similarity judgments. *Cognitive Psychology, 23,* 222–264.

Goodman, N. (1972). Seven strictures on similarity. In N. Goodman (Ed.), *Problems and projects.* New York: Bobbs-Merrill.

Griggs, R. A. (1983). The role of problem content in the selection task and THOG problem. In J. St. B. T. Evans (Ed.), *Thinking and reasoning: Psychological approaches.* London: Routledge.

Griggs, R. A., & Cox, J. R. (1982). The elusive thematic-materials effect in Wason selection task. *British Journal of Psychology, 73,* 407–420.

Griggs, R. A., & Cox, J. R. (1983). The effects of problem content and negation on Wason's selection task. *Quarterly Journal of Experimental Psychology, 35A,* 519–533.

Hahn, U., & Chater, N. (1998). Similarity and rules: Distinct? Exhaustive? Empirically distinguishable? *Cognition, 65,* 197–230.

Halford, G. S. (1987). A structure-mapping approach to cognitive development: The neo-Piagetian theories of cognitive development: Toward an interpretation [Special issue]. *International Journal of Psychology, 22*(5–6), 609–642.

Halford, G. S. (1992). Analogical reasoning and conceptual complexity in cognitive development. *Human Development, 35*(4), 193–218.

Halford, G. S. (1993). *Children's understanding: The development of mental models.* Hillsdale, NJ: Erlbaum.

Halford, G. S., Bain, J. D., & Maybery, M. T. (1994). Analogies in intra-domain and inter-domain transfer of learning. In K. J. Holyoak & J. A. Barnden (Eds.), *Connectionist approaches to analogy, metaphor and case-based reasoning.*

Hayes-Roth, F., & McDermott, J. (1978). An interference matching technique for inducing abstractions. *Communications of the ACM, 21*(5), 401–411.

Heit, E., & Rubinstein, J. (1994). Similarity and property effects in inductive reasoning. *Journal of Experimental Psychology: Learning, Memory, and Cognition, 20*(2), 1–12.

Henle, M. (1962). On the relation between logic and thinking. *Psychological Review, 69,* 366–378.

Hoch, S. J., & Tschirgi, J. E. (1985). Logical knowledge and cue redundancy in deductive reasoning. *Memory & Cognition, 13*(5), 453–462.

Hofstadter, D. R., & Mitchell, M. (1994). The Copycat project: A model of mental fluidity and analogy-making. In K. J. Holyoak & J. A. Barnden (Eds.), *Advances in connectionist and neural computation theory: Vol. 2. Analogical connections* (pp. 31–112). Norwood, NJ: Ablex.

Holland, J. H., Holyoak, K. F., Nisbett, R. E., & Thagard, P. R. (1986). *Induction: Processes of inference, learning, and discovery.* Cambridge, MA: MIT Press.

Holyoak, K. J., & Cheng, P. W. (1995). Pragmatic reasoning about human voluntary action: Evidence from Wason's selection task. In S. E. Newstead & J. St. B. T. Evans (Eds.), *Perspectives on thinking and reasoning: Essays in honour of Peter Wason.* London: Erlbaum.

Holyoak, K. J, & Koh, K. (1987). Surface and structural similarity in analogical transfer. *Memory & Cognition, 15,* 332–340.

Holyoak, K. J., Novick, L. R., & Melz, E. R. (1994). Component processes in analogical transfer: Mapping, pattern completion, and adaptation. In K. J. Holyoak & J. A. Barnden (Eds.), *Advances in connectionist and neural computation theory: Vol. 2. Analogical connections.* (pp. 113–180). Norwood, NJ: Ablex.

Holyoak, K. J., & Spellman, B. A. (1993). Thinking. *Annual Review of Psychology, 44,* 265–315.

Holyoak, K. J., & Thagard, P. (1989). Analogical mapping by constraint satisfaction. *Cognitive Science, 13*(3), 295–355.

Hummel, J. E., & Holyoak, K. J. (1997). Distributed representations of structure: A theory of analogical access and mapping. *Psychological Review, 104*(3), 427–466.

Inagaki, K. (1989). Developmental shift in biological inference processes: From similarity-based to category-based attribution. *Human Development, 32,* 79–87.

Inagaki, K. (1990). The effects of raising animals on children's biological knowledge. *British Journal of Developmental Psychology, 8,* 119–129.

Inagaki, K., & Hatano, G. (1987). Young children's spontaneous personification as analogy. *Child Development, 58,* 1013–1020.

Inagaki, K., & Hatano, G. (1991). Constrained person analogy in young children's biological inference. *Cognitive Development, 6,* 219–231.

Inagaki, K., & Sugiyama, K. (1988). Attributing human characteristics: Developmental changes in over- and underattribution. *Cognitive Development, 3,* 55–70.

Inhelder, B., & Piaget, J. (1964). *The early growth of logic in the child.* London: Routledge & Kegan Paul.

Jacobs, R. A., Jordan, M. I., Nowlan, S. J., & Hinton, G. E. (1991). Adaptive mixtures of local experts. *Neural Computation, 3*(1), 79–87.

Johnson-Laird, P. N. (1983). *Mental models.* Cambridge University Press.

Johnson-Laird, P. N. (1989). Mental models. In M. I. Posner (Ed.), *Foundations of cognitive science.* Cambridge, MA: MIT Press.

Johnson-Laird, P. N., & Byrne, R. M. J. (1989). Only reasoning. *Journal of Memory and Language, 28,* 313–330.

Johnson-Laird, P. N., & Byrne, R. M. J. (1990). Meta-logical reasoning: Knights, knaves, and rips. *Cognition, 36,* 69–84.

Johnson-Laird, P. N., & Byrne, R. M. J. (1991). *Deduction.* Hove, UK: Erlbaum.

Johnson-Laird, P. N., & Byrne, R. M. J. (1993). Rules or models? *Behavioral and Brain Sciences, 16.*

Johnson-Laird, P. N., Byrne, R. M. J., & Schaeken, W. (1992). Propositional reasoning by model. *Psychological Review, 99*(3), 418–439.

Johnson-Laird, P. N., Byrne, R. M. J., & Schaeken, W. (1994). Why models rather than rules give a better account of prepositional reasoning: A reply to Bonatti and to O'Brien, Braine, and Yang. *Psychological Review, 101,* 734–739.

Johnson-Laird, P. N., Legrenzi, P., & Legrenzi, M. S. (1972). Reasoning and a sense of reality. *British Journal of Psychology, 62*(3), 395–400.

Johnson-Laird, P. N., Oakhill, J., & Bull, D. (1986). Children's syllogistic reasoning. *Quarterly Journal of Experimental Psychology, 38A*(1), 35–58.

Johnson-Laird, P. N., & Wason, P. C. (1970). A theoretical analysis of insight into a reasoning task. *Cognitive Psychology, 1,* 134–148.

Kahneman, D., & Miller, D. T. (1986). Norm theory: Comparing reality to its alternatives. *Psychological Review, 93,* 136–153.

Kahneman, D., Slovic, P., & Tversky, A. (1982). *Judgment under certainty: Heuristics and biases.* Cambridge, England: Cambridge University Press.

Kass, A. (1994). Tweaker: Adapting old explanations to new situations. In R. Schank, A. Kass, & C. K. Riesbeck (Eds.), *Inside case-based explanation* (pp. 263–295). Hillsdale, NJ: Erlbaum.

Keane, M. T. (1988). *Analogical problem solving.* Chichester, England: Ellis Horwood (New York: Halsted Press).

Keane, M. T. (1996). On adaptation in analogy: Tests of pragmatic importance and adaptability in analogical problem solving. *Quarterly Journal of Experimental Psychology, 49A*(4), 1062–1085.

Keane, M. T., & Brayshaw, M. (1988). The incremental analogical machine: A computational model of analogy. In D. Sleeman (Ed.), *Third European Working Session on Machine Learning* (pp. 53–62). San Mateo, CA: Kaufmann.

Keil, F. C. (1989). *Concepts, kinds, and cognitive development.* Cambridge, MA: MIT Press.

Keil, F. C. (1991a). The emergence of theoretical beliefs as constraints on concepts. In S. Carey & R. Gelman (Eds.), *The epigenesis of mind* (pp. 3–36). Hillsdale, NJ: Erlbaum.

Keil, F. C. (1991b). Theories, concepts, and the acquisition of word meaning. In J. Byrnes & S. Gelman (Eds.), *Perspectives on language and thought: Interrelations in development* (pp. 197–224). Cambridge, England: Cambridge University Press.

Kempton, W. (1986). Two theories of home heat control. *Cognitive Science, 10,* 75–90.

Kempton, W., Boster, J. S., & Hartley, J. (1994). *Environmental values in American culture.* Cambridge, MA: MIT Press.

Kieras, D. E., & Bovair, S. (1984). The role of a mental model in learning to operate a device. *Cognitive Science, 8,* 255–273.

Klaczynski, P. A., Gelfand, H., & Reese, H. W. (1989). Transfer of conditional reasoning: Effects of explanations and initial problem types. *Memory & Cognition, 17,* 208–220.

Kotovsky, L., & Gentner, D. (1996). Comparison and categorization in the development of relational similarity. *Child Development, 67,* 2797–2822.

Kroger, J. K., Cheng, P. W., & Holyoak, K. J. (1993). Evoking the permission schema: The impact of explicit negation and a violation-checking context. *Quarterly Journal of Experimental Psychology, 46A,* 615–635.

Kurtz, K. J., & Gentner, D. (1998). *Category learning and comparison in the evolution of similarity structure.* 20th annual meeting of the Cognitive Science Society, Madison, WI.

Lassaline, M. E. (1996). Structural alignment in induction and similarity. *Journal of Experimental Psychology: Learning, Memory, and Cognition, 22*(3), 754–770.

Lopez, A., Atran, S., Coley, J., Medin, D. L., & Smith, E. E. (1997). The tree of life: Universal and cultural features of folkbiological taxonomies and inductions. *Cognitive Psychology, 32,* 251–295.

Lopez, A., Gelman, S. A., Gutheil, G., & Smith, E. E. (1992). The development of category-based induction. *Child Development, 63,* 1070–1090.

Manis, M., Dovalina, I., Avis, N. E., & Cardoze, S. (1980). Base rates can affect individual predictions. *Journal of Personality and Social Psychology, 38,* 287–298.

Manktelow, K. I., & Evans, J. St. B. T. (1979). Facilitation of reasoning by realism: Effect or non-effect? *British Journal of Psychology, 70,* 477–488.

Manktelow, K. I., & Over, D. E. (1990). Deontic thought and the selection task. In K. J. Gilhooly, M. Keane, R. Logie, & G. Erdos (Eds.), *Lines of thought: Reflections on the psychology of thinking.* Chichester, England: Wiley.

Manktelow, K. I., & Over, D. E. (1991). Social roles and utilities in reasoning with deontic conditionals. *Cognition, 39,* 85–105.

Marcus, S. L., & Rips, L. J. (1979). Conditional reasoning. *Journal of Verbal Learning and Verbal Behavior, 18,* 199–233.

Markman, A. B. (1997). Constraints on analogical inference. *Cognitive Science, 21*(4), 373–418.

Markman, A. B., & Gentner, D. (1993a). *All differences are not created equal: A structural alignment view of similarity.* Proceedings of the 15th annual conference of the Cognitive Science Society, Boulder, CO, pp. 682–686.

Markman, A. B., & Gentner, D. (1993b). Splitting the differences: A structural alignment view of similarity. *Journal of Memory and Language, 32,* 517–535.

Markman, A. B., & Gentner, D. (1993c). Structural alignment during similarity comparisons. *Cognitive Psychology, 25,* 431–467.

Markman, A. B., & Gentner, D. (1996). Commonalities and differences in similarity comparisons. *Memory & Cognition, 24*(2), 235–249.

Markman, A. B., & Wisniewski, E. (1997). Similar and different: The differentiation of basic-level categories. *Journal of Experimental Psychology: Learning, Memory, and Cognition, 23*(1), 54–70.

McCloskey, M. (1983). Intuitive physics. *Scientific American, 248*(4), 122–130.

McCloskey, M., Caramazza, A., & Green, B. (1980). Curvilinear motion in the absence of external forces: Naive beliefs about the motion of objects. *Science, 210*(4474), 1139–1141.

Medin, D. L., Goldstone, R. L., & Gentner, D. (1993). Respects for similarity. *Psychological Review, 100*(2), 254–278.

Medin, D. L., Lynch, E. B., & Coley, J. D. (1997). Categorization and reasoning among tree experts: Do all roads lead to Rome? *Cognitive Psychology, 32,* 49–96.

Medin, D. L., & Ortony, A. (1989). Psychological essentialism. In S. Vosniadou & A. Ortony (Eds.), *Similarity and analogical reasoning* (pp. 179–195). New York: Cambridge University Press.

Medin, D. L., & Ross, B. H. (1989). The specific character of abstract thought: Categorization, problem-solving, and induction. In R. J. Sternberg (Ed.), *Advances in the psychology of human intelligence* (Vol. 5, pp. 189–223). Hillsdale, NJ: Erlbaum.

Miyake, N. (1986). Constructive interaction and the iterative process of understanding. *Cognitive Psychology, 10*(2), 151–177.

Murphy, G. L., & Medin, D. L. (1985). The role of theories in conceptual coherence. *Psychological Review, 92,* 289–316.

Newell, A., & Simon, H. A. (1972). *Human problem solving.* Englewood Cliffs, NJ: Prentice-Hall.

Novick, L. R. (1988a). Analogical transfer, problem similarity, and expertise. *Journal of Experimental Psychology: Learning, Memory, and Cognition, 14,* 510–520.

Novick, L. R. (1988b). Analogical transfer: Processes and individual differences. In D. H. Helman (Ed.), *Analogical reasoning: Perspectives of artificial intelligence, cognitive science, and philosophy* (pp. 125–145). Dordrecht, The Netherlands: Kluwer.

Oaksford, M., & Chater, N. (1993). Reasoning theories and bounded rationality. In K. I. Manktelow & D. E. Over (Eds.), *Rationality.* London: Routledge.

O'Brien, D. P., Braine, M. D. S., & Yang, Y. (1994). Propositional reasoning by mental models? Simple to refute in principle and in practice. *Psychological Review, 101,* 711–724.

Osherson, D. N. (1975). Logic and models of logical thinking. In R. J. Falmagne (Ed.), *Reasoning: Representation and process in children and adults.* Hillsdale, NJ: Erlbaum.

Osherson, D. N., Smith, E. E., Wilkie, O., Lopez, A., & Shafir, E. (1990). Category-based induction. *Psychological Review, 97*, 185–200.

Overton, W. F., Ward, S. L., Noveck, I. A., Black, J., & O'Brien, D. P. (1987). Form and content in the development of deductive reasoning. *Developmental Psychology, 23*, 22–30.

Platt, R. D., & Griggs, R. A. (1993). Darwininan algorithms and the Wason selection task: A factorial analysis of social contract selection task problems. *Cognition, 48*, 163–192.

Politzer, G., & Nguyen-Xuan, A. (1992). Reasoning about conditional promises and warnings: Darwinian algorithms, mental models, relevance judgments or pragmatic schemas? *Quarterly Journal of Experimental Psychology, 44*, 401–412.

Polk, T. (1993). Mental models, more or less. *Behavioral and Brain Sciences, 16.*

Pollard, P. (1982). Human reasoning: Some possible effects of availability. *Cognition, 12*, 65–96.

Pollard, P. (1990). Natural selection for the selection task: Limits to social exchange theory. *Cognition, 36*, 195–204.

Pollard, P., & Evans, J. St. B. T. (1987). On the relationship between context and context effects in reasoning. *American Journal of Psychology, 100*, 41–60.

Quine, W. V. (1969). *Ontological relativity and other essays.* New York: Columbia University Press.

Ratcliff, R., & McKoon, G. (1989). Similarity information versus relational information: Differences in the time course of retrieval. *Cognitive Psychology, 21*, 139–155.

Reed, S. K. (1987). A structure-mapping model for word problems. *Journal of Experimental Psychology: Learning, Memory, and Cognition, 13*, 124–139.

Reich, S. S., & Ruth, P. (1982). Wason's selection task: Verification, falsification and matching. *British Journal of Psychology, 73*, 395–405.

Revlis, R. (1975). Two models of syllogistic inference: Feature selection and conversion. *Journal of Verbal Learning and Verbal Behavior, 14*, 180–195.

Rips, L. J. (1975). Inductive judgments about natural categories. *Journal of Verbal Learning and Verbal Behavior, 14*, 665–681.

Rips, L. J. (1983). Cognitive processes in propositional reasoning. *Psychological Review, 90*, 38–71.

Rips, L. J. (1988). Deduction. In R. J. Sternberg & E. E. Smith (Eds.), *The psychology of human thought.* New York: Cambridge University Press.

Rips, L. J. (1989). The psychology of knights and knaves. *Cognition, 31*, 85–116.

Rips, L. J. (1990). Reasoning. *Annual Review of Psychology, 41*, 85–116.

Rips, L. J. (1994a). *The psychology of proof: Deductive reasoning in human thinking.* Cambridge, MA: MIT press.

Rips, L. J. (1994b). Deduction and its cognitive basis. In R. J. Sternberg (Ed.), *Thinking and problem solving.* San Diego, CA: AcademicPress.

Rips, L. J. (1995). Deduction and cognition. In E. E. Smith & D. N. Osherson (Eds.), *Thinking: An invitation to cognitive science* (Vol. 3). Cambridge, MA: MIT Press.

Rips, L. J., & Conrad, F. G. (1983). Individual differences in deduction. *Cognition and Brain Theory, 6*, 259–285.

Rosch, E., Mervis, C. B., Gray, W. D., Johnson, D. M., & Boyes-Braem, P. (1976). Basic objects in natural categories. *Cognitive Psychology, 8*, 382–439.

Ross, B. H. (1984). Remindings and their effects in learning a cognitive skill. *Cognitive Psychology, 16*, 371–416.

Ross, B. H. (1987). This is like that: The use of earlier problems and the separation of similarity effects. *Journal of Experimental Psychology: Learning, Memory, and Cognition, 13*(4), 629–639.

Ross, B. H. (1989). Distinguishing types of superficial similarities: Different effects on the access and use of earlier examples. *Journal of Experimental Psychology: Learning, Memory and Cognition, 15*(3), 456–468.

Ross, B. H., & Murphy, G. L. (1996). Category-based predictions: Influence of uncertainty and feature associations. *Journal of Experimental Psychology: Learning, Memory, and Cognition, 22*(3), 736–753.

Rumain, B., Connell, J., & Braine, M. D. S. (1983). Conversational comprehension processes are responsible for reasoning fallacies in children as well as adults. *Developmental Psychology, 19,* 471–481.

Rumelhart, D. E. (1989). Toward a microstructural account of human reasoning. In S. Vosniadou & A. Ortony (Eds.), *Similarity and analogical reasoning* (pp. 298–312). New York: Cambridge University Press.

Rumelhart, D. E., Durbin, R., Golden, R., & Chauvin, Y. (1996). Backpropagation: The basic theory. In P. Smolensky, M. C. Mozer, & D. E. Rumelhart (Eds.), *Mathematical perspectives on neural networks.* Mahwah, NJ: Erlbaum.

Rumelhart, D. E., Smolensky, P., McClelland, J. L., & Hinton, G. E. (1986). Schemata and sequential thought processes in PDP models. In J. L. McClelland & D. E. Rumelhart (Eds.), *Parallel distributed processing: Explorations in the microstructure of cognition.*

Schwartz, D. L., & Black, J. B. (1996). Analog imagery in mental model reasoning: Depictive models. *Cognitive Psychology, 30,* 154–219.

Shafir, E., Smith, E. E., & Osherson, D. (1990). Typicality and reasoning fallacies. *Memory & Cognition, 18,* 229–239.

Sloman, S. A. (1993). Feature-based induction. *Cognitive Psychology, 25,* 231–280.

Sloman, S. A. (1996). The empirical case for two systems of reasoning. *Psychological Bulletin, 119*(1), 3–22.

Sloman, S. A. (1998). Categorical inference is not a tree: The myth of inheritance hierarchies. *Cognitive Psychology, 35*(1), 1–33.

Smith, E. E., Langston, C., & Nisbett, R. E. (1992). The case for rules in reasoning. *Cognitive Science, 16,* 1–40.

Smith, E. E., & Medin, D. L. (1984). *Categories and concepts.* Cambridge, MA: Harvard University Press.

Smith, E. E., & Osherson, D. N. (1989). Similarity and decision making. In S. Vosniadou & A. Ortony (Eds.), *Similarity and analogical reasoning* (pp. 60–75). New York: Cambridge University Press.

Smith, L. B. (1984). Young children's understanding of attributes and dimensions: A comparison of conceptual and linguistic measures. *Child Development, 55,* 363–380.

Smith, L. B. (1989). A model of perceptual classification in children and adults. *Psychological Review, 96,* 125–144.

Smith, L. B. (1993). The concept of same. In H. W. Reese (Ed.), *Advances in child development and behavior* (Vol. 24, pp. 215–252). San Diego, CA: Academic Press.

Smolensky, P. (1988). On the proper treatment of connectionism. *Behavioral and Brain Sciences, 11,* 1–23.

Smolensky, P., Mozer, M. C., & Rumelhart, D. E. (1996). *Mathematical perspectives on neural networks.* Mahwah, NJ: Erlbaum.

Tversky, A., & Kahneman, D. (1973). Availability: A heuristic for judging frequency and probability. *Cognitive Psychology, 5,* 207–232.

Tversky, A., & Kahneman, D. (1981). The framing of decisions and the psychology of choice. *Science, 211,* 453–458.

Tversky, A., & Kahneman, D. (1983). Extensional versus intuitive reasoning: The conjunction fallacy in probability judgment. *Psychological Review, 90*(4), 293–315.

Tversky, B. (1991). Distortions in memory for visual displays. In S. R. Ellis, M. Kaiser, & A. Grunewald (Eds.), *Spatial instruments and spatial displays* (pp. 61–75). Hillsdale, NJ: Erlbaum.

Ward, S. L., & Overton, W. F. (1990). Semantic familiarity, relevance, and the development of deductive reasoning. *Developmental Psychology, 26,* 488–493.

Wason, P. C. (1966). Reasoning. In B. M. Foss (Ed.), *New horizons in psychology* (Vol. 1). Harmondsworth, Middlesex: Penguin.

Wason, P. C. (1968). Reasoning about a rule. *Quarterly Journal of Experimental Psychology,* 273–281.

Wason, P. C. (1969). Regression in reasoning? *British Journal of Psychology, 60,* 471–480.

Wason, P. C., & Johnson-Laird, P. N. (1970). A conflict between selecting and evaluating information in an inferential task. *British Journal of Psychology, 61,* 509–515.

Wason, P. C., & Johnson-Laird, P. N. (1972). *Psychology of reasoning: Structure and content.* London: Batsford.

Wason, P. C., & Shapiro, D. (1971). Natural and contrived experience in a reasoning problem. *Quarterly Journal of Experimental Psychology, 23,* 63–71.

Wisniewski, E. J. (1995). Prior knowledge and functionally relevant features in concept learning. *Journal of Experimental Psychology: Learning, Memory, and Cognition, 21*(2), 449–468.

Wittgenstein, L. (1953). *Philosophical investigations.* New York: Macmillan.

Wu, M. L., & Gentner, D. (1998). *Structure in category-based induction.* Twentieth annual meeting of the Cognitive Science Society, Madison, WI.

Yachanin, S. A. (1986). Facilitation in Wason's selection task: Contents and instructions. *Current Psychological Research and Review, 5,* 20–29.

Yachanin, S. A., & Tweney, R. D. (1982). The effect of thematic content on cognitive strategies in the four-card selection task. *Bulletin of the Psychonomic Society, 19,* 87–90.

CHAPTER 5

Cognitive Development

Susan Carey
Ellen M. Markman

To account for human knowledge, one must specify the innate initial state and the mechanisms intervening between birth and the stable adult state. Thus, several of the foundational issues in cognitive science are developmental questions at heart. These include all facets of the nativist–empiricist debate. Philosophers who sharpened the debate were not interested in development per se, but rather were interested in fundamental issues within epistemology. They saw that no account of human knowledge could stand if one cannot imagine, at least in principle, how that knowledge is acquired. Nativists such as Kant and empiricists such as Hume appealed to learnability (among other things) as a criterion for accepting any given account of the nature of the human mind.

The modern study of cognitive development engages these same debates. In doing so, studies of development provide one source of data relevant to characterizing cognitive architecture. Developmental studies provide evidence for specialized learning mechanisms in different content domains, and also provide a unique window on such classic issues as how to draw a principled distinction between perception and cognition. In addition to constraining our theories of adult cognition, development poses problems of its own. Those discussed in this chapter include continuity versus discontinuity within cognitive development, the existence of critical periods in development, and the role of maturation in cognitive development.

I. THE NATIVIST–EMPIRICIST DEBATE

We begin this chapter with two classic cases from the historical empiricist–nativist debate: the origin of physical knowledge (especially the concept *physical object*) and the origin of mathematical knowledge (especially the concept *integer*).

The essence of the empiricist position is that knowledge is grounded in sensory, perceptual, or sensorimotor primitives, and that domain-general learning mechanisms such as association, prototype abstraction, and correlation detection suffice to account for the construction of more complex knowledge from perceptual primitives. Captured under this broad characterization are the British empiricists such as Locke, Berkeley, and Hume, modern behaviorists, modern philosophers such as Quine, many nonbehaviorist psychologists, such as Piaget, and many connectionist modelers (e.g., Elman et al., 1996). One particularly striking developmental example comes from Saffran, Aslin, and Newport's (1996) demonstration of statistical learning in infants. They had 8-month-old infants listen to 2 min of a tape of a steady stream of nonsense syllables. They manipulated the transitional probabilities of the sound sequences the babies listened to, but the continuous stream of syllables had no pauses, stress, or other acoustic information about how to segment the stream. Transitional probabilities between syllables were used to distinguish potential "words," defined as syllable strings with very high transitional probabilities, from "nonwords," defined as strings with low transitional probabilities. Babies preferred to listen to the "words" over the "nonwords," thus demonstrating their ability to extract the statistical regularities from a short exposure to the input. Whether this kind of learning mechanism is available to babies across a wide range of domains or whether it is limited to speech segmentation remains to be seen. But it is an intriguing candidate for a domain-general mechanism.

The nativist notion of domain-specific cognition to be pursued here is articulated most clearly by Chomsky (1980). On this view, humans are endowed with a number of systems of knowledge, such as knowledge of language, knowledge of physical objects, knowledge of persons, and knowledge of space. Each system of knowledge applies to a distinct set of entities and phenomena. For example, knowledge of language applies to sentences and their constituents; knowledge of physical objects applies to macroscopic material bodies and their behavior; knowledge of space applies to places in the layout and geometrical relations among them. More deeply, each knowledge system is organized around a distinct set of core principles. For language, these are the principles of universal grammar; for physical objects, the principles might include Newton's axioms or the principles of continuity and solidity; for space, the principles might include the axioms and postulates of Euclidean geometry. These domain-specific cognitive structures are *learning mechanisms*. This is seen most clearly in contemporary theories of syntax acquisition, which debate the nature of the evidence that triggers parameter settings among innately constrained values (e.g., Roeper & Williams, 1987).

For the purposes of this chapter, we take the distinction between the empiricist and the nativist positions to be the commitment to the existence of domain-specific learning mechanisms.

Just as in the historical debate, appeals to learnability are still current within cognitive science, most overtly in research on language acquisition. Whether some syntactic device would be learnable or not is one consideration in decisions between different syntactic proposals. In a classic work within this tradition, Wexler and Cullicover (1980) proved that under certain assumptions about the syntax to be learned (i.e., Chomsky, 1965), the initial state of a language acquisition device, the input to it, and its learning mechanisms, this system would converge on English. Anybody is free to challenge any of the assumptions of this proof, but then must assume the burden of providing a mechanism that would converge on English under different assumptions. See, for example, Morgan's (1986) argument that Wexler and Cullicover underestimated the evidence for syntactic structure from prosodic information, his evidence that children have access to such information, and his characterization of how a learning device that made use of such information would differ from that proposed by Wexler and Cullicover. See also Gibson and Wexler's (1994) discussion of the learnability of a different syntactic theory (i.e., Chomsky, 1981).

Today's versions of learnability arguments differ from those of the philosophers in several respects. First, they are couched in terms of much richer accounts of the representations that constitute knowledge, and much richer ideas about possible learning mechanisms. Second, they are constrained by actual empirical study of children, even infants. Learnability arguments are no longer strictly a priori.

A. Case 1: The Object Concept

Adults represent the world in terms of enduring solid physical objects. People, rocks, and tables are all conceptualized in the same ways with respect to certain core principles: all physical objects are subject to the constraints that one of them cannot be two places at the same time, and that two of them cannot coincide in space and time. Objects do not come into and out of existence, and they occupy unique points in space and time. These aspects of our representation of the world are certainly deeply entrenched in the adult conceptual system. How do they arise?

On the empiricist position, babies begin by representing perceptual properties of objects—their shapes, colors, textures, and patterns of motion. Domain-general learning mechanisms can easily account for the detection of co-occurrence of such perceptual properties. For instance, babies can come to expect that entities with a certain symmetrical configuration (two round shapes above a triangular shape above an oval shape) are usually of a certain texture and/or color, are flexible, mobile, emit sounds, and so on. The learnability question, though, is whether babies can derive such principles as that objects do not go into and out of existence (object permanence), or do not intersect in space and time, from domain-general learning mechanisms operating on perceptual data.

Consider object permanence. When an object goes behind a barrier, what evidence is available to a baby that the object does not cease to exist? Note that this way of posing the problem already grants the baby a representation in terms of the concept *object,* and thus begs part of the question. The problem should be posed: when a perceived entity of a certain size, color, and shape, moves on a trajectory that takes it behind a different perceived entity, what happens to the first entity? Does the baby represent its continued existence? Learnability considerations suggest that there could be no conclusive evidence that would lead the baby to infer continued existence. The baby's observation that an entity with the same perceptual properties later appears from behind the screen, or that an entity with the same perceptual properties is revealed if the barrier is removed, is certainly not conclusive evidence. In principle, such evidence would be consistent with two interpretations—the entity continued to exist, or another similar one came into existence behind the barrier.

Empiricists accept this learnability argument. Quine (1960), for example, argued that the concept of an object central to our worldview is a cultural construction, embodied in our language, and that children do not construct it until they master the quantificational system of nominal syntax (i.e., quantifiers such as "a, one, . ." and particles such as "same"). Piaget (1955) was the first to attempt to bring empirical data to bear on the question. In his famous studies of object permanence, he found that below around 8 months of age, babies will not retrieve objects that have been placed under or behind barriers, and he interpreted this finding as revealing that they did not represent the objects' continued existence. After that age, Piaget found that babies will search behind or under a barrier for an object that has gone out of view, but he did not conclude that this success showed that they represent the absent object as still existing. Rather, he thought they have learned a generalization—search where you see something disappear and something interesting will happen. The reason he came to this conclusion was the existence of the "A not B error." If babies of 8–11 months see an object disappear in location A, they will search in location A and retrieve it. Subsequently, if the object is then hidden in location B, the baby will search again in location A! Piaget argued that the A not B error shows that the baby is not actually tracking the object and representing its continued existence when it went out of view, but simply has learned a rule—search where you see something disappear.

What evidence, other than that from searching for and finding objects that disappeared behind barriers, might be available to the child? The child might reason that since most entities that are visible or tangible are spatiotemporally continuous (i.e., do not disappear and reappear), this is a property that holds even when the child is not in perceptual contact with them. That is, the child induces spatiotemporal–temporal continuity of objects from perceptual experience of visible, tangible objects. This inductive inference is just probabilistic, but it is deeply entrenched through massive experience with physical objects. One consequence of this empiricist proposal is that the adult intuition that spatiotemporal-temporal continuity is *constitutive* of our concept of an object (part of what it is to *be* an object) is wrong; it is not a necessary truth, merely a well-confirmed one.

This position differs from Spelke's nativist proposal that spatiotemporal continuity is one of the core principles that *determines* the entities in the world that are objects (cf. Carey & Spelke, 1994). On Spelke's view, this property does not have to be learned; it is part of the innate principles that define what objects are in the first place.

In the past 15 years or so, methods for providing reliable information of how young infants represent the world have become available, and have yielded data that inform the nativist–empiricist debate concerning the origin of the concept *object*. Research with infants requires a very sensitive, noninvasive, measure of how they are representing the world. The new methods rely on babies' selective attention to novelty. The basic idea is simple. Under most circumstances babies will look longer at what is unfamiliar or unexpected compared to what is familiar or expected. Researchers use this fact to diagnose how babies represent some situation, especially what babies consider surprising given their current state of knowledge.

The first use of this method to explore infant conceptual knowledge was a pioneering experiment by Ball (1973), which has subsequently been replicated by Spelke, Phillips, and Woodward (1995). In this study, infants were shown a screen that partially occluded a green ball protruding out one side of it. They were habituated to events in which a second, red, ball rolled behind the screen, followed by the first, green, one going into motion (see Figure 1). After repeatedly being shown this event, the screen was removed, and babies were shown one of the two following events: the red ball rolling up and hitting the green ball, setting it in motion, or the red ball rolling up and stopping short of the green ball, which, after a suitable

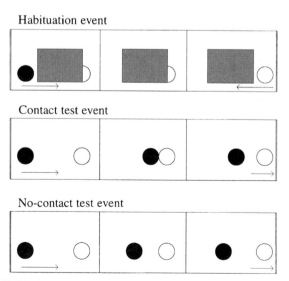

FIGURE 1   Schematic of Ball's (1973) study of infant causal reasoning.

pause, moved as if the red ball had continued, hit it, and set it in motion. Babies as young as 8 months generalize habituation to the first of these two events (the event involving contact) and dishabituate to the second (the event not involving contact). This outcome is interpreted as revealing the following aspects of the babies original representation of what was happening behind the screen:

1. They represented the red ball as continuing to exist behind the screen.
2. They extrapolated its trajectory.
3. They interpreted the motion of the green ball as being caused by contact from the red ball.

In sum, these data suggest not only that 8-month-old babies expect the ball to continue to exist behind the screen, but also that they understand Michotte-type contact causality (see also Leslie, 1988, 1994; Oakes & Cohen, 1990).

Studies based on this methodology have revealed object permanence in babies as young as 3.5 months. Baillargeon and colleagues habituated babies to a screen rotating 180° in front of the baby. It rotated toward and away from the infant (see Figure 2). After habituation, an object was placed behind the screen and the screen rotated toward it. In "possible events" the screen stopped when it would hit the object behind the screen and then rotated back toward the infant (now traversing 135° rather than 180°). In "impossible events" the screen rotated the full 180°, apparently rotating through the object that was behind it. Babies as young as 3.5 months generalize habituation to the possible events and dishabituate to the impossible events (Baillargeon, 1987; Baillargeon, Spelke, & Wasserman, 1985). This phenomenon is interpreted as showing the following:

1. Babies know that the object continues to exist behind the screen.
2. Babies know that one solid object cannot pass through the space occupied by another solid object.

Thus, besides demonstrating knowledge of object permanence, these data suggest that young infants also know that two objects cannot be in the same place at the same time. Other data also document this latter knowledge, at least in babies of 4 months of age (Spelke, Breinlinger, Macomber, & Jacobson, 1992).

Dramatic results such as these do not settle the empiricist–nativist debate, of course. It is always possible that babies *learn* the relevant properties of objects during the first few months of life. However, these results certainly constrain our theories about how these principles may be learned, for many sources of potential evidence are not available to such young babies. They rule out Quine's speculation that mastery of the quantificational devices of natural languages is part of the mechanism through which the schema of the enduring object is constructed, because 3.5-month-olds are over 2 years away from such mastery. They also rule out any learning procedures in which evidence from baby's successful reaching for and obtaining hidden objects is necessary, because 3.5-month-old babies are still several months from being able to reach for and obtain objects fully in view, let alone hidden

Habituation Event

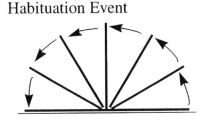

Test Events
Possible Event

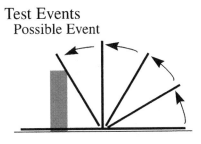

Impossible Event

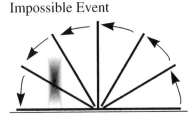

FIGURE 2 Schematic of Baillargeon, Spelke, and Wasserman (1985) study of object permanence.

objects. At this point in the debate, we must again pose the learnability question. If the capacity for representing objects as existing when out of view is not innate, then what aspects of the representation of objects *are* innate, and what evidence to which learning devices yields this knowledge by 3.5 months?

Data from infant studies bear on the debate in other ways than establishing the ages at which different representations are available. For example, there are data which suggest that by 4.5 months, the spatiotemporal–temporal properties that are constitutive of objects for adults also play this role in babies' representations. That is, babies do not merely expect objects to continue to exist through time, but rather, interpret apparent evidence for spatiotemporal discontinuity as evidence for two numerically distinct objects. Spelke, Kestenbaum, Simons, and Wein (1995) showed 4.5-month-old babies two screens, from which objects emerged as in Figure 3. The objects were never visible together; their emergences were timed so that the move-

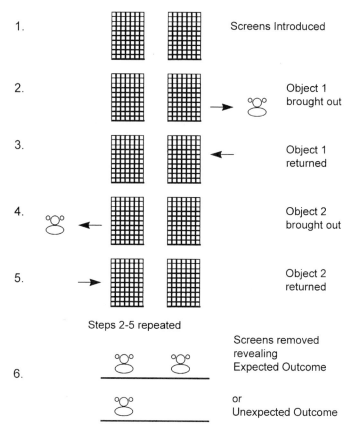

1.   Screens Introduced

2.   Object 1
                                                brought out

3.   Object 1
                                                returned

4.   Object 2
                                                brought out

5.   Object 2
                                                returned

Steps 2-5 repeated

6.   Screens removed
                                                revealing
                                                Expected Outcome

                                                or
                                                Unexpected Outcome

FIGURE 3   Schematic of Spelke, Kestenbaum, Simons, and Wein's (1995) study of infant's representation of spatiotemporal continuity.

ments would be consistent with a single object going back and forth behind the two screens. However, no object ever appeared in the space between the screens. Rather, one object emerged from the left edge of the left screen and then returned behind the screen, and after a suitable delay, a second object emerged from the right edge of the right screen and then returned behind it. Babies were habituated to this event. Adults draw the inference from this array that there must be two numerically distinct objects in this display, because objects trace spatiotemporal-temporally continuous paths—one object cannot get from point A to point B without tracing some continuous trajectory between the points. Spelke, Kestenbaum et al.'s babies made the same inference. If the screens were removed and only one object was revealed, they were surprised, as shown by longer looking at outcomes of one object than at the expected outcome of two objects. Thus, by 4.5 months, the spatiotemporal–temporal properties that are constitutive of the adult concept of object are also constitutive of the baby's representation of object; babies use them to establish representations of objects in their mental models of what they are seeing (see Xu & Carey, 1996, for a replication with 10-month-olds).

Experiments such as these have led Spelke and others (see also Leslie, 1988, 1994) to conclude that the concept of an enduring object that uniquely occupies space is innate. It is always possible, however, that an empiricist account of these phenomena may be forthcoming. The challenge is clear: one must specify what *is* innate, a learning mechanism, and the evidence available to babies in the first few months of life that could yield the knowledge revealed in the infant habituation experiments. The issue will be settled through a combination of empirical studies and learnability arguments.

B. Case 2: The Origin of Mathematical Knowledge

The British Empiricist, Mill, speculated that knowledge of basic number facts, such as that $2 + 1 = 3$, is arrived at by induction. A child notes that if two cows are joined by one other, the resultant group contains three cows, that two marbles plus one marble yields three marbles, and so on, finally inducing that two plus one is always three. This account is unlikely to be right for several reasons. It leaves unexplained our feeling of *necessity* that two plus one makes three. But most importantly, it leaves unexplained the origin of the capacity for representing numbers in the first place. The child could not induce this regularity without the capacity to represent the integers 2, 1, and 3. But, as we shall see, all of the currently available proposals for how young children represent numbers have the consequence that two plus one is three. No inductive process is needed for the child to come to represent this fact.

What is known about children's earliest representations of numbers? When are they formed? What is their nature? We consider here four possible answers to the question of the nature and origin of the human capacity for number representation.

The first proposal is that children must master a culturally constructed counting system before they have a way of representing numbers. On this view, numbers are mentally represented by an internalized version of natural language count words, "one, two, three . . ." To employ this internalized list to represent number, one must statisfy what Gelman and Gallistel (1978) called the counting principles: one must always apply the list in a fixed order, assigning one count word to each item in a set to be enumerated. The last count word reached represents the cardinal value of the set; its value is determined by its ordinal position in the mentally represented list.

This proposal could account for the origin of number representations in each child, but it would leave unexplained the original construction of this system. Further, evidence for prelinguistic representations of number conclusively rule out this proposal. There are now many demonstrations that, in at least some situations, both animals and preverbal human babies can base responses on number of objects or events. The animal studies most typically require that the animal make some fixed number of responses in order to get a reward. To give just one example, a rat may be trained to press one lever a fixed number of times before switching to a second one to be rewarded. Rats can learn to do this, and have been shown to discriminate numbers up to 49 (the highest that has been tried so far). It is clear that it is number that is being tracked, rather than some other property of the lever pressing correlated with number (e.g., length of time, amount of effort), because after the behavior has been learned, the levers can be changed in various ways that will change all other parameters of the task. That is, it can be arranged so that it is now much harder to press the lever, so that pressing it 49 times will take much longer and much more effort. The animal still presses 49 times before switching, or 15 times if he has been trained to press 15 times, or how many times it has been rewarded for (see Gallistel, 1990, for an extensive review of studies of animal representations of number).

These studies require keeping the animals very hungry and highly motivated to learn to get the food. Thousands of trials are required to train the animals. Obviously, these methods cannot be used with human infants, but the habituation technique described earlier provides a measure of how infants are representing the world. There are two types of studies using this methodology that show that babies represent number, at least small numbers from 1–3 or 4. In the first type, babies are simply presented with arrays containing a fixed number of objects, say 2 of them, one after another. For example, 2 cups, followed by 2 shoes, 2 bottles, 2 hats, 2 pens, and so on. The pairs of objects are never repeated, so the arrays have nothing in common but twoness. The baby's looking is monitored, and after a while, the baby's attention to each new array decreases, relative to his or her original looking time. The baby is getting bored. After looking time has decreased to half its original level, the baby is presented with an array containing 1 object, or 3 objects. In both cases, looking time recovers to its original level. The baby notices the difference between two objects, on the one hand, and a single object or three objects, on the other (Starkey & Cooper, 1980). This result, at least one very like it, has been obtained with neonates (Antell & Keating, 1983). Evidence for numerical representations in neonates conclusively rules out learning of culturally constructed symbols, or any experience with objects in the world, such as cows or marbles, as being necessary for their construction. At least some aspects numerical representations are innate.

A second source of evidence that babies represent number derives from data showing that babies can add and subtract. Wynn (1992a) showed 4-month-olds events in which an object is placed on an empty stage while the baby watched and then a screen was raised that covered the object. A hand carrying a second object was shown going behind the screen and returning empty. The screen was then lowered, revealing either one object (the unexpected outcome, even though that was what the baby had last seen) or two objects (expected outcome, if the baby knows $1 + 1 = 2$). Babies looked longer at the unexpected outcome of one object.

A further experiment showed that babies expected exactly two objects, rather than simply more than one object. In this study, the expected outcome was two objects, as before, but the unexpected outcome was three objects. Again, babies were bored at seeing two objects, and looked longer at the unexpected outcome of three objects. Wynn's results have been replicated with 4–5-month-olds (Koechlin, Dehaene, & Mehler, in press; Simon, Hespos, & Rochat, 1995), and parallel results have been found with 8-month-olds (Uller, Huntley-Fenner, Carey, & Klatt, 1999) and 10-month-olds (Baillargeon, Miller, & Constantino, 1993).

Finally, the Spelke, Kestenbaum, et al. (1995) experiment summarized earlier also provides evidence that young infants represent number. Recall that the unexpected outcome in the split screen experiment was one object; the expected outcome two objects. Success in this study shows that the 5-month-old distinguishes two numerically distinct but physically similar objects from one object seen in two different locations over time.

In sum, there must be some nonlinguistic representation of number; both babies and animals are sensitive to the number of objects and events in their environment. Thus, the origin of numerical representations in individuals cannot derive from learning natural language count systems; indeed, the results from neonates show that learning is not necessary at all.

Three other proposals for the representation of number are potentially available to infants and non-verbal babies:

1. *The numeron list proposal* (Gelman & Gallistel, 1978). Babies and animals establish numerical representations through a counting procedure that works as follows. There is a mentally represented list of symbols &, ˜, @, # . . . (Of course, we do not know what such symbols might actually be. Given the animal work, the list must be at least 49 items long). Gelman and Gallistel dub these mentally represented symbols "numerons." Entities to be counted are put in 1–1 correspondence with items on this list, always proceeding in the same order through the list. The number of items in the set being counted is represented by the last item on the list reached, its numerical value determined by the ordinal position of that item in the list. For example, in the above list, "˜" represents 2, because "˜" is the second item in the list.

2. *The accumulator proposal* (Meck & Church, 1983). Meck and Church propose that animals and babies represent number with a magnitude that is an analog of number. The idea is that the nervous system has the equivalent of a pulse generator that generates activity at a constant rate, and a gate that can open to allow energy through to an accumulator that registers how much has been let through. When the animal is in a counting mode, the gate is opened for a fixed amount of time (say 200 ms) for each item to be counted. The total energy accumulated will then be an analog representation of number. This system works as if length were used to represent number, "--" being a representation of 1, "----" a representation of 2, and so on. See Gallistel (1990) for a summary of evidence for the accumulator model of animal representation of number.

3. *Object-file model* (Simon, 1997; Uller et al., 1999). Babies may be establishing a representation of the array, with one object file (Kahneman, Triesman, & Gibbs,

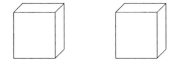

FIGURE 4   Object-file representation of two blocks.

1992) for each object. The representation of two blocks may be the equivalent of Figure 4. It has long been recognized that a representation of the state of affairs that there are exactly two blocks in some array may not actually contain a symbol for "2." In first-order logic, this is accomplished with the formula, "∃x, ∃y, block(x), block(y), x /= y, ∀z, (z = x) or (z = y)." In English, this states that "there is an entity, and there in an entity numerically distinct from the first, and that each entity is a block, and there isn't any other entity." This formula in first-order logic is logically equivalent to (has the same truth conditions as) the sentence "There are two blocks." Note that in such a representation, there is no single symbol for two at all, not "˜" nor "----" nor "2" nor any other. The object-file model is another representational system in which two blocks, for example, are represented in a code in which each block is represented as a numericaly distinct individual, but there is no symbol for two.

These three proposals for nonlinguistic representational systems for number are genuinely different from each other. The first two (the numeron list system and the accumulator system) embody distinct symbols for each integer. These differ in the nature of the symbols they use. In the accumulator model an analog representational system exploits the fact that the symbols are magnitudes linearly related to the numbers they represent. In the numeron list model, in contrast, each symbol bears an arbitrary relation to the number it represents. And, as previously noted, in the object-file model, there is no distinct symbol that represents each integer at all.

For our present purposes, it is sufficient to note that we have an embarrassment of riches here—three proposals for possible innate nonlinguistic representations of number, and each could derive the fact that two plus one is three follows deductively.

We now turn to a consideration of which of these systems most likely underlies animal and infant representations of number. We use this discussion to illustrate one of the most important questions that faces developmental psychology: whether there are discontinuities in cognitive development.

C. The Representation of Number—Continuity or Discontinuity

Many students of language acquisition and cognitive development argue that the *continuity hypothesis* should be the default, to be defeated only in the face of extraordinary evidence (e.g., Macnamara, 1982; Pinker, 1984). Most simply, the continuity hypothesis is that young children do *not* differ from adults cognitively in any fundamental ways. People who accept the continuity hypothesis agree that young children know less than adults about just about every imaginable topic, but argue that this is no different from one adult's knowing less than another one does about some particular topic.

In order to even begin exploring the continuity hypothesis, we would have to agree on what it means to differ in *fundamental* ways. Usually, this is taken to mean that the child lacks some logical or representational capacities that the adult has. To endorse the continuity hypothesis is to assume that infants have innately the logical and conceptual resources to represent their world as do adults. The continuity hypothesis denies stage changes of the sort envisioned by Piaget. If children's representations are continuous with those of adults, it cannot be that babies' representations are sensorimotor, whereas adults' are conceptual, or that preschool children are incapable of logical thought.

Of course, whether the continuity hypothesis is true or not is an empirical question, and to examine it, one must entertain possibilities as to what types of discontinuities *could* occur in the course of development. If evidence for discontinuities is found, several further questions are then licensed, including what processes cause the change—a maturational process or some kind of learning process by which new representational resources are constructed. A second question is the role of culture in the change. That is, are the new representational resources culturally constructed, and then mastered by each new generation of individual children, or are they constructed by each child independently as he or she interacts with the world?

The domain of number concepts, as expressed by the integers of the standard count sequence, "one, two, three . . ." allows us to explore the continuity hypothesis. The numeron list proposal for nonlinguistic representations of number is a clear case of a continuity proposal. Gelman and Gallistel have since modified their position (e.g., see Gallistel, 1990; Gallistel & Gelman, 1992). However, we will explore the original Gelman and Gallistel position because it is a serious empirical possibility, and because it allows us to see what the issues of continuity come to.

This numeron list system for representing number should be very familiar to you, for it is exactly how natural languages represent number. This is why the Gelman and Gallistel numeron list hypothesis (hereafter, *the numeron list hypothesis*) for nonlinguistic representations of numbers is a paradigm example of continuity over development; the baby's representational system is hypothesized to be exactly the same as the adult's. Learning to count in English, on this view, involves identifying the relevant list ("one, two, . . .") and mapping it to the list of numerons. Learning to count does not require the construction of any new types of mental representations.

There are several considerations in favor of the numeron list hypothesis. All natural languages that have words for numbers exploit a representational system that works exactly like the numeron list system. For example, in English, the list is "1, 2, 3, 4 . . ." Even languages that employ body part words as a mnemonic aid to ordering the symbols in the proper sequence (e.g., "finger, wrist, elbow, shoulder . . ." might be the words for "one" through "four") employ the same counting principles to establish a numerical representation of a set. This is what would be expected on the continuity hypothesis, because natural languages are merely expressing verbally the system of representation all complex animals, including humans, are hypothesized to share.

Gelman and Gallistel's major source of evidence for the numeron list hypothesis was their research on very young children (age 2 to 4) learning to count. They showed that from the very beginning of learning to count, children honor 1–1 correspondence; that is, they attempt to count each item in the set to be enumerated once and only once. And whereas they may not have mastered the standard count list (e.g., they might count "one, two, four, seven, eleven . . ."), they always use their nonstandard sequence in the same order, emphasizing the last word in the count. All of this is consistent with the hypothesis that young children have identified the English count list as corresponding to the list of numerons, and their knowledge of how to use the numerons to establish a representation of number is guiding their use of the English count words. And the most surprising piece of evidence was the extremely rare, but telling, phenomenon in which some children when asked "How many?" counted with the wrong list: "a, b, c, . . ." or "Monday, Tuesday, Wednesday . . ."

These data are exactly what would be expected on the continuity hypothesis, whereby a nonlinguistic system of numerons is guiding the search for the corresponding list in language, and, once identified, guiding the child in its use. But it is also possible that the early activity of counting is a meaningless game, like pattycake. Other data support this latter possibility. These data suggest that for about a year children engage in the activity of counting without understanding what the words "two, three, four . . ." mean, that is, without understanding that the activity of counting results in a representation of the number of items in the set.

Consider first a phenomenon we could call the "recount phenomenon." After children have counted the items in a small array (e.g., three items), if the experimenter asks how many there were, the child recounts, rather than merely saying "3." Indeed, a 2-year-old child will recount as many times as asked, "How many?" This is what would be expected if this question were simply the prompt to engage in this meaningless (for the child) game. However, this is not a decisive observation—after all, the child might think he or she made a mistake; otherwise, why is the adult asking how many there are again?

Two other observations confirm that very young counters do not know the numerical meanings of the words in the count sequence. First, if given a pile of objects, and asked to give the adult "two" or "three" or any other number the child can use in the game of counting, the 2.5–3.5-year-olds fail (Wynn, 1990, 1992b). What the child does is grab a random number of objects and hand them to the experimenter. Also, shown two cards, one depicting, for example, two balloons and the other three balloons, and asked to indicate which one has two balloons on it, the child responds at chance. Of course *some* children between ages 2.5 and 3.5 years succeed at these tasks, but these are just the same children who do not show the recount phenomenon. Rather, these children simply provide the numeral that provides the answer to the question, "How many?" when they have just completed a count of a small array. That is, analysis of within-child consistency on these three tasks bolsters the conclusion that most young children count for over a year before they learn what the words in the count sequence *mean*.

One further observation from Wynn's studies is important to our evaluation of the Gelman and Gallistel continuity hypothesis. Wynn (1990, 1992b) showed that from the beginning of learning to count, children know what "one" means. They can pick *one* object from a pile when asked, and they correctly distinguish a card with "one fish" from a card with "three fish." Furthermore, they know that the other words in the count sequence contrast with one. They always grab a random number of objects greater than one, when asked to hand over "two, three, four . . ." objects, and they also successfully point to a card with three fish when this is contrasted with a card with one, even though their choices are random when three is contrasted with two.

The following conclusions can be drawn from this brief empirical review. First, toddlers identify the English count list as relevant to number from very early on (earlier than age 2.5). They know what "one" means and they know that "two, three, four, etc." contrast with "one" and refer to numbers greater than one. They are in this state of knowledge for a full year before they work out how the English count system represents number—before they work out the principle that allows them to determine which number each numeral refers to. But this state of affairs is unlikely on the continuity hypothesis: according to this hypothesis, the English count list need only be identified and mapped onto the preexisting nonlinguistic count list that the infant already uses to represent number.

To sum up the argument so far: Some nonlinguistic representation of number must underlie animals' and human babies' capacity to respond on the basis of the number of bar presses or the number of objects in an array. However, there must be some kind of discontinuity between this nonlinguistic representational system and that expressed in natural languages. What might this be?

Both the accumulator model and the object-file model are candidates for nonlinguistic representational systems for number that are qualitatively different from natural language numeral lists. In each system the animal or child does not have to learn *which* number a given state of the system represents. In the accumulator system, each state is a direct linear function of number. In the object-file model, there is no distinct symbol for numbers at all. If either of these two proposals is correct, then mastering natural language count systems *does* require constructing a new representational resource. Specifically, the child must internalize a system for representing number based on a list of symbols. And the child must learn *which* number the word "two" represents, must learn the rule relating ordinal position in the list and cardinal value of the numeral. The demands in language of expressing each number as a distinct symbol force the construction of a different representational system from the Meck and Church accumulator model or from the object-file model.

Do we have any reason to choose between the accumulator model and the first-order logic model? We believe some of the choices differ for animals' numerical representations, on the one hand, and babies' numerical knowledge on the other. There is substantial evidence for the accumulator model in animals. The accumulator model can also be used to represent time, if the animal opens the gate for as long as the event to be timed, instead of for a fixed time for each event to be counted. Drugs that plausibly change the rate of pulse generation throw off the representation of time and number by the same factor. Also, under certain conditions, transfer based on a common state of the accumulator from a temporal duration task to a number task is observed (see Gallistel, 1990, for a review of these studies). Also, the object-file model places a demand on working memory; it is limited by the number of entities that can be simultaneously represented in a mental model of an array. This limit is likely to be quite severe for human adults (around 3 or 4; see Trick & Pylyshyn, 1994). There is no such limit in animal sensitivity to numerosity. Thus, the accumulator model is favored for the representations underlying animal numerical capacity.

For babies, in contrast, we favor the object-file model. First of all, there are severe set size effects in the numerical representations of babies and young preschoolers; infant studies reveal sensitivity only to one, two, and three (and sometimes four); behavior always breaks down with sets larger than four. This result is not expected on the accumulator model. Second, if babies are constructing models of the objects in an array that embody number only in the sense of the object-file model, then any manipulations that make it more difficult to construct such models should interfere with performance. There are preliminary data from studies of infant addition that suggest that this result obtains. Uller et al. (1999) compared two versions of Wynn's addition experiments with 8-month-old infants. One was a fairly close replication (the object-first condition): babies were shown an object placed on an empty stage, a screen was raised, and then a second object was lowered behind the screen. The screen was then removed, revealing either two objects (the expected outcome) or one object (the unexpected outcome). Not surprisingly, given Wynn's results with 4.5-month-old babies, the 8-month-old babies succeeded. The second condition (the screen-first condition) differed only in that the screen was placed on the empty stage before the first object was lowered. Then a second object was also lowered behind the screen, and the screen removed. Babies failed in this condition.

We interpret the difference between the object-first and the screen-first conditions as reflecting the difficulty in constructing a model of the objects behind the screen. In the object-first condition, the baby sees one object on the stage, and must update that representation in imagery only once. In the screen-first condition, the baby must create an image of the first object behind the screen, and then operate on this image-generated representation to create a representation with two objects on the stage. Apparently, it is more difficult to update a representation created in imagery than one based on perceptual experience. Baillargeon et al. (1993) found that 10-month-old babies succeed in the screen-first version of an adding study in the case of $1 + 1 = 2$, but they fail in the case of $1 + 1 + 1 = 3$. This latter condition apparently places too high an information-processing demand on their capacity to update their representations of the objects behind the screen.

These results would not be expected on the accumulator model. If the baby is incrementing the accumulator for each new object, why should it matter whether they see the first object before or after the screen is introduced? Clearly, the matter of the nature of babies' numerical representations is very much open. It seems extremely unlikely to us that people would not have the accumulator system for representation of number that animals have, but as yet there is no evidence for this in infants. There is, however, substantial evidence for an analog system of number representation in adults (see Dehaene, 1997, for a review). It is possible that the roots of numerical *concepts* are the object-file model, and that it is only after the child has mastered the count system, and has come to have explicit representations of numbers greater than 3 or 4, that the conceptual representation of number is integrated with the accumulator model.

Whatever the outcome of the debate concerning infant representation of number, the following conclusions from the empirical data already are warranted:

1. There is a prelinguistic representational system for number. Children and animals do not have to induce that $1 + 1 = 2$, or that $2 + 1 = 3$.
2. The representational system available to infants differs from the linguistic system for numerical representation.
3. Mastering the linguistic system requires the construction of a new representational resource.

We see, then, that the nativist position does not entail a commitment to the continuity assumption; the existence of innate domain-specific representational systems is not incompatible with the construction of genuinely new representational resources. In this case (the numeral list representation of number) it is very likely that the symbolic representational system for integers based on ordinal position in a list was a cultural construction, and that each child must discover how such a system works anew, in the process constructing a new representational resource. This process is most likely repeated many times; culturally constructed representational systems for rational numbers, real numbers, the calculus of limits, and so on, must be mastered by each child learning mathematics, and in doing so, the child goes beyond his or her current concepts of number (see Gelman, 1991, for a discussion of rational numbers from this perspective).

II. CONSTRAINTS ON LEARNING—LESSONS FROM ETHOLOGY

As can be seen from the discussion so far, our construal of the nativist–empiricist controversy is not tantamount to a debate over whether knowledge is learned or not. Nativist accounts of knowledge acquisition are themselves learning theories.

The real distinction is in how learning is accounted for, for example by domain-general versus domain-specific learning mechanisms. The literature on the ethology of learning highlights this distinction, arguing that learning itself should be thought of as a biological adaptation—one solution among many for a given problem an animal faces (Rozin & Schull, 1988; Shettleworth, 1972, 1983, 1984). Moreover, learning mechanisms differ in what they require for input and in which kinds of problems they can potentially solve. As Shettleworth (1984) points out, even such general learning mechanisms as habituation, classical conditioning, operant conditioning, trial-and-error learning, one-trial learning, and so on, each have their own advantages and disadvantages, so it is an oversimplification to invoke "learning" as an explanation for a given acquired behavior.

One way that learning is enhanced in animals is through domain-specific learning mechanisms that give the animal a head start in solving a given problem. Animals may be predisposed to consider some solutions to problems over others. These predispositions are not guarantees of the correct solution—if that were possible, learning might not be needed. But they trade on some advance probabilities—some solutions are more probable than others, and the animal may start out better prepared to learn these. If the odds work in the animal's favor, it will have a head start on solving the problem. On the other hand, the animal also has a way of overriding these prior hypotheses when they turn out to be wrong. These predispositions have been called "constraints" on learning, which in some ways is an unfortunate terminology (see Golinkoff, Mervis, & Hirsh-Pasek, 1994; Rozin & Schull, 1988). The idea is that rather than having to consider all possible solutions to a problem as equally probable, the hypothesis space is narrowed or constrained, and thereby simplifies the problem for the animal.

Bees' foraging for food provides one example of how this kind of mechanism works (Gould & Marler, 1984). Bees searching for food try out different flowers, selected partly on the basis of color. Although they are capable of learning to approach flowers of a wide range of colors, they are best able to learn to approach purple flowers. In experimental tests, bees have been shown to prefer purple flowers over all others. Gould and Marler (1984) argue that purples serve as a "default parameter—a probabilistic bias which helps guide bees when they experiment with various flowers while searching for food" (p. 65).

The hypotheses animals try out can often be ordered hierarchically with one playing a role only if another fails. Take the problem of learning which entity is one's mother. Since the classic work of Lorenz (1937), we have known of the imprinting mechanisms chickens and geese use for this purpose—follow the first moving object seen and imprint on that. M. H. Johnson, Bolhuis, and Horn (1985) have recently shown that this is only a fall-back mechanism, and that chicks are born with a schematic representation of what hens look like. It is only if no entity that fits that template is available that chicks fall back on following a moving entity; newborn chicks will huddle next to a stuffed hen and ignore a moving block, person, or other entity that they would imprint to if there were no hen present.

III. CONSTRAINTS ON WORD LEARNING

The insights gained from the ethology of learning can be fruitfully applied to learning in humans. We argued earlier that infant learning about objects and number is constrained by principles that allow the identification of the individual objects in the world. Word learning is another domain where children's success is, in part, attributable to constraints on the hypotheses children consider. There is now quite a lot of controversy about both whether or not such constraints exist (Markman, 1992, 1994; Nelson, 1988; Tomasello, 1992) and, if they do, how to best formulate them (Bloom, 1994; Clark, 1991; Gathercole, 1989; Golinkoff et al., 1994; Merriman & Bowman, 1989; Woodward & Markman, 1991). For our purposes here, we will summarize a selected set of findings to illustrate the way in which such constraints on learning could help children solve the inductive problem that word learning poses.

Imagine, as Quine (1960) asks us to do, that the only information you have about the meaning of an unfamiliar word in an unfamiliar language comes from a linguistic informant who points to something in the world and then utters something in the novel language. This serves as a rough analogy to what infants first learning a language encounter. To take Quine's (1960) example, the informant points in the direction of a rabbit and says "gavagai." "Gavagai" could mean "rabbit," of course, but it could also mean "brown," "fast," "furry," "jumping," "alive," "pet," "attractive," and many other such routine meanings, not to mention meanings such as "where rabbithood is manifested," or "undetatched rabbit parts" that Quine uses to argue that ostension alone cannot yield a unique solution to this induction problem. How then do we, as speakers of a language, come to agree on the meanings of terms and how do infants and young children rapidly acquire their early vocabulary? The answer is in part that we share certain biases, assumptions, or constraints that lead us to converge on the same hypotheses. Rather than sampling evenly among all the logically possible alternatives, children elevate some hypotheses over others. These hypotheses serve as a good first guess as to the meaning of a novel term.

One of these initial hypotheses is the whole-object assumption. Children first suppose that the a novel term applied to an object is a label for the object as a whole, instead of its parts, substance, color, texture or other possible attributes, or other things in the environment. Even under circumstances where an object per se is not the most salient thing around, children will still assume that the term refers to the object. The strongest test of this hypothesis has been provided by Woodward (1992). In her study, 18- and 24-month-old babies viewed two monitors. On one, they saw a static novel object. On the other they saw a dynamic swirling substance such as two different colored liquids diffusing, or lava flowing. These displays contrasted in two important ways. First, one depicted an object and one depicted an unbounded, moving substance that was clearly not an object. Second, the dynamic substances were selected to be more interesting and more salient than the static object, and this was verified by the greater amount of time children spent looking at the substances over the objects. The critical test of the whole object assumption was to see what would happen when children heard a novel term while watching these displays. If children map labels to what is most salient, rather than to objects per se, then labeling should increase children's attention to the dynamic substance. If, however, children map labels to whole objects, rather than to what is salient, then labeling should increase children's attention to the (less salient) object. As predicted on the basis of the whole-object assumption, when babies heard a novel term, they shifted their attention away from the more salient display to focus somewhat more on the object.

Once a child assumes that a given novel term refers to a given object, there is still the question of how to extend that term to other objects. A second assumption that governs children's interpretation of novel terms is the *taxonomic assumption,* which leads children to extend terms to things of like kind. Markman and Hutchinson (1984) first proposed this assumption to help reconcile the findings from early word learning with those of early categorization tasks. When asked to organize an array of objects into things that are alike, young children often sort objects "thematically." They group objects together on the basis of their participation in some event or theme, rather than on the basis of shared taxonomic categories. A child might place a man and a car together, for example, because the man drives the car, rather than placing vehicles and people into separate categories. Given that children find these thematic relations so salient, one might assume that children's early word meanings would reflect this. Children's early category terms do differ from the standard adult forms, sometimes by being more broad and sometimes by being more narrow, but not by having a completely different basis as would be needed for thematic meanings. Thus, we need to be able to account for how children readily acquire category *terms*—words that refer to things of like kind—if they find thematic relations more salient than taxonomic relations. Markman and Hutchinson (1984) proposed the taxonomic assumption to account for children's success at word learning in the face of a thematic bias. When children hear a word, they assume it refers to things of like kind. There are now a large number of studies using oddity tasks, free classification tasks, and habituation tasks among others that demonstrate that hearing a novel label heightens children's attention to taxonomic relations (Baldwin, 1989, 1992; Becker & Ward, 1991; Markman, 1994; Waxman, 1994).

A third proposed constraint on word learning is the mutual exclusivity assumption, which leads children to prefer only one category label for each object. One important role that mutual exclusivity plays is to help override the whole-object assumption. According to the whole-object assumption, children should assume that each novel label they hear is an object label. Yet, children must be able to acquire terms for many other aspects of objects including parts, substances, colors, sizes, textures, and so on; as well as terms referring to actions, spatial locations, and other relational terms. By overriding the whole-object assumption, mutual exclusivity frees children to begin to consider other potential meanings for terms. If children do not yet know a term for a given object then they should interpret a novel word as a label for the object, on the whole-object assumption. But if children already know a label for an object, then they will resist learning a second label for that object (Liitschwager & Markman, 1994) and will thus be freed to consider alternative meanings. This predicts that children should be better able to learn a part term or a substance term, for example, for objects whose labels are known relative to objects whose labels are unknown. This prediction has been supported (Markman & Wachtel, 1988). Following this same logic, Hall (1991) argued that children should be better able to learn proper names (which violate the taxonomic assumption) for objects whose labels are known compared to objects whose labels are unknown. Again, the prediction was confirmed. Thus by preventing children from treating every term as another category label, mutual exclusivity prepares children to acquire a wider range of vocabulary.

Mutual exclusivity can also provide an indirect means of word learning for children. Suppose a child sees a ball and a whisk on the table and knows the term *ball* but not *whisk*. Someone saying "Could you please bring me the whisk" might be sufficient for the child to infer the correct referent of "whisk." By virtue of mutual exclusivity, children could reason that "whisk" doesn't refer to the ball because that is a "ball," so it likely refers to the other thing. In this way, children infer the referents of novel terms without anyone explicitly pointing to the appropriate object (Golinkoff et al., 1994; Markman & Wachtel, 1988; Merriman & Bowman, 1989, but see Merriman and Bowman, 1989, for an alternative explanation).

In sum, the whole-object, taxonomic, and mutual exclusivity assumptions appear to serve as default assumptions, guiding children's initial hypotheses about what words mean. One point that is worth emphasizing is that this is a first stab at a theory about how children *learn* word meanings. These constraints do not obviate the need to learn—they are part of the presumed learning mechanism.

IV. LESSONS ABOUT COGNITIVE ARCHITECTURE FROM DEVELOPMENTAL STUDIES OF DOMAIN SPECIFICITY

There are many different debates within cognitive science concerning cognitive architecture. Debated is the question of what the subsystems of cognition are (perception/cognition, attention, different memory systems, executive function) and how they are interrelated. Also debated is how to draw the distinction between symbolic (classical) information-processing systems and nonsymbolic (connectionist) information-processing systems, and what role in cognition each plays.

The literature reviewed in this chapter suggests that part of the task of characterizing cognitive architecture will be specifying the *content* domains that are the subsystems of higher cognition. If Spelke (1990) and Leslie (1988, 1994) are right, then our knowledge of objects and of physical causality constitutes an innate domain. Spelke argues that a small set of principles enable the baby to pick out the objects in an array, and guide reasoning and learning about them. These principles include the following:

1. Cohesion: objects maintain their boundaries as they move through space.
2. Continuity: two objects cannot occupy the same space at the same time; objects move on spatiotemporally continuous trajectories.
3. Contact: objects causally affect each other only if in contact.

Note that on Spelke's formulation (see also Leslie, 1994), mechanical causality is part of the domain in which *object* is the core kind—"no action at a distance" is the converse principle of Michotte's causality upon contact. And if, as argued earlier, the infant representation consists of one object file for each distinct object in the array, then number is also initially part of this same domain. The principles of cohesion and continuity provide criteria for individuation of objects, and "individual" is a numerical concept. Language is a second candidate for an innate content domain as the work on learnability theory exemplifies and possibly the research just reviewed on word-learning constraints, though how domain specific these word learning constraints are is an interesting question (cf. Markman, 1992).

A third candidate for an innate content domain has the concept of "person" as its core. The evidence for there being a distinct cognitive module that picks out the people in the world, and guides reasoning and learning about people, parallels that for the object/mechanical causality module—emergence in early infancy, some innate mechanisms (as shown by studies of neonates), and concepts that cannot be reduced to perceptual primitives. In addition, this case offers yet another type of evidence—the existence of a developmental disorder (autism) that selectively disrupts reasoning in this cognitive domain.

Humans have an innate representation of the human face that guides neonates to selectively attend to faces (Goren, Sarty, & Wu, 1975; Morton, Johnson, & Maurer, 1990). Babies will follow a moving schematic face over a moving nonface, scrambled face, or even face-like configuration in which the parts are squares instead of ovals for the eyes and mouth. Morton and Johnson (1991) show that it is the actual configuration of the face that is determining the baby's attention, and not some lower level property of the stimulus such as a preferred spatial frequency (but see Banks & Ginsberg, 1985).

That babies have some innate perceptual mechanism that ensures that they attend to faces does not show that they have any knowledge of what faces *are*. Neonatal imitation documents that babies can map what they see somebody else's face do to their own facial motions. Neonates will imitate a model's opening and closing its mouth, or sticking its tongue out (Meltzoff & Borton, 1979). Although we cannot conclude that neonates have any conceptual understanding of the relation between self and others' faces, at a minimum, they have a powerful perceptual mechanism that establishes correlations between visual information about someone's face and motoric movements of one own's face. This correlation could constitute important input to a later developing conceptual system, with people at its core. In a similar vein, very young infants discriminate emotional expressions on faces, and recognize the intermodal correspondence between a facial expression and vocal intonation contour (Walker-Andrews, 1986).

To understand people's causal interactions with the world, babies must suspend some of the principles that guide understanding of other objects, especially the contact principle. In fact, it is the extreme violation of such principles that might motivate babies' organization of a distinct domain of animate beings (Gelman, 1990; Premack, 1990). People move without having been contacted by other objects, and babies know this at least by 8 months of age. Spelke, Phillips, & Woodward (1995) report a replication of the Ball (1973) study reviewed earlier in which babies' expectancies about the interactions of rolling balls behind screens was contrasted with their expectancies about the interactions of walking people. Only in the former case did babies expect the motion of a second object to depend upon being contacted by the first.

Babies' concepts of people go beyond spatiotemporally available information in several ways. Some of the earliest involve the attribution of attentional states and goals to people, which babies begin doing by the end of the first year of life. Starting at around 7 months of age, babies follow the gaze of a person facing them (Scaife & Bruner, 1975), and they begin to follow pointing gestures some months later (Bates, Benigni, Bretherton, Camaioni, & Voltera, 1979). Although some investigators have interpreted this to mean that babies understand that people are capable of attending to objects in the world (e.g., Baron-Cohen, 1995), others point out that following eye gaze and pointing could be accounted for by lower level associative processes or evolutionarily adapted signal releasers (e.g., Butterworth, 1991; Corkum & Moore, 1995). Some stronger evidence that babies may understand the importance of people's focus of attention comes from a recent study on babies monitoring the focus of attention in goal-directed activities (Spelke, Phillips, & Woodward, 1995). In this study, 8- and 12-month-old babies watched an adult seated in front of two stuffed toys. The adult repeatedly looked at one of the toys and expressed joy and interest. A curtain closed on the scene, then opened again to reveal the adult holding the toy she had been looking at. Babies were habituated to this event. The test trials consisted of two kinds of events. In one, the adult looked toward and smiled at the second of the stuffed toys and when the curtain was opened was seen holding that toy. In the second kind of test trial, the adult was seen looking and smiling at the second toy, but when the curtain opened was seen holding the original toy from the habituation trials. From one vantage point, this second test scene was more familiar to the babies who had been habituated to it. On the other hand, this scene is inconsistent with an understanding that people tend to reach for objects they attend to (and desire). The 8-month-olds showed no difference in looking times to the two test events. In contrast, the 12-month-olds looked longer when the adult was seen holding the toy she had not previously looked at.

When Spelke, Phillips, and Woodward (1995) split the 8-month-old data according to whether the babies followed the gaze during the habituation events, they found that those that did so also succeeded on the test trials. These data, if replicable, suggest that as early as babies follow eye gaze, they expect that people's actions are guided by, or at least predicted by, their focus of attention and emotional expression.

Adults automatically attribute intentions and goals to entities that move in certain ways—even animated dots (Gelman, Durgin, & Kaufman, 1995; Heider & Simmel, 1994). Apparently, so do babies. Gergeley, Nadasdy, Csibra, and Biro (1995) habituated 10-month-old babies to a display in which a dot apparently jumped over a barrier to get to another dot; after habituation, the barrier was removed and the baby was shown two displays in alternation—the dot following the same trajectory as before (jumping now for no apparent reason), or the dot going directly to the goal in a straight line. In spite of the former's being the familiar motion, babies looked longer at it, just as adults found it strange.

Further evidence that 1-year-olds treat attentional and emotional signals as being referential—as being about a particular object—is provided by studies of social referencing (see Baldwin & Moses, 1994, 1996, for reviews). Babies look to adults, especially parents, for clues about safety in uncertain situations, such as being placed on visual cliffs (Sorce, Emde, Campos, & Klinnert, 1985) or presented with unusual toys (Mumme, Fernald, & Herrera, 1996). Baldwin, Moses, and Tidball (1999; Baldwin & Moses, 1994) showed 12- and 18-month-olds a pair of toys selected because babies would be uncertain as to whether or not to handle them, for example, a furry black plastic spider. One toy from the pair was placed within reach of the baby and once the baby attended to that toy the adult either emitted positive emotional signals such as "Oh! Nice!" or negative ones such as "Iiuu! Yeech!" The critical manipulation in this study concerned the adult's focus of attention as she produced the emotional reactions. In some cases, the adult looked toward the same toy the baby was examining, while in some cases the adult looked toward the other toy—the one the baby was not engaged with. With this design, one can ask whether the emotional reactions of another person are seen as having a referent in which case babies will monitor the focus of attention of others, or whether babies are simply affected by the emotional display and will associate the positive or negative reactions to whatever they themselves happen to be attending to. Baldwin et al. (1999) found that even 1-year-olds took into account the adult's focus of attention even when it was discrepant from their own. Babies reacted more positively to the toy that was the object of the adult's focus of attention when the adult had displayed pleasure than when she had displayed disgust. In particular, babies reacted appropriately to the toy that was the object of the adult's attention even when it differed from the toy they had been examining.

Thus, 12-month-olds treat other people's emotional reactions as having reference and monitor attentional cues such as eye gaze to determine the object of other people's emotional reactions.

Language learning is another domain in which understanding reference is critical. Object labels *refer* to objects and are not simply associated with them. Baldwin found that by 15 months of age, babies expect that a new word uttered by an adult refers to the object the adult is looking at, even if the baby is looking at another unfamiliar object at the time of the utterance (Baldwin, 1993).

To summarize some of the conclusions so far:

1. From birth babies are adept at perceptual analyses, such as face recognition and neonatal imitation, that could provide a pretheoretical organization of information pertaining to people.

2. By 1 year of age, babies have a richer conceptualization of mental states.

3. Attention is an intentional state—it has "aboutness"; a person's attention is directed to entities in the world. Another intentional relation is reference, and this is central to understanding people's emotional states as well as language.

4. Babies show evidence of appreciating the referential component of attention and emotion by 1 year of age and of object labels by 15 months.

5. In attributing attentional and intentional states to entities, babies go beyond information that is available in the perceptual array; these concepts are contributed by the babies' representations of their perceptual input.

The baby's initial concept of people becomes greatly elaborated during the toddler and preschool years. By 18 months or so, babies begin to understand pretense, and by age 2 they have begun to understand people's actions in terms of perceptions and desires. And as outlined later, by age 4 they have constructed a fully representational understanding of belief (Flavell, 1988; Perner, 1991; Wellman, 1990). They have constructed the everyday folk psychology in which behavior is understood in terms of the actors' beliefs and desires. These achievements in the preschool years have their roots in the infants understanding of people as agents capable of self-generated motion, attentionally connected to the world, and pursuing goals.

The status of intuitive folk psychology as a specialized domain within the cognitive system receives support from evidence that autistic children are selectively impaired on tasks that draw on it. Compared to other retarded children, matched on overall IQ to autistic subjects, autistic children have been shown not to engage in pretense, to be extremely delayed in pointing or following eye gaze, to be selectively impaired in their use of mental state verbs, and to tend to fail the theory-of-mind tasks solved by 3- and 4-year-olds (Baron-Cohen, 1995). Here we describe two results from this literature to give a flavor for it.

Baron-Cohen (1995) describes four studies of subjects' inferences from the direction of gaze. Subjects were autistic adolescents (with mental ages of 6 or higher), retarded matched controls, and normally developing 3-year-olds. All subjects could report the direction of gaze (where is the person looking?). The retarded subjects and normal 3-year-olds realized that direction of gaze predicted which object a person wanted, which object the person was about to reach for, and which object the person was referring to when he said, "There's a blicket." Autistic subjects utterly failed to make any of these inferences.

Leslie and Thais (1992) compared subjects' performance in a standard false belief task with a closely matched "false photograph task" (Zaitchik, 1990). In the false belief task, the subject and a confederate watch an object being hidden in one place, the confederate leaves, and the object is moved to a new hiding place. The confederate returns and the subject is asked where the confederate thinks the object is, and where he will look for it. High functioning autistic subjects typically fail this task (success rates around 20%), whereas normally developing 4-year-olds and retarded controls pass (success rates around 80%). The false photograph task (Zaitchik, 1990) is structurally similar: a Polaroid is taken of a doll on a box, the Polaroid is turned face down while it develops, the doll is removed and a dog placed on the box, and the critical question posed: "In the photograph [touching the developing print], who is on the box, the doll or the dog?" Zaitchik found that normally developing 4-year-olds, even those who pass the false belief task, fail the false photograph task. Leslie and Thais (1992) found that their autistic adolescents, who failed the false belief task, succeeded on the photograph tasks. Apparently, the autistic subjects' problem is limited to the domain of *mental* representation; they have no particular problems reasoning about representations in general.

Some developmental disorders, such as specific language impairment (SLI) and autism, selectively impair a subset of cognitive mechanisms. Just as the existence of SLI adds to the weight of evidence for language as a specialized cognitive domain, a module in Fodor's (1983) sense, so the nature of autism supports the claim that folk psychology requires a specialized learning mechanism on top of the domain-general learning devices humans are endowed with.

In sum, a full characterization of cognitive architecture will include specifying the content domains for which specialized learning mechanisms exist. Developmental studies, both of normally developing children and abnormal populations, are a crucial source of evidence concerning this aspect of cognitive architecture.

V. BEYOND INNATE CONSTRAINTS—THEORY CHANGE, CONCEPTUAL CHANGE

As exemplified in the case of the child's representations of number, the existence of domain-specific learning devices does not preclude the construction of genuinely new representational resources. Development within cognitive domains can sometimes be thought of as a process of theory change (Carey, 1985; Gopnik & Meltzoff, 1997), and theory change sometimes requires the construction of new concepts, concepts incommensurable with those that articulate the earlier theory (see Carey, 1988, 1991; Kitcher, 1978; Kuhn, 1962, 1982, for a characterization of incommensurability).

Many have claimed that such a change occurs within the child's theory of mind between ages 3 and 4 (e.g., Flavell, Green, & Flavell, 1995; Gopnik & Wellman,

1994; Perner, 1991; but see Fodor, 1992; Harris, 1992, for contrary views of the developmental changes during these ages). Wellman and Wooley (1990) argue that the shift within the child's theory of mind should be thought of as a shift from a desire psychology to a belief-desire psychology, and that this shift is a compelling example of discontinuity in development. A simple desire psychology postulates an internal state and causal mechanisms that explain and predict both human behavior and human emotion. Two-year-olds understand that if someone wants a given goal they will perform a relevant act to achieve that goal. They understand that people will persist in a goal-directed activity if the goal is not yet achieved and that they will cease the activity when the goal is achieved. Two-year-olds also understand that people are happy when they achieve their goal and disappointed or sad when they fail to achieve their goal. To take a simple concrete example, 2-year-olds will judge that someone who wants an apple might look in the refrigerator for an apple. They predict that the person will continue looking until the apple is found. They expect the person to be happy upon finding the apple and to be sad upon failing.

All of this seems very straightforward and similar to how anyone might construe human action. But there is a striking dissimilarity as well. Although 2-year-olds construe action and emotion as we might in terms of how desire motivates human behavior, they do not take into account how people's beliefs affect their behavior. To continue with the simple example of searching for an apple, we assume that someone is searching in the refrigerator because that is where they believe the apple is. On Wellman and Woolley's account, 2-year-olds have no notion of belief. They explain someone searching in the refrigerator not in terms of where the actor believes apples are, but in terms of where the apples are in fact. There is no intervening mental representation such as belief or thought that governs behavior—there is only the desire and reality. Although 2-year-olds have a coherent framework for interpreting behavior when the actor's beliefs are accurate, they have no way of construing actions based on false beliefs. If the actor believes the apples are in the refrigerator but they are really on the table, 2-year-olds predict the actor will search on the table, not the refrigerator.

To document this developmental shift, Wellman and Woolley (1990) had young children predict the behavior of characters who were described in brief scenarios. In some cases the predictions would be based on the characters' desires and in other cases on the characters' beliefs. In each case, the experimenter first had the children state their own desire or belief. The character in the story was then said to have a desire or belief that differed from the child's. In this way, the task demands of the questions were nicely equated, and in both cases children needed to understand that other people's desires or beliefs could differ from their own. An example that focuses on desire is, "At Betsy's school they can play with puzzles in the classroom or they can play with sand on the playground." The child would then be asked which they would play with. A child who selected the sand would be told, "Betsy wants to play with puzzles today; she doesn't want to play with the sand." The child would then be asked to predict where Betsy will go. An analogous example that focuses on belief is, "Mary's ball might be by the porch or it might be by the garage." The children were then asked where they thought it was. A child who thought the ball was by the porch would be told, "Mary thinks the ball is by the garage. She doesn't think the it's by the porch." The child would then be asked to predict where Mary will go. Young children could readily reason about a character's behavior from information about the character's desire, with 85% of the young 3-year-olds answering three out of three of the discrepant desire questions correctly. In marked contrast, these children had difficulty reasoning about a character's behavior from information about the character's belief. Only 25% of the children answered all three discrepant belief questions correctly. From a simple desire psychology, children can recognize that others can have desires that differ from their own and reason accordingly about their behavior. But because these young children have no concept of belief they cannot register that beliefs can differ.

From the young child's point of view behavior that is based on false beliefs is inexplicable. Why someone would search for an apple in the refrigerator when it is on the table is beyond comprehension for a desire psychologist. Without an intervening notion of belief, children cannot make sense of such mistakes. Early on the child's reaction to witnessing such an anomalous event is to simply deny it. As with scientists who overlook counterevidence to their theories, young children lacking a notion of belief, deny evidence that contradicts their desire psychology. Striking examples of this come from the well-studied false belief tasks described above (Leslie & Thais, 1992). In one version of this task children are shown, say, a Band-aid box and asked what they think is inside it. They answer "Band-aids," of course. When the box is opened it turns out to have, say, a toy car inside instead. Having seen the unexpected contents of the box, children are now asked to predict what someone else coming into the room would think was in the box. Three-year-olds predict that someone entering the room would think that a car was in the Band-aid box. What is even more amazing is that they now state that then knew all along a car was in the box and deny ever thinking that Band-aids were in the box. This phenomenon is remarkably robust and appears across many variations of the task (Gopnik & Astington, 1988; Perner, Leekam, & Wimmer, 1987).

This shift from a desire psychology to a belief-desire psychology constitutes a radical change in the conceptual system that interprets human behavior. Events that are routine to the point of being pedestrian for someone with a belief-desire psychology, are true anomalies for someone with only a desire psychology. The addition of a new ontological category of belief enables children to represent, understand, and explain a set of phenomena that they could not conceptualize before. How the concept of belief emerges remains one of the critical unanswered questions in this field.

Other cases in which developmental discontinuity has been likened to theory change (change within intuitive theories, that is) include intuitive biology (Carey, 1985; Keil, 1989), an intuitive theory of matter (Carey, 1991; Piaget & Inhelder, 1941; Smith, Carey, & Wiser, 1985), and intuitive cosmology (Vosniadu & Brewer, 1992).

VI. INFANT REPRESENTATIONS—PERCEPTUAL OR CONCEPTUAL?

Characterizing the structure of the mind involves much more than discovering the domain-specific learning mechanisms that constrain knowledge acquisition. We also seek to distinguish among different kinds of cognitive processes, and must assign various cognitive tasks to those processes responsible for their solution. The developmental literature we have reviewed raises a fundamental problem within current debates concerning cognitive architecture: are the representations of objects, persons, causality, number, and so on, perceptual or conceptual? To address this question we must agree on how to draw the distinction. Working this issue out for infant representations contributes to the debate on how do to so.

The question of the status of infants' representational abilities is particularly acute because of the widespread belief that young infants are incapable of conceptual thinking. Traditionally, the developmental question has been formulated as when do infants become capable of thought at all, rather than asking whether a given ability is handled at a perceptual versus conceptual level. Piagetian theory is quite explicit in denying infants conceptual thought, dubbing much of infancy the "sensorimotor" period of development (e.g., see Piaget, 1954, 1966). According to this view, even into the second year of life infants are thought to be capable only of sensorimotor actions which, although they form the basis for later conceptual thought, are not themselves conceptual.

Recently, however, this assumption about infants has been called into question, and investigators have argued that conceptual thinking is available well before babies' first birthday and maybe even at birth. We will concentrate on arguments put forward by Mandler, Spelke, and Leslie, who have been very explicit about the criteria they use to argue for an early conceptual ability.

At issue in this debate is the source of infants' longer looking times at unexpected events in the kinds of studies reviewed throughout this chapter. There is fairly high agreement in the field that *some* representations of objects, numbers, and persons underlie performance, but if these representations are not conceptual, then these studies do not challenge Piaget's characterization of infancy as a period of sensorimotor representations, nor do they challenge his denial that infants lack *concepts* of number, object, or persons. In what follows, we present arguments by Spelke, Leslie, and Mandler that contrary to Piaget's claims, infants' representations *are* conceptual. We are interested in how each writer draws the perceptual–conceptual distinction, as well as the evidence they present that infants have conceptual representations.

A. Spelke's Arguments for Conceptual Abilities in Infancy

Spelke (1988) identifies the distinction between perceptual and conceptual mechanisms with the distinction between peripheral and central mechanisms, and reviews the extensive evidence that infant representations of objects are central. She shows that the same principles that operate on visual information to determine the objects in an array also operate on tactual information, and, more to the point, that there is transfer from one modality to another. For example, Kellman and Spelke (1983) found that if infants saw two parts of (what might be) a single rod that was partly occluded by a block moved together, they assumed it was indeed a single rod. That is, they were surprised if the block was removed, revealing a broken rod in two pieces with a gap that had been hidden by the block. They did not have this expectation if the original rod was stationary, or if the two parts moved independently behind the block. Seeing parts that move together, then, leads babies to expect a single object (the cohesion principle). To explore whether this tactual evidence for this principle is interpreted in the same way, Streri and Spelke (1988) positioned babies so that their hands were under a cloth and obscured from view. A ring was placed in each hand. In one condition, the two rings were connected by a rigid rod, so that the rings could not move independently. In the other, the rings were connected by a flexible wire. After babies habituated to this haptic exploration of the objects, they were presented with one of two visual displays in alternation. One depicted a single object—two rings connected by a rod, while the other depicted two objects—two unconnected rings. Infants who had tactually explored the rings that formed a rigid object generalized their habituation to the visual display of a single object, looking longer at the visual display of two rings. Infants who had tactually explored the rings that moved independently generalized their habituation to the visual display of two objects, looking longer at the visual display of one object. Spelke concludes that the mechanisms that establish whether principles such as cohesion are satisfied are indifferent to whether the information is from the haptic or visual modality, and therefore qualify as cognitive rather than perceptual.

Spelke (1988) argues that there is another reason to conclude that infants' representations of objects are conceptual, and that is evidence that infants are capable of reasoning. The studies reviewed above (e.g., the Ball, 1973 study and Spelke, Phillips, & Woodward's 1995 replication of it) often require babies to infer the nature and consequences of interactions between objects that are out of view. This is evidence for conceptual thought that Piaget accepted, which is why his experiments on the object concept involved infants' reasoning about hidden displacements of objects. Many of the studies require complex inferences. For example, Baillargeon, Graber, DeVos, and Black (1990) designed an habituation study to explore whether infants' failures on Piaget's object permanence tasks can be accounted for by a lack of knowledge about what sequence of events is necessary to retrieve an object that is behind or under a second object, say a cup. That is, they assessed whether babies know that the cup must be removed before the object can be retrieved. Baillargeon et al. (1990) showed 5.5-month-old babies displays where an attractive object was positioned in a variety of ways. In one case, infants saw a display where a bucket was placed over an object and then the whole display was screened from view. In a second version, infants saw the bucket placed to the right of the object before the display was screened. A hand was then seen to reach behind the left side of the screen and remove the object. In the case where the bucket was placed to the right of the toy, this direct retrieval is possible, unlike the case where the bucket was placed over the toy. Infants' patterns of looking time suggested that they did in fact view the impossible events as surprising. These 5.5-month-olds are, therefore, reasoning about the sequence of actions required to obtain an object that is hidden from view.

According to Spelke, then, infant representations operate on and integrate input from different perceptual systems, suggesting a central system at work rather than mechanisms tied to specific peripheral perceptual systems. Second, that babies can reason about the properties, positions, and behavior of unseen objects also implies the existence of a conceptual system in early infancy.

Whether we accept Spelke's conclusions depends upon whether we accept her criteria for conceptual representations. Perceptual mechanisms may well integrate information from distinct modalities. For example, McGurk and MacDonald (1976) showed that information about lip shape and movement is integrated with auditory information during speech perception to allow listeners to distinguish "ba" from "da." And at least since the time of Helmholz the existence of unconscious perceptual inference has been debated. Thus there is room for disagreement as to whether Spelke has shown that infants' representations of objects are conceptual.

B. Mandler's Arguments for Conceptual Representations in Infancy

Mandler (1988) distinguishes conceptual from perceptual knowledge along lines closely related to those of Piaget. Piaget argued that symbolic activity is the hallmark of conceptual representation. All representations are symbolic in some sense, of course. A representation is a symbol. So Piaget's (and Mandler's) task is to distinguish perceptual representations from conceptual symbols. One dimension of difference is arbitrariness. Following Marr (1982) and Fodor (1983), Mandler sees perceptual representations as the output of hard-wired, cognitively inpenetrable, input modules, whereas conceptual symbols are freely chosen, either by cultural convention or by the person herself. Another dimension of difference is accessibility to conceptual processes. The outputs of perceptual input modules can be consciously accessible, but they arise only when driven by the relevant sensory input. Conceptual symbols, in contrast, are promiscuously available to thought; they can be activated whenever reasoning, or desire, or association, or whatever executive function drives thinking, calls for them. For this reason, Piaget took evidence for recall and delayed imitation as hallmarks of conceptual representations. Mandler agrees that in order to conclude that infants' representations are partly conceptual, we need demonstrations of symbolic activity on the part of the baby, and offers evidence for symbolic use of gestures, and also evidence of recall and delayed imitation, from babies much younger than Piaget would predict.

1. Gestures

Mandler (1988) cites Piaget's observation that at around 5 or 6 months his children used a kind of motor recognition of objects. Suppose, for example, a baby typically kicked a mobile to make it shake. The baby might then be observed to make slight kicking movements while viewing the mobile from across the room. This could be interpreted as the baby using the kicking as a means of symbolizing or categorizing the object. Mandler offers this as evidence that the baby has an accessible code in which to think about the object.

Piaget, of course, would agree, but would counter that the code is sensorimotor, not conceptual. The code is a reduced form of the typical motor response the mobile elicits. Piaget's objection does not, however, apply to the finding that some of the first manual signs by babies acquiring American Sign Language (ASL) have been seen in 5.5–7-month-olds. If babies this young are using signs as words, to request or indicate objects, this would be very good evidence indeed for an arbitrary, culturally constructed, symbolic code in much younger infants.

In fact there is now considerable evidence that hearing children begin assigning meaning to words as young as 9 months of age. Parental report measures put the beginnings of language comprehension between 9 and 12 months of age (Fenson et al., 1994). At as young as 9–12 months of age, words serve as an invitation to categorization, beyond the capacity of infant-directed speech or auditory stimulation in general, to recruit attention (Balaban and Waxman, 1997; Waxman & Markow, 1995).

2. Imagery—Recall and Delayed Imitation

Mandler (1988) argues that if infants did not have the capacity for symbolic representations, they could not recall objects or events (as opposed to merely recognizing them). The ability to recall something previously experienced or known in the absence of perceptual support implies that the baby must have an accessible knowledge system (if not imagery, per se) that subserves thought.

As evidence for recall, Mandler cites Piaget's descriptions of delayed circular reactions, which first appear around 6 months of age. If an object is placed behind a baby, the baby will turn to reach for it even after some delay. Because there is no perceptual information available at the time of search, babies must be acting on the basis of some representation of the object.

The capacity for deferred imitation was first put forward by Piaget as evidence for symbolic representation; he claimed this ability did not appear until Stage 6 of sensorimotor development—roughly 18 months of age. Contrary to Piaget's claim, Meltzoff (1988) found that 9-month-olds were able to imitate actions that they first viewed 1 day earlier.

Finally, Mandler (1988) argues that the habituation studies that involve babies' reasoning about the interactions of objects hidden from view provide evidence for recall. Examples of these studies include Baillargeon et al. (1985, 1990), Ball (1973), Spelke (1988), Spelke, Kestenbaum, et al. (1995), and Wynn (1992a), all reviewed earlier. Such studies implicate recall because the baby is drawing inferences about represented objects and imagined interactions among them.

In sum, Mandler has marshalled evidence for delayed imitation, recall, and use of arbitrary, culturally constructed symbol systems well before age 18–24 months, the age at which infants were granted conceptual representations by Piaget. However, the last argument of Mandler's (that the infant violation of expectancy results themselves provide evidence for recall) is subject to the same counter argument as Spelke's appeal to babies' reasoning as a criterion for conceptual representations. These studies certainly imply representations of objects; at issue is whether the representations are perceptual or conceptual. If perceptual inferential processes exist, then the existence of inference provides, in itself, no evidence for symbolic, conceptual representations (see Jones & Smith, 1993, for a related point).

3. Perceptual Redescription

Mandler (1988, 1992) offers a third argument in favor of the proposition that perceptual development and conceptual development occur in parallel from the earliest stages of infancy. She argues that babies have a mechanism for perceptual analysis whereby some subset of perceptual information is recoded into a form that is accessible to reasoning processes. The kinds of concepts that are encoded in the early developing conceptual code are thought to be fundamental universal cognitive notions. For ideas about what these might be, Mandler (1992) looked toward the work of cognitive linguists whose goal has been to characterize some of the basic semantic notions required to express the concepts encoded in language (Lakoff, 1987; Talmy, 1988). Two examples of the kinds of concepts Mandler (1992) postulates for infants are *path* (the representation of movement from one place to another), and *containment*. These representations are more coarsely grained, simpler, and contain much less information than the perceptual information from which they are derived.

The infant habituation studies reviewed above certainly provide evidence for representations of path and containment, as well as providing evidence for representations of causality, object, number, goal, agency, and persons (other candidates for basic semantic notions). Mandler seems to be suggesting that one consideration that bears on the nature of these representations (perceptual or conceptual) is an examination of their content. The fact that these basic semantic notions are part of the universal cognitive backbone for human language, Mandler suggests, shows that they are good candidates for cognitive representations.

Of course we agree that they are good *candidates* for cognitive representations. But the question at hand is whether during early infancy these representations are conceptual rather than perceptual.

4. An Aside

Mandler (1992) also assumes that early perceptual redescription results in a dynamic analog code ("image schemas") rather than a propositional code. Her justification for this assumption is that a propositional code uses symbols that themselves must be interpreted. This in turn implies either that the symbols must be innately specified or that there must be some other mechanism for interpreting them. Mandler (1992) believes that an image-schema finesses this problem because "its meaning resides in its own structure." Thus, Mandler is suggesting that the process of perceptual redescription provides a source of conceptual representations that obviates the need for positing innate concepts.

The same questions about interpretation that Mandler raises about propositional codes arise in the case of imagistic codes. As Mandler (1988, 1992) argues, because image-schemas are schematic they contain much less information than their corresponding perceptions. But no matter how abstract the image, more is encoded than abstractions such as *path, containment,* and *goal.* To take Mandler's example, suppose all that children represent from an event is *path*—that an object has moved from one place to another. Direction and speed are not represented. In a given dynamic iconic representation, however, the path must have some direction, speed, and so on. How does the child know to interpret that iconic image as representing *path* alone, ignoring speed, location, and local details for direction? Thus, even iconic representation of the sort Mandler proposes requires interpretation of symbols and thus is not, in that sense, an advantage over a propositional system (Fodor, 1975).

In sum, Mandler (1988) argues that early use of gestures and evidence of recall and delayed imitation in very young infants suggests an accessible conceptual system that develops in parallel to the sensorimotor system from very early infancy. This development occurs through a process of perceptual analysis whereby some information is abstracted from the rich perceptual information and redescribed in a simpler, coarser grained code that constitutes the symbols that are accessible to thought.

C. Leslie's View on Conceptual Abilities in Infants

Of the three positions, Leslie's (1988) view demands the most stringent criteria for attributing a conceptual ability to infants. In particular, Leslie is willing to grant some ability to recall and to reason about objects to a specialized perceptual system. Nevertheless, Leslie also concludes that there is evidence for a symbolic, conceptual system during the first year of life.

Leslie begins his discussion of the mental architecture of the infant mind by laying out a position he aims to refute, namely, that the beginning state should be characterized as a homogeneous system lacking symbolic capabilities. Through some general processing mechanism, such as associative learning, the initially homogeneous system begins to acquire structure.

Leslie (1988) argued that specialized perceptual mechanisms may involve inferential processes that operate over representations, so that evidence for infant reasoning and recall cited by Spelke (1988) and Mandler (1988) does not conclusively favor the position that infants' representations are conceptual.

Leslie makes it clear that two questions about infant cognitive architecture must be sharply distinguished—the question of domain-specificity and the question of perceptual versus conceptual domains. Those who deny domain-specific learning mechanisms hold that the beginning state should be characterized as a homogeneous system lacking symbolic capabilities. Through some general processing mechanisms, such as associative learning, the initially homogeneous system begins to acquire structure. Throughout this chapter we have reviewed arguments in favor of some domain-specific learning mechanisms. Leslie (1988) develops related arguments, focusing on the representation of causality. He shows that infants represent the causal structure in some Michotte-like interactions among entities, even though alternative noncausal spatiotemporal descriptions are possible. For example, babies view a scene in which a red block moves towards and touches a green block after which the green block is seen to move off in the same direction. The scene could be represented merely as directional movement of blocks with no representation of causality. Instead, young infants interpret the event as the red block pushing the green block. He stresses, however, that the ability to impose causal structure on events does not require a conceptual system that is interpreting the more basic perceptual information. This kind of physical causality could be apprehended by a specialized perceptual system.

If the apprehension of causal relations can be handled by a specialized mechanism, would causal reasoning about unseen objects require a conceptual system? Recall that both Mandler and Spelke argued that Baillargeon et al.'s rotating screen study provides evidence for a conceptual system in babies. For babies to be surprised that the screen appears to pass through the space that was occupied by a solid object, they must both represent and reason about the object behind the screen. Leslie argues, however, that a rich enough perceptual system could, in principle, account for these results. Perceptual systems designed to obtain information about the current state of the world could be designed to maintain a representation of the state over some modest delay to allow organisms to act appropriately on current knowledge, and to integrate information from distinct sources. What then would provide evidence for a conceptual system operating? Leslie's proposal is that the existence of illusions provides the needed evidence.

1. Illusions

In perceptual illusions, we perceive an event or scene in a way that conflicts with the true state of the world, often in the face of explicit knowledge about that true state. Knowing that some interpretation of what we are seeing is an illusion does not prevent us from experiencing it, even repeatedly. The existence of illusions argues for the modularity of perception (Fodor, 1983). The perceptual mechanism that generates the illusion is operating independently of other mechanisms and is unaffected by knowledge obtained from other sources. Leslie (1988) argues that in addition to providing evidence for the modularity of perception, illusions can establish the existence of a conceptual system. It is the conceptual system that detects the inconsistency between two sources of knowledge. Although we cannot modify the illusion, we recognize the incongruity.

With this analysis in mind, Leslie (1988) reconsiders the infant's behavior in the Baillargeon et al. rotating screen study. The babies' heightened interest in a screen that appears to pass through a solid object would qualify as conceptual if it could be shown that the perceptual mechanism involved does not detect such inconsistencies. What is required, Leslie argues, is evidence that the perceptual system will allow that one solid object can pass through another. Babies' interest in Baillargeon et al.'s (1985) rotating screen could not then be generated by the perceptual mechanism itself. Leslie (1988) argues that Wilson and Robinson's (1986) Pulfrich double pendulum illusion provides the needed evidence. In this illusion, one solid rod appears to pass through another. The visual system, then, accepts the idea of one object passing through another. Thus, when babies are surprised that a screen appears to pass through a solid object, they are detecting an incongruity between input from their perceptual system and knowledge of a principle that one solid object cannot occupy the space of another. Both the principle and the detection of the incongruity can now be said to have a conceptual basis.

Leslie's elegant analysis, like Mandler's, draws on Fodor's (1983) distinction between the representations internal to encapsulated perceptual input systems and representations that are freely accessible to thought. If there is a weak point in Leslie's argument, it is the assumption that the workings of an encapsulated perceptual input system are inviolable; if a perceptual system cannot build a representation of one object passing through another, then we should not be able to *see* one object passing through another. Perhaps the input system, although still impenetrable to top-down influences from conceptual knowledge, is more probabilistic in its operation. If the perceptual evidence for one object's passing through another is strong enough, as in the Pulfrich double pendulum illusion, the input system can build a perceptual experience under that description (as Wilson & Robinson have shown). But still, the information that objects do not ususally interact this way may still be represented within an input system, in the form of probabilistic constraints on the models of the world that the system constructs.

D. Perceptual versus Conceptual Representations—Conclusions

Spelke (1988), Mandler (1988), and Leslie (1988) all come to the same conclusion— that young infants have the capacity for conceptual representations, and that experiments such as Baillargeon et al.'s (1985) rotating screen study exploit such conceptual representations. They reach this conclusion via subtly different analyses of the distinction between perceptual and conceptual representations, appealing, therefore, to slightly different sorts of evidence. The arguments and analyses offered so far may not be conclusive, but they are addressing a fundamental question about the rich body of infant research we have sketched in this chapter. Without settling this issue, we are not licensed to speak of infant "beliefs being violated," or infant "concepts" of number, causality, person, and object. And settling it will certainly clarify for the whole field of cognitive science whether, and how, the distinction between conceptual and perceptual representations should be drawn.

VII. MATURATION, CRITICAL PERIODS, AND THE "LESS-IS-MORE" HYPOTHESIS

To account for adult cognitive architecture, and adult knowledge, we must characterize the initial state of the infant's conceptual system, describe how it changes over time, and characterize the processes that cause the change. To this end, we have emphasized so far the need for studying specific content domains and domain-specific learning mechanisms. Some of the candidate domains are the domains of number, with *integer* at its core; lay physics with *physical object* as its core; language learning, with *word* as one core concept; and folk psychology, with *person* at its core. We have argued that a characterization of the initial state will include specification of domain-specific learning mechanisms, and that development involves transcending the initial constraints that allow learning to get off the ground. An important challenge is to understand the learning mechanisms that underlie theory change, especially theory changes that require conceptual change (see Carey & Spelke, 1994, for suggestions). Although such domain-specific analyses are critical for understanding cognitive development, there are important domain-general contributions to cognitive change. And although we believe understanding of cognitive development requires an analysis of learning mechanisms, not all cognitive advances can be attributed to learning. Maturational change may underlie some important developments, both domain-specific and domain-general. In the remaining sections of this chapter we discuss an example of a maturational change that helps account for early cognitive development, an example of a critical period in development, and an example of a domain-general phenomenon that would be hard to discover without a developmental perspective.

VIII. APPEALS TO MATURATION IN EXPLAINING DEVELOPMENTAL CHANGE

The data reviewed earlier on the infant's concept of objects raised a problem not yet resolved: why do babies of 5 to 11 months fail in Piaget's object permanence and A/not B tasks when results from the habituation paradigm indicate that babies well below these ages can track objects through visible and invisible displacements, and represent them as continuing to exist when out of sight behind barriers? Several general observations serve as partial answers to this question. First, having a concept is not an all-or-none matter. Representations are graded in strength (see the difference in outcomes between the object-first and screen-first versions of the addition studies reviewed earlier. Besides being graded in strength, it is possible that there is modularity within systems of object representation that is, the representations underlying looking may actually differ in some respects from those underlying reaching. Finally, there is evidence that Piaget's tasks require executive function contributed by the frontal cortex that is undergoing maturation in the second half of the first year of the human baby's life. That is, there are maturational constraints on success on Piaget's tasks that do not contribute to the data from the habituation paradigm.

Thus, resolving the paradox from the two classes of data on the object concept (habituation vs. Piagetian problem solving tasks) allows us to explore what sorts of considerations support a maturational contribution to behavioral change. For the sake of this illustration, we focus on a maturational account of the A/not B error (Diamond, 1990; Diamond & Goldman-Rakic, 1989). This account begins with the observation that the A/not B task closely resembles a task used to diagnose frontal function in monkeys: delayed response (DR). In DR, an item (usually food) is hidden in one of two wells, a delay is imposed in which the animal is not allowed to orient toward the correct well, and the animal is then allowed to search for the item. This is essentially the same as the A/not B task, with the exception that in the delayed response task, placement of the item is randomly determined, whereas in A/not B, the crucial trials are those that follow a successful search at one well with placing the item in the different well. These trials occur in the DR task, of course, and Diamond (1990) reports that these are the trials on which monkeys with frontal lesions make errors.

The evidence for frontal involvement in DR is extremely strong (see Diamond, 1990, for a review). Lesions in prefrontal cortex (specifically dorsolateral prefrontal cortex) of adult monkeys disrupt performance on DR. Monkeys with such lesions can still succeed at the task when there is no delay, but performance falls apart at delays as short as 2 s. Lesions in other memory or visual systems (such as the hippocampus, or parieto-temporal areas) do not affect DR. Also, there is excellent evidence for a maturational contribution to the development of DR during infancy. In rhesus monkeys, 1.5-month-old infants perform on DR as do adults with lesions in the dorsolateral prefrontal regions. Between this age and 4 months of age, the delay that can be tolerated increases from 2 s to 10 s or more; 4-month-old infant rhesus monkeys perform as well as do adults with intact prefrontal cortex. That maturational changes in prefrontal cortex underlie this improvement is shown by the fact that lesions in this area at 1.5 months preclude the developmental improvement in DR, and the same lesions at 4 months have the same effect on performance on DR as do such lesions in adulthood—to wit, disrupt it to the level of 1.5-month-old infants.

Diamond (1990) has amassed considerable evidence that the maturational changes in prefrontal dorsolateral cortex taking place in infant rhesus monkeys between ages 1.5−4 months occur in infant humans between ages 7.5 and 11 months, and underlie the developmental changes seen in Piaget's Stage IV of the object concept. Diamond gave the same version of the A/not B task to human infants at this age, to infant rhesus monkeys, and to adult rhesus monkeys who had been lesioned in the prefrontal dorsolateral cortex. She found that the developmental changes in human infants matched, in parametric detail, those of the monkeys, except that the development was a bit slower in humans (over 2.5 months in monkeys, over 4.5 months in humans). In both species, the delay at which the A/not B task was solved increased from 2 s at the youngest age to 10 s or more at the oldest age. In humans, the rate of increase was about 2 s per month (e.g., 9-month-olds erred in the A/not B task only at delays over 5 s). In both species, errors were predominantly on trials in which the correct choice differed from the correct choice of the previous trial (i.e., switch trials). In both species, details of the infants' behavior on the switch trials suggested they *knew* where the object was; sometimes they did not even look in the well they had uncovered before reaching for the correct well, and sometimes they stared at the correct well even as they reached for the incorrect one. These behaviors occurred at comparable rates in the two species. Finally, the adult rhesus monkeys with lesions in the prefrontal dorsolateral areas, as expected, failed the A/not B task at delays over 2 s (like 1.5-month-old rhesus infants), and made errors predominantly in the crucial switch trials in which the bait was placed in a different well from that of an immediately preceding successful trial.

Diamond (1990) reasoned that if immaturity of dorsolateral prefrontal cortex underlies the 7.5-month-old's failure on the A/not B task, and if maturation of this structure underlies the parametric improvement on this task over the next 5 months or so, then other tasks that diagnose prefrontal dorsolateral function in primates should show a parallel developmental pattern. She confirmed this prediction in a series of elegant studies of babies reaching for objects in transparent plexiglas boxes. Problems of differential difficulty are posed for the infant as a function of where the opening of the box is placed. Young infants (7.5-month-olds) cannot solve this problem unless the direct line of sight between the infant and the object is through an opening. If the opening is to the side, for example, the infant of this age keeps reaching directly for the object, hitting the plexiglas wall, and trying again until giving up in frustration. Diamond charted a series of stages infants between 7.5 months go through before complete success at this task at age 11 months, and showed that infant rhesus monkeys go through parallel stages between ages 1.5 months and 4 months, and that adult rhesus monkeys with lesions in prefrontal dorsolateral cortex fail at this task, performing like 1.5-month-old infants of their species.

There is no obvious conceptual similarity between the A/not B task and the transparent box task. In the former, the object is hidden, and memory is a critical component (performance is a function of delay). In the latter, the object is visible through the box, so memory plays no role whatsoever. What unifies these two tasks is their reliance on intact, functioning, dorsolateral prefrontal cortex. We would like to know, of course, the computational function of this part of the brain, in order to answer the question posed at the beginning of this section: *why* does an infant who knows where the object is reach under the wrong cover? Based on analyses of executive function served by frontal cortex, Diamond suggests a few possible answers. First, success at both the A/not B task (switch trials) and the transparent box task require inhibition of a prepotent response (a previously reinforced reach in the A/not B task, and a reach directly at the target in the transparent box task). Also, both tasks involve coordinating responses over temporal or spatial gaps. Diamond argues that these are aspects of executive function supported by the prefrontal cortex, and these are not required in the habituation studies. On Diamond's story, then, the A/not B error does not reflect a limit in the infants' concept of an object, but rather reflects limits in executive function that limit the means/end problem solving of infants under 1 year of age.

IX. CRITICAL PERIODS IN DEVELOPMENT: LANGUAGE ACQUISITION

Maturation does not result only in improvement. Some maturational changes can result in a loss of functioning. With respect to cognitive development, many abilities increase with age. This improvement with age is taken for granted as the standard developmental pattern. There are behaviors that violate this pattern, however, where there are critical periods during which the sensitivity to input is maximum and the ability to benefit from the input declines at the end of this period. Although there is some controversy about how narrowly to define critical periods as opposed to sensitive periods, we will follow Newport's broad use of the term. Critical periods for a given ability are limited periods during which the sensitivity to input is at its peak. The ability declines with maturation once the boundary of the period has been passed.

Language is the most obvious candidate for a cognitive ability that has a critical period for its development. Despite the enormous complexity of natural language, for the most part it is babies and very young children who acquire language. Some theorists have argued, in fact, that children are not only capable of acquiring language but that they are better able to acquire language than adults. Lenneberg (1967) first put forward the hypothesis that there is a critical period for language acquisition that ends around the time of puberty. More recently, Newport and her colleagues (J. S. Johnson & Newport, 1989, 1991; Newport, 1988, 1990, 1991; Newport & Supalla, 1990) have provided some impressive tests of this hypothesis.

Deprivation experiments provide the most compelling evidence for critical periods. Relevant input or experience is withheld from the organism until provided at precise times by the experimenter. Because it is not possible to conduct deprivation experiments on humans, however, the arguments about whether there are critical periods in language acquisition have had to rely on indirect kinds of evidence, such as how well children of different ages recover an ability to speak after damage to the left hemisphere (Lenneberg, 1967) or how successfully children who have been severely isolated acquire language (e.g., Curtiss, 1977). Newport and her colleagues, however, have made a compelling case that the critical period hypothesis can be better tested by examining the acquisition of ASL by the deaf.

Most babies who are born deaf (90–95%) are born to hearing parents who do not know ASL. Many of these parents were advised not to allow their children to learn to sign but to instruct them instead in oral methods of lipreading and speaking English. These profoundly deaf children were sent to residential schools for the deaf for this instruction in English. ASL functions as a kind of underground language at the residential schools, so once a child was sent to school, he or she would pick up ASL on the playground and in the dorms. Before being sent to the school, these children were not able to learn a spoken language at home, nor were they exposed to sign language. Thus their move to the residential school marks the first time they were exposed to language. Newport (1991) asked whether the children's ultimate ability to acquire ASL depended on the age at which children were first exposed to the language. The test of the critical period hypothesis involved examining the linguistic proficiency of deaf adults, plotted as a function of the age of exposure to ASL. The adults in the sample ranged in age from 35 to 70 years old. The range in age of first exposure to ASL was from birth (for the rare deaf children born to deaf parents) to age 12 or later. All of the participants had been using ASL as their primary language for at least 30 years by the time of testing. All of the adults were given a test of knowledge of ASL morphology developed by Newport and Suppalla (1990).

The results were that the adults' knowledge of ASL morphology declined as a function of the age at which they were first exposed to ASL. Early exposure to the language, from birth through age 6 or so, resulted in better mastery than exposure at age 8–10 years, which in turn was superior to exposure at 11–15 years. There was no sudden drop off at any age. Rather, there was a gradual decline in the ability to acquire language until around puberty. After puberty there is no further decline with age. These findings provide a striking demonstration of a maturational decline in the ability to acquire language. Late learners who have been signing for 30 or 40 years or more, still did not reach the proficiency achieved by early learners.

Following the logic that was used in these studies, J. S. Johnson and Newport (1989, 1991) asked whether the same maturational decline is found in one's ability to acquire a second rather than a first language. All of their subjects were native speakers of Korean or Chinese who had acquired English as a second language and were now either graduate students or faculty at a major university in the United States. J. S. Johnson and Newport (1989, 1991) plotted these speakers' proficiency in English as a function of the age at which they immigrated to the United States and were thus immersed in English. The same maturational decline seen in people acquiring ASL as a first language was found in people acquiring English as a second language. The age at which speakers were first exposed to English predicts their ultimate proficiency with the language. As before, there was a decline in the ability to acquire language until about puberty, and no further decline after that.

In sum, both in first and second language acquisition, there is a gradual decline with age in children's ability to acquire language. The younger the age of first exposure to a language, the better the language is learned.

X. POSSIBLE COGNITIVE BENEFITS OF IMMATURITY: THE LESS-IS-MORE HYPOTHESIS

A. Language Acquisition

The work just described on language acquisition suggests that younger children are better at acquiring language than older children and adults. This superiority of younger children is greatly puzzling given that in most cognitive tasks children become more, not less, proficient with age. (Even if younger children are not superior at language learning, they clearly are proficient language learners and this is just as puzzling.) A common explanation for this maturational change in the ability to acquire language is that there is a language-specific learning mechanism that deteriorates with age. Newport (1988, 1990, 1991) has suggested a quite different resolution to this paradox. Instead of searching for a mechanism that could compensate for young children's limited information-processing abilities, Newport suggests that the limitations themselves are part of the solution to the problem. Part of the problem in acquiring language is that the learner needs to impose structure on an enormously complex database. Information-processing limitations could serve to reduce the amount of data that needs to be organized. To acquire the morphological system of a language, for example, learners need to take the stream of speech, segment it into words and syllables, then determine which of the syllables are morphemes. Adults, with their superior memory spans, can retain more of the input sentences than can young children. They retain whole words and phrases that need to then be decomposed. Children's more limited short-term memory could, in effect, accomplish the decomposition for them. Take the morpheme *-ing* for example. Adults hearing a word *walking* will retain the entire word, just as they'd retain *sing* or *swing* for example. But very young children may only retain the stressed syllable of a word, and so from the input *walking* would only retain *walk*. Children's initial failure to encode or retain *-ing* might ultimately help them acquire this morpheme. The segmentation of the word *walking* would have already been accomplished in that the stem is represented apart from (without) the morpheme *-ing*. The same will be true for the past-tense morpheme *-ed* where from *walked* children might only retain *walk*. For a range of verbs, then, children might begin by representing only the stem. As their information-processing abilities improve they may be able to retain and add morphemes to the stems and to notice that *-ing* and *-ed* are being systematically added.

Newport argues that this kind of a mechanism is consistent with what is known about developmental differences in acquiring morphemes. The errors that children make differ from those made by adults. Children tend to produce incomplete forms (entire morphemes are omitted), whereas adults tend to produce "frozen" forms, suggesting a lack of analysis. Adults tend to be more inconsistent in their use of morphemes. On the other hand, some of the data presented in J. S. Johnson and Newport (1989) comparing early and late learners does not seem fully consistent with this position. One of the items that distinguished late versus early learners of English best was their acquisition of past tense. Examples of test items given are "Yesterday the hunter (shot vs. shoots) a deer," "A bat (flew vs. flewed) into our attic last night." Yet these are irregular past-tense forms, and the holistic strategies of late learners should be well suited to learning this.

The less-is-more hypothesis needs to be defined relative to some standard; otherwise we would have to predict that the less intelligent a child the better their language should be and other obviously wrong hypotheses. Some domain-specific learning mechanism for language may still be required to guide the process of data reduction, for example, and these learning mechanisms might deteriorate with age. Although it is not the full story, Newport's argument provides a partial resolution of the long-standing puzzle of how it could be that it is the children of our species who acquire language. Early cognitive limitations could serve as selective filters that reduce and maybe even analyze the data that need to be organized.

Goldowsky and Newport (1993) provided a test of the less-is-more hypothesis by modeling the learning of morphemes. The learning mechanism in their model correlates linguistic forms and meanings. The linguistic forms were meant to be words that were represented by a set of features that could be thought of as syllables. As in natural languages, some, but not all, of these syllables would turn out to be morphemes. Similarly, the meanings were decomposed into a set of features that could be thought of as semantic features or concepts. The learning problem is to identify the morphemes of the language that are the smallest meaningful units. This boils down to the problem of finding which of the small linguistic units consistently correlates with a given unit of meaning. As input, the learning device was presented with word-meaning pairs, or more precisely, the set of features that constituted the units of the word and the set of semantic features that constituted the units of meaning. From the set of input pairs provided, the device will generate a table of co-occurrences, with the linguistic forms on one axis and meanings on the other. When presented with the linguistic form consisting of features ABC, for example, and the meaning XYZ, the system would generate the following co-occurrences: AX, AY, AZ, BZ, BY, BZ, and CX, CY, CZ as well as ABXY, ABXZ, and other higher level mappings. These co-occurrences are for a single input pair. It is easy to see how complex and how noisy the co-occurrence matrix can become as input increases. There are many spurious correlations that will be generated that will interfere with the ability to discover the true correlations in the language.

To test the less-is-more hypothesis, Goldowsky and Newport (1993) compared the performance of the device when it was allowed to retain all the information it had generated in the co-occurrence table versus when it operated with a reduced memory capacity. To simulate reduced capacity, the input was processed through a filter that randomly deleted 50% of the features presented. Random deletion provides a theory-neutral and conservative test of this hypothesis. Stronger results might be obtained if the filter retained only stressed or only final syllables, for example. The filter representing a limited short-term memory capacity results in significant data loss. It results in more single-unit mappings (e.g., AX) being retained compared to higher order units (e.g., ABXY). This focus on small units is more likely to reveal the morphemes that are the smallest meaningful elements in a language. Another advantage of the data loss is that it improves the signal-to-noise ratio. This is because the random loss deletes items evenly across the entire co-occurrence table. Some of the spurious correlations will drop to very low levels while the true correlations will be strengthened with additional input. In another simulation, Goldowsky and Newport (1993) modeled developmental change in capacity by allowing the filter to expand after a time. This resulted in the device becoming capable of finding a high-level co-occurrence that it would have otherwise missed, but not at the expense of hypothesizing spurious high-level co-occurrences. In sum, Goldowsky and Newport (1993) have demonstrated that, at least in principle, reducing processing capacity can improve a learner's ability to detect correlations in a complex problem space.

In a similar vein, Elman (1993) has demonstrated that a connectionist network was better able to learn components of English grammar when the network's short-term memory capacity was reduced. Elman began by training a network with a memory capacity meant to simulate adult capacity. The network was presented with sentences that exhibited (a) number agreement between the subject and verb, (b) several kinds of verbs argument structure, and (c) relative clause embeddings. Examples of sentences used are "Boys who chase dogs see girls" and "Mary feeds John" and "Dogs see boys who cats who Mary feeds chase." The task of the network was to take words one at a time and predict what the next word will be. This is an odd measure of language comprehension, but Elman (1991) justifies it on several grounds. Part of the rationale for using ability to predict the next word as a measure of comprehension was that in order to predict the next word appropriately, the network must have represented the grammatical structure of the portion of the sentence that had been presented. Another reason for Elman's use of prediction is that covert predictions are believed to have psychological reality, and violated predictions can provide a source of indirect negative evidence (Elman, 1991). But for naturally occurring word-by-word predictions, often the best one could do would be to predict a class of words or a semantic domain, not a single word. Hearing "the" for example, one could predict the remainder of a noun phrase might follow, but the next word could be an adverb (incredibly), adjective (ugly), singular or plural count noun (spoon or spoons), or mass noun (clay). Yet the task for Elman's network is to predict the exact word. To make this feasible, the vocabulary would have to be greatly restricted. In fact, as reported in Elman (1991), the entire lexicon was only 23 words including 8 nouns, 12 verbs, and the relative pronoun "who." The results were that the network failed to acquire the language.

Given that the network failed when presented with the full range of sentences as input, Elman tried training the network by beginning with simple sentences and gradually increasing the complexity of the sentences until the full range was presented. This proved much more successful. Elman pointed out that although in some ways the network's achievement here may resemble that of children acquiring natural language in that both master complex constructions after simpler ones, there is an important difference. In the case of the simulation the order is determined entirely by structuring the input, but in the case of the humans, the input may not be so neatly organized, and maturational changes in the cognitive capacities of the child might be accounting for the developmental changes seen.

To address this, another simulation was run, this time providing the network with the full range of input sentences from the start but reducing the memory capacity of the network. The memory capacity was set at 3–4 words, later increased to 4–5, then 5–6, 6–7, and then not restricted at all. Note that the unit of memory here is presumed to be a word, rather than a syllable, for example. The network's task continued to be to predict the next word in the sentence one word at a time. When the number of words in short-term memory exceed the capacity one word was deleted. Although the word was lost and could play no further role in generating the predictions, its influence on the hypothesized grammatical structure up to that point remained. Restricting the memory capacity of the network in this way resulted in successful learning.

Elman's explanation, like Newport's, is that restricting the memory capacity reduces the amount of data that need to be processed, thereby constraining the solution space to a smaller region. Elman argues that the unrestricted data set is so complex that the primitive notions such as lexical category or subject–verb agreement are obscured. Moreover, the network can hit upon some hypotheses that, though wrong, predict enough of the data that they tend to remain and even to strengthen over time. Limitations on capacity simplify the input and thus avoid these problems. To quote Elman (1993): "Limited capacity acts like a protective veil, shielding the infant from stimuli which may either be irrelevant or require prior learning to be interpreted" (p. 95).

In sum, both Goldowsky and Newport (1993) and Elman (1993) have provided simulations of learning that demonstrate that under some circumstances, limiting the information-processing capacity of a system can paradoxically improve its ability to learn. In both cases, the simulations focus on language—morphology in the case of Goldowsky and Newport and components of syntax in the case of Elman.

We turn now to consider ways in which this "less-is-more" principle might be more widely applicable. We speculate on domains other than language where limitations in information-processing capacities might improve rather than impede initial learning (see Bjorklund & Green, 1992, for some different ideas). To begin we consider an argument put forward by Turkewitz and Kenny (1982) that Newport (1988, 1990) credits as influencing her ideas about language acquisition.

B. Perceptual Development

Turkewitz and Kenny (1982) argue that in some cases, perceptual organization is facilitated by initial limitations on sensory systems. In support of this position, they review findings from prenatal as well as postnatal development, from animals as well as humans, and from studies of neural organization as well as of behavior.

Here is one example Turkewitz and Kenny cite from the development of the human visual system. At birth, babies' visual acuity is limited such that babies can resolve only relatively large objects and features. In addition, babies' accommodation is restricted such that they can focus best on objects roughly 10 inches away. One implication of these limitations is that they greatly reduce the amount of information in the visual environment that needs to be processed at first. Another possible advantage is that this initial state could promote cross-modal associations for objects, because the objects that the baby sees best are those that are within reach. A third possible advantage is that the babies' limited visual acuity serves as a substitute for kinds of perceptual organization. In particular, Turkewitz and Kenny (1982) argue that these limitations could substitute for size constancy. The problem for the perceptual system is how to judge the relative size of objects given that the retinal projections of objects vary as a function of the object's distance to the observer. The problem should be much less severe for babies who can focus on objects only within a very limited range of distances. Wide disparities between retinal projections and actual size won't exist. Babies may thus be able to accurately judge the relative size of objects within the narrow range that they can perceive. Having some knowledge of relative size might then later help the development of size constancy.

C. Inhibition: Development of the Frontal Cortex

Adele Diamond's work on the development of the frontal cortex served as an example of how a maturational change can affect cognitive development. An immature frontal cortex results in an inability to inhibit ongoing action and may explain in part children's failure on certain object permanence tasks. More broadly, the ability to inhibit actions is fundamental to the execution of planned, intentional, goal-oriented activity. Yet, there may be some benefits to the lag in the ability to inhibit ongoing action. Lack of inhibition results in perseveration, but perseveration might serve as a form of practice. Repetition of a behavior promotes its acquisition. In fact, one of the dominant themes in Piaget's early description of the sensorimotor phase of development in infancy was the appearance at several different levels of development of what he called "Circular Reactions." Some action would be executed by the baby and then repeated, again and again. Which action and what kind of repetition varied with the developmental level of the child. During the first few months of life, babies exhibit Primary Circular Reactions. These actions are oriented towards the child's own body rather than to objects in the world. A baby might accidentally rub his or her eye, for example, then continue rubbing it over and over again. During the phase of Secondary Circular Reactions a baby might shake a rattle he or she was holding and then shake it repeatedly. Or a baby might throw an object on the floor and continue to throw it as long as a parent is willing to retrieve it. Parents tire of this game long before their babies do. These circular reactions were interpreted as evidence that the developing schemas had a built-in motivational component causing them to be exercised. This exercise resulted in schemas being strengthened and consolidated. Instead of invoking some motivational component, lack of inhibition could explain why babies tend to repeat actions so much, but with the same result that the behaviors become more skilled with this practice.

It could be advantageous for inhibition to lag behind the development of a given behavior even past early infancy. A new skill could be practiced and not be prematurely interrupted before it has a chance to consolidate. Young children learning to count, for example, will spontaneously count all kinds of things in their environment—steps in the staircase, toes on their feet. Children learning to talk will repeatedly request labels for things asking many "what's that?" questions. Children's "why" questions often seem nonstop. Some of these later examples of repetition of an activity might also be caused by a lag in inhibitor function. Here too lack of inhibition could provide some benefit in promoting the smooth, skilled, automated execution of a behavior.

D. Holistic versus Analytic Approaches to Categorization

Some speculations about how the less-is-more hypothesis might be useful in thinking about the acquisition of object categories can be found in Markman (1989). One developmental trend that has been postulated to account for children's categorization of objects is a shift from holistic to analytic strategies (e.g., Kemler, 1983; Kemler-Nelson, 1984; Smith & Kemler, 1977; see Medin & Heit, chapter 3, this volume, for a discussion). It is argued that young children are less able to analyze objects into their component dimensions and thus are less able to acquire certain kinds of categories. In keeping with the less-is-more hypothesis, however, this inability to perform the appropriate analyses may in some ways be beneficial. One possible benefit, pointed out by Wattenmaker, Nakamura, and Medin (1988), is that use of holistic strategies might prevent children from prematurely settling on an incorrect hypothesis. A related advantage of nonanalytic strategies is that they can prevent one from prematurely discarding information (Brooks, 1978; Kossan, 1981). Analytic strategies can lead one to focus on a dimension or even a set of dimensions at the expense of other potentially relevant ones. If all that is retained is the hypothesis under consideration and if that proves wrong, little progress has been made. In sum, exemplar-based or other holistic strategies prevent children from settling on erroneous hypotheses and allow them to retain potentially useful information.

Another potential advantage of limited information-processing abilities is that it may simplify the inductive problem that categorization poses (Markman, 1989). In principle, categories could be based on any discriminable dimension or Boolean combination of dimensions. Given a positive exemplar of a given category, say a dog, there are an infinite number of possible categories that could be exemplified (e.g., brown, furry, four-legged, two-eyed, friendly, brown and furry, less than 50 pounds, less than 55 pounds, etc). One main challenge to understanding conceptual organization and development is how from an infinite set of possibilities, children learn the conventional categorization system of their culture. If early on, children are less likely to analyze objects into their component dimensions, that would prevent the mushrooming of hypotheses. Children will treat an exemplar as the dog itself, for example, rather than its color, size, ferocity, or other dimensions because they are not as capable of analyzing the object into such dimensions. Very early in development this holistic tendency might be established and reinforced by the perceptual limitations discussed by Turkewitz and Kenny (1982). Infants will focus on whole objects rather than details because the contours of objects are visible and the details not. Thus both cognitive and perceptual limitations that prevent children from analyzing complex objects into their component dimensions might help in the initial acquisition of categories.

XI. SOME FINAL CONCLUDING REMARKS

The study of cognitive development is essential to the enterprise of characterizing cognitive architecture. We have presented evidence for early emerging content domains that ground conceptual understanding, including representations of physical object, person, number, and for early emerging language-specific learning mechanisms. We also outlined ways in which developmental studies highlight classic architectural conundrums, such as how to draw the perceptual–conceptual representation distinction.

Thus, cognitive development is an arena to explore problems central to all of cognitive science. Other examples we have touched on include the nature of theory construction and the fact that human beings are capable of constructing representations that are qualitatively different from those with which they began, as occurs in the course of development of an integer list representation of number and the concept of belief within the theory of mind. Understanding the mechanisms that underlie representational discontinuities such as these is a major challenge for cognitive science in the future.

And finally, the study of development evokes its own mysteries, such as the role maturational processes play in the construction of the human mind. We considered the maturation of frontal structures as underlying developments in executive function, and we considered critical periods in language learning. Finally, we concluded with a meditation on the uses of immaturity, the ways in which nature may have taken advantage of the limited information-processing capacity of the immature human mind in fashioning a solution to the learning problems human beings face.

We have only scratched the surface of the huge, rich, literature on cognitive development and language acquisition. The philosophers saw clearly that an account of development is one standard to which any characterization of human knowledge must be held. Now, perhaps for the first time in history, we have the empirical, computational, and conceptual tools to bring evidence to bear on age-old debates, as they are transformed in ways we cannot yet anticipate.

References

Antell, S., & Keating, D. (1983). Perception of numerical invariance in neonates. *Child Development, 54,* 695–701.

Baillargeon, R. (1987). Object permanence in 3.5- and 4.5-month-old infants. *Developmental Psychology, 23,* 655–664.

Baillargeon, R., Graber, M., DeVos, J., & Black, J. C. (1990). Why do young infants fail to search for hidden objects? *Cognition, 36,* 255–284.

Baillargeon, R., Miller, K., & Constantino, J. (1993). *Ten-month-old infants' intuitions about addition.* Unpublished manuscript, University of Illinois at Urbana, Champaign.

Baillargeon, R., Spelke, E., & Wasserman, S. (1985). Object permanence in 5-month-old infants. *Cognition, 20,* 191–208.

Balaban, M. T., & Waxman, S. R. (1997). Do words facilitate object categorization in 9-month-old infants? *Journal of Experimental Child Psychology, 64,* 3–26.

Baldwin, D. (1993). Infants' ability to consult the speaker for clues to reference. *Journal of Child Language, 20,* 395–418.

Baldwin, D. A. (1989). Priorities in children's expectations about object label reference: Form over color. *Child Development, 60,* 1291–1306.

Baldwin, D. A. (1992). Clarifying the role of shape in children's taxonomic assumption. *Journal of Experimental Child Psychology, 54,* 392–416.

Baldwin, D. A. (1993). Infants' ability to consult the speaker for clues to reference. *Journal of Child Language, 20,* 395–418.

Baldwin, D. A., & Moses, L. J. (1994). Early understanding of referential intent and attentional focus: Evidence from language and emotion. In C. Lewis & P. Mitchell (Eds.), *Origins of an understanding of mind* (pp. 133–156). Hillsdale, NJ: Erlbaum.

Baldwin, D. A., & Moses, L. J. (1996). The ontogeny of social information gathering. *Child Development, 67,* 1915–1939.

Baldwin, D. A., Moses, L. J., & Tidball, G. (1999). Social referencing versus social receptiveness: Infants' use of others' attentional cues to clarify the reference of emotional displays. Manuscript in preparation.

Ball, W. A. (April 1973). *The perception of causality in the infant.* Presented at the meeting of the Society for Research in Child Development.

Banks, M. S., & Ginsberg, A. P. (1985). Infant visual preferences: A review and new theoretical treatment. In H. W. Reese (Ed.), *Advances in child development and behavior* (Vol. 19). New York: Academic Press.

Baron-Cohen, S. (1995). *Mindblindness: An essay on autism and theory of mind.* Cambridge, MA: MIT Press.

Bates, E., Benigni, L., Bretherton, I., Camaioni, L., & Volterra, V. (1979). Cognition and communication from 9–13 months: Correlational findings. In E. Bates (Ed.), *The emergence of symbols: Cognition and communication in infancy.* New York: Academic Press.

Becker, A. H., & Ward, B. T. (1991). Children's use of shape in extending novel labels to animate objects: Identity versus postural change. *Cognitive Development, 6,* 3–16.

Bjorklund, D. F., & Green, B. L. (1992). The adaptive nature of cognitive immaturity. *American Psychologist, 47*, 46–54.

Bloom, P. (1994). Possible names: The role of syntax-semantics mappings in the acquisition of nominals. *Lingua, 92*, 297–329.

Brooks, L. (1978). Nonanalytic concept formation and memory for instances. In E. H. Rosch, & B. B. Lloyd (Eds.), *Cognition and Categorization*. Hillsdale, NJ: Lawrence Erlbaum Associates.

Butterworth, G. (1991). The ontogeny and phylogeny of joint visual attention. In A. Whiten (Ed.), *Natural theories of mind: Evolution, development, and simulation of everyday mindreading*. Oxford, England: Blackwell.

Carey, S. (1978). The child as word learner. In J. Bresan, G. Miller, & M. Halle (Eds.), *Linguistic theory and psychological reality* (pp. 264–293). Cambridge, MA: MIT Press.

Carey, S. (1985). *Conceptual change in childhood*. Cambridge, MA: MIT Press.

Carey, S. (1991). Knowledge acquisition: Enrichment or conceptual change?. In S. Carey & R. Gelman (Eds.), *The epigenesis of mind: Studies in biology and cognition* (pp. 257–291). Hillsdale, NJ: Erlbaum.

Carey, S., & Spelke, E. (1994). Domain-specific knowledge and conceptual change. In L. A. Hirschfeld & S. A. Gelman (Eds.), *Mapping the mind: Domain specificity in cognition and culture* (pp. 169–200). Cambridge: Cambridge University Press.

Chomsky, N. (1965). *Aspects of the theory of syntax*. Cambridge, MA: MIT Press.

Chomsky, N. (1980). *Rules and representations*. New York: Columbia University Press.

Chomsky, N. (1981). *Lectures on government and binding*. Dordrecht, The Netherlands: Foris Publications.

Clark, E. V. (1991). Acquisitional principles in lexical development. In S. A. Gelman & J. P. Byrnes (Eds.), *Perspectives on language and thought: Interrelations in development* (pp. 31–71). Cambridge, England: Cambridge University Press.

Corkum, V., & Moore, C. (1995). Development of joint visual attention in infants. In C. Moore & P. Dunham (Eds.), *Joint attention: Its origin and role in development*. Hillsdale, NJ: Erlbaum.

Curtiss, S. (1977). *Genie: A psycholinguistic study of a modern-day "wild child."* New York: Academic Press.

Dehaene, S. (1997). *The number game*. Oxford, England: Oxford University Press.

Diamond, A., & Goldman-Rakic, P. S. (1989). Comparison of human infants and rhesus monkeys on Piaget's AB task: Evidence for dependence on dorsolateral prefrontal cortex. *Experimental Brain Research, 74*, 24–40.

Elman, J. L. (1991). Distributed representations, simple recurrent networks, and grammatical structure. *Machine Learning, 7*, 195–225.

Elman, J. L. (1993). Learning and development in neural networks: The importance of starting small. *Cognition, 48*, 71–99.

Elman, J. L., Bates, E., Johnson, M. H., Karmiloff-Smith, A., Parisi, D., & Plunkett, K. (1996). *Rethinking innateness: A connectionist perspective on development*. Cambridge, MA: MIT Press.

Fenson, L., Dale, P. S., Reznick, J. S., Bates, E., Thal, D., & Pethick, S. J. (1994). Variability in early communicative development. *Monographs of the Society for Research in Child Development, 59*, (5, serial no. 242).

Flavell, J. H. (1988). The development of children's knowledge about the mind: From cognitive connections to mental representations. In J. Astington, P. Harris, & D. Olson (Eds.), *Developing theories of mind*. New York: Cambridge University Press.

Flavell, J. H., Green, F. L., & Flavell, E. R. (1995). Young children's knowledge about thinking. *Monographs of the Society for Research in Child Development, 60*(1).

Fodor, J. A. (1975). *The language of thought*. New York: Crowell.

Fodor, J. A. (1983). *Modularity of mind: An essay on faculty psychology*. Cambridge, MA: MIT Press.

Fodor, J. A. (1992). A theory of the child's theory of mind. *Cognition, 44*, 283–296.

Gallistel, C. R. (1990). *The organization of learning*. Cambridge, MA: MIT Press.

Gallistel, C. R., & Gelman, R. (1992). Preverbal and verbal counting and computation. *Cognition, 44*, 43–74.

Gathercole, V. C. (1989). Contrast: A semantic constraint? *Journal of Child Language, 16,* 685–702.

Gelman, R. (1990). First principles organize attention to and learning about relevant data: Number and the animate-inanimate distinction as examples. *Cognitive Science, 14,* 79–106.

Gelman, R. (1991). Epigenetic foundations of knowledge structures: Initial and transcendent constructions. In S. Carey & R. Gelman (Eds.), *The epigenesis of mind: Essays on biology and cognition* (pp. 293–322). Hillsdale, NJ: Erlbaum.

Gelman, R., Durgin, F., & Kaufman, L. (1995). Distinguishing between animates and inanimates: Not by motion alone. In D. Sperber, D. Premack, & A. J. Premack (Eds.), *Causal cognition* (pp. 150–184). Oxford, England: Clarendon Press.

Gelman, R., & Gallistel, C. R. (1978). *The child's understanding of number.* Cambridge, MA: Harvard University Press.

Gergely, G., Nadasdy, Z., Csibra, G., & Biro, S. (1995). Taking the intentional stance at 12 months of age. *Cognition, 56,* 165–193.

Gibson, E., & Wexler, K. (1994). Triggers. *Linguistic Inquiry, 25,* 407–454.

Goldowsky, B. N., & Newport, E. L. (1993). Modeling the effects of processing limitations on the acquisition of morphology: The less is more hypothesis. In E. Clark (Ed.), *Proceedings of the twenty-fourth annual Child Language Research Forum.* Stanford, CA: CSLI.

Golinkoff, R. M., Mervis, C. B., & Hirsh-Pasek, K. (1994). Early object labels: The case for a developmental lexical principles framework. *Journal of Child Language, 21,* 125–155.

Gopnik, A., & Astington, J. W. (1988). Children's understanding of representational change and its relation to the understanding of false belief and appearance-reality distinction. *Child Development, 59,* 26–37.

Gopnik, A., & Meltzoff, A. N. (1997). *Words, thoughts, and theories.* Cambridge, MA: MIT Press.

Gopnik, A., & Wellman, H. M. (1994). The theory theory. In L. A. Hirschfeld & S. A. Gelman (Eds.), *Mapping the mind: Domain specificity in cognition and culture* (pp. 257–293). New York: Cambridge University Press.

Goren, C. C., Sarty, M., & Wu, P. Y. K. (1975). Visual following and pattern discrimination of face-like stimuli by newborn infants. *Pediatrics, 56,* 544–549.

Gould, J. L., & Marler, P. (1984). Ethology and the natural history of learning. In P. Marler & H. S. Terrace (Eds.), *The biology of learning* (pp. 47–74). Berlin: Springer-Verlag.

Hall, D. G. (1991). Acquiring proper nouns for familiar and unfamiliar animate objects: Two-year-olds' word-learning biases. *Child Development, 62,* 1142–1154.

Harris, P. L. (1992). From simulation to folk psychology: The case for development. *Mind and Language, 7,* 120–144.

Heider, F., & Simmel, M. (1994). An experimental study of apparent behavior. *American Journal of Psychology, 57,* 243–259.

Johnson, J. S., & Newport, E. L. (1989). Critical period effects in second language learning: The influence of maturational state on the acquisition of English as a second language. *Cognitive Psychology, 21,* 60–99.

Johnson, J. S., & Newport, E. L. (1991). Critical period effects on universal properties of language: The status of subjacency in the acquisition of a second language. *Cognition, 39,* 215–258.

Johnson, M. H., Bolhuis, J. J., & Horn, G. (1985). Interaction between acquired preference and developing predispositions during imprinting. *Animal Behavior, 33,* 1000–1006.

Jones, S. S., & Smith, L. B. (1993). The place of perception in children's concepts. *Cognitive Development, 8,* 113–140.

Kahneman, D., Treisman, A., & Gibbs, B. (1992). The reviewing of object files: Object specific integration of information. *Cognitive Psychology, 24,* 175–219.

Katz, N., Baker, E., & Macnamara, J. (1974). What's in a name? On the child's acquisition of proper and common nouns. *Child Development, 45,* 269–273.

Keil, F. C. (1989). *Concepts, kinds, and cognitive development.* Cambridge, MA: MIT Press.

Kellman, P. J., & Spelke, E. S. (1983). Perception of partly occluded objects in infancy. *Cognitive Psychology, 15,* 586–593.

Kemler, D. (1983). Holistic and analytic modes in perceptual and cognitive development. In T. Tighe & B. E. Shepp (Eds.), *Perception, cognition, and development: Interactional analyses* (pp. 77–102). Hillsdale, NJ: Erlbaum.

Kemler-Nelson, D. (1984). The effect of intention on what concepts are acquired. *Journal of Verbal Learning and Verbal Behavior, 23,* 734–759.

Kitcher, P. (1978). Theories, theorists and theoretical change. *Philosophical Review, 87,* 519–547.

Koechlin, E., Dehaene, S., & Mehler, J. (1996). Numerical transformations in five month old infants. *Journal of Mathematical Cognition.*

Kossan, N. E. (1981). Developmental differences in concept acquisition strategies. *Child Development, 52,* 290–298.

Kuhn, T. S. (1962). *The structure of scientific revolutions.* Chicago: University of Chicago Press.

Kuhn, T. S. (1982). Commensurability, comparability, communicability. *PSA 1982* (Vol. 2, pp. 669–688). East Lansing, MI: Philosophy of Science Association.

Lakoff, G. (1987). *In women, fire, and dangerous things: What categories reveal about the mind.* Chicago: University of Chicago Press.

Lenneberg, E. H. (1967). *Biological Foundations of Language.* New York: John Wiley and Sons.

Leslie, A. M. (1988). The necessity of illusion: Perception and thought in infancy. In L. Weiskrantz (Ed.), *Thought without language* (pp. 185–210). Oxford, England: Oxford Science Publications.

Leslie, A. M. (1994). ToMM, ToBy, and Agency: Core architecture and domain specificity. In L. Hirschfeld & S. Gelman (Eds.), *Mapping the mind: domain specificity in cognition and cultural* (pp. 119–48). New York: Cambridge University Press.

Leslie, A. M., & Thaiss, L. (1992). Domain specificity in conceptual development: Evidence from autism. *Cognition, 43,* 225–251.

Liitschwager, J. C., & Markman, E. M. (1994). Sixteen- and twenty-four-month-olds' use of mutual exclusivity as a default assumption in second-label learning. *Developmental Psychology, 30,* 955–968.

Lorenz, K. (1937). The companion in the bird's world. *Auk, 54,* 245–273.

Macnamara, J. (1982). *Names for things.* Cambridge, MA: MIT Press.

Mandler, J. M. (1988). How to build a baby: On the development of an accessible representational system. *Cognitive Development, 3,* 113–136.

Mandler, J. M. (1992). How to build a baby: II. Conceptual primitives. *Psychological Review, 99,* 587–604.

Markman, E. M. (1989). *Categorization and naming in children: Problems of induction.* Cambridge, MA: MIT Press, Bradford Books.

Markman, E. M. (1992). Constraints on word learning: Speculations about their nature, origins, and domain specificity. In M. R. Gunnar, & M. P. Maratsos (Eds.), *Modularity and Constraints in Language and Cognition: The Minnesota Symposia on Child Psychology* (pp. 59–101). Hillsdale, NJ: Erlbaum.

Markman, E. M. (1994). Constraints on word meaning in early language acquisition. *Lingua, 92,* 199–227.

Markman, E. M., & Hutchinson, J. E. (1984). Children's sensitivity to constraints on word meaning: Taxonomic vs. thematic relations. *Cognitive Psychology, 16,* 1–27.

Markman, E. M., & Wachtel, G. F. (1988). Children's use of mutual exclusivity to constrain the meanings of words. *Cognitive Psychology, 20,* 121–157.

Marr, D. (1982). *Vision.* San Francisco: W. H. Freeman.

McGurk, H., & MacDonald, J. (1976). Hearing lips and seeing voices. *Nature (London), 264,* 746–748.

Meck, W. H., & Church, R. M. (1983). A mode control model of counting and timing processes. *Journal of Experimental Psychology: Animal Behavior Processes, 9,* 320–334.

Meltzoff, A. N. (1988). Infant imitation and memory: Nine-month-old infants in immediate and deferred tests. *Child Development, 59,* 217–225.

Meltzoff, A. N., & Borton, R. W. (1979). Intermodal matching by human neonates. *Nature (London), 282,* 403–404.

Merriman, W. E., & Bowman, L. L. (1989). The mutual exclusivity bias in children's word learning. *Monographs of the Society for Research in Child Development, 54* (3–4, Serial No. 220).

Morgan, J. L. (1986). *From simple input to complex grammar.* Cambridge, MA: MIT Press.

Morton, J., & Johnson, M. H. (1991). Conspec and conlern: A two-process theory of infant face recognition. *Psychological Review, 98*(2), 164–181.

Morton, J., Johnson, M. H., & Maurer, D. (1990). On the reasons for newborns responses to faces. *Infant Behavior and Development, 13,* 99–103.

Mumme, D. L., Fernald, A., & Herrera, C. (1996). Infants' responses to facial and vocial emotional signals in a social referencing paradigm. *Child Development, 67,* 3219–3237.

Nelson, K. (1988). Constraints on word learning? *Cognitive Development, 3,* 221–246.

Newport, E. L. (1988). Constraints on learning and their role in language acquisition: Studies of the acquisition of American sign language. *Language Sciences, 10,* 147–172.

Newport, E. L. (1990). Maturational constraints on language learning. *Cognitive Science, 14,* 11–28.

Newport, E. (1991). Contrasting concepts of the critical period in syntax acquisition. In S. Carey & R. Gelman, *Epigenesis of mind,* Hillsdale, NJ: Erlbaum, 111–132.

Newport, E., & Suppalla, T. (1990). A possible critical period effect in the acquisition of a primary language. Unpublished manuscript. University of Rochester.

Oakes, L. M., & Cohen, L. B. (1990). Infant perception of a causal event. *Cognitive Development, 5,* 193–207.

Perner, J. (1991). *Understanding the representational mind.* Cambridge, MA: MIT Press.

Perner, J., Leekam, S. R., and Wimmer, H. (1987). Three-year olds' difficulty with false belief: The case for a conceptual deficit. *British Journal of Developmental Psychology, 5,* 125–137.

Piaget, J. (1954). *The construction of reality in the child.* New York: Basic Books.

Piaget, J. (1955). *The child's construction of reality.* London: Routledge & Kegan Paul.

Piaget, J. (1966). *Psychology of intelligence.* New Jersey: Littlefield, Adams.

Piaget, J., & Inhelder, B. (1941). *The child's construction of quantities: Conservation and atomism* (A. J. Pomerans, Trans.) New York: Basic Books.

Pinker, S. (1984). *Language learnability and language development.* Cambridge, MA: Harvard University Press.

Premack, D. (1990). The infant's theory of self-propelled objects. *Cognition, 36,* 1–16.

Quine, W. V. O. (1960). *Word and object.* Cambridge, MA: MIT Press.

Roeper, T., & Williams, E. (1987). *Parameter setting.* Dordrecht, The Netherlands: D. Reidel.

Rozin, P., & Schull, J. (1988). The adaptive-evolutionary point of view in experimental psychology (Vol. 1). In R. C. Atkinson, R. J. Herrnstein, G. Lindsey, & R. D. Luce (Eds.), *Perception and motivation* (2nd ed., pp. 503–546). New York: Wiley.

Saffran, J. R., Aslin, R. N., & Newport, E. L. (1996). Statistical learning by 8-month-old infants. *Science, 274,* 1926–1928.

Scaife, J. F., & Bruner, J. S. (1975). The capacity for joint visual attention in the infant. *Nature (London), 253,* 265–266.

Shettleworth, S. J. (1972). Constraints on learning. In D. Lehrman, R. Hinde, & E. Shaw (Eds.), *Advances in the study of behavior* (pp. 1–68). New York: Academic Press.

Shettleworth, S. J. (1983). Function and mechanism in learning. In M. D. Zeiler & P. Harzem (Eds.), *Advances in analysis of behavior* (Vol. 3, pp. 1–39). New York: Wiley.

Shettleworth, S. J. (1984). Natural history and evolution of learning in nonhuman mammals. In P. Marler & H. S. Terrace (Eds.), *The biology of learning* (pp. 419–433). New York: Springer-Verlag.

Simon, T. J. (1997). Reconceptualizing the origins of number knowledge: A "non-numerical" account. *Cognitive Development, 12,* 349–372.

Simon, T., Hespos, S., & Rochat, P. (1995). Do infants understand simple arithmetic? A replication of Wynn (1992). *Cognitive Development, 10,* 253–269.

Smith, C., Carey, S., & Wiser, M. (1985). On differentiation: A case study of the development of the concepts of size, weight, and density. *Cognition, 21,* 177–237.

Smith, L. B., & Kemler, D. G. (1977). Developmental trends in free classification: Evidence for a new conceptualization of perceptual development. *Journal of Experimental Child Psychology, 24,* 279–298.

Sorce, J. F., Emde, R. N., Campos, J., & Klinnert, M. D. (1985). Maternal emotional signaling: Its effect on the visual cliff behavior or 1-year-olds. *Developmental Psychology, 21,* 195–200.

Spelke, E. S. (1988). Th eorigins of physical knowledge. In L. Weiskrantz (Ed.), *Thought without language* (pp. 168–184). Oxford, England: Clarendon Press.

Spelke, E. S. (1990). Principles of object perception. *Cognitive Science, 14,* 29–56.

Spelke, E. S., Breinlinger, K., Macomber, J., & Jacobson, K. (1992). Origins of knowledge. *Psychological Review, 99,* 605–632.

Spelke, E. S., Kestenbaum, R., Simons, D. J., & Wein, D. (1995). Spatio-temporal continuity, smoothness of motion and object identity in infancy. *British Journal of Developmental Psychology, 13,* 113–142.

Spelke, E. S., Phillips, A., & Woodward, A. L. (1995). Infants' knowledge of object motion and human action. In D. Sperber, D. Premack, & A. J. Premack (Eds.), *Causal Cognition: A Multidisciplinary Debate.* Oxford, UK: Clarendon Press.

Starkey, P., & Cooper, R. (1980). Perception of numbers by human infants. *Science, 210,* 1033–1035.

Streri, A., & Spelke, E. S. (1988). Haptic perception of objects in infancy. *Cognitive Psychology, 20,* 1–23.

Talmy, L. (1988). Force dynamics in language and cognition. *Cognitive Science, 12,* 49–100.

Tomasello, M. (1992). In *First verbs: A case study of early grammatical development.* Cambridge, MA: Cambridge University Press.

Trick, L., & Pylyshyn, Z. (1994). Why are small and large numbers enumerated differently? A limited capacity preattentive stage in vision. *Psychological Review, 101,* 80–102.

Turkewitz, G., & Kenny, P. (1982). Limitations on input as a basis for neural organization and perceptual development: A preliminary theoretical statement. *Developmental Psychobiology, 15,* 357–368.

Uller, C., Carey, S., Huntley-Fenner, G., & Klatt, L. (in press). What representations might underlie infant numerical knowledge. *Cognitive Development.*

Vosniadou, S., & Brewer, W. F. (1992). Mental models of the earth: A study of conceptual change in childhood. *Cognitive Psychology, 24,* 535–585.

Walker-Andrews, A. S. (1986). Intermodal perception of expressive behaviors: Relation of eye and voice? *Developmental Psychology, 22,* 373–377.

Waxman, S. R. (1994). The development of an appreciation of specific linkages between linguistic and conceptual organization. *Lingua, 92,* 229–257.

Waxman, S. R., & Markow, D. R. (1995). Words as invitations to form categories: Evidence from 12- to 13-month-old infants. *Cognitive Psychology, 29,* 257–302.

Wellman, H. M. (1990). *The child's theory of mind.* Cambridge, MA: Bradford Books/MIT Press.

Wellman, H. M., & Woolley, J. D. (1990). From simple desires to ordinary beliefs: The early development of everyday psychology. *Cognition, 35,* 245–275.

Wexler, K., & Culicover, P. (1980). *Formal Principles of Language Acquisition.* Cambridge, MA: MIT Press.

Wilson, J. A., & Robinson, J. O. (1986). The impossibly twisted Pulfrich pendulum. *Perception, 15,* 503–504.

Woodward, A. L. (1992). *The role of the whole object assumption in early word learning.* Unpublished doctoral dissertation, Stanford University, Stanford, CA.

Woodward, A. L., & Markman, E. M. (1991). Constraints on learning as default assumptions: comments on Merriman & Bowman's "The mutual exclusivity bias in children's word learning." *Developmental Review, 14,* 57–77.

Wynn, K. (1990). Children's understanding of counting. *Cognition, 36,* 155–193.

Wynn, K. (1992a). Addition and subtraction by human infants. *Nature, 358,* 749–750.

Wynn, K. (1992b). Children's acquisition of the number words and the counting system. *Cognitive Psychology, 24,* 220–251.

Xu, F., & Carey, S. (1996). Infants' metaphysics: The case of numerical identity. *Cognitive Psychology, 30*(2).

Zaitchik, D. (1990). When representations conflict with reality: The preschooler's problem with false beliefs and "false" photographs. *Cognition, 35,* 41–68.

CHAPTER 6

The Brain Basis of Syntactic Processes
Architecture, Ontogeny, and Phylogeny

Michael D. Patterson
Benjamin Martin Bly

I. INTRODUCTION

Human language differs from any other form of animal communication. It is often claimed that the greatest difference between human language and animal communication is the syntactic structure in language (Bickerton, 1995). The apparent uniqueness of syntax leads to three questions: How does the human brain process syntax, what genetic predispositions allow the brain to be syntax-capable, and how did these predispositions originate? To answer the first question we will examine neuropsychological and neuroimaging data concerning the neural substrates of syntactic processing in adults. To identify the genetic predispositions for syntax, we will examine the neural and environmental requirements for children to acquire syntax, and compare the syntactic abilities of humans and other animals. Finally, we will discuss theories of brain adaptation and the evolution of the brain basis of syntax in humans.

II. PART 1: THE BRAIN ARCHITECTURE OF SYNTACTIC PROCESSES HISTORICAL BACKGROUND

The Wernicke-Geschwind model is the most influential model of the neural substrates of language processing. Although this model has been modified since its introduction, none of the research that will be reviewed in this chapter contradicts

Cognitive Science

the general outlines of the model. However, the model can only be used as a general guide as to how language is processed in the brain because it leaves some important problems unaddressed. The model does not specify the separate neural substrates of different subcomponents of language processing, such as phonological, lexical, semantic, and syntactic processing. It only divides language processing into comprehension and production. Although, researchers now often search for the neural substrates of these subcomponents separately, most models of language processing in the brain are based upon the Wernicke-Geschwind model. Since the Wernicke-Geschwind model influences how researchers discuss language and the brain, it is useful to briefly review it (for a more detailed description of the Wernicke-Geschwind model see Damasio & Geschwind, 1984; Geschwind, 1972).

The Wernicke-Geschwind model stresses the importance of two areas in the brain, named for researchers who played a major role in explaining their functional role in language. Historically, most information about language processing in the brain came from studies of adults with acquired cerebral lesions, which could only be localized posthumously. The use of lesions to localize language areas in modern neurolinguistics began with Paul Broca, who made two important discoveries: patients with language deficits usually have lesions on the left side of the brain, and lesions in the posterior inferior frontal gyrus,[1] also known as Brodmann's area (BA) 44, lead to a deficit in language production. Patients with lesions in the posterior inferior frontal gyrus, or Broca's area, have difficulty producing speech, and the speech they produce has abnormal articulation. Broca's area is located next to the motor area, which controls the organs involved in vocalization, so it was assumed that the calculation of the motor plans for speech took place in Broca's area.

In 1874, Wernicke published a paper noting the co-occurrence of damage in another area of the brain with a different linguistic deficit. Patients with lesions in the posterior cortex (in BA 22) could produce speech easily, but their speech often lacked meaning since they used words incorrectly or produced neologisms. Wernicke noted the importance of the arcuate fasciculus between Broca's and Wernicke's areas and theorized that this was the pathway through which language is processed. Wernicke proposed that spoken language first entered the primary auditory cortex and was converted into meaning in Wernicke's area. If a patient wanted to speak then they first had to convert the meaning they wished to express in Wernicke's area to a phonetic form and then send that information to Broca's area so that the motor plan for vocalizing the words could be expressed. Further additions were made to this theory so the pathways used during reading and writing could be explained. Dejerine (1892) proposed that information from the visual system passed through the angular gyrus before connecting to Wernicke's area, where it would be converted into phonetic representation before being translated into a meaning.

---

[1] Alexander Hood noted the relation between a lesion in Broca's area and difficulties with language production in 1824, but explained the deficits within a phrenological framework. See Whitaker (1998) for a detailed review of the history of neurolinguistics.

The Wernicke-Geschwind theory explained in more detail what deficits would follow if lesions occurred in Broca's or Wernicke's areas, or in the pathways between these areas, and included predictions that led to the discovery of several novel language disorders. Some disorders that the Wernicke-Geschwind theory can explain include conduction aphasia, sensory transcortical aphasia, motor transcortical aphasia, alexia, and agraphia. For example, conduction aphasia occurs when the connection between Broca's and Wernicke's area is damaged. As the theory predicts, patients comprehend language because Wernicke's area is undamaged, but they make many lexical errors when they attempt to speak since meanings translated into phonological forms cannot reach Broca's area to be converted into speech. Overall, the Wernicke-Geschwind theory has proven quite predictive; its localization of language components has been largely confirmed by subsequent lesion and imaging studies. This includes the angular gyrus, which was not involved during reading in initial positron emission tomography (PET) studies, but whose involvement has recently been detected using functional magnetic resonance imaging (fMRI) (Bavelier et al., 1998).

Language is made up of many subcomponents, including the interpretation of sounds into phonemes, phonemes into words, and strings of words into sentences. It is remarkable that the subcomponents of language were not mentioned in either Geschwind's 1972 or later (1984) paper. The focus on Wernicke's area in language comprehension draws plausible support from its location near the primary auditory cortex, and the Wernicke-Geschwind theory describes how sounds are converted into phonemes, but not what happens afterwards. After language is converted from its auditory form into phonetic representation, many levels of processing remain before the meaning of a sentence can be decoded. Similarly, the focus of Broca's area centers on its role in speech production and not on any of the necessary preprocessing to ready the sentence for conversion into speech. Rather than study only comprehension or production, in the past 15 years, researchers have searched for the brain areas involved in the processing of each language subcomponent.

A. Separating Syntax from Other Language Subcomponents

This chapter is concerned with the neural substrates of syntactic processing, but controversy remains concerning the elements of language that distinctly constitute syntax. One definition relies on separating two subcomponents of syntax, morphosyntax and sentence-level syntax, which is based on word order and function words. Damasio and Damasio (1992) define the syntax subcomponent as including, "the admissible combinations of words and phrases in sentences." Morphosyntax is placed in the lexicon, which is defined as "the collection of all words of a given language. Each lexical entry includes all information with morphological or syntactic ramifications but does not include conceptual knowledge" (p. 90). However, different languages use either morphosyntax or sentence-level syntax based on word order and function words to accomplish the same task of identifying the agent and the patient in the sentence. For example, word order is more important for this function in English, but in Korean affixes label the patient and agent. Thus one controversy is whether morphosyntax and syntax based on word order and function words rely upon the same neural subprocesses.

The autonomy of syntactic and semantic processing is also a controversial issue. It is often assumed that the syntactic and semantic subcomponents are processed in different neural pathways. One argument used to support the case that syntax is separate is that we can make grammatically correct but semantically meaningless sentences,[2] even though these kinds of sentences are not usually produced (for review, see Chomsky, 1957; Wray, 1998, p. 58). Another opinion is that the trend of separating syntactic and semantic subcomponents has gone too far. According to Bates and Goodman (1997):

> We suggest that the heterogeneous set of linguistic forms that occur in any natural language (i.e. words, morphemes, phrase structure types) may be acquired and processed by a unified processing system, one that obeys a common set of activation and learning principles. There is no need for discontinuous boundaries. (p. 510)

Although this chapter will focus on syntactic processing, it is not yet known how autonomous syntax is from other language subcomponents, or whether morphosyntax and sentence-level syntax use the same neural processes. Thus, we will take a broader perspective and discuss the interaction of other cognitive and linguistic processes with syntactic processing.

B. Role of Broca's, Wernicke's, and Other Areas of the Brain in Syntactic Processing

Due to the prominence of the Wernicke-Geschwind theory, most imaging and lesion studies concerning syntactic processing have focused on Broca's and Wernicke's areas. In the next section we will review what these studies reveal about the architecture of the neural substrates of syntax. The review will focus on anterior regions of the brain near Broca's area, and posterior regions near Wernicke's area. Since few imaging and lesion studies have addressed the role of other brain areas in syntactic processing, the role of other brain areas, including subcortical areas, will only be discussed briefly.

C. Role of Broca's and Other Anterior Brain Areas in Syntactic Processing

According to the Wernicke-Geschwind theory, Broca's area is vital for speech production (Geschwind, 1972). Several researchers have claimed that Broca's area is also

---

[2] The most famous example is, "Colorless green ideas sleep furiously," coined by Noam Chomsky (1957).

necessary for other linguistic and cognitive processes, including the production and comprehension of syntax. The most extreme claim is that Broca's area is important for general temporal and hierarchical structuring used in general planning, motor planning, syntax, and phonology (e.g., Wilkins & Wakefield, 1995). Evidence used to support Broca's syntactic role includes the fact that Broca's aphasics have difficulty understanding sentences that can only be resolved by the knowledge of syntax[3] (Zurif, Caramazza, & Meyerson, 1972). In addition, Broca's aphasics use many fewer function words and produce much shorter sentences than normals.

Recent research has revealed that the role of Broca's area in language may have been misunderstood. Broca's aphasics can incorrectly identify whether a sentence is grammatically correct, which might indicate that Broca's aphasics have difficulty accessing syntactical forms, and not that syntactic processing takes place in Broca's areas (Bates & Goodman, 1997, p. 556). In addition, lesions completely outside of Broca's area can lead to Broca's aphasic symptoms, including purely subcortical lesions (Caplan, 1992; Lieberman, 1991). Thus, syntactic functions originally attributed to Broca's area require the participation of other areas besides Broca's area.

Even Broca's postulation of an area necessary for speech production appears to be overly broad. Dronkers (1996) reported a 100% double disassociation between patients with damage in the left precentral gyrus of the insula who had persisting speech apraxia,[4] and other patients with damage only in other areas of the brain, who did not have persisting speech apraxia. Although the precentral gyrus of the insula is in the frontal cortex, it is not in Broca's area. Dronkers notes several reasons why speech articulation was previously mistakenly localized to Broca's area. First, the left precentral gyrus is near Broca's area, and both areas are often damaged together. Furthermore, in previous studies, no distinction was drawn between persistent and transitory speech apraxia effects of lesions. Transitory effects may be due to the pathways used for articulation being temporarily disabled and not to damage in the cortical systems responsible for articulation.

Imaging studies indicate that Broca's area may at least play a role in speech articulation, but it is not clear whether Broca's area or proximal regions are being affected during these studies (see section below on imaging methods). One hypothesis is that Broca's area is involved during tasks that require the conscious manipulation of items in the phonological loop, since it is involved during repetition and tasks that require rhyming judgments, but not during passive listening or phonological detection tasks (Paulesu et al., 1993; Price et al., 1996). This view is consonant with one of the roles attributed to the entire frontal cortex, which a number of researchers claim is involved in conscious, controlled processing (Caplan & Waters, 1999; Deacon, 1997;

---

[3] An example of a sentence that can only be understood correctly by knowing syntax: The boy was kicked by the girl. If asked the question "Who kicked whom?" Broca's aphasics would respond half the time that the boy kicked the girl.

[4] Patients with speech apraxia have difficulty producing the motor movements necessary for speech.

Kolb & Wishaw, 1996, chapter 14). Is the function of Broca's area similar for syntactic processing: to keep track of the relationships of lexical items in a sequence?

Unfortunately, our knowledge concerning the areas of the brain necessary for syntactic processing is not as well developed as it is for phonetic processing. In addition, most researchers examine syntactic processing with the assumption that it is completely autonomous from semantic processing. One theory is that the frontal cortex, including Broca's area, and the basal ganglia-frontal cortex loop, are needed for rule-based syntactic processing, in contrast to the role proposed for the posterior cortex of processing irregular syntactic forms (Ullman et al., 1997). This argument is interesting, even though the paper in which the argument is proposed suffers from several flaws, including the amorphous definition of rule-based syntactic processing and the presentation of inconclusive supporting evidence.

Rule-based syntactic processing is not defined by the authors except as the addition of the past tense to regular verb infinitives. It is not clear whether rule-based syntactic processing would include only verb conjugation or the addition of all affixes that can be regularly applied. In addition, Ullman et al. (1997) did not comment on whether rule-based morphosyntax is similar to sentence-level syntax. However, there is evidence that the two levels cannot be separated because in Broca's aphasia, symptoms can vary depending on the patient's maternal language. According to one group of researchers, "Patients affected by Broca's aphasia may omit free-standing grammatical morphemes in English, but add or substitute bound grammatical morphemes in Italian" (Aglioti, Beltramello, Girardi, & Fabbro, 1996).

Neuroanatomically, there are also limitations to the Ullman et al. (1997) paper. To support their claim that rule-based syntactic processing relies on anterior areas of the brain, Ullman et al. (1997) compared the performance of an anterior lesion group, and a control group on conjugating the past tense of regular and irregular verbs. Subjects in the "anterior lesion group" had more difficulty defining the past tense of regular verbs than irregular verbs. However, this group was very heterogeneous. Only one subject in the "anterior lesion group" had a strictly anterior lesion. Other patients had lesions that reached as far as temporal and temporo-parietal areas. Furthermore, patients varied in recovery from the lesions from only 9 months to 17 years, which suggests a large potential variation in the degree to which the brain has adapted. In addition, the particular functions of the frontal cortex, Broca's area, and the basal ganglia are not delineated in this article. However, the lack of specific details is a general problem faced by articles in this field, suggesting again how little is known about how what each area of the brain does in syntactic processing. Despite these limitations, the plausibility of some form of Ullman and colleagues' hypothesis certainly suggests a viable direction in which to proceed empirically.

Parametric analysis is the most promising technique for locating the neural substrates of syntactic processing and, specifically, for determining what role the anterior brain regions play in syntax (see section II. K). In the few studies that have used the parametric approach to study syntactic processing, the conditions termed more syntactically complex have a greater memory load than conditions termed less syntactically complex. In these studies changes during the processing of right branching sentences has been compared to those occurring during center-embedded sentences. Here is an example of a center-embedded sentence: The boy who the teacher scolded was sleeping. An example of a right-branching sentence: The teacher scolded the boy who was sleeping. The assumption is that center-embedded sentences are more syntactically complex than right-branching sentences (Caplan, Alpert, & Waters, 1998; Just, Carpenter, Keller, Eddy, & Thulborn, 1996; Stromswold, Caplan, Albert, & Rauch, 1996).[5] Before examining imaging results, we will examine the evidence that the kind of syntactic variation in these experiments generally affects syntactic complexity separately from other kinds of processing complexity, such as working memory load. Center-embedded sentences impose a greater memory load than right-branching sentences because two agents must be held in memory before they can be matched with their verbs in the center-embedded sentence, whereas in a right-branching sentence only one verb-less agent needs to be held in memory at a time (Caplan & Waters, 1999; Stromswold et al., 1996).

Caplan and Waters (1999) claim that the memory used during syntactic processing is one of at least two kinds of memory used during sentential processing. They claim memory used during syntactic processing is different from the memory for the semantic content of the sentence used for relating the meaning of the sentence with previously acquired knowledge. Syntactic, or "interpretive processing" is defined as using the syntactic structure to extract the meaning of a sentence. Propositional processing or "postinterpretive processing" involves relating the meaning of a sentence to other information stored in the brain. According to Caplan et al. (1998),

> The propositional content of a sentence includes information about events and states in the world such as who is doing what to whom (thematic roles), which adjectives are associated with which nouns (attribution of modification), and other similar semantic information. Propositions can have truth values and can therefore enter into logical systems and be important in planning actions. (p. 541)

According to the examples provided by Caplan and colleagues, a proposition usually consists of a verb with an agent and optional complements.[6] Evidence from several sources is used to support the argument of separate propositional and syn-

---

[5] These attempts to vary syntactic complexity parametrically in order to avoid problems with more traditional imaging studies (see section II. K) face a common problem. Because the variation of complexity is coarse and discontinuous ("high" vs. "low"), it may be that the conditions in these studies are not varied on a continuous parameter (complexity), but instead differ qualitatively and invoke a different collection of strategies.

[6] Example of a two-proposition phrase: "The magician performed the stunt that included the joke." Example of a one-proposition phrase: "The magician performed the stunt and the joke." (From Caplan et al., 1998.)

tactic processing, including the performance of normal patients during concurrent memory tasks, patients with working memory deficits, and imaging results as propositional and syntactic complexity are varied. First we will review this evidence and then note some alternate interpretations.

One way to determine how distinct propositional and syntactic memory processes are from other memory processes is to test the effect of concurrent verbal memory distraction tasks on the performance of sentence processing. If syntactic processing and verbal memory both use the same resources, then verbal memory tasks such as the digit span task should reduce the amount of resources available for syntactic processing. Although the digit load did affect the accuracy of subjects matching sentences to pictures, it had no interaction with syntactic complexity. These results are compatible with the hypothesis that the effect of digit load on the performance of the sentence task was due to the constraints of a system used by both sentential processing and syntactic processing, but not specific to syntactic processing. On the other hand, there was a digit span interaction with the number of propositions in a sentence. Digit span has a larger effect with two propositions than with one. According to Caplan and Waters (1999),

> This suggests that, unlike syntactic processing in sentence comprehension, operations on the propositional content of a sentence such as matching it to knowledge in semantic memory or depictions of events or using it to plan and execute actions share resources with span tasks. (p. 85)

Importantly, some alternative conclusions have been offered. Miyake et al. (1999) noted that Caplan and Waters' experiment may have lacked the sensitivity to detect an interaction between memory and syntactic complexity. Miyake et al. (1994) did detect interaction between syntactic form and memory load in an earlier experiment that Caplan and Waters failed to replicate. Blackwell and Bates (1995) also found evidence of an interaction between memory and morphosyntactic processes suggesting that not all syntactic processes are equally vulnerable to interference from memory load.

Another source of evidence used by Caplan and Waters to examine the separability of syntactic and propositional memory is the performance of patients with working memory deficits. In aphasic patients with deficits in syntactic comprehension (as measured by a picture matching task using similar sentences to those in footnote 3), but still with the ability to perform above chance, a concurrent digit span task did not exacerbate their errors. One individual had a working memory span of 1 as measured by the Daneman-Carpenter task (Daneman & Carpenter, 1980), a task commonly used to assess working memory. Nevertheless, the patient could understand the individual sentences. However, the number of propositions in each sentence affected comprehension more than in normal controls, which confirms the hypothesis that propositional and digit span processing tasks share the same resources. These results are also controversial. There has been a case reported of a patient with working memory deficits but normal performance on sentences with increasing syntactic complexity or number of propositions (Kotz & von Cramon, 1999.)

Finally, to confirm the disassociation between syntactic and propositional processing, imaging tests were performed while subjects were viewing sentences that varied by syntactic complexity and propositional load. If syntactic processing is different from propositional processing, then parametric imaging results depending on the amount of syntactic complexity should differ from the results depending on the number of propositions. If one small area of the brain is found that is involved in only syntactic processing, this would fit Chomsky's theories about a special syntactic "module," but since propositional "postinterpretive" processes involve relating knowledge that was encoded in the sentence with knowledge gained from other senses, they should involve many areas in the brain (Caplan et al., 1998).

The area that was affected most strongly and consistently as syntactic complexity increased was the pars opercularis of Broca's area (Caplan et al., 1998; Just et al., 1996; Stromswold et al., 1996). Imaging studies using subtraction provide indirect evidence of the importance of Broca's area in syntactic processing. Broca's area was implicated in studies using the subtraction technique where the goal was to isolate sentential processing that occurs at a higher level than phonetic analysis (Bavelier et al., 1997; Neville et al., 1998). In the parametric study, other areas were also involved, including the anterior cingulate and medial frontal gyrus. However, these areas were not as strongly associated with the two different syntactic processing conditions as was Broca's area (Caplan et al., 1998).

In comparison to conditions based on syntactic complexity, as the number of propositions in a sentence increased from one to two, effects increased in different brain areas. Caplan et al. (1998) reported "a significant increase in rCBF [regional cerebral blood flow] in a large contiguous posterior region that included the occipital poles and inferior temporal cortex bilaterally" (p. 546). rCBF changes also increased bilaterally in the inferior occipital lobe, and inferior and medial temporal gyri. Caplan, et al. hypothesize that the increase is due to increased visualization requirements needed to perform the semantic plausibility task. The inferior temporal cortex involvement indicates that semantic information is being accessed, since the inferior temporal cortex in particular has been linked to the long-term memory of different categories of objects (Tranell et al., 1997).

Although Caplan and Waters present substantial evidence that the memory used during syntactic processing is different from other kinds of memory, there is evidence that the components of function localized to Broca's area may also be used by several other memory processes. Broca's area has been implicated in several kinds of nonsyntactically varying stimuli (Courtney, Ungerleider, Kell, & Haxby, 1997; MacLeod, Buckner, Miezin, Peterson, & Raichle, 1998). For example, Broca's area has been a locus of rCBF change during tasks that required the subjects to remember visual objects and during phonetic processing (Ungerleider, Courtney, & Haxby, 1998; Cohen et al., 1997; Paulesu et al., 1993). These imaging results led to some new questions about the neural substrates of syntactic processing.

Why would Broca's area be involved during all of these tasks? What relationship does syntactic processing have with other memory processes? To attempt to answer these questions, we will examine memory in more detail, specifically the relationship between memory used for general processing and memory used for syntactic processing. Working memory has traditionally been divided into two subsystems: slave subsystems and central executive (CE) subsystems. In the original theory, there were only two slave systems (a visuospatial sketch pad, and phonological loop) and a CE system (Baddeley & Hitch, 1974). The items in the various single-modality slave subsystems are linked and compared with each other or items temporarily retrieved from long-term memory by one or many CEs. How the CE is organized is still controversial. It is not known whether it is localized to one area of the brain, or results from interconnections between different memory areas (Deacon, 1997). Due to recent advances in the methodology of *in vivo* neuroimaging, the systems (slave and central executive) thought to be involved in memory processes have been continuously subdivided in the past several years (Baddeley, 1998). There is evidence that CEs may be divided into at least two different types: automatic, subconscious CEs and conscious, controlled CEs.[7] Syntactic processing may be classified as an automatic CE because people do not consciously plan which syntactic structures they use. Postinterpretive memory appears to require a conscious, controlled CE, since they do plan what content to include. Frequent modifications of theories of memory organization are expected as new experimental results become available and neuroimaging techniques are further refined.

It has been proposed that Broca's area may be important for the CE function (Goldman-Rakic, 1997). An alternative possibility is that syntactic processing relies upon the same CE as other cognitive processes but that the memory tasks did not require the use of the CE. If syntactic processing is also reliant on CE processing, then it would explain why digit span working memory does not appear to correlate well with syntactic processing. This may be true because the digit span task only tests the phonetic slave system, and syntactic processing requires CE processing. Digit span appears to only test the phonetic slave system because subjects only have to remember the numbers verbatim and do not have to compare or process the numbers. However, this argument does not explain why digit span processing affects propositional memory unless conscious CE processing needs attentional resources, which Caplan and Waters use to support their hypothesis that syntactic processing memory may be separate from other memory systems.

One way to test this hypothesis is to use a concurrent task that depends upon a central memory allocation resource. The most commonly used task for measuring working memory is the Daneman-Carpenter task. Caplan and Waters (1999) failed to find a difference in sentence-processing performance depending on syntactic complexity between patients who scored high and those who scored low on the

---

[7] Automatic and controlled CEs may of course represent two extremes in a continuum rather than qualitatively distinct classes.

Daneman-Carpenter task. However, there was a correlation as the propositional content increased. One study found a high correlation between the Western Aphasia Battery (WAB) morphosyntactic score of aphasics and their score on a slightly modified Danemann and Carpenter working memory task (Casapari, Parkinson, LaPointe, & Katz, 1998).[8] However the Danemann-Carpenter task may not be a reliable measurement of working memory, and the WAB measures morphosyntax and not the sentence-level syntax used by Caplan and Waters. According to Caplan and Waters, the Daneman-Carpenter working memory test is not a reliable measure of working memory because the results vary significantly from test to test within the same subject (Waters & Caplan, 1996).

One critique of Caplan and Waters (1999) is that the authors only consider the relationship of propositional complexity and syntactic complexity during sentence comprehension, not during production. In addition, they only consider syntax that is dependent on word order, and not the relation of morphosyntax to propositions. There are several other methods for testing syntactic processing, including comparing passive with active, and negative with affirmative sentences. Passive and negative sentences take longer to process than affirmative and active sentences (Baddeley & Hitch, 1974). A possible alternative to Caplan and colleagues' explanation of the separability of syntactic processing from other cognitive processing, proposed by Dick, Bates, Wulfeck, and Dronkers (1998), is that syntactic forms are just one kind of regularity perceived in the environment, stored differently than the propositional content, but similar to other regularities. This proposal explains the difference in syntactic and propositional processing without hypothesizing a separate working memory system for syntactic processing. Due to the lack of specific predictions in Dick et al.'s article, their proposal serves primarily as a starting point for a competing theory of the organization of syntactic processes in the brain.

D. Role of Prefrontal Cortex

As noted, several imaging studies based on parametric analysis indicate that the pars opercularis of Broca's area is the most important brain area for syntactic processing. However, lesion evidence indicates that the prefrontal cortex also plays a role in syntactic processing. Support for involvement in syntactic processing comes from studies of patients with agrammatic Broca's aphasia, who usually have lesions that include Broca's area and the prefrontal cortex. If the lesion is limited to Broca's area, then the aphasic patients are much more likely to recover their language and have less severe agrammatism (Caplan, 1992). One reason why lesion and imaging evidence appear to be contradictory is that the current imaging techniques do not have the resolution to detect every area involved in syntactic processing. One possible

---

[8] The modifications included shortening the average sentence length and separating out the words to be remembered from the sentences. The task was reported to be equally reliable as the original Daneman-Carpenter task, but allowed easier measurement of aphasics (Caspari et al., 1998).

interpretation of their proposal is that interpretive and post-interpretive processing may use the same memory processes but that memory traces for syntactic and propositional memory may be subject to different levels of interference, with propositional traces less resistant to the memory tasks used to test the interaction. There are currently many limitations of imaging studies of syntactic processing (see section II.K, for review).

Other imaging studies, wherein the focus is not only syntactic processing, have detected cerebrovascular changes in and around the dorsal lateral prefrontal cortex (DLPFC). Some subtraction imaging experiments indicate that the DLPFC has at least a role in sentential processing, but it is unclear if the effect is due to syntactic processing or another component of sentential processing (Bavelier et al., 1997; Neville et al., 1998). In one experiment it was possible to use cross-correlational fMRI data to interpret the time course of sentential processing. The prefrontal cortex (BA 46) showed modulation after Broca's area and the inferior portion of prefrontal sulcus, suggesting that the prefrontal cortex may have a different role in processing than Broca's area (Bavelier et al., 1997). In another subtraction experiment, BA 46 was seen to be involved when changes during the control word repetition tasks were subtracted from the experimental sentence-generation task (Mueller et al., 1997). It is not clear, however, if this result indicates syntactic, propositional processing, or participation in both functions. An indication that the DLPFC is important for propositional processing comes from an experiment which showed that the more difficult the task was semantically, the more the DLPFC was involved (for review, see Gabrieli, Poldrack, & Desmond, 1998).

The DLPFC has also been implicated in executive functioning, although it is not clear if it is part of the same executive function system used by syntactic processing. In one task requiring the CE where the subject was instructed to compare a newly presented consonant with a previously seen consonant held in memory, the DLPFC and not Broca's area responded differently as the memory load increased (Cohen et al., 1997). When subjects are instructed to remember numbers and the order of numbers, then the DLPFC is more strongly involved, but just the pure detection of a target normally does not lead to changes in the DLPFC (see Gabrieli et al., 1998). All these experiments are similar to the digit span task and may not use working memory, but instead test the phonetic slave system.

E. Summary of Role of Anterior Areas of Brain in Syntactic Processing

Working memory in humans has been divided into an increasingly larger number of subsystems. How these different memory systems interact is still being worked out. There is evidence from imaging of several different kinds of separate short-term memory systems in the frontal cortex (for reviews, see Baddeley, 1998; Frackowiak, 1994; Ungerleider, 1995). Evidence of several separate memory systems has been confirmed by studies in monkeys. For example, cells were found in different locations in the frontal cortex that responded preferentially during a delay period to either "what" characteristics like color or "where" characteristics like the location of an object (Wilson, Scalaidhe, & Goldman-Rakic, 1993; see also Fuster et al., 1982). Not addressed by any of the studies reviewed is a possible division between the memory systems used during syntactic production and comprehension. There is some evidence of a dissociation between the storage and retrieval of word lists, with the left frontal region involved more strongly during initial encoding of memory, and the right frontal region during retrieval (Baddeley, 1998).

The preliminary results from imaging and behavioral studies of syntactic processing appear to support the idea that there is a separate memory system for syntactic processing, and that the area of the brain most closely associated with this system is located in or near Broca's area. A specialized working memory system for syntactic processing would not be unprecedented. Evidence has also been found of a separate unconscious, automated working memory system for decision making based on emotional value (Bechara, Damasio, Tranel, & Anderson, 1996). However, it is now known whether this area is used only for syntactic memory processing or is involved in a subprocess used by both syntactic memory processing and other memory processes. More research is necessary to determine the role of Broca's area and anterior regions of the brain, to test the hypothesis that these areas are also involved in rule-based syntactic processing.

It is important to note that Broca's area is only one part of the brain involved in language. Besides lesion evidence that the DLPFC may be involved in syntactic processing, several researchers have claimed that every part of the brain involved in language appears to play some general role in language processing. According to Bates and Goodman (1997), "anomia is the one symptom (or class of symptoms) that is present in every form of aphasia that has been documented to date" (p. 551). These authors also claim that patients with lexical deficits also have syntactic deficits either in comprehension or production: "Studies of speech production in richly inflected languages show that Wernicke's aphasics make grammatical errors that are similar in quantity and quality to the errors produced by Broca's aphasics" (p. 552). Caplan et al. (1996) confirmed this claim, by noting that damage in any cortical area leads to a syntactic deficit. However, the claims made by Bates and Goodman (1997) are still strongly debated. It is possible that the measurements used were not fine-grained enough to detect qualitative differences between different kinds of aphasias. Although there are many similarities to all kinds of aphasia, there is evidence of different kinds of anomia in Wernicke's and Broca's patients (for review, see Gainotti, 1998). Nevertheless, the differences are not sharp enough to support localization of linguistic subcomponents divided by syntax or semantics into specific areas. The lesion data does support a different division based upon the characteristics of the word, whether it is used to describe actions (which most verbs are) or to objects with visual or auditory properties (which many nouns do). Combining imaging and lesion data, we can temporarily conclude that syntactic processing is spread over a nonlocalized network of neurons, with a higher density of neurons in the anterior areas, particularly Broca's area. In order to refine this hypothesis, the methods in imaging and neuropsychological studies need to be improved. A critique of the current methods used in these studies will be offered below after a more thorough review of the evidence that nonanterior areas of the brain are involved in syntactic processing.

F. Role of Posterior Areas in Syntactic Processing

Evidence for the role of the posterior areas is much more limited than for anterior areas because researchers studying the neural substrates of syntax have focused more on the anterior areas. However, lesion evidence indicates that the posterior areas are important for syntactic processing. As noted, several authors claim that Wernicke's aphasics who often have posterior lesions also make similar syntactic errors as Broca's aphasics (Bates & Goodman, 1997). The only experiments that specifically examined the role of the posterior areas in syntactic processing using parametric analysis found involvement near Wernicke's area (Just et al., 1996; Stromswold et al., 1996). In these studies an increase in the effect on the left and right temporal middle gyrus was reported as the syntactic complexity of sentences increased (Just et al., 1996; Stromswold et al., 1996). The right hemisphere change was surprising because it is thought that linguistic processing is lateralized to the left hemisphere, because people with lesions in the left hemisphere show aphasic symptoms much more often than patients with lesions in the right hemisphere. However, Caplan et al. (1998) did not replicate their earlier results, and the pattern of function-related changes in the right hemisphere reported by Just et al. was much less than that recorded in the left hemisphere.

Posterior areas and, in particular, the superior temporal sulcus (STS) were implicated during sentence-level processing of several imaging studies of general language processing. Similar to the Stromswold et al. (1996) and Just et al. (1996) imaging experiments, Bavelier et al. (1997) also found that the right "midportion" of the STS was implicated during sentence processing as compared to consonant viewing. In a subtraction experiment, the right "midportion" of the STS was involved when consonant viewing was subtracted from sentence viewing (Bavelier et al., 1997). The anterior temporal lobe, especially the anterior STS, was involved during sentence-processing tasks, but not during single word tasks, which may indicate that it is involved in syntactic processing or at least some part of sentential processing (for review see Bavelier et al., 1997). The timing of effects in one study shows that functional connectivity appears to proceed from the posterior STS to anterior STS (Bavelier et al., 1997). The authors of this study hypothesize that "the anterior and middle portions of the STS participate in syntactic and semantic analysis respectively" (Bavelier et al., 1997, p. 675). Like Caplan and colleagues, the assumption is made that syntactic processing occurs before semantic processing (but cf. Marslen-Wilson & Tyler, 1987). Mueller et al. (1997) also found effects in the superior and middle temporal gyrus during sentence comprehension when a resting condition was subtracted. How do posterior areas interact with anterior areas to process syntax?

A literature review revealed two different theories about the role of posterior brain areas in syntactic processing. One theory is that posterior areas are involved in the storage of irregular morphosyntactic forms (Ullman et al., 1997). Another theory is that they are involved in relating individual words with other words in a sentence (Posner & Pavese, 1998). To support the theory that irregular forms are stored in the posterior areas of the brain, Ullman et al. (1997) claim that patients with posterior lesions have more difficulties conjugating the past tense of irregular than regular verbs. However, this interpretation is premature, because the "posterior lesion group" of subjects used in this study have differing degrees and locations of damage spreading beyond posterior areas, but in all subjects the dorsolateral frontal cortex was spared. Some of the patients that were placed in the posterior group had lesions large enough that parts of the basal ganglia were damaged. According to Ullman et al.'s theory, these patients should have had deficits in conjugating the past tense for both regular and irregular verbs, but the results of these subjects with posterior and basal ganglia damage were not listed separately. Ullman et al. do not specify in more detail what particular posterior area of the brain could be responsible for the storage of past tense forms.

Another hypothesis is that Wernicke's area has a role in relating words to the context of a sentence and not just in the lexical access of individual words. In an event related potential (ERP) study, Posner and Pavese (1998) found that the posterior area appeared to be the most important area for tasks requiring integration at the sentence level and that the anterior area is more involved during a task requiring only single-word processing. Although the task showed that the posterior areas are involved in sentential semantic processing, it is not clear whether the posterior areas are also important to syntactic processing. Posner and Pavese's task measures propositional processing rather than syntactic processing. Thus, Posner and Pavese's hypothesis does not contradict the theory that Broca's area is most important for purely syntactic processing.

In summary, there are several sources of evidence that posterior areas, and in particular the superior temporal sulcus, is involved in sentential and possibly syntactic processing, but more evidence is needed to specify the role. We reviewed two theories about the specific role of the posterior brain areas in linguistic processing, but the theories did not discuss the role of posterior areas in general syntactic processing. A few imaging studies of syntactic processing showed that right posterior areas were involved, but this was not supported by later studies.

G. Nonclassical Areas Involved in Syntactic Processing

In the Wernicke-Geschwind model, only the role of Broca's area, Wernicke's area, and the connections between these areas are emphasized. Since the importance of these areas in language processing has been stressed for more than 100 years, these areas are known as "classical" language areas. As researchers have searched for the neural substrates of language subcomponents, an increasing number of nonclassical brain areas have been implicated in language processing. Although Geschwind noted that there were some other areas of the brain besides Broca's or Wernicke's area that if damaged could cause aphasia, including the supplemental motor cortex and subcortical loops (especially the basal ganglia and the thalamus), the role of these areas was not explained or integrated into a new model. In the next section, we will examine what role several nonclassical areas play in syntactic processing, including the basal ganglia, cerebellum, and right hemisphere.

1. Role of Basal Ganglia in Processing Syntax

Although several of the following sources of evidence support the basal ganglia's role in language, most researchers do not specifically examine the role of the basal ganglia in syntactic processing. Lieberman (1998) noted that people camping on Mount Everest have delays in voice onset time and syntactic deficits that appear similar to Broca's aphasics. Since the basal ganglia is one of the most vulnerable areas in the brain-to-oxygen deprivation, the climber's performance is an indication that when the basal ganglia cannot function normally, syntactic processing is disturbed. However, this data is only indirect, and it is possible that the climbers are suffering from a general processing deficit, not specific to language or syntax, because they also have difficulty in general cognitive tasks. Even subjects without brain impairments or exposure to low oxygen levels show similar aphasic symptoms under stress (Blackwell & Bates, 1995; Miyake, Carpenter, & Just, 1994; Dick et al., 1998).

In a study of a patient with a purely subcortical lesion in the basal ganglia (bilaterally in the putamen and caudate nucleus), syntactic deficits were found in the absence of apparent semantic or naming deficits (Pickett, Kuniholm, Protopapas, Friedman, & Lieberman, 1998). However, increases in syntactic complexity did not lead to more errors. Similar stimuli were used by Caplan and colleagues (Caplan & Waters, 1999; Caplan, Alpert, & Waters, 1998), and center-embedded sentences were considered the most syntactically complex stimuli, so syntactic complexity was again linked with memory load. The authors hypothesize that syntactic complexity did not lead to an increase in errors, because the subject had normal verbal memory, but some other component of syntactical processing used in both simple and complex sentences was affected by the lesion (Pickett et al., 1998). Note that it is possible that the basal ganglia is involved more strongly in postinterpretive (propositional) processing than the initial syntactic interpretation of sentences. Pickett et al. did not test the patient only by varying the number of propositions in each sentence. Because the patient also had difficulty both with producing articulatory gestures in the right sequence while speaking and with a cognitive task that involved choosing which objects should be grouped together, it is possible that the subject's ability to sequence was impaired by the lesion, or that CE processing was impaired (Pickett et al., 1998).

Two diseases that affect the functioning of the basal ganglia, Huntington's disease and Parkinson's disease, indicate a role for the basal ganglia in syntactic processing. Several syntactic deficits have been documented in Parkinson's patients. Parkinson's patients have syntactic comprehension deficits and use simpler syntax and shorter sentences than age-matched controls (Lieberman, 1992). Parkinson's patients also make significantly more mistakes in conjugating the past tense of regular verbs than irregular verbs, which may indicate that regularly applied morphosyntax requires the basal ganglia more than irregularly applied morphosyntax (Ullman et al., 1997). Interestingly, there were no overregularizations recorded for irregular verb errors in Parkinson's patients. However, these results do not necessarily mean that there is a separate rule system for irregular and regular verbs. In a connectionist study that used only a single algorithm for learning regular and irregular verbs, after lesioning some connections in the neural net, the system was able to recover irregular verbs more fully than regular verbs (for review, see Plunkett & Marchman, 1996).

Contrary to Parkinson's patients, Huntington's patients overregularize and misconjugate significantly more irregular verbs than controls (Ullman et al., 1997). Since basal ganglia functioning is disturbed differently in Huntington's patients than in Parkinson's patients, they should be expected to show different syntactic deficits than Parkinson's patients. In Huntington's patients it appears that the motor and frontal cortical circuits are more involved than in normal subjects, whereas Parkinson's patients have less active frontal cortices than normals (Ullman et al., 1997). Ullman and colleagues claim that the past-tense verb conjugation performance of Huntington's and Parkinson's patients shows that the role of the frontal cortex–basal ganglia loop is to process regular syntactic forms. However, other possible explanations for the performance of the patients are equally plausible. Another possible interpretation of the Huntington's patients' performance is that the deficits are not a specific problem with language, but with the selection of motor programs, and in this case with the selection of the correct articulatory gesture. The regular "-ed" suffix is used far more commonly than other past-tense suffixes, and thus the Huntington's patients produced this past-tense suffix more often. This hypothesis is supported by the fact that there were several cases where the Huntington's patients said both a correct and incorrect conjugation. These answers were scored as wrong and could make the syntactic deficits appear larger than they were.

Finally, an unusual case of persistent asymmetric bilingual aphasia provides evidence that the basal ganglia's role may not be in syntactic processing, but in a more general process of automatization. Aglioti, Beltramello, Girardi, and Fabbro (1996) report a patient who had similar qualitative deficits in L1 (maternal language) and L2 (second language), but had much greater quantitative deficits in L1 that still persisted 5 years after a purely subcortical lesion. This may be because L1 was much more automatized because it was used more and acquired at an earlier age.

In summary, although several sources of evidence indicate that the basal ganglia is important for syntactic processing, the syntactic deficits are always accompanied by other cognitive or motor deficits. Whether the deficits are due to damage in several subsystems in the basal ganglia, or if all of these behaviors require similar processing requires further study to determine. One interesting candidate is that all of these behaviors are reliant on the role the basal ganglia plays in automatization.

2. Role of Cerebellum in Syntactic Processing

The role of the cerebellum in syntactic processing is even less clear than the basal ganglia. There are two sources of evidence that signal at least a role in cognition: evidence from anatomical studies and evidence from behavioral studies. Neuroanatomically, the cerebellum is expanded in humans compared to other primates, indicating that it is responsible for some aspect of human behavioral uniqueness. The dentate nucleus in particular is expanded in humans (Deacon, 1997). An indication that the cerebellum plays a greater role in cognition in humans than in other animals is also given by the expanded cerebro-cortical connections in humans.

Patients with cerebellar lesions in the dentate nucleus of the cerebellum do suffer some verbal deficits, such as difficulty in learning new word-generation tasks. However, patients with cerebellar lesions also have nonlinguistic deficits, including difficulty learning new nonverbal tasks, such as the tower of Hanoi (for a review of the cerebellum's role in cognition, see Bloedel, 1993; Desmond & Fiez, 1998; Fiez, 1996; Glickstein, 1993; Leiner, Leiner, & Dow, 1993).

According to three recent reviews, the imaging evidence that the cerebellum has a role in linguistic processing comes from only one experiment. In this PET experiment, when the subjects were asked to read a noun, and in a comparison task to generate a verb after a noun was read, the cerebellum was affected (Petersen et al., 1989). However, the same areas are also affected during nonlanguage tasks (Desmond & Fiez, 1998). Some researchers have attempted to name one computational process that is common to all tasks that produce function-related changes in the cerebellum, and it appears that tasks that require novel movements involve the cerebellum more than tasks that are practiced and automatic. With practice on novel tasks, the effect in the cerebellum decreases (van Mier, Tempel, Perlmutter, Raichle, & Peterson, 1998). Leiner et al. (1993) claim that the cerebellum is involved in the manipulation and ordering of symbols, although the authors make no attempt to define exactly what these symbols are or what the exact role of the cerebellum would be in the "manipulation of these symbols." They also make the rather vague statement that "the cerebellum can improve the performance of any parts of the brain to which it is reciprocally connected" (p. 446). As pointed out by Fiez, the attempt to find a function for what all the tasks that involve the cerebellum have in common may be misguided if the cerebellum performs many functions, instead of just one. Ito (1993) suggests that the dentate nucleus is involved in planning, and that other areas of the cerebellum are involved in the performance of automated movement sequences. The PET experiments do not provide the spatial resolution to examine this hypothesis. No experiments have been done to determine whether the cerebellum plays a role specifically in syntactic processing. Based on (a) the cerebellum's anatomical uniqueness in humans, (b) evidence from one imaging experiment on language, and (c) evidence from patients with cerebellar lesions who have deficits in word generation tasks, it is possible to assume that the cerebellum, if not involved in syntactic processing, is useful for acquiring syntax.

3. Role of the Right Hemisphere in Syntactic Processing

Evidence from imaging and neuropsychological research of right hemisphere involvement in syntactic processing is a little stronger than evidence for the cerebellum. As noted in the section reviewing involvement of posterior areas during syntactic processing, the right STS has been implicated in several language imaging studies. Neuropsychological evidence also indicates that the right hemisphere appears to play some role in syntactic comprehension. Patients with right hemisphere lesions had a deficit in syntactic interpretation (Caplan, Hildebrandt, & Makris, 1996). However, it is not clear if the deficit is due to damage to syntactically specific or more general cognitive processing resources. Caplan et al. (1996) hypothesized that "[t]he roles of the right hemisphere might be to provide a less specialized working memory capacity that makes a lesser contribution to syntactic processing" (p. 944). The imaging study of Caplan et al. (1998) supports this hypothesis, since the right cortical areas were involved much more strongly during tasks that varied the amount of propositional memory than during tasks comparing the effects of varying the load on syntactic memory.

4. Other Nonclassical Areas Implicated in Syntactic Processing

Another brain area, the anterior cingulate, was implicated during a language imaging study. Caplan et al. (1998) found rCBF changes in the anterior cingulate in more syntactically complex versus less complex sentences. They hypothesized that the changes in the anterior cingulate might be due to increased attentional and processing resource requirements.

5. Summary of Nonclassical Areas Involved in Syntactic Processing

Due to the biases of the Wernicke-Geschwind theory, the roles of nonclassical areas in syntactic processing have not been examined in detail. Of the nonclassical areas examined in this paper, the basal ganglia and the right hemisphere appear more likely to be used for syntactic processing. However, it is not clear if they are involved directly in syntactic processing or in a general cognitive process that is also used during syntactic processing. Caplan et al.'s (1996) lesion study confirmed Bates and Goodman's claim (1997) of a widely distributed neural network involved in syntactic processing, and indicated that a lesion anywhere in the cortex may affect syntactic processing. In summary, although it appears that nonclassical areas of the brain are important for syntactic processing, thus far, the evidence appears to indicate that they are important because of their role in either earlier processes that occur before syntactic processing, or later processes after syntactic processing is performed relating to the expression of syntactic knowledge, but not necessarily directly in syntactic processing itself. Further examination of all these areas will be necessary to determine their importance in syntactic processing, but the strongest evidence of a specialized area is still in the anterior cortex, in Broca's area.

H. Role of Imaging and Lesion Data in Determining Brain Areas Involved in Syntactic Processing

Why have researchers not been able to more precisely localize the neural substrates of syntactic processing? One reason is the limited power of the techniques used to study the architecture of the neural substrates of syntactic processing. Historically, researchers relied on lesion studies for probing the neural substrates of language. In the past few decades, *in vivo* imaging techniques have been developed to supplement lesion studies. Because the techniques of lesion and imaging studies are still being perfected, both general limitations and specific limitations of using these methods to determine the architecture of the neural substrates of syntactic processing will be examined.

I. General Limitations of Lesion Studies

In initial lesion studies, because the analysis of the lesions was done post mortem, lesion localization was not very accurate. Subsequently, after better scanning techniques were developed it became possible to more precisely visualize the lesion location in living patients. Unfortunately for researchers interested in studying the relationship of specific anatomical areas to behavior, lesions are rarely limited to one anatomical area. Even if the lesion is limited to one anatomical area, it is difficult to determine if the damaged area is involved in the processing of the cognitive component being studied, or if the lesion interrupts a pathway that sends input needed by another area for processing. One way to resolve this dilemma is to check if the patient eventually recovers the behavior lost after the lesion, or if the behavioral deficit is persistent. Only persistent deficits may indicate that an area is necessary for a patient to be able to perform a behavior. If the deficit is not persistent then the lesion may be in a pathway (Dronkers, 1999). However, the ability of the brain to recover from damage is not yet well known, so this hypothesis may be incorrect, because it is possible that undamaged areas of the brain may be able to adapt to take over the functions of the damaged area. To address this problem, more longitudinal studies of patients with lesions must be done. Another limitation of lesion studies is that most patients suffer lesions due to cerebral vascular accidents (CVAs), and because CVAs tend to happen only in certain areas with heavy vasculature, the importance of many areas that are rarely affected (especially in isolation) is not usually shown by lesion studies. Thus lesion studies must be supplemented by other methods, such as imaging studies (Dronkers, 1998).

J. Limitations of Using Lesions to Study the Neural Substrates of Syntactic Processing

Most neuropsychological studies characterize one or a few patients in great detail. Only a very few researchers have attempted to define the relationship between lesion sites and the resulting syntactic deficits in a large group of identically tested patients (Caplan et al., 1996; Berndt, Mitchum, & Haendiges, 1996; Grodzinsky, Pinango, Zurif, & Drai, 1999.) In the first two of these studies, no correlation was found between a specific syntactic processing deficit and damage to a particular anatomic region. Grodzinsky et al. (1999) claimed that Broca's aphasics with inferior frontal abnormalities have a very specific syntactic deficit but Berndt and Caramazza (1999) have noted that the selection criteria may have excluded several reported Broca's aphasics that contradict this obervation. Even in the largest of these studies (Caplan et al., 1996), involving over 60 patients, they still did not have enough patients to make detailed comparisons about the importance of small neural regions in syntactic processing, such as the hypothesis made by Dronkers about the site (the insula) needed for articulation (Dronkers, 1996). Because of a large degree of interindividual variability in lesion size and location, the patients were only classified depending on whether they had an anterior or posterior lesion, and whether the lesion was in the left or right hemisphere. Despite this low level of granularity, there were not even enough patients to compare the effects of left posterior and left anterior lesions. The difficulty of finding a large group of subjects with lesions limited to the area in which researchers are interested was also demonstrated by Ullman et al.'s (1997) study. These authors also could not locate patients with lesions limited to either anterior or posterior areas. Because the interruption of connections between regions can have a similar effect as lesions in the gray area of these regions, it is important to take into account whether the lesions include white matter. Caplan et al. (1996) note that although in their study they did not examine whether the lesions included white matter, future studies will need to take this consideration into account.

Even with many more subjects, deciding how to divide the subjects into groups would remain difficult, as there are few hypotheses about what anatomical areas are most important specifically for syntactic processing besides Broca's area. An example of the difficulty of choosing how to divide subjects into groups while studying the neural substrates of a cognitive process comes from one study of the neural substrates of decision making (Bechara et al., 1998). Initially, subjects were grouped depending on whether they had lesions in the ventral medial (VM) or dorsal medial (DM) division of the prefrontal cortex, but the authors noticed later that they had to divide the VM group into subgroups with either anterior VM or posterior VM lesions because that grouping matched the behavioral results better. An analysis based upon a different grouping of patients in the Caplan et al. (1996) study would possibly show clearer results. Despite the limitations of lesion studies, they are useful for providing corroboration of data gathered using other methods. As mentioned in the previous section, they may also be useful for detecting areas involved in syntactic processing that are not shown by imaging.

K. Limitations of Imaging Syntactic Processing in the Brain

1. Temporal Limitations

Similar to lesion studies, there are currently many limitations in using imaging techniques for studying the neural substrates of syntactic processing. Because the role of syntax is to indicate relationships between lexical elements in a sentence, syntactic processing must occur over a period of several seconds during which the sentence is pronounced or read. Currently there is no imaging technique with the combined spatial and temporal resolution necessary for determining architecture of the neural substrates of syntactic processing. Imaging techniques with relatively good spatial resolution, such as fMRI, and PET do not have enough temporal resolution to map areas involved during different points of processing a sentence. Thus these techniques cannot be used to examine which areas are affected during different stages of syntactic processing, such as whether the patient or the agent in a sentence is being read. Researchers using imaging techniques with high spatial resolution, including PET and fMRI, have been limited to studying patterns of change in blood flow or blood oxygenation during either the presentation of a series of single words or whole sentences.

Imaging techniques with a sufficiently high temporal resolution for examining effects in the brain of individual stages of syntactic processing have very low spatial resolution. These techniques include electroencephalography (EEG) and magneto-electroencephalography (MEG). Event-related EEG and MEG techniques are useful for determining what subprocesses are included in syntactic processing because the performance of activities with similar subprocesses results in similar waveforms. However, MEG and EEG are not useful for precisely determining where in the brain the processing occurs. Thus, this chapter has focused mainly on the results from PET and fMRI studies.

The refinement of these techniques will be necessary to elaborate the spatial and temporal dimensions of syntactic processing. One promising new technique involves using PET or fMRI to determine the order in which different areas of the brain participate (Bavelier et al., 1997; McIntosh & Gonzalez-Lima, 1994).

2. Spatial Resolution Limits

Although fMRI has the best spatial resolution of any technique used for in vivo imaging of behavior, presently the highest spatial resolution of fMRI is limited to around 2 mm^2 (Brodal, 1998). However, a typical resolution used in studies of language processing is $2.5 \times 2.5 \times 5$ mm (Bavelier et al., 1997). This resolution is far removed for the level needed to chart the activity of individual neurons thought to be the unit of computation in the brain (Kandel, Schwartz, & Jessel, 1991, p. 20). Even if the spatial resolution were not constrained by MRI technology, the fact that the effects observed are based on blood-oxygenation and are therefore vascular, rather than electrochemical, makes it unlikely that the increased resolution would yield more revealing data. Another reason comparisons between individuals can only be done on a general level is due to interindividual variation in human brain anatomy and the lack of knowledge on how these variations affect syntactic processing. The relation of interindividual variation to behavioral variation is not yet known, because researchers have only begun to quantify the amount of anatomical interindividual variation. In one of the few papers where interindividual variation was examined, the changes in blood oxygenation relative to the location of different landmarks in the brain varied considerably (Bavelier et al., 1997). Researchers currently performing imaging studies make the assumption that interindividual anatomical variation does not affect organization of the neural substrates of syntax, but further study is needed.

The spatial resolution of PET is even more limited than fMRI. PET relies on averages across subjects so that it is not possible to compare interindividual variation. Using PET it is easy to overestimate the size of a rCBF change because of the anatomical variability among subjects (Ungerleider, Courtney, & Haxby, 1998). The spatial resolution is so limited that it may not even be possible to distinguish effects among areas 44, 45, 46, or 47, which includes Broca's area and the prefrontal cortex, areas that are often damaged in aggrammatics (Warburton et al., 1996). Researchers using the fMRI technique have proposed some methods to mitigate the problem of interindividual variation. One way to get around the problem of interindividual variation and overestimating the size of regional changes, and thus the difficulty of comparing different studies done with different people, is to do several tests within the same subjects to determine how tasks are related to each other. Another more practical technique often used in fMRI is to report the patterns of function-related changes within individuals and not averaged across subjects.

An unresolved question is how to report the location of patterns of blood flow and oxygenation change from imaging studies. Methods vary across experiments. For example, in one experiment the implicated area is simply referred to as the left prefrontal cortex (Gabrieli et al., 1998). In another experiment, the cortex was divided into the arbitrary number of 31 different areas based on anatomical landmarks (Neville et al., 1997). The lack of a standardized method for reporting results makes it difficult to determine precisely whether change occurs in the same area in different studies.

The regions reported are likely to be more generic and larger than the underlying loci of change, because in any anatomically based taxonomy of cortical regions, only part of that area must be affected before the entire area is taken to be "activated." In the experiment where the brain was divided into 31 different areas, only 5–10% of each of these areas was involved during any one time, and in each individual subject variations in effect in each area were as high as 47% from trial to trial (Bavelier et al., 1997). In most imaging studies, data from many subjects is combined and spatial filtering is used, with the underlying assumption that large areas of the brain, several voxels across, are affected at once. Bavelier et al. (1997) note that an alternate possibility is that many small focal areas may be involved. They pointed out in their fMRI study that, "highly correlated voxels did not appear as the peaks of a broad area of activation, but were directly surrounded by voxels with low correlation values" (Bavelier et al., 1997, p. 668).

In summary, there is no agreed upon method for reporting the results of imaging experiments, because it is not yet known how cognitive functions are instantiated in the brain. Although more is known about how sensory information is stored and how behavioral tasks affect the size of these maps in the brain, the processing done beyond the initial sensory interpretation is not known (for a recent review, see Buonomano & Merzenich, 1998).

3. Difficulty of Choosing Behavioral Tasks to Study Syntactic Processing

In order to determine which areas of the brain are used by language, some researchers have had subjects perform an experimental task while they are viewing, or listening to, a sentence and a control task including all the sensory and motor components of the sentence task except the sentence. Next, the patterns of blood flow or oxygenation recorded during the control task are subtracted from the pattern recorded during the sentence task. A problem with this kind of experiment is the assumption of "pure insertion" (Smith et al., 1998). Researchers using subtraction assume that the cognitive processes used in both the experimental and control task are exactly the same except for the process they want to examine. This assumption may not be valid because subjects may use different strategies during the experimental and the control task. In addition, researchers who use subtraction make the assumption that processing in the brain occurs in a unidirectional hierarchy with little top-down input, which would alter earlier stages of processing and invalidate the subtraction.

Because the temporal resolution of fMRI is too slow to analyze what is occurring during a sentence, most researchers have either used experimental tasks that are simplified compared to natural language, or chosen a control task to subtract out what they are not interested in. Even if the assumption of "pure insertion" is correct, it is very difficult to choose which tasks to subtract, so that, theoretically, only syntactic processing would be examined.

One example of the subtraction approach was studied by Neville and colleagues, who used the presentation of a group of consonants placed in random order as the control task, and full sentences as the experimental condition. The authors claimed that the sensory effects during the control condition could be subtracted from the experimental condition, leaving purely linguistic processing effects (Bavelier et al., 1997; Neville et al., 1998). However, as noted above, this claim is controversial. It is likely that the subjects use an entirely different strategy during the experimental task than when processing consonants. Second, it is not possible to determine what subcomponents of language are being visualized, because even if effects could be subtracted from the sentence tasks, many language subcomponents are being imaged at once, including syntactic processing.

A different strategy from the subtraction technique used to study syntactic processing is to use experimental tasks instead of natural language. Van Turrenout, Hagoort, and Brown (1998) claimed that their experimental results were evidence for separate, parallel processing of phonology and syntax. They also claimed that syntactical characteristics may be retrieved faster than phonetic characteristics. However, there are some possible design flaws in the ERP experiment, which make this interpretation premature. To represent syntactic processing, the authors instructed subjects to label the gender of nouns. Gender may not be a good example for syntactical processing, as gender-labeling morphosyntax is not present in many languages in the world and thus generalization to other syntax is questionable. The phonological task was to name the first sounds of noun phrase. This task may be more difficult than naming the gender, which may explain why the syntactic task according to the ERP measurements occurred approximately 40 ms faster than the phonetic task. This experiment shows the limitations of any artificial task used to represent language processing. It is difficult to determine if any artificial task is generalizable to a natural situation, because the artificial tasks only examine one small aspect of the natural tasks. Because language includes so many interacting levels of processing, both at the linguistic and cognitive levels, choosing artificial tasks to represent language is especially difficult. Many studies of linguistic processing have been done at the single word level, but because syntactic processing occurs at the sentence level, one-word tasks like generating a noun for a verb will not be reviewed in this chapter (for a review of word-level studies, see Price et al., 1996, 1998; Warburton et al., 1996).

Another common strategy used by language imaging researchers is to choose one language-like task to represent all language processing. The bias not to separate out different subcomponents of language processing may originate from the Wernicke-Geschwind model, which does not separate out individual subcomponents of language. This strategy is evident in the title of Binder et al.'s (1998) paper "Human brain language areas identified by functional magnetic resonance imaging," even though Binder and colleagues only measured BOLD effects during a semantic judgment task after the presentation of individual words.

A recently developed technique, parametric analysis, appears better suited for imaging cognitive processes in humans because it does not have the limitations of "pure insertion," and does not require the subjects to perform artificial tasks. In order to perform parametric analysis of syntactic processing, it is necessary to create several tasks that require progressively more complex syntactic processing. The assumption behind parametric analysis is that areas involved in syntactic processing will be more strongly involved in tasks that require more syntactic processing compared to tasks that require less syntactic processing. Another assumption is that only one process is being varied at a time during the task. There are only a few imaging studies using this method, and so far it has been difficult to find tasks that vary only the syntactic processing load. So far, in imaging studies, parametric analysis has only been performed by comparing patterns of cerebrovascular change during the reading of center-embedded sentences and right-branching sentences (Caplan et al., 1998; Just et al., 1997; Stromswold et al., 1996).

During any behavioral task, it is important to confirm that the subjects are performing the task as they have been instructed. To confirm that subjects are paying attention to the sentence stimuli, researchers usually give subjects a question about the sentence. However, this question biases the way the subjects process the sentences and may affect which areas of the brain are affected. One method is to ask the subjects to judge whether the sentences are semantically plausible, which is probably not what people normally do when they hear a sentence, because we assume that sentences will be semantically plausible (see Caplan et al., 1998; Stromswold et al., 1996). Another method that has less relation to natural language processing is to test the subjects' posttest recognition memory of the sentences shown during the experimental task (Bavelier et al., 1997; Neville et al., 1998). A better method and the most natural task used to confirm subjects' participation is to ask the subjects questions about the sentences similar to what could be asked during a typical conversation for clarification (i.e., "Who did what to whom?") (Pickett et al., 1998).

4. Other Methodological Limitations of Imaging Studies

Besides the difficulties of choosing a task, confirming that the subject is performing the task correctly, and analyzing the results, several other questions about imaging techniques have not yet been resolved. The following is a brief list of some other methodological problems in imaging that need to be addressed. First, no imaging method allows researchers to determine whether an affected area is involved in inhibition or excitation. Another question that has not been seriously considered by any of the studies reviewed in this chapter is how gender, handedness, and right hemisphere lateralization for language functions affect the results of these studies (Gabrieli et al., 1998). In one study that analyzed the fMRI results by gender, the pattern of rCBF change in females as syntactic processing load increased was more anterior and higher than in male subjects (Caplan et al., 1998). Furthermore, most imaging experiments have presented stimuli in blocks, so that subjects may change their strategies when presented with a block of control or experimental stimuli. The recent development of event-related fMRI allows the presentation of different stimuli in a random order. Event-related studies are only possible using fMRI and EEG, but not PET. In summary, because of all the limitations of imaging, it is important to complement imaging data with data from other studies and to focus on improving imaging techniques. It is expected that as this technique improves, more knowledge will accumulate about the architecture of syntactic processing in the brain.

III. PART 2: ONTOGENY OF THE NEURAL SUBSTRATES OF SYNTACTIC PROCESSING

The previously reviewed studies were performed in adults. Before we can examine what evolutionary pressures led to the development of brain areas for syntactic processing, we need to examine how much knowledge of syntax children are born with, and how much of the brain architecture devoted to syntactic processing is due to learning. Obviously, because of the variability of words, grammatical structures, and prosodic patterns across languages, much of language is learned.

A. Evidence from Language Acquisition

1. Poverty of Stimulus Argument

Many researchers claim that syntax learning is a much more difficult problem than learning word meaning or other language subcomponents. The argument that children are not given enough feedback to learn syntax and thus must be born with some knowledge of syntax, is known in the language acquisition literature as the poverty of the stimulus (POS) argument. Other researchers argue that syntax *is* learnable without an innate special purpose syntax-specific learning algorithm. Recent research on language acquisition in normal children with atypical or typical language input, and in children with focal lesions, has been used by both supporters and detractors of the POS argument.

2. Why Syntax Is Difficult to Learn

Syntax is harder to learn than other components of language. Syntax appears more difficult to learn than the finite number of phonemes in each language, prosody patterns, or word meanings. Words appear to be easier to learn than syntax because they can be learned by observing the correlation between the word and the context in which it is used. The relation between syntax use and the environment is more abstract. However, learning a large number of arbitrary sound-to-meaning mappings is still a difficult problem, and not all words have a simple relationship to the environment (Oliphant, in press). Thus, children acquire the meaning of concrete words more accurately and sooner than abstract words (Holzman, 1997, p. 127). If observational learning was always required for learning a word meaning, then an infant would always have to observe the meaning being used in the context of that object to learn it. A system where children could learn words without observational learning would be much more powerful. It is likely that the ability to express the relationship between words, or syntax, greatly facilitates the learning of a large number of meaning-to-sign pairs. Children as young as 20 months old can use syntactic context to aid in determining the meaning of a word (i.e., whether it is a noun or a verb) (MacWhinney, 1998). How do children learn these syntactic rules?

Researchers who claim that syntax is not learnable using general cognitive strategies argue that parents do not explicitly teach grammar to their children, and even if they tried, that syntactic rules are just too complex to be learned. Two quotations typify the POS argument.

> Given that the rules of syntax are too complex for a general purpose learner to deduce without training and that children do not require training, children cannot be general-purpose learners when it comes to language. They must come equipped with

special-purpose learning algorithms that allow them to learn language in a rapid and error free manner. (Ganger & Stromswold, 1998, p. 200)

Newmeyer (1991) claims that for some grammar rules, "it seems beyond the realm of possibility that anything on the order of generalization from observed environmental input could have led to this conclusion [to learn the Empty Category Principle in Universal Grammar]" (p. 14). The rules of syntax are so complicated that linguists working for almost 50 years have not been able to either produce a list of rules or a computer program that describes how to make every syntactically well-formed phrase in even one language (Ganger & Stromswold, 1998).

Another argument that is used to support the hypothesis that children have knowledge of syntax is that syntax develops like an organ, and not like an acquired skill. "[T]he fact that most children acquire the components of language in essentially the same order suggests that language development is largely the result of innate processes" (Ganger & Stromswold, 1998).

One component for which there is strong evidence of innateness is babbling. The process of babbling[9] seems to be innate and specific to language development, not just tied to the development of the vocal apparatus, since deaf children exposed to sign language from birth also manually babble in a manner that is very similar to vocal babbling (Petitto & Marentette, 1991). There seems to be a tendency to use speech for language because even deaf children babble vocally (for review, see Harley, 1995, p. 353). However, there is also evidence of a similar tendency to use manual gestures for communication. Blind speakers use as many gestures as sighted speakers, even when the blind speakers are talking to a blind listener (Iverson & Goldin-Meadow, 1998). Although the fact that blind speakers gesture as often as sighted speakers supports the hypothesis that humans have an innate tendency to gesture to communicate, another possibility as Iverson and Goldin-Meadow point out, is that gesturing helps the speakers to organize their thoughts while communicating.

Although there is a stronger consensus that the tendency to babble is innate, another possible aspect of language that appears to be innate is the naming insight, or a desire to learn the names of things that are in the environment (Aitchison, 1996). However, neither the innate tendency of babbling nor the naming insight is good evidence that a part of syntax is innate because syntax is very different from both. Preliminary evidence from one research group shows that all children acquire grammatical structures in the same order (Granger & Stromswold, 1998). It is important to note, however, that this evidence is preliminary and not reported in detail. However, many studies of this issue are underway.

In summary, evidence to determine how much knowledge of syntax children are born with still needs to be gathered. Due to the complexity of syntax, lack of

---

[9] Babbling begins in infants around 6 months of age and ends around 10 months when they acquire their first words. It is different from crying or cooing because it consists of strings of a combination of vowels and consonants (for review see Harley, 1995, pp. 352–353).

feedback, the speed and order of syntax acquisition in children exposed to language, many researchers have argued that children must be born with some knowledge of syntax.

B. Arguments That Syntax Is *Learned* by Normal Children with Typical Language Input

On the other hand, several researchers claim that syntax is learnable starting without a specialized syntax learning algorithm and with only typical language input. Recent research has revealed that children actually do receive instruction from their caregivers about syntax. When children first use words, usually the words are only used in certain contexts and in set structures. Caregivers then take a child's utterances and use them in longer and more syntactically complex sentences (Holzman, 1997). They also use words in different contexts from the children. According to one study, the caregivers were not consciously aware that they were adapting their child's utterances into their own speech (Holzman, 1997). Humans, as young as 4 years old, appear to automatically adopt their speech to the level of the recipient (Holzman, 1997). Thus, humans appear to naturally adapt their speech so that it is more easily understood and learned. Because it is done subconsciously, this tendency itself may be an instinct.

Some researchers have noted that language does not develop like other innate skills such as motor development, because the rate of language acquisition is variable (Bates & Goodman, 1997). This is true for both syntax and vocabulary acquisition. Children acquire vocabulary at different rates, and syntax acquisition correlates strongly with vocabulary acquisition. This correlation appears consistent cross-linguistically because the correlation was found in both Italian- and English-speaking children even though these languages have very different syntax (Bates & Goodman, 1997). According to Bates and colleagues, there is no stage where syntactic development separates from lexical development—as if the syntax acquisition device was turned on, contrary to Bickerton's claims that "the mechanism that generates syntax does not come online until two" (Bickerton, 1995). Furthermore, the relationship between syntactic and lexical development is similar in the 10th to the 90th percentile of children acquiring vocabulary in both longitudinal and cross-sectional studies. This correlation applies for all syntactic structures measured, including the acquisition of past-tense endings in English (albeit, there have only been a few syntactic constructions measured). Vocabulary development can be used to predict when past-tense overregularization will occur (Bates & Goodman, 1997, p. 521). This evidence supports an argument against a separate device for acquiring the past tense of regularly conjugated verbs because it does not appear to be a system that matures when the child reaches a certain age (p. 525). These results are consistent with Ganger and Stromswold's (1998) preliminary evidence that children tend to acquire the same syntactic structures in order. A possible interpretation of this data that would support the POS argument is that the acquisition of vocabulary "triggers" innate syntactic knowledge that the child is born with.

More evidence that detailed expectations about the structure of syntax are not necessary to acquire syntax comes from experiments with neural nets that have been more successful than previously predicted at learning syntactic rules (for review, see Elman et al., 1996). Neural networks generalize rules after being exposed to several instances of a rule. The training approach of giving examples of syntactically correct sentences contrasts with the approach of explicitly listing rules, like a computer program—the method that many linguists have attempted. Although, the POS argument is that syntax rules are not explicitly taught well enough for syntax to be learned, it is possible that more structure exists in the environmental input than previously realized and children, like neural nets, can detect regularities (Bates & Elman, 1996). For example, it has been discovered that children appear to use statistical learning to detect word boundaries, which had not been suspected earlier (Saffran et al., 1996).

In summarizing studies of language acquisition in children receiving typical language input, the evidence is not detailed enough yet to decide the validity of the POS argument. Although it has been discovered that children receive some feedback from their caregivers, and neural networks have been able to learn some syntactic rules with exposure only to sentences, it is not clear if the amount of feedback and the learning capability of a general learning device (like neural networks) are powerful enough for syntax acquisition. In addition, although syntax does not develop like other innate skills, because it does not develop according to a set time scale, it is possible that syntactic ability is triggered by vocabulary acquisition.

C. Evidence from Language Acquisition in Children without Typical Language Input

A difficulty in resolving the POS debate and determining how much syntactic knowledge children are born with is to separate out the structure that is in the environment from the structure the children are born knowing. To solve this problem, researchers ideally would be able to raise several groups of children, exposing each group to varying amounts of syntax, and then record how much syntax the children in each group produced. These studies could be used to determine the amount of syntax exposure children need before they have a fully functional language, with as much ability to express relationships as any human language. Morally, this experiment can not be performed, but there have been several natural experiments of deaf children who were isolated within their families, and were not exposed to language, or who were exposed to language at an older age than normal.

Some researchers have argued that the way that children learn spoken pidgins also gives evidence of innate syntactic knowledge (Bickerton, 1995). We will not examine evidence from spoken creolization because in spoken Creoles it is difficult to determine the influence of the different language inputs that children were exposed to, or the role of the varied language inputs for creating the Creoles (see Kegl & McWhorter, 1997; for an alternate view, see Bickerton, 1995). Deaf children provide much cleaner evidence of language innateness than studies of hearing children because they often receive only limited language input. They can only receive language input from the visual modality. In the United States, only 6% of deaf children learn sign language from deaf parents, so other children must either receive input from parents who have acquired sign language relatively late, from schooling, or not at all (Kegl & McWhorter, 1997). Some children may not be exposed to sign language until they are too old to acquire it fully.

It has been claimed that children whose parents are not "native" signers can surpass the input of their parents (for review, see Kegl & McWhorter, 1997). They produce sign forms with complex word-internal morphology, more consistent use of spatial relations, and more consistent use of grammar than their parents (Newport, 1982; Singleton, 1989). However, as Kegl and McWhorter (1997) point out, these data may also be corrupted because the children are exposed to "sign language native" peers, and so are exposed to the full, richer form of American Sign Language (ASL). Even if there is a case of a child being exclusively exposed to the fractured language of his deaf parents who had acquired ASL past the critical period, or "non-native peers," it could be argued that he was able to surpass their input by detecting and reassembling the remnants of ASL and using them more regularly (Kegl & McWhorter, 1997). The main evidence examined was gathered as a new sign language in Nicaragua was formed, because it is the closest real case to the forbidden experiment researchers would like to theoretically perform (Kegl, Senghas, & Coppola, 1999). In no previous study of the beginning of a new language is the role of the children's language expectations clearer. Only in Nicaragua were there no remnants of language or inputs from another language to aid the children when forming a new language. However, they did need language-like input to form a language.

Before reviewing how a new language emerged in Nicaragua, we will review what happens when children receive no language input. Some deaf children are never exposed to language at all. They only learn to communicate using a set of idiosyncratic gestures with a small number of people. These natural experiments show that children need some language input to develop language because without sufficient language input, they only develop a home sign system but not a full language. The home sign systems that children use are different from language for several reasons. First of all, home signs must remain very transparent so that other community members will be able to communicate with them because the gestures are not used regularly by others. Although iconic, the home sign gestures still remain relatively arbitrary and difficult for anyone but family members or close friends to interpret, and thus successful communication requires many repetitions and confirmations (Kendon, 1995; Morford, 1996). Unlike language, the form of each home sign varies from individual to individual, and even within each individual from utterance to utterance different signs are used to express the same meaning. Finally, the number of lexical items in each home signer's vocabulary is extremely small. For example, home signers often use the same sign to express all kinds of food or all kinds of drinks (Morford & Kegl, 1996).

The differences between home sign and language show that most of language cannot develop like an organ, and requires at least some environmental input before it can be learned. Nevertheless, there are some regularities across home sign systems that are not present in the input the children receive and may indicate some natural tendencies children have to use language. Although, home signers generally use only two to three word productions, children use regular syntactic structure by ordering the patient, agent, and verb consistently, and seem to use a stem differently if the word is a verb or a noun (Morford, 1996). These regularities are not nearly as complicated or regular as syntax in language. In one study that included home-signing children up to age 5 years and 9 months old, it was found that the children only used 170 to 180 different signs (Goldin-Meadow, 1993). Thus, the amount of syntax appears to correlate with the lack of vocabulary during acquisition.

When home signers past the sensitive period for language acquisition are exposed to a sign language, they can acquire a large vocabulary, but have difficulty acquiring syntactic rules (Kegl et al., 1999). One interpretation of the fact that children past the critical period easily acquired lexical items but not syntax is that syntactic and lexical processing are separate. However, it could also be argued that because the children were past the sensitive period for language acquisition, they did not acquire language like normal children would have.

In Nicaragua, language emerged when isolated home signers were brought together for schooling. Many of the first generation of home-signing children that were brought together for schooling were past the sensitive period, and only developed a "pidgin"[10] without a regular syntax. Pidgin users differed from home sign system users by having a greatly increased vocabulary. Younger children who were not past the sensitive period then entered the school with the older home signers and changed the pidgin into a full language. There is an abrupt division between the pidgin and the creole. The pidgin looks like each utterance could be separated into linear segments consisting of individual signs, but in the full language each sign overlaps with the next. The grammatical rules in the Nicaraguan Sign Language also are applied much more regularly and are easier to define (Kegl et al., 1999; Senghas, 1995). In addition, the full version of Nicaraguan Sign Language allows the expression of more units of information per second and can be more consistently interpreted by listeners than the Nicaraguan home sign pidgin or home sign (Kegl et al., 1999).

---

[10] A pidgin is usually defined as the stage when a new spoken language is being formed, but does not contain regular grammar, and has an unstable lexicon. When discussing Nicaragua, the stage when home signers expanded the lexicon, but before syntactic rules regularized, is called a "pidgin" in this paper, even though it may be different than spoken pidgins because spoken pidgins have fully formed languages as their substrates, and Nicaraguan Sign Language only had home-sign systems as its substrate.

In summary, due to the limited amount of input before the sensitive period, home signers do not acquire full language with syntax. Although there are a few regularities in home sign systems, they are much less complex than language. Research on deaf children in Nicaragua revealed that when children are exposed to input that resembles language strongly enough, they will take that input and modify it so that it becomes language (Kegl et al., 1999; Senghas, 1995). It appears that children are born with the expectation that there will be regularly applied syntactic rules in language, and even when the input is not completely regular, they choose some rules from the input and apply them more faithfully. Not only do they use the rules in the environment but they systematically extend the rules so that they are more powerful than those used by the pidgin users (Kegl et al., 1999; Senghas, 1995). Thus, Kegl et al. argue that the children did not only select regularities from the environment, but they also "were able to draw upon their innate language capabilities" to insert regularity that was not present in the environment.

Another alternative interpretation of the studies of the emergence of Nicaraguan Sign Language is that language rules stabilize through the interaction of a community. This interpretation is similar to what some researchers of spoken Creoles have concluded. While studying spoken Creoles, one researcher came to the conclusion that rather than inventing structures, a child tends to select structures and use them more regularly than adults (Aitchison, 1996). Thus it is possible that the rules of language are not present in one individual and that there is not one set default for the way language is structured that children revert to if they do not receive enough input (see Bickerton, 1990, 1995). The difference between a home signer in a family and the signing community in Nicaragua is the size, and the fact that the other signers were relying on sign language as their only means of communication. Both of these factors are important so that enough attempts at communication will be in the environment so rules can be extracted, which children appear to have the tendency to do, or alternatively so that children's innate syntactic knowledge is retrieved. Another indication that rules emerge through interaction is from spoken languages, in that creolization occurs over time, not with the birth of the first generation young enough to be exposed to the pidgin before the sensitive period (Aitchison, 1995; Bickerton, 1995). In Nicaragua, the language has emerged much faster than was previously thought possible, but it has continued to change rapidly, with influence from other sign languages.

D. Language Acquisition in Children with Focal Lesions but Regular Language Input

Another source of evidence of how much syntactic information children are born with comes from studies of language acquisition in children with focal lesions. If focal lesions in a specific area in the brain prevent children from acquiring syntax correctly but do not interfere with other cognitive or linguistic abilities, then it could be argued that the specific area is specialized for syntactic processing. On the other hand, the ability of children to recover from a lesion anywhere in the brain would be evidence that more general cognitive learning mechanisms were being used to acquire language, and that no one area of the brain was necessary for syntax acquisition.

Because language in most adults appears to be localized to the left side of the brain, it appears that the left side of the brain is specialized at processing language. However, the results of language acquisition of children with focal lesions show that this is only a bias, and the left hemisphere is not so specialized that children cannot acquire syntax without it. In children there is evidence that they can recover language and syntax so that they fall within normal range, no matter where the lesion is located, although there are periods of vulnerability where damage in a specific area of the brain (i.e., the left temporal cortex) can lead to a temporary delay in language acquisition (for review, see Elman et al., 1996, chapter 5). Because there are some periods of vulnerability in specific areas, it appears areas of the brain are biased to be used for acquiring language. The bias was not specifically linked with syntactic processing alone. In children with focal lesions, there is no evidence of syntax or vocabulary acquisition selective deficits (Reilly et al., 1998). The results that no area of the brain is strongly specialized for language could be due to the fact that children were grouped together who had multifocal lesions over more than one lobe or neuroanatomical area (Cohen & Le Normand, 1998). Groupings based on neuroanatomically smaller regions might lead to stronger results, but a lack of subjects makes this grouping difficult. Bates and colleagues did not examine the effect of early cerebellar lesions. ERP studies of normal children also support the hypothesis that the brain is only slightly biased for language acquisition. In infants, known words evoke ERPs bilaterally throughout anterior and posterior regions, but after 20 months, the ERP response is localized to left temporal areas (Mills, Coffey-Corina, & Neville, 1994). These results indicate that the brain areas become specialized for language over time, and the brain maintains flexibility in adapting for language processing, because initially language involves a large brain area. At this stage, children retain a much greater plasticity for recovering their language after lesions. The effect in adults is much more localized than in children, and it is much more difficult for adults to recover from lesion-induced language deficits. However, it is important to note that although these results are compatible with the hypothesis that language can be learned using general cognitive learning mechanisms, an alternative interpretation could be that the brain is specialized for language, but their are redundancies so that if one specialized area is damaged, another specialized area can take over (see also Thulborn, Carpenter, & Just, 1999).

E. Summary of Language Acquisition Studies

Previously, many researchers argued that syntax was too difficult to learn because of its complexity and the lack of input that the children received about what syntactic forms are correct. However, children receive more guidance than was thought, and there is more structure than expected in language that can be acquired by statistical learning algorithms. Some evidence for some preconceptions about language exists because children in Nicaragua and home signers structured language more regularly than their language input, and all children appear to babble and have a desire to name things. The preconceptions about syntax that children are born with do not appear to be very detailed because of the variability among languages. Children simply expect that patterns will be found in language, and automatically extract them from their input. It is not clear whether they also have expectations about the exact syntactic structures that exist in language, as many POS proponents claim (i.e., Bickerton, 1995). Language acquisition in children with focal lesions confirms the hypothesis of only general expectations about language because they appear to be able to recover from lesions anywhere in the brain with only some areas causing a temporal delay in language acquisition. In other words, some areas of the brain are biased to acquire language, but other areas can take over if necessary.

IV. PART 3: PHYLOGENY

A. Evolutionary Origins of Syntax

The results of language acquisition studies showing the lack of details in children's expectations about language and syntax are not surprising, when the amount of time that evolution has had to develop these expectations is considered.

> The relative slowness of evolutionary genetic change compared to language change guarantees that only the most invariant and general features of language will persist long enough to contribute any significant consistent effect on long-term brain evolution. (Deacon, p. 329)

The field of study focused on determining evolutionary origins of language and syntax is a multidisciplinary field that can be termed evolutionary linguistics. The goal of evolutionary linguistics is to explain how evolutionary pressures lead to the adaptation of the brain for linguistic processing. Evolutionary linguistics differs from historical linguistics because historical linguists only examine remnants of past languages, either by comparing vocabulary or syntactic structures across languages. Historical linguistics is limited because it is only possible to trace back linguistic changes to around 10,000 years ago at the farthest, or with a newer method of comparing syntactic structures, perhaps 30,000 years ago, which is not early enough to reach the time when language was in a more primitive state than it is today (Aitchison, 1996, p. 166). Nevertheless, some researchers claim that they can trace all languages back to the one original language, assuming monogenesis (see Ruhlen, 1994).

Evolutionary linguistics must rely on more than historical linguistics for evidence of language origins. Besides historical linguistics, evolutionary linguistics includes the contributions from several other fields, including comparative neuroanatomy, animal communication, archeology, and evolutionary biology. The focus of evolutionary linguistics is not only on what forms of communication predated language like historical linguistics, but also how the brain co-evolved with language evolution.

Even though evolutionary linguistics includes contributions from many different fields, there is no direct evidence of what early language was like. There is no way to know how the first words or first syntactical constructions formed, as there are no written records or recordings from this time. Researchers are forced to rely on indirect evidence that has degraded due to the passage of time. From examining the evidence, two main theories about language origins have been proposed. The first theory is that language emerged gradually, adding different parts over many hundreds of thousands of years. At the extreme end of the gradualist theories, Deacon (1997) claims that vocal tract changes and connections to it may have been forming 1–2 million years ago. The second theory is that language emerged suddenly over a very short period.

Until recently, most data supported the sudden emergence theory. One source of supporting evidence is the quality of tools found at ancient hominid's sites. For millions of years, tool technology appeared to stagnate, with remarkably similar tools found at sites separated by as much as a million years (Gibson & Ingold, 1993; Semaw et al., 1997). The archeological record shows that cultural and tool diversification did not accelerate until around 60,000 years ago (Bickerton, 1995). In addition, 60,000 years ago humans first colonized Australia, which indicates that humans were capable of planning repeated journeys across long spans of water (Davidson & Noble, 1993). Several researchers have argued that the changes in human behavior approximately 60,000 years ago happened because humans acquired language at this time. They argue that language was needed for cultural transmission of tool technology, and for coordinating and planning community activities (Bickerton, 1995; Davidson & Noble, 1993).

More evidence that language developed only recently comes from the analysis of hominid remains, showing that only modern humans, and not even Neanderthals, have descended larynxes, which are necessary to make the variety of sounds used in language. A descended larynx is evolutionarily disadvantageous because humans can choke when eating. Thus, it has been argued that there would be no selection pressure for a descended larynx unless it greatly aided humans in using language (Lieberman, 1991). Because the larynx only appears to have descended recently, early hominids may not have had enough language for a descent to be advantageous. Another argument given for the sudden language emergence theory is the large gap between the language ability of humans and animals. Some researchers argue that the gap is so great that to get to human language appears to require a sudden change, and not just a slight improvement of other animals' communication abilities (King, 1996; Lieberman, 1991).

Most theories of language evolution do not try to explain the emergence of each of the subcomponents of language. The focus tends to be on the lexical and syntactic levels. The most extreme sudden emergence hypothesis is that the brain became capable of all syntactic processing after only a single genetic mutation, although the author who made this claim now supports a theory of slightly more gradual emergence (Bickerton, 1990). Most proponents of the sudden language emergence theory do not argue that language with syntax emerged in one step in its complete form. Language appears too complex to originate recently and fully formed or as a consequence of only a single mutated gene (Ganger & Stromswold, 1998; Newmeyer, 1991; Pinker & Bloom, 1990; Ujhelyi, 1996). The most popular sudden emergence theory assumes that the lexicon developed before syntax (Bickerton, 1995). This hypothesis still matches the archeological data if the existence of the lexicon alone did not allow the transfer of cultural information necessary for tool or cultural development.

The gradual theory predicts that if language emerged over time, hominids with partial language should have been able to exchange cultural information, and tool technology should not have stagnated for so long. Although it appeared that archeological evidence did not support this hypothesis, archeological evidence is still being gathered and in the last few years there have been discoveries that a wider variety of tools existed earlier than previously thought. Remnants of wooden spears and evidence of organized hunting were discovered in Germany that were dated to 400,000 years ago (Thieme, 1997). In addition, evidence was discovered that *homo erectus* were capable of making extended water crossings as early as 800,000 to 900,000 years ago (Morwood, O'Sullivan, Aziz, & Raza, 1997). Future archeological findings may further erode the theory of sudden emergence of tool technology and planning abilities, and thus weaken the case of sudden emergence language theorists.

Although indirect evidence can only give a hint of when humans started using language, at the very least human ancestors must have had the neural substrates necessary for language 150,000 to 200,000 years ago. All ethnic groups appear to have equal language and syntactic abilities, and the most unrelated humans have common ancestors dating back to this time (for review see Fischman, 1996). Thus sudden emergence theorists who claim that language emerged 60,000 years ago must claim that early modern humans had the capacity for language but did not use it, and thus that natural selection could not have shaped the brain specifically for syntactic processing, or alternatively, that similar evolutionary pressures led to the similar brain adaptions in widely separated human groups.

Proponents of the gradualist theory assume that once a simple communication system developed that could be used to express relationships between symbols, evolutionary selection would perfect this system of communication, as it would be advantageous to the survival of an individual for a wide variety of reasons, including improving social relationships and exchanging general environmental knowledge. How similar to language does a simple communication system need to be so that changes can lead to language? Some gradualist theorists do not address this question. Pinker and Bloom (1990) argue for a continuous emergence of syntax, but they do not make a hypothesis about the initial conditions that led to the gradual selection for syntax and language. Other theorists argue that syntax must have emerged fully formed because any forms of communication with simpler syntax than the syntax found in today's language would not be useful. Bickerton argues that less syntax than we have now would not be useful because then it would take more repetition to explain the same ideas (Bickerton, 1995). He argues that less syntax is disadvantageous because if there were more than two participants in a sentence, then there would be a confusion about which role each noun played in the sentence. However, he does not note that word order could be used for case marking instead of grammatical morphemes, and that the word order could develop due to social convention. Even if social convention could not be used, if the syntax in primitive languages was maladapted for expressing all relationships, it would still be more useful than no syntax, and evolutionary pressures could lead to a more developed syntax. Among gradualists, at the most extreme end are the theorists who claim that human language developed by modifying the systems used for animal communication. Theorists who hypothesize that human language evolved from animal communication look for similarities between human language and animal communication. Showing that the gap between human and animal language abilities is small enough to be crossed with only a few changes would give support to the gradual emergence theory. On the other hand, a large gap would support theories that argue that other neural systems must have been reappropriated for syntactic processing.

B. Evidence of Linguistic and Syntactic Precursors in Living Species

If language evolved by modifying animal communication systems of ancestors we have in common with other animals, then language homologs should exist in animal communication. Generally, researchers searching for language homologs have focused on two properties of language, learned arbitrary sign to signal mapping, or the use of symbols, and a way to combine a string of signs in order to communicate relationships between these symbols. The latter property is more similar to syntax, but the combination of these properties is necessary for a true homology of syntax because the role of syntax is to communicate the relations between lexical items. Starting from the least phylogenetically related animal, we will compare several animal communication systems to check for the existence of these properties.

1. Comparison of Language and Bird Song

Some researchers have claimed that of all natural animal communication systems, bird song most resembles human language (Aitchison, 1996). Bird song has many similarities to language, including, at first glance, many properties of syntax. In both birds and humans, the individual sounds have no meaning by themselves; the combination of sounds is more important (Aitchison, 1996). However, when compared in more depth to human language, bird song is only similar to the phonetic and not the syntactic level. In human language, words are made up of combinations of phonemes, but each isolated phoneme has no inherent meaning. The finite number of phonemes used in each language depends upon the language and dialect. Birds also combine sounds according to rules, and there are different dialects in the same species depending on the location where the bird lived (for review, see Aitchison, 1996). Although, bird song is similar to the phonetic subcomponent of human language, it lacks properties of other subcomponents of language, including syntax and semantics that give language its expressive power. Unlike syntax, the songs are not used for communicating relationships between symbols, as there are no units of meaning at the symbol level in the birds' utterances. In most species, the male birds sing much more than the females. They sing in order to attract female birds who base their selection partially on song complexity and quality, but not on the informational content of the song (Aitchison, 1996). Bird song only has a few specialized uses and is not as flexible as language. In order for something similar to bird song to become a precursor to language, the songs would need to be made up of units of meaning. In addition, there are no hierarchical tree-like structures present in the organization of bird song, which is present in the syntactic structure of language.

Because other species that descended from common ancestors of humans and birds do not use combinations of sounds for communication, it appears that humans and birds evolved this ability independently. However, some researchers claim that at the beginning of language, proto-hominids may also have sung like birds, so that bird song is one stage closer to language than other kinds of animal communication (Ujhelyi, 1996). Some apes and monkeys, more phylogenetically related to humans, also sing to communicate.

2. Language Homologs in Nonhuman Primates

To find possible language and syntax homologs it is better to examine more closely phylogenetically related species, like monkeys or apes. Chimpanzees (including bonobos) are the most phylogenetically related living species to humans, so they are most likely to have the most neural and behavioral similarities to humans, and possibly a homolog to the area used for syntactic processing. Chimpanzees have 98.5% similar DNA to humans, and much of the variation occurs in noncoding segments (Gibbons, 1998). Other species which are as genetically related are not as anatomically and behaviorally different as humans and chimps: "The molecular similarity between chimpanzees and humans is extraordinary because they differ far more than many other sibling species in anatomy and way of life" (King & Wilson, 1975, as quoted by Gibbons, 1998, p. 1432). How these molecular genetic differences link to biochemical and anatomical differences between chimps and humans has only begun to be explored. One difference that has been found is that all apes have a cell surface molecule not found in humans, but what importance this has is not known (Gibbons, 1998).

Besides questions about genetic differences at the microbiological level, the importance for language processing of neuroanatomical differences between primates and humans is not yet understood. Comparative anatomists interested in language have focused mainly on searching for anatomical homologs of Broca's and Wernicke's area and the connections between them. According to Hauser (1996), "In both New and Old World monkey species, anatomical homologues to Broca's and Wernicke's areas exist" (p. 36). The Wernicke's area homolog appears to have similar properties to Wernicke's area in humans, at least for interpreting species-specific calls. Although when these areas are lesioned they do not appear to affect the character of vocal outbursts, as occurs in humans, in monkeys the homologous Wernicke's area responds best to species-specific call stimuli (Rauschecker, Tian, & Hauser, 1995). Not all researchers agree that monkeys have true homologs to Broca's areas. At least one research group claims that macaques do not have areas similar to BA44 and BA45 (Broca's area) (Aboitiz & Garcia, 1997). It is not possible to interpret how the neuroanatomical homologs found in monkeys relate to syntactic processing until we learn more about the neural substrates of syntactic processing in humans. Instead of focusing solely on Wernicke's and Broca's areas homologs, future researchers will also search for other homologs to nonclassical language areas found in human neuroimaging and neuropsychological experiments.

Among primate communication, the vocalizations of gibbons, tamarind, and indris are particularly interesting as candidates for behavioral homologs to syntax because these species produce songs that consist of individual notes, and there are rules for combining these notes (for review, see Ulhelyi, 1996). However, like birds, the primary function of the songs does not appear to be for general communication. Instead, the function of the songs appears to be mate attraction, and to indicate territory, as male songs are much more complicated than female songs and are used in mating and territorial defense situations. The songs, however, do have some information content because they can indicate whether a male is mated or not, but there are no arbitrary sign to meaning mappings. These complex songs only develop in species that bond monogamously and defend territories in pairs, but not in species that defend a group territory. However, animals that defend individual territories do not appear to have as complex social relationships as animals who defend group territories. Ujhelyi (1996) predicts that human ancestors may have been monogamous at one time to allow the development of songs, which could then be adapted into language in animals who lived in groups:

> It seems that it is just the territorial singing vocalization that provides the basic preconditions for language to arise. A minimal language system can develop on this basis, although the territoriality itself does not exist, but a complex social network does. It seems that both preconditions are necessary, because neither monogamous species, nor group-living species without monogamous traditions could achieve the level that can be found in great apes. (p. 75)

Although Ujhelyi's hypothesis is interesting because it attempts to explain how the large gap between gibbon vocalizations and human language could be crossed, because gibbon vocalizations are like bird song, it does not explain how the combinations of sounds could be broken up into words that have individual meaning. How the development of a social system based on group living could lead to the development of words will be examined later in this chapter.

Vervet alarm calls are an example of another possible language precursor. Vervet alarm calls appear to show a limited arbitrary sign-to-meaning mapping. Unlike other species that appear to have innately mapped alarm calls, vervet infants must learn which signal to use for each type of predator (Hauser, 1996, pp. 306–307; Seyfarth & Cheney, 1986). However, vervets' signal-to-meaning mapping is very limited. They only use this communication system for alarm calls, and only in the presence of predators. It is as if the vervets are only discussing predators in the present tense (Deacon, 1997, p. 57). Vervets have also not been observed combining utterances. Thus, a large gap remains between vervet alarm calls and human language, and in particular the lack of anything similar to syntax.

Preliminary studies of chimp communication indicate that it is not as complicated as human language. Chimps naturally use gestures to communicate, but the meaning can be easily guessed, and the gestures-to-meaning mapping is not arbitrary as are vervet alarm calls (for review, see Oliphant, in press). However, chimps use very simple symbolic communication by dragging branches across the ground to indicate in which direction the group should travel (King, 1996). Another form of chimpanzee communication is long calls. Long calls (used to keep the group together when spread over a long distance) are made up of segments (Ujhelyi, 1996). The information content calls is not yet known, but it is possible that they contain combinations of units of meaning.

In summary, none of the primate communication systems examined approach human language in complexity of structure or flexibility for transmitting information. However, researchers have not yet decoded many animal communication systems, including our genetically closest relatives, chimpanzees (Hauser, 1996, p. 38). Because a homology to human language has not been found in nonhuman primates in the wild, researchers have attempted to teach nonhuman primates human language in experimental settings, to see if primates have the ability to learn language but do not use this ability in the wild.

C. Language Teaching Experiments in Chimps

If chimps were found capable of acquiring language including syntax, it would support the hypothesis that language is learnable without a specialized language-learning device because nonhuman primates do not appear to use a language-like system in the wild and thus their brains were not subjected to evolutionary pressure to acquire language. Initial language teaching experiments of raising an infant chimp alongside an infant child were not successful. The chimp was unable to produce more than a few barely comprehensible words. Later researchers discovered that chimps lacked the vocal apparatus necessary for producing the range of sounds used in spoken language. Thus, for the past 20 years, attempts have been made to teach language via a simplified system of sign-language-influenced gestures or via a computerized lexigraphic keyboard (for review, see Lieberman, 1998).[11] These attempts have only had limited success.

The animal that has been cited as the most successful language user is a bonobo named Kanzi, trained by Savage-Rumbaugh and colleagues. Savage-Rumbaugh and Lewin (1994) go as far as to claim that Kanzi's performance shows that chimpanzees are nearly as intelligent as humans:

> This [the results of the Kanzi experiments] raises the possibility that more of the apparent intellectual gap between *Pan* and *homo* may be attributable to learning than is commonly acknowledged. A small physical difference, such as one which conferred the ability to control the expiration of air, could have permitted a complex ape-like intelligence to take advantage of this new found physical ability by inventing a crude vocal language. (p. 87)

However, even when Kanzi is freed from vocalization limitations by a computerized keyboard, Kanzi's communication skills are so limited that they can hardly be called language. Kanzi's mean length utterance (MLU), which is typically used to measure grammatical complexity, is only 1.7 symbols per utterance after more than 8 years of training (Bates & Goodman, 1997). Since the MLU is so low, it is evident that Kanzi uses very little syntax, which was measured by checking how regularly Kanzi put words together in the same order. Only 10% of Kanzi's utterances were combinations of two or more words, and could be examined for regularities. Just a few syntax-like rules were reported in Kanzi's grammar: that he tended to put an action verb before an agent, that he referred to distal objects before proximal objects, and that he combined two action verbs in a row (Savage-Rumbaugh & Rumbaugh, 1993). However, these rules are very simple and do not resemble the nested tree-like structures present in every human language. Kanzi often did not follow these "grammatical rules," so his rules are not as consistent as human grammar (King, 1996). In addition, humans do not use two verbs without indicating the patients or agents like Kanzi does (i.e., "tickle-bite"), nor do humans use two nouns in a row with no verbs or grammatical morphemes like "food-blackberry" (Beaken, 1996, p. 67).

There are a few possible reasons Kanzi's syntactic ability is limited. First, he may simply be incapable of learning more than a combination of a few words, or alternatively, he may not have been given sufficiently language-like input. The first possibility is supported by the fact that Kanzi seems able to learn only a limited amount

---

[11] A lexigraphic keyboard is a keyboard with lexigraphs instead of letters. Each lexigraph is a geometric shape and stands for a word. The keyboards used by Savage-Rumbaugh and colleagues to train chimpanzees contain a few hundred lexigraphs.

of lexical items. So far, the most learned chimpanzee has acquired between 200 and 300 lexical items, which correlates with a very small amount of syntactical development in children, according to Bates and Goodman (1987, p. 545):

> Chimpanzees do not attain the 'critical mass' that is necessary for grammar in normal children; instead, they appear to be arrested at a point in lexical development when grammar is still at a very simple level in the human child. Hence the putative dissociation between lexical and grammatical abilities in non-human primates may be an illusion.

The second possibility is that chimpanzees have simply not been exposed to sufficiently language-like input. Savage-Rumbaugh had the goal to teach the chimpanzees three things that she claims are essential for communication: the ability to request, the comprehension of symbols as the referent of objects, and the ability to name objects (Savage-Rumbaugh & Lewin, 1994, p. 64). As pointed out by Savage-Rumbaugh (quoted in Bates & Goodman, 1997), the chimpanzees were taught few signs in their lexicon which relate to syntax. In her list of essentials for communication, Savage-Rumbaugh does not discuss anything about specifying relationships between objects, or about learning how strings of signs can be combined. The chimpanzees that have trained with gestures have also been exposed to a very syntactically reduced input made up of morphemes taught in isolation, not in syntactically normal sentences (for review, see Lieberman, 1998).

The hypothesis that a chimpanzee can acquire more language with better input is given support by the fact that Kanzi had a surprising amount of comprehension of spoken English grammar that he was not intentionally taught. To assess Kanzi's linguistic ability, he was compared on a spoken English comprehension test with a 2.5-year-old child. Kanzi could understand many grammatical constructions as well or better than the child (Savage-Rumbaugh & Rumbaugh, 1993).[12] However, Kanzi never progressed beyond this stage, and he only learned to comprehend a few hundred English words. Children have already learned thousands of words by the time they are 5 or 6 years old (Pinker, 1994).

In summary, language acquisition studies in chimps, and in particular bonobos, have revealed that they are at least capable of acquiring some learned sign-to-meaning mappings and at least the comprehension of some simple syntactic structures. Because chimpanzee's brains could not be specialized for acquiring language, they must have learned using general cognitive strategies. However, it is possible that to learn a greater amount of lexical items and syntax may still require more than general cognitive learning methods. How much syntax chimpanzees can acquire is not yet known owing to flaws in chimpanzee language teaching experiments.

---

[12] The sentences were manipulated so that word order alone could not be used to understand the sentences. For example: "Put the doggie in the refrigerator," and "Go get the doggie that's in the refrigerator." (Examples are from Savage-Rumbaugh & Rumbaugh, 1993).

D. Future Ape Language Teaching Study Suggestions

Several suggestions have been made for improving language teaching studies in chimpanzees, and they could be used to conclusively determine chimpanzees' language learning abilities. One additional step could be to teach the chimpanzees word order. Györi (1995) further recommends that

> What really would be of interest for the study of competence of grammar in the ape, is an ape language project trying to teach not simply word order to an ape but some kind of markers of semantic roles that correspond to case endings in some languages. (p. 115)

One example is Korean, where endings added to the words indicate whether the word is the patient or the agent in the sentence, and can be used to indicate stress, compared to English where tone is used for stress. Besides omissions at the syntactic level of language input, note also that no nonhuman primate has been exposed to the phonetic rules of a language. The lexigraphs Kanzi was taught had one symbol to one meaning mappings without orthographic regularities to indicate the ties to the phonetic rules of spoken English. The ideal input would be a human language, perhaps sign language with native signers, because, as noted, the chimpanzees are not capable of producing human speech sounds (Lieberman, 1991).[13] Although there have been several experiments using input that has been influenced from sign language, in each case the input was extremely simplified compared to sign language and mainly consisted of individual signs in isolation (for review, see Lieberman, 1998). In addition, researchers ideally would encourage interactions between each chimpanzee *and* their offspring and reward them for transmitting information via language. This might allow the chimpanzees to adapt the linguistic input to their chimpanzee-specific learning strategies. If these studies are performed and chimps are more successful at acquiring language and syntax, it would support the hypothesis that a specialized device to acquire language is not necessary, and that just a general cognitive learning strategy can be used for language acquisition. If, however, even with further experiments, chimpanzees are not capable of learning syntactic relations, the results would support the idea of a specialized area of the brain in humans for processing syntax, or at least a general learning strategy unavailable to chimps that can be used to acquire syntax and/or a large lexicon.

E. Origins of the First Words

As noted, the separability of syntactic and lexical processing is still controversial. However, most language evolution theories assume that lexical and syntactic processing evolved separately. The stage before the development of syntax, when only the lexicon existed, has been termed *protolanguage* by Bickerton (Bickerton, 1995). He claims that a way to relate individual items to each other was lacking from pro-

---

[13] The idea of using natural sign language as input was suggested by Judy Kegl.

tolanguage. Bickerton explains how protolanguage changed into full language with syntax, but he does not explain how or why protolanguage emerged (Hauser, 1996). Is it possible to have a large lexicon without syntax? To answer this question, we will examine the formation of a lexicon-only protolanguage in more detail.

The only natural existing data of how oral languages form comes from creole studies, but Creoles are influenced from pre-existing languages (Kegl & McWhorter, 1997). Aitchison (1996) notes that during the formation of a new language via creolization, a new sound is only rarely spontaneously generated and matched with a meaning. Words are usually borrowed from other languages; even if the meaning is not borrowed, the sound of the word is borrowed and used to represent another meaning. Nicaraguan sign language vocabulary began in home signers and was initially iconic. However, it is more difficult to think of iconic representations using vocalization. Thus neither spoken creole studies nor Nicaraguan Sign Language indicate how words used in spoken language were initially formed. The fact that home signers who have passed the sensitive period that are exposed to language can acquire a large vocabulary but limited syntax might indicate that a syntactically less organized protolanguage could have existed before language (Kegl et al., 1997). It shows that there is the probability of communication without a regularly applied grammar. However, they still do use some grammar, so it does not support the hypothesis of a completely syntax-free, lexicon-only protolanguage.

At the word level, it is impossible to avoid all syntactic properties. Words could be used to symbolize objects (nouns), or describe an action (verbs) or a property that objects have in common (adjectives). What did the protolanguage lexicon consist of? Aitchison (1996) argues that nouns came first in protolanguage, because during language acquisition children appear to acquire nouns before adjectives and verbs (Bates & Goodman, 1997, p. 543). Aitchison (1996) claims that it is easy to make a noun into a verb, but not vice-versa. Nouns can be translated to verbs: "I handed her the book." However, it is also easy to make a verb into a noun: "The runners started the race before the walkers."

Bickerton does not explain whether nouns, verbs, or adjectives came first. Instead of addressing this question, he names other general properties of protolanguage. According to Bickerton (1995), protolanguage had no regular grammar, and is restricted to a few syllables. In addition, protolanguage is also repetitive, nonfluent, and *not* context-free. Bickerton contrasts protolanguage with natural languages, which are fluent, fast, efficient, allow context-free expression, and have a regular grammar with many more grammatical items.

Bickerton claims that examples of protolanguage can be found by observing the output of language-trained apes, pidgin speakers, and infants. However, closer examination of Bickerton's examples of protolanguage reveals that these examples do not have all the properties he claims. In addition, there are several differences between the utterances of language-trained apes, pidgin speakers, and infants, which makes it invalid to place them together in one group (Aitchison, 1995). In particular, pidgin utterances are the most dissimilar from infant's or language-trained ape's utterances. In pidgins, repetition appears to be used for clarification, but in apes and infants it is used to please adult listeners. Furthermore, pidgin utterances are much longer than a few syllables, and are much longer and context free than infant or chimp utterances. Both pidgins and infant utterances include much more syntax than apes have thus far demonstrated. Bickerton's theory of language evolution is that the development of a separate syntactic processor was necessary so that pro-tolanguage could become language. None of the examples show a complete lack of syntax, and thus the necessity for the development of a separate syntactic proces-sor to explain the emergence of syntax is not supported.

Wray (1998) proposed an alternative to protolanguage that does not assume a priori a separation of lexical and syntactic processing. She asserts that before lan-guage developed, each signal did not map to the meaning of just one object, but mapped to the more complex meaning of an entire phrase. For example, when vervets give an alarm call, an interpretation of the meaning is not just "snake," but "climb a tree quickly, or else a snake will come eat you!" A need to make finer dis-tinctions could lead to breaking down these utterances, or a large memory load caused by the number of individual utterances that must be remembered could lead to pressure to regularize the formation of related utterances. If by chance two holis-tic utterances with similar meanings also had similar forms, then a hominid ances-tor searching for a pattern might find a rule to use for creating new utterances (Wray, 1998). This theory is tenuous because it relies on chance regularity between two strongly meaning-related utterances before reanalysis can occur, and it also requires that individuals have expectations that patterns existed in utterances.

Nevertheless, this theory is supported by the fact that both children and adults still use language holistically, which could indicate that language was once holistic. Children often learn a phrase before learning how to use the individual words of the phrase (Bates, Bretherton, and Snyder, 1988). Even when infants only use sin-gle words, they use them as if they were phrases, in several different contexts with different meanings. Thus even though children tend to acquire nouns first, they do not use the nouns like adults use nouns. Adults also still use holistic utterances, espe-cially in formal social situations.[14]

Wray argues that holistic utterances were initially vocal, but it is also possible that language was initially reliant on gesture, as it is easier to make an iconic utterance with gesture than a vocalization (Morford, Singleton, & Goldin-Meadow, 1995). Gestures are inherently holistic, containing an agent, a patient, and a verb (Arm-strong, Stokoe, & Wilcox, 1995, quoted by King, 1996). Any gesture of an action also contains information about who initiated and who was the recipient of the action. One difficulty with the gestural theory of language origin is explaining how language became oral. It is more likely that language was initially multimodal. Stud-ies of language acquisition support the theory that children expect language to

---

[14] Examples of holistic phrases adults still use are "Can I help you?" "Can I take a message?" "How do you do?" (from Wray, 1998).

include both vocal and gestural components (see part III). If language was initially multimodal and the vocal utterances could be supplemented with gestures, then gestures would provide the regularity that hominids could use to relate phonetically unrelated vocalizations, and thus provides support for the holistic protolanguage theory. The holistic protolanguage theory also offers a solution for some of the problems in Ujhelyi's (1996) proposal about language beginning from songs. If songs could initially have general meanings, then Wray's proposal offers a solution of how they could eventually be broken down into more specific meanings.

In summary, what language looked like before humans started to use combinations of words to communicate remains unknown. Which of these theories is correct, the existence of a holistic, or lexicon-only protolanguage as a precursor to a fully syntactic language, is still controversial and possibly unresolvable because there is no record remaining of protolanguage. Computer simulations are being used to address this debate, but the methodology is still being developed, and the focus has been on testing the plausibility of language starting from a syntax-free, lexicon-only protolanguage (see Steels, 1998, for review). As is evident in the review of the following theories of the evolutionary origin of syntax, most evolutionary linguists still assume that protolanguage began as a syntax-free lexicon.

F. Language and Syntax Were Originally Selected for What Survival Purpose?

Unless language developed strictly by modifying the areas originally involved in animal communication, the areas of the brain that are used in processing language initially emerged serendipitously through the selection of a neural system for a non-linguistic reason. Many of the following theories are based on the assumption that a protolanguage with only arbitrary signal–meaning matched pairs alone could never develop into language as it exists today without the addition of a separate syntactic processor. Thus most theories focus on the function of the areas thought to be used for syntax now, before it was reappropriated for syntactic processing. One controversy is how similar the area would need to be to today's syntactic processing to be capable of forming a primitive but useful form of syntax. If a simpler form of syntax is not useful, then syntax must have emerged in its full form and could be considered a spandrel. Most theorists assume that a precursor must at least be able to account for rules for combining symbols *and* explain how symbols can be related to each other in a sentence.

G. Similarity of Categorical Processing and Syntactic Processing

According to Bickerton (1995), the structures that are now used for language were not originally selected due to the communicative advantages it gave individuals, but instead for improving how the brain stores and organizes information. When humans were placed in a changing environment, it was important to be able to quickly categorize the regularities in the environment. Two requirements for categorizing well are the ability to store a large amount of information about individual items in an environment, and the ability to find relationships between these items. These two requirements are very similar to the processing that occurs at the lexical and syntactic levels of language.

Bickerton (1995) hypothesizes that the brain first increased in size to store more lexical items (symbols that stand for objects in the environment), and then there was a separate selection pressure for the development of an organizing module, or the conceptual system, for relating lexical items. One proposal is that language began when the conceptual system became connected with the system for mapping sign–meaning pair combinations (Bickerton, 1995; Newmeyer, 1991). The conceptual system is syntax-like because it allows the relating of a few objects. This is done by comparing what properties that they have in common. How the conceptual system could be used for processing the more abstract syntactic relations is not explained by Bickerton or Newmeyer.

It is interesting that Kanzi seemed to be developing some very simple rules (which were not taught) after acquiring only 200–300 items of vocabulary. These rules could be a first step towards syntactic processing. This evidence is compatible with the hypothesis that conceptual processing did not develop separately, but instead developed as part of the system whose development led to an increase in memory for lexical items. Being able to find relationships between objects might actually save storage space, since characteristics of an item would not have to be listed separately, but instead each item could have connections.[15]

Understanding that there are relationships between concepts is a vital precursor to language development (Deacon, 1997). Human brains appear programmed to look for abstract relationships and not only to focus on details of individual items. Thinking abstractly about the future is a skill that humans appear to be far superior at than any other species. One possible reason other animals did not develop the ability of humans to think abstractly is that more abstract levels of categorization may be disadvantageous, because they are less useful for predicting what will happen in the present (Deacon, 1997). Thus, Deacon argues that the ability to symbolize may have initially developed by accident. Practice is also an example of abstract thinking because it is an example of imagining how to react to a possible future removed from the present, something only humans appear to do (Bickerton, 1995). The fact that language can be used to discuss more than the present gives human language its power. Being able to use a sign without evoking a response, or without requiring the right stimuli to use a sign represents one important step in symbolic thinking (Deacon, 1997; Newmeyer, 1991).[16]

---

[15] Another way to think of the memory for an item is as consisting of a series of pointers to the memory for different characteristics; for example, the entry for "rose" might be pointers to flower, romantic, thorny, and so on.

[16] Language would not be very useful if every time one person spoke the word *tiger* the other person would run away, or if people could only talk about tigers in the presence of tigers (Newmeyer, 1991).

The roots of the ability to categorize the environment are phylogenetically old, as there is evidence of categorization abilities in New World monkeys that are only distantly related to humans. Hauser (1997) noted that cotton-top tamarins had the ability in an experimental task to choose tools that were best suited for retrieving food. Nevertheless, humans have better categorization abilities than nonhuman primates. Humans group objects into categories spontaneously, which has not been observed in chimps until they are 5 or 6 years old (Gibson, 1993). In addition, language-trained chimpanzees appear to have to relearn a category every time that something new is added to it (Deacon, 1997).

In summary, because none of the authors, who claim that the ability to categorize and the syntactic processing are similar, compares the formation of syntactic structures and categorization in detail, it is difficult to determine whether the processing used during categorization was subsequently reappropriated for syntactic processing. However, the ability to relate items in memory is an important precursor for syntactic and linguistic development, whether or not the areas of the brain originally developed for categorization were reappropriated for syntactic processing. The ability to group different items into categories is important so that language can be used to discuss general events, and not just specific objects or instances.

H. Role of Theory of Mind in Language and Syntax Development

It is likely that there is more than one precursor for syntactic processing; syntax may have been able to emerge only after the development of several cognitive processes. Besides having unique categorization abilities, humans also seem to be the only animal with a theory of mind (TOM). A simple definition of TOM is the ability to make inferences about the mental state of another (Povinelli & Eddy, 1996). Povinelli and Eddy suggest that there is a relation of TOM to language and possibly hypothetical thinking (imagining what actions would be taken in a certain situation). It seems unlikely that useful complex communication could occur without TOM because one animal would not realize that another could have something important to say. In addition, to communicate effectively, it is necessary to determine what the recipient does not know. As noted earlier, humans as young as 4 years old adopt their speech to the level of the recipient, although they do appear not to understand how to react appropriately to others as well as adults (Holzman, 1997).

One possible reason that chimpanzees seem to have limited language ability may be that they lack a theory of mind. There is anecdotal evidence that chimpanzees have a theory of mind due to the observed exhibition of deceptive behavior, but not good experimental evidence that they have even a limited theory of mind (for review, see Aitchison, 1996). However, the lack of experimental evidence may be due to the difficulty of demonstrating nonverbally that a subject has a TOM. Preliminary results from one series of experiments by Povinelli and Eddy (1996) support the theory that TOM is important at least for separating humans from other animals, and possibly for language, as the results indicate that chimpanzees have only a very limited TOM. These experiments are also good examples of the limitations of current methods for measuring chimp TOM.

I. Povinelli and Eddy (1996) Experiment

Povinelli and Eddy (1996) designed an experiment with the goal of determining whether a chimpanzee can "understand that as a result of seeing, others can form opinions about the world." The chimps were trained to make a food begging gesture to either an experimenter whose eyes were covered, or an experimenter whose eyes were unobstructed. The chimpanzees were only rewarded if they gestured to the trainer whose eyes were not covered. The experimenter's eyes were covered in a variety of ways throughout the experiments, by buckets over her head, blindfolds, hands over her eyes, etc. Which experimenter's vision was obstructed varied. Povinelli and Eddy hypothesized that if the chimpanzees could immediately determine which experimenter to gesture to, it would provide strong evidence that the chimpanzees had a theory of mind. However, the only condition that the chimpanzees immediately performed well on was when one experimenter had her back turned and the other did not, and the chimps correctly begged to the person facing forward. The chimpanzees did not perform well when the only difference between the experimenters was that one experimenter had her eyes closed and the other did not, so it appeared that the chimpanzees were using a face-viewable strategy for choosing who to beg to, but were not aware of the relationship between the obstruction of the experimenter's vision, and the ability of the experimenter to see their begging gesture. Thus, it appeared that the chimpanzees did not have a TOM.

J. Critiques of Povinelli and Eddy (1996) Experiment

Several critiques have been made about Povinelli and Eddy's (1996) experiments to explain why the chimpanzees were not successful, and that even if they had been successful the results would not demonstrate that they had a theory of mind. One possible reason that the chimpanzees failed the experiments was because they were too young (Povinelli & Eddy, 1996). At the beginning of the experiment all the subjects were between 4 and 5 years old. Nevertheless, the chimpanzees did not improve as they grew older, and there is not another similar experiment where older chimpanzees have performed better. In addition, the chimps may have had theory of mind but not have used it during the experiment. The chimps spontaneously played games by themselves where they covered their eyes and walked until crashing into a wall. These games are evidence that they did understand that seeing was important to perceive the world, even though it was not be measured by an experiment (Povinelli & Eddy, 1996). Even if the chimpanzees had understood that eyes are important for choosing a person, it would only show that chimpanzees could appreciate the fact that they must choose the person whose eyes are visible, not that they had a theory of mind (Heyes, 1998). In conclusion, even though evidence is limited about other animals' TOM, preliminary evidence from Povinelli and Eddy supports the hypothesis that humans have a much more developed TOM than other animals. The connection between TOM and linguistic and syntactic abilities needs to be more fully specified. It is not clear if the connection is direct or indirect, whether only the addition of TOM allowed humans to learn language, and limits the language acquisition ability of other species, or whether TOM is only one of several abilities that separates humans from other animals and allow language acquisition.

K. Comparison of Processing Used to Maintain Social Relationships and Syntactic Processing

Several theorists have argued processing used to keep track of social relationships could have been readapted for syntactic processing, and that pressure to develop better social relationships led to the development of language. Again, the ability to have complex social relationships may be one of several cognitive precursors necessary for language and syntax development. Animals that could develop TOM would be able to manipulate their way into a better position on the social hierarchy, and animals with TOM would be able to have more complex social relationships. Unfortunately, like theories linking TOM emergence to language emergence, in none of the papers reviewed is the link between language and social development explained in detail. Instead, the authors attempt to explain what environmental conditions led to the development of more complex social relationships, and assume those explanations also have some explanatory power towards language emergence, because language allows more complex social relationships.

One hypothesis of why social relationships developed is that increased cooperation was necessary for survival. Humans are much more efficient in gathering food when tasks are divided among a group, and language may have developed to help members of a group coordinate what each member did (Beaken, 1996; Hildebrand-Nishon, 1995). Many animals use pheromones to coordinate activities, and a proposal of why humans developed language instead is that humans lacked well-developed pheromones (Deacon, 1997). However, it seems easier to have simply developed the pheromones then to have developed language. None of these researchers attempts to explain in detail how the leap was made from cooperation to language, although they offer some general theories.

Hildebrand-Nishon (1995) suggests that the structure for keeping track of social relationships developed in the brain because of the need to figure out who did what to whom, and then the structure for keeping track of social relationships could be adapted for syntactic processing. The more complex social relationships became, the more complex social hierarchies an animal would need to keep track of, including genetic relationships, and positions in the social dominance hierarchy. Although keeping track of social relationships requires maintaining information about relationships between individuals, it is not clear whether it may have been useful as a primitive syntactic processor. A more detailed comparison between syntactic processing and the processing used to maintain social relationships is necessary.

To maintain social relationships, primates spend a lot of time grooming. Dunbar proposes that language evolved to replace grooming. Individuals are required to groom other individuals and make an investment in maintaining and earning social relationships. This investment makes it less likely the primates will betray established relationships in the future. Human social groups are too large to allow grooming between every individual in a social relationship. Dunbar argues that language in the form of gossip could fulfill the role of grooming to establish social relationships and leave humans time to do other things besides grooming, like searching for food.

However, grooming does not involve the exchange of any information, so the jump from grooming to gossip is not clear (Wray, 1998). Dunbar does not explain how "gossip" turned into language. Furthermore, his definition of gossip allows the exchange of information on things like food preferences and personal experiences. Dunbar's definition of gossip is very close to a definition of general communication. A more typical definition of gossip would be a discussion of social relationships with or concerning third parties.

Note that several theories of language origin rely on the assumption that evolutionary selection occurs at the group level. Dunbar and Newmeyer argue that language gave a survival advantage to the groups using it. Newmeyer (1991) claims that groups that had better language would have an advantage over other groups. Dunbar claims that humans developed dialects to isolate themselves from other groups. Newmeyer's theory of how syntax developed is also based on the assumption of group-level evolutionary selection. Newmeyer noted that there is a conflict between the speaker and the hearer: the speaker wants to spend less time organizing her thoughts, whereas the listener wants to spend less time interpreting the message the speaker is sending. Universal grammar, Newmeyer claims, may have originated so that less time was spent struggling between the speaker and hearer over who should do more work. All of these theories assume that evolutionary selection occurs above the level of the individual. However, most evolutionary biologists believe that selection occurs very rarely at the group level, and mainly at the individual level (for review, see Dawkins, 1992). It is more likely that language represents a compromise between the speaker and hearer, due to constant competition between their conflicting demands. Despite the fact that language was probably not selected at the group level, competition between individuals within a group may still have led to syntax and the development of language, because individuals who could communicate better or understand better may have had an advantage over other individuals.

If there is a strong relationship between social and linguistic abilities, neuropsychological data should confirm it. As mentioned earlier, the anterior areas of the brain appear to play an important role in syntactic processing. People with frontal lobe damage also often have difficulty maintaining normal social relationships. At first glance, William's syndrome patients also seem to confirm the link between social and linguistic skills, since they have lower than average general intelligence, but relatively advanced social and linguistic skills (Deacon, 1997). However, William's patients do not provide a clear dissociation between linguistic processing and general intelligence because their intelligence level is typically equivalent to an average 4 or 5 year old, and children that age have a well-developed grasp of how to use language, including the ability to make most syntactically correct sentences that adults can (for reviews see Bellugi, Lichtenberger, Mills, Galaburda, & Korenberg, 1999; Bates & Goodman, 1997). Although both syntactic processing and the ability to maintain social relationships are often damaged at the same time in patients with acquired lesions, the patients' lesions may be large enough to damage separate areas needed for social and syntactic processing. There are cases when the patient's linguistic ability apparently remains intact while the ability to maintain normal social relationships is damaged. In summary, neuropsychological evidence indicates that social and linguistic processes are at least partially separate, although the fact that both their neural substrates are nearby indicates the possibility that they may have once shared more neural resources.

L. Link between Tool Use and Syntactic Processing

Another theory of syntax emergence is that the areas originally shaped by the pressure to develop better tools were reappropriated for syntactic processing (Gibson, 1993; Wilkins & Wakefield, 1995). To make tools, like making a sentence, requires planning a sequence. To form a tool often requires attaching parts together, and planning what the tool will be needed for in the future (Gibson, 1993). To make a sentence also requires attaching several parts together, and being able to separate the contents of the sentence from the present moment. Support that the neural loops developed for tool making may have been important for subsequent language, and syntax development comes from comparison of human and nonhuman primates. Nonhuman primates appear to have limited language and tool-making abilities. Apes are very limited in their constructional tool use, and do not attach things together to make a tool, whether by weaving or using an adhesive substance to hold them together (Gibson, 1993). Apes do not seem able to plan out a series of steps to accomplish a task. In addition, only humans make tools for use in the future (Savage-Rumbaugh & Lewin, 1994).

Even though humans appear to have better tool-making abilities than other primates, syntax may not use the neural systems originally developed for tool making. A problem with the theory that tool planning served as a precursor to syntactic processing is that individual tool parts do not relate to each other in the same embedded tree structures that lexical items do in syntactically formed sentences. In addition, to plan in the future is not limited to tool making, but is a general advantage of humans compared to other animals. The ability to plan in the future may have emerged while another ability was selected.

Another hypothesis of how tool making led to improved syntactic and linguistic abilities is that the development of tool use led to the emergence of more cortico-cortical connections, which were then used for syntactic processing (Aboitiz & Garcia, 1997; Wilkins & Wakefield, 1995). The selection for improved hand-eye coordination for making tools may have led to the development of a circuit between Broca's area and Wernicke's area that could be used later for language (Wilkins & Wakefield, 1995). Besides connections specified in the Wernicke-Geschwind theory, selection for improved tool making ability also may have lead to the development of connections in other areas that could be used for syntactic processing, including connections between unimodal areas to allow more multimodal processing (Aboitiz & Garcia, 1997). However, a large increase in the amount of amodal processing areas would be unprecedented in evolutionary history (see below for discussion).

M. Summary of Possible Neural Preadaptions for Syntactic Processing

Several other theories of evolutionary precursors to syntax have not been reviewed here, but all suffer from the same problems of not enough detail of the kind of processing done in the area of the brain, so that it could be readapted for syntactic processing. For example, another theory is that brain areas responsible for interpreting visual scenery were adapted for language (Sereno, 1990). The author does not specify how linguistic processing is similar to visual scenery interpretation. Although it is possible that the neural substrates important for categorization, social relationships, TOM, tool use, and visual scenery integration may have been reappropriated for syntactic and linguistic processing, the lack of specificity in all of these theories makes them very difficult to verify or falsify. It appears that one common strategy in evolutionary linguistics is to look for another unique aspect of human behavior and assume that both syntactic processing and the processing used during that behavior are linked. Future theories need to provide more direct comparison about specific examples of linguistic and syntactic processing, and how this processing relates to what processing the reappropriated area originally performed.

N. Areas of the Brain That Changed to Support Syntactic Processing

As in any multidisciplinary field, evolutionary linguists have sometimes oversimplified their nonprimary field. A common mistake is to be too general when describing the neural substrates of language and syntactic processing. For example, in an article on language origins Elman (1999) claims that "the uniqueness [of language] emerges out of an interaction involving small differences in domain-nonspecific behaviors" (p. 19). It is difficult to determine the validity of this statement without more details about what behaviors have changed.

Another oversimplification is the theory that language and syntax emerged as a side effect of brain encephalization because an increase in brain size led to a capacity for more complex processing (Beaken, 1996; Gibson, 1993). Thus chimps also would have language if they just had larger brains. Beaken writes, "We possess, in other words, a typical primate brain, proportioned the way a very large primate brain would be expected to be proportioned" (p. 14). In fact, the cerebellum, cerebral cortex, and in particular the prefrontal cortex have expanded in humans much more than would be expected by simply making a chimpanzee brain larger (Deacon, 1997). The human prefrontal cortex is two times larger than would be expected if a chimpanzee brain had been enlarged to human size, and six times larger than chimpanzees even though they have a similar body size compared to humans. In addition, brain size does not correlate directly with intelligence either between or within species. The brain size of humans varies between 1000 and 2000 cc, and yet there is not a correlation between an individual human's brain size and their intelligence when humans with different brain sizes are compared with each other (Bickerton, 1995). Humans have neither the largest brains nor the highest brain-to-body weight ratio among animals. Elephants and whales have bigger brains, more neurons, and more connections, and mice have a brain-to-body ratio almost twice as big as humans (see Deacon, 1997, especially chapter 5). Neanderthals had larger average brain sizes than humans, but that did not keep them from going extinct. Their brains may have been larger, but may not have been organized for language (Lieberman, 1998). Although humans have comparatively large brains for their body size, the unique organization of human brains is more important for allowing syntactic processing than size alone. We are not claiming that the entirely new brain areas were created uniquely in the human brain. As Deacon said, "though we are on the large end of the range of body and brain sizes, this is not the result of adding new organs, but merely enlarging existing ones with slight modifications" (Deacon, 1997, p. 29). More specific hypotheses about what brain areas became modified for syntactic processing are needed.

Rather than hypothesizing that brain encephalization led to a language-capable brain, a hypothesis by Dunbar (1996) is slightly more specific, but still not specific enough to make useful predictions. Dunbar noted that average group size within a species and average individual neocortex size are positively correlated. Thus he concluded that the pressure to create larger group sizes leads to a larger neocortex so that individuals have better social skills, with language being the ultimate social skill. However, correlation alone should not be confused with cause. Another evolutionary pressure could have selected for the expansion of the neocortex, and increased possible group size may have been a side effect. Even assuming that Dunbar's hypothesis is correct, he does not attempt to pinpoint which area of the neocortex expanded or how the expansion could improve social and linguistic function.

Some researchers claim that for language to be possible the neocortical association cortices had to expand so that both amodal processing could occur, and multimodal associations could be made (Aboitiz & Garcia, 1997; Wilkins & Wakefield, 1995). If some parts of syntactic processing are entirely separate from semantic interpretation, then they would require amodal processing, and thus the expansion of association cortex could lead to an improved syntactic processing ability. Preliminary evidence indicates that only humans make multimodal associations in the cortex, whereas apes must rely on the limbic system (mainly the amygdala to make associations) (Aboitiz & Garcia, 1997). However, a large expansion of association cortices in humans would be evolutionarily unprecedented since association cortices did not expand considerably from small mammals to primates even as brain size increased (Merzenich and Kaas, 1980). Instead, as the neocortex has increased in size, more specialized areas for processing different aspects of a single modality have appeared. Although an increase in multimodal processing capable areas of the brain would be important for categorization, and symbolization, the link to the emergence of syntactic processing is still tenuous.

An alternative to the expansion of association cortices is the development of connections between unimodal working memory buffers, allowing information from various senses to be compared (Aboitiz & Garcia, 1997). According to neuroimaging and neuropsychological studies, working memory appears to rely strongly on the frontal cortex. No equivalents to many of these frontal areas (i.e., 46 and 9) has been found in prosimians (Aboitiz & Garcia, 1997).

An indication of the role of memory systems in language has come from the work of Elman (1993, 1999). In a computer simulation, neural nets could learn syntactic relations only if "memory" for words in sentences that served as training stimuli was initially limited and gradually increased throughout training. Initially limited memory may help infants focus on certain aspects of language, such as phonology and word boundaries, before gradually learning more complex linguistic relationships, including sentence level syntax. Thus change in the maturational course of memory circuits may also have been important for language acquisition. However, it is not clear if memory for linguistic processing would be separate from memory from other kinds of cognitive processing, or if the memory used for linguistic processing emerged due to the development of a novel set of connections between existing working memory circuits. As noted, preliminary evidence indicates that there is at least a separate memory system for syntactic processing.

Another hypothesis of how the brain changed for syntactic processing is that one area of the brain became specialized for general hierarchical or motor processing and can be used for syntactic and phonetic processing, as well as motor planning and general planning (Wilkins & Wakefield, 1995). Lieberman (1991, 1992, 1998) has proposed a similar hypothesis that one area of the brain controls multiple functions, including syntax. Lieberman hypothesizes that the area that controls orofacial movements is also needed for syntactic, phonologic, phonetic, and motor planning processing. Others have claimed that phonology and syntax have similar neural substrates claiming that phonology is similar enough to syntax that it was originally used as a primitive syntax (Aboitiz & Garcia, 1997; Newmeyer, 1991). However, there is evidence that not all of these functions rely on the same neural substrates. The differences between syntax and phonology indicate that if phonology was once used as a primitive syntax, it has lost many of its syntactic qualities because individual phonetic elements do not signify relations to other phonetic elements, and there is no recursive tree-like hierarchical structure. Individual phonemes do not have meanings and cannot exist separate from other phonemes. In addition, the number of words in a language is several orders of magnitude greater than the number of phonemes used in language. It is not clear whether some of the areas for controlling articulation overlap with the areas used for syntactic processing. There are at least some areas used separately for syntactic processing and not phonology, since articulation and syntactic processing deficits can occur separately. However, they are also often affected simultaneously (i.e., Broca's aphasia), so they may have common subprocesses. There are also differences between the processes involved in other kinds of hierarchical processing and syntactic processing, as King stated:

> The cognitive underpinnings for understanding "something did something to something else" are present in monkeys and apes, and in my view are more significant precursors to the evolution of syntactic ability than a sensitivity to sequence or an ability to pattern one's symbolic output." (King, 1996, p. 201).

It is possible that despite the differences in processing mentioned between all the functions hypothesized to use Broca's area, there may be an as of yet unknown common process between all of these functions that does rely on Broca's area, but if this was true then a patient with a lesion only in Broca's area should display deficits in all of these functions, and there is no reported case of such a patient that we are aware of.

Some theories are specific about what area of the brain changed to allow syntax and language. An early hypothesis about how the posterior brain area changed so that syntactic processing became possible was that the planum temporale expanded in the left hemisphere (Damasio & Geschwind, 1984). However, more recently it was discovered that chimpanzees also have similarly lateralized planum temporales (Gannon et al., 1998). Newer proposals about posterior regions claim that the development of the phonological loop in the supramarginal gyrus (area BA40) was important for syntax, because only with the capability to keep long vocalizations in memory can syntactic processing occur at the sentential level. The development of a slave phonetic loop would require pressure to produce and remember long vocalizations (Aboitiz & Garcia, 1997). This could occur if humans went through a stage of evolution similar to gibbons, or birds, where songs were used and there was a pressure to learn songs. If the phonological loop could become connected with other working memory circuits and if items within the phonological loop could be manipulated and related to other items, then syntactic processing may have become possible.

Connections between the anterior and posterior areas of the brain are better developed in humans than in other species (Aboitiz & Garcia, 1997). Many researchers have hypothesized that humans became capable of language once Broca's area and Wernicke's area became connected (i.e., Wilkins & Wakefield,

1995). Although in the Wernicke-Geschwind theory, only one loop from Wernicke's area to Broca's area via the arcuate fasciculus is mentioned, there are actually at least three loops between these areas, which could indicate different stages of linguistic processing. However, in macaque monkeys there are no connections between Broca's area and Wernicke's area homologs like there are in humans (Aboitiz & Garcia, 1997). These connections are important because they allow both Wernicke's and Broca's areas to influence the development of the other. Changes in one area of the brain will affect other areas because there will be more axons from the area that increased in size competing with the axons from other areas, so the whole pattern of connectivity may change (Deacon, 1997). Thus changes in the size of one area may lead to changes in the organization of connections throughout the brain. Finding how these changes led to a syntax-capable brain is an important area of future research.

V. CONCLUSION

Although we would like to conclude with clear answers to the questions posed at the start of this chapter, because all of these fields are still in their infancy we have only been able to arrive at preliminary answers. Much remains to be learned about the architecture, ontogeny, and phylogeny of the neural substrates of syntactic processing. There are still large knowledge gaps separating these studies from each other. Nevertheless, researchers in each field would benefit from collaboration. Studies of the architecture of the neural substrates of processing in adults could help refine hypotheses of what previous processing the areas involved in syntactic processing performed before being reappropriated. Studies in language acquisition could be used to test the link between the development of syntactic processing and other processes, as well as determine how much detail about syntactic processing is encoded in the genome. New more precise evolutionary theories about how syntax originated could help define how syntactic processing and cognitive processing are broken up into smaller subprocesses in the brain. More precise evolutionary theories could lead to the discovery of more areas involved in syntactic processing.

References

Aboitiz, F., & Garcia, V. R. (1997). The evolutionary origin of the language areas in the human brain. A neuroanatomical perspective. *Brain Research Reviews, 25,* 381–396.

Aglioti, S., Beltramello, A., Girardi, F., & Fabbro, F. (1996). Neurolinguistic and follow-up study of an unusual pattern of recovery from bilingual subcortial aphasia. *Brain, 119,* 1551–1564.

Aitchison, J. (1995). Chimps, children, and Creoles: The need for caution. In S. Puppel (Ed.), *The biology of language* (pp. 1–18). Philadelphia: John Benjamins.

Aitchison, J. (1996). *The seeds of speech: Language origin and evolution.* Cambridge, UK: Cambridge University Press.

Aitchison, J. (1997). *The language web.* Cambridge, UK: Cambridge University Press.

Baddeley, A. (1998). Recent developments in working memory. *Current Opinion in Neurobiology, 8,* 234–238.

Baddeley, A. D., & Hitch, G. (1974). Working memory. *The Psychology of Learning and Motivation, 8,* 47–89.

Bates, E., Bretherton, I., & Snyder, L. (1988). *From first words to grammar: individual differences and dissociable mechanisms.* New York: Cambridge University Press.

Bates, E., & Elman, J. (1996). Learning rediscovered. *Science, 274,* 1849–1850.

Bates, E., & Goodman, J. C. (1997). On the inseparability of grammar and the lexicon: Evidence from acquisition, aphasia and real-time processing. *Language and Cognitive Processes, 12*(5/6), 507–584.

Bavelier, D., Corina, D., Jezzard, P., Padmanabhan, S., Clark, V. P., Karni, A., Prinster, A., Braun, A., Lawlani, A., Rauschecker, J. P., Turner, R., & Neville, H. J. (1997). Sentence reading: A functional MRI study at 4 tesla. *Journal of Cognitive Neuroscience, 9,* 664–686.

Beaken, M. (1996). *The making of language.* Edinburgh, UK: Edinburgh University Press.

Bechara, A., Damasio, H., Tranel, D., & Anderson, S. W. (1998). Dissociation of working memory from decision making within the human prefrontal cortex. *Journal of Neuroscience, 18*(1), 428–437.

Bellugi, U., Lichtenberger, L., Mills, D., Galaburda, A., & Korenberg, J. R. (1999). Bridging cognition, the brain and molecular genetics: Evidence from Williams Syndrome. *Trends in Neurosciences, 22*(5) 197–207.

Berndt, R. S., Mitchum, C. C., & Haendiges, A. N. (1996). Comprehension of reversible sentences in "aggramatism": A meta-analysis, *Cognition, 58,* 289–308.

Berndt, R. S., & Caramazza, A. (1999). How "regular" is sentence comprehension in Broca's aphasia? It depends how you select the patients. *Brain and Language, 67,* 242–247.

Bickerton, D. (1990). *Species and Language.* Chicago: Chicago University Press.

Bickerton, D. (1995). *Language and human behavior.* Seattle, WA: University of Washington Press.

Blackwell, A., & Bates, E. (1995). Inducing aggramatic profiles in normals: Evidence for the selective vulnerability of morphology under cognitive resource limitation. *Journal of Cognitive Neuroscience, 7*(2), 228–257.

Bloedel, J. R. (1993). 'Involvement in' versus 'Storage of'. *Trends in Neurosciences, 16,* 451–452.

Brodal, P. (1998). *The central nervous system: Structure and function* (2nd ed.). New York: Oxford University Press.

Buonomano, D. V., & Merzenich, M. M. (1998). Cortical plasticity: From synapses to maps. *Annual Reviews in Neuroscience, 21,* 149–186.

Caplan, D. (1992). *Language: Structure, processing, and disorders.* Cambridge, MA: The MIT Press.

Caplan, D., Alpert, N., & Waters, G. S. (1998). Effects of syntactic structure and propositional number on patterns of regional cerebral blood flow. *Journal of Cognitive Neuroscience, 10*(4), 541–552.

Caplan, D., & Waters, G. S. (1999). Verbal working memory and comprehension. *Behavioral and Brain Sciences, 22*(1), 77–126.

Caplan, D., Hildebrandt, N., & Makris, N. (1996). Location of lesions in stroke patients with deficits in syntactic processing in sentence comprehension. *Brain, 119,* 933–949.

Casapari, I., Parkinson, S. R., LaPointe, L. L., & Katz, R. C. (1998). Working memory and aphasia. *Brain and Cognition, 37,* 205–22.

Chomsky, N. (1957). *Syntactic structures.* The Hague: Mouton.

Cohen, J. D., Peristein, W. D., Braver, T. S., Nystrom, L. E., Noll, D. C., Jonides, J., & Smith, E. E. (1997). Temporal dynamics of brain activation during a working memory task. *Nature, 386,* 604–607.

Cohen, H., & Le Normand, M. (1998). Language development in children with simple-partial left-hemisphere epilepsy. *Brain and Language, 64,* 409–422.

Courtney, S. M., Ungerleider, L. G., Kell, K., & Haxby, J. V. (1997). Transient and sustained activity in a distributed neural system for human working memory. *Nature, 386,* 608–611.

Crain, S., & Thornton, R. (1998). *Investigations in universal grammar: A guide to experiments on the acquisition of syntax and semantics.* Cambridge, MA: MIT Press.

Damasio, A. R., & Geschwind, N. (1984). The neural basis of language. *Annual Reviews on Neuroscience, 7,* 127–147.

Damasio, A. R., & Damasio, H. (1992). Brain and language. *Scientific American,* (September), 89–95.

Daneman, M., & Carpenter, P. A. (1980). Individual differences in working memory and reading. *Journal of Verbal Learning and Verbal Behavior, 19,* 450–466.

Davidson, I., & Noble, W. (1993). Tools and language in human evolution. In K. R. Gibson & T. Ingold (Eds.), *Tools, language and cognition in human evolution* (pp. 363–388). Cambridge, UK: Cambridge University Press.

Dawkins, R. (1992). *The selfish gene* (2nd ed.). Oxford, UK: Oxford University Press.

Deacon, T. W. (1997). *The symbolic species: The co-evolution of language and the brain.* New York: W. W. Norton & Company.

Dejerine, J. (1892). Contribution à l'étude anato-clinique et clinique des différentes variétés de cécité verbale. *Mémoires de la Société de Biologie, 4,* 61–90.

Desmond, J. E., & Fiez, J. A. (1998). Neuroimaging studies of the cerebellum: Language, learning, and memory. *Trends in Cognitive Sciences, 2,* 355–362.

Dick, F., Bates, E., Wulfeck, B., & Dronkers, N. F. (1998). Simulating deficits in the interpretation of complex sentences in normals under adverse processing conditions. *Brain and Language, 65,* 57–59.

Dronkers, N. F. (1996). A new brain region for coordinating speech articulation. *Nature, 384*(6605), 159–161.

Dronkers, N. (1999). The neural basis of language. *The Encyclopedia of Cognitive Neuroscience.* Cambridge, MA: MIT Press.

Dunbar, R. (1996). *Grooming, gossip, and the evolution of language.* Cambridge: Harvard University Press.

Elman, J. (1999). Origins of language: a conspiracy theory. In B. MacWhinney (Ed.), *The emergence of language.* Hillsdale, NJ: Erlbaum Associates.

Elman, J., Bates, E., Johnson, M., Karmiloff-Smith, A., Parasi, D., & Plunkett, K. (1996). *Rethinking innateness: A connectionist perspective on development.* Cambridge, MA: MIT Press/Bradford Book.

Fiez, J. A. (1996). Cerebellar contributions to cognition. *Neuron, 16,* 13–15.

Fischman, J. (1996). Evidence mounts for our African origins and alternatives. *Science, 271,* 1364.

Frackowiak, R. S. J. (1994). Functional mapping of verbal memory and language. *Trends in Neurosciences, 17*(3), 109–115.

Fuster, J. M., Bauer, R. H., & Jervey, J. P. (1982). Cellular discharge in the dorsolateral prefrontal cortex of the monkey in cognitive tasks. *Experimental Neurology, 77,* 679–694.

Gabrieli, J. D., Poldrack, R. A., & Desmond, J. E. (1998). The role of the left prefrontal cortex in language and memory. *Proceedings of the National Academy of Sciences (USA), 95,* 906–913.

Gainotti, G. (1998). Category-specific disorders for nouns or verbs: A very old and very new problem. In B. Stemmer & H. A. Whitaker (Eds.), *Handbook of neurolinguistics* (pp. 27–54). San Diego: Academic Press.

Ganger, J., & Stromswold, K. (1998). Innateness, evolution, and genetics of language. *Human Biology, 70*(2), 199–213.

Gannon, P. J., Holloway, R. L., Broadfield, D. C., & Braun, A. R. (1998). Asymmetry of chimpanzee planum temporale: Humanlike pattern of Wernicke's brain language area homolog. *Science, 279,* 220–222.

Geschwind, N. (1972). Language and the brain. *Scientific American, 226*(4), 76–83.

Gibbons, A. (1998). Which of our genes makes us human? *Science, 281*(5382), 1432–1434.

Gibson, K. R. (1993). Tool use, language and social behavior in relationship to information processing capacities. In K. R. Gibson & T. Ingold (Eds.), *Tools, language and cognition in human evolution* (pp. 251–270). Cambridge, UK: Cambridge University Press.

Gibson, K. R., & Ingold, T. (1993). *Tools, language and cognition in human evolution.* Cambridge, UK: Cambridge University Press.

Glickstein, M. (1993). Motor skills but not cognitive tasks. *Trends in Neurosciences, 16*(11), 450–451.

Goldin-Meadow, S. (1993). When does gesture become language? A study of gesture used as a primary communication system by deaf children of hearing parents. In K. R. Gibson & T. Ingold (Eds.), *Tools, language, and cognition in human evolution* (pp. 63–85). New York: Press Syndicate of the University of Cambridge.

Goldman-Rakic, P. S. (1997). Space and time in the mental universe. *Nature, 386,* 559–560.

Grodzinsky, Y., Piñango, M. M., Zurif, E., & Drai, D. (1999). *Brain and Language, 67*(2), 134–147.

Grodzinsky, Y. (in press). The neurology of syntax: Language use without Broca's area. *Behavioral and Brain Sciences, 23.*

Györi, G. (1995). Animal communication and human language: Searching for their evolutionary relationship. In S. Puppel (Ed.), *The biology of language* (pp. 99–126). Philadelphia: John Benjamins Publishing Company.

Harley, T. A. (1995). *The psychology of language: From data to theory.* East Sussex, UK: Psychology Press.

Hauser, M. D. (1996). *The evolution of communication.* Cambridge, MA: The MIT Press.

Hauser, M. D. (1997). Artifactual kinds and functional design features: What a primate understands without language. *Cognition, 64,* 285–308.

Heyes, C. M. (1998). Theory of mind in nonhuman primates. *Behavioral and Brain Sciences, 21,* 101–148.

Hildebrand-Nishon, M. (1995). From protolanguage to grammar: Psychological considerations for the emergence of grammar in language evolution. In S. Puppel (Ed.), *The biology of language* (pp. 127–147). Philadelphia: John Benjamins Publishing Company.

Holzman, M. (1997). *The language of children* (2nd ed.). Cambridge, MA: Blackwell Publisher.

Ito, M. (1993). Movement and thought: Identical control mechanisms by the cerebellum. *Trends in Neurosciences, 16*(11), 448–450.

Iverson, J. M., & Goldin-Meadow, S. (1998). Why people gesture when they speak. *Nature, 396,* 228.

Just, M. A., Carpenter, P. A., Keller, T. A., Eddy, W. F., & Thulborn, K. R. (1996). Brain activation modulated by sentence comprehension. *Science, 274,* 114–116.

Kandel, E. R., Schwartz, J. H., & Jessell, T. M. (1991). *Principles of neural science* (3rd ed.). Norwalk, CT: Appleton & Lange.

Kegl, J., & McWhorter, J. (1997). Perspectives on an emerging language. In E. V. Clark (Ed.), *The Proceedings of the 28th Annual Child Language Research Forum:* Center for the Study of Language and Information.

Kegl, J., Senghas, A., & Coppola, M. (1999). Creation through contact: Sign language emergence and sign language change in Nicaragua. In M. Degraff (Ed.), *Comparative grammatical change: The intersection of language acquisition, creole genesis, and diachronic syntax.* Cambridge, MA: MIT Press.

Kendon, A. (1993). Human gesture. In K. R. Gibson & T. Ingold (Eds.), Tools, language, and cognition in human evolution (pp. 43–62). New York: Press Syndicate of the University of Cambridge.

King, B. J. (1996). Syntax and language origins. *Language & Communication, 16*(2), 193–203.

Kolb, B., & Whishaw, I. Q. (1996). *Fundamentals of human neuropsychology.* (4th ed.). New York: W. H. Freeman and Company.

Kotz, S. A., & Yves von Cramon, D. (1999). Is it timing after all? *Behavioral and Brain Sciences, 22*(1), 103–104.

Leiner, H. C., Leiner, A. L., & Dow, R. S. (1993). Cognitive and language functions of the human cerebellum. *Trends in Neurosciences, 16*(11), 444–447.

Lieberman, P. (1985). On the evolution of human syntactic ability. Its pre-adaptive bases—motor control and speech. *Journal of Human Evolution, 14,* 657–668.

Lieberman, P. (1991). *Uniquely human: The evolution of speech, thought and selfless behavior.* Cambridge, MA: Harvard University Press.

Lieberman, P. (1992). Could an autonomous syntax module have evolved? *Brain and Language, 43,* 768–774.

Lieberman, P. (1998). *Eve spoke.* New York: W. W. Norton.

Linebarger, M., Schwartz, M., & Saffran, E. (1983). Sensitivity to grammatical structure in so-called agrammatic aphasics. *Cognition, 13,* 361–392.

MacLeod, A. K., Buckner, R. L., Miezin, F. M., Petersen, S. E., & Raichle, M. E. (1998). Right anterior prefrontal cortex activation during semantic monitoring and working memory. *Neuroimage, 7,* 41–48.

MacWhinney, B. (1998). Models of the emergence of language. *Annual Reviews in Psychology, 49,* 199–227.

Marslen-Wilson, W. D., & Tyler, L. K. (1987). Against modularity. In J. L. Garfield (Ed.), *Modularity in knowledge representation and in natural language understanding.* Cambridge, MA: MIT Press.

McIntosh, A. R., & Gonzalez-Lima, F. (1994). Structural Equation Modeling and its application to network analysis in functional brain imaging. *Human Brain Mapping, 2,* 2–22.

Merzenich, M. M., & Kaas, J. H. (1980). Principles of organization of sensory-perceptual systems in mammals. *Progress in Psychobiology and Physiological Psychology, 9,* 1–41.

Mills, D. L., Coffey-Corina, S. A., & Neville, H. J. (1994). Variability in cerebral organization during primary language acquisition. In G. Dawson & K. W. Fischer (Eds.), *Human behavior and the developing brain* (pp. 427–455). New York: The Guilford Press.

Miyake, A., Carpenter, P., & Just, M. (1994). A capacity approach to syntactic comprehension disorders. Making normal adults perform like aphasic patients. *Cognitive Neuropsychology, 11,* 671–717.

Miyake, A., Emerson, M. J., & Friedman, N. P. (1999). Good interactions are hard to find. *Behavioral and Brain Sciences, 22*(1), 108–109.

Morford, J. P., Singleton, J. L., & Goldin-Meadow, S. (1995). The genesis of a language: How much time is needed to generate arbitrary symbols in a sign system? In K. Emmory & J. S. Reilly (Eds.), *Language, gesture, and space* (pp. 313–332). Hillsdale, NJ: Laurence Earlbaum Associates, Inc.

Morford, J. P. (1996). Insights to language from the study of gesture: A review of research on the gestural communication of non-signing deaf people. *Language & Communication, 16*(2), 165–178.

Morford, J. P., & Kegl, J. (1996). Grammaticization in a newly emerging signed language in Nicaragua. *Fifth International Conference on Theoretical Issues in Sign Language Research, Montreal, Canada.*

Morwood, M. J., O'Sullivan, P. B., Aziz, F., & Raza, A. (1997). Fission-track ages of stone tools and fossils on the east Indonesian island of Flores. *Nature, 392,* 173–176.

Mueller, R. (1996). Innateness, autonomy, universality? Neurobiological approaches to language. *Brain and Behavioral Sciences, 19*(4), 616.

Mueller, R., Rothermel, R. D., Behen, M. E., Muzik, O., Mangner, T. J., & Chugani, H. T. (1997). Receptive and expressive language activations for sentences: A PET study. *NeuroReport, 8,* 3767–3670.

Neville, H. J., Bavelier, D., Corina, D., Rauschecker, J. P., Karn, A., Lalwani, A., Braun, A., Clark, V., Jezzard, P., & Turner, R. (1998). Cerebral organization for language in deaf and hearing subjects: Biological constraints and effects of experience. *Proceedings of the National Academy of Sciences (USA), 95,* 922–929.

Newmeyer, F. J. (1991). Functional explanation in linguistics and the origins of language. *Language & Communication, 11*(½), 3–28.

Newport, E. (1982). Task specificity in language learning? Evidence from speech perception and American Sign Language. In E. Wanner & L. Gleitman (Eds.), *Language acquisition: The state of the art* (pp. 450–486). New York: Cambridge University Press.

Nobre, A. C., & Plunkett, K. (1997). The neural system of language: Structure and development. *Current Opinion in Neurobiology, 7,* 262–268.

Oliphant, M. (in press). Rethinking the language bottleneck: Why don't animals learn to communicate? Submitted to Knight et al. (Eds.), Volume arising form the *Second International Conference on the Evolution of Language.* London, April 1998.

Paulesu, E., Frith, C. D., & Frackowiak, R. S. J. (1993). The neural correlates of the verbal component of working memory. *Nature, 362,* 342–345.

Petersen, S. E., et al. (1989). Positron emission tomographic studies of the processing of single words. *Journal of Cognitive Neuroscience, 1,* 153–170.

Petitto, L. A., & Marentette, P. F. (1991). Babbling in the manual mode: Evidence of the ontogeny of language. *Science, 251,* 1493–1496.

Pickett, E. R., Kuniholm, E., Protopapas, A., Friedman, J., & Lieberman, P. (1998). Selective speech motor, syntax and cognitive deficits associated with bilateral damage to the putamen and head of the caudate nucleus: A case study. *Neuropsychologia, 30*(2), 173–188.

Pinker, S. (1994). *The language instinct.* New York: Morrow.

Pinker, S., & Bloom, P. (1994). Natural language and natural selection. *Behavioral and Brain Sciences, 13,* 707–784.

Plunkett, K., & Marchman, V. A. (1996). Learning from a connectionist model of the acquisition of the English past tense. *Cognition, 61,* 299–308.

Posner, M. I., & Pavese, A. (1998). Anatomy of word and sentence meaning. *Proceedings of the National Academy of Sciences (USA), 95,* 899–905.

Povinelli, D. J., & Eddy, T. J. (1996). What young chimpanzees know about seeing. *Monographs of the Society for Research in Child Development* (Vol. 61, p. 3). Chicago: The University of Chicago Press.

Price, C. J. (1998). The functional anatomy of word comprehension and production. *Trends in Cognitive Sciences, 2*(8), 281–288.

Price, C. J., Wise, R. J. S., Warburton, E., Moore, C. J., Howard, D., Patterson, K., Frackowiak, R. S. J., & Friston, K. J. (1996). Hearing and saying: The functional neuroanatomy of auditory word processing. *Brain, 119,* 919–931.

Puppel, S. (1995). *The biology of language.* Philadelphia: John Benjamins Publishing.

Rauschecker, J. P., Tian, B., & Hauser, M. D. (1995). Processing of complex sounds in the macaque nonprimary auditory cortex. *Science, 268,* 111–114.

Raichle, M. E. (1998). Behind the scenes of functional brain imaging: A historical and physiological perspective. *Proceedings of the National Academy of Sciences (USA), 95,* 765–772.

Reilly, J. S., Bates, E., & Marchman, V. (1998). Narrative discourse in children with early focal brain injury. *Brain and Language, 61,* 335–375.

Ruhlen, M. (1994). *The origin of language: Tracing the evolution of the mother tongue.* New York: John Wiley & Sons.

Saffran, J. R., Aslin, R. N., & Newport, E. L. (1996). Statistical learning by 8-month-old infants. *Science, 274,* 1926–1928.

Savage-Rumbaugh, E. S., & Lewin, R. (1994). *Kanzi: An ape on the brink of the human mind.* New York: Doubleday.

Savage-Rumbaugh, E. S., & Rumbaugh, D. M. (1993). A comparative approach to language parallels. In K. R. Gibson & T. Ingold (Eds.), *Tools, language, and cognition in human evolution* (pp. 86–108). New York: Press Syndicate of the University of Cambridge.

Semaw, S., Renne, P., Harris, J. W. K., Feibel, C. S., Bernor, R. L., Fesseha, N., & Mowbray, K. (1997). 2.5-million-year-old stone tools from Gona, Ethiopia. *Nature, 385,* 333–336.

Senghas, A. (1995). *Children's contribution to the birth of Nicaraguan Sign Language.* Unpublished Doctoral Dissertation. MIT, Cambridge, MA.

Sereno, M. I. (1990). Language and the primate brain. *Center for Research in Language Newsletter, 4*(4).

Seyfarth, R. M., & Cheney, D. L. (1986). Vocal development in vervet monkeys. *Animal Behaviour, 34,* 1640–1658.

Singleton, J. (1989). *Restructuring of language from impoverished input.* Unpublished doctoral dissertation, University of Illinois at Urbana-Champaign.

Smith, E. E., Jonides, J., Marshuetz, C., & Koeppe, R. A. (1998). Components of verbal working memory: Evidence from neuroimaging. *Proceedings of the National Academy of Sciences (USA), 95,* 876–882.

Steels, L. (1998). The synthetic modeling of language origins. *Evolution of Communication, 1*(1), 1–34.

Stromswold, K., Caplan, D., Alpert, N., & Rauch, S. (1996). Localization of syntactic comprehension by positron emission tomography. *Brain and Language,* (52), 452–473.

Thieme, H. (1997). Lower palaeolithic hunting spears from Germany. *Nature, 385,* 807–810.

Thulborn, K. R., Carpenter, P. A., & Just, M. A. (1999). Plasticity of language-related brain function during recovery from stroke. *Stroke, 30,* 749–754.

Tomasello, M. (1995). Language is not an instinct. *Cognitive Development, 10,* 131–156.

Tranel, D., Damasio, H., & Damasio, A. R. (1997). A neural basis for the retrieval of knowledge. *Neuropsychologia, 35,* 1319–1327.

Ujhelyi, M. (1996). Is there an intermediate stage between animal communication and language? *Journal of Theoretical Biology, 180,* 71–76.

Ullman, M. T., Corkin, S., Coppola, M., Hickock, G., Growdon, J. H., Koroshetz, W. J., & Pinker, S. (1997). A neural dissociation within language: Evidence that the mental dictionary is part of declarative memory, and that grammatical rules are processed by the procedural system. *Journal of Cognitive Neuroscience, 9*(2), 266–276.

Ungerleider, L. G. (1995). Functional brain imaging studies of cortical mechanisms for memory. *Science, 270,* 769–775.

Ungerleider, L. G., Courtney, S. M., & Haxby, J. V. (1998). A neural system for human visual working memory. *Proceedings of the National Academy of Sciences (USA), 95,* 883–890.

van Mier, H., Tempel, L. W., Perlmutter, J. S., Raichle, M. E., & Petersen, S. E. (1998). Changes in brain activity during motor learning measured with PET: Effects of hand of performance and practice. *Journal of Neurophysiology, 80,* 2177–2199.

van Turrenout, M., Hagoort, P., & Brown, C. M. (1998). Brain activity during speaking: From syntax to phonology in 40 milliseconds. *Science, 280,* 572–574.

Warburton, E., Wise, R. J. S., Price, C. J., Weiller, C., Hadar, U., Ramsay, S., & Frackowiak, R. S. J. (1996). Noun and verb retrieval by normal subjects Studies with PET. *Brain, 119,* 159–179.

Washabaugh, W. (1986). *Five fingers for survival.* Ann Arbor: Karoma Publishers, Inc.

Waters, G., & Caplan, D. (1996). The measurement of verbal working memory and its relation to reading capacity. *Quarterly Journal of Experimental Psychology, 49,* 51–79.

Whitaker, H. A. (1998). Neurolinguistics from the Middle Ages to the pre-Modern era: Historical vignettes. In B. Stemmer & H. A. Whitaker (Eds.), *Handbook of neurolinguistics* (pp. 27–54). San Diego: Academic Press.

Wilkins, W. K., & Wakefield, J. (1995). Brain evolution and neurolinguistic preconditions. *Behavioral and Brain Sciences, 18,* 161–226.

Wilson, F. A. W., Scalaidhe, S. P. O., & Goldman-Rakik, P. S. (1993). Dissociation of object and spatial processing domains in primate prefrontal cortex. *Science, 260,* 1955–1957.

Wray, A. (1998). Protolanguage as a holistic system for social interaction. *Language & Communication, 18,* 47–67.

Zurif, E. B., Caramazza, A., & Meyerson, R. (1972). Grammatical judgements of agrammatic aphasics. *Neuropsychologia 10:* 405–417.

CHAPTER 7

The Cognitive Neuroscience Approach

Kevin N. Ochsner
Stephen M. Kosslyn

Imagine that you are a physician trying to understand how digestion is accomplished; you want to know how the structure and function of internal organs cause food input to be converted into energy output. How might you begin and what types of information might you seek? You might begin by observing the problems experienced by people who have suffered injuries to particular internal organs, which could give you a general idea of what functions each helps to carry out in digestion. However, you might soon notice that damage to different organs results in similar, but not identical difficulties. Furthermore, you find that damage to a given organ does not always result in a single, consistent dysfunctional pattern, and the particular observed pattern seems to depend upon the integrity of related organs. Understanding digestion becomes an increasingly complex task as each new observation reveals a host of new questions. Moreover, each organ may participate in more than one aspect of digestion, and observations of deficits and locations of damage are not enough to identify the functions uniquely.

Happily, you can use information from other domains to help you interpret the data. Anatomical studies reveal that the organs in question, such as the stomach, intestines, liver and pancreas, are not connected haphazardly; in fact, they appear to be connected in a precise fashion, each organ connected to a specific set of other organs. These data help you piece together the notion of a "digestive tract" or system in which each organ carries out a particular process upon food as it passes through the system. This insight might help explain why the pattern of deficits following damage to one organ depends upon the integrity of others. You realize further that in order to understand the functional relationships among these organs you need to know more about how they communicate, what they do, and which aspects of their operation might be shared by all organs in the digestive tract. For example, you learn that a chemical called insulin is produced by the pancreas, is found in the liver, and has been linked to changes in blood sugar levels in rats. How does insulin relate to different aspects of digestion? How and when does the liver use it? Might insulin be influenced by, or itself influence, other processes? In answering these questions you may develop an understanding of digestion that draws on many levels of analysis, from the molecule to the system, ultimately providing a coherent description of the digestive process in general, and the role of specific components of the process, like insulin, in particular.

From this perspective, the digestive tract and the brain may have a lot in common. The goal of cognitive neuroscience is to understand how brain function gives rise to mental abilities such as memory, reasoning, vision, or movement, and to understand how such abilities interact with the systems underlying emotion. Our analogy illustrates one way in which multidisciplinary research on such a complex problem might proceed. Unfortunately, the task of understanding the relation of behavior to the structure and function of the brain is much more complex than that of understanding the relation of digestion to the structure and function of the liver, stomach, and other organs in the digestive tract. Not only is the brain structurally more complex than the digestive tract, it also carries out many more functions, and each function is both more complex and more difficult to describe operationally than are aspects of the digestive process.

Nevertheless, the same multidisciplinary approach that has proven successful in medical research has been incorporated in cognitive neuroscience. In cognitive neuroscience, we consider data collected by researchers studying behavior, cognition, neurophysiology, neuroanatomy, and computation, and each new finding provides additional fodder for theories of brain function. Theory building thus becomes a process of trying to fit together a wide variety of different types of information into a complex, but integrated whole. Thus the different types of information must be explained by the same theory; the theory is not simply "constrained" by different types of data, but rather it is an attempt to explain diverse phenomena with a single set of assumptions and principles.

Perhaps the most significant difference between cognitive neuroscience and cognitive science is that cognitive neuroscience aims to understand the neural implementation of mental abilities. Cognitive science focuses only on function, independently of the organ that gives rise to the function. From a cognitive science perspective, there are many ways that digestion could in principle take place, and the goal of research is seen as an attempt to specify them. But even though studying the function in its own right may implicate only a few candidate digestive processes, there is only one way that the body actually converts food input into energy output. If our goal is to understand how digestion works, viewing it as a functional property of the physiology and anatomy of the digestive tract focuses and delimits the problem. Similarly, research in cognitive neuroscience characterizes function as a property of the brain itself, and in so doing necessarily integrates across physical and functional levels of analysis. Given that the human brain is currently the only system capable of producing the complex functions we call memory, emotion, and so forth, it makes sense to try to understand how its design is related to these abilities.

The purpose of this chapter is to illustrate the cognitive neuroscience approach in several problem domains. We selected domains that pertain to visual analyses of the world: attention, high-level vision, and visual memory. We focus on vision in large part because much of the research on the neural bases of cognition and behavior, especially using animals, has focused on vision. Our focus on vision also allows us to illustrate a key feature of the cognitive neuroscience approach: A major goal of cognitive neuroscience is the construction of integrated theories of cognition and behavior, and we wanted to illustrate the process of theory construction not simply within a single domain, such as attention, but across several related domains. Vision is thus the tie that binds several domains together.

Nevertheless, the reader should be aware that the cognitive neuroscientific approach outlined here is being profitably applied to the study of many topics, such as language (Caplan, 1993), movement (Georgopoulos, 1994), and emotion (J. E. LeDoux, 1994). Some of the topics we touch upon are reviewed in greater depth, from a different perspective, elsewhere in this volume (e.g., see chapters in this volume by Martin, 8, on language, LaBerge, 2, on attention, Gallistel, 1, on action).

With these considerations in mind, we discuss first key historical developments and general principles that have motivated research in cognitive neuroscience, and then consider briefly how research on attention, high-level vision, and visual memory has benefited from an application of the cognitive neuroscience perspective.

I. FOUNDATIONS OF COGNITIVE NEUROSCIENCE

A number of important advances in neurobiology, experimental psychology, and computer science laid the foundations for the emergence of cognitive neuroscience (see Kosslyn & Andersen, 1993).

In the late 1960s researchers began recording the electrical activity of cortical neurons in awake, behaving monkeys (Evarts, 1966). This technique allowed precise correlation of behavioral and physiological data, and researchers were able to characterize the functional organization of some parts of the brain. For example, Hubel and Wiesel (1968) discovered that the primary visual cortex is composed of a series of columns of cells, and the cells in each column are sensitive to the presence of bars or edges with particular orientations located in specific parts of the visual field. Although the parcellation of the brain into discrete functional components had been suggested by earlier work with brain-damaged patients and animals (e.g., Broca, 1863), direct measurement of neural activity allowed researchers systematically to map stimulus parameters onto the function of individual or groups of neurons.

A similar emphasis on understanding complex functions in terms of constituent processes also emerged in the cognitive psychology of the late 1960s and 1970s (e.g., see Neisser, 1967), but this approach had a very different origin: the computer metaphor. Researchers in psychology began to conceive of internal processing in humans by analogy to internal processing in a computer. For example, Sternberg (1969) developed a technique for isolating distinct information-processing stages that were characterized in terms of how information is stored, encoded, interpreted, or compared. Similarly, Posner developed tasks to tap simple component processes of complex abilities such as attention (e.g., Posner, Nissen, & Ogden, 1978). In addition, Shepard and his colleagues (e.g., Shepard & Feng, 1972; Shepard & Metzler, 1971) provided evidence that the brain can perform analog computations in some situations. Together, these findings led researchers to conceptualize behavior as arising when specific types of processing are performed upon specific internal representations.

However, cognitive psychologists recognized that descriptions of behavior are not enough to implicate one set of underlying mechanisms. Indeed, it was proved that any set of behavioral data could be explained by a number of theories (e.g., Anderson, 1978). Anderson argued that data from neurophysiology, such as that collected by Hubel and Wiesel, could provide critical insights into the nature of internal representations and the processes that operate upon them, thereby limiting our choices among theories to those that could accommodate these data.

Further key developments came from the rapidly developing field of artificial intelligence within computer science. Von Neumann (1958) and McCulloch and Pitts (1943) suggested that neural processes could be usefully conceptualized as computational processes. Early computational models demonstrated that neural activity could in fact be conceptualized as information processing. Combined with Hebb's (1949) associative model for learning in networks of neurons, and new findings of circumscribed learning deficits following focal brain damage (e.g., Scoville & Milner, 1957), there seemed good reason to believe that mental abilities could be viewed in terms of discrete processing stages operating upon internal representations.

Thus, links between mental abilities and sets of distinct processes were becoming apparent, and links between brain function and computation were becoming clear. But the whole was not greater than the sum of its parts until researchers saw how to combine the different sorts of information so that they mutually informed each other.

A. The Cognitive Neuroscience Approach

A comprehensive framework for understanding how the brain carries out computations was developed by David Marr (1982). Marr's work focused on vision, but his approach can be generalized to any type of biological information processing.

He posited that vision should be studied at three levels of analysis, which in turn must be integrated. These levels varied in abstraction: At the most abstract level, a theory specifies *what* is computed by a specific module; at an intermediate level, a theory specifies *how* a given computation is actually carried out (i.e., it specifies an algorithm); and at the most concrete level, a theory specifies how a set of processes is actually implemented in the brain. Marr argued that the three levels, particularly the more abstract ones, could be studied independently. This perspective is clearly compatible with the notion that the mind is like a computer program, which can be understood independently of the machine on which it runs. This view has recently been questioned, however, and many researchers are now impressed more by the close relationships among the levels than by their independence (e.g., Kosslyn & Maljkovic, 1990).

Indeed, the dominant paradigm in experimental psychology appears to be shifting because of two factors. First, many researchers have been impressed by the power of the connectionist ("neural network") method of modeling cognitive abilities; such models conflate Marr's levels of analysis (see Grossberg, 1980; Kosslyn & Koenig, 1992; J. L. McClelland & Rumelhart, 1986). Second, research in neurobiology has revealed a close relationship between the structure and function of the brain (for a review, see Kosslyn & Koenig, 1992). The brain is not a general purpose machine that can be programmed in any arbitrary way; rather, key aspects of the structure of the brain apparently have been tailored (via natural selection) for the specific types of computations that it performs. Cognitive neuroscience has emerged in part because researchers realized that facts about the evolution and biology of the brain could provide insight into the nature of cognition.

Research in neuroscience has led to several generalizations that in turn have guided much theorizing in the field. These generalizations can be summarized as follows.

1. *Limitations on "optimal" performance.* Brains have limited processing capacities because they are part of a biological system. Therefore, there can be no "optimal" or "logically correct" solution to a computational problem without reference to available hardware and resources; each computational step requires metabolic energy and must interact with the resource requirements of other processes. In addition, the brain was not engineered to perform optimally all computations; rather it is the product of hundreds of thousands of years of selection pressures that have added particular functions to those already present (Sherry & Schacter, 1987) if such functions enhanced the reproductive capability of the organism (but also sometimes even if they did not; see Gould & Lewontin, 1979). Thus any theory of the computation, algorithm, or implementation that does not take into account these limitations may make unfounded assumptions about what is possible, and therefore risks biological implausibility.

2. *Anatomical structure.* As will be discussed in more detail below, the brain is not a homogeneous "wonder net"; rather, different parts do different things. Moreover,

anatomical connectivity leads some sets of processes to take place in parallel, and other sets to take place in series (e.g., see DeYoe & Van Essen, 1988; Ungerleider & Mishkin, 1982). In addition, information typically does not flow in only one direction in the brain. In the vast majority of cases, every projection from a lower (i.e., closer to sensory input) area to a higher (i.e., further from sensory input) cortical area is accompanied by connections running in the opposite direction—and the two kinds of connections are of comparable size (Felleman & Van Essen, 1991). Furthermore, it appears that these reciprocal, feedback, connections have more diffuse target regions than the feed-forward connections; this anatomical fact may suggest that a given process can be modulated by many others. Thus it may not make sense to consider a single computation or algorithm in isolation because computations are carried out by systems of interacting subsystems (Kosslyn & Koenig, 1992; Posner & Petersen, 1990; Schacter, 1994). Connectionist (neural network) models are useful in part because they can be constructed to mimic the interactive nature of cortical processing; they consist of interacting layers of neuron-like nodes that can be designed to involve extensive bidirectional cross-talk between input and output levels.

3. *Physiological observations.* Basic facts about neural dynamics also shape the way the brain can process information. For example, the brain can carry out only about 10 serial steps to produce a response 250 ms after a stimulus has appeared (Churchland & Sejnowski, 1992; Feldman, 1985). Considering data from neuropsychology, neurophysiology, and other branches of neuroscience not only helps us understand existing data and evaluate theories of cognition, but also helps develop new theories and collect various types of additional data.

As illustrated in Figure 1, the cognitive neuroscience approach can be represented as an equilateral triangle with *abilities* at the apex, and *neuroscience* and *computation* at the two bottom corners (see also Kosslyn, 1994). Abilities is at the top because that is what one is trying, ultimately, to explain, and neuroscience and computation are at the bottom because the explanations rest on conceptions of how the brain computes. The equal length of the connections between each vertex reflects the fact that there is no privileged level of analysis or means of constraining or generating hypotheses. Explanations derived from multidisciplinary analyses necessarily turn on a confluence of facts about abilities (usually as manifested in observable behavior), the brain, and computation.

Many theories in cognitive neuroscience aim to specify the functional architecture for a specific type of processing. Such theories have two components: First, they may specify a set of processing subsystems, which either store or transform information in some way, and how information flows from one component of the system to another (e.g., see Kosslyn, 1994). Second, theories in cognitive neuroscience may specify the precise nature of processing within a single component subsystem. Such theories typically specify a type of neural network, which transforms input to a particular kind of output (e.g., Hasselmo, 1993; Hasselmo & Bower, 1993).

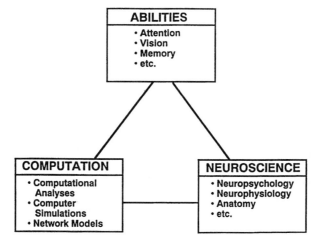

FIGURE 1   The cognitive neuroscience triangle.

B. The Isolable Systems Problem

Cognitive neuroscience thus is inherently multidisciplinary. Disciplines such as cognitive psychology, linguistics, and psychophysics are all concerned with delineating the nature of human abilities. The challenge here is to describe abilities in a way that can make contact with available data about brain function. A fundamental question researchers must answer in order to understand an ability has been termed the *isolable systems problem* (Posner, 1978): Does a given ability (or behavior that follows from it) come about through the function of a single system or many systems, and if many are involved, how do they coordinate their operations? This problem leads one to formulate and test a theory of a functional architecture. This problem is difficult to grapple with using behavioral data alone because any behavioral measure reflects the performance of the system as a whole (Posner & Carr, 1992). Even task-analytic procedures that rely on patterns of interaction between experimental variables (e.g., Sternberg, 1969) are subject to multiple interpretations (e.g., see Anderson, 1978; Townsend, 1974).

One approach to solving the isolable systems problem rests on the concept of convergent evidence. No one study provides conclusive evidence for a specific neurofunctional decomposition, but the results from a set of studies using diverse methods may point the way towards a single decomposition that explains all of them. Such studies have more power when the methods interlock, as occurs when one designs cognitive studies to investigate issues about the brain, and designs neuropsychological studies to investigate issues about cognition (Kosslyn, 1994). This is where neuroscientific data and techniques can be particularly important. For example, one can simultaneously record activity of neurons in different parts of the brain while an animal performs a task that has been designed to require a specific type of processing; such findings may suggest which areas perform what computations and at what time (e.g., see Andersen, 1987). In humans, brain imaging techniques such as positron emission tomography (PET) and functional magnetic resonance imaging (fMRI) allow us to determine which sets of brain areas are most active when a person performs a specific task (e.g., Posner, Petersen, Fox, & Raichle, 1988). If tasks are designed to tap specific types of processing, one can learn about the neural bases of such processing by comparing results from different tasks. The key is that

> both brain imaging and neurophysiology add (on top of behavioral measures) the ability to break the system down into spatially defined parts in which the amount and timing of processing changes as a function of experimenter controlled manipulations of variables such as difficulty, type of task, decision rules, load, accuracy, etc.
>
> *(Posner & Carr, 1992, p. 8)*

Given the truly staggering range of possibilities, it is no small thing to design tasks appropriately and to know where to look for specific effects in the brain. But these problems are more tractable if one has an hypothesis in hand. This hypothesis specifies one or more potentially isolable systems, and may or may not specify a candidate anatomical localization. Both parts of the hypothesis can be motivated in part by anatomical data that specify the connections between different areas. Such information not only can suggest separate processing components, as will be illustrated shortly, but also can be used to generate hypotheses about the flow of information in a system. These hypotheses can then be tested using brain imaging techniques, including time-sensitive measures such as event-related potentials (ERP) (e.g., Mangun, Hilyard, & Luck, 1992).

In addition to studying behavior and the brain, two types of computational data can help one to solve the isolable systems problem. First, *computational analyses* can lead one to formulate theories of how a given input can produce a given output. Such analyses rely on a careful consideration of the "problem" to be solved by an information-processing system, which often hinges on a consideration of the information that is available in the input (see Kosslyn & Koenig, 1992; Marr, 1982). Computational analyses typically result in hypotheses about the decomposition of a system into subsystems. These analyses must be informed by neurophysiology and neuroanatomy because we want to know how our cognitive system—not just any possible system—functions.

Second, one can construct *computational* models of hypothesized functional systems. These models are computer programs designed to mimic the operation of a dynamic system, and as such can help one to understand behavioral and neurobiological data in a number of ways. Models can lead one to discover unforeseen implications of a theory; by observing the behavior of an intact or "lesioned" model one can generate hypotheses about how the normal system functions, which can then be examined experimentally (e.g., predictions of Ambros-Ingerson, Granger, & Lynch, 1990, were tested by McCollum et al., 1991; see also S. Keele & Jennings,

1992). In addition, computational models can help address the isolable systems problem by specifying conditions under which it is more efficient to break a function down into component parts, each computed by a separate system, than to have the function carried out by a single system. For example, Rueckl, Cave, and Kosslyn (1989) demonstrated that some types of complex input–output mappings can be computed more efficiently by two networks rather than one, with each subnetwork specialized for carrying out different aspects of the mapping. By examining such models, one can experimentally determine when two mappings are "computationally incompatible," and hence likely to interfere with each other if carried out within a single unified network.

In short, cognitive neuroscience can be characterized as having two general goals: First, it aims to carve the cognitive system at its functional and anatomical joints, along the way specifying the nature of, and interactions among, the component subsystems. Second, it aims to specify the ways specific neural networks operate to produce the requisite output when provided with an input. In both cases, the ultimate aim is to understand how computation in the brain confers specific abilities.

In the following three sections we consider how the cognitive neuroscience approach has begun to bear fruit in the study of some of our most fundamental mental abilities: selectively attending to objects, visual perception, and memory. There are several comprehensive cognitive neuroscience theories of attention (e.g., LaBerge, 1990; Posner & Petersen, 1990), visual perception (e.g., Hummel & Biederman, 1992; Kosslyn, 1994), and memory (e.g., Cohen & Eichenbaum, 1994; Schacter, 1990; L. R. Squire, 1987, 1992; see Schacter & Tulving, 1994a, 1994b, for summary of many recent theories). Space limitations preclude our considering each of these theories in detail. Our goal is not to review the literature exhaustively, but rather to convey the flavor of the cognitive neuroscience approach in action. Thus for each of the three content areas we will provide an overview of current theory, and illustrate the utility of a multidisciplinary approach and converging evidence.

II. ATTENTION

Attention is the selective aspect of information processing. This function allows us to focus on some information at the expense of other information. We typically are aware of what we attend to, and only specified pieces of information enter our conscious experience. Traditional conceptions of attention have posited either a limited "energy" resource or a structural bottleneck (Allport, 1992). Debate has focused on specifying exactly which types of processing do or do not require attention, which task variables play critical roles in demanding and directing attention, and exactly how far into the cognitive system information is processed before attention operates upon it (e.g., Broadbent, 1971; Shiffrin, 1988). However, as we have learned more about neural information processing, at least some of these questions have begun to appear ill posed (Allport, 1992). In particular, these questions are in large part predicated on the assumption that attention operates on information flowing through the cognitive system in a precise, linear, increasingly abstract manner. However, the neuroanatomy suggests strongly that information processing in the brain is anything but simply linear and unidirectional (e.g., Felleman & Van Essen, 1991). Questions about capacity and the putative locus of attentional selection may be considered best with respect to particular types of information processed by particular components of neural systems (Allport, 1992; Posner & Petersen, 1990).

Attention has also been approached as a particular example of the isolable systems problem (Posner, 1978). Research in this mode begins with an analysis of the processing steps necessary for selective attention, which are then investigated by collecting a combination of behavioral and neurobiological data. Working within this paradigm, Posner and Petersen (1990) offer three general conclusions about attention: (a) the attention system is neurally distinct from, but interacts with, other processing systems of the brain; (b) this system consists of a network of different brain areas; and (c) each area carries out different computations that can be specified in cognitive terms. A series of seminal studies conducted by Posner and his colleagues (e.g., see Posner, Inhoff, Friedrich, & Cohen, 1987; Posner et al., 1988; Posner & Petersen, 1990) illustrates the utility of the cognitive neuroscience approach and will serve to flesh out our understanding of these three basic tenets.

A. Subsystems of Attention

At the computational level, attention can be viewed as involving the interaction of separable systems for (a) orienting to a stimulus; (b) detecting a stimulus; and (c) alerting and remaining vigilant for the appearance of a stimulus. The systems for orienting can be further distinguished as being used for overt (when the body, head, or eyes are moved) or covert (when no overt movement is made) shifts of attention. Furthermore, such shifts of attention appear to involve three processing subcomponents: in order to shift attention one must first disengage it from its current location, move it, and then engage attention at a newly specified location. The functional architecture of attention is illustrated in Figure 2.

1. Orienting to a Stimulus

An impressive amount about the mechanisms underlying spatial attention has been learned from a simple cuing task (e.g., Posner et al., 1978; Posner, Snyder, & Davidson, 1980). In this task, subjects first fixate on a cross and are cued to attend to a box that is either to the left or right of fixation. An asterisk then flashes in either the attended or the unattended box, and the subject simply presses a key as soon as he or she sees the asterisk. Subjects typically respond faster on validly cued trials, when the asterisk appears on the attended side, than on invalidly cued trials, when the asterisk appears in the box on the unattended side. The response time "cost" for invalidly cued trials has been interpreted as reflecting the time it takes to disengage

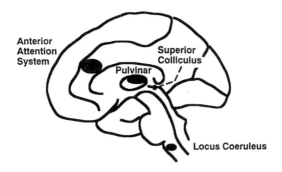

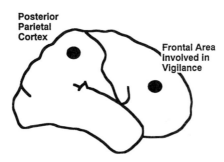

FIGURE 2   The functional architecture of attention shown superimposed on medial (top) and lateral (bottom) views of the right cerebral hemisphere. The neural locus of each subsystem is indicated by a solid black circle. These subsystems allow us to orient attention (posterior attention subsystem, which includes the posterior parietal cortex, pulvinar nucleus of thalamus, and superior colliculus), detect target stimuli (anterior attention subsystem), and maintain an alert, vigilant state (locus coeruleus and right hemisphere).

attention from the attended location in order to detect a target at the unattended location.

Neurophysiological studies have indicated that neurons in areas of the posterior parietal cortex (Wurtz, Goldberg, & Robinson, 1980), lateral pulvinar nucleus of the thalamus (D. L. Robinson & Petersen, 1992), and superior colliculus (Posner & Petersen, 1990) increase their firing rates when a monkey attends to a target stimulus to the exclusion of other distracting stimuli. These data suggest that these areas of the brain may be involved in attention, and in fact, patients with damage to any of these areas are impaired in the cuing task described above. Indeed, depending on the precise locus of the damage, patients are impaired at different aspects of the cuing task. First, patients with damaged parietal lobes have difficulty on invalidly cued trials, in which attention is initially focused in the incorrect location (Posner et al., 1987; Posner, Walker, Friedrich, & Rafal, 1984). These patients appear to have particular difficulty moving attention away from an ipsilesional (same-side) cue to detect a target in their neglected visual field. Subsequent brain-imaging data have confirmed that the parietal lobes are activated when subjects shift their attention (Corbetta, Miezin, Shulman, & Petersen, 1993). These findings are consistent with the fact that damage to the parietal lobes often causes a deficit known as visual neglect (Bisiach & Luzzatti, 1978; Bisiach, Luzzatti, & Perani, 1979). For example, patients with right parietal damage appear unaware of or may not be able to respond to stimuli on the left side of space (Bisiach et al., 1979). Such patients typically exhibit *extinction,* or the loss of awareness of a stimulus appearing on the side contralateral to their lesion when it appears simultaneously with a stimulus on the same side as the lesion.

This deficit in disengaging attention differs markedly from the impairments exhibited by patients with lesions of the pulvinar nucleus of the thalamus (see Figure 2). Such patients are slow to respond to targets at cued locations (D. L. Robinson & Petersen, 1992), and similar results have been found with monkeys. Furthermore, PET scanning has revealed that the pulvinar becomes more active when subjects must attend to one aspect of a display to the exclusion of others (LaBerge & Buchsbaum, 1990). Thus the pulvinar seems to play a special role in engaging attention at a target location.

Finally, the ability to shift attention may be selectively disrupted by damage to the midbrain. In progressive supranuclear palsy, damage to the superior colliculus (see Figure 2) results in a slowing of responses to targets that appear at cued and uncued locations; the advantage for targets at cued locations appears only if the subjects are given a long time to focus on the cue before the asterisk appears; these patients apparently need extra time to shift attention to the cue (Posner, Choate, Rafal, & Vaughan, 1985).

2. Detecting a Stimulus

Researchers have also begun to understand the neural mechanisms that allow primates to detect behaviorally significant target events. However, theories of these mechanisms rest primarily on post hoc explanations of data; computational analyses that can motivate theory-driven research on the processes that underlie target detection are only now beginning to take shape. One reason for this is that studies have only recently revealed an area of the brain, anterior cingulate cortex, that appears to play a special role in target detection (see Figure 2). By examining the connectivity between the anterior cingulate and other parts of the brain, researchers can formulate hypotheses about interactions among specific subsystems (e.g., Ochsner & Baker, 1994). This is an example of how neuroscientific data can motivate a theory, which in turn prompts researchers to design behavioral experiments that bear on this new hypothesis.

Our knowledge about the function of the anterior cingulate in attention rests in large part on results from PET studies. For example, Petersen, Fox, Posner,

Mintun, and Raichle (1988) found anterior cingulate activation when subjects generated verbs that describe functions of nouns (e.g., when given "hammer" they might say "pound"), decided whether an animal was dangerous, or passively listened to words read aloud. Hypothesizing that this area might be involved in detecting targets, or selecting stimuli relevant to task demands, these researchers predicted, and found, that activity increased when greater numbers of targets were presented in the "dangerous animal detection" task. Anterior cingulate cortex is also active during performance of the Stroop task (Pardo, Pardo, Janer, & Raichle, 1990), during diffuse attention, as opposed to focal attention (Corbetta, Miezin, Dobmeyer, Shulman, & Petersen, 1991), when painful stimuli are applied to the forearm (Talbot et al., 1991), when subjects generate attention-based visual mental images (Kosslyn, Alpert et al., 1993), and when subjects generate finger movements from memory (Dieber et al., 1991). In contrast, anterior cingulate activity decreases when subjects become more practiced in the verb generation task (Raichle et al., 1993), or when they mentally manipulate forms (Haier et al., 1988, cited in LaBerge, 1990); it also decreases when subjects are in a vigilant state, waiting to detect an infrequently presented target tone (see Posner & Rothbart, 1992).

The almost ubiquitous changes of activation in the anterior cingulate during task performance may suggest that it is something of a general-purpose attentional area, which is recruited whenever relevant stimuli cannot be detected on the basis of simple stimulus features or automatized routines (cf. Corbetta et al., 1991; LaBerge, 1990; Petersen & Fiez, 1993; Posner & Petersen, 1990; Posner & Rothbart, 1992). Posner and colleagues have used dual-task methods to test the generality of the anterior cingulate's role in attention. When subjects shadowed speech while they also performed the cued probe-detection task described earlier, the response time difference between valid and invalid trials disappeared when the cues were presented to the left hemisphere. Passive listening to spoken words has been shown to activate the left anterior cingulate by Petersen et al., 1988, thus the anterior cingulate may have been engaged by the shadowing task, and hence was not able to confer an advantage for valid trials. Similarly, a concurrent auditory task can slow engagement of attention in parietal patients (Posner et al., 1987). Hence, there is evidence that language and visual spatial attention may share some common attentional mechanisms, although the nature of the shared computation(s) remains unclear.

Insights into the possible computations carried out by the anterior cingulate can also be garnered by examining the pattern of behavioral deficits that occurs when it is lesioned. Psychiatric patients for whom other interventions have failed sometimes receive bilateral stereotactic lesions in the rostral portions of anterior cingulate cortex, just above the genu of the corpus callosum. This operation is thought to alleviate anxiety (Ballantine, Cassidy, Brodeur, & Giriunas, 1972). Janer and Pardo (1991) examined the performance of one such patient on three tasks found in PET studies to activate anterior cingulate cortex: verb generation, identifying dangerous animals, and the Stroop task. Compared to her preoperative level of performance, the cingulotomy patient had deficits on all three tasks 2 weeks after the operation.

However, the deficits on the Stroop and identifying dangerous animals tasks disappeared 6 weeks later, which suggests that the attentional system can compensate (somehow) for small lesions. It is clear, however, that whatever the anterior cingulate does, that computation or computations is normally drawn upon when one performs these tasks.

Additional information about the role of the anterior cingulate comes from research on discriminative aversive conditioning in rats. Although it is always dangerous to generalize across species, basic sensory and motor processes (and at least some forms of attention may be included in these categories) are often similar among different mammals; in any case, findings about rat brains are a good source of plausible hypotheses about processing in the human brain. Such research has shown different patterns of firing in neurons in anterior cingulate cortex to a conditioned stimulus than to a stimulus that was not conditioned, and lesions of this area impair acquisition—but not expression—of discriminative avoidance behavior (Gabriel, 1990). These results suggest that the anterior cingulate cortex helps to identify behaviorally significant stimuli. This function is consistent with the fact that this area has major connections to the amygdala—which plays a critical role in emotion (Amaral et al., 1992).

We might expect that a system playing a general role in detecting target events would enjoy widespread connections with cortical areas involved in attention, memory, and motor control. And in fact, Goldman-Rakic (1988) has documented the connections between the anterior cingulate and some of the other areas known to be involved in attention, specifically the posterior parietal cortex and possibly the pulvinar nucleus; the anterior cingulate is also connected to the dorsolateral prefrontal cortex and parahippocampal cortex, which are involved in short-term visual-spatial and long-term object memory, respectively. In addition, within the cingulate sulcus, the anterior cingulate has reciprocal connections with primary and supplementary motor cortices (Barbas & Pandya, 1981; V. B. Brooks, 1986; Vogt & Miller, 1983), and the neurons there are sensitive to errors made during motor skill learning (V. B. Brooks, 1986).

Thus the anatomy and neurophysiology of the anterior cingulate suggest that it has a general role in attention. Posner and Petersen (1990) have termed anterior cingulate cortex "the anterior attention system," distinct from the "posterior attention system," which consists of posterior parietal cortex, pulvinar thalamus, and the superior colliculus (as summarized earlier). Posner and Petersen conceptualize the anterior system as a general purpose target detector, which gates various components of the posterior system as well as mediates attention to other functions such as language. Recent research suggests that the cingulate may be specialized not just for detecting targets, but for monitoring the relationship of stimuli to the goals of the individual (for discussion see Ochsner & Feldman-Barrett, in press). This is suggested by the finding that painful stimulation (e.g., Rainville et al., 1997) and attention to one's current emotional state activates the cingulate (Lane et al., 1998), and by event-related potential (Gehring et al., 1993) and functional magnetic resonance imaging studies (Carter et al., 1998) that show cingulate activity when participants make an error in simple reaction time tasks (cf. Brooks, 1986). It is possible that different areas of the anterior cingulate subserve slightly different, but related functions (Posner & DiGirolamo, 1998) and future work will serve to differentiate them.

3. Maintaining Vigilance

The brain stem and right hemisphere apparently play key roles in alerting and maintaining a vigilant, aroused, state (see Figure 2). Norepinephrine (NE) released by the locus coeruleus (a structure in the brain stem) apparently modulates the alert state (Aston-Jones, Foote, & Bloom, 1984), and right-hemisphere lesions lead to depletion of NE in *both* hemispheres (R. G. Robinson, 1985). Furthermore, NE strongly innervates the thalamus and parietal cortex (Morrison & Foote, 1986), and NE agonists (which facilitate the uptake of NE by receptors) may enhance processing in the parietal cortex, speeding the disengage operation (Clark et al., 1989) and thereby speeding the process of attentional selection (Posner & Petersen, 1990). Given these data, we would predict that patients with damage to the right—but not patients with damage to the left—hemisphere would have a deficit in alerting (Coslett, Bowers, & Heilman, 1987). As expected, Posner et al. (1987) found that patients with damage to the right parietal lobe had an increasingly smaller benefit from validly cued targets as the delay between cue and target increased: the patients were unable to keep attention engaged at the cued location over a short delay. Furthermore, PET studies have shown that regions of the right frontal lobe are activated during maintenance of a vigilant state (Corbetta et al., 1991, 1993).

B. Summary

Attention can be divided into three major systems, and at least one of these systems can in turn be divided into two subsystems (for a caveat, however, see Farah, 1994). The emerging theories have been built on a convergence of findings from different patient populations, brain-imaging techniques, and behavioral results from normal subjects. Advances thus made have the effect of systematizing and concretizing our notions of attention and "attentional resources" while at the same time providing a testable framework that makes contact with research in other domains. Such a framework provides a starting point for examining the roles of other brain areas in attention. For example, recent work indicates that the basal ganglia (Alexander, Crutcher, & DeLong, 1990; Clark et al., 1989; Jackson & Houghton, 1995) may modulate interactions between the anterior and posterior attention systems. As we shall see in the following section, attention plays an important role in perceiving the visual world.

III. HIGH-LEVEL VISION

A hallmark of the human visual system is the ability to recognize and identify objects presented in various orientations, from different perspectives, and in many different viewing conditions (such as poor lighting or partial occlusions; see Kosslyn, 1994, for a taxonomy of these abilities). It is useful to distinguish between low-level and high-level vision. Low-level visual processing is bottom-up, driven solely by properties of the perceptual input that strikes the retina. It is concerned with specifying information such as edges, regions of homogeneous color or texture, and depth. In contrast, high-level visual processing makes use of stored information to help one identify an object or use stored knowledge to guide reaching and navigation. We focus here on the mechanisms that underlie high-level vision, which are of most interest to cognitive scientists.

A. Subsystems of High-Level Vision

Kosslyn (1994; see also Kosslyn & Koenig, 1992) has argued that the system subserving high-level vision can be broken down into a set of major subsystems, each of which is instantiated in a discrete cortical area. These subsystems are illustrated in Figure 3. We briefly describe each subsystem below.

1. Visual Buffer

When viewing an object, information from the eyes is passed through the brain stem and thalamus to the primary visual cortex. From the primary visual cortex, information is distributed to over a dozen distinct visual areas in the occipital lobe (see Felleman & Van Essen, 1991). These areas are "retinotopically organized": their

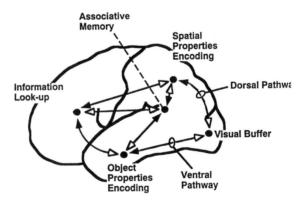

FIGURE 3   The functional architecture of high-level vision shown superimposed on a lateral view of the left cerebral hemisphere. A set of subsystems (described in text) allow one to recognize and identify objects. The putative location of each subsystem is indicated by a solid black circle. Arrows indicate possible directions of information flow between subsystems. Information flowing in a bottom-up fashion from lower to higher level areas follows paths marked with solid arrowheads. Information can also flow between higher level areas or in a top-down fashion from higher to lower level areas, following paths marked with open arrowheads.

spatial structure corresponds (approximately) to that of the retina itself; however, these maps typically are distorted so that there is a disproportionately large area devoted to the high-resolution central portion of the retina, and not all of the remainder of the visual field is represented equally well. A particularly vivid demonstration of the existence of such areas was reported by Tootell, Silverman, Switkes, and DeValois (1982), who had monkeys view a flashing circular spoked pattern after injection of radioactive sugar. The more a neuron fired while the animal watched the pattern, the more sugar the neuron took up, and hence the more radioactivity was taken up. The monkeys were then sacrificed and their cortices "developed" so that cells that had taken up the tracer were visible. Tootell et al. showed that in the primary visual cortex (in addition to other areas) there was a physical pattern of active cells laid out on the surface of the cortex in roughly the same shape as the spoked pattern; the map was distorted so that parts of the pattern that fell on or near the fovea received larger representation.

Kosslyn (1994) groups into a single functional structure the set of retinotopically mapped areas that work together to segregate figure from ground. This structure is called the "visual buffer." It is clear that this component can be decomposed into more specialized components; indeed, in the monkey some of the constituent areas include a preponderance of neurons that are sensitive to wavelength (area V4), others to motion (e.g., area MT), and so on. Nevertheless, patterns of activity in the set of areas that comprise the visual buffer preserve key features of the local geometry of images that strike the retina. Data from patients with occipital lobe damage who cannot see in particular regions of the visual field (e.g., Holmes, 1918), and more recent data from PET studies (e.g., Fox et al., 1986) confirm that this conclusion can be extended to the human brain.

2. Attention Window

There is much more information in the visual field than can be processed at any one time; hence some of this information must be selected over others. The mechanisms that orient attention (discussed in the previous section) not only shift one's body, head, and eyes so that a specific stimulus is fixed, but also can shift the locus of attention covertly. An internal "attention window" selects patterns in the visual buffer for further processing (for a review of supporting evidence, see Kosslyn, 1994). We are led to infer the existence of such a mechanism by the fact that subjects can covertly shift attention over an ionic image (Sperling, 1960) or display (e.g., Posner et al., 1980) to search for a particular item. Furthermore, A. M. Treisman and Gelade (1980) have shown that in some circumstances such covert attention is necessary to bind together the location and form of an object.

The position of the attention window gates the information that is passed along for further processing. For example, consider the results from an experiment reported by Moran and Desimone (1985). They first located neurons in monkeys that responded selectively to a certain stimulus (e.g., a vertical green bar). They then mapped out the receptive fields of these neurons; a receptive field is the area of space where a stimulus will drive the neuron. Moran and Desimone then rewarded the monkeys for responding to stimuli that appeared only in one quadrant of the receptive field of a cell. After such training the cell fired vigorously to stimuli in the reinforced quadrant and would still show some response to stimuli appearing in other quadrants—but responses to stimuli in nonreinforced quadrants were quickly squelched. In this case at least, it seems clear that the "engage" component of attention is operating via inhibition: stimuli in the unselected regions begin to evoke increased neural activity, but this activity is soon suppressed.

3. Ventral and Dorsal Systems

Information selected by the attention window is sent along two parallel cortical pathways, one specialized for processing the "object properties" of a stimulus, such as its shape and color, and the other specialized for processing the "spatial properties" of a stimulus, such as its location and orientation. Ungerleider and Mishkin (1982) term these the "what" and "where" pathways, or ventral and dorsal systems because they are located in the inferior temporal and posterior parietal lobes, respectively. This distinction between the ventral and dorsal systems is motivated by a number of different findings. In the monkey, removing the inferior temporal lobes devastates the ability to recognize shapes of objects but not the ability to recognize location; in contrast, removing the parietal lobes devastates the ability to recognize spatial locations but not the ability to recognize shape. For example, Ungerleider and Mishkin (1982) trained monkeys to select food hidden under one of two lids; if the monkeys had to select a lid with a particular pattern in order to get the food, inferior temporal lobe lesions impaired performance, whereas if they had to select the lid closest to a visual landmark, parietal lobe lesions impaired performance. Consistent with these findings in monkeys, damage to the posterior inferior temporal lobes of humans may impair perception of the visual form of objects, whereas parietal damage impairs orientation in space (e.g., Farah, 1990; Kosslyn, 1994; Levine, 1982).

In addition, single-cell recording studies in monkeys have found neurons in inferior temporal cortex that are sensitive to shape and color (Desimone, Albright, Gross, & Bruce, 1984; Gross, Desimone, Albright, & Schwartz, 1984; Maunsell & Newsome, 1987; Perrett et al., 1985). These neurons typically have very large receptive fields, and are relatively insensitive to an object's location (Gross & Mishkin, 1977); such cells may underlie our ability to recognize objects regardless of their spatial location (see also Kosslyn, 1994). In contrast, cells in posterior parietal cortex fire in response to the location, size, and motion of an object (Andersen, 1987; Andersen, Essick, & Siegel, 1985; Hyvarinen, 1982; Maunsell & Newsome, 1987).

In addition, PET studies of face comparison (Haxby et al., 1993), face recognition (Sergent, Ohta, & MacDonald, 1992), and object recognition (Kosslyn, Alpert et al., 1994) have documented activation in inferior portions of the temporal lobes. In contrast, PET studies that require encoding spatial relations have shown activation of the posterior parietal lobes (typically the inferior portion; e.g., Corbetta et al., 1993). Further support for this distinction comes from psychophysical studies in humans. These studies have shown that information about location and shape can independently influence perception (Sagi & Julesz, 1985; A. Treisman & Gormican, 1988).

The division of higher-level visual processing into two major processing streams makes sense from a computational point of view. As noted earlier, Rueckl et al.'s (1989) computational models showed that a single network that identified both an object's form and spatial location is substantially less efficient than two subnetworks, one for each computation (provided that enough resources were allocated to the subnetworks). Just as in humans, the single-network model needed to ignore location to recognize the shape in different locations, but needed to encode location to specify it in the output. Encoding object identity and spatial relations apparently were "computationally incompatible" processes, and hence were difficult to compute in the same system.

4. Associative Memory

Processing in the ventral system can allow one to *recognize* an object; recognition occurs when the shape matches the stored representation of another shape. But the ventral system is modality-specific: it only encodes visual input. One knows that an object is familiar after it has been recognized, but knows nothing else about it. In order to *identify* an object, one needs to access representations of its categories, its name, and various other kinds of nonvisual information. Identification can occur even if recognition is not very good, provided that the object has strong spatial cues (e.g., such as occurs when one encodes the size of an ant). Thus, information from the ventral (what) and dorsal (where) pathways must make contact with information stored in a long-term "associative memory" (which may or may not be further divisible into an "episodic" and "semantic" memory; for our purposes, we need not take a position on this issue). This memory system stores relations among object and spatial properties, as well as other attributes such as names and categories to which an object belongs. The same information in associative memory can be accessed when an object is recognized in any modality, as would occur if one heard a cat meow, felt it caress one's shin, or saw it walking towards one.

The literature is vague with respect to the locus of associative memory. However, the object and spatial properties systems are known to converge on the dorsolateral prefrontal cortex as well as regions of the parietal-temporal junction (Goldman-Rakic, 1988). The dorsolateral prefrontal regions appear to store information temporarily, as part of "working memory" (e.g., Goldman-Rakic, 1988), and hence this region is not a good candidate for the site of a long-term associative memory structure. In contrast, lesions in the region of the parietal-occipital junction can result in deficits in linguistic and semantic processing (e.g., see Geschwind, 1965).

5. Information Look-up

Under ideal conditions, one can identify an object via the route described thus far. However, if the input image of an object is degraded, or the object projects a novel shape (perhaps because it is contorted or seen from an unusual viewpoint), it may not correspond well to a representation in the ventral system. In such circumstances, the bottom-up input may lead only to a tentative hypothesis about an object's identity. In such straits, one can look up information in memory that would support this hypothesis, but has not yet been detected. This information can then guide one to search "top down" for this decisive part or characteristic (e.g., such as a particular dimple on the bottom of a Delicious apple; see Gregory, 1970; Kosslyn, 1994).

The frontal lobes are the likely locus of systems used to look up possibly diagnostic information in memory. PET studies have found activation of regions in the frontal lobe when subjects are retrieving from memory information about objects (Petersen et al., 1988; Tulving et al., 1994). In addition, retrieving stored information and holding it temporarily on-line are important for formulating and testing hypotheses, and a substantial literature indicates that lesions to the frontal lobe impair this ability. For example, the Wisconsin Card Sort test requires subjects to infer a rule that relates patterns on successively presented cards. This rule changes periodically, and patients with damaged frontal lobes perseverate, or get stuck, using one rule even when they realize that the rule has changed (e.g., Milner, 1964).

6. Attention Shifting

In the previous section we discussed the mechanisms underlying attention shifting. In addition to those mechanisms, the frontal lobes play a role in using information accessed from memory to shift attention. The frontal eye fields (also known as Area 8) direct voluntary eye movements, and frontal lesions disrupt systematic visual search and visual working memory (Alexander et al., 1990; Luria, 1980; D. L. Robinson & Petersen, 1986). Frontal lesions can also cause a form of unilateral neglect (Heilman & Valenstein, 1985), which might be expected given their rich connections with the anterior and posterior attention systems (Posner & Petersen, 1990).

Once one has shifted one's attention to the location where a diagnostic part or property should be located, that pattern is recognized and identified. If the expected part or property is present, one may have enough information to identify the object. If not, additional information may need to be encoded.

B. Summary and Extensions of the Theory

In summary, information striking the retina sets up a pattern of activation in a set of retinotopically mapped regions of cortex, which we call the visual buffer. Some of this information is selected by an attention window for further processing, and this information is passed to the object-properties and spatial-properties encoding systems, which operate in parallel. The outputs from these systems are sent to a long-term associative memory structure. If the set of information reaching associative memory is not consistent with the properties of a single object, the best matching description in associative memory is treated as an hypothesis. This hypothesis in turn guides a top-down search for a distinctive part or characteristic, which will either confirm or reject the hypothesis. The frontal lobes play a key role in this top-down search process; mechanisms implemented there retrieve information from memory, that guides attention to select disambiguating information. This process is repeated until the object is identified.

Each of the major component processes just described can in turn be divided further. For example, the dorsal (spatial-properties encoding) system consists of at least three distinct subsystems, which have different functions. The "spatiotopic mapping" subsystem converts the retinotopic coordinates of the visual buffer, which depend on where one's eye is positioned, to spatiotopic coordinates, which are anchored in external space. The "categorical spatial relations encoding subsystem" encodes spatial relations such as above/below, left/right, and on/off; this subsystem operates more effectively in the left than in the right cerebral hemisphere. And the "coordinate spatial relations encoding subsystem" encodes metric spatial relations, and it operates more effectively in the right cerebral hemisphere (see Hellige & Michimata, 1989; Kosslyn, 1987; Kosslyn et al., 1989; Laeng, 1994; but see also Sergent, 1991, versus Kosslyn, Chabris, Marsolek, & Koenig, 1992, and Cook, Fruh, & Landis, 1995, versus Kosslyn, Chabris, Jacobs, Marsolek, & Koenig, 1995). Similarly, the ventral (object-properties encoding) system can be divided into more specialized subsystems that extract distinctive features, that match such features to stored memories, and so on.

The theory of high-level vision is more detailed than the theory of attention, in large part because of the enormous volume of research on vision. What do such detailed theories buy us? For one, they allow us to interpret a large body of data, which addresses computational, neural, and behavioral properties. Because such a theory must accommodate a wide range of different types of findings, it is likely to have more general and powerful principles than a theory that is restricted to only one type of data. In addition, we have seen that a multicomponent theory of attention can help us understand the deficits exhibited by patients and make predictions about the roles components of the system should play in different tasks; the same is true for the theory of high-level vision (e.g., Kosslyn & Koenig, 1992). The following two examples illustrate the utility of such a theory.

Warrington and her colleagues have found that patients with posterior cortical lesions have difficulty recognizing objects that are seen from unusual (noncanonical) points of view, but not objects seen from a usual (canonical) perspective (e.g., Warrington & James, 1991; Warrington & Taylor, 1973, 1978). This finding makes sense within the framework just developed because posterior lesions may disrupt the spatial properties encoding system; damage to this system may impair one's ability to recognize objects shown in unusual views because their three-dimensional structure cannot be reconstructed. However, Warrington also found that patients with frontal lobe lesions were not impaired when asked to recognize objects seen from unusual views, and this finding is not as predicted by the theory: presumably objects shown from unusual views are difficult to recognize initially, and hence one would typically identify them only after engaging in top-down search—and this process is putatively guided by the frontal lobes.

Kosslyn et al. (1994) suggested that the reason Warrington and her colleagues did not find deficits in frontal lobe patients in this task was because they failed to record response times: One can locate a distinctive part or characteristic by random search, but this method would take longer than when top-down search can be employed (and hence one can use knowledge to search immediately for distinctive parts or characteristics). To test the hypothesis that the frontal lobes play a role in top-down search when objects are viewed from unusual perspectives, Kosslyn et al. used PET to compare the brain areas that were active when subjects identified objects that were seen from typical points of view with the areas that were active when they identified objects seen from unusual points of view. In one condition the subjects decided whether objects shown from a typical perspective matched an object name; in another condition the subjects performed the same task with objects seen from unusual perspectives. To isolate the brain areas that were activated selectively when the subjects identified objects seen from unusual points of view, which the theory predicts should reveal evidence of the role of the frontal lobes in top-down search, Kosslyn et al. subtracted cerebral blood flow recorded in the typical-view condition from that recorded in the unusual-view condition.

As predicted, dorsolateral prefrontal cortex in both hemispheres was more active when subjects identified objects seen from unusual points of view. This is good evidence that this region plays an important role in looking up information in memory to test hypotheses. The specific locus of activation was similar to that reported by Petersen et al. (1988) when subjects accessed information about uses and functions of objects. Furthermore, as was also expected, the set of brain areas predicted to be involved in object identification was also activated: the occipital cortex corresponding to the visual buffer was active, as were areas of the parietal lobe associated with shifting attention, and areas of the parietal lobe associated with encoding spatial properties (part of the dorsal system), and the inferior and middle temporal lobes (part of the ventral system). Moreover, an area at the occipital-temporal-parietal junction was activated, which may play a critical role in implementing associative memory.

A second example illustrates how knowledge of the systems involved in high-level vision can inform cross-domain hypothesis testing (Schacter, 1992). This study used the theory of visual perception to illuminate the nature of the neural mechanisms involved in visual mental imagery. Historically, much debate has surrounded the status of mental images; in recent years, much interest has focused on questions about the nature of the representation underlying imagery and the relation of imagery to perception. Marshaling evidence from various disciplines, Kosslyn (1980,

1994) argued that visual mental images are depictive (i.e., that they use space to represent space, thereby preserving geometric properties of imaged objects), and furthermore that such images correspond to patterns of activation in the visual buffer. In fact, according to this theory, imagery relies on many of the same neural mechanisms as high-level visual perception. Specifically, frontal lobe mechanisms access stored information from associative memory, which is used to activate visual information stored in the ventral system; this information in turn engenders an image proper by causing a pattern of activation in the visual buffer—this inverse mapping procedure apparently is necessary because visual memories are not stored as topographic representations, but rather as "population codes" (e.g., Fujita, Tanaka, Ito, & Cheng, 1992). Additional parts can be added to an imaged object by shifting the attention window over it, and activating stored representations of parts or properties so that they are positioned in the correct relative locations (see Kosslyn, 1994, for a detailed theory of how such processing may occur).

According to this theory, once the geometric properties of an object have been reconstructed in the visual buffer, the object properties and spatial properties of the imaged object can be reinspected. For example, once one has formed an image of a German shepherd dog, one can "see" the shape of its ears (an object property) and also determine which is longer, its tail or rear leg (a spatial property).

Some researchers have challenged this theory. Not only have some (e.g., Pylyshyn, 1973, 1981) suggested that image representations are language-like propositions (and the depictive properties evident to introspection are epiphenomenal, like the heat of a lightbulb while one is reading), but others have questioned the commonality of the neural systems underlying imagery and perception (e.g., Roland & Gulyas, 1994, versus Kosslyn & Ochsner, 1994). Kosslyn, Alpert et al. (1993) tested these claims using several PET studies of imagery. In one, the subjects closed their eyes and visualized letters at either small or large sizes. Not only was the topographically organized visual cortex activated during this task, but the locus of activation depended on the size of the imaged letters; indeed, the precise coordinates of the activated regions were close to what one would predict if subjects were actually viewing objects at the corresponding sizes.

Other studies in this series were designed to study image generation, the process of building up an image from stored information. The theory predicts that the same areas used to encode objects when top-down hypothesis testing is used should be activated when an image is built up from parts. In this case, instead of searching for a distinctive party or property at a particular location, one searches for the location in order to add another part or property to the image. Subjects viewed a 4 × 5 grid with a lowercase cursive letter printed underneath. An X mark occupied one cell of the grid. Subjects either simply saw the stimuli and responded (in a baseline condition), or visualized the corresponding uppercase letter in the grid and decided whether it would cover the X if it were actually in the grid. As predicted, a very similar set of brain areas was activated when visual mental images are formed and when top-down search is used in visual perception: when blood flow in the baseline condition was subtracted from blood flow in the imagery condition, very much the same areas were identified as were identified when blood flow in the typical-point-of-view condition was subtracted from blood flow in the unusual-point-of-view conditions in the object-identification task described above (the same subjects participated in both sets of tasks; see Kosslyn, Thompson, & Alpert, 1997). The fact that such similar patterns of activity were observed in such seemingly different tasks (evaluating names of pictures versus visualizing letters in grids) is strong evidence that the theory is on the right track.

In the following section we will consider how research on memory reveals additional properties of some systems used in both vision and imagery.

IV. MEMORY

Memory allows us to use knowledge gained from previous experience to guide current and future actions, and is the cornerstone of many cognitive processes. Indeed, memory is crucial for identifying and recognizing objects that our attentional systems have selected for further processing. Memory, like visual perception and attention, is accomplished by a set of subsystems working together. One not only can store and recall the meanings of and associations among words, images, and concepts, but also can recognize objects and encode relationships among particular stimuli and visceral or motor responses. Each of these abilities is accomplished primarily by a distinct system or set of systems. In this section we consider more fully the memory encoding and storage systems that play critical roles in visual perception and attention, and we also consider memory systems involved in encoding and storing other types of information. The view presented here draws on and is consistent with aspects of many contemporary theories of memory (e.g., Schacter, 1990; Squire, 1992), but is derived primarily from the analysis offered by Kosslyn and Koenig (1992). The functional architecture of memory is illustrated in Figure 4.

A. Perceptual Encoding Subsystems

In order to recognize an object we must have previously stored a representation of its object properties. These representations are stored in perceptual encoding subsystems that store the structural and feature properties of modality-specific inputs (Kosslyn & Koenig, 1992; Schacter, 1990). Examples are the object-properties-encoding ventral system and spatial-properties-encoding dorsal systems discussed above, although every sensory modality has its own perceptual encoding subsystems.

1. Object Properties Encoding Subsystem

After initial processing by the visual buffer in the occipital lobe, information is passed along to the object properties encoding subsystem in the inferior temporal

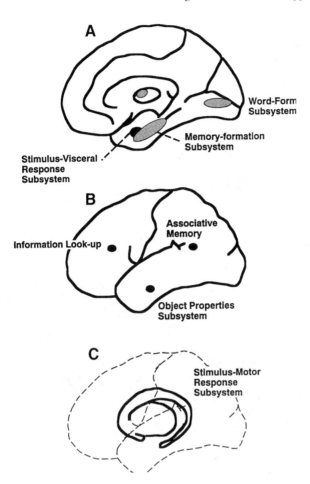

FIGURE 4 The functional architecture of memory shown superimposed on (A) a medial view of the right hemisphere, (B) a lateral view of the left cerebral hemisphere, and (C) a transparent view of the left hemisphere. A set of subsystems (described in text) encode and/or store different types of information. The putative neural locus of each subsystem is indicated.

lobe (see Figure 4B). Research in monkeys has revealed some of the basic characteristics of representations in this subsystem. Neurons in this area are sensitive to the form, color, and shape, but not orientation or size of objects (Desimone et al., 1984; Gross et al., 1984; Gross & Mishkin, 1977; Maunsell & Newsome, 1987; Perrett et al., 1985), and lesions impair memory for the form of an object but not memory for its relationship to other objects in space (Levine, 1982; Pohl, 1972; Ungerleider & Mishkin, 1982).

Much has been learned about the nature of object representations in normal human subjects from studies of priming. In a typical priming task, subjects first are shown a set of objects or words and asked to make some simple decision about their perceptual or semantic attributes; this task requires them to look at each stimulus and produces an "incidental" memory representation. Later, degraded versions of these stimuli are presented along with degraded versions of new objects, and the subjects are asked to identify, read, or make some decision about them; priming is assessed by measuring the gain in performance for the previously seen stimuli compared to the new ones. The notion is that when a stimulus is encoded initially, one or more representations are activated in memory; this activation decays rather slowly, and hence subjects can subsequently encode the stimulus more easily if it appears soon enough after it was shown initially. Similar to the neurophysiological findings in monkeys, studies of priming for familiar objects (e.g., a shoe) have shown that primed identification of pictures is long-lasting (Cave & Squire, 1992; Mitchell & Brown, 1988) and is unaffected by study-to-test changes in object size or reflection in both normal subjects (Biederman & Cooper, 1992) and amnesics (Cave & Squire, 1992). Although we will discuss amnesia in more detail below, this latter finding is important because it indicates that perceptual representations can guide performance even when they are not accessed consciously.

Schacter, Cooper, and their colleagues (e.g., Schacter, Cooper, & Delaney, 1990) have used an object decision priming task to study the nature of the representations stored in memory. In their task, subjects decide whether drawings depict structurally possible or impossible three-dimensional objects. These objects are novel, and hence a new representation must be encoded for all of them during the initial exposure phase; priming is measured by comparing the errors when previously shown and new objects are subsequently presented very briefly, and the subjects are asked to determine whether the object is structurally possible or impossible. Priming in this task is found only for possible objects (Schacter, Cooper, & Delaney, 1990), is preserved in amnesics (Schacter, Cooper, Tharan, & Rubens, 1991), and depends upon encoding the global three-dimensional structure of the object when it was first shown (Schacter, Cooper, Delaney, Peterson, & Tharan, 1991). Thus it appears that representations in the object-properties encoding subsystem incorporate regularities that characterize actual objects. As one would expect given the properties of interior temporal lobe neurons in monkeys, priming in this task is not affected by changes in the size of an object or changes in the direction it faces; however, priming is reduced by changes in orientation on the picture plane (Cooper, Schacter, Ballesteros, & Moore, 1992; Schacter, Cooper, & Treadwell, 1993; for a review and interpretation of these and similar findings, see chapter 5 of Kosslyn, 1994).

The fact that the object-properties encoding subsystem cannot represent impossible objects easily does not imply that it can only represent well-formed objects. Rather, it appears to store perceptual representations of objects and parts of objects. For example, when a subject is shown a picture of an object that has had many of its recognizable features eliminated, and the global structure of the object itself is very difficult to recover based on this picture, subjects show greater subsequent priming for that picture of the fragmented object than for a picture of the whole, undegraded object—even though the picture of the whole object is in some sense "less degraded" (Srinivas, 1993).

We earlier distinguished between modality-specific perceptual representations that underlie recognition and amodal representations in "associative memory." If this distinction is correct, then we might predict that brain damage can disrupt one structure while leaving the other intact. And in fact, when the cortical areas that implement the object-properties encoding subsystems are damaged, subjects may have a "visual object agnosia" (see Farah, 1990; Kosslyn & Koenig, 1992): They cannot identify the object visually, but can identify it via other sensory modalities (e.g., by touching it). This disorder was originally characterized as "mind blindness." Such damage impairs recognition of objects, but not access to their semantic attributes. In contrast, selective brain damage may produce the opposite pattern of deficits: one may lose the ability to access semantic, but not perceptual characteristics of objects. The neuropsychological literature includes many reports of patients with cortical lesions who perform normally when asked to match or copy pictures, to decide whether a design represents a real object or is nonsensical, and similar visual tasks, but are impaired when asked to display knowledge of the semantic attributes of pictured objects, such as naming or describing an object's function (e.g., Farah, 1990; Riddoch & Humphreys, 1987; Warrington & Taylor, 1978; see Kohn & Friedman, 1986, for analogous deficits in audition).

2. A Word Form System?

Recognizing letters or words is similar to recognizing objects, but is not exactly the same: Compared to objects, words are defined solely by patterns of lines whose meaning has been arbitrarily assigned; recognizing them does not require computation of global, three-dimensional structure, and for many adults words are more familiar than are most objects. Such observations have led some to argue that word forms are stored in a distinct visual memory (e.g., J. L. McClelland & Rumelhart, 1981; Petersen & Fiez, 1993; Petersen, Fox, Synder, & Raichle, 1990). It is possible that frequent exposure to words biases the object-properties encoding subsystem to dedicate part of its structure to encoding words; if so, we might expect word recognition to involve a brain area distinct from those used in object recognition. Consistent with this view, Petersen et al. (1990) found that both real words and nonwords that could be words (according to the rules of English) activated an area of left medial extrastriate cortex; this area is distinct from areas of the temporal lobe that are activated when one recognizes objects or faces (Kosslyn, Alpert et al., 1994; Sergent et al., 1992). In addition, some brain-damaged patients have difficulty accessing word meanings but can recognize word forms and identify objects (Warrington & Shallice, 1980). Thus, part of the object properties pathway may be specialized for representing highly familiar words; we do not yet know, however, whether this pathway deals with all highly familiar stimuli, or words per se. Various researchers have posited a *word form subsystem* (see Figure 4A) that represents the perceptual or orthographic properties of words (e.g., Schacter, 1990; Warrington & Shallice, 1980).

Priming studies have revealed properties of the representations of word shapes in memory. These tasks often require the subjects first to view a set of words, and later to complete three-letter "word stems" or fragments with the first words that come to mind. Alternatively, a subject might be asked to identify a briefly presented word. The increased probability of completing the fragments to form one of the initially seen words or of identifying the briefly presented stimulus is the measure of priming. By and large, the findings with these tasks dovetail nicely with the findings for objects, though there are some important differences. As has been reported with object priming, word priming is long lasting (MacAndrews, Glisky, & Schacter, 1987; Sloman, Hayman, Ohta, Law, & Tulving, 1988), and semantic encoding during the initial exposure phase (e.g., having the subjects judge the number of meanings of each word on the list) enhances recall, but has little or no effect upon priming (e.g., Graf, Squire, & Mandler, 1984; Jacoby & Dallas, 1981; H. L. I. Roediger, Weldon, Stadler, & Riegler, 1992). Moreover, priming is substantially reduced when the presentation modality is changed (e.g., auditory to visual; Jacoby & Dallas, 1981; H. L. Roediger & Blaxton, 1987). Like objects, studies of word priming have shown that the object properties subsystem encodes highly specific features of perceptual input. For example, changes in typefont or letter case can reduce priming (e.g., Hayman & Tulving, 1989; Jacoby & Hayman, 1987; H. L. Roediger & Blaxton, 1987), but usually only when the incidental encoding task (administered when subjects are given a list of words at the outset of the experiment) focuses the subjects on the perceptual characteristics of the words (e.g., counting the number of T-junctions in the letters of a word; Graf & Ryan, 1990).

Additional findings suggest that the enhanced priming when the identical form is presented during the initial exposure phase and the test phase arises from a particular type of word form system, which is localized in the right cerebral hemisphere. Marsolek, Kosslyn, and Squire (1992) found that changes in typefont had no effect upon word-stem completion priming when word stems were presented to the left hemisphere at test (this is done by having the subject stare straight ahead and flashing the stem to the left or right—which causes the input to be encoded initially by the right or left hemisphere, respectively). In contrast, preserving the typefont enhanced the amount of priming when word stems were presented to the right hemisphere at test. This led Marsolek et al. to infer that a right-hemisphere system stores form-specific representations, and a left-hemisphere system stores more abstract visual form representations. Furthermore, PET investigations of word-stem completion priming have found a decrease in activation of right extrastriate occipital cortex when typefont is unchanged between study and test, which may reflect that priming has facilitated processing (Squire et al., 1992). Similar studies of object priming have yet to be reported.

B. Associative Memory

As discussed earlier, all perceptual encoding systems send input to associative memory (see Figures 3 and 4B; see Kosslyn & Koenig, 1992, for extended discussion). Three characteristics of associative memory are of interest in the context of memory per se. First, although it encodes relations among perceptual representations, associative memory represents this information in an abstract or propositional format. These propositions can specify complex relations such as "is a," "has a," and so on. These relations are qualitatively distinct and often abstract, and so could not be implemented by simple direct connections between perceptual representations.

Second, relations in associative memory appear to involve pointers back to representations in the perceptual subsystems, and in that sense have "meaning." These pointers are bidirectional, allowing perceptual input to activate associative memory, and vice-versa. Thus associative memory is distinct from the systems that provide it input, and as one would expect, dissociations between impaired access to semantics and intact access to perceptual features, and vice versa, can be found in different sensory modalities (e.g., Schacter, Cooper, Delaney, Peterson, & Tharan, 1991; Warrington & Taylor, 1978). In addition, patients with category-specific associative memory deficits have been described (e.g. Hart, Berndt, & Caramazza, 1985; McCarthy & Warrington, 1986); for example, a patient might be unable to identify pictures of living things, but has no trouble identifying nonliving things. Although such findings may sometimes reflect damage to associative memory per se, in many cases the deficits may reflect disruptions of the pointers from associative memory to perceptual memories. Careful analysis of these deficits and results from neural network models has revealed that such deficits may arise from damage to modality-specific representational systems, rather than damage to a special "living things" memory system (Farah & McClelland, 1991).

Third, it is not clear where in the brain associative memory is implemented. Although the occipital-temporal-parietal area appears to play a critical role in associative memory (e.g., Geschwind, 1965; Kosslyn & Koenig, 1992), deficits in associative memory have been described after lesions to many different brain areas (e.g., Hart et al., 1985; Tulving, Hayman, & MacDonald, 1991). A problem in localizing this subsystem is that activation of areas associated with semantic processing may reflect either the memory structure itself or the processes that access it.

C. Information Look-up Subsystem

When encoding new information into memory or looking up information to help identify an object, generate a mental image, or answer a question, one can use the look-up subsystem to access associative memory. As noted earlier, the frontal lobes play a key role in implementing this subsystem (see Figures 3 and 4B). PET investigations have shown that various tasks that involve accessing semantic information in memory activate the left frontal lobe; such tasks include verb generation (Petersen

et al., 1988), verbal fluency (Frith, Friston, Liddle, & Frackowiak, 1991), completion of nonstudied word stems (Buckner et al., 1996), image generation (Kosslyn,
Alpert et al., 1993), and identifying objects seen from unusual views (Kosslyn et
al., 1994). Left frontal lesions may also impair short-term semantic priming that
depends on the strength of association between word pairs (Milberg & Blumstein,
1981). In addition, accessing semantic information in memory often activates the
left anterior cingulate cortex, part of the anterior attention system discussed earlier
(e.g., Frith et al., 1991; Kapur et al., 1994; Kosslyn, Daly et al., 1993; Petersen et al.,
1988).

In some situations, however, the right-frontal lobe—not the left—is activated
when people access information in memory. Retrieval of episode-specific memories for auditory sentences (Tulving, Kapur, Markowitsch et al., 1994), words from
three-letter cues (Buckner et al., in press; Squire et al., 1992), faces (Haxby et al.,
1993), or scents (Jones-Gotman, Zaforre, Evans, & Meyer, 1993) activate the right
frontal lobe. Kosslyn (1994) suggests that different look-up subsystems are implemented in the left and right frontal lobes, which access categorical information
(such as that specified by words) and specific information (such as specific events),
respectively.

D. Memory Formation Subsystem

When the term *memory* is used in common parlance, it usually refers to memory for
specific events (a person who has difficulty encoding or retrieving such memories is
often referred to as having a "bad memory"). We can encode various types of new
information: new perceptual representations, new associations between items in associative memory, new associations between items in associative memory and perceptual representations, and all of this information is often embedded in a particular spatio-temporal context. How do we flexibly and quickly encode these new memories?

The ability to store new facts in memory depends upon the integrity of the diencephalon, and medial temporal lobe structures that include the mammillary bodies,
the hippocampus, and the surrounding perirhinal, entorhinal, and parahippocampal cortices (although findings in monkeys suggest that the contributions to memory of these latter four areas may differ in interesting ways; for discussion, see Gaffan
& Murray, 1992; Squire, 1992; Zola-Morgan, Squire, Amaral, & Suzuki, 1989). The
hippocampal region and medial dorsal thalamic nucleus, part of the diencephalon,
are indicated in Figure 4A. The hippocampal formation receives inputs from a variety of cortical areas in the frontal, parietal, and temporal lobes, and seems ideally
positioned to encode relations among cues and context (Squire, 1992). Indeed, hippocampal lesions impair a rat's ability to learn to navigate in a water maze or eight-
arm radial maze, to learn to discriminate among locations containing food, and to
acquire conditioned responses that are specific to a spatial context (Jarrard, 1993).
Similar lesions impair a monkey's ability to recall a rewarded object across delays
lasting from minutes to days (Squire, 1992).

Results from studies of brain-damaged humans converge with the findings from nonhuman animals. In a series of classic studies of patient H. M., Milner and her colleagues (e.g. Milner, Corkin, & Teuber, 1968; Scoville & Milner, 1957) discovered that bilateral medial temporal lobe removal caused permanent anterograde amnesia (i.e., disrupted memory for new events) and slight retrograde amnesia (i.e., disrupted memory for past events), but spared short-term memory and prior semantic knowledge. After his operation, H. M. could not remember events beyond a few minutes; for example, after more than a few minutes, he would consistently forget ever having met the experimenter. Squire and his colleagues later showed that damage confined exclusively to the CA1 region of the hippocampus causes marked memory impairment, but not as severe as that of H. M. (who had complete removal of the medial temporal area; see Squire, 1992; Squire, Amaral, & Press, 1990; Zola-Morgan, Squire, & Amaral, 1986). Memory deficits have been found following CA1 damage in rats (Auer, Jensen, & Whishaw, 1989) and monkeys (Zola-Morgan & Squire, 1990a).

The memory formation subsystem is needed for normal encoding of information into associative memory: amnesics typically cannot acquire new semantic information (e.g., Rozin, 1976; Squire & Shimamura, 1986), such as word meanings (Gabrieli, Cohen, & Corkin, 1988) or paired associates (D. N. Brooks & Baddeley, 1976). If they do acquire semantic information, it is usually tied to specific aspects of the learning environment, and occurs only after a slow and laborious training (Glisky & Schacter, 1988; MacAndrews et al., 1987; Schacter, Harbluk, & McLachlan, 1984; Shimamura & Squire, 1987, 1988; Tulving et al., 1991). In contrast, damage to the medial temporal lobe does not substantially impair encoding of representations by the perceptual encoding subsystems: amnesic patients show normal priming on both visual object (e.g., Cave & Squire, 1992; Schacter, Cooper, Tharan, & Rubens, 1991) and visual word and nonword priming tasks (word identification, Cermak, Talbot, Chandler, & Wolbarst, 1985; word stem completion, Graf et al., 1984; word fragment completion, Tulving et al., 1991; Warrington & Wieskrantz, 1974; nonwords, Cermak, Verfaellie, Milberg, Letourneau, & Blackford, 1991; Haist, Musen, & Squire, 1991; see, however Cermak et al., 1985; Smith & Oscar-Berman, 1990).

One important aspect of the memory encoding subsystem is that it takes time to complete the encoding process. Damage to the hippocampus causes a temporally graded retrograde amnesia: there is a large loss of memory when the lesions occur soon after learning, but memory loss tapers off as the time between learning and lesion increases (Kim & Fanselow, 1992; MacKinnon & Squire, 1989; Zola-Morgan & Squire, 1990b). Computational models of the hippocampus have provided insights into why such a delay might be necessary for memory encoding. J. L. McClelland, McNaughton and O'Reilly (1994; see also Gluck & Meyers, 1993) argue that typically we do not want the influence of any one learning event to have a large effect on representations in associative memory. Rather, it would be more useful to have the connections among items in an associative memory network change slowly and gradually as a function of events that recur in time. But we still want to be able to take a quick "snapshot" of the environment, so that relations among cues can be encoded if necessary. The memory encoding subsystem takes this "snapshot," which allows rapid encoding and orthogonalization (i.e., creation of distinct representations) of memories in a sparse, compact code. This code specifies spatial, temporal, and other contextual variables and can later be used to "train" cortical areas to store a structural representation of the information. This training is slow in order to reduce interference among cortically based memory representations (cf. McCloskey & Cohen, 1989).

This model accounts for findings of retrograde amnesia in humans and animals following damage to the hippocampus: these memory problems arise because recently acquired memory traces have yet to be stored as structural representations in the cortex. This model also suggests why it is so difficult for amnesics to acquire new semantic information: the connections in associative memory change only very slowly in the face of perceptual input without training by the memory formation subsystem. It is also possible that loss of an orthogonalization process underlies some aspects of human amnesia.

E. Stimulus–Motor Response Connection Subsystem

We not only can store representations of facts, but also can store relatively direct connections between stimuli and motor responses. Stimulus–response (SR) learning is akin to behaviorist notions of a direct link between eliciting stimuli and consequent actions without any mediating internal representations (Skinner, 1957). Typically these associations are built over the course of many repeated pairings of a stimulus and a response. A particularly clear example of such learning was provided by Mishkin and his colleagues (Mishkin & Appenzeller, 1987). These researchers presented monkeys with an object discrimination task in which pairs of items were presented once per day for a period of about 4 weeks. Upon presentation of each pair the monkey had to choose the item that was consistently paired with the reward. Not only could monkeys with lesioned hippocampi acquire the correct response, eventually choosing the rewarded object in each pair, but they did so at the same rate as normal monkeys. The memory formation subsystem is not necessary for acquiring this sort of information.

This object discrimination task involves a consistent mapping of a single stimulus onto a response and depends upon integrity of a set of subcortical structures known as the neostriatum (often simply called the striatum). The striatum has two parts, the caudate and the putamen (both of which are parts of the basal ganglia), which have connections to the perceptual encoding systems and motor output systems (see Figure 4C). Lesions of the striatum impair learning of brightness discriminations, avoidance learning, reversal learning, and alternation (McDonald & White, 1993).

It is important to note that tasks that tap the stimulus–motor response subsystem can be disrupted independently of tasks that tap the memory formation subsystems, and vice versa (this type of pattern of results is called a "double dissociation"; Teuber, 1955). Researchers have contrasted performance in two types of tasks, which superficially may appear similar: In the win–stay task, a rat must learn to return to a single arm of an eight-arm radial maze in order to receive food; in the win–shift task, food is available in any of the eight arms, and a rat must learn to visit each arm only once, noting the spatial location of each arm visited so as not to visit it a second time. Lesions of the stratum impair learning in the win–stay task, but not the win–shift task, and fornix lesions (disrupting input to the hippocampus) have the opposite effect (Packard, Hirsh, & White, 1989; Packard & McGaugh, 1992). Thus, it appears that the striatum is necessary for coding consistent S-R mappings built up over time.

The stimulus-motor response subsystem may also be involved in the control of sequences of successive S-R mappings. Striatal lesions can disrupt production of sequences of rat instinctual grooming behaviors, although the individual constituent movements can still be elicited (Berridge & Whishaw, 1992). Furthermore, neurophysiological recordings of activity in the striatum have revealed that such neurons are active only when the animal produces grooming sequences (Aldridge, Berridge, Herman, & Zimmer, 1993).

Similarly, humans with Parkinson's disease (which reflects impaired functioning of the striatum, due to a depletion of the neurotransmitter dopamine) also have deficits in sequential processing, such as the timing of vocal utterances and syntactic comprehension (Lieberman et al., 1992). In addition, patients with Huntington's disease (caused by degeneration of the striatum) may show deficits in a variety of tasks that require either acquisition of simple S-R mappings or acquisition of sequences of such mappings. In contrast, amnesics do not show such impairments. For example, in the serial reaction time (SRT) task subjects press keys in response to visual cues that appear in one of four locations. Cues may appear at these locations in either a random order or in a repeating sequence (usually 10 items long). Learning is indexed by a decrease in reaction time as more trials are completed, and acquisition of the sequence is shown by greater improvement in repeating blocks as compared to random blocks of trials. Amnesics acquire the sequence normally, but patients with Huntington's disease fail to show this learning (e.g., Knopman & Nissen, 1991). A similar dissociation is revealed by a weight judgment task, in which prior exposure to a set of weights biases subsequent judgments of them: amnesics show normal biases, whereas patients with Huntington's disease do not (Heindel, Salmon & Butters, 1991). Moreover, patients with Huntington's disease are also impaired on the pursuit rotor task in which subjects must hold a stylus on a disk located near the edge of a rapidly rotating platter (Heindel, Salmon, Shults, Walicke, & Butters, 1989). Abnormal metabolic activity in the striatum has been linked to psychiatric syndromes involving repetitive thoughts or actions, such as obsessive-compulsive disorder (Rauch et al., 1997) and Tourette's syndrome (Witelson, 1994).

F. Stimulus-Visceral Response Subsystem

In some situations it is necessary to form an association between an external, neutral stimulus and an internal state evoked by an event with negative consequences. This type of learning is different from that involved in S-R learning because the association is formed between a stimulus and a physiological state resulting from a stimulus, rather than between a stimulus and an overt motor response. For example, in the fear-conditioning paradigm a rat is shocked following presentation of a light or tone (J. LeDoux & Hirst, 1986). Over time, the rat comes to exhibit fearful behavior to the light alone, as evidenced by changes in sympathetic and parasympathetic nervous system activity when the light is presented. Lesions of the striatum do not impair conditioning in this paradigm, whereas lesions to the central and lateral nuclei of the amygdala do (see Figure 4A for location of this subsystem). These two amygdaloid nuclei have proven crucial for learning to occur in a variety of tasks that involve association of an aversive stimulus and a neutral stimulus, such as fear-potentiated startle (Davis, 1992), passive avoidance (Cahill & McGaugh, 1990), and conditioning of autonomic responses such as heart rate or blood pressure (Kapp, Whalen, Supple, & Pascoe, 1992). What is common across all these tasks, even though the motor responses may differ, is the link between a stimulus and a visceral, internal state.

This subsystem is also important for acquiring associations between stimuli and appetitive events, though different amygdaloid nuclei may be involved (basolateral and lateral; Everitt et al., 1992; McDonald & White, 1993). Thus, damage to the amygdala may impair acquisition of a variety of conditioned reward tasks in which a neutral stimulus is paired with reward. McDonald and White (1993) showed that rats with lesions of the amygdala, but not the striatum or fornix, were impaired in learning a task in which rats were allowed to feed in different, although perceptually similar, locations whenever a light was present. Other rats were fed only in dark areas. Learning was assessed by the amount of time spent in the lighted or darkened area that had been associated with food. In this task, the only memory that could underlie the animals' preference was the association of the cue and the internal state generated by food. The amygdala lesions did not impair learning of the win-stay or win-shift tasks, although performance in these tasks is impaired following striatal and hippocampal damage, respectively.

G. Summary and Extensions

Like other complex mental abilities, memory is subserved by a host of specialized subsystems. Perceptual encoding subsystems represent modality-specific inputs at a presemantic level; associative memory stores relational, identifying, and classifying information in a propositional format; information look-up subsystems access information in associative memory; the memory formation subsystem enables flexible, rapid encoding of episodes and events; and the stimulus-motor response and stimulus-visceral response subsystems encode pairings of stimuli and behaviors or stimuli and physiological states.

This conceptualization of memory not only allows one to account for a wide range of experimental findings, but also leads to predictions that follow from specific interactions among different subsystems. For example, consider a task that is impaired following hippocampal damage, but may involve the stimulus-motor response subsystem as well. In the negative patterning paradigm, an animal is rewarded if it presses a bar when a tone is presented or when a light is on. However, the animal is not rewarded if it presses when the tone and light appear simultaneously. Normal animals learn not to respond when both cues are present. Hippocampal lesioned animals, however, cannot withhold responses to the tone-light pairing, although they respond normally to each of the stimuli in isolation (McDonald and White, 1993). Presumably, the intact stimulus-motor response system mediates responses to the individual stimuli, but the hippocampus is necessary to encode the association between the two simultaneous cues and the lack of reward. If this account is correct, then animals with striatal lesions should also show impairments on this task, even when only a single stimulus is present. Future work may address this prediction.

Similar analyses may inform and motivate research with human subjects. Most of the work on the learning of S-R sequences in the SRT in humans has employed sequences in which responses predict each other with unequal probability. For example, key 1 might be followed by key 2 with .67 probability, by key 3 with .33 probability, and by key 4 with .00 probability. Having some responses predict the occurrence of others may reduce the number of S-R mappings that must be acquired. These probabilistically *unbalanced* sequences are the type that patients with striatal damage have been shown to be unable to acquire (Knopman & Nissen, 1991), which has led to the conclusion that the striatum alone may participate in sequence learning and performance.

However, some researchers suggest that the memory formation subsystem may participate in some forms of sequence learning that cannot be learned on the basis of predictive S-R chains but require hierarchical grouping of response sequence clusters (Keele & Curran, 1995; but see also Keele et al., 1998). It is possible that a stimulus-motor response subsystem may allow expression of only a few simple S-R chains, and when more complex mappings are required the memory formation subsystem is recruited as necessary (cf. Squire & Frambach, 1990).

Finally, consider an example in which a cognitive neuroscientific view of memory can lead one to infer properties of previously unstudied subsystems, which in turn may lead to novel results that can be explained with reference back to the systems that generated the initial hypotheses. This process is being played out in investigations of the auditory perceptual encoding subsystem. Given that there are modality-specific, cortically based systems that represent the structure and form of objects and words at a "presemantic" level (i.e., the level of recognition, as opposed to identification), we expect similar systems to exist in various sensory modalities.

Indeed, neuropsychological and PET research has shown that encoding phonological information involves the posterior superior temporal lobe (Ellis & Young, 1988; Petersen et al., 1988).

Such findings led Schacter and Church (1992) to infer the existence of an auditory word form subsystem that is dedicated to representing the acoustic, but not the semantic, properties of spoken words. Support for this claim comes from studies of priming on tests in which subjects identify perceptually degraded spoken words that have had their low frequencies removed, and in tests of auditory stem completion, in which subjects complete an auditory stem to form the first word that comes to mind. Consistent with the notion that auditory priming is modality-specific and presemantic, word identification priming is reduced when the presentation modality is changed from the initial exposure to the test phases of the experiment (A. G. R. McClelland & Pring, 1991); moreover, such priming is not affected by semantic encoding tasks that enhance explicit memory (Schacter & Church, 1992). Such priming is also specific to the acoustic properties of the input. Church and Schacter (1994) found that changing the emotional tone, gender, or fundamental frequency of a speaker's voice from exposure to test phases reduces priming. Furthermore, auditory priming is preserved in amnesia (Schacter, Church, & Treadwell, 1994) as well as in patients who suffer from word meaning deafness (Schacter, McGlynn, Milberg, & Church, 1993).

V. CONCLUSIONS

In this chapter we have tried to illustrate the ways in which cognitive neuroscientific analyses make use of multiple, converging streams of evidence to inform theory construction. There are five general points about cognitive functions revealed by this analysis:

1. Many of the subsystems that confer a specific ability such as attention, vision, or memory, can interact in multiple ways.
2. These systems consist of networks that are implemented in distinct brain areas.
3. Each area carries out computations that can be characterized specifically enough to be implemented in a simulation model.
4. Each system processes information both serially and in parallel.
5. Processing is highly interactive, with higher-level areas sending feedback to lower level areas.

At the present stage of research, different types of data carry more or less weight in different domains. For instance, in the study off visual perception, theorizing rests in large part on the results of studies of monkeys. Only recently have neuroimaging studies begun to confirm and extend some of the basic findings from the animal literature; theories have also gained leverage by attempting to explain the effects of focal brain damage in humans. In the case of attention, recent neuroimaging findings are beginning to gather force as well, complementing early work with brain-damaged patients. And in the study of memory, the multiple systems account offered here is guided primarily by work with human subjects, using data from animals to help address specific questions.

There are perhaps two major reasons for the differences in approaches among the fields. First, the study of each topic is strongly influenced by the first disciplines to make significant contributions to theory in that area. Second, and this is especially true for study of various forms of attention and memory, we currently do not have the techniques to study some human abilities, such as priming, in animal populations. But the day is still young. The term *cognitive neuroscience* was only coined in 1970 (Kosslyn & Andersen, 1993) and the Cognitive Neuroscience Society had its inaugural meeting in 1994. Despite its relative infancy, the field is making steady progress in many areas, and the rapid development and increased availability of new imaging techniques will help to address the functional anatomy of abilities.

This chapter has surveyed theoretical advances in only a handful of areas that currently are being explored from a cognitive neuroscience perspective. Emotion, language, categorization and reasoning, movement, and audition are but a few of the topic domains in which theories of this sort are now being advanced (Gazzaniga, 1995; Kosslyn & Koenig, 1992; LeDoux & Hirst, 1986; Ochsner & Schacter, in press; Weingartner & Lister, 1991). Current work is extending the cognitive neuroscience approach to problems of interest to social psychologists, such as attitude change (Lieberman, in press; Lieberman et al., 1999; Ochsner & Lieberman, 1999). We anticipate that future work will only broaden the horizons of these exciting research programs.

Acknowledgments

Completion of this article was supported by a National Science Foundation Graduate Research Fellowship awarded to K. N. Ochsner, and National Institutes of Health grant NINDS 2 PO1 17778-09 and AFOSR grant F49620-99-1-0114 awarded to S. M. Kosslyn. We thank Daniel L. Schacter and Tim Curran for helpful discussion of relevant issues.

References

Aldridge, J. W., Berridge, K. C., Herman, M., & Zimmer, L. (1993). Neuronal coding of serial order: Syntax of grooming in the neostriatum. *Psychological Science, 4*, 391–395.

Alexander, G. E., Crutcher, M. D., & DeLong, M. A. (1990). Basal ganglia-thalamocortical circuits: Parallel substrates for motor, oculomotor, "prefrontal" and "limbic" functions. In H. B. M. Uylings, C. G. Van Eden, J. P. C. De Bruin, M. A. Corner, & M. G. P. Feenstra (Eds.), *Progress in brain research* (pp. 119–146). Amsterdam: Elsevier.

Allport, A. (1992). Attention and control: Have we been asking the wrong questions? A critical review of twenty five years. In D. E. Meyer & S. Kornblum (Eds.), *Attention and performance XIV* (pp. 187–213). Cambridge, MA: MIT Press.

Amaral, D. G., Price, J. L., Pitkanen, A., & Carmichael, S. T. (1992). Anatomical organization of the primate amygdaloid complex. In J. P. Aggleton (Ed.), *The amygdala: neurobiological aspects of emotion, memory, and mental dysfunction* (pp. 1–66). New York: Willey Liss.

Ambros-Ingerson, J., Granger, R., & Lynch, G. (1990). Simulation of paleocortex performs hierarchical clustering. *Science, 247,* 1344–1348.

Andersen, R. A. (1987). Inferior parietal lobule function in spatial perception and visuomotor integration. In F. Plum (Ed.), *Handbook of physiology* (Sect. 1, Vol. 5, pp. 483–518). Bethesda, MD: American Physiological Society.

Andersen, R. A., Essick, G. K., & Siegel, R. M. (1985). Encoding of spatial location by posterior parietal neurons. *Science, 230,* 456–458.

Anderson, J. R. (1978). Arguments concerning representations for mental imagery. *Psychological Review, 85,* 249–277.

Aston-Jones, G., Foote, S. L., & Bloom, F. E. (1984). Anatomy and physiology of locus coeruleus neurons: Functional implications. In M. G. Ziegler (Ed.), *Frontiers in clinical neuroscience.* Baltimore, MD: Williams & Watkins.

Auer, R. N., Jensen, M. L., & Whishaw, I. Q. (1989). Neurobehavioral deficit due to ischemic brain damage limited to half of the CA1 section of the hippocampus. *Journal of Neuroscience, 9,* 1641–1647.

Ballantine, H. T., Cassidy, W. C., Brodeur, J., & Giriunas, I. B. (1972). Frontal cingulotomy for mood disturbance. In E. Hitchcock, L. Laitinen, & K. Vearnet (Eds.), *Psychosurgery* (pp. 221–228). Springfield, IL: Charles C. Thomas.

Barbas, H., & Pandya, D. N. (1981). Frontal lobe afferent input to area 6 in the rhesus monkey. *Society for Neuroscience Abstracts, 7,* 414.

Berridge, K. C., & Whishaw, I. Q. (1992). Cortex, striatum and cerebellum: Control of serial order in a grooming sequence. *Experimental Brain Research, 90,* 275–290.

Biederman, I., & Cooper, E. E. (1992). Size invariance in visual object priming. *Journal of Experimental Psychology: Human Perception and Performance, 18,* 121–133.

Bisiach, E., & Luzzatti, C. (1978). Unilateral neglect of representational space. *Cortex, 14,* 129–133.

Bisiach, E., Luzzatti, C., & Perani, D. (1979). Unilateral neglect, representational scheme, and consciousness. *Brain, 102,* 609–618.

Broadbent, D. E. (1971). *Decision and stress.* London: Academic Press.

Broca, P. (1863). Localisations des fonctions cérébrales. Siège du langage articule. *Bulletins de la Societe d'Anthropologie, 4,* 200–204.

Brooks, D. N., & Baddeley, A. D. (1976). What can amnesic patients learn? *Neuropsychologia, 14,* 111–122.

Brooks, V. B. (1986). How does the limbic system assist motor learning? A limbic comparator hypothesis. *Brain, Behaviour and Evolution, 29,* 29–53.

Buckner, R. L., Petersen, S. E., Ojemann, J. G., Miezin, F. M., Squire, L. R., & Raichle, M. E. (1996). Functional anatomical studies of explicit and implicit memory retrieval tasks. *Journal of Neuroscience, 16,* 6219–6235.

Cahill, L., & McGaugh, J. L. (1990). Amygdaloid complex lesions differentially affect retention of tasks using appetitive and aversive reinforcement. *Behavioral Neuroscience, 104*(4), 532–543.

Caplan, D. (1993). *Language.* Cambridge, MA: MIT Press.

Carter, C. S., Braver, T. S., Barch, D. M., Botvinick, M. M., Noll, D., & Cohen, J. D. (1998). Anterior cingulate cortex, error detection, and the online monitoring of performance. *Science, 280,* 747–749.

Cave, C. B., & Squire, L. R. (1992). Intact and long-lasting repetition priming in amnesia. *Journal of Experimental Psychology: Learning, Memory, and Cognition, 18,* 509–520.

Cermak, L. S., Talbot, N., Chandler, K., & Wolbarst, L. R. (1985). The perceptual priming phenomenon in amnesia. *Neuropsychologia, 23,* 615–622.

Cermak, L. S., Verfaellie, M., Milberg, W., Letourneau, L., & Blackford, S. (1991). A further analysis of perceptual identification priming in alcoholic Korsakoff patients. *Neuropsychologia, 29*(8), 725–736.

Church, B. A., & Schacter, D. L. (1994). Perceptual specificity of auditory priming: implicit memory for voice intonation and fundamental frequency. *Journal of Experimental Psychology: Learning, Memory, and Cognition, 20,* 521–533.

Churchland, P. S., & Sejnowski, T. J. (1992). *The computational brain.* Cambridge, MA: MIT Press.

Clark, C. R., Geffen, G. M., Geffen, L. B. (1989). Catecholamines and the covert orientation of attention in humans. *Neuropsychologia, 27*(2), 131–139.

Cohen, N. J. (1984). Preserved learning in amnesia: Evidence for multiple memory systems. In L. R. Squire & N. Butters (Eds.), *Neuropsychology of memory* (pp. 83–103). New York: Guilford Press.

Cohen, N. J., & Eichenbaum, H. (1994). *Memory, amnesia and the hippocampal system.* Cambridge, MA: MIT Press.

Cohen, N. J., & Squire, L. R. (1980). Preserved learning and retention of pattern analyzing skill in amnesics: Dissociation of knowing how and knowing that. *Science, 210,* 207–210.

Cook, N. D., Frueh, H., & Landis, T. (1995). The cerebral hemispheres and network simulations: Design considerations. *Journal of Experimental Psychology: Human Perception and Performance, 21,* 410–422.

Cooper, L. A., & Schacter, D. L. (1992). Dissociations between structural and episodic representations of visual objects. *Current Directions in Psychological Science, 1,* 141–146.

Cooper, L. A., Schacter, D. L., Ballesteros, S., & Moore, C. (1992). Priming and recognition of transformed three-dimensional objects: Effects of size and reflection. *Journal of Experimental Psychology: Learning, Memory, and Cognition, 18,* 43–57.

Corbetta, M., Miezin, F. M., Dobmeyer, S., Shulman, G. L., & Petersen, S. E. (1991). Selective and divided attention during visual discriminations of shape, color, and speed: Functional anatomy by positron emission tomography. *Journal of Neuroscience, 11*(8), 2383–2402.

Corbetta, M., Miezen, F. M., Schulman, G. L., & Petersen, S. E. (1993). A PET Study of visuospatial attention. *Journal of Neuroscience, 13,* 1202–1226.

Coslett, H. B., Bowers, D., & Heilman, K. M. (1987). Reduction in cerebral activation after right hemisphere stroke. *Neurology, 37,* 957–962.

Davis, M. (1992). The role of the amygdala in conditioned fear. In J. P. Aggleton (Ed.), *The amygdala: Neurobiological aspects of emotion, memory, and mental dysfunction* (pp. 255–306). New York: Wiley-Liss.

Desimone, R., Albright, T. D., Gross, C. G., & Bruce, C. J. (1984). Stimulus selective properties of inferior temporal neurons in the macaque. *Journal of Neuroscience, 4,* 2051–2062.

DeYoe, E. A., & Van Essen, D. C. (1988). Concurrent processing streams in monkey visual cortex. *Trends in Neurosciences, 11,* 219–226.

Dieber, M. P., Passingham, R. E., Colebatch, J. G., Friston, K. J., Nixon, P. D., & Frackowiak, R. S. J. (1991). Cortical areas and the selection of movement: A study with PET. *Experimental Brain Research, 84,* 393–402.

Ellis, A. W., & Young, A. W. (1988). *Human cognitive neuropsychology.* Hove, UK: Erlbaum.

Evarts, E. V. (1966). Methods for recording activity of individual neurons in moving animals. In R. F. Ruhmer (Ed.), *Methods in medical research* (pp. 241–250). Chicago: Chicago Year Book.

Everitt, B. J., & Robbins, T. W. (1992). Amygdala-ventral striatal interactions and reward-related processes. In J. P. Aggleton (Ed.), *The amygdala: Neurobiological aspects of emotion, memory, and mental dysfunction* (pp. 401–429). New York: Wiley–Liss.

Farah, M. J. (1990). *Visual agnosia: Disorders of object recognition and what they tell us about normal vision.* Cambridge, MA: MIT Press.

Farah, M. J. (1994). Neuropsychological inference with an interactive brain: A critique of the "locality" assumption. *Behavioral and Brain Sciences, 17,* 43–104.

Farah, M. J., & McClelland, J. L. (1991). A computational model of semantic memory impairment: Modality-specificity and emergent category-specificity. *Journal of Experimental Psychology: General, 120,* 339–357.

Feldman, J. A. (1985). Four frames suffice: A provisional model of vision and space. *Behavioral and Brain Sciences, 8,* 265–289.

Felleman, D. J., & Van Essen, D. C. (1991). Distributed hierarchical processing in the primate cerebral cortex. *Cerebral Cortex, 1,* 1–47.

Fox, P. T., Mintun, M. A., Raichle, M. E., Miezen, F. M., Allman, J. M., & Van Essen, D. C. (1986). Mapping human visual cortex with positron emission tomography. *Nature (London), 323,* 806–809.

Frith, C. D., Friston, K. J., Liddle, P. F., & Frackowiak, R. S. J. (1991). A PET study of word finding. *Neuropsychologia, 29,* 1137–1148.

Fujita, I., Tanaka, K., Ito, M., & Cheng, K. (1992). Columns for visual features of objects in monkey inferotemporal cortex. *Nature (London), 360,* 343–346.

Gabriel, M. (1990). Functions of anterior and posterior cingulate cortex during avoidance learning in rabbits. In H. B. M. Uylings, J. P. C. Van Eden, M. A. De Bruin, & M. G. P. Feenstra (Eds.), *Progress in brain research* (pp. 467–483). Amsterdam: Elsevier.

Gabrieli, J. D. E., Cohen, N. J., & Corkin, S. (1988). The impaired learning of semantic information following bilateral temporal lobe resection. *Brain and Cognition, 7,* 157–177.

Gaffan, D., & Murray, E. A. (1992). Monkeys (*Macaca fascicularis*) with rhinal cortical ablations succeed in object discrimination learning despite 24-hr intertrial intervals and fail at matching to sample despite double presentations. *Behavioral Neuroscience, 106,* 30–38.

Gazzaniga, M. S. (Ed.). (1995). *The cognitive neurosciences.* Cambridge, MA: MIT Press.

Gehring, W. J., Goss, B., Coles, M. G., Meyer, D. E., & Donchin, E. (1993). A neural system for error detection and compensation. *Psychological Science, 4*(6), 385–390.

Georgopoulos, A. P. (1994). Motor cortex and cognitive processing. In M. S. Gazzaniga (Ed.), *The cognitive neurosciences* (pp. 507–517). Cambridge, MA: MIT Press.

Geschwind, N. (1965). Disconnexion syndromes in animals and man. *Brain, 88,* 237–294.

Glisky, E. L., & Schacter, D. L. (1988). Long-term retention of computer learning by patients with memory disorders. *Neuropsychologia, 26,* 173–178.

Gluck, M. A., & Meyers, C. E. (1993). Hippocampal mediation of stimulus representation: A computational theory. *Hippocampus, 3,* 491–516.

Goldman-Rakic, P. S. (1988). Topography of cognition: Parallel distributed networks in primate association cortex. *Annual Review of Neuroscience, 11,* 137–156.

Gould, S. J., & Lewontin, R. C. (1979). The spandrels of San Marco and the Panglossian paradigm: A critique of the adaptationist paradigm. *Proceedings of the Royal Society of London, Series B, 205,* 581–598.

Graf, P., & Ryan, L. (1990). Transfer-appropriate processing for implicit and explicit memory. *Journal of Experimental Psychology: Learning, Memory, and Cognition, 16,* 978–992.

Graf, P., Squire, L. R., & Mandler, G. (1984). The information that amnesic patients do not forget. *Journal of Experimental Psychology: Learning, Memory, and Cognition, 10,* 164–178.

Gregory, R. L. (1970). *The intelligent eye.* London: Weidenfeld & Nicholson.

Gross, C. G., Desimone, R., Albright, T. D., & Schwartz, E. L. (1984). Inferior temporal cortex as a visual integration area. In F. Reinoso-Suarez & C. Ajmone-Marsan (Eds.), *Cortical integration.* New York: Raven Press.

Gross, C. G., & Mishkin, M. (1977). The neural basis of stimulus equivalence across retinal translation. In S. Harnad, R. Doty, J. Jaynes, L. Goldstein, & G. Krauthamer (Eds.), *Lateralization in the nervous system.* New York: Academic Press.

Grossberg, S. (1980). How does a brain build a cognitive code? *Psychological Review, 87,* 1–51.

Haier, R. J., Siegel, B. V., Neuchterlein, K. H., Hazlett, E., Wu, J. C., Paek, J., Browning, H. L., & Buchsbaum, M. S. (1988). Cortical glucose metabolic rate correlates of abstract reasoning and attention studied with positron emission tomography. *Intelligence, 12,* 199–217.

Haist, F., Musen, G., & Squire, L. R. (1991). Intact priming of words and nonwords in amnesia. *Psychobiology, 19,* 275–285.

Hart, J., Berndt, R. S., & Caramazza, A. (1985). Category-specific naming deficit following cerebral infarction. *Nature (London), 316,* 439–440.

Hasselmo, M. E. (1993). Acetylcholine and learning in a cortical associative memory. *Neural Computation, 5,* 32–44.

Hasselmo, M. E., & Bower, J. M. (1993). Acetylcholine and memory. *Trends in Neurosciences, 16,* 218–222.

Haxby, J. V., Horwitz, B., Maisog, J. M., Ungerleider, L. G., Mishkin, M., Schapiro, M. B., Rapoport, S. I., & Grady, C. L. (1993). *Journal of Cerebral Blood Flow and Metabolism, 13*(Suppl. 1), S499.

Hayman, C. A. G., & Tulving, E. (1989). Is priming in fragment completion based on "traceless" memory system? *Journal of Experimental Psychology: Learning, Memory, and Cognition, 14,* 941–956.

Hebb, D. O. (1949). *The organization of behavior.* New York: Wiley.

Heilman, K., & Valenstein, K. M. (1985). *Clinical neuropsychology.* New York: Oxford University Press.

Heindel, W. C., Salmon, D. P., & Butters, N. (1991). The biasing of weight judgments in Alzheimer's and Huntington's disease: A priming or programming phenomenon? *Journal of Clinical and Experimental Neuropsychology, 13,* 189–203.

Heindel, W. C., Salmon, D. P., Shults, C. W., Walicke, P. A., & Butters, N. (1989). Neuropsychological evidence for multiple implicit memory systems: A comparison of Alzheimer's, Huntington's, and Parkinson's disease patients. *Journal of Neuroscience, 9,* 582–587.

Hellige, J. B., & Michimata, C. (1989). Categorization versus distance: Hemispheric differences for processing spatial information. *Memory & Cognition, 17,* 770–776.

Holmes, G. (1919). Disturbances of visual space perception. *British Medical Journal, 2,* 449–468, 506–615.

Hubel, D. H., & Wiesel, T. N. (1968). Receptive fields and functional architecture of monkey striate cortex. *Journal of Physiology (London), 195,* 215–243.

Hummel, J. E., & Biederman, I. (1992). Dynamic binding in a neural network for shape recognition. *Psychological Review, 99*(3), 480–517.

Hyvarinen, J. (1982). Posterior parietal lobe of the primate brain. *Physiological Review, 62,* 1060–1129.

Jackson, S., & Houghton, G. (1995). Sensorimotor selection and the basal ganglia: A neural network model. In J. Howe (Eds.), *Models of information processing in the basal ganglia* (pp. 336–367). Cambridge, MA: MIT Press.

Jacoby, L. L., & Dallas, M. (1981). On the relationship between autobiographical memory and perceptual learning. *Journal of Experimental Psychology: General, 110,* 306–340.

Jacoby, L. L., & Hayman, C. A. G. (1987). Specific visual transfer in word identification. *Journal of Experimental Psychology: Learning, Memory, and Cognition, 13,* 456–463.

Janer, K. W., & Pardo, J. V. (1991). Deficits in selective attention following bilateral anterior cingulotomy. *Journal of Cognitive Neuroscience, 3*(2), 231–241.

Jarrard, L. E. (1993). On the role of the hippocampus in learning and memory in the rat. *Behavioral and Neural Biology, 60,* 9–26.

Jones-Gotman, M., Zatorre, R. J., Evans, A. C., & Meyer, E. (1993). *Society for Neuroscience Abstracts, 19,* 1002.

Kapp, B. S., Whalen, P. J., Supple, W. F., & Pascoe, J. P. (1992). Amygdaloid contributions to conditioned arousal and sensory information processing. In J. P. Aggleton (Eds.), *The amygdala: Neurobiological aspects of emotion, memory, and mental dysfunction* (pp. 229–254). New York: Wiley-Liss.

Keele, S. W., & Jennings, P. (1992). Attention in the representation of a sequence: Experiment and theory. *Human Movement Science, 11,* 125–138.

Keele, S. W., & Curran, T. (1995). On the modularity of sequence learning systems in humans. In E. Covey (Ed.), *Neural representation of temporal patterns* (pp. 197–225). New York: Plenum Press.

Keele, S. W., Ivry, R. B., Hazeltine, E., Mayr, U., & Heuer, H. (1998). *The cognitive and neural architecture of sequence representation.* (Technical Report 98-03 REVISED). University of Oregon: Institute of Cognitive and Decision Sciences.

Kim, J. J., & Fanselow, M. S. (1992). Modality-specific retrograde amnesia of fear. *Science, 256,* 675–677.

Knopman, D., & Nissen, M. J. (1991). Procedural learning is impaired in Huntington's disease: Evidence form the serial reaction time task. *Neuropsychologia, 29,* 245–254.

Kohn, S. E., & Friedman, R. B. (1986). Word-meaning deafness: A phonological-semantic dissociation. *Cognitive Neuropsychology, 3,* 291–308.

Kosslyn, S. M. (1980). *Image and mind.* Cambridge, MA: Harvard University Press.

Kosslyn, S. M. (1987). Seeing and imagining in the cerebral hemispheres: A computational approach. *Psychological Review, 94,* 148–175.

Kosslyn, S. M., Koenig, O., Barrett, A., Cave, C. B., Tang, J., & Gabrieli, J. D. E. (1989). Evidence for two types of spatial representations: Hemispheric specialization for categorical and coordinate relations. *Journal of Experimental Psychology: Human Perception & Performance, 15,* 723–735.

Kosslyn, S. M. (1994). *Image and brain.* Cambridge: MIT Press.

Kosslyn, S. M., Alpert, N. A., Thompson, W. L., Chabris, C. F., Rauch, S. L., & Anderson, A. K. (1994). Identifying objects seen from canonical and noncanonical viewpoints: A PET investigation. *Brain, 117,* 1055–1071.

Kosslyn, S. M., Alpert, N. M., Thompson, W. L., Maljkovic, V., Weise, S. B., Chabris, C. F., Hamilton, S. E., Rauch, S. L., & Buonanno, F. S. (1993). Visual mental imagery activates primary visual cortex: PET investigations. *Journal of Cognitive Neuroscience, 5,* 263–287.

Kosslyn, S. M., & Andersen, R. A. (1993). General introduction. In S. M. Kosslyn & R. A. Andersen (Eds.), *Frontiers in cognitive neuroscience* (pp. xv–xxix). Cambridge, MA: MIT Press.

Kosslyn, S. M., Chabris, C. F., Jacobs, R., Marsolek, C., & Koenig, O. (1995). [reply to Cook, Fruh & Landis]. *Journal of Experimental Psychology: Human Perception and Performance, 21,* 423–431.

Kosslyn, S. M., Chabris, C. F., Marsolek, C. J., & Koenig, O. (1992). Categorical versus coordinate spatial representations: Computational analyses and computer simulations. *Journal of Experimental Psychology: Human Perception and Performance, 18,* 562–577.

Kosslyn, S. M., Daly, P. F., McPeek, R. M., Alpert, N. M., Kennedy, D. N., & Caviness, V. S. J. (1993). Using locations to store shape: An indirect effect of a lesion. *Cerebral Cortex, 3,* 567–582.

Kosslyn, S. M., & Koenig, O. (1992). *Wet mind.* New York: Free Press.

Kosslyn, S. M., & Maljkovic, V. M. (1990). Marr's metatheory revisited. *Concepts in Neuroscience, 1,* 239–251.

Kosslyn, S. M., & Ochsner, K. N. (1994). In search of occipital activation during visual mental imagery. *Trends in Neurosciences, 17,* 288–290.

Kosslyn, S. M., Thompson, W. L., & Alpert, N. M. (1997). Neural systems shared by visual imagery and visual perception: A positron emission tomography study. *NeuroImage, 6,* 320–334.

LaBerge, D. (1990). Thalamic and cortical mechanisms of attention suggested by recent positron emission tomographic experiments. *Journal of Cognitive Neuroscience, 2*(4), 358–372.

LaBerge, D., & Buchsbaum, M. S. (1990). Positron emission tomography measurements of pulvinar activity during an attention task. *Journal of Neuroscience, 10,* 613–619.

Laeng, B. (1994). Localization of categorical and coordinate spatial functions: A study of unilateral stroke patients. *Journal of Cognitive Neuroscience, 6,* 189–203.

Lane, R. D., Reiman, E. M., Axelrod, B., Yun, L.-S., Holmes, A., & Schwartz, G. E. (1998). Neural correlates of levels of emotional awareness: Evidence of an interaction between emotion and attention in the anterior cingulate cortex. *Journal of Cognitive Neuroscience, 10,* 525–535.

LeDoux, J. E. (1994). In search of an emotional system in the brain: Leaping from fear to emotion and consciousness. In M. S. Gazzaniga (Ed.), *The cognitive neurosciences* (pp. 1049–1061). Cambridge, MA: MIT Press.

LeDoux, J. E., & Hirst, P. (Eds.). (1986). *Mind and brain: Dialogues in cognitive neuroscience.* New York: Cambridge University Press.

Levine, D. N. (1982). Visual agnosia in monkey and man. In D. J. Ingle, M. A. Goodale, & R. J. W. Mansfield (Eds.), *Analysis of visual behavior* (pp. 629–670). Cambridge, MA: MIT Press.

Lieberman, P., Kako, E., Friedman, J., Tajchman, G., Feldman, L. S., & Jimenez, E. B. (1992). Speech production, syntax comprehension, and cognitive deficits in Parkinson's disease. *Brain and Language, 43,* 169–189.

Lieberman, M. D. (in press). Intuition: A social cognitive neuroscience approach. *Psychological Bulletin.*

Lieberman, M. D., Ochsner, K. N., Gilbert, D. T., & Schacter, D. L. (1999). *Attitude change: A social cognitive neuroscience approach.* Cambridge, MA: Harvard University Manuscript.

Luria, A. R. (1980). *Higher cortical functions in man.* New York: Basic Books.

MacAndrews, M. P., Glisky, E. L., & Schacter, D. L. (1987). When priming persists: Long-lasting implicit memory for a single episode in amnesic patients. *Neuropsychologia, 25,* 497–506.

MacKinnon, D., & Squire, L. R. (1989). Autobiographical memory in amnesia. *Psychobiology, 17,* 247–256.

Mangun, G. A., Hilyard, S. A., & Luck, S. J. (1992). Electrocortical substrates of visual selective attention. In D. E. Meyer & S. Kornblum (Eds.), *Attention and performance XIV: Synergies in experimental psychology, artificial intelligence, and cognitive neuroscience* (pp. 219–244). Cambridge, MA: MIT Press.

Marr, D. (1982). *Vision: A computational investigation into the human representation and processing of visual information*. New York: Freeman.

Marsolek, C. J., Kosslyn, S. M., & Squire, L. R. (1992). Form-specific visual priming in the right cerebral hemisphere. *Journal of Experimental Psychology: Learning, Memory, and Cognition, 18*, 492–508.

Marsolek, C. J. (1995). Abstract visual-form representations in the left cerebral hemisphere. *Journal of Experimental Psychology: Human Perception & Performance, 21*, 375–386.

Maunsell, J. H. R., & Newsome, W. T. (1987). Visual processing in monkey extrastriate cortex. *Annual Review of Neuroscience, 10*, 363–401.

McCarthy, R. A., & Warrington, E. K. (1986). Visual associative agnosia: A clinico-anatomical study of a single case. *Journal of Neurology, Neurosurgery, & Psychiatry, 49*, 1233–1240.

McClelland, A. G. R., & Pring, L. (1991). An investigation of cross-modality effects in implicit and explicit memory. *Quarterly Journal of Experimental Psychology, 43A*, 19–33.

McClelland, J. L., McNaughton, B. L., & O'Reilly, R. C. (1994). *Why we have complementary learning systems in the hippocampus and neocortex: Insights from the successes and failures of connectionist models of learning and memory* (Tech. Rep. No. PDP.CNS.94.1). Pittsburgh, PA; Carnegie-Mellon University.

McClelland, J. L., & Rumelhart, D. E. (1981). An interactive activation model of context effects in letter perception: Part 1. An account of basic findings. *Psychological Review, 88*, 375–407.

McClelland, J. L., & Rumelhart, D. E. (1986). *Parallel distributed processing: Explorations in the microstructure of cognition: Vol. 2. Psychological and biological models*. Cambridge, MA: MIT Press.

McCloskey, M., & Cohen, N. J. (1989). Catastrophic interference in connectionist networks: The sequential learning problem. In G. H. Bower (Ed.), *The psychology of learning and motivation*. Orlando, FL: Academic Press.

McCollum, J., Larson, J., Otto, T., Schottler, Granger, R., & Lynch, G. (1991). Single unit processing in olfactory cortex. *Journal of Cognitive Neuroscience, 3*, 293–299.

McCulloch, W. S., & Pitts, W. (1943). A logical calculus of the ideas imminent in nervous activity. *Bulletin of Mathematical Biophysics, 5*, 115–133.

McDonald, R. J., & White, N. M. (1993). A triple dissociation of memory systems: Hippocampus, amygdala, and dorsal striatum. *Behavioral Neuroscience, 107*, 3–22.

Milberg, W., & Blumstein, S. E. (1981). Lexical decision and aphasia: Evidence for semantic processing. *Brain and Language, 14*, 371–385.

Milner, B. (1964). Some effects of frontal lobectomy in man. In J. M. Warren & K. Akert (Eds.), *The frontal granular cortex and behavior*. New York: McGraw-Hill.

Milner, B., Corkin, S., & Teuber, H. L. (1968). Further analysis of the hippocampal amnesic syndrome: Fourteen year follow-up study of H.M. *Neuropsychologia, 6*, 215–234.

Mishkin, M., & Appenzeller, T. (1987). The anatomy of memory. *Scientific American, 256*, 80–89.

Mitchell, D. B., & Brown, A. S. (1988). Persistent repetition priming in picture naming and its dissociation from recognition memory. *Journal of Experimental Psychology: Learning, Memory, and Cognition, 14*, 213–222.

Moran, J., & Desimone, R. (1985). Selective attention gates visual processing in the extrastriate cortex. *Science, 229*, 782–784.

Morrison, J. H., & Foote, S. L. (1986). Noradrenergic and serotonergic innervation of cortical, thalamic and tectal structures in old world and new world monkeys. *Journal of Comparative Neurology, 243*, 117–128.

Neisser, U. (1967). *Cognitive psychology*. New York: Appleton-Century-Crofts.

Nordahl, T. E., Benkelfat, C., Semple, W. E., & Gross, M. (1989). Cerebral glucose metabolic rates in obsessive compulsive disorder. *Neuropsychopharmacology, 2*, 23–28.

Ochsner, K. N., & Baker, D. P. (1994). *An integrative neural systems approach to motivation and emotion.* Unpublished manuscript, Harvard University, Cambridge, MA.

Ochsner, K. N., & Feldman-Barrett, L. (in press). The neuroscience of emotion. In T. Mayne & G. Bonnano (Eds.), *Emotion: Current issues and future directions.* Oxford: Oxford University Press.

Ochsner, K. N., & Lieberman, M. D. (1999). *The social cognitive neuroscience approach.* Cambridge, MA: Harvard University Manuscript.

Ochsner, K. N., & Schacter, D. L. (in press). Constructing the emotional past: A social cognitive neuroscience approach to emotion and memory. In J. Borod (Ed.), *The neuropsychology of emotion.* Oxford: Oxford University Press.

Packard, M. G., Hirsh, R., & White, N. M. (1989). Differential effects of fornix and caudate lesions on two radial maze tasks: Evidence for multiple memory systems. *Journal of Neuroscience, 9,* 1465–1472.

Packard, M. G., & McGaugh, J. L. (1992). Double dissociation of fornix and caudate nucleus lesions on acquisition of two water maze tasks: Further evidence for multiple memory systems. *Behavioral Neuroscience, 106,* 439–446.

Pardo, J. V., Pardo, P. J., Janer, K. W., & Raichle, M. E. (1990). The anterior cingulate cortex mediates processing selection in the Stroop attentional conflict paradigm. *Proceedings of the National Academy of Sciences of the U.S.A., 87,* 256–259.

Perrett, D. I., Smith, P. A. J., Potter, D. D., Mistlin, A. J., Head, A. S., Milner, A. D., & Jeeves, M. A. (1985). Visual cells in the temporal cortex sensitive to face view and gaze direction. *Proceedings of the Royal Society of London, Series B, 223,* 293–317.

Petersen, S. E., & Fiez, J. A. (1993). The processing of single words studied with positron emission tomography. *Annual Review of Neuroscience, 16,* 509–530.

Petersen, S. E., Fox, P. T., Posner, M. I., Mintun, M., & Raichle, M. E. (1988). Positron emission tomographic studies of the cortical anatomy of single-word processing. *Nature (London) 331,* 585–589.

Petersen, S. E., Fox, P. T., Snyder, A. Z., & Raichle, M. E. (1990). Activation of extrastriate and frontal cortical areas by visual words and word-like stimuli. *Science, 249,* 1041–1044.

Petersen, S. E., Robinson, D. L., & Morris, J. D. (1987). *Neuropsychologia, 25,* 97–105.

Posner, M. I. (1978). *Chronometric explorations of mind.* Hillsdale, NJ: Erlbaum.

Posner, M. I., & Carr, T. H. (1992). Lexical processing and the brain: Anatomical constraints on cognitive models of word recognition. *American Psychologist, 105,* 1–27.

Posner, M. I., Choate, L., Rafal, R. D., & Vaughan, J. (1985). Inhibition of return: Neural mechanisms and function. *Cognitive Neuropsychology, 2,* 211–228.

Posner, M. I., & DiGirolamo, G. J. (1998). Executive attention: Conflict, target detection, and cognitive control. In R. Parasuraman (Ed.), *The attentive brain* (pp. 401–423). Cambridge, MA: The MIT Press.

Posner, M. I., Inhoff, A. W., Friedrich, F. J., & Cohen, A. (1987). Isolating attentional systems: A cognitive-anatomical analysis. *Psychobiology, 15,* 107–121.

Posner, M. I., Nissen, M. J., & Ogden, W. C. (1978). Attended and unattended processing modes: The role of set for spatial location. In H. L. Pick & I. J. Saltzman (Eds.), *Modes of perceiving and processing information* (pp. 137–158). Hillsdale, NJ: Erlbaum.

Posner, M. I., & Petersen, S. E. (1990). The attention system of the human brain. *Annual Review of Neuroscience, 13,* 25–42.

Posner, M. I., Petersen, S. E., Fox, P. T., & Raichle, M. E. (1988). Localization of cognitive operations in the human brain. *Science, 240,* 1627–1631.

Posner, M. I., & Rothbart, M. K. (1992). Attentional mechanisms and conscious experience. In M. Rugg & A. D. Milner (Eds.), *Neuropsychology of consciousness* (pp. 91–111). San Diego, CA: Academic Press.

Posner, M. I., Snyder, C. R. R., & Davidson, B. J. (1980). Attention and the detection of signals. *Journal of Experimental Psychology: General, 109*(2), 160–174.

Posner, M. I., Walker, J. A., Friedrich, F. J., & Rafal, R. D. (1984). Effects of parietal lobe injury on covert orienting of visual attention. *Journal of Neuroscience, 4,* 1863–1874.

Pylyshyn, Z. W. (1973). What the mind's eye tells the mind's brain: A critique of mental imagery. *Psychological Bulletin, 80,* 1–24.

Pylyshyn, Z. W. (1981). The imagery debate: Analogue media versus tacit knowledge. *Psychological Review, 87,* 16–45.

Raichle, M. E., Fiez, J. A., Videen, T. O., MacLeod, A. K., Pardo, J. V., Fox, P. T., & Petersen, S. E. (1993). Practice-related changes in human brain functional anatomy. *Society for Neuroscience Abstracts, 17*, 21.

Rainville, P., Duncan, G. H., Price, D. D., Carrier, B., & Bushnell, M. C. (1997). Pain affect encoded in human anterior cingulate but not somatosensory cortex. *Science, 277*, 968–971.

Rauch, S. L., Savage, C. R., Alpert, N. M., Dougherty, D., Kendrick, A., Curran, T., Brown, H. D., Manzo, P., Fischman, A. J., & Jenike, M. A. (1997). Probing striatal function in obsessive-compulsive disorder. A PET study of implicit sequence learning. *Journal of Neuropsychiatry & Clinical Neurosciences, 9*, 568–573.

Riddoch, M. J., & Humphreys, G. W. (1987). Visual object processing in optic aphasia: A case of semantic access agnosia. *Cognitive Neuropsychology, 4*, 131–186.

Robinson, D. L., & Petersen, S. E. (1986). The neurobiology of attention. In J. LeDoux & P. Hirst (Eds.), *Mind and brain: Dialogues in cognitive neuroscience.* New York: Cambridge University Press.

Robinson, D. L., & Petersen, S. E. (1992). The pulvinar and visual salience. *Trends in Neurosciences, 15*, 127–132.

Robinson, R. G. (1985). Lateralized behavioral and neurochemical consequences of unilateral brain injury in rats. In S. G. Glick (Ed.), *Cerebral lateralization in nonhuman primates.* Orlando, FL: Academic Press.

Roediger, H. L. III., & Blaxton, T. A. (1987). Effects of varying modality, surface features, and retention interval on priming in word fragment completion. *Memory & Cognition, 15*, 379–388.

Roediger, H. L. III., Weldon, M. S., Stadler, M. L., & Riegler, G. L. (1992). Direct comparison of two implicit memory tests: Word fragment and word stem completion. *Journal of Experimental Psychology: Learning, Memory, and Cognition, 18*, 1251–1269.

Roland, P. E., & Gulyas, B. (1994). Visual imagery and visual representation. *Trends in Neurosciences, 17*, 281–287.

Rozin, P. (1976). The psychobiological approach to human memory. In M. R. Rosenzweig & E. L. Bennet (Eds.), *Neural mechanisms of learning and memory.* Cambridge, MA: MIT Press.

Rueckl, J. G., Cave, K. R., & Kosslyn, S. M. (1989). Why are "what" and "where" processed by separate cortical systems? A computational investigation. *Journal of Cognitive Neuroscience, 1*, 171–186.

Sagi, D., & Julesz, B. (1985). "Where" and "what" in vision. *Science, 228*, 1217–1219.

Schacter, D. L. (1990). Perceptual representation systems and implicit memory: Toward a resolution of the multiple memory systems debate. *Annals of the New York Academy of Sciences, 608*, 543–571.

Schacter, D. L. (1992). Understanding implicit memory: A cognitive neuroscience approach. *American Psychologist, 47*, 559–569.

Schacter, D. L. (1994). Priming and multiple memory systems: Perceptual mechanisms of implicit memory. In D. L. Schacter & E. Tulving (Eds.), *Memory systems 1994.* Cambridge, MA: MIT Press.

Schacter, D. L., & Church, B. (1992). Auditory priming: Implicit and explicit memory for words and voices. *Journal of Experimental Psychology: Learning, Memory, and Cognition, 18*, 915–930.

Schacter, D. L., Church, B. A., & Treadwell, J. (1994). Implicit memory in amnesic patients: Evidence for spared auditory priming. *Psychological Science, 5*, 20–25.

Schacter, D. L., Cooper, L. A., & Delaney, S. M. (1990). Implicit memory for unfamiliar objects depends on access to structural descriptions. *Journal of Experimental Psychology: General, 119*, 5–24.

Schacter, D. L., Cooper, L. A., Delaney, S. M., Peterson, M. A., & Tharan, M. (1991). Implicit memory for possible and impossible objects: Constraints on the construction of structural descriptions. *Journal of Experimental Psychology: Learning, Memory, and Cognition, 17*, 3–19.

Schacter, D. L., Cooper, L. A., Tharan, M., & Rubens, A. B. (1991). Preserved priming of novel objects in patients with memory disorders. *Journal of Cognitive Neuroscience, 3*, 118–131.

Schacter, D. L., Cooper, L. A., & Treadwell, J. (1993). Preserved priming of novel objects across size transformation in amnesic patients. *Psychological Science, 4*, 331–335.

Schacter, D. L., Harbluk, J. L., & McLachlan, D. R. (1984). Retrieval without recollection: An experimental analysis of source amnesia. *Journal of Verbal Learning and Verbal Behavior, 23*, 593–611.

Schacter, D. L., McGlynn, S. M., Milberg, W. P., & Church, B. A. (1993). Spared priming despite impaired comprehension: Implicit memory in a case of word meaning deafness. *Neuropsychology, 7,* 107–118.

Schacter, D. L., Rapcsak, S. Z., Rubens, A. B., Tharan, M., & Laguna, J. M. (1990). Priming effects in a letter-by-letter reader depend on access to the word form system. *Neuropsychologia, 28,* 1079–1094.

Schacter, D. L., & Tulving, E. (Eds.). (1994a). *Memory systems 1994.* Cambridge, MA: MIT Press.

Schacter, D. L., & Tulving, E. (1994b). What are the memory systems of 1994? In D. L. Schacter & E. Tulving (Eds.), *Memory systems* (pp. 1–38). Cambridge, MA: MIT Press.

Scoville, W. B., & Milner, B. (1957). Loss of recent memory after bilateral hippocampal lesions. *Journal of Neurology and Neurosurgery and Psychiatry, 20,* 11–21.

Sergent, J. (1991). Judgments of relative position and distance on representations of spatial relations. *Journal of Experimental Psychology: Human Perception and Performance, 91,* 762–780.

Sergent, J., Ohta, S., & MacDonald, B. (1992). Functional neuroanatomy of face and object processing: A positron emission tomography study. *Brain, 115,* 15–36.

Shepard, R. N., & Feng, C. (1972). A chronometric study of mental paper folding. *Cognitive Psychology, 3,* 228–243.

Shepard, R. N., & Metzler, J. (1971). Mental rotation of three-dimensional objects. *Science, 171,* 701–703.

Sherry, D. F., & Schacter, D. L. (1987). The evolution of multiple memory systems. *Psychological Review, 94,* 439–454.

Shiffrin, R. M. (1988). Attention. In R. C. Atkinson, R. J. Herrnstein, G. Lindzey, & R. D. Luce (Eds.), *Steven's handbook of experimental psychology* (pp. 739–811). New York: Wiley.

Shimamura, A. P., & Squire, L. R. (1987). A neuropsychological study of fact memory and source amnesia. *Journal of Experimental Psychology: Learning, Memory, and Cognition, 13,* 464–473.

Shimamura, A. P., & Squire, L. S. (1988). Long-term memory in amnesia: Cued recall, recognition memory, and confidence ratings. *Journal of Experimental Psychology: Learning, Memory, & Cognition, 14,* 763–770.

Skinner, B. F. (1957). *Verbal behavior.* New York: Appleton-Century-Crofts.

Sloman, S. A., Hayman, C. A. G., Ohta, N., Law, J., & Tulving, E. (1988). Forgetting in primed fragment completion. *Journal of Experimental Psychology: Learning, Memory, and Cognition, 14,* 223–239.

Smith, M. E., & Oscar-Berman, M. (1990). Repetition priming of words and pseudowords in divided attention and amnesia. *Journal of Experimental Psychology: Learning, Memory, and Cognition, 16,* 1033–1042.

Sperling, G. (1960). The information available in brief visual presentations. *Psychological Monographs, 74* (11, Whole No. 498).

Squire, L. R. (1987). *Memory and brain.* New York: Oxford University Press.

Squire, L. R. (1992). Memory and the hippocampus: A synthesis from findings with rats, monkeys, and humans. *Psychological Review, 99,* 195–231.

Squire, L. R., Amaral, D. G., & Press, G. A. (1990). Magnetic resonance measurement of hippocampal formation and mammillary nuclei distinguish medial temporal lobe and diencephalic amnesia. *Journal of Neuroscience, 10,* 3106–3117.

Squire, L. R., & Frambach, M. (1990). Cognitive skill learning in amnesia. *Psychobiology, 18,* 109–117.

Squire, L. R., Ojemann, J. G., Miezin, F. M., Petersen, S. E., Videen, T. O., & Raichle, M. E. (1992). Activation of the hippocampus in normal humans: A functional anatomical study of memory. *Proceedings of the National Academy of Sciences of the U.S.A., 89,* 1837–1841.

Squire, L. R., & Shimamura, A. P. (1986). Characterizing amnesic patients for neurobehavioral study. *Behavioral Neuroscience, 100,* 866–877.

Srinivas, K. (1993). Perceptual specificity in nonverbal priming. *Journal of Experimental Psychology: Learning, Memory, & Cognition, 19,* 582–602.

Sternberg, S. (1969). Memory scanning: Mental processes revealed by reaction-time experiments. *American Scientist, 57,* 421–457.

Talbot, J. D., Marret, S., Evans, A. C., Meyer, E., Buswell, M. C., & Duncan, D. H. (1991). Multiple representations of pain in human cerebral cortex. *Science, 251,* 1355–1358.

Teuber, H. L. (1955). Physiological psychology. *Annual Review of Psychology, 6,* 267–296.

Tootell, R. B. H., Silverman, M. S., Switkes, E., & DeValois, R. L. (1982). Deoxyglucose analysis of retinotopic organization in primate striate cortex. *Science, 218,* 902–904.

Townsend, J. T. (1974). Issues and models concerning the processing of a finite number of inputs. In B. H. Kantrowitz (Ed.), *Human information processing: Tutorials in performance and cognition* (pp. 133–185). New York: Wiley.

Treisman, A. M., & Gelade, G. (1980). A feature integration theory of attention. *Cognitive Psychology, 12,* 97–136.

Treisman, A. M., & Gormican, S. (1988). Feature analysis in early vision: Evidence from search asymmetries. *Psychological Review, 95,* 15–48.

Tulving, E., Hayman, C. A. G., & MacDonald, C. (1991). Long-lasting perceptual priming and semantic learning in amnesia: A case experiment. *Journal of Experimental Psychology: Learning, Memory, and Cognition, 17,* 595–617.

Tulving, E., Kapur, S., Craik, F. I. M., Moscovitch, M., & Houle, S. (1994). Hemispheric encoding/retrieval asymmetry in episodic memory: Positron emission tomography findings. *Proceedings of the National Academy of Science, 91,* 2016–2020.

Tulving, E., & Schacter, D. L. (1990). Priming and human memory systems. *Science, 247,* 301–306.

Ungerleider, L. G., & Mishkin, M. (1982). Two cortical visual systems. In D. J. Ingle, M. A. Goodale, & R. J. W. Mansfield (Eds.), *Analysis of visual behavior* (pp. 549–586). Cambridge, MA: MIT Press.

Vogt, B. A., & Miller, M. W. (1983). Cortical connections between rat cingulate cortex and visual, motor, and postsubicular cortices. *Journal of Comparative Neurology, 216,* 192–210.

von Neumann, J. (1958). *The computer and the brain.* New Haven, CT: Yale University Press.

Warrington, E. K., & James, M. (1991). A new test of object decision: 2D silhouettes featuring a minimal view. *Cortex, 27,* 377–383.

Warrington, E. K., & Shallice, T. (1980). Word-form dyslexia. *Brain, 30,* 99–112.

Warrington, E. K., & Taylor, A. M. (1973). The contribution of the right parietal lobe to object recognition. *Cortex, 9,* 152–164.

Warrington, E. K., & Taylor, A. M. (1978). Two categorical stages of object recognition. *Perception, 7,* 695–705.

Warrington, E. K., & Weiskrantz, L. (1974). The effect of prior learning on subsequent retention in amnesic patients. *Neuropsychologia, 12,* 419–428.

Weingartner, H., & Lister, R. (1991). *Perspectives on cognitive neuroscience.* New York: Oxford University Press.

Witelson, S. F. (1994). Clinical neurology as data for basic neuroscience: Tourette's syndrome and human motor systems. *Neurology, 43,* 859–861.

Wurtz, R. H., Goldberg, M. E., & Robinson, D. L. (1980). Behavioral modulation of visual responses in the monkey: Stimulus selection for attention and movement. In J. M. Sprague & A. N. Epstein (Eds.), *Progress in psychobiology and physiological psychology* (pp. 48–83). New York: Academic Press.

Zola-Morgan, S., & Squire, L. R. (1990a). The neuropsychology of memory: Parallel findings in humans and nonhuman primates. *Annals of the New York Academy of Sciences, 608,* 434–456.

Zola-Morgan, S., & Squire, L. R. (1990b). The primate hippocampal formation: Evidence for a time-limited role in memory storage. *Science, 250,* 288–290.

Zola-Morgan, S., Squire, L. R., & Amaral, D. G. (1986). Human amnesia and the medial temporal lobe region: Enduring memory impairment following a bilateral lesion limited to field CA1 of the hippocampus. *Journal of Neuroscience, 6,* 2950–2967.

Zola-Morgan, S., Squire, L. R., Amaral, D. G., & Suzuki, W. A. (1989). Lesions of perirhinal and parahippocampal cortex that spare the amygdala and hippocampal formation produce severe memory impairment. *Journal of Neuroscience, 9,* 4355–4370.

CHAPTER 8

Emotion

George Mandler

The field of emotion has not achieved a consensus of basic knowledge and core paradigms across the various cognitive sciences. In its place, I shall try to give the reader a general overview of a much divided field. Since the 1960s the field of emotion, in its various guises, has attracted increasing numbers of investigators, and sooner or later some kind of paradigm is likely to be agreed upon and further developed. In the meantime, here is a *vade mecum* into a large and often disorganized territory. There is much still to be done, and the enterprising reader should be encouraged to follow some of the often tantalizing leads that the field presents.

I. INTRODUCTION

The cognitive sciences have inherited a number of natural language categories that are believed to denote more or less unitary collections of phenomena. These categories include intelligence, information, development, and, of course, emotion. Similarly, at least until sometime in the 20th century, the traditional view has been that emotion is a unitary phenomenon, and that the only question to be resolved was which theoretical account best explains that unitary phenomenon.[1]

Until the 19th century the dominant belief was based on the notion that most

---

[1] For a contemporary introduction to problems of emotion see Strongman (1987), and for more extended discussion of some of the historical themes see Mandler (1979).

Cognitive Science

emotions represent some concatenation of bodily or visceral arousal and cognitive or belief states—a position that goes back to Aristotle and was repeatedly revived over the centuries, most notably by Descartes. Aristotle saw the emotions as a combination of cognitive and sensual functions and, very much in the modern mold, defined emotions in terms of the beliefs (cognitions) that engendered them. Descartes saw things somewhat more complicatedly, with the human soul organizing both the cognitive and the bodily sensual reactions. The major impetus for the contemporary renewed interest in that position came from the work of Stanley Schachter (first in Schachter & Singer, 1962).

The traditional approach was concerned primarily with the factors, events, and variables that generate the feelings that are popularly included under the title of "emotions." There was relatively little scientific or quasi-scientific interest in the conditions that produce or elicit the states that concatenate into emotion. Although there was always some interest in the conditions responsible for *specific* emotions such as fear or anger, it was not until the end of the 19th century that any attempt was made to describe general antecedent conditions responsible for the collection of phenomena called emotion. Here again, the general thrust was the belief in a unitary phenomenon, explicable by a single set of principles. The main concept employed was the notion that conflict produced emotional reactions. Among the early conflict theorists were the French philosopher F. Paulhan (1887) and the American philosopher/psychologist John Dewey (1894), who made reference to the conflict or tensions arising out of the inadequacy of available reactions and responses. Sigmund Freud presented the single most important conflict theory of emotion. He ascribed most emotional phenomena (and particular anxiety) to conflicts among primitive impulses, social constraints, and reality demands (Id, Superego, and Ego).[2]

The unitary view of emotion could well have held sway, possibly in combination with conflict approaches. Major changes until the middle of the 20th century dealt with new techniques, new data, and input from different relevant fields of knowledge, but not with radically different views of the psychology of emotion. However, even a cursory examination of our contemporary technical and popular literature demonstrates that "emotion" is no longer a term that commands immediate assent as to its domain or definition. The question then arises how one should investigate emotion, and specifically whether any single approach can possibly do justice to all the different definitions and functions that have accumulated under the umbrella concept. As different investigators and different theorists have tried to unpack the natural language concept, a large number of different interpretations of emotion have emerged. Is it even possible to attempt to answer William James's question: What is an emotion? (James, 1884).

---

[2] I will not discuss Freud's contribution any further here, primarily because many of his ideas have been absorbed by other more contemporary approaches, and also because such a presentation would require a chapter of its own (as an introduction to relevant work, see Freud (1916/1975, 1926/1975).

II. WHAT IS AN EMOTION?

The question that William James posed over a hundred years ago has, on the one hand, had the beneficial effect of encouraging the study of whatever-it-is, and, on the other hand, produced a search for an answer to a pseudoquestion, or invited a confusion between "a semantic or metaphysical question with a scientific one" (McNaughton, 1989, p. 3). As we know—and as I hope to show—different people answer the question differently, as behooves a well used umbrella term from the natural language. Everybody wishes to unpack "emotion" idiosyncratically.

William James (1884, 1890, 1894), more than anyone else, established the tradition of unpacking common-sense notions about the emotions, though in the process he misled several generations of psychologists into believing that his "What is an emotion?" admitted of an unequivocal answer. Remember, though, that James was primarily interested in the relation between emotional feeling and bodily expression. He criticized the received knowledge of the day which described emotion as a "mental affection" which "gives rise to the bodily expression." He noted that common experience suggests instead that our feeling of the bodily changes that follow the perception of some "exciting fact," *is* the emotion.[3] He argued that if all feelings of bodily symptoms were abstracted from the felt emotion, all that would remain would be a "cold and neutral state of intellectual perception" (1884, p. 193). In illustration James noted, *inter alia,* that it would be impossible to think of an emotion of fear if "the feelings neither of quickened heart-beats nor of shallow breathing, neither of trembling lips nor of weakened limbs, neither of goose-flesh nor of visceral stirring, were present" (1884, p. 194).[4] James misled psychologists to believe that an exhaustive account of such natural language descriptions was possible. James was probably wrong in assigning the feelings of a particular emotion to a specific concatenation of visceral and muscular activities (Fridlund, 1991; Mandler, 1975, 1984; Ortony & Turner, 1990). Many current theoretical accounts still wish to answer James's question "What is an emotion?", but his central question about visceral and muscular involvement has become peripheral for many positions.

All this is irrelevant of course if all that we wish to address is the fact that within any language or social community people seem to know full well, though they have difficulty putting into words, what emotions are, what it is to be emotional, what experiences qualify as emotions, and so forth. However, these agreements vary from language to language and from community to community (Geertz, 1973). Given that the emotions are established facts of everyday experience, it behooves us to determine what organizes the common language of emotion in the first place, and then to find a reasonable theoretical account that provides a partial understanding of these language uses. Given the vagaries of the common language, it is of course

---

[3] Ten years later, James (1894) started to turn to the problem of defining, the "exciting facts," a problem central to cognitive accounts of emotion today (e.g., Ortony, Clore, & Collins, 1989).

[4] I note, though, that the same bodily experiences have been known to accompany passionate love, extreme guilt, and other emotions.

useless to try to give a *full* account; the common language is neither exact nor universal.

I turn to the common language to see if there is a common core to the various uses and misuses of emotion language. Is there anything that is essential to the use of the term *emotion* some aspect that represents the core, without necessarily doing justice to all the nuances and implications of the concept? Lexicographers perform an important function for the social sciences; they circumvent the need for extensive surveys and interviews by distilling the meanings of our language. Their work is cumulative and, in general, responds to the nuances and the changing customs of the common language. What do the lexicographers tell us? *Webster's New Collegiate Dictionary* (1969) tells us that emotion is "a psychic and physical reaction subjectively experienced as strong feeling and physiologically involving changes that prepare the body for immediate vigorous action," and that affect is defined as "the conscious subjective aspect of an emotion considered apart from bodily changes."

Here is the traditional definition, including an approach to James's pure abstracted emotion. Presumably under the influence of the received wisdom that dominated thinking about emotion since Aristotle, emotions are seen as having two components, a psychic and a physical one. The scientific task is to go beyond, and below, such knowledge, to determine what it is that psychological science needs to explain. And once we have satisfactorily completed the task of simplification, we can and need to return to an attempt to understand the complexities of the real world.

All science is—in the first instance—an extension of common sense and common knowledge. Scientific knowledge started—historically—with everyday observations couched in the natural language, and it develops ontogenetically in the same fashion. In the natural sciences the shift toward special observations and languages occurred early and is easily maintained against the evidence of everyday observations. In the social sciences—and particularly in psychology—refined ("scientific") observations coexist to a large extent with common experience and common myth and lore. Emotions are taken to be unitary experiences, they occur in more or less well-defined categories (such as fear, love, etc.), they are supposedly expressed in the face and body, and—being apparently not under rational, voluntary control—seem to be primitive and animal-like. In the face of such concurrent folk beliefs, the scientific labors of constructing, deconstructing, decomposing, and unpacking the natural phenomena is daunting indeed. The challenge of this task can best be illustrated by the attempts that have come from the various cognitive sciences. I now turn to some illustrative examples of these attempts.

III. DEFINITIONS AND THEORIES

I present here some of the most popular and representative positions on emotion—mostly by psychologists. This survey will serve the reader as an illustration of both the diversity of the field and the complexities that it must face.

Izard's (1972) approach is typical of the advocates of a unitary emotional complex. He says that emotion "is a complex process that has neurophysiological, motor-expressive, and phenomenological aspects" (p. 51). Each "fundamental" emotion has its own innate program, whose neurochemical activity "produces patterned neuro-muscular responses of the face and body and the feedback from these responses is transformed into conscious form" (p. 52). At the core is an unanalyzed "innate pro-gram"—the essence of the emotion. Autonomic nervous system activity plays a part as do all the components as "part of the structure underlying the emotion process" (p. 11). Autonomic activity is said to be patterned differentially for differ-ent emotions. When we ask what are the conditions that produce these emotion complexes, the answer lies "in the situation." There are fear situations and interest situations, grief situations, and so forth. Complex emotions are mixtures of a lim-ited number of basic emotions. More specifically, "an internal or external event changes . . . the pattern of . . . activity in the nervous system," and that "change directs" an "innately determined facial expression" (Izard & Buechler, 1980, p. 169) that activates the emotion. And once an emotion is activated other glandular, car-diovascular, and other systems are involved in its "amplification or regulation."

Frijda (1986) may be the most wide-ranging and ambitious of contemporary theorists. He starts off with a working definition of emotion as the occurrence of noninstrumental behavior, physiological changes, and evaluative experiences (or their inner determinants). In the process of trying a number of different proposals and investigating action, physiology, evaluation, and experience, Frijda arrives at a definition that is broad indeed. Frijda (1986, p. 473) describes emotion as a set of mechanisms that ensure the satisfaction of concerns, compare stimuli to preference states, and by turning them into rewards and punishments, generate pain and plea-sure, dictate appropriate action, assume control for these actions and thereby inter-rupt ongoing activity, and provide resources for these actions. The question is whether such mechanisms do not do too much, and leave nothing in meaningful action that is not emotional. That may well be Frijda's intention, but it leaves the topic of emotion burdened with supporting practically all of psychology.

Ortony, Clore, and Collins (1988) are straightforward. They define emotions as "valenced reactions to events, agents, or objects, with their particular nature being determined by the way in which the eliciting situation is construed" (p. 13). Such a definition is of course subject to James's critique; it is abstracted from the "bod-ily felt" emotions. But as a definition of "affect" (the cognitive part of the emo-tions) it is the most consistent approach that is seriously concerned with James's "exciting facts."

Oatley and Johnson-Laird's (1987) theory of emotion is the only one specifically claiming direct ties to the computational cognitive science enterprise. Their approach is more complex and elaborate than most and it introduces new termi-nologies (though often for old concepts). They propose a system of modular proces-sors in the human information-processing system with emotion modes that are nonpropositional communications setting the whole system for appropriate action, including the switching on and off of appropriate modules. These nonpropositional signals can function without higher level cognitive evaluations and without conscious intervention. There are five basic emotion modes (in keeping with other basic emotion models). Complex emotions are not mixtures of the basic ones, but cognitive elaborations of them. In addition, the emotion modes coordinate the modular nervous system, and the cognitive system "adopts an emotion mode at a significant juncture of a plan" (p. 35). These junctures are the equivalent of particular cognitive structures specific to the five basic emotions, and as cognitive structures not much different from the kind of structures envisaged by Ortony et al. For example, for anger the "juncture" is "active plan frustrated" and a transition occurs to a state of "try harder, and/or aggress."

Richard Lazarus and his co-workers (Folkman & Lazarus, 1990; Lazarus, 1991) define emotion as organized reactions that consist of cognitive appraisals, action impulses, and patterned somatic reactions. Emotions are seen as the result of continuous appraisals and monitoring of the person's well-being. The result is a fluid change of emotional states indexed by cognitive, behavioral, and physiological symptoms. Central to their position is the notion of cognitive appraisal that is an integral part of the emotional state, and it leads to actions that cope with the situation. Coping is an important concept in this position, and it can be centered on problems faced or on emotions experienced. *Primary* appraisal asks what is at stake in a situation and defines the quality and intensity of emotion, whereas *secondary* appraisal asks questions about how to cope with a stressful situation and about the response of the environment to such reactions.

A. Topical Approaches

There are a number of other important directions and amendments in the field that I can only characterize briefly:

1. Development of Emotion

There are no significant theories devoted entirely to the early development of emotion. It is generally agreed that the same factors apply to early emotional experience as apply to adult emotions, given the inability to determine the infant's subjective experiences. It is also the case that early emotional development follows the general pattern of infant development (i.e., showing increasing differentiation). In contrast there has been extensive work on the way children acquire and use emotional labels and concepts (e.g., Bullock & Russell, 1986), how they begin to understand emotions in others, and how such understanding is mediated by the social context (Harter & Whitesell, 1989; N. L. Stein & Levine, 1987, 1989; N. L. Stein, Trabasso, & Liwag, 1993).

2. Emotion and Artificial Intelligence

Given the heterogeneity of approaches to emotion, it is not surprising that relatively little work has been done in the artificial intelligence (AI) modeling of emotion.

Pfeifer (1988) has extensively discussed various symbolic AI models and their differences and shortcomings. He concluded that none of the computational approaches meets the requirement of an emotional system, having particular difficulty in representing physiological systems and subjective experience. Furthermore, Pfeifer emphasized how closely emotions are tied to common-sense reasoning—a particularly difficult problem for AI. In a subsequent summary, Ortony (1992) stressed the importance of using modeling for testing potential theories of emotion, for developing reasonable representation of naive psychology notions, and exploring the use of emotional mechanisms in the control of ongoing processes. Much of this has yet to be done.

Detailed attention to *positive emotions* has been provided by Ellen Berscheid and her innovative ways of looking at love and related symptoms (Berscheid, 1982, 1983; Berscheid & Walster, 1978), and by Alice Isen in detailing the facilitative effects of positive emotions (Isen, 1990; Isen, Daubman, & Nowicki, 1987; Isen & Means, 1983). Dysfunctional and *clinical aspects* of emotion have been described by Oatley and Jenkins (1992), and investigated from various aspects in D. J. Stein and Young (1992).

IV. CENTRAL ISSUES IN THE STUDY OF EMOTION

I have tried to show that different theorists see different conditions, situations, concerns, stresses, and junctures central in creating emotional reactions. There is also disagreement whether the felt emotion itself depends on significant sympathetic nervous system participation. Given such diversity, are there any overarching issues that all theories address—or should address? I turn to several issues that have been of concern to students of the emotions and that cut across disciplinary lines, ranging from the relation of cognition to emotion to the definition of emotion by the social context.

A. Cognition and Emotion

It has been several decades since the notion of cognition was reintroduced into the analysis of emotion. The central question raised by the cognition approach is, "What is it that the organism needs to know and perceive in order to react emotionally? During the behaviorist hegemony in America (ca. 1920–1950), it was convenient to look only at behavior as such (e.g., lashing out = anger) and to look at the environment for the causes of emotion (blocked action/goal → anger/frustration). In that context, a continued adherence to an orthodox Jamesian view was acceptable (i.e., that an emotion was [the perception of] bodily reactions). But even James in a later paper (1894) realized that something has to set the behavior going, and today essentially all theories and positions that deal with human emotions are cognitive in the sense that they require some analysis of the environment and social setting to produce the required "emotional" state. The one exception is Zajonc's position (1980, 1984) that postulates a set of "sensory" events, called *preferenda,* that act directly on preferences that set the stage for emotions and that produce their effect prior to and independent of cognitive analyses. There is no direct evidence for such events and some negative evidence (e.g., Mandler & Shebo, 1983), which leaves that position in limbo until more evidence is adduced.

B. Neurophysiology

Much of the work on the neurophysiology of the emotions has been done with nonhuman animals. That, probably unavoidable, emphasis has created a serious methodological problem in distinguishing between emotional behavior and emotional experience. Experimenters working with nonhumans have as their object of interest the behavior of animals, whereas most investigators of human emotion deal with the (reported) experience of emotion. Is aggressive behavior the same as anger, as some investigators would have it, and is, for example, defensive rage more or less than the experience of rage—or just the elicitation of a certain class of behavior? After all, humans can be angry without being aggressive, can other animals be aggressive without being "angry"? Nor is it very convincing to argue that the effectiveness of drugs for humans "developed through the study of fear behavior in animals . . . attests to the conservation of fear mechanisms across species" (LeDoux, 1992, p. 24). If, for example, these drugs primarily regulate or modulate autonomic nervous system products and their precursors, then it seems premature to talk about the conservation of "fear mechanisms."

One of the major dividing lines between functional psychological approaches and physio/biologically based ones has to do with the role of sympathetic nervous system arousal. We have seen that many psychological approaches, ranging from psychological arousal and cognition models to constructivist ones, assign a causal or quasi-causal role to such arousal, most neuroscientific approaches see such arousal as a result rather than a determiner of emotional evocation. Thus, Panksepp (1991) endorses the notion that visceral changes are support systems that "facilitate the behavioral ends of emotion;" thus a reified anger energizes behavior because of an "accompanying" increase in heart rate (p. 64). Such strong statements draw the line quite clearly, and probably usefully in trying to distinguish these different models. Panksepp in the same context of trying to bring psychological and physiological approaches together advocates a common language of "basic emotions," using existing natural language expressions of folk psychology.

Panksepp's chapter provides a useful summary of current neurobiological speculations about some few emotional states, with most of the evidence derived from animal studies. These states include separation/panic, fear and rage, but because animal studies are opaque on the question of subjective emotional experiences, it seems premature to assume that feeling states as well as emotional behavior emerge from the same "primal executive substrates of the brain" (Panksepp, 1991, p. 89).

An attractive attempt to bridge functional and physiological speculations can be found in the work of LeDoux (1989). In a specific approach to cognition-emotion problems, LeDoux suggested that separate systems mediate affective and cognitive computations, with the amygdala being primarily responsible for affective computation, whereas cognitive processes are centered in the hippocampus and neocortex. The (conscious) experience of emotion is the product of simultaneous projections of the affective and cognitive products into "working memory." Whereas much detail is missing, such as the functions of consciousness, it is at least one attempt to combine apparently disparate approaches.

A further illustration of the still existing gulf between animal models and human emotion can be found in the kind of neurophysiology that is stressed by the two strands of research. Whereas the animal models are primarily concerned with an understanding of brain mechanisms that mediate fear and related states, a recent compendium on human emotion has four chapters on the physiology of emotion, all of which are concerned to some extent with hemispheric differences and differentiation in emotion—not a topic ever approached by animal modelers.[5]

Finally, a look at the peripheral physiology of emotion. Whereas the notion of visceral involvement in the human emotions has always been an important concern, it became central with William James's (1884) view that different subjective emotional states arise out of the perception of different bodily (including autonomic nervous system) states. A number of different emotion theories claim that different emotions consist in part of, or are caused by, specific patterns of sympathetic nervous system activity (cf. Ekman, 1982; Izard, 1977). The strong position (i.e., that different patterns *cause* the emotional state) is at present not only without support, but probably beyond our current technical abilities to test. To show this effect one would have to produce experimentally particular autonomic patterns and then show that these patterns causally produce particular subjective emotional states. At the present time, it would be difficult to know how these patterns could be produced experimentally. The weak versions, (i.e., that each specific emotion is accompanied by specific autonomic patterns) has some support. In this case one needs to show that the pattern occurs as soon as and not later than the onset of the subjective state. Much of the evidence that has been amassed shows that different emotions may differ in some ways physiologically *after* the emotion has been induced. Only few cases pass the test of simultaneity, which is important since different emotional states involve different behaviors (fighting, fleeing, attacking, jumping up and down, and other unusual concatenations) that may produce different subsequent patterns. In any case, whatever pattern may have been shown to be the case is always superimposed on higher levels of sympathetic arousal for *all* emotional states. Those theorists that have embraced the position that emotions are a function of a general undifferentiated state of sympathetic arousal (Cannon, 1927; Mandler, 1975; Schachter,

---

[5] But it was not always thus, during the behaviorist interlude in American psychology, much of the work on human emotion was primarily concerned with emotions such as fear and anxiety—partly because of the general commitment to developing human psychology out of animal models (see, for example, Mowrer, 1939, 1960).

1970) have usually responded to the preponderance of evidence. None of their positions depends on such a state of affairs; arousal theories can function with patterned or unpatterned states.

C. Social Construction Views

The view that emotions are socially constructed states has been advocated by both psychologists and anthropologists. The major advocate among psychologists has been James Averill (cf. Averill, 1980, 1990). Averill considers emotions to be both behavioral syndromes (i.e., systematic behavioral repertories) and also social roles enacted by individuals. Important in the development and enactment of these roles is the appraisal of the situation and the experience of the state as a passion (i.e., as a passive rather than active state). Intensity of emotional experience is seen as a function of the person's involvement in emotional roles. And whereas biological factors obviously contribute to the emotional syndromes, social constructivists reject any notion of basic or fundamental emotions. In general, social constructivists are more sensitive to the variety of possible human emotional experiences than the usual approach to emotions envisages.

Anthropologists like Catherine Lutz have contributed to the constructivist position (e.g., Lutz, 1988; see also Lutz & Abu-Lughod, 1990). From the vantage point of looking at different cultures and the different experiences of emotions within those cultures, the constructivist point of view tries to account for variations in human experience, and in particular of emotions, by reference to a psychosocial reality that is constructed by an individual's position within and understanding of his or her culture and the culture's emotional knowledge systems and structures. In that context, Rimé, Philippot, and Cisamolo (1990) have shown that reported patterns of physiological response in emotions are at least to some considerable extent a function of social expectations and construction.

D. Do Facial Expressions Express Emotion?

Apart from folk observations of daily experience, the linking of emotions and facial expression has its origins in Darwin's (1872) book. Unfortunately, the linking of Darwin and facial expression has left the impression that Darwin considered these facial displays as having some specific adaptive survival value. In fact, the major thrust of Darwin's argument is that the vast majority of these displays are vestigial or accidental or, at best, what would in modern parlance be called preadaptive. In fact, Darwin specifically argued against the notion that "certain muscles have been given to man solely that he may reveal to other men his feelings" (cited in Fridlund, 1992b, p. 119). Fridlund (1992b) has explored Darwin's (1872) motive and message and notes that his antiadaptationist view of facial displays also prevented Darwin from viewing these displays as primarily communicative.

The contemporary intense interest in facial expression started primarily with the work of Tomkins (1962–1992, 1981), who placed facial expressions at the center of his theory of emotion and the eight basic emotions that form the core of emotional experience. The work of both Ekman (e.g., 1982) and Izard derives from Tomkins's initial important exposition.

The notion that facial displays *express* some underlying mental state forms a central part of many arguments about the nature of emotion. Apart from the fact that it needs to be made clear how the outward expression of inner states is adaptive (i.e., how it could contribute to reproductive fitness), important arguments can and have been made that facial displays are best seen (particularly in the tradition of behavioral ecology) as communicative devices as such, independent of emotional states (Fridlund, 1991, 1992a; Mandler, 1975, 1992a). Facial displays can be interpreted as remnants of preverbal communicative devices and as displays of values (indicating what is good or bad, useful or useless, etc.). That original position is more or less identical with the extensive and original work recently presented by Fridlund on the function of facial displays (Fridlund, 1991). Fridlund notes, *inter alia,* that facial displays are consonant with current evolutionary views of signaling, and that even displays previously considered involuntary, are in fact social and communicative. Fridlund has shown how a social interpretation of these displays best fits with existing knowledge about the function of displays in emotion and their presumed universality. He has elaborated a scenario of the evolutionary origin and utility of facial displays in which these displays function to communicate intentions and situational evaluations in the absence of verbal devices. The work of Janet Bavelas and her colleagues has shown the importance of communicative facial and other bodily displays. The conclusion, in part, is that the "communicative situation determines the visible behavior" (Bavelas, Black, Lemery, & Mullett, 1986). In the construction of emotions, facial displays are important contributors to the evaluative cognitions (see below) and appraisals (Lazarus, Kanner, & Folkman, 1980) of the current scene, similar to verbal, imaginal, or unconscious evaluative representations. Facial displays occur in many situations where emotions are inferred or asserted. However, they also occur in many situations that one would not call emotional at all; facial and body language frequently provides important social communications. In fact, the original position of some inexorable link between face and emotion has been softened in recent years, as when Ekman in an important summary of his position notes that facial expressions may serve a variety of different purposes, including the transmission of information (Ekman, 1989). Furthermore, if emotions are conceptualized as a concatenation of evaluative cognitions and sympathetic arousal (see below), then seeing facial displays as displays of values can make them often (but not always or inevitably) part of the emotional complex. I leave open for the time being the evolutionary history of these displays, and their relationship to the apparently similar displays of nonhuman animals that so fascinated Darwin.

E. The Question of Basic Emotions

An important part of the argument for the impenetrability of emotions is the postulation of basic or fundamental emotions. Constructivist approaches have usually rejected such a view. The lead for such a rejection was taken by William James, and it has received important support from recent detailed expositions (Averill, 1980; Fridlund, 1991, 1992a; Ortony & Turner, 1990). Ortony and Turner (1990) have noted that a rejection of basic emotion does not prevent one from looking for basic elements that constitute emotions, except that such basic elements are not in themselves emotions. Even though many tales have been spun about the evolution and origins of the separate emotions (e.g., Izard, 1977; Plutchik, 1980), there is little agreement or consistency to be found. One of the difficulties that faces speculators about the origins of discrete emotions is that they have not yet agreed on what the discrete fundamental emotions are (see Mandler, 1984, p. 36). Thus, Ortony and Turner (1990) note that the number of basic emotions can vary from 2 to 18, depending on which theorist you read. If there is an evolutionary basis to the primary emotions, should they not be more obvious?

The emotions that one finds in most lists of basic emotions are fear/anxiety, happiness/joy, and anger. Again, the list is heavily weighted toward the negative emotions. Two "emotions" sometimes included are interest and surprise as distinct and separate emotions. To call surprise an emotion depends on one's interpretation of the common usage of emotion. And because many different "emotions," such as fear and happiness, may involve some degree of surprise, how does one deal with surprise as a separate emotion. On the other hand, surprise is an excellent example of the reaction to discrepancies (see below). To insist that interest is an emotion is a more extreme position. There seems to be little basis in experience or theory to consider the expression of interest indicative of an emotional state; to call interest an emotion moves such a position far from the general understanding. On the other hand, it is equally puzzling that the emotion of "love" (much less "lust") is never found among the basic emotions. Is it because no distinct facial "expression" can be found for love? For the time being, we need to consider the various alternative points and in particular to await the outcome of the various views on facial displays that interact with the issue of basic emotions.[6]

V. A PERSONAL INTERLUDE

I decided some time ago to follow the lead of the traditional dual process approach and of Stanley Schachter (e.g., Schachter & Singer, 1962) by advocating an analytic, constructivist position that handles many, but not all, of the symptoms and effects of the common emotions. I put here my personal view of human emotions, developed over the past 20+ years. The approach owes much to the oldest

---

[6] For a survey of this contentious issue, see Ortony and Turner's original paper (1990) and the rejoinders (Ekman, 1992; Izard, 1992; Panksepp, 1992; Turner & Ortony, 1992).

tradition in the investigation of emotion—the combination of arousal and cognition.

Another tradition that informs my views is concerned with some of the conditions that produce emotional states. It suggests that many occasions for emotional experiences are represented by some discrepancy between expectation and actuality, some interruption to the usual or habitual way of acting or thinking. The best representatives of that tradition were F. Paulhan (1887) and J. Dewey (1894). To the extent that functional psychological theories postulate the occurrence of sympathetic nervous system arousal as a necessary part of the emotional complex, they face a critical problem, succinctly put by LeDoux (1989): "How is it that the initial state of bodily arousal . . . is evoked? . . . Cognitive theories require that the brain has a mechanism for distinguishing emotional from mundane situations prior to activating the autonomic nervous system" (p. 270). I have suggested that it is discrepancy or interruption that provides that mechanism. Discrepant situations are rarely mundane and usually emotional.

Constructivist analyses see the experience of emotion as "constructed" or composed of underlying processes. My approach is constructivist for the emotions as well as for the nature of conscious experience in general. Holistic conscious events are constructed out of activated underlying representation, and represent the best "sense" that can be made out of currently important concerns (cf. Mandler, 1985, ch. 3).

Discrepancy-evaluation theory only claims explanatory power for specified instances of emotional experience. There are aspects of human emotion that the theory cannot handle at present—or possibly ever. The theory proposes two basic underlying processes, autonomic (sympathetic) nervous system arousal and evaluative cognitions. In addition it suggests that the majority of occasions for sympathetic nervous system arousal come about by the occurrence of discrepancies in perception, action and thought. In particular, arousal accounts for the physical dimension (body), whereas evaluation incorporates the socially situated aspects of emotion (mind).

I have also tentatively suggested that emotion—however prevalent and seemingly crucial to the human state—may be the result of preadaptive processes. The notion is that different evolutionary stories account for the development of the sympathetic nervous system, the presence of difference and discrepancy detection, and the cognitive and evaluative faculties of human beings. These then become combined at a later stage into the modern "emotions." This still leaves open separate evolutionary sequences for the reaction to threat (i.e., fear), the evocation of lust, and other emotional states.[7]

---

[7] It is interesting to note in this connection that concerns are frequently voiced that modern humans are saddled with the remains of their animal ancestry in the expression of anger, aggression, and similar emotional states. The implication is that overcoming those states would be helpful, but these suggestions forget that an abandonment of such emotional states might also involve the abandonment of positive states such as joy and ecstasy.

The motivational impact of the resulting subjective states is obvious, and my account is similar to other theoretical views. Organisms will seek out occasions that make them feel good, and avoid those that produce noxious states; they will act to generate positive states and to eliminate negative ones.

I have not considered interruptions or discrepancies themselves to be emotions. All these do is set the stage for emotional experience by providing the passionate contribution of the sympathetic nervous system. Nor do I consider discrepancies as valenced; they are value neutral. Discrepancies exist in positive as well as negative situations, and provide the fuel for both types of emotions. Positive emotions also arise out of the opportunity to complete interrupted or discrepant actions and thought (Berscheid, 1983). On the other hand, discrepancy is not the only source of "emotional" arousal; emotions can be energized by arousal arising from a variety of sources, such as effort, exercise, drugs, and so on.

Discrepancy-evaluation theory has been developed and elaborated since 1964. Emotions are too diverse all to have come from a single source or even a single set of evolutionary developments. They are also too important in the daily life of homo sapiens to have a single evolutionary origin. Emotions emphasize our values, color our actions, and motivate much of our behavior, and are likely to have several sources. However, there might be something useful about an analysis of the emotions that not only deals with some of the usual aspects of emotional experience, but also is able to inform related topics ranging from stress to mood and memory and the experience of freedom (Mandler, 1992b, 1992c, 1993).

VI. HOW MANY EMOTIONS?—DO WE NEED A CLUSTER OF EXPLANATIONS?

Given that different lists of emotions and definitions seem to appeal to different sets of emotions, one might have to consider the possibility that the emotion chapter contains so many disparate phenomena that different theories might be needed for different parts of the emotion spectrum. Such a possibility was hinted at even by William James (1884) who, in presenting his theory of emotion, noted that the "only emotions . . . [that he proposed] expressly to consider . . . are those that have a distinct bodily expression" (p. 189). He specifically leaves aside aesthetic feelings or intellectual delights, the implication being that some other explanatory mechanism applies to those. On the one hand, many current theories of human emotion restrict themselves to the same domain as James did—the subjective experience that is accompanied by bodily "disturbances." On the other hand, much current work deals primarily with negative emotions—and the animal work does so almost exclusively. Social and cognitive scientists spend relatively little time trying to understand ecstasy, joy, or love (but see, for example, Berscheid, 1982, and Isen, 1990). Must we continue to insist that passionate emotional experiences of humans, ranging from lust to political involvements, from coping with disaster to dealing with grief, from the joys of creative work to the moving experiences of art and music, are all cut from the same cloth, or even that that cloth should be based on a model of negative emotions?

There are of course regularities in human thought and action that produce general categories of emotions, categories that have family resemblances and overlap in the features that are selected for analysis (whether it is the simple dichotomy of good and bad, or the appreciation of beauty, or the perception of evil). These families of occasions and meanings construct the categories of emotions found in the natural language (and psychology). The emotion categories are fuzzily defined by external and internal situations, and the common themes found within the categories of emotions vary from case to case, and they have different bases for their occurrence. Sometimes an emotional category is based on the similarity of external conditions, as in the case of some fears and environmental threats. Sometimes an emotional category may be based on a collection of similar behaviors, as in the subjective feelings of fear related to avoidance and flight. Sometimes a common category arises from a class of incipient actions, as in hostility and destructive action. Sometimes hormonal and physiological reactions provide a common basis, as in the case of lust, and sometimes purely cognitive evaluations constitute an emotional category, as in judgments of helplessness that eventuate in anxiety. Others, such as guilt and grief depend on individual evaluations of having committed undesirable acts or trying to recover the presence or comfort of a lost person or object. All of these emotional states involve evaluative cognitions, and their common properties give rise to the appearance of discrete categories of emotions.

It can also be argued with considerable justification that different theories and theorists are concerned with different aspects of an important and complex aspect of human existence. Thus, the animal research is concerned with possible evolutionary precursors or parallels of some few important, usually aversive, states. Others are more concerned with the appraisal and evaluation of the external world (Lazarus, 1991; Ortony et al., 1988), whereas some theories focus on the cognitive conjunction with autonomic nervous system reactions (James, Schachter). And the more ambitious try to put it all together in overarching and inclusive systems (e.g., Frijda).

It may be too early or it may be misleading to assume common mechanisms for the various states of high joy and low despair that we experience, or to expect complex human emotions to share a common ancestry with the simple emotions of humans and other animals. In any case, no simple answer is likely to resolve the question of what emotions *are*. Cognitive science, from its multifaceted vantage point, can only continue in pursuit of some agreement among theorists, some common ground from which to proceed.[8]

---

[8] Preparation of this chapter was concluded in June 1993.

References

Averill, J. R. (1980). A constructivist view of emotion. In R. Plutchik & H. Kelleman (Eds.), *Theories of emotion.* New York: Academic Press.

Averill, J. R. (1990). Emotions in relation to systems of behavior. In N. S. Stein, B. L. Leventhal, & T. Trabasso (Eds.), *Psychological and biological approaches to emotion* (pp. 385–404). Hillsdale, NJ: Erlbaum.

Bavelas, J. B., Black, A., Lemery, C. R., & Mullett, J. (1986). I *show* how you feel: Motor mimicry as a communicative act. *Journal of Personality and Social Psychology, 50,* 322–329.

Berscheid, E. (1982). Attraction and emotion in interpersonal relationships. In M. S. Clark & S. T. Fiske (Eds.), *Affect and cognition: The seventeenth annual Carnegie Symposium on Cognition* (pp. 37–54). Hillsdale, NJ: Erlbaum.

Berscheid, E. (1983). Emotion. In H. H. Kelley, E. Berscheid, A. Christensen, J. H. Harvey, T. L. Huston, G. Levinger, E. McClintock, L. A. Peplau, & D. R. Peterson (Eds.), *Close relationships* (pp. 110–168). San Francisco: Freeman.

Berscheid, E., & Walster, E. (1978). *Interpersonal attraction* (2nd ed.). Reading, MA: Addison-Wesley.

Bullock, M., & Russell, J. A. (1986). Concepts of emotion in developmental psychology. In C. E. Izard & P. B. Read (Eds.), *Measuring emotions in infants and children: Vol. 2. Cambridge studies in social and emotional development* (pp. 203–237). New York: Cambridge University Press.

Cannon, W. B. (1927). The James-Lange theory of emotions: A critical examination and an alternative theory. *American Journal of Psychology, 39,* 106–124.

Darwin, C. (1872). *The expression of the emotions in man and animals.* London: John Murray.

Dewey, J. (1894). The theory of emotion. I. Emotional attitudes. *Psychological Review, 1,* 553–569.

Ekman, P. (1982). *Emotion in the human face* (2nd ed.). New York: Cambridge University Press.

Ekman, P. (1989). The argument and evidence about universals in facial expressions of emotion. In H. Wagner & A. Manstead (Eds.), *Handbook of social psychophysiology* (pp. 143–164). Chichester, England: Wiley.

Ekman, P. (1992). Are there basic emotions? *Psychological Review, 99,* 550–553.

Folkman, S., & Lazarus, R. S. (1990). Coping and emotion. In N. S. Stein, B. L. Leventhal, & T. Trabasso (Eds.), *Psychological and biological approaches to emotion* (pp. 313–332). Hillsdale, NJ: Erlbaum.

Freud, S. (1975). Introductory lectures on psychoanalysis. In J. Strachey (Ed. and Trans.), *The standard edition of the complete psychological works of Sigmund Freud* (Vols. 15 & 16). London: Hogarth Press. (Original work published 1916).

Freud, S. (1975). Inhibitions, symptoms, and anxiety. In J. Strachey (Ed. and Trans.), *The standard edition of the complete psychological works of Sigmund Freud* (Vol. 20). London: Hogarth Press. (Original work published 1926).

Fridlund, A. J. (1991). Evolution and facial action in reflex, social motive, and paralanguage. *Biological Psychology, 32,* 3–100.

Fridlund, A. J. (1992a). The behavioral ecology and sociality of human faces. In M. S. Clark (Ed.), *Review of personality and social psychology* (Vol. 13, pp. 90–121). Beverly Hills, CA: Sage.

Fridlund, A. J. (1992b). Darwin's anti-Darwinism in *The expression of the emotions in man and animals.* In K. T. Strongman (Ed.), *International review of studies on emotion* (Vol. 2, pp. 117–137). Chichester, England: Wiley.

Frijda, N. H. (1986). *The emotions.* Cambridge, England: Cambridge University Press.

Geertz, C. (1973). *The interpretation of cultures: Selected essays.* New York: Basic Books.

Harter, S., & Whitesell, N. R. (1989). Developmental changes in children's understanding of single, multiple, and blended emotion concepts. In C. Saarni & P. L. Harris (Eds.), *Children's understanding of emotion* (pp. 81–116). New York: Cambridge University Press.

Isen, A. M. (1990). The influence of positive and negative affect on cognitive organization: Some implications for development. In N. S. Stein, B. L. Leventhal, & T. Trabasso (Eds.), *Psychological and biological approaches to emotion* (pp. 75–94). Hillsdale, NJ: Erlbaum.

Isen, A. M., Daubman, K. A., & Nowicki, G. P. (1987). Positive affect facilitates creative problem solving. *Journal of Personality and Social Psychology, 52,* 1122–1131.

Isen, A. M., & Means, B. (1983). Positive affect as a variable in decision making. *Social Cognition, 2,* 18–31.

Izard, C. E. (1972). *Patterns of emotion.* New York: Academic Press.

Izard, C. E. (1977). *Human emotions.* New York: Plenum Press.

Izard, C. E. (1992). Basic emotions, relations among emotions, and emotion-cognition relations. *Psychological Review, 99,* 561–565.

Izard, C. E., & Buechler, S. (1980). Aspects of consciousness and personality in terms of differential emotion theory. In R. Plutchik & H. Kellerman (Eds.), *Theories of emotion.* New York: Academic Press.

James, W. (1884). What is an emotion?. *Mind, 9,* 188–205.

James, W. (1890). *The principles of psychology.* New York: Holt.

James, W. (1894). The physical basis of emotion. *Psychological Review, 1,* 516–529.

Lazarus, R. S. (1991). *Emotion and adaptation.* New York: Oxford University Press.

Lazarus, R. S., Kanner, A. D., & Folkman, S. (1980). Emotions: A cognitive-phenomenological analysis. In R. Plutchik & H. Kellerman (Eds.), *Theories of emotion.* New York: Academic Press.

LeDoux, J. E. (1989). Cognitive-emotional interactions in the brain. *Cognition and Emotion, 3,* 267–289.

LeDoux, J. (1992). Brain systems and emotional memory. In K. T. Strongman (Ed.), *International review of studies on emotion* (Vol. 2, pp. 23–29). Chichester, England: Wiley.

Lutz, C. (1988). *Unnatural emotions: Everyday sentiments on a Micronesian atoll and their challenge to Western theory.* Chicago: University of Chicago Press.

Lutz, C., & Abu-Lughod, L. (1990). *Language and the politics of emotion.* Cambridge, England: Cambridge University Press.

Mandler, G. (1975). *Mind and emotion.* New York: Wiley.

Mandler, G. (1979). Emotion. In E. Hearst (Ed.), *The first century of experimental psychology* (pp. 275–321). Hillsdale, NJ: Erlbaum.

Mandler, G. (1984). *Mind and body: Psychology of emotion and stress.* New York: Norton.

Mandler, G. (1985). *Cognitive psychology: An essay in cognitive science.* Hillsdale, NJ: Erlbaum.

Mandler, G. (1992a). Emotions, evolution, and aggression: Myths and conjectures. In K. T. Strongman (Ed.), *International review of studies on emotion* (Vol. 2, pp. 97–116). Chichester, England: Wiley.

Mandler, G. (1992b). Cognition and emotion: Extensions and clinical applications. In D. J. Stein & J. E. Young (Eds.), *Cognitive science and clinical disorders* (pp. 61–78). San Diego, CA: Academic Press.

Mandler, G. (1992c). Memory, arousal, and mood: A theoretical integration. In S.-A. Christianson (Ed.), *Handbook of emotion and memory* (pp. 93–110). Hillsdale, NJ: Erlbaum.

Mandler, G. (1993). Emotions and the psychology of freedom. In S. H. M. van Goozen, N. E. van de Poll, & J. A. Sergeant (Eds.), *Emotions: Essays on emotion theory.* Hillsdale, NJ: Erlbaum.

Mandler, G., & Shebo, B. J. (1983). Knowing and liking. *Motivation and Emotion, 7,* 125–144.

McNaughton, M. (1989). *Biology and emotion.* Cambridge, England: Cambridge University Press.

Mowrer, O. H. (1939). Stimulus–response analysis of anxiety and its role as a reinforcing agent. *Psychological Review, 46,* 553–565.

Mowrer, O. H. (1960). *Learning theory and behavior.* New York: Wiley.

Oatley, K., & Jenkins, J. M. (1992). Human emotions: Function and dysfunction. *Annual Review of Psychology, 43,* 55–85.

Oatley, K., & Johnson-Laird, P. N. (1987). Towards a cognitive theory of emotion. *Cognition and Emotion, 1,* 29–50.

Ortony, A. (1992). Emotion modeling. In S. C. Shapiro (Ed.), *Encyclopedia of artificial intelligence* (2nd ed., pp. 446–448). New York: Wiley.

Ortony, A., Clore, G. L., & Collins, A. (1988). *The cognitive structure of emotions.* New York: Cambridge University Press.

Ortony, A., & Turner, T. J. (1990). What's basic about basic emotions? *Psychological Review, 97,* 315–331.

Panksepp, J. (1991). Affective neuroscience: A conceptual framework for the neurobiological study of emotions. In K. T. Strongman (Ed.), *International review of studies on emotion* (Vol. I, pp. 59–99). Chichester, England: Wiley.

Panksepp, J. (1992). A critical role for "affective neuroscience" in resolving what is basic about basic emotions. *Psychological Review, 99*, 554–560.

Paulhan, F. (1887). *Les phénomènes affectifs et les lois de leur apparition.* Paris: F. Alcan.

Pfeifer, R. (1988). Artificial intelligence models of emotion. *NATO ASI Series, Series D, 44*, 287–320.

Plutchik, R. (1980). *Emotion: A psychoevolutionary synthesis.* New York: Harper & Row.

Rimé, B., Philippot, P., & Cisamolo, D. (1990). Social schemata of peripheral changes in emotion. *Journal of Personality and Social psychology, 59*, 38–49.

Schachter, S. (1970). The assumption of identity and peripheralist-centralist controversies in motivation and emotion. In M. B. Arnold (Ed.), *Feelings and emotions.* New York: Academic Press.

Schachter, S., & Singer, J. E. (1962). Cognitive, social and physiological determinants of emotional state. *Psychological Review, 69*, 379–399.

Stein, D. J., & Young, J. E. (1992). *Cognitive science and clinical disorders.* San Diego, CA: Academic Press.

Stein, N. L., & Levine, L. (1987). Thinking about feelings: The development and use of emotional knowledge. In R. E. Snow & M. Farr (Eds.), *Aptitude, learning, and instruction.* Hillsdale, NJ: Erlbaum.

Stein, N. L., & Levine, L. J. (1989). The causal organisation of emotional knowledge: A developmental study. *Cognition and Emotion, 3*, 343–378.

Stein, N. L., Trabasso, T., & Liwag, M. (1993). The representation and organization of emotional experience: Unfolding the emotional episode. In M. Lewis & J. M. Haviland (Eds.), *Handbook of emotions.* New York: Guilford.

Strongman, K. T. (1987). *The psychology of emotion.* Chichester, England: Wiley.

Tomkins, S. S. (1962–1992). *Affect, imagery, and consciousness* (Vols. 1–4). New York: Springer.

Tomkins, S. S. (1981). The quest for primary motives: Biography and autobiography of an idea. *Journal of Personality and Social Psychology, 41*, 306–329.

Turner, T. J., & Ortony, A. (1992). Basic emotions: Can conflicting criteria converge? *Psychological Review, 99*, 566–571.

Webster's Seventh New Collegiate Dictionary. (1969). Springfields, MA: G & C Merriam.

Zajonc, R. B. (1980). Feeling and thinking: Preferences need no inferences. *American Psychologist, 35*, 151–175.

Zajonc, R. B. (1984). On the primacy of affect. *American Psychologist, 39*, 117–123.

Index

385